Jews: A People's History of the Lower East Side

Volume III

Jews: A People's History of the Lower East Side

Volume III

Clayton Patterson
Editor-in-Chief and Soliciting Editor

Jim Feast, Monica Uszerowicz
Senior Editors

Kenny Petricig
Assistant Editor

Clayton Books, LLC

CLAYTON BOOKS, LLC, TRADE PAPERBACK EDITION OCTOBER 2012
Jews: A People's History of the Lower East Side, VOLUMES I, II AND III
copyright © 2012 by Clayton I. Patterson; Volume II by Clayton I. Patterson

Published in the United States by Clayton Books, LLC,
161 Essex Street, New York, NY 10002.

Library of Congress Cataloging-in-Publication Data
Patterson, Clayton I.
Jews: A People's History of the Lower East Side, VOLUMES I, II AND III
First Edition/First Printing
Printed in Canada

ISBN 978-0-9857883-0-8 Vol. I
ISBN 978-0-9857883-1-5 Vol. II
ISBN 978-0-9857883-2-2 Vol. III

book design by Monica Ponomarev

DEDICATION

Volume III of *Jews: A People's History of the Lower East Side* is dedicated to those Jews on the Lower East Side who have influenced me and contributed to who I am. The connection or inspiration may relate to a measurable, intense period of time in the past or that started in the past and is ongoing in the presence and the persistence of memory. Because of the density of the flow of electricity between us, the depth and intensity of our friendship, the give and take of Yes and No!, the shared inspirations, the magical overlaps, the conscious and unconscious levels of communication, Boris Lurie (RIP), Rabbi Lionel Ziprin (RIP) and I entered into some kind of brotherhood. It connected us somewhere out there in the deep, far reaches of inner space, removed from the grounds of the normal or the mainstream. And there are those who created and exposed channels of thought that led to possibilities and once-in-a-lifetime experiences – Sol Fried, Mrs. Miller (RIP), Ben Booksinger (RIP), Ralph Feldman, Al Orensanz. And there are those who opened doors or extended a needed hand – Rabbi Spiegel (RIP), Rabbi Joseph Singer (RIP), Rabbi Feinstein, Rabbi Kline (House of Sages of Israel), Danny Stein, Elissa Sampson, Efroim Snyder, the sisters Agathe Snow and Anne Apparu. And there are those non-religious Jews who made valuable contributions to my life, showing me that being a Jew may have nothing to with the idea of G-d, but to being a part of the tribe starting with Moses: Frances Golden, Sun PK (nee Peter Kwaloff), Mickey (the Pope of Dope) Cezar, Thom Paul DeVita. And to those outlaw, street philosopher, slumlord, creative types, between Houston and Delancey, who made it possible for the survival of a Lower East Side artist's existence to work – if the artist understood the rules of the game: Jerry the Electrician, Eliot, David and his brother Nathan – these men who gave space to the outsiders who would have trouble surviving as artists anywhere else.

TABLE OF CONTENTS

PART 7: PHOTOGRAPHY

PART 8: LOOSE ENDS

ACKNOWLEDGMENTS

I could never have gotten volume II and III together if not for a number of people. In terms of editing and preparing the documents, Dr. Jim Feast, to me, was the backbone. Assisting Jim edit was Monica Uszerowicz, and sometimes with the help of her father Professor Uszerowicz. I am indebted to Monica Ponomarev the designer for her patience as we struggled through the changes and she stayed with the project. This anthology would have never made it to completion without the help of Ethan Swan who guided me through the Kickstarter process which allowed me to make the money needed to produce this book. Without the able of assistance of Suzanna Wasserman Kickstarter may not have ever gotten kickstarted. Without the assistance of Steve Dalachinsky a number of hard to get to creative individuals would not be in this anthology. Then there was Joyce Mendelsohn always there ready with a kind word as well as an intelligent response to solving a problem. Elissa Sampson's help was invaluable to navigating different aspects of the LES Jewish Left and Orthodox shul history. I am thankfully that Kenny Petricig took it upon himself to learn how to make an index and then indexed all three volumes. Kenny was also invaluable with final editing and helping us cross the finish line. I say a thank you to Julius Klein the cover artist. I appreciate that Howie Seligman, and the Solo Foundation, held the money between Kickstarter and paying the bills. Thanks to Ron Kolm for his guidance on how to finish the project. And to Aishling Labat for helping with the finishing touches. I am indebted to all the people who contributed to Kickstarter without them this project would never have happened. For the noticeable contributions by Aaron Sosnick, Michael Rosen, and Robert Perl, and then later, a needed contribution from Serge Hoyda. Then came the team of Jody Carl Weiner and Nancy Sue Calef. Jody providing the legal intelligence and expertise which got this book into production and Nancy for her help getting the logo done.

Of course, none of this would be possible to even exist if not for the support and love from Elsa Rensaa my partner since 1972, and now my wife.

There are numerous others who made countless silent contributions to the making of this anthology and to all of them I say thank you.

In terms of paying respect to the people who contributed to the making of this anthology, it somehow seems fitting that I am wrapping this up on the eve of September 11, 2012. It brings to mind how much we have to be grateful for and no matter the trials and hardships we face "We the People" can overcome whatever adversity gets thrown into our path.

My last note of thanks, gratitude, respect, and honor, is wrapped up in my one political statement. A statement which was extremely important to me: Made In the USA.

Forever grateful to all who made this book possible.
thanks
Clayton Patterson

PREFACE

It might seem that there is a great hiatus within the history of the Lower East Side, separating the politics of the largely socialist, Jewish culture of the turn of the century from the later, more ethnically mixed and anarchistically inclined social action of the 1960s through the '90s. The early books in this collection, *Captured* and *Resistance*, which profile the later period and are centered on the Tompkins Square homeless encampment and the riot of 1988 that dispersed it, might seem deviant in the light of earlier immigrant struggles, which focused on the unionization of the needle trades, the rise of such leaders as Morris Hillquit (Jewish LES lawyer and founder of the Socialist Party), and the fight against abusive conditions in the sweated trades. I think, though, even the Jewish period pivots on Tompkins Square, 1988, since the activists of the earlier period laid out the exact organizational methods and utopian considerations that went into the creation of that incendiary moment.

Briefly let me sketch in the basis for this last claim. Preceding that, however, I want to offer a few thoughts on how Volume III is to be distinguished from the others in this study of Jewish life. After that and the presentation of the reasoning behind my claim to continuity, I will end with a mention of how the organizational and editorial plan of the five books correspond to the vision laid out in a rough way in the LES ghetto by Jewish radicals so many generations ago.

First, then, how are we to understand this third volume, particularly as it focuses on cultural activities such as art, theater, and film. It seems to me that if anyone reads through this book, going, for example, from Seth Tobocman's tales of anarchist glory to Judith Malina on the early days of the Living Theater to Eve Packer's discussion of the Yiddish theater, one finds a daredevil exuberance beyond what is normally found in countercultural activity. This distinction is central.

I define alternative cultural products as reformist and dependent on money while resistant art, that largely represented here, is of a more radical nature and depends on time.

An alternative cultural activity, at its best, will harshly criticize existing institutions or practices while (in the case of theater or dance, for instance) charging people admission as a way to accrue funds to continue its projects. Resistant art while often equally critical will tend to focus on a vision of another society or set of intimate relations that would be superior (less hierarchical and less sexist, for example) to those that presently exists. Moreover, to the extent possible, providers of resistant culture will downplay profit.

To expand on this last point in relation to people and institutions profiled in this and Volume II, I might mention the Living Theater, which always has a night, once a week, when audience members can pay whatever they can afford to attend. I should also mention the Stone, a music club founded by John Zorn. He takes care of the expenses for rent, heat, etc., and everyone working there is a volunteer; so every penny that comes in at the door is divided between the musicians performing that night. The Unbearables, too, profiled in the last volume, mounted some of their largest, gliztiest productions – such as the séance at FusionArts Gallery, which that featured smoke machines, strange audio/visual effect, and all the poets dressed as corpses – for no charge.

To put this realistically, in resistant endeavors turning a profit is downgraded in importance in relation to other considerations having to do with community formation and inspiration. A detailing of what these considerations are will be presented below. Here we only need to emphasize that what this form of culture puts uppermost in terms of audience reception is the seizure and enlacement of time. At present the average American is swamped by a wrap-around ideology that does its best to occupy her or his every moment with praise for a commodity-ensnared individualism and demonization of social movements that use collective, democratic practices to change social norms and institutions. Resistant culture sets great store by the fact that its audience is temporarily removing itself from this zone of ruling class conditioning. Ideally, as long as the audience occupies this space, the themes and images of resistance are so implanted that, soon enough, when the participants are back awash in the sea of hurtful propaganda, the new messages will enlace with, hence weakening and subverting, the ruling class's philosophy. Time is of the essence in the sense that the more exposure an individual has to resistant art and practice, the greater her or his ability to overcome the induced alienation of mainstream culture.

The themes and images of resistant culture are taken from the doctrine and visions elaborated by progressive organizations. Those on the Lower East Side found them in the Jewish labor and social movement of the 1880s through the 1920s. These themes, which unite all five books, have four core production values, which in intent do not aim to overthrow existing state and capitalist structures, but to set up a base area that would function by, in part or in total, breaking away from relationships governed by private property and commerce, replacing them with ones arranged around communal structures, the carnivalesque and the gift economy. Let me elaborate.

1) One key point in the resistant philosophy was to transfer housing away from the landlord/tenant locus. Take the Jewish housing projects on the Lower East Side, alluded to in a few places in this anthology, which were usually put up by unions. For instance, the Amalgamated Dwellings on Grand Street, begun in 1930, was financed by the Amalgamated Clothing Union, as was its companion, the Hillman Houses, named for the Amalgamated's founder and opened in

1947. The East River Houses, by contrast, begun in 1950, were bankrolled by the Ladies Garment Workers Union.

These housing projects were cooperatively owned, with each tenant having a share and a vote in how the building was run. The avowed motive for these ventures was that the only landlords would be individual dwellers/owners so that, ultimately, a person would own only her or his own domicile. There would be no non-tenant owners of real estate. This desire to eliminate landlords was understandable given the frequency of evictions in the quarter. As Moses Rischin notes in *The Promised City*, "Uncertainty of employment, nonpayment of wages, unexpected obligations, dependents, and adversities contributed to the high incidence of evictions. In the year 1891-1892 alone, in two judicial districts of the Lower East Side, 11,550 dispossess warrants were issued by the presiding magistrates."

Still, as is the way of the world, those who prospered did not necessarily hold onto the more progressive ideas on landlordism, and many prosperous Jews bought tenements. There are profiles of such landlords in these three volumes. However, the old philosophy still applied to the degree that these were live-in (as opposed to absentee) landlords, who generally had a live-and-let-live attitude to their tenants. As Clayton Patterson writes, in a private communication, "It was the Jewish landlords who made it possible for artists to live in their space because they had a philosophy: if you never bother us, we would not bother you." Patterson goes on to pointedly link the two types of Jewish housing mentioned so far, "There were 2 streams of housing: the cooperative housing and the privately owned homes. BUT, what made the difference here was the landlord lived in the property as well. You had both private and cooperative housing, both forms were connected to community and face to face interactions."

By the 1960s, the LES playing field had shifted radically. While some Jews clung on, many moved to more upscale neighborhoods as immigrant Hispanics filled in the gaps. Housing stock deteriorated, and by the late '70s many landlords forfeited their buildings to the city, in lieu of paying outstanding property taxes and plowing in more money for necessary repairs to keep the habitation viable. The city kept operating a few of these properties (called in-rem buildings), but shut many others down, leaving the neighborhood filled with boarded-up tenements. Faced with this geography, squatting became the new tactic for moving homes into the hands of those who would rehabilitate them. Squatters simply took over empty apartment buildings and made them livable.

The same working principle was behind the homeless encampment in Tompkins Square Park. The homeless saw a public space where it appeared they could camp undisturbed. They learned that, aside from very infrequent crackdowns, the police did not try to roust them, and they were allowed to set up housekeeping for more than a year in the park.

So, in different ways, both Jewish and squat activists sought (at their most radical) to purge the LES of landlords or (for the more conservative) to do away with absentee and corporate landlords.

2) Let me make clear that not every one of the four core principles are given lengthy or even explicit discussion in these three volumes, but they are the dominant background factors that pervaded and influenced artistic, professional and religious striving catalogued in the texts.

It can't be put too strongly that the turn-of-the-century Jewish unions were far to the left of other AFL-affiliated labor organizations. Their aim was not simply to ameliorate the lives of their members but to replace capitalism with the cooperative commonwealth. As this new, coming social form was pictured, one's housing and one's workplace would be one's own in a very real sense. There would be minimal private ownership. The stores, factories, farms and houses would belong to those who worked and lived in them. The power to decide what was done in each would be democratically shared by those who participated in its functioning.

Let me note that there were profound historical factors behind this orientation. It was not that Eastern European Jews had some special radical essence, but rather that two elements in their background pressed in that direction. First, many had experience in militant unions (particularly in Poland, which had begun industrializing in the 1880s, funded by German capital) as well as in underground political organizations that were fighting the disenfranchisement and murderous oppression of the czarist tyranny. Second, the type of labor in which they engaged in New York was particularly suited to stoke radicalism.

Now, it's often said truthfully that the Jews dominated the garment trades as if this were one of many fields they might have prevailed in. Against this, we need to stress that the garment industry was the largest manufacturing sector in New York, and its lineaments shaped the city's work force as a whole. Two facts about this trade stand out. Garment making was seasonal, and it was arranged, contra the emerging situations in the other major American industries of the time, in small workshops, not giant plants. On this last point, Rischin notes, "In no other industry could so many shops numbering so few employees be found. In 1913 the clothing industry in New York City numbered 16,552 factories and 312,245 employees. The factories ... averaged eighteen employees."

This is not the replace to rehearse an argument I have made in the political journal Fifth Estate, but let me say that I believe tendentially (not exclusively) seasonal employment inclines workers toward anarchism while more sure, full-time employment usually associates workers with socialism. As we know, both anarchism and socialism flourished on the Lower East Side, though socialism eventually gained the upper hand. This was a socialism that had an anarchist tinge, nonetheless. Many traits separated these two left movements – socialists believed highly in electoral politics, for instance, which anarchists disdained – but one differentiator is of relevance here. Socialists looked to gradual reform, quickened as workers gained class consciousness, to replace capitalism. As explained by Tony Michels in *Socialist Politics and the Making of Yiddish Culture in New York City, 1890-1923*, "Socialists did believe [with the anarchists] that capitalism would [eventually] be overturned by violent revolution … Yet they also maintained that strikes, trade-unions, and the ballot box could achieve meaningful gains and heighten workers' class-consciousness along the way." Anarchists, by contrasted, repudiated any truck with the economic system, calling for its quick overthrow. This latter attitude, I believe, is linked (for one) to workers who were part timers and had less stake in current arrangements than those who were in more stable positions.

In line with this anarchist edge, as I understand the visions of such people as Hillman, Hillquit and Emma Goldman, if all went well, the Lower East Side would become a conquered beachhead within capitalism. The neighborhood's cooperative housing projects would be surrounded by cooperatively owned and managed factories and stores. Newly opened and added park space would create a landscape of strange, vacuumed beauty.

Again, there is a continuity that ties the cooperative kosher butcher shop, opened in 1902 at 245 Stanton, the Jewish Cooperative League, which opened a LES hat factory in 1909, and (as noted by Rischin, the "sons and daughters of Odessa, Kiev, and Vilna [who] experimented with cooperative living and even formed a cooperative laundry" to the 1960s Motherfuckers' Free Store and other such enterprises that existed in the neighborhood from then through the '80s.

3) Obviously, for this cooperative paradise to be born, there would have to be the change of many hearts, and the distillation of an ethnic of solidarity. Many episodes described in Volume I of this Jewish book, ably put together by Mareleyn Schneider, center on synagogues, and how the maintenance of the building and the keeping together of the congregation became a collective project of great focus, energy and scope, in which personal concern and convenience took a back seat. The activists who defended and supplied the Tompkins Square homeless encampment were inspired by quite similar ideals. This was the ideology.

4) The best way to keep these ideals afloat was through practice, such as in working together to rebuild or preserve a shul or synagogue. But there also has to be educational part, so youth can learn and grasp the vision. In a wider

sense, there needs to be a whole set of institutions backing and pushing these views. So, as a final component, the tradition called for the eventual transfer of educational, policing, medical, judicial and other functions to the democratically managed, cooperative context. For the time being, a parallel state would be set up to supplement and partially supplant the existing organs of social reproduction.

It seems to me the multipurpose Workmen's Circle (not in the LES) or Delancey Street Labor Lyceum, which opened in 1892 and is described by Michels as a place that housed two Yiddish journals, "a café, and a hall for lectures and Socialist Party meetings," places which provided many services, such as insurance, medical consulting, education, counseling, and rooms to hold social and political gatherings, offer a good sketch of some of the probable contours of such a replacement structure.

And, to me, this structure was re-envisioned in Tompkins Square's Tent City. This large gathering of the homeless, ignored for a year by the city, was supplied with food, cooking equipment, clothes, blankets and other supplies by a loosely organized network of self-organized volunteers. There were clean-up squads, outreach progra ms to connect the residents to city services, and political ties formed with various progressive movements, including the national homeless rights organization. Ironically enough, by the way, Jewish organization still existing in the neighborhood were conspicuous by their absence from engagements with the homeless enclave. Certainly, such organizations no longer had the importance they once did and so were less involved in all the neighborhood's doings. More pragmatically, Patterson has suggested, that the reason "in all of the Tent City struggles, there was a noticeable lack of Jewish presence" was because "the Grand Street organizations, the orthodox, were too Republican while the leftists and Socialists about Delancey, in places like Cooper Square and the Met Council on Housing, were hooked into the bureaucracy. Remember this fact. The city was all Democratic at that time."

Even so, these Jewish attitudes in the late 1980s hardly modify the fact that the revolutionary patterns of broad solidarity and the establishment of massive alternative structures were the bequeathal of treasures of the Jewish LES labor and social movements.

And, to sum up, taken together, these four components suggest the underground continuity of the immigrant labor and social movements and the later flowering of dissent in the same community from the 1960s through early 1990s, times of anarchist-flavored protests and the creation of a replacement structure. This suggests also where lay the roots of a resilient resistant culture, one far different from a generalized alternative art, that can be filtered through capitalist structures in a way that resistant practices cannot.

And this reflection moves me directly to my last point: the form of these books. The genius of Clayton Patterson in organizing the early books, and the combined genius of Schneider and Patterson in these three new volumes, is that the book's selections and structure have broadly mimed certain key aspects of the social movements the writers in the book describe.

I'm thinking of two. The first is that the books have no settled program. They do not reflect one perspective on the past nor seek to hype one component of the social world above another. Rather what is created is a network of differing ideologies, lives and experiences. The path is not that different from that cleared by de Souza-Santos in his six anthologies on new practices. He says his goal is to set adjoining, leftist viewpoints in dialogue, not in order to reach a shared conclusion but to establish a unified (and diverse) front. So, to focus on the three Jewish texts, the editors establish a rapport between voices within the Jewish diaspora, mixing conservatives and radicals, performance artists and deli owners, so as to connect at all levels. For these editors, it is almost as if they were putting the past in motion. And this mirrors the LES's social struggles, which, as we saw, attempted to concert different institutions and multiple identities under a generous umbrella.

But there is another ricochet here. The books purposely offer little overall editorial guidance to the reader. There is no opening introduction to each section; no hierarchy within sections, whereby a famous person or event is given more attention than a less known woman, man or tradition; no exclusion of views that might seem too extreme or complacent.

Instead, if preferences are to be expressed; some arguments counted as heavier than others; some memoirs felt to be more authentic; such evaluations are left to the reader as she or he travels through this vast expanse, this steppe, of vital and rich material. And this is another example of parallelism, for, despite later attempts to pigeonhole and schematicize the history of the Jewish Lower East Side, the struggles taking place there were so multi-pronged and open-ended – for, as seen, the assault on the reigning business and state arrangement was total in the sense that a complete separate system was envisioned to replace it – that only a book that presents a near-chaotic jumble of texts, each one filled with insight but also with unique views that are incompatible with many others beside them, can yield a sense of the wild diversity, livid passion and a daring quest to craft a newer, truer world that was the Jewish Lower East Side.

Jim Feast

1.Identity

What makes Jewish identity unique and what remains always as the connective tissue is that Jews whether they be self-hating secularists, zealous Zionists, or fanatical Chassidim all have the word JEW as their common denominator be they in a group or just single lonely unattached intellectuals. Unlike other groups, the Jew is classified as the JEW, not because of his race (we are neither black, white, yellow, brown etc.), religion or other so-called socially defining terms but simply because one was born a JEW. Therefore being a JEW is that rare species defined by a multitude of "identities"/ labels, tribe being one, that can contain both positive and negative connotations and qualities causing wider prejudices as well as both shaky and superficial "identity" crises.

An Irishman comes from Ireland. An African comes from Africa, etc etc. Where does a Jew come from? Jewland? Get my point? This also leads to labels. Am I a Jewish American poet or an American Jewish poet? Does this connote my race? My religion? My genre? My IDENTITY? My affiliations ? Is it a group identity that reveals some sordid solidarity or schism between me and the "Others"? Is religion or labeling an artificial unifier? Is this multiplicity one of the main reasons why Jews are so multi-faceted and all encompassing and may I add in some cases, neurotic. Many of these answers are in this book as it takes us on a journey across continents and through neighborhoods crisscrossing geographies both internal and external.

Jew. Judaica. Judaism. Jewish identity vs. assimilation re: World War 2. Why was specifically putting an end to the Jewish race/religion called the Final Solution? Weren't there other ways for the Nazis to win the war?

Does to have a specific identity equal community, commodifying, quantifying, ghettoizing, solidarity, security or a possible false sense of security as in "artificial" unifier and/or qualifier?

I have no faith I have no identity but...being Jewish has on some levels fostered and forged despite "ME" an identity which for myself and many has become the common denominator. WE ARE THE CHOSEN PEOPLE, but chosen for WHAT?

How does identity work for us?? Race, religion, food, customs, behavioral patterns, history, lore, caricatures, stereo-types all explored in these volumes. How one observes traditions as well as one's self. Many Jews are locked into or always struggling with these IDENTITY issues. Always viewing, exploring and questioning one's surroundings even one's own inhabited SHELL as both insider and outsider.

2. Culture

What makes a Jew and Jewish culture so rich, is a keen sense of fairness, the good/evil dichotomy (amongst a host of other dualities), leadership (albeit for the corruption which permeates everything), persecution, freedom and yearning for knowledge through reading, and as stated above, searching, arguing and questioning (as in the Talmud), be it through religion, the arts, education or simply complex philosophical meandering. As the editors state in their preface to volume 1, the aim of this anthology is a kind of manumission from myth, artificially induced death, disregard and blatant erasure of fact by bringing "to life" a "lost world," with "its remnants, and its successors" thereby creating "an unusual popular" and may I add newly revised and re-invigorated "history of" what was for all intents and purposes, outside perhaps museums, synagogues, private memorabilia and souvenirs, that relatively forgotten and in many cases discarded "lost world" through the eyes, ears, minds and souls of those "acquainted with nontraditional as well as conservative Jewish life and persons." The authors, storytellers, poets and thinkers of all ilk in these 3 volumes make "this project a learning experience," an expansive, heart-rending journey, with each step taken, each tale told, each revealing chapter, story and verse as rich, diverse, introspective, entertaining and wide ranging as the Bible itself. Adding to, expanding and (im)parting, like the Red Sea, a way for the reader, the searcher with an inquisitive mind, to escape the "philistines" and cross the great divide between religions, cultures, prejudices, personalities, converging, diverging and newly emerging histories.

The essence of Jewish law is about knowing, teaching, exploring, debating and sharing, its central rivet and rite of passage being Mentschlekeit, which, if practiced by all, might possibly be humanity's and the world's saving grace. What we have here in the pages of this beyond-valuable-of-almost-biblical-proportions three volume set is the continuation of the search and many relevant insights into it, both personal and objective, secular and religious, from gangsters to peddlers to kibitzers to politicos to grandmas, stories of family, food, edifice, music, theater, rebellion and legend. And like the essence of Judaism itself and the "word" Jew with all the implications and mystery it invokes, they are filled with insight, seriousness, wit, intellect and kvetching...

According to that law we need not seek heaven for heaven is right here on earth... so peruse these pages...open them gently as you would a scroll...take the plunge...awaken.

3. Conclusions

Recently while standing on the Brighton Beach subway platform after a nice day at the beach I was approached by 2 Chassid followers of the great Chabad Rebbe Menachem Mendel Schneerson. One asked me if I was Jewish. I said yes but that I was a secular Jew. To this he responded "There is no such thing as a secular Jew. A Jew is a Jew is a Jew," to which my wife answered, He's right. Everyone says the same thing. He looked at my wife who is Asian. I remarked "She's not a Jew," whereupon he replied "That's O.K. Non-Jews are O.K. too," and he handed her some literature as well about The Seven Universal Laws – The True Way to Peace. He seemed like a real Mentsch. We both thanked him and as he turned to leave us reminded me once again, "ALWAYS REMEMBER. A JEW IS A JEW IS A JEW." "Thanks," I said, "I will."

steve dalachinsky - nyc - june 2012

FOREWORD

I suspect that I met Clayton Patterson the way most people do. Recommended by a (Jewish) friend in the neighborhood, I rang the bell on his graffiti-covered metal door next to the gated storefront windows behind which are usually displayed strange and wonderful pieces of art and sculpture cluttered amongst other detritus of the Clayton Patterson Gallery and Outlaw Art Museum on the Lower East Side of New York City.

For many years Patterson, along with his partner in crime, Elsa Rensaa, have continuously documented the evolving history of the LES, photographing and videotaping police actions, fires, evictions, and political and legal proceedings, while also chronicling the Neighborhood's counter- and subcultures of art, poetry, religion, music, body art and mutilation. Patterson's life spent observing, collecting and creating the living-breathing historical art of New York's streets is not some ultimate contrivance designed to garner him fame or fortune. Patterson is the real deal, living his art because of this marvelous obsession with humanity in all its forms and shapes, stretched to our limits of wonder and desperation.

In this three volume anthology, Patterson has amassed a reasonable representative cross-cultural and historical documentation of the Jewish experience in Lower Manhattan spanning the last one hundred and fifty years. A true people's history, this compilation of nearly two hundred essays from an international array of historians, neighborhood preservationists, activists, artists, poets, journalists, filmmakers, regular people who grew up in the neighborhood, and other scholars provides an investigation and explanation of how this tiny, shrinking race/religion of fifteen million people has influenced not only New York City but every aspect of global society.

The first volume put together with Mareleyn Schneider examines the social and moral history of Judaism on the LES, from the public baths to the Jewish Defense Organization, to the peddlers, "tough guys" and politically powerful lifelong Lower East Siders, to "living the synagogue lifestyle." The second and third volumes are organized according to the artistic, political, business and professional contributions to modern culture made by the individuals or socio-political groups and other movements described in each essay. The wildly diverse collection of writers, left to draw from their own experience, unfiltered by editorial agenda, has laid open the seldom seen guts of contemporary urban Jewish life from the sacred to the profane.

A huge debt is owed to Clayton Patterson, compassionate and Jewish by LES injection. He has managed to keep alive so many direct links in the history of an otherwise endangered people, much like the twelve original tribes who had embraced literacy, writing down and passing on their knowledge since the old testament. This anthology is a treasure trove of enduring wisdom that would otherwise disappear.

Jody Weiner

Jody Weiner wrote the novel Prisoners of Truth, *co-authored* Kinship With Animals, *and co-edited* Resistance: A Radical Social and Political History of the Lower East Side; Raise Your Other Right Hand is his new novel on the way.

http://www.jodyweiner.com

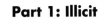

Part 1: Illicit

Some Meanings of MJ
in Lower East Side Jewish Culture

Eric Miller

This essay discusses what MJ has meant to certain Lower East Side Jews: those Jews who are basically atheist and progressive, and who have respect for the MJ experience. What MJ symbolizes to these people provides a key to the worldviews of this culturally significant group.

To begin with, let us consider atheist, progressive Lower East Side Jewish culture in general. New York City's Lower East Side has been the proverbial and actual gateway to the USA for many generations of people entering the country from Europe and elsewhere. Many of these immigrants settled in the LES. Today in 2008, the LES continues to have a strong international atmosphere. The LES has long been a center of progressive thought and activism, Jewish and other. This culture has been based on the ideals of equality and of people helping each other. This is a particular vision of a "more perfect union" (in the words of the USA Constitution). It is a utopian vision.

Many groups that settled in the LES have retained their group cohesiveness, and have remained relatively exclusionary of others. But this could not be the case with atheist progressive Jews. It has been said that one of the contributions of Jews to world culture has been skepticism.[1] However, when this approach of doubting and questioning is applied to the group's own religion – including the existence of the group's divine figure – the result can, to some degree, be a dissolving of one's Jewishness. Thus, an atheist progressive Jewish family is often just a one- or two-generation phenomenon. For the further one moves from religious belief, and from living in the midst of a community of believers, the more likely it is that one's children may also grow away from the traditional culture and may marry outside the group. This is especially so in the case of atheist progressive Jews, who tend to feel that the ideal society is multicultural and multiracial.

Despite their belief that there are no divine figures, atheist Jews may still be very aware of the story of their tribe, and may even relate to aspects of this story. For example, a defining moment in Jewish history is Moses leading the Jews out of slavery, out of Egypt. This episode is exemplified by the expression, "Let my people go!" This motif supplies a basic aspect of Jewish identity, and may partly explain the "liberation mentality" that has been especially ascribed to progressive Jews. The "liberation mentality" refers to a mindset that seeks to help liberate oneself and all others, on all levels.

Two other motifs central to the Jewish experience are the tribe, having left Egypt, 1) wandering in the desert, and 2) entering the "promised land," the "land of milk and honey" (like socialism/communism, this is also a utopian vision).

Throughout much of history, most Jews have lived away from the culture's place of origin. Thus, the expression, the "wandering Jew." Although Jews have partly been of the other cultures in which they have lived, to some extent they have also remained detached from those cultures.

Jews tend to emphasize the importance and value of reading. Reading aloud before the community marks entry to adulthood. Traditionally, Jews have especially read and discussed the 613 laws that are pronounced in the Torah (the first five books of the Old Testament: Genesis, Exodus, Leviticus, Numbers, and Deuteronomy), and the writings of the many generations of commentators on these 613 laws.

These factors – the partial non-involvement with local cultures, and the incessant reading of the group's laws and commentaries on these laws – have, culturally speaking, contributed to the formation of sharp minds, with (on certain levels) highly developed reasoning skills and much skepticism.

Two of the intellectual founders of modernism were Jews: Karl Marx (1818-1883, founder of communism, who lived mostly in London), and Sigmund Freud (1856-1939, founder of psychoanalysis, who lived mostly in Vienna). Both of these thinkers can be seen as outsiders to the European societies in which they lived, who pointed out disquieting underlying factors in these societies – alienated peasants and workers in Marx's case, and a dangerous unconscious in Freud's case. In so doing, they exposed tension and turmoil that had until then been hidden under neat and pleasant surfaces.[2]

The analysis and criticism of, and detachment from, certain conventional social norms is thus a longstanding tradition among atheist Jews. An uncompromising desire for truth is part of Jewish culture – especially atheist Jewish culture. Sentimentality, comfort, and conventional community, are not the highest priorities (at least in principle) among atheist progressive Jews. The model for behavior, for Jews in general, is rather: leaving what has been one's home, and wandering in the wilderness – for the sake of achieving freedom and fulfilling one's destiny.

The Torah tells the story of humanity from the beginning of the universe, to Jews escaping from Egypt, wandering in the desert, and reaching the Holy Land. The Jewish cultural experience involves reliving this epic story each year, week by week. The Jewish new year—the anniversary of G-d's creation of the cosmos—begins on September 5 at the earliest, and October 5 at the latest. Each Saturday, sections of the Torah relating to successive episodes of the story are read aloud in synagogues. Even though atheist Jews deny the objective truth of various aspects of the Torah, the epic story it tells in the yearly cycle forms a background of the existence of such individuals, if they are at all related to Jewish culture.

To what long-term future does the atheist progressive Jew typically look forward? Not a "return" to the Holy Land (the state of Israel being seen as a problematic and largely-failed effort to live side-by-side with Arab peoples); nor a divinely-wrought heaven on earth; nor the flourishing of the Jewish tribe; nor entrance to heaven (which is not stressed in Judaism anyway). What remains, then, is the desire and hope for a global egalitarian society, in which no one automatically accepts any traditions or conventions. The urge for this utopia can be seen as a transformed, secular version of the traditional Jewish urge to reach the Holy Land. In this transformed vision, instead of what is now the state of Israel, it is the international-flavored LES—and beyond, the rest of the USA, and the rest of the world—that is the (potential) "land of milk and honey."

Now that we have a general picture of the atheist progressive LES Jewish mindset, let us see how MJ fits into the picture.

First of all, it should be noted that many atheist progressive LES Jews today do not respect the MJ experience in the least; and that MJ was abhorred by the "Old Left" (that which was associated with the Communist Party), every bit as much as it was by the "Right":

> For years the great centers of Puritanism of consciousness, of blackout and persecution of the subtle vibrations of personal consciousness catalyzed by [mj], have been precisely Moscow and Washington, the centers of the human power war. Fanatical rigid mentality pursuing abstract ideological obsessions make decisions in the right-wing mind of America, pursuing a hateful war against a mirror-image of the same "sectarian, dogmatic" ideological mentality in the Communist camp. It is part of the same pattern that both centers of power have the most rigid laws against [MJ].[3]

In contrast, the "New Left," which came into its own in the Sixties, idealized flexibility and independence of thought, the escape from all dogma. Within New Left culture, to a large extent the MJ experience symbolized these ideals. Here, MJ was often perceived as "a catalyst to self-awareness,"[4] involving a discovery of one's personal sensory, emotional, and reasoning functions:

> [MJ] is a useful catalyst for specific optical and aural aesthetic
>
> perceptions.[5]
>
> [MJ] consciousness is one that, ever so gently, shifts the center of attention from habitual shallow purely verbal guidelines and repetitive secondhand ideological interpretations of experience to more direct, slower, absorbing, occasionally microscopically minute engagement with sensing phenomena.[6]
>
> [MJ catalyzes] ... a useful area of mind-consciousness to be familiar with, a creative show of the silly side of an awful big army of senseless but habitual thought-formations risen out of the elements of a language world.[7]

These observations came from Allen Ginsberg, a professional poet, who knew well both the powers and the limitations of words!

There have been many famous LES Jews who have spoken out on behalf of MJ. Among them are Abbie Hoffman, AJ Weberman, Aron Kay, Michael Cezar, and Ed Rosenthal. None have been as articulate as Allen Ginsberg. His 1966 article about MJ has, 42 years later, supplied most of the ideas reported on in the present essay.

Allen Ginsberg described how he enjoyed observing certain modern paintings while he was high on MJ, especially those of artists such as Cézanne, Picasso, and Klee. These works involve a shift from attention to actual objects to how the painter and viewer perceive those objects. While looking at these paintings and also at scenes of actual nature, "through the use of [MJ], awe and detail were made conscious."[8]

Especially in the Sixties, MJ was perceived to threaten "the mundane world of order."[9] This challenge to order was perceived positively by some, and negatively by others. MJ's proponents tended to feel that it had been criminalized in part because the MJ experience was a threat to intellectual and social control by authorities. As Steve Stollman puts it, MJ is illegal because "the system wants worker ants."[10] From this point of view, MJ is a catalyst by which people may de-program themselves from de-humanizing aspects of the dominant culture.

While the MJ experience was cast by its critics as mindless and selfish hedonism (pleasuring the senses), it was cast by its proponents as mind-expanding and community-building:

> By dissolving the firm hold of the logico-rational mind over the perception of reality, entheogens[11] propitiate, on the one hand, the appearance and observation of contents arising from pre-personal levels (their regressive aspect) and, on the other, the appearance and observation of contents arising from transpersonal levels (their transcendental aspect).[12]

Many proponents of the MJ experience believe it can help one to become aware of, comment upon, and develop alternatives to, the hollow competition, the materialism, and the lack of community, empathy, and love in the dominant culture (often referred to as "the rat-race").

It must be remembered that this vision of MJ crystallized in the late Sixties, in the time of the Vietnam War, which many felt had been based on lies (the USA's justification for entering the war, the Gulf of Tonkin incident, was indeed shown to have been a fabricated event). To many LES atheist progressive Jews, MJ represented Vietnam's opposite: truth, peace, non-violence, and the exploration of feelings, creativity, sensitivity, and one's own vulnerability:

> The Vietnam War may have convinced those who opposed it of the immorality of corporate American imperialism, but it was the emerging drug culture that helped frame an alternative to the system.[13]

> [Many] saw in capitalist consumerism a jittery wilderness of commercially generated false needs reinforcing (and in turn reinforced by) a false con-

sciousness, despoiling the environment in return for more stress than happiness.[14]

[The MJ experience exposed] the hollowness of the consumerist game. From this perspective, stoned thinking acts like the little boy noticing that the Emperor's new clothes are merely a birthday suit. It is not insignificant that from coast to coast, head shops of the period offered reproductions of the now-classic print of an alchemist breaking through the confines of his worldview and throwing back his arms in wonder at the sight of a new, unimagined sphere beyond.[15]

An "important aspect of this break-through in consciousness was that it could be shared."[16] The sense of a community of true seekers—who often had little more than (what they perceived to be) the truth, and each other—has been a large part of the MJ legend:

[Many] knew instinctively that distinguishing True from Bogus at the cosmic level involved a more meaningful exercise of personal responsibility than the blind acceptance of the Puritan paradigms of Right and Wrong that tumbled America into the Vietnam War. At the same time, truth-questing could not be purely solitary; it demanded a degree of reality-checking unattainable without the engagement of one's most reliable peers. "I get high with a little help from my friends" says it best... Underground papers, alternative bookstores, and radical spirituality spread from coast to coast, and beyond.[17]

Of course, unlike Transcendentalism, transformational drug mysticism wasn't primarily an intellectual movement, and in this lay both its power and its weakness. The subtlety and fluidity of the drug experience, along with its unpredictability, opened the minds of initiates to a flowing, intuitive level of awareness not dependent on conventional education and thus broadly universal, but hard to communicate in words and highly vulnerable to verbal attack. Control freaks of the Left as well as the Right dismissed as incoherent what was merely inarticulate.[18]

The steady refusal of government and media to heed the urgent message of drugs drove them increasingly underground and eventually corrupted the drug culture as well. Not only did a rapacious black market drive the nickel bag off the streets and replace it with crack, but the entire context of drug use shifted from good vibes, exploration, and social engagement in the Sixties to violence, crime, and anomie in the Nineties.[19]

Some believe that MJ use promotes "associative intelligence, which William James calls the source of all genius."[20] Associative intelligence sees connections. It is an intelligence of empathy and love:

The drug culture awakened this connective consciousness in any number of ways, of which the rock festival, happening, and spontaneous eruption of community known as Woodstock became the immediate symbol.[21]

A circle of friends, or strangers, passing a joint around got high on more than the smoke. There was ritual involved in the shared defiance of law and convention; trust and solidarity in affirming the value of a forbidden alteration of consciousness; welcome into an officially despised class of mainstream pariah for whom inhibition could magically dissolve into hilarity. Above all, there was the act of sharing, giving away the illicit substance itself in rogue communion.[22]

"Dope" in this sense represents free-circulating, spontaneous Dionysian energy, just as "money" represents the reverse: hoarding, quantifying, and hierarchical disconnection. In times without money, there is always community to fall back on, as "poor" cultures repeatedly demonstrate; in times without community, the comforts of property are few and cold, as "rich" cultures have shown with equal regularity.[23]

In the Sixties, some atheist progressive LES Jews especially associated MJ with certain aspects of African-American culture:

The suppression of Negro rights, culture, and sensibility in America has been complicated by the [MJ] laws. African sects have used [MJ] for divine worship (much as I have described its sacred use in India). And to the extent that jazz has been an adaptation of an African religious form to American context ... , [mj] has been closely associated with the development of this indigenous American form of chant and prayer. Use of [MJ] has always been widespread among the Negro population in this country, and suppression of its use, with constant friction and bludgeoning of the law, has been one of the major unconscious, or unmentionable, methods of suppression of Negro rights.[24]

Thus, for some atheist progressive Jews, MJ was associated with the Civil Rights Movement, and buying MJ from African-Americans and smoking it with them was part of this Movement.

Among LES Jews who believed in the positive qualities of the MJ experience, criminalization of MJ was associated with both the psychological suppression of aspects of one's self, and the social-economic-political suppression of communities of color (and the dominant culture's efforts to keep people apart). On all of these levels then, the embrace of MJ was an aspect of liberation mentality.

Had it not fostered an awakening of community, the drug culture would have been no more than the exercise in hedonism its detractors have always branded it. They failed to see its wider implications, or else have felt actively threatened by them.[25]

> In the main, [MJ's] effect was ... fostering reappraisal and radicalism by uncorking regions of the mind long suppressed by the dominant culture of materialism.[26]

> The usurpation [by economics] had prevailed so thoroughly in the industrialized world that it might have continued unnoticed but for a social revolution fueled on the one hand by revulsion toward an unjust war, and on the other by drugs. *The Doors of Perception*, as Aldous Huxley titled the book recounting his mescaline experiences, were flung open, and life in the West has never been the same.[27]

> Of course, there are regressive forces in our society who would like nothing better than to shut those doors and pretend they never opened, and they have succeeded to the degree that they completely set the terms of debate about drugs... If drugs are so awful, why are they popular? There are no ad campaigns in their behalf comparable to those promoting alcohol and tobacco. On the contrary, they are fervently damned from every electronic pulpit, though their opponents dare not call them subversive outright, for fear of being asked what is it they subvert.[28]

One may ask: "Shall our children pray to an authoritarian Sky Daddy who will keep them in line, or to an inner source of Wisdom who will help their souls to flower?"[29] Proponents of the MJ experience might likely choose the latter option, and might feel that MJ use can correspond to this path, as the center of authority that MJ tends to direct one to is the self—both to one's body, and to one's own intellectual and moral processes and decisions. There seems to be something about the chemical components of MJ that facilitate many people to perceive the artificialness, the constructed quality, of ideologies, governments, nations, and hierarchical social situations in general. As mentioned, the MJ experience seems, among its proponents, to be associated with a feeling of escaping boundaries (including relating to belief systems and cultural norms that one had previously accepted without question), and of achieving a mystical sense of oneness with others and with nature. One aspect of this escape can involve the feeling that one had previously been brainwashed into believing untruths, including about MJ itself:

> When the citizens of this country see that such an old-time, taken-for-granted, flag-waving, reactionary truism of police, press, and law as the "reefer menace" is in fact a creepy hoax, a scarecrow, a national hallucination ... , what will they begin to think of the whole of taken-for-granted public REALITY?... What of other issues filled with the same threatening hysteria? The spectre of Communism? Respect for the police and courts? Respect for the Treasury Department? If [MJ] is a hoax, what is Money? What is the War in Vietnam? What are the Mass Media?[30]

In short:

> There's nothing quite as effective in undermining a young person's respect for the law as when one tries [MJ] and finds it to be benign and fun and at times profound.[31]

While doing research for this essay in October 2007, I visited the Yippie Museum Cafe on the LES one evening.[32] Although I did not know if they were atheist, progressive, Jewish, or of the LES, I asked some of those present, "What does MJ mean to you?"

One person said, "MJ helps me to remember what is important. It helps me to keep perspective, and to not be distracted or overwhelmed by the little problems in life."

Another said, "For me, smoking MJ is like taking off the top half of my skull, and just letting my brain and mind air out for a while. It is a meditative experience."

One young lady said enthusiastically, "Wholesome living!" At first I was shocked. How could a substance that is considered just the opposite of that by the dominant culture be thought of as wholesome? But then I thought about where her statement seemed to be coming from. For many progressive people, especially those who have lived in the countryside, MJ is part of the lifestyle of growing one's own vegetables, often organically, and of producing what one needs with one's own labor. After all, MJ is an herb, which can be made into a tea, or eaten. From this perspective, MJ is antithetical to synthetic and processed drugs, and to inauthentic living in general.

In this culture, MJ is not associated with "partying," but rather with thinking and talking, with imagining and planning improvement of relationships and society. To review, from this point of view MJ symbolizes 1) psychological freedom, 2) the primacy of personal experience and thought, 3) a community of adherents to truth and tolerance, and 4) the unity of races. Here, MJ is not generally associated with addiction: addiction is thought to flourish primarily in the realms of nicotine (tobacco), alcohol, white-powder drugs such as cocaine and heroin, many synthetic/artificial/manufactured drugs, and money and capitalism. "Who would dispute that the number one out-of-control abused substance in America today is money?"[33] Actually, in this context the MJ experience is sometimes seen as a potential antidote to all of these addictions, and to addictiveness in general.

As for the idea of MJ facilitating paranoia: Proponents of the MJ experience have suggested that such thoughts arise in people largely due to their government's criminalization of the substance, and thus also of the experience; as well as to the fact that the MJ altered-state-of-mind tends to facilitate a thoughtful facing of one's self, and this can be a harrowing experience.

While it has been a great joy to atheist progressive Jews to have found that many aspects of the USA are in sympathy with their ideals (of course, many aspects of the USA have helped to shape these ideals), it has greatly frustrated them to have found that other aspects of the USA are not in sympathy with their ideals. The coming-of-age process of atheist progressive Jews in the USA has been described well by Mark Rudd:

> It was on or about my bar mitzvah that it occurred to me, like happens to so many other Jewish kids, that God probably doesn't exist, that He's a social construct, just like all other gods.[34]

> Morally and emotionally we could not fit into the civilized world of the racist, defense-oriented modern university. Such was our ordeal of civility.[35]

> We were good Jewish kids, the cream of the crop, who had accepted the myths of America—democracy, opportunity for all, good intentions toward the world—and of the university—free and open inquiry toward the truth. We were betrayed by our country and the university when we learned, in a relative instant, that the reality wasn't even close to these myths.[36]

> Perhaps our anger was derived in some unconscious way from the famed prophetic tradition in Judaism.[37]

> I proudly acknowledge the drive for education in Jewish culture which made me want to read about the world and to understand it and to become a teacher. I also recognize that in my social activism I am one of thousands working in the grand tradition of Jewish leftists, the Trotskys and the Emma Goldmans and the Goodmans and Schwerners of the twentieth century. I honor this lineage. As Jews our advantage in the past, though, was that we were outsiders critically looking in; today Jews sit at the right hand of the goy in the White House advising him whom to bomb next in order to advance the Empire. To be outsiders in a nation or an empire is not such a terrible thing. Keeping critical and alert has allowed the Jewish people to survive all sorts of imperial disasters over the millennia.[38]

Although progressive Jews who respect the MJ experience may be non-religious themselves, many are aware that

> Religious communities worldwide are at the vanguard of wise entheogen use. In the United States the Native American population uses plant entheogens (peyote) for its ceremonies. In West Africa the psychedelic plant iboga is used in rituals. In India, the religious use of a psychedelic called soma was featured in the Rig Veda, and entheogens have been a part of south Asian religious practice for millennia. For two thousand years, initiates into the Greek Eleusinian Mystery School would consume a powerful vision-enhancing drug called kykeon.[39] In South America the sacred use of the psychedelic ayahuasca[40] has moved from the native populations of the Amazon Basin into the urban centers where it is the central sacrament in their religious praxis.[41]

In India, MJ has been used since time immemorial by tribal people for a variety of recreational, medical, and spiritual purposes; and by saddhus, especially in relation to the worship of Siva.

Religions of the Roman empire included Mithraism, which exists today as Zoroastrianism. This religion's birthplace was Persia (modern-day Iran):

> Mithraism's sacrament, haoma, was virtually identical to ... soma, in Brahmanism [in what today is India]. Worshipped as a god, soma was a

plant without leaves or roots that needed little light and induced religious ecstasy. It was most likely amanita muscaria: a magic mushroom. In ancient Rome, sharing the haoma cemented the bond of brotherhood of emperors, bureaucrats and soldiers.[42]

The Jewish people

have a long tradition of altering consciousness for spiritual purposes. The ritual use of wine in Judaism is ubiquitous for organizing blessings and celebrations. It is a sacrament that has been used for centuries as an adjunct to prayer precisely for its consciousness-shifting qualities. Fasting is another ancient tradition of the Jewish people that is used as a means to alter consciousness in order to access places of deep grief and heightened moral introspection.[43]

In 1935, a Slovakian linguist identified the plant known as "fragrant cane" in the English Bible as flowering [MJ]... Ancient people were fascinated by herbs and their healing powers, and knew much more about them than we do; at least about mixing herbs to release their potency.[44]

Ancient wines were always fortified, like the "strong wine" of the Old Testament, with herbal additives: opium, datura, belladonna, mandrake and henbane. Common incenses, such as myrrh, ambergris and frankincense are psychotropic; the easy availability and long tradition of [MJ] use would have seen it included in the mixtures. Modern medicine has looked into using [MJ] as a pain reliever and in treating multiple sclerosis. It may well be that ancient people knew, or believed, that [MJ] had healing power.[45]

An important starting point of the Jewish people's mission was Moses' receiving a great truth in the form of an overpowering blast from a burning bush (through which it is said that G-d spoke to Moses). This episode is somewhat evocative of the smoking of MJ.

In Judaism, then, there are: the anointed oils, the incense, the burning bush, and the wine that goes with numerous ritual celebrations. There was also manna. As the story has it, manna was the Jews' exclusive food during their 40 years in the desert, after the provisions they took with them from Egypt were exhausted. Manna, it is said, formed on the ground. It was considered to be a supernatural substance, descended during the night, and associated with the morning dew. It needed to be collected before sunrise, as it dissolved in the sun. It has been suggested that manna was in fact hallucinogenic mushrooms.[46]

In Jewish culture, the past is composed of the story of the beginning of the cosmos, up to the Jews' enslavement in Egypt. The present holds the opportunity for escape, and for achieving utopia: the MJ high, which often involves some feeling of euphoria, can be seen as corresponding to this sense of escape and utopia.

Atheist progressive Jews may relate at times to aspects of the Jesus figure, who, like them, was a Jew who broke certain Jewish rules. It may even be that the historical Jesus was not a stranger to the MJ experience:

> The word Christ does mean "the anointed one" and [it may be] that Christ was anointed with chrism, a [MJ] based oil that caused his spiritual visions. The ancient recipe for this oil, recorded in Exodus, included over 9 pounds of flowering [MJ] tops (known as kaneh-bosem in Hebrew), extracted into a hin (about 11 pints) of olive oil, with a variety of other herbs and spices. The mixture was used in anointments and [incenses] that ... allowed the priests and prophets to see and speak with Yahweh.[47]

> Residues of [MJ], moreover, have been detected in vessels from Judea and Egypt in a context indicating its medicinal, as well as visionary, use. Jesus is described by the apostle Mark as casting out demons and healing by the use of this holy chrism. Earlier, from the time of Moses until the later prophet Samuel, holy anointing oil was used by the shamanic Levite priesthood to receive the "revelations of the Lord." The chosen ones were drenched in this potent [MJ] oil.[48]

> Indeed, [some scholars posit] that Jesus was probably not born the messiah but acquired the title when he was anointed with [MJ] oil by John the Baptist. The baptism in the Jordan was probably to wash away the oil after it had done its work. The early Christians fought hard for followers in the ancient world, recognizing the similarity of their own "foreign" god and his eucharistic meal to the Greek gods. Various sects and even the elite in what would eventually become the Roman Catholic church probably used the full range of available entheogens for baptism, ordination and the eucharistic meal.[49]

Eating bread and drinking wine together is at the heart of Christian ritual.[50] Drinking wine together is also an important aspect of Jewish ritual. Wine is an intoxicant, and, as mentioned above, both wine and wheat were often "fortified" in the ecstatic religious practices of the ancient world.

The questions then arise:

> Would the Psalmist who saw "the mountains skip like rams, the hills like young lambs," be kicked out of the canon if he turned out to have been tripping? Would the visions of Isaiah and Ezekiel, images of singing trees and clouds filled with cherubim, lose their validity if sacred mushrooms had brought them on? Or would they retain their power as symbols of the ravishingly beautiful spiritual energy latent within physical form, beckoning timelessly to the captive human mind, teasing it out of the solemn prisons of fear and calculation, tickling it with enchantment and mirth, and guiding it into a new sphere, no longer unimagined, of harmony, community, and love?[51]

> What is it about drugs that, like sex, so fiercely vexes the Puritan mind? Why is it a given in our culture that religious ecstasies, creative visions, or just simple elation, are more discredited if drug-induced than if laid to the influence of music, poetry, nature, a page of Scripture, or a pretty face?[52]

The culture of atheist, progressive, MJ-respecting LES Jews continues to develop. From this culture's point of view:

Following the Sixties—which was a seminal golden age for the MJ experience—the "subsequent burgeoning of environmental reverence, of non-sectarian and body-affirming spirituality, of holistic therapies and egalitarian liberationist politics," have in part been the MJ experience's offspring.[53]

"Despite unwavering governmental, societal, and parental disapproval, the consciousness scouts of the Sixties found and supported each other, confirmed one another's resolve, and laid the foundations of a transformed global culture."[54]

And, "[MJ] and versions of the African ritual music (rock and roll) are slowly catalyzing anti-ideological consciousness of the new generations."[55]

Works Cited

Chadwick, David. "Psychoactivism." In *Zig Zag Zen: Buddhism and Psychedelics*, Allan Hunt Badiner and Alex Grey, eds., San Francisco: Chronicle Books, 2002, pp. 115-123.

Cuddihy, John Murray. *The Ordeal of Civility: Freud, Marx, Levi-Strauss and the Jewish Struggle With Modernity.* New York: Basic Books, 1974.

Ginsberg, Allen. "The Great [Mj] Hoax." *Atlantic Monthly*, Nov 1966, 8 pages. http://tinyurl.com/2wrw6m .

Mo Hanan, Stephen. "Out of the Psychedelic Closet." *Tikkun*, Sept 1995, Vol. 10, Issue 5, 15 pages.

Ruck, Carl. "Was There a Whiff of [Mj] about Jesus?" *The Sunday Times*, 12 Jan 2003, p. 9.

Rudd, Mark. "'Why Were There So Many Jews in SDS?': A Talk for the New Mexico Jewish Historical Society." 2005. (SDS is Students for a Democratic Society, founded in the Sixties.) http://tinyurl.com/yrcffj .

Ziegler, Michael. "Psychedelic Religious Experience." *Tikkun*, Jan/Feb 2004, Vol. 19, Issue 1, 4 pages.

Eric Miller is a native New Yorker transplanted to Chennai (on India's southeast coast), where he has co-founded the World Storytelling Institute (www.storytellinginstitute.org). His website is titled Storytelling and Videoconferencing *(www.storytellingandvideoconferencing.com).*

[1] Steve Stollman, personal communication, October 2007.

[2] Cuddihy; as cited by Rudd, p. 5.

[3] Ginsberg, p. 8.

[4] Ibid.

[5] Ibid., p. 6.

[6] Ibid., p. 1.

[7] Ibid.

[8] Ibid., p. 6.

[9] Ibid., p. 3.

[10] Personal communication, October 2007.

[11] The word, "entheogen," is derived from the Greek word, entheos, which means "god-inspired within" (Ruck, p. 9). Entheogens are (mostly plant-based) sacramental consciousness-altering substances, especially those used by shamans to assist in achieving mystical/spiritual ecstasy.

[12] Zeigler, p. 2.

[13] Mo Hanan, p. 3

[14] Ibid.

[15] Ibid.

[16] Ibid.

[17] Ibid.

[18] Ibid.

[19] Ibid. p. 4.

[20] Ibid., p. 5.

[21] Ibid.

[22] Ibid.

[23] Ibid.

[24] Ginsberg, p. 6.

[25] Mo Hanan, p. 5.

[26] Ibid., p. 6.

[27] Ibid.

[28] Ibid.

[29] Ibid., p. 15.

[30] Ginsberg, p. 7.

[31] Chadwick, p. 122.

[32] Yippie Museum Cafe, 9 Bleeker Street, New York, NY 10012. The Yippie Museum documents the history of the Yippie Movement, which was founded by people of the culture discussed in this essay (such as Abbie Hoffman), and others, in the Sixties.

[33] Mo Hanan, p. 6.

[34] Rudd, p. 1.

[35] Ibid., p. 3.

[36] Ibid.

[37] Ibid.

[38] Ibid., p. 5.

[39] Kykeon may have contained ergot, an hallucination-inducing fungus that grows on wheat.

[40] Derived from vines native to the Amazonian rainforest.

[41] Zeigler, p. 1.

[42] Ruck, p. 9.

[43] Zeigler, p. 2.
[44] Ruck, p. 9.
[45] Ibid.
[46] http://en.wikipedia.org/wiki/Manna
[47] Ruck, p. 9.
[48] Ibid.
[49] Ibid.
[50] Ibid.
[51] Mo Hanan, p. 6.
[52] Ibid.
[53] Ibid., p. 5.
[54] Ibid., p. 3.
[55] Ginsberg, p. 8.

Jews With Guns:
The Jewish Gangster On The Lower East Side

David H. Katz

Tough and ruthless, the Jewish gangster was as murderous as any Irish street thug, as Machiavellian as any Castellammarese capo, as crazy as any Serbian anarchist. Blessed with chutzpah (aka: nerve, big balls) and seichel (Yiddish for smarts, brains; the kind of cunning and cleverness you don't find in shul) the matzo Mafia proved as dexterous with a .38 and an ice pick as with a pencil and an eyeshade, as gifted at extortion, loan sharking, prostitution, gambling, murder, and all 'round gangland mayhem as their more respectable co-religionists were at medicine, science, business and law.

"The very idea of a Jewish gangster goes against basic stereotypes of Jews, stereotypes that explain the place of Jews in the world. Jews are physically unthreatening office creatures,"[56] writes Rich Cohen in *Tough Jews*, his invaluable history of, and meditation upon, Jews as gangsters and gangsters as Jews, and their impact on Jewish culture and identity, especially for American Jews that came of age during World War II. To their descendants, second- or third-generation American Jews, comfortably middle class or better and well assimilated into the fabric of American life, the notion of Jews as mobsters and murderers, steeped in vice, running rackets, peddling drugs, and perpetrating the kind of extreme, remorseless violence seen in Mafia movies and on Discovery channel documentaries, seemed unthinkable. It was an affront to their core belief, perhaps naïve, perhaps chauvinistic, that Judaism and Jewish life is essentially righteous, law abiding, ordered, Godly, kind, compassionate and just; ethical, in concordance with the spirit and the dictates of the Torah. With so much violence historically perpetrated on the Jewish people, for them, this may well be, if not a moral truth, then an emotional one. And within life's uncertainties and vicissitudes, despite the daily personal shortcomings common to all, for most Jews, this paradigm more or less holds true. The idea that Jews can be as amoral, as down and dirty, as nasty and sadistic as the rest of humanity is not an idea that resonates well in the larger Jewish community, where assimilation and respectability, achievement and social mobility, are the goals and rewards for a righteous life. Denial is strong; just as many Jews cannot bring themselves to believe that a Jewish army, like any army of any race, creed, politics or religion, is capable of repression, occupation or atrocity, thereby holding Jews to an unrealistic, unattainable moral superiority that is, ironically, another philosophical trap door in the illogical edifice of anti-Semitism, the Jewish gangster is more often than not portrayed as a mere advisor, an accountant or a misplaced business consultant. As Cohen points out, "They are seen as number crunchers, financial geniuses, who could have worked their craft as easily on Wall Street as on Hester Street."[57]

As well they did. But in the reality of early 20th century urban American life, that didn't mean that when called upon by circumstance or necessity, Jews weren't just as capable, or as willing, as any other ethnic group, as any other tribe of human beings, to shoot, knife, garrote, club, poison or strangle their enemies, and dump the bodies in the East River.

While the fabled Hebraic flair for finance, organization and management, from tracking the odds in a floating crap game to fixing the vig on a "personal" loan, to laundering of millions of dollars of "dirty" money, runs like the blue thread of a tzitzit though the tallis of 20th century organized crime, the logic of the gun also runs close beside it. "Nothing personal, it's just business," the apocryphal final comment many a "business competitor" might have heard at the end of a less-than-fruitful "transaction," is a quintessentially Yiddishkeit understatement regarding commercial enterprises that happen to settle financial misunderstandings with bullets and shivs. The phrase was coined by Otto "Abbadabba" Berman, born Otto Biederman, an accountant and advisor to Dutch Schultz (born Arthur Flegenheimer). It has entered the popular consciousness through film and fiction; its dual meaning signifies that when push came to shove, a man like Meyer Lansky, who could track dice games and calculate complex mathematical equations and algebraic expressions in seconds, using neither pen or paper, just his yiddisha kup, also had no qualms about having troublesome individuals "taken for a ride"—even if his personal involvement was limited to the unspoken agreement, signaled with a nod, a wink, a handshake or a glance.

And the crucible for these kinds of men, these kinds of Jews, dangerous Jews, Jews With Guns, and the guts to use them—was far and away the Lower East Side of Manhattan.

The Teeming Streets

Between roughly 1880 and 1924, when massive emigration from Eastern Europe was choked off by an increasingly xenophobic America, the teeming streets of the Lower East Side—Division, East Broadway, Canal, Allen, Ludlow, Orchard, Houston and their immediate environs, contained—just barely—the largest population of Jews outside Warsaw. In 1881 the assassination of Tsar Alexander II of Russia unleashed a vitriolic campaign of government-led anti-Semitism, and the "huddled masses, yearning to breath free" left in droves to come to the New World. Two-thirds of Eastern Europe's Jewish population, nearly two million people, came from beyond the Jewish Pale of Russia (which then included what is now Poland), fleeing prejudice, pogroms and compulsory conscription (at age 12) into the Tsarist army; seeking refuge and riches, if not on streets paved with gold, then through the promises and protections of "liberty" or whatever that abstract concept might mean in America; hopefully, religious freedom, reasonable employment, decent education and opportunity for their children.

What they found on New York's Lower East Side were densely packed slums, exploitive factory owners, crowded sweatshops with draconian working conditions, grinding poverty and new forms of squalor unimaginable even for the former inhabitants of Eastern Europe's impoverished shetls. "It is said that nowhere in the world are so many people crowded together on a square mile as here," wrote Jacob Riis of what was called "Jewtown" in his landmark 1890 study, *How The Other Half Lives*, describing downtown's densely packed slums:

> The densest crowding of Old London, I pointed out before, never got beyond a hundred and seventy-five thousand. Even the alley is crowded out. Through dark hallways and filthy cellars, crowded, as is every foot of the street, with dirty children, the settlements in the rear are reached. Thieves know how to find them when pursued by the police, and the tramps that sneak in on chilly nights to fight for the warm spot in the yard over some baker's oven. They are out of place in this hive of busy industry and they know it. It has nothing in common with them or with their philosophy of life, that the world owes the idler a living. Life here means the hardest kind of work almost from the cradle. The world as a debtor has no credit in Jewtown. Its promise to pay wouldn't buy one of the old hats that are hawked about Hester Street, unless backed by security representing labor done at lowest market rates.[58]

As with all the great immigrant populations—Irish, German, Italian, Asian—the vast majority of Jews in America were not necessarily perfect citizens of their adopted country, but at least they tried to *be* citizens, people who went to work, obeyed the law, paid taxes, and voted (at times more than once, and at times from the grave) for their benefactors in Tammany Hall, the Democratic political machine that dominated New York politics. They strove to assimilate, to speak English, which they learned in the great Settlement Houses and other institutions of the Lower East Side, like the Henry Street Settlement and the Educational Alliance on East Broadway. They sought employment, the unskilled congregating at the chazar mark, the work market, on the corner of Ludlow and Hester every morning, seeking day labor in the garment industry; others contracted to do poorly paid piecework, fabricating belts, buckles or shirt collars at home, for a pittance. Still others labored at factory lofts under horrifying conditions eighteen hours a day, for equally meager wages. Yet despite their economic plight, most of them were eager to adopt the customs and methods of their new home and grateful to be in America; they were patriotic, at times to extremes, and sought to pursue that often amorphous, elusive, loosely defined, sometimes triumphant, sometimes tragic American Dream.

However, there was perhaps a small minority who had other ideas, inclinations and methods. As reported by the great Herbert Asbury, and depicted on film by Martin Scorsese in *Gangs of New York*, (loosely derived from Asbury's book, among others) criminality has always flourished, and criminal gangs have operated in New York since the at least the early 1800s; colorful, strange and deadly, with oddball punk rock names like The Roach Guards, The Plug Uglies, The Whyos, The Dead Rabbits, The Gophers, The Forty Thieves, Shirt Tails, True Blue Americans and The Bowery Boys. Like fashion-forward gangs today, they wore distinctive outfits and colors: The True Blue Americans paraded about in stove-pipe hats and long black frock coats. The Plug Uglies sported crude football helmets, The Roach Guards wore blue striped pantaloons, The Dead Rabbits arrived in red stripes. They operated in and out of New York City's most wretched slum, the Five Points, located at the intersection of Anthony (now Worth), Orange (now Baxter), and Cross (now Park) Streets. The area formed a triangle about one mile square, bounded by Canal Street, the Bowery, Chatham Street (now Park Row), Pearl and Centre

Streets. The incongruously named Paradise Square, a small triangular park, located between Anthony (now Worth) and Cross (now Park) Streets and converged into Orange Street (now Baxter), served as a battleground, as did the Bowery. Most of the conflicts—bloody street battles—were territorial, ethnic and sectarian: Protestant versus Catholic, Native versus Immigrant, WASP versus Irish versus Italian. Later they became political: Irish gangs—the True Blue Americans, O'Connell Guards and Atlantic Guards supported the Democratic Party and its consummate political machine, Tammany Hall. The Bowery Boys and American Guards, headquartered in the Bowery, thugged for the Whigs or for anti-immigrant, anti-Irish Catholic Nativist groups, such as the American Party, which ran former President Millard Fillmore for the Presidency in 1856, and the secret Order of The Star Spangled Banner, also known as the Know Nothings (as in: "I know nothing," when questioned about their secret society.) The Irish dominated the Five Points until the Italians, mostly from southern Italy and Sicily in the 1880s, arrived, followed by the Jews beginning in the 1890s. Each new wave of immigrants fought to stymie the rise of their successors, invariably viewed as rivals for their slice of the American Dream. They each operated under the cruel yet not uncommon historical tradition of yanking up the ladder before their potential rivals could climb aboard.

The last to settle into Five Points in the late 1890s were Chinese and other Asians, and in the early 1900s, as reformers like Riis publicized the appalling conditions of these areas, slum clearance, the turn-of-the-century term for urban renewal, gradually gained momentum. Displaced Jews and the other members of 'the other half' were pushed up into the tenements of the Lower East Side; the Chinese remained in what came to be known as Chinatown, and the rest of the Five Points ironically became the area now known as Foley Square, home to city, state and federal courthouses and offices, where the jail known as The Tombs serves as the last remnant of the reign of The Whyos, the Plug Uglies, The True Blue Americans and the Roach Guards.

Monk Eastman and His Gang

The large Irish gangs waned in the 1890s, as many of the second- and third-generation Irish found a respectable if ironic niche in the Police and Fire Departments, Newly arrived Italians and Jews formed gangs to take their place, first for protection, then for crime. The first major Jewish criminal organization was the Eastmans Gang, led by Monk Eastman, born Edward Osterman around 1873.

Eastman came not out of poverty, but out of Brooklyn, where his respectable parents owned a restaurant. His father set Edward up in a pet shop, and he developed a lifelong affection for animals. However, business, in the conventional sense, proved not to be his calling. Around 1895 Eastman appeared in Manhattan, where he became a "sheriff" at New Irving Hall, a social club in Lower Manhattan linked with Tammany Hall. "Sheriffs" were jack-of-all-trade thugs responsible for keeping order in the social clubs, gambling parlors, whorehouses and urban resorts owned and frequented by gangster/politicians and their cronies. Eastman soon established a reputation for dispensing rough justice with a large wooden club, which bashed in the heads of unruly patrons. He would then gorge a ceremonial notch for every smashed skull. Forty-nine notches later the ambulance drivers nicknamed Bellevue's emergency room "the Eastman Pavilion."

Eastman left New Irving Hall to start his own gang, and by 1900 his organization numbered more than 1200 professional thugs, thieves, pickpockets, pimps and other less-than-savory, less-than-law-abiding characters. Income came from whorehouses (many on Chrystie, Allen and Grand Streets) and stuss games (a form of faro, similar to baccarat), and from providing a cruder, more rigorous form of "security" for political gatherings. There were also blackjacking services, handy for sending a message to a business competitor, a romantic rival, or both; along with the cut from a floating army of pickpockets, thieves and burglars. The gang called a dive on Chrystie Street home, where a frightening arsenal of slingshots, revolvers, blackjacks and brass knuckles, Eastman's favorite implement of assault, stood stockpiled for use. Eastman was now nicknamed Monk, short for "Monkey," due to his odd, fearsome, simian appearance. His face, smashed, twisted, mangled and scarred from street battles and other, more personal encounters, belied his inordinate fondness for cats, dogs, and birds. Going about his murderous rounds, gang in tow, Monk was easily recognizable, an undersized derby perched precariously on his head, shirt opened, a trained pigeon on his shoulder, a blackjack in his pants and a set of brass knuckles on each hand, which he boasted had never been used on a woman, although that is in dispute.

The origins of the gang were political: According to Albert Fried's excellent study *The Rise and Fall of the Jewish Gangster in America*, Eastman got his start as an organizer for Tammany: he made speeches, in a mocked yet much-imitated slang that became standard LES gangster patois, then led the fired-up crowd to a saloon and bought drinks for everyone, one of the kinder, gentler ways he insured that new citizens exercised their right to vote early and often. In return for political services like rounding up the "repeaters," intimidating recalcitrant voters and stuffing ballot boxes, Tammany Hall bailed him out when he got arrested, giving Monk protection, an essential element in any large-scale criminal enterprise. While fully capable of extreme violence, including murder, (Fried calls him "malevolence incarnate"), Eastman was not just a violent thug with a street gang to back him up, he was the forerunner of the more organized, more businesslike mobsters who were soon to take his place:

> "But to emphasize this side of his career, the side displayed by his 'ferocious and unusual appearance,' is to lose sight of what made Eastman what he was. . . In fact, Eastman's career was on the whole quite prosaic, and businesslike. Early on in life he was part of the Tenth Ward, clubhouse organization, an organic part of the system that controlled the city. He worked as bouncer in "Silver Dollar Smith's" famous saloon—the floor of which was inlaid with silver dollars—situated, not accidentally, across from the Essex Street Courthouse, the organization's home base and source of power. Silver Dollar Smith, a Jew whose real name was Charles Solomon (or was it Finklestein? Or Goldschmidt? No one knew for sure), was one of its high-ranking members, a status conferred upon him and them by their ability to round up votes."[59]

Eastman's main rival for control of the LES was The Five Pointers Gang, run by a dapper Italian immigrant and former professional boxer named Paolo Vaccarelli, who had adopted the Irish moniker of Paul Kelly. Kelly's gang was well regarded by the criminal cognoscenti of its day. In fact, young Chicago punks like Al Capone, Frankie Yale and Johnny Torrio traveled to New York to serve as apprentice gangsters in Kelly's organization. Kelly was urbane and educated; he could move smoothly in a more refined stratum of society. His New Brighton Dance Hall, a flashy club on Great Jones Street, was where, then as now, New York's moneyed classes came downtown to "slum" with the colorful criminal culture of the LES. Society matrons reveled in the perverse thrill of discussing the merits of Matisse with a man they suspected of being a murderer. The Five Pointers and the Eastmans Gang soon became rivals for the same territory, basically the area in and around the Bowery from Fourteenth Street down. In 1901 a Five Pointer shot Eastman in the stomach; he recovered. His gang soon retaliated. By 1903 open gang warfare raged on the streets of the Lower East Side; some skirmishes involved more than a hundred men; there were with shootouts on Rivington and Chrystie Streets. Tammany brokered sporadic peace agreements after an appalled citizenry demanded action. The quaint notion of a boxing match between Kelly and Eastman was floated and took place in an abandoned warehouse in the Bronx. The men fought to a bloody draw, and the war went on. Tammany finally sided with Kelly, cutting off the political protection Eastman and his gang needed to survive; shortly thereafter, Eastman, beaten to a pulp by a cop after a failed robbery, was convicted of the crime and sent to Sing Sing for ten years.

Zweibach and Zelig

His top lieutenant, the vicious Max Zweibach—a.k.a. Kid Twist, a.k.a. Kid Sly Fox— succeeded him. Zweibach earned his nickname by knocking off his main rival, Richie Fitzpatrick. In true latter day Godfather fashion, he invited Richie to a bar on Chrystie Street to settle their problems amiably over a few drinks; the "come, let us reason together" ruse. The lights went out; a shot rang out; when they came up, Fitzpatrick was extremely dead. Zweibach henceforth vowed that "no 'wop' and no 'mick' would rule over the Lower East Side of New York." In addition to gambling and protection rackets, the Kid swiftly cornered the monopoly on celery tonic, the Jewish soft drink of choice at the time.

Providing much of the muscle for these enterprises was one Samuel Teitsch, also known as Vach Lewis, also known as Cyclone Lewis, a former Coney Island strongman. His preferred method of execution was to twist, Superman style, iron rods around the victim's neck, similar to the ones he bent around his own neck in his act, without, of course, killing himself. (You can take the killer out of the circus but you can't take the circus out of the killer.) Cyclone systematically knocked off the rest of Fitzpatrick's cronies, blowing a troublesome gambling operator named The Bottler away in full view of twenty players at a stuss parlor on Suffolk Street, where he then became a partner.

Zweibach's reign was short-lived. On May 14, 1908, along with Cyclone, he was murdered outside a Coney Island bar by "Louie the Lump" Pioggi, reportedly in a dispute over a woman, although the presence of a horse-drawn carload of Five Pointers at the scene of the crime would perhaps indicate otherwise.

Zweibach's murder brought the Eastmans Gang to an end, but new gangs, new coalitions and entirely new organizations were forming, precursors to the explosion of much more highly organized crime that was to soon accompany Prohibition.

Monk himself had a curious destiny. Paroled from Sing-Sing in 1909, he returned to the LES to reestablish his gang, but descended to pickpocketing, robbery and selling opium. He floated in and out of prison between 1912 and 1917; then, at the age of 44, he assumed the name of William Delaney and enlisted in the New York National Guard. The doctor at the recruiting station noted Monk's battered, knife- and bullet-scared body and asked him what war he had served in; he mentioned some skirmishes on the Lower East Side. Sent to France, Monk distinguished himself with the 106th Infantry of the 27th Division, "O'Ryan's Roughnecks," and proved as fearless in the trenches as he was on Avenue A. Discharged in 1919, his citizenship was restored by Governor Al Smith, but the lure of dope peddling and, with Prohibition, bootlegging, proved too strong. On December 26, 1920 Eastman was shot to death in front of the Blue Bird Café on 14th Street, between Broadway and 4th Avenue, by a corrupt Prohibition Enforcement Agent. He was buried with full military honors at Brooklyn's Cypress Hill Cemetery, where he rests today.

With Zweibach gone, the largest remaining faction of the Eastmans Gang fell to his protege, Big Jack Zelig. Zelig was born in 1882, grew up on the Lower East Side and began as a thief and a pickpocket. His family of hardworking Russian Jews was reportedly affluent and educated; there seemed no reason for him to fall into a career of crime. Perhaps he just enjoyed it.

Zelig moved steadily up the ranks in the Eastmans Gang and, after the death of Kid Twist, solidified control with the help of a troika of murderous thugs: Jacob "Whitey Lewis" Seidenschnier, Louis "Lefty Louie" Rosenberg, and the infamous Harry "Gyp the Blood" Horowitz, whose specialty, despite his diminutive size, (five foot seven, 140 pounds) was grabbing a random passerby and breaking his back over his knee, usually on a bet. Along with Lewis, Lefty Louie, and a particularly nasty Italian named Francisco "Dago Frank" Cirofisi, Horowitz eventually moved uptown and started his own operation, The Lenox Hill Gang, committing muggings, burglaries and an occasional contract murder for Zelig.

The gang met its end when they were hired—probably by Zelig—to murder gambler Herman "Beansie" Rosenthal, a suspected police informant. He was shot several times outside the Metropole Hotel on July 16, 1912, in front of dozens of witnesses. The gang was quickly arrested. Once questioned, they told police that a corrupt NYPD detective named Charles Becker had hired them to silence Rosenthal, who had been blabbing about Becker's ties to brothels and gambling parlors. After a highly publicized trial, Gyp the Blood and his co-conspirators were convicted and put to death in the electric chair on April 13, 1914; Becker followed in 1915.

"Big" Jack Zelig was a complex figure: tough, resilient, expansive, smart and, in his time, legendary, particularly for his determination to push the Italian gangs out of the LES. Zelig personally iced a gunman named Julius Morrello who had been ordered to kill him. Not the brightest banana in the bunch, Morello barged through the door of the Stuyvesant Casino on Second Avenue, yelling "Where's that big Yid Zelig? I gotta cook that big Yid!" Morrello got "cooked" instead, in front of a roomful of witnesses. Amazingly, no one saw anything; in business matters, Big Jack was relentless and lethal. From a hospital bed with a bullet wound to the head, he had sent men to shoot up the Bowery headquarters of rival gangster Chick Trickster, and he had also survived another bullet wound to the neck in 1912.

All this gunplay on the Lower East Side finally prompted Tammany to pass the Sullivan Act, sponsored by Tammany boss Big Tim Sullivan, the leader of the same politicians and fixers who had used the gangs to enforce order in their brothels and casinos, and to bring out the voters as many times as possible for their crooked candidates on Election Day. The act banned the possession of unlicensed weapons, and remains to this day the primary instrument of gun control in the City of New York.

But it proved fatal to Big Jack Zelig. Fearing arrest or harassment, Zelig had sewed his pockets up and handed his gun off to an underling. Thus, on October 5, 1912, he was defenseless when a petty hoodlum shot and killed him on a Lower East Side trolley. A packet of letters found on his body implicated him in the murder of "Beansie" Rosenthal, and helped send his pals Whitey, Lefty and Gyp the Blood to the chair.

Dopey Fein, and Schtarkers and Schlammers

What was left of Zelig's organization was now taken over by one of its members, Benjamin "Dopey Benny" Fein, another intriguing and enigmatic character. Fein operates at the early intersection of the criminal underworld and the labor movement, beginning the pattern of collusion and symbiosis between organized crime and organized labor that, for better or worse, expanded and extended through the 20s, 30s and 40s with Meyer Lansky and Lucky Luciano, and on through the 50s, 60s and 70s with racketeers like Frank Costello, Jack Dragna, Sidney Korshak, and, of course, Jimmy Hoffa. Born circa 1887, he was nicknamed Dopey because of his slow speech and heavy eyelids, but Fein was no fool; he all but dominated labor racketeering in the late 1910s. Albert Fried called him a "specialist nonpareil in 'labor' or 'industrial relations.'"[60] Like so many of his fellow gangsters, Benny rose from abysmal poverty on the LES and became a thief and pickpocket at an early age, compiling an arrest record that included petty theft, assault, grand larceny and murder, of which he was acquitted twice for lack of evidence. He did time in Elmira Reformatory and Sing Sing for armed robbery and other offenses. Around 1905 Fein formed his own gang of pickpockets and pushcart thieves; in 1910 Fein joined Zelig's gang as a labor "slugger," a goon for hire by either labor or management.

By then the garment industry was undergoing rapid and radical change. Packed tenement sweatshops with extended families producing piece goods had given way to large corporate manufacturers who now dominated the apparel industry. They set up even larger sweatshops, in huge lofts, tightly regimented factories that churned out huge volumes of clothing for a national market at the lowest prices on earth, for some of the lowest wages on earth. For clothing, the Lower East Side was basically the China of its day. A seemingly endless tsunami of cheap immigrant labor was paid a meagerly daily or hourly rate and worked like animals under abysmal conditions: bad sanitation and ventilation, low light, long hours, no sick leave, no vacations. There was no such thing as unemployment insurance, medical benefits, disability insurance or worker's compensation; you're injured on the job, you starve; you complain, you're fired. There were no food stamps, or welfare: you don't work, you don't eat, and people did literally starve to death. Union strike funds were meager, if they existed at all; every branch of government—local, state and federal, along with the courts—was firmly in the pockets of big business, the trusts and the banks, who were murderously hostile to the interests of organized labor, working people, minorities and immigrants; there was little or no regulation of food, drugs or consumer goods. In short, it was the ideal world of the unfettered, unregulated and unchallenged free market, the plutocrat paradise today's Republican Party has been tirelessly working to restore.

In response, garment industry workers, many of them immigrants influenced by the ideals and methods of European—that is Russian, Polish and Austrian—socialism, organized trade unions to demand higher wages and better working conditions. Their only tool was strikes, a dangerous and at times lethal course of action in the early 20th century. In 1909 female shirtwaist workers struck and stayed out for six months; there were strikes by furriers and cloak makers; in 1913 and 1914 men's clothing unions walked off their jobs. Manufacturers hired scabs—nonunion labor—to break the strikes, along with "schlammers" and "bolagulas"—paid goons—to terrorize workers; unions hired "schtarkers" (their own goons) to terrorize the scabs, sabotage factories and fight the industry goons.

Zelig and his predecessors often played both sides of the fence, and while Big Jack had put the protection rackets he had inherited from Kid Twist on a more orderly and business like footing, Fein entirely revolutionized the relationship between criminality and class struggle by, as Fried puts it in Marxian terms, "rationalizing" the protection racket. He transformed it from ad hoc thuggery, akin to piece work, to a reasonably efficient business enterprise, like a cheese store, a restaurant or a garage, except the business was extortion, intimidation and at times murder. He established an agreed-to fee schedule; contracts were drawn up by lawyers for approval by clients. Services were specific, and all aspects of street mayhem were broken down and covered, everything from clipping an ear off, to breaking an arm, to tossing someone down a flight of stairs or worse. For $150 Fein and his thugs would destroy a small business, for $200 take out the foreman on a large one. Nothing personal, just business.

The Yiddish Black Hand

Fein also formed alliances with non-Jewish gangs, and set up distinctly drawn territories where other gangs were free to run their own extortion schemes as long as Dopey got his cut. In fact, Fein employed some of the management techniques that have come to be known as outsourcing, especially with regard to a crew of extortionists known as the Yiddish Black Hand, after the Sicilian Mafia group of the same name.

The YBH formed sometime around 1906, led by a man named Jacob "Johnny" Levinsky (aka "Harry McGurk"). Levinsky, a man named Charles "Charlie The Cripple" Vitoffsky, and Joseph "Yoski Nigger" Toblinsky operated from a saloon on Suffolk Street. They would deliver anonymous letters to pushcart vendors and other businessmen, threatening, to "drop"—i.e. poison — their horses unless they were paid off. From this enterprising start, working both jointly and independently (Toblinsky himself was rumored to have personally poisoned over 200 horses), the gang extended its tentacles to a variety of enterprises. Levinsky squeezed the ice cream trade; by 1913 the manufacturers' association had to create a slush fund for annual payments. Vitoffsky extracted cash from rivals in the lucrative seltzer and soda trade; Toblinsky from the produce market, as well as from truckmen and livery stables. From time to time Fein would tap the organization for nasty jobs such as assault, theft, and murder, an early model of the kind of independent contracting Meyer Lansky and Lucky Luciano would later develop with Murder, Inc. The YBH had its own "menu" of services and rates. Poisoning one horse was a rather steep $35, dispatching a team of horses cost $50. (You may as well go wholesale). In the human category, nonlethal gunplay cost you $100, broken noses, arms, legs, and clipped ears were less; the "Big Job", that is, homicide, set you back $500. (Variations of the YBH "menu" now appears on 100% all cotton T-shirts for sale at the Tenement Museum Bookstore on Orchard Street; proving once again that the bloody mayhem of yesteryear is the clever marketing angle of today.)

Fein "rationalized" his own business as well, taking a strict salary of 12 bucks a day for himself, while paying his men a generous $7.50 a day, plus bonuses.

> "Though he worked by the job he demanded regular salaried payments for himself and his men as insurance against the hazards common to his occupation, he himself having once been stabbed in the line of union duty and laid up for four months without income. Gangsters, he argued, also needed protection."[61]

There was even a kind of ad hoc gangland due process to assure Fein's orders were carried out. If a gang member or client got out of line, Fein convened a "General Sessions Court," which "decided" whether and how the offender should be punished: a broken thumb, an arm, or a leg, an ear severed, or perhaps the ultimate penalty with, it goes without saying, no appeal.

Brutal as Fein could be, women were nonetheless appreciated in his organization and received equal pay for equal work. They were utilized as gunrunners, concealing weapons under an orthodox wig or inside a bouffant hairdo known as a "Mikado tuck-up." They would wield weighted umbrellas and hatpins against scabs, and would infiltrate garment factories to make sure strike orders were obeyed.

These quasi-socialist touches led some to believe Fein's sympathies were with the working classes, that he was sort of a Jewish Gangster Eugene Debs. An apocryphal story has him allegedly refusing $15,000 to break a strike for a manufacturer. "My heart lay with the workers," he reportedly said.

But it is far more likely that money, not ideology, was the bottom line for Fein. Or perhaps he just farmed out "labor slugging" — attacks on union picket lines and demonstrations; assaults on union leaders —to a fellow LES gangster who was both an ally and later a rival, during the first of a series of conflicts that became known as the Labor Slugger Wars.

Joe The Greaser and The First Labor Slugger's War

Romanian-born Joe "The Greaser" Rosenzweig had worked as a tailor's presser before breaking into the business of breaking heads around 1907. He led a hundred or so men in breaking strikes and disrupting demonstrations. Like Fein, Rosenzweig was protected by Tammany Hall and, parallel to Fein's coercive efforts on the labor end, he established an iron monopoly on strikebreaking until 1913, when Philip "Pinchey" Paul, a schtarker for the Furriers Union, challenged Benny and "The Greaser" in a pitched gun battle that took place on either Rivington or Grand and Forsyth Streets; accounts differ. Participants included such colorfully named thugs as

Billy Lustig, Paul Phili, Little Rhody and Moe Jewbach. While there were no casualties on either side, this, along with other altercations, including one between Paul and Rosenzweig in a Rivington Street movie house in May of 1914, launched the first Labor Slugger War, running roughly from 1913 to 1917.

Pinchey was eventually gunned down on Norfolk Street by Benjamin Snyder and several other gunmen, including Jacob Heiseman and Hyman Berthstein, under orders from Rosenzweig. Arrested by the police, Snyder confessed, and fingered Rosenzweig. He in turn ratted out the rest of the gang. Despite turning state's evidence, The Greaser was convicted of the murder, and in December 1915, along with Snyder, received ten years in Sing Sing. Released in 1925, Rosenzweig was warned by his ex-lieutenant Waxey Gordon not to try to restart his gang; his time had long passed and Prohibition had changed the criminal landscape beyond recognition. Rosenzweig left New York and retired from crime—one of a select and fortunate group of gangsters to actually leave the profession alive.

Battles continued with remnants of the Five Pointers, now a predominantly Italian gang led by a mobster and rival labor racketeer named Paul Sirroco; Sirroco had built his own slugging organization, challenging both Fein and Rosenzweig, who allied in this instance to fight the Italian encroachment on their mutual monopolies. There were gunfights on Broome Street, the informal dividing line between the Five Pointers' downtown territory and the Lower East Side, dominated by Dopey and The Greaser. In October 1913 Sirroco's men gunned down Max Greenwalt, one of Fein's most trusted lieutenants, during a strike at a downtown hat company. Vowing revenge, a few months later Fein staked his men out at the Arlington Dance Hall at 21-25 St. Marks Place near Second Avenue; in the '60s it was home to the Dom, later the Electric Circus; today it's a Quiznos. Sirroco's gang was expected to attend a ball there. A gunfight ensued and an innocent bystander named Frederick Strauss, who happened to be a city court clerk, was cut down in the crossfire. Righteous indignation immediately ensued. The Mayor vowed to crack down on organized gangs and Fein was arrested for the murder; when witnesses could not place him at the scene of the crime, he was released, but a systematic campaign of harassment had begun against him and his gang. An unprovoked assault on a policeman led to another arrest and Fein was quickly sentenced to five years, but his conviction was overturned after four months by the Appellate Court. Fein and nine of his gang were then fingered for Strauss's murder by Joe The Greaser. Fein, incarcerated in the Tombs, expected his men to rat him out but, surprisingly, they didn't. Two of his men, Irving Wexler, later to become Waxey Gordon, and Isadore "Jew Murphy" Cohen, were tried for the murder but acquitted.

Fein the Canary

Ironically enough, it was Fein himself who eventually turned against his own gang, following his arrest on a separate assault charge in 1914. After a business agent for the butcher's union named B. Zalamanowitz refused to pay Benny his standard $600 protection fee, Benny paid him a personal visit and threatened to kill him. Knowing Benny's reputation for violence, Zalamanowitz, in a panic, went to the police. They eavesdropped on the pair's next meeting, where Fein repeated his threats. Benny was promptly busted, charged with first degree extortion and taken to the Tombs. He assumed his Tammany pals would bail him out in time for dinner, but this time no such luck. No one showed. Possibly because as a result of Dopey's previous arrests, bail was now a whopping eight grand, but it was also likely that Tammany saw an opportunity to rid themselves of what had become a political liability. Or perhaps Rosenzweig or some other upcoming rivals had cut a deal with the corrupt Democratic machine. Or both.

Whatever the reason, being screwed did not sit will with Fein; unbeknownst to both his gang and the politicians, Fein, ever the meticulous businessman, had kept a diary of every corrupt transaction, every dirty deal. Exceedingly pissed off, he named names, illuminating the fine points of the labor slugging racket in voluminous testimony running to several hundred pages. This led to the arrest of 23 labor leaders and eleven gang members, who faced charges ranging from assault to extortion to murder and riot in the succeeding months. Though none were convicted due to lack of evidence and, in no small measure, political connections, the sensational publicity surrounding the case undoubtedly made life on the street difficult for Fein. And with the strengthening of various reform movements, the establishment of new, more wholesome Jewish institutions, and particularly the entry of America into World War I, much of the animosity between labor and capital was set aside, abated or defused in the general prosperity that wartime production created, as well as in the hot flush of wartime patriotism (often enforced with repressive vigor by the Wilson Administration and the media). The era of coercion, extortion and labor slugging was coming to an end, and more prosperous Jews began migrating to the newer, nicer neighborhoods near the new subway stations in Brooklyn and the Bronx.

Statistics as cited by Fried bear this out:

> With the steady rise in incomes and expectations the flight from the great ghetto swelled to a mass exodus. Immigration, meanwhile was slowing to a trickle and would soon end altogether. The statistics tell much of the story: at its height around the turn of the century and through its first decade the Lower East Side contained over 500,000 Jews, by 1916 it was down to 313,000, by 1925, to 264,000 and declining swiftly. . . The prostitutes and cadets and gamblers and gangsters—many, perhaps most of them, were swept along on this cataract of redemption; they too settled into anonymous respectability in the newer habitations of the Bronx and upper Manhattan and Brooklyn and elsewhere, leaving only the ghosts of their wayward past to walk the streets of the old neighborhood.[62]

Fein retired to Brooklyn and became a successful garment manufacturer. There was a court appearance in 1931 on assault charges. In 1941, he and several "associates" were arrested for running a ring that allegedly stole over 250 million dollars' worth of garments in three years. Again he went to Sing Sing, and that was the end of his criminal career. After his release, he returned to the garment industry as a tailor and died in 1962 from cancer and emphysema.

Kid Dropper and Johnny Spanish and the Second Labor Sluggers War

But while many Jews did move out of the LES in the years during and after the First World War, and the attention of police and politicians, especially with the decline of Tammany and Big Tim Sullivan, shifted elsewhere, plenty of Jews remained, and of course, new men and new opportunities soon presented themselves, especially when it came to making a fast buck.

Among the men were Nathan Kaplan, also known "Kid Dropper," born in the LES around 1891. Kid got his nickname from his proficiency at the Drop Swindle, the classic con in which the "dropper" drops a wallet with counterfeit money near the mark. The mark tries to pick up the wallet only to find the "dropper" reaching for it at the same time. Pretending to be in a hurry, the "dropper" generously offers to give up the wallet in exchange for money; the mark can then claim the reward from the owner. (Yes, this actually worked, and is still successfully practiced today. There *is* a sucker born every minute.)

By 1910 Kaplan had formed his own gang, pulling together remnants of the Five Pointers, including a thug named Johnny Spanish. Born John Weyler, or Wheiler, he was Jewish, but claimed to be related to a Cuban dictator named Valeriano Weyler; hence the moniker Spanish. A violent man given to unrestrained gunplay, Johnny Spanish swiftly moved up the criminal food chain from pickpocket to pushcart extortionist, acquiring a nasty reputation for mayhem, especially involving gunplay. A policeman of the day noted that he was "remorseless in his treatment of foes." Spanish organized his own gang within the Five Pointers, and became known for bloody holdups and daring robberies. In one, he visited a Norwalk Street saloon owned by another tough guy named Merscher the Strong Arm. Vowing openly to return and rob the bar, he showed up exactly when he said he would, and shot the place up, pistol whipping several patrons who resisted.

Spanish joined forces with Kid Dropper around 1909, but a rivalry soon developed over Spanish's girlfriend. This led to a street fight in which Dropper nearly knifed Spanish to death; he recovered and shifted his attention to struss games on the LES. A gunfight over a disputed gambling joint led to the death of an eight-year-old girl, and Spanish fled the city, returning after several months to discover that Kaplan had stolen his girlfriend, who was now pregnant. Spanish kidnapped the woman, drove her to Long Island, tied her to a tree and shot her in the abdomen. The woman survived, and eventually gave birth to a three-fingered baby.

Spanish went to prison for the crime in 1911 for seven years; oddly enough, upon his release, he rejoined Kaplan as a labor slugger, but soon started organizing other Five Points veterans into his own gang. The ensuing conflict became known as the Second Labor Sluggers War, which revolved around a garment workers' strike in 1919.

While battling Kaplan, Spanish also became one of the most notorious drug dealers in Manhattan, pushing heroin and cocaine along with his brother, Joey Spanish, out of an eatery at 19 Second Avenue, near East 1st Street. On July 29, 1919, Johnny Spanish was shot to death entering the restaurant by three unidentified men. Kaplan was later arrested for the murder but released for lack of evidence; the crime was never solved. Kid Dropper now presided over all labor slugging operations in New York, working mainly for the unions but occasionally providing services for employers, for the right price.

However, his reign didn't last long. By 1923, as Prohibition got underway, The Kid began to feel the heat from a number of rising young newcomers—mainly Jacob "Little Augie" Orgen, whose gang included Jack "Legs" Diamond, the murderous Louis "Lepke" Buchalter, and Jacob

"Gurrah" Shapiro, deadly hoods in their own right, who would each go on to make their mark in the history of organized crime as the linchpins of Murder, Inc. Orgen, born around 1901, worked as a slugger for Dopey Fein, then formed his own gang, the "Little Augies," after Fein's conviction in 1917. During the gang war between Kaplan and Johnny Spanish in 1919, Orgen quietly built his organization, and Kaplan and Orgen were soon warring over protection of wet wash laundry workers, resulting in more violent shootouts on the Lower East Side, which again commanded the attention of politicians and the police.

Arrested On August 28, 1923 for carrying a concealed weapon, Kaplan was arraigned at Essex Market Courthouse (on Essex and the now-vanished Market). Police Captain Cornelius W. Willemse, who had warned Kaplan to get out of town, posted a heavy guard at the Courthouse and personally accompanied Kaplan in a taxi. As he sat in a cab between Willemse and another cop, a diminutive 17-year-old named Louis Kushner, a/k/a Cohen, came up from behind and pumped five shots through the rear window, four killing Kaplan, one going through Willemse's hat. Caught at the scene, Kushner claimed Little Augie's gang had plied him with booze and drugs and put him up to the killing. He managed to avoid the chair (with future mayor James J. Walker as his attorney), and instead served 15 years in Sing-Sing. He was paroled in 1937; in January of 1939 he was shot to death on a Manhattan street corner.

The Gift of Prohibition

With Kaplan gone, the "Little Augies" took complete control of labor racketeering, and here is where the tale begins to twist its way to the modern era of highly centralized, highly organized and wildly profitable criminal enterprise. With the passage of the Volstead Act in 1917, and its ratification by the states as the 18th Amendment to the Constitution in 1919, organized crime in America changed radically, as traditional rackets like gambling, prostitution, labor racketeering and extortion took a backseat to the United States government's greatest gift to crime: Prohibition. By banning the manufacture, sale and transportation of alcoholic beverages, the Feds transformed a lucrative legitimate business into a wildly lucrative criminal enterprise. The insatiable demand of Americans for booze and the magic of the marketplace led to the establishment of a vast illicit infrastructure, with fleets of smuggling vessels and caravans of trucks filling secret warehouses, from which liquor was distributed to "blind pigs" and speakeasies, which by 1925 were estimated to number anywhere between 30,000 and 100,000 in New York City alone. And at every level of production and distribution, they were more often than not run by increasingly powerful criminal organizations that became, with LES Jewish ingenuity, as sophisticated at the subtleties of business as they were at the mechanics of murder.

As with drugs in the 60s and 70s, banning liquor only served to glamorize its use, creating a culture of lawlessness and defiance, especially among the young and the disaffected, the Lost Generation that had gone through World War I and its disillusioning aftermath. The profits from bootlegging were enormous, more than enough to provide plenty of protection money to state, local and even federal officials. As an engine of corruption, Prohibition was unparalleled. Overseeing the provision of thirsty Americans with the booze they demanded were some of the greatest criminal figures in history—men who, by ingenuity, intimidation and, when necessary, horrific violence, put the "Organized" in Organized Crime. And the most significant figures were either from, or produced by, Jewish life and the Jewish criminal subculture found below 14th street.

"Money Talks": The Rise of Arnold Rothstein

Arnold Rothstein was born in 1882, and raised in a townhouse on the Upper East Side. His father, Abraham, "had one of those dark, haunted Jewish faces that seemed to disappear with the last century, or else survived just long enough to die in Treblinka or Auschwitz."[63] A wealthy, successful, well-connected businessman, with a reputation for honesty and generosity, Abraham at one point served as the chairman of the board of Beth Israel Hospital. Governor Al Smith and Justice Louis Brandeis both attended a dinner in his honor in 1919; within the Jewish community, where he settled disputes and mediated political problems between the uptown Protestant establishment and impoverished downtown working class Jews, he was known as Abe The Just, a nickname bestowed upon him by his friend, Governor Smith.

Rothstein's older brother became a rabbi, but Arnold was cut from a different cloth. At fifteen he began sneaking downtown to the fleshpots of the Lower East Side, where the action was. And the action, for Arnold, was gambling: open air crap games, the dying struss parlors, covert basement casinos, smoke-filled, all-night poker games, pool, and all the racy mishigass that went along with it: girls, booze, good food, the fast life of the forbidden. Rothstein discovered he loved gambling, loved to bet, and that he was good at it: He had mathematical precocity, nerves of steel, a gambler's instincts, and the plain old luck that makes a winner. Rothstein loved taking big risks on big bets, relished the action and, even when losing, rarely lost his cool. Flunking out of school, he headed downtown, made money and finally broke with his father, and like many Jews of his generation, his religion, when he married a shiksa:

> . . .when the girl told the old man no, she was not Jewish, and no, she would not convert, the old man shook his head and said, "Well, I hope you'll be happy." And after the wedding, when the old man pronounced his boy dead, when he covered the mirrors and read the Kaddish, it was a great development in American crime. It set Arnold free.[64]

By 1911, Rothstein was known as a comer in the gambling parlors and pool halls of lower Manhattan. He already had enemies. To knock Rothstein down a peg, they imported a young pool shark named Jack Conway from Philadelphia. Conway was purposely introduced to Arnold and immediately challenged him to a game of pool. Rothstein, of course, immediately accepted. John McGraw, the manager of the New York Giants, a great New York sports figure, a betting man and a friend of Rothstein's, ran a fancy pool hall near Herald Square. The two began playing there on a Thursday evening. As word spread, a growing audience of New York's top gangsters and gamblers gathered to watch, lay odds and place bets. The game went on and on and on, nonstop, until Saturday morning, when McGraw halted it, fearing the players would drop dead of exhaustion or simply bug out. Rothstein, in a tremendous display of will and self-confidence had, against all the odds, bet on himself, and he was up more than $10,000, a small fortune at the time (easily $100,000 or more today). Conway graciously conceded, and Rothstein, always the gentleman, took him downtown in a cab to relax at a Turkish bath.

It was all very exciting and very civilized, and his classy, cool performance both during the game and after made Arnold Rothstein a New York legend. His celebrity status swiftly propelled him to wealth and power. In his late 20s he opened his first gambling parlors; by the age of 30, in 1912, he was a millionaire. Under Tammany Hall's protection, his swanky Midtown casino raked in $10,000 a week. He ran all-night poker games, floated crap games and pulled ingenious stock scams down on Wall Street. He bought into a racetrack in Maryland; the races were allegedly fixed. His philosophy was in step with the Roaring Twenties: "Look out for Number One," he told a reporter. "If you don't, no one else will. If a man is dumb, someone is going to get the best of him, so why not you? If you don't, you're as dumb as he is." And: "Money talks. The more money the louder it talks."

He also had that elusive and essential element of style. Arnold Rothstein became the suave archetype of the modern gangster, replacing the ragged, eccentric garb and boorish vulgarity of the downtown thug with the fashion-forward panache and easy charm of a successful 1920s entrepreneur, and the rakish glamour of a silent movie star. Impeccably groomed, Rothstein cut a dapper figure, appearing only in handmade silk suits, cashmere coats, wingtips and top-quality hats. He was smooth and well spoken, which made him seem even more menacing; he moved effortlessly in wealthy, respectable upper crust society. Lucky Luciano said he learned how to dress, how to impress a classy dame, how to behave at fancy parties, in addition to more practical skills and certain financial practices, from Rothstein. Arnold ran with many nicknames: A. R., Mr. Big, The Man Uptown, The Brain (a title that would later devolve to one of his protégés, Meyer Lansky) and The Big Bankroll. He would peel off fifty-dollar tips for apple vendors and shoeshine boys from a wad of cash he always carried in his pocket. His operations—high-stakes gambling in hotel suites and on ocean liners, huge stock and bond frauds on Wall Street, hidden interests in betting parlors and nightclubs, fixed horse races—could rarely be traced back to him. He left no fingerprints, put nothing in writing. Everything was done through intermediaries.

In 1920, he was accused of fixing the 1919 World Series. It was said his agents paid off eight members of the Chicago White Sox some $100,000 to throw the series. Called to testify before a Grand Jury in Chicago, he played the innocent businessman, outraged and intent on clearing his good name. No evidence was ever found and he was never indicted. After the dust settled, he threatened to sue his accuser, the president of the American League, for libel. More likely, Rothstein probably knew of the fix and allowed his name to be used, and then, betting accordingly, made a fortune. Which was more his style, though it never hurt his reputation that he became known as "the man who fixed the World Series." In 1925 he was fictionalized by F. Scott Fitzgerald, with a somewhat anti-Semitic gloss, in The Great Gatsby as "Broadway character" Meyer Wolfsheim:

> As he shook hands and turned away his tragic nose was trembling. I wondered if I had said anything to offend him.
>
> 'He becomes very sentimental sometimes,' explained Gatsby. 'This is one of his sentimental days. He's quite a character around New York—a denizen of Broadway.'
>
> 'Who is he anyhow, an actor?'

'No.'

'A dentist?'

'Meyer Wolfsheim? No, he's a gambler.' Gatsby hesitated, then added coolly: 'He's the man who fixed the World's Series back in 1919.'

'Fixed the World's Series?' I repeated.

The idea staggered me.[65]

Rothstein also perfected the floating crap game (a game that moves to a different location every night), thus becoming the inspiration for Nathan Detroit in Damon Runyon's novel *The Idyll of Miss Sarah Brown,* which eventually became the musical *Guys and Dolls.*

But far more critical for the future of crime in America, Rothstein became known as The Fixer, a man whose police contacts and political influence, mainly with Tammany Hall leader Charles Murphy, could "rectify" any "sticky situation." Thousands of prostitution, gambling and, after Prohibition, bootlegging cases were literally "fixed" by Rothstein, through his personal connections with police captains, judges and the politicos of Tammany Hall. The mechanism, of course, was envelopes of cold cash passed "under the table" in restaurants, casinos and speakeasies; markers canceled, favors given and repaid. In a quantum leap for municipal corruption, Rothstein reversed the flow of graft in New York City: Whereas politicians formerly purchased the services of the criminals, the huge revenues obtained from bootlegging enabled Rothstein to purchase the politicians on behalf of the criminals. The fox was now guarding the henhouse; the inmates ran the asylum. Greedy politicos "on the take" were also vulnerable to blackmail, another potent lever of control and coercion. The police still received payoffs to insure their cooperation, but now their bosses, the politicians, owned directly by Rothstein, discreetly dictated overall policies, much to the benefit of his criminal empire.

A.R. also saw no problem with strategic alliances among fellow thugs and thieves, apportioning territories and making deals with Irish or Italian gangs, so long as he got his cut. Everybody was happy, and while the threat of violence was always there, it was now more implied then actually brought to fruition—utilized, hopefully, only as a last resort. Rothstein was also, for his time, somewhat of an equal opportunity employer, hiring Jews, Irishmen, Blacks, Italians, even women, and paying them equitably, so long as they made him money. To Rothstein, the dollar had but one nationality and one religion: profit. He was known to pay well for information, especially inside information, the lifeblood of business. For crime was a business, soon to become one of the biggest in America.

He was, as his biographer, Leo Katcher put it, "the J. P. Morgan of the underworld; its banker and master of strategy," an early version of today's venture capitalist, albeit a crooked one. Like any shrewd entrepreneur, Rothstein was always on the lookout for new talent, new opportunity, new ideas, new rackets, and fresh, well-heeled suckers to separate from their money. His lawyer once characterized him as "a man who dwells in doorways . . . A gray rat, waiting for his cheese."

Bootlegging and Rum Running with Arnold and Waxey

The cheese—the big cheese—was the Eighteenth Amendment to the Constitution, the Volstead Act, ratified in January 1919, universally known as Prohibition. It banned the general manufacture, sale and transportation of intoxicating liquors and beers in the United States. It was a dreadfully misguided social experiment rammed through Congress by opportunistic Republicans backed by straight-laced rural Protestant denominations and groups like the Woman's Christian Temperance Union and the Anti-Saloon League. These self-righteous, self-appointed guardians of public morality were aghast at what they saw as a postwar explosion of drinking and drunkenness, and with it whoring, gambling and violent crime, particularly among the returning veterans of the First World War. While the evils of alcohol were not to be underestimated, these groups were also frightened—and politically challenged—by what they saw as the pernicious and immoral influence of the growing immigrant populations, mostly Italian Catholics and Eastern European Jews, who crowded socially progressive, increasingly libertine urban areas, where it seemed like people other than the rich—"those people"—might—heaven forbid!—be having a good time. As motion pictures and other modern means of mass communication brought more glimpses of the wild and licentious urban culture to the countryside, these prudish and provincial fundamentalists essentially freaked out. Prohibition was a way of asserting both their moral superiority and their God-given political entitlement over the unkempt, alien masses in the cities, traditionally distrusted in rural America as debased cesspools of decadence and depravity—which, more often than not, was not so far from the truth.

It did not take long for a man of Rothstein's intelligence and business acumen to grasp the enormous opportunities inherent in Prohibition. While Italian bootleggers on the Lower East Side, under the control of the much-feared old school Mafia Don Joe "The Boss" Masseria were making and selling cheap rotgut liquor and sweet crappy wine, Rothstein's vision extended way beyond the basement and backyard distilleries of Little Italy. And with the financial capital at his command, he set out to make his dream a reality.

Sometime in the fall of 1920, he was approached by a man who had also, almost at the same time, perceived the vast profits to be made importing booze into the United States. His name was Waxey Gordon.

Born Irving Wexler around 1889 to impoverished immigrant parents on the Lower East Side, he earned the nickname Waxey for the ease with which he could slip a wallet out of someone else's pocket, as if it were "waxed." He picked Gordon from many aliases, perhaps from a fondness for English gin. A big, robust, intimidating man, Waxey had worked as a labor slugger for Benny Fein, sold dope and ended up in Sing-Sing for robbing and beating a man. Upon his release in 1916, Gordon went freelance, peddling drugs and hiring himself out to various gangs as a goon, strike breaker and dope peddler until Prohibition began in 1920, when he met a man from Detroit named Max "Big Maxie" Greenberg. Greenberg had begun smuggling Canadian whiskey across the Great Lakes into Detroit, and needing funds to expand his operation, he asked Gordon to approach Rothstein, who knew of Gordon through his dealings with Benny Fein. Greenberg and Gordon wanted $175,000. In the fall of 1920, the three men met on a bench in Central Park, and an era was born.

The next day they gathered in Rothstein's office. Rothstein would finance their plan, but with some major changes. True to form, The Brain had been thinking big. Instead of cheap downtown rotgut or mediocre Canadian booze coming across the Great Lakes in small boats, Rothstein insisted on only the highest quality Scotch whiskey bought over the Atlantic by the shipload from Britain. Large cargo vessels packed with the high-quality contraband would anchor just outside US waters, off Montauk Point on Long Island, then a sleepy beachhead. A fleet of speedboats would carry hundreds of cases of liquor to the shore; from there a caravan of trucks would move the cargo—"liquid gold"—to a warehouse in Manhattan; it would then be distributed to clubs and speakeasies throughout the city.

Waxey asked for and received a small piece of the action and was soon running all of Rothstein's bootlegging operations in New York and New Jersey, as well as moving Canadian whiskey over the U.S.-Canadian border. He was clearing an estimated $2 million a year, buying into breweries, distilleries and several speakeasies. In 1921 Rothstein ended his explicit partnership with Gordon to, as we will see, move into a more lucrative and extensive business relationship with Meyer Lansky and Charlie Luciano (when it came to Rothstein, the left hand never knew what the right hand was doing). But he continued to finance Waxey's operations, taking his usual cut. Gordon was also said to have introduced Rothstein to the large profit potential of narcotics, specifically heroin, which was also smuggled in on his speedboats, and later diamonds. Rothstein planned to expand and control both of these businesses; even at the beginning of Prohibition, he was already foreseeing its end. His eventual goal was the establishment of a nationwide crime syndicate. Gordon could not compete with The Brain's connections, muscle, financial resources or the scope of his vision. Few could.

Waxey put together a gang from his old neighborhood in Philadelphia to help him smuggle in the Scotch. The liquor would be retrieved from "Rum Row," a fleet of ships anchored just outside the three-mile limit (later extended to 12) off the coast of New York and New Jersey. It would then be brought ashore, transferred by truck caravans to the warehouses where it would be—contrary to Rothstein's directives—cut with cheaper whiskey and distributed. Top clientele, however, always received the top-shelf, uncut product.

Modeling himself and his operation on Rothstein, for a time Gordon ran his business from the Knickerbocker Hotel on 42nd Street and Broadway, lived large in a lavish 10-room apartment on the Upper West Side, and built himself a mansion on the Jersey shore, adopting the persona of a wealthy businessman with interests in real estate and financing. Like his mentor, Waxey dressed to kill and tooled about town in a limousine, entourage in tow. To complete the facade of legitimacy, when among "civilians" he returned to his given name of Irving Wexler, lending a patina of respectability to the thuggish reality.

Both men and their illicit businesses continued to thrive, but there were a number of problems, some long range, some immediate. The size and scope of Gordon's operations were too small to propel Rothstein's ultimate ambition of a nationwide crime syndicate, and a number of Waxey's business practices, like adulterating the booze, were not to Rothstein's liking. Then there was ultimately Joe "the Boss" Masseria, and the entire old-school, old-style Italian Mafia to deal with; first-generation "Moustache Petes" who, like Roman emperors, demanded obsequious obedience, exorbitant tribute and the complete domination of every aspect of every racket, solving any major business dispute or loyalty issue with beatings and bullets. To Rothstein and, later, Lucky Luciano and Meyer Lansky, this was, above all, a counterproductive, foolish management style whose time had passed.

But Rothstein's most pressing concern in the first heady months of Prohibition was simply that other gangs and other gangsters all wanted in on his action, and were willing to use force to get what they wanted.

Sure, local cops and magistrates, mainly on the backcountry Long Island roads where the liquor shipments were trucked, were easily bribed: an envelope here, a bottle there or, if need be, hookers or a whole case of whiskey; but even the master fixer could hardly complain to the authorities when gunmen interfered with the illegal trafficking of a legally banned commodity. As Big Paulie explains to Henry Hill in Martin Scorsese's *Goodfellas*, the mob is just a police force for people who can't go to the police.

When Rothstein needed protection for his most lucrative racket, he turned—or returned—to the Lower East Side, where two tough young Jews, in alliance with a rising young Sicilian hood, were making a much-feared name for themselves shaking down pushcart operators, small businesses and factory owners; hiring themselves out as labor sluggers, perhaps even as hit men; renting out stolen cars for robberies; providing stolen trucks to bootleggers, then hijacking their shipments, then offering them protection from hijackers (i.e., from themselves); all of which may be accurately defined by that all-encompassing Yiddish term *chutzpah*.

In fact, Arnold Rothstein had already met one of these young men in 1920:

> His thoughts turned to a small, lean, hungry-looking young man he had met quite by chance at the Bar mitzvah of the son of old family friends in Brooklyn.
>
> The young man had struck Rothstein as being smart and ambitious. The well-groomed gambler was highly amused as Lansky told him how much he envied his sophistication and way of life. Lansky confided to Rothstein that he read about his exploits in the newspapers and admired the way he had crashed upper class New York society and become a powerful figure in it. The young man had implied that he too had dreams of becoming a man of power, a man as successful as Rothstein. Arnold Rothstein had forgotten the name of the youth. He glanced at his notebook and read the name he had scrawled: 'Meyer Lansky.'
>
> That moment was another turning point in the life of the boy from Grodno, who was still working as a tool-and-die-maker by day and at night building up his loyal following.[66]

Meyer Lansky: From Poland to The Lower East Side

Meyer Lansky was born Maier Suchowljansky, in Grodno, Russia (now Hrodna, Belarus) to Polish-Jewish parents. As a young boy, he experienced first hand the virulent, often state-sponsored anti-Semitism that pervaded Czarist Russia like a foul odor. His experience was even more telling due to the unique position of his family, and the unique nature of the town he was born and raised in.

His grandfather Benjamin was wealthy and educated, a successful businessman and a devout Jew. Meyer's family, his father, mother, brother and sister, lived in the same house with their grandfather. It was large, well appointed, made of stone. Lansky remembers his grandfather recounting the rich history of Grodno, then a major center of Jewish life, where Jews had lived for more than 800 years, invited by the Lithuanians in the fourteenth century to establish commerce and trade. There were merchants and skilled craftsmen, shops, markets, an impressive synagogue, even a hospital and a Jewish cemetery. While still a ghetto, with Jews confined to an area between the castle and the marketplace, they nonetheless prospered, creating a vibrant, educated community that only saw its final end at the hands of the Nazis during the Second World War.

Nonetheless, the town was deeply affected by the anti-Semitism of the late 19th and early 20th centuries. Meyer's grandfather would recount in vivid detail how hoards of Cossacks would rape, pillage, plunder, and burn Jewish communities, especially during Easter, Passover and other holidays, all with the encouragement of the authorities. Russian soldiers would go from house to house in search of Jewish boys as young as twelve for conscription into the Czar's army for periods of up to 25 years. Jews were expelled from surrounding villages where they had lived for centuries, then came to Grodno in poverty and despair. Lansky himself often witnessed and endured many daily slights, deprivations and insults, as well as several pogroms, which got progressively more violent and vicious during the reigns of the openly anti-Semitic Alexander III, and Nicolas II, the last Czar before the Russian Revolution of 1917.

It was during one such moment of peril that a speech made by a Jewish soldier at a meeting in his grandfather's house had a profound effect on Lansky; it was a speech he remembered the rest of his life, one he quoted, seemingly verbatim, to biographer Uri Dan:

> 'Jews!' he shouted at the people who had gathered there. 'Why do you just sit around like stupid sheep and allow them to come and kill you, steal your money, kill your sons and rape your daughters? Aren't you ashamed? You must stand up and fight. You are men like other men. I have been a soldier in the Turkish army. I was taught to fight. A Jew can fight. I will teach you how. We have no arms, but it doesn't matter. We can use sticks and stones. Even if you are going to die, at least do it with honor. Fight back! Stop being cowards. Stop lying down like stupid sheep. Don't be frightened. Hit them and they'll run. If you are going to die, then die fighting. Protect your beloved ones. Your womenfolk should be able to rely on you.' Lansky's voice was louder now. The words still thrilled him.[67]

Grodno went on to become a center of the Jewish resistance to Czarist rule; one of the very few places in Eastern Europe where Jews, in defiance of the laws, actively amassed weapons and practiced armed resistance against their oppressors; at one point deliberately planning the murder of a Russian police inspector touring the region to organize massacres against the Jews.

Nonetheless, along with many other Jews throughout Eastern Europe during the early 1900s, Jews left Grodno in increasing numbers. Lansky's father left sometime around 1909 or 10, after bitter arguments with his father (Lansky's grandfather, Benjamin) over whether to emigrate to Palestine or America; Benjamin chose Palestine, Max Suchowljansky America. His wife, Meyer and Meyer's younger brother and sister soon followed him, arriving in New York in April 1911, after what Lansky remembers as a harrowing passage in steerage aboard a vessel called the S. S. *Kursk*. Coming through Ellis Island, immigration officials listed Meyer Lansky's birthday as July 4th, 1902. "I guess they wanted to make a patriot out of me,"[68] he reflected later.

After a brief period in Brooklyn, Lansky's family moved to a tenement at 546 Grand Street, which was demolished after the World War II and replaced by high-rise urban renewal projects. According to one of his biographers, Robert Lacey, Lansky now divided his time between the Seward Park branch of the New York Public Library, the reading rooms of The Educational Alliance and, as he grew older, the vice-filled streets of the Lower East Side:

> Just a few blocks away from 546 Grand Street was some of the most colorful and disreputable street life in New York.

> "On sunshiny days the whores sat on chairs along the sidewalks," Michael Gold was later to write in his vivid and moving memoir of Lower East Side life, *Jews Without Money*. "They sprawled indolently, their legs taking up half the pavements . . . "

> "It is better to stray away from Allen, Chrystie and Forsyth streets if you go walking with your wife, daughter or fiancée," cautioned the Jewish daily Forward in 1898, "There is an official flesh trade in the Jewish Quarter."[69]

In addition to the whores, the "dancing academies"—bordellos—and other nodes of corruption, there were plenty of street thieves, pickpockets and loan sharks amid the general all 'round chaos that spilled out onto the street. On Broome, down the block from the public schools Meyer attended with his brother Jake, were gambling parlors that did double duty as fences for stolen goods. The street boasted five saloons, each with its own category of dubious clientele, and a notorious whorehouse run by a madam named Jenny the Factory, for the boundless enthusiasm and energy she brought to her work. And above all there was gambling, in alleys, in stuss parlors, in basements and on the street. Open-air street corner dice games run by wiseguys, policed by *shtarkes*, and crowded with chumps attracted Meyer's attention and, according to some, set the inexorable direction of his life.

This is another story that has become part of the Lansky legend, and its outcome is often cited as one of the motivating factors that led him into a life of crime, or at least gambling, as if any single incident could propel such a complex individual, like a flicked marble, down a particular path. As with so many other Jewish stories, it involved the Sabbath, and food, particularly cholent, the thick, filling bean, beef and barley stew traditionally prepared for the midday Sabbath meal two or even three days before Shabbat, then left to simmer in an oven on Friday before sundown until lunchtime the next day.

Since the Lansky oven wasn't big enough to accommodate the large cholent pot, after school on Friday Meyer's mother would entrust him with the meal and a nickel for the local baker, who would cook the dish in his oven. On his way to the bakery, Meyer would pass the crap games and, inevitably, curiosity would get the better of him. But curiosity wasn't all young Meyer brought to the game:

> Lansky could look at a crap game and sum it up in figures. It made sense to him; it had a shape of its own. One player throws the dice in craps, trying to make a particular score, or "point." Onlookers bet, as if at a horse race, for or against the chances of the shooter making his point, and as the probabilities ebbed and flowed, the young A student discovered that he could chart the progress of the game in his head, as the best gamblers can, in terms of the odds.[70]

As Meyer carried the cholent pot down from Grand Street to the bakery, he hit Delancey Street, where the Williamsburg Bridge, a modern, all-steel structure completed a little more than a decade before, emptied out onto the LES. The entire gaudy tableaux of street life on the Lower East Side sprawled out before his young, curious eyes; every inch of the sidewalk was occupied, rented or appropriated by pushcart vendors, prostitutes, scam artists, cardsharps and crapshooters. On Friday, payday, there was dough to gamble; Lansky was undoubtedly tempted by what must have seemed a fortune in nickels and dimes lying in piles on stoops and street corners waiting to be won.

Lansky, finally succumbing to temptation, put his sole nickel down at a crap game and promptly lost. Devastated, he wandered the streets with his cold pot of cholent in despair and anger. Finally he went home and confessed to his mother. When he told her what had happened she burst into tears. It was the family's last nickel, specifically saved for the cholent. The next day, after synagogue, there was no hot noonday meal, and the family sat in silence while Meyer sat in shame.

Other boys might have drawn the obvious lesson from this misadventure—not Lansky. First, he vowed to himself never, ever to lose again. To anybody. Then, with the fierce determination he brought to anything he cared about, he stalked the streets of the Lower East Side, quietly observing, carefully studying the game of craps, paying particular attention to how the games were organized, and especially how they were rigged, with loaded dice and a "shill" who secretly worked for the bank and repeatedly won big, in order to entice the suckers into placing their own big bets, which they would invariably lose.

After much study, on a Friday night he later termed "one of the most fateful moments of my life," Lansky followed a game carefully and, precisely at the crucial moment, bet with the shill. It didn't endear him to the banker or the gangs running the game, but they couldn't stop him, at least during the game, for fear of raising the suspicions of the other players. They had to let him win.

> 'My timing was perfect, but my hands trembled so much that I thought I was going to drop the cholent dish. But I won. I knew I won.
>
> That victory taught me a great lesson: that if you think ahead and carefully plan what you are going to do, whatever activity it is, then you can win. It's the fools who rush in unprepared, who try to get rich because they are greedy—they are life's suckers. That was a golden moment, a lesson that has lasted me to this very day. I was hooked on gambling from that moment on and I have remained a gambler ever since. The difference of course is that I gamble only when I know I can win, when the odds are stacked in my favor. And that's the only way you can win.'[71]

He won his lost nickel back and more, and began to build up a bankroll, which he hid in his mattress. But far beyond learning how to outgame the gamesters, Lansky had learned an essential truth about gambling: "There is no such thing as a lucky gambler, there are just the winners and the losers. The winners are those who control the game, the professionals who know what they're doing. All the rest are the suckers."[72] Lansky would never gamble, in the sense suckers understand it. He would always win, by running the game.

He began to observe not only the games themselves, but also the shadowy men who actually controlled the rackets and cons that flourished on every street corner and in every alleyway; his keen intelligence soon penetrated the means and methods these men used to separate the suckers from their money and control the people who worked for them:

> "Slowly I began to notice that the men who actually ran the dice games and street gambling with cards were only the pawns. Other men, well dressed and looking much more prosperous, used to come and watch from time to time. I could see secret signs pass between the rich bosses and the men running the game. I used to follow them, making sure they didn't notice me. I would see the banker pull out of his pockets all the money he had won from the suckers, as they called the gamblers, and hand it over to the man with the good suit and the nice clean shoes.[73]

In addition to the technicalities of gambling on the Lower East Side, Lansky also received an education in the brutality with which the bosses ran their rackets and punished transgressors:

> "Once down an alley I saw a man who collected the money hit the banker across the face and scream at him, 'So you want to cheat us! Next time you'll get a bullet in the head.' Two men with him pulled out knives and slashed the gambler across the face. As he fell to the ground pleading for his life, with the blood streaming all over his clothes, the one with the silk suit stepped back and shouted at him, 'You pig! Your blood has stained my trousers.' Then he kicked the bleeding man hard in the ribs and in the genitals. As the man on the ground coughed up blood, the silk-suited man and his two assistants laughed and walked away as if nothing in the world had happened. I was too frightened to

come out from behind the garbage can where I was hiding until they had gone.[74]

He witnessed beatings, shootouts, acts of prostitution and pimping; at one point he witnessed the brutal murder of a pretty streetwalker he had observed and grown fond of (it is doubtful there was any intimate relationship); the incident left him with a lifelong antipathy toward prostitution, even though his best friends Lucky Luciano and Busgy Siegel were both notorious bordello patrons and owners, and voracious lovers whose liaisons ranged from classy call girls and street hookers to movie stars and European royalty. Before marriage, Lansky kept romance strictly separate from business; at times nobody even knew if he had a girlfriend. Once married, in 1929, to Anne Citron, the daughter of a successful produce dealer from Hoboken, Lansky's reputation as a solid family man remained intact throughout his life; his father-in-law's business operations, which Meyer's managerial talents improved considerably, served as fronts for his less-than-legal undertakings.

By the time of his bar mitzvah, Lansky led a double life: by day an A student at PS 34, by night a student of vice and gambling on Delancey, Orchard, Allen and Ludlow.

To please his family he remained religiously observant, at least until his bar mitzvah. At 15, after the 8th grade, he dropped out of school. It was 1917, during the war. His father, a garment presser horrified at the prospect of Meyer going into the schmatta business he was trapped in, found his young son work in the burgeoning automobile industry as an apprentice in a tool and die shop. It made sense: the wartime demand for skilled automobile mechanics was intense. He worked 52 hours a week for ten cents an hour. The foreman, struck by Meyer's mechanical aptitude, told him he had "golden hands." If he played his cards right and stuck to his job, in 20 years he would be making good money—a dollar an hour! Meyer must have rolled his eyes. He was already reeling in that much and more roughing up scabs or demonstrators as a slugger, or playing dice, or acting as muscle for crap games run by two local hoodlum friends of his, Yudie and Willie Albert. Generally, he avoided trouble though, almost inexplicably, he ends up on the police blotter for allegedly beating up a prostitute on Madison Street, perhaps in an atypical and bizarre effort to pass himself off as a pimp.

Meyer, Benny and Charlie

There are several quite different stories; alternate narratives if you will, as to how Meyer Lansky met his two lifelong friends, blood brothers, and (quite literally) partners in crime: Benjamin Siegel, who became Bugsy (but never to his face), and Salvatore Lucania, later Luciano, who changed his first name to Charlie, when his Jewish pals had trouble pronouncing Salvatore, and was later christened "Lucky", in 1929, after he survived, with an ominous facial scar and a permanently droopy right eye, a "ride" from which he was never intended to return.

One legend has it that Lansky met them both men at the same time; which seems a bit far-fetched, but it makes for a ripe story that well captures the milieu of the times. Albert Fried writes that Lansky was walking home from his job in the tool-and-die shop on the Lower East Side when:

". . .he heard screams coming from an abandoned tenement house. The good Samaritan, crowbar in hand, found his way to the apartment where the cries had come from. He flung open the door and beheld a little drama in progress: a woman was lying on the floor, her face bloodied, while a young man chased a boy around the room. Without a second's hesitation Lansky leaped into the fray and brought the crowbar down on the young man's head. As he did so, the police arrived and arrested everyone.

At the Fifth Street station house the police pieced together the following story. The young man, Salvatore Lucania, resident of Little Italy . . . had caught his girl making love in the empty apartment with the lad, Benjamin Siegel, resident of Williamsburg, Brooklyn, and was taking revenge on both when Lansky burst in on them. The police pressed charges against Lansky; his was the only crime they had witnessed. But thanks to Siegel's testimony Lansky was let off by the kindly judge with a two-dollar fine and an admonition to behave himself."[75]

This seems a little too pat; Fried even fixes a date for the auspicious meeting: October 24, 1918.

A far more nuanced and more plausible narrative of Meyer Lansky's introduction to Luciano is provided by Lansky himself, in what remains the most authoritative—though biased—account of his life and times: *Meyer Lansky: Mogul of The Mob*, a sympathetic 1979 biography by Israeli journalists Uri Dan, Eli Landau and Dennis Eisenberg. Aside from documentary evidence compiled from sources in Washington, Havana and Jerusalem, and eight years of interviews with law enforcement officials and many major and minor gangsters, Dan conducted extensive conversations with Lansky from 1971 on, after he had fled to Israel, where he sought asylum and citizenship under the Law of Return; asylum ultimately denied under pressure—literally blackmail—by the Untied States government, which held shipments of Phantom jet fighters hostage to Lansky's deportation. Much of the biography is reputedly in Lansky's own words, and thus the book has become a primary source for any study of Meyer Lansky and the crucial role he, and the Lower East Side, where so much of his early story takes place, played in the creation of the modern criminal infrastructure of America.

Of course, seeing as Lansky was in exile, fearing incarceration, and seeking asylum from Israeli authorities, the book, and the manner in which he frames his own narrative, is obviously self-serving to say the least, although the authors—and Lansky as well—certainly do not shy away from their subject's amoral, illegal or violent activities. But if the biography is sympathetic, it also vividly illuminates how strongly Lansky's attitudes toward life and crime were influenced by two major factors: his identification with the Jewish culture and, to some extent the religion, both in Russia and America, and his formative years on the streets of the LES. Indeed, as we have seen, many aspects of Lansky's unique personality—his toughness and determination, his powers of observation, his mathematical acumen, his amorality, his acute business sense, his tragic knowledge of human nature—were developed between Canal and East Houston Streets, on Delancey, Rivington, Orchard, Stanton, Allen and Ludlow, as well as on streets that have vanished forever, between the years 1914 and 1930.

According to Dan, it was on Hester Street one cold January day that Lansky first encountered Charles Luciano:

> "Lansky remembers that it was a bitterly cold January day. Fresh snow was falling onto the gray sludge of the previous night's fall. Meyer was walking along with no buddies around when he suddenly found himself surrounded by a gang of Sicilian boys, all older and much bigger than he.
>
> 'If you wanna keep alive, Jew boy, you gotta pay us five cents a week protection money,' the leader told the puny-looking victim. Salvadore was sure the kid was so frightened he was wetting his pants. But Lucania was mistaken.
>
> Looking at the menacing faces that surrounded him, and hearing their leader's heavy accent, Meyer stared back and replied, 'Go fuck yourself.'"[76]

Taken aback, but impressed by the little Yid's defiance, Luciano told his gang to forget the beating, and, to save face with his gang, told Meyer they would "come back for you when milk from your mother's tits has dried on your face."[77]

The incident was the beginning of an almost telepathic and lifelong friendship that would change the face of organized crime. As Luciano later put it:

> "We both had a kind of instant understanding. It was something that never left us. Later we didn't always have to talk to explain things to each other. He knew I was getting him off the hook and insulting him purely to keep my gang members quiet. He detected the tone of sympathy in my voice, though none of my gang could pick it up. In the later days I would think of something and he would have the same thought at the same time, you know how it is with some women sometimes, but of course we were men. The feeling was still the same though, it was as though we were twins and our minds were connected in some way. It may sound crazy, but if anybody wants to use the expression 'blood brothers,' then surely Meyer and I were like that even though we had come from totally different backgrounds."[78]

According to *Mogul of the Mob*, years later a perceptive Benny Siegel, speaking to another of Lansky's loyal lifelong friends, Joseph "Doc" Stacher, also noted the extraordinary intimacy of the small, brainy Jew from Russia and the tough Italian from Sicily, in remarks that were perhaps unconsciously too revealing:

> "They were more than brothers, they were like lovers, Charlie Luciano and Meyer, although of course there was nothing sexual between them. They would just look at each other and you would know that a few minutes later

> one would say what the other was thinking. I never heard them argue. I
> never heard them quarrel. . . . . Charlie was tough and ruthless in an open
> way. Meyer was just as tough, just as ruthless, but he never showed it.
> Charlie was the brains of the organization and he knew how to handle the
> gunmen and the soldiers who worked for us. Lansky was the financial
> genius and could keep in his head how to move from one business to
> another, what to do with the money and where the future prospects lay.
> They were an unbeatable team. . . . . . I suppose if they had wanted to they
> could have conquered the whole of the United States, starting anywhere
> they wanted to. If they had become president and vice-president of the
> United States, they would have run the place far better than the idiot politi-
> cians that did it."[79]

They met again a few months later, and after a confrontation with Irish gangs during a swim in the East River. Luciano and Lansky formed a silent, loose alliance against the Hibernian remnants of the Five Pointers, who preyed on both Jews and Italians, and with whom Lansky had had several earlier, violent run-ins on the streets of the LES. That winter, after several street fights in which Lansky gave as good as he got, Luciano surprised the tough young Jew and offered his hand, a gesture that formally began their friendship: "The day the Sicilian boy who was to become my lifelong friend sought me out for a handshake is one I will never forget."[80]

Luciano once described his unique business relationship with Meyer Lansky, including the place of Benjamin Siegel in their organization. "We were like analyzers. We didn't hustle ourselves into a decision before we had a chance to think it out. Siegel was just the opposite, and I guess that's what made him good for us, because he would make his move on sheer guts and impulse."[81] Luciano's respect and warm affection for Lansky was genuine and lifelong, and Lansky conscientiously ran many of Luciano's operations after Luciano was deported in 1946 (following his behind-the-scenes-service to US intelligence during World War II) making sure his friend lived very comfortably in Italy while his business interests were well looked after in America. Luciano once said that Lansky "could look around corners," and that "the barrel of his gun was curved," meaning that he could see trouble coming but knew how to avoid it. "I learned a long time before that Meyer Lansky understood the Italian brain almost better than I did. . . . I used to tell Lansky that he may've had a Jewish mother, but someplace he must've been wet-nursed by a Sicilian." Which was perhaps the highest tribute the most important gangster America has ever produced could pay to his Jewish friend and partner, the man most responsible for his spectacular and lucrative success.

The Bugs and Meyer Mob

The origin of Lansky's other great association, with Benjamin "Bugsy" Siegel, is also the stuff of legend.

Siegel was born in Williamsburg, Brooklyn as Benjamin Siegelbaum; his parents were Austrian and dirt poor. Siegel's father worked for pennies, a circumstance that made no small impression on his Benjamin, one of five children. Siegel launched his criminal career as a boy, shaking down pushcart vendors and other merchants on Lafayette Street with his running buddy, a compliant lackey named Moe Sedway. They carried around squirt guns of kerosene; if the vendors didn't cough up a dollar or two, the pushcart, newsstand or table of schmattas outside a dry goods store would be torched on the spot. Next time, payment would be swiftly forthcoming, and the experience taught Siegel the value of intimidation and violence as a useful tool of persuasion. As Al Capone, (another veteran of Lower East Side gangland) is said to have put it: "A kind word and a gun will get you further than a kind word." From simple extortion and robbery, Benny moved onto protection, taking payments from vendors as "insurance" so that copycat shakedown artists, as well as he and his comrades, wouldn't victimize them. A beating or a knifing would insure compliance, both for the merchant and potential competitors.

Siegel grew up to be extremely good looking and extremely hot tempered, with a reputation for irrationality and sudden outbursts of violence that eventually earned him the nickname "Bugsy," as in "bugging out" or "crazy as a bedbug." Either way, if you wanted to keep your teeth, and perhaps your life, you never uttered the word in his presence. Even as a teenager he was known as a fearless street fighter with a schizoid personality. Your best friend one moment, he could inexplicably explode with furious malevolence the next. On the street he was called *chaye*, Yiddish for "untamed," meaning really "an animal." Movie star handsome, he could seduce almost any girl he set his sights on, and did. Devoid of conscience, a classic sociopath, Benny Siegel had committed dozens of heinous crimes, including assault, arson, burglary, bookmaking, bootlegging, hijacking, armed robbery, dealing drugs, rape, running prostitutes, numbers rackets, extortion and numerous murders—by the time he was 21.

In *Mogul of the Mob,* Lansky says that he first encountered Siegel in a dispute over a crap game, really a battle for territory between two criminal gangs that spiraled into a pitched gun battle:

> Just then another boy rushed into the middle of the carnage. Weaving his way among the battling men, he went straight for a revolver which had fallen to the ground. Just as his fingers reached for the weapon came the sound of police whistles. At the same time one of the gang members leaped at the boy and tried to grab back the revolver. The police were now running straight for the contestants. The youngster held his ground and took careful aim at the gangster. He was about to pull the trigger when Meyer jumped out of his hiding place and took hold of his arm.

> Lansky had suddenly recognized the boy as the son of a woman his mother knew. She used to cry and complain about the problems she was having with her Benny. "You're crazy," he shouted, holding onto Benny Siegel. "Drop that gun and run." Obeying without question, the young boy flung down the weapon and scampered away with Meyer, dodging around the cops. Minutes later, when they had lost themselves in the crowded market, Meyer was astonished to hear the boy curse him. "Why didn't you let me kill that bastard?" he said. "I needed that gun."

> Meyer answered calmly, "The police were right on the scene. If you had been caught with the gun you'd be in deep trouble. Only an idiot, a schlemazel, would shoot with the cops in sight. Use your head." Still complaining bitterly, Benny went home, but from that moment on the two boys were friends.[82]

Thus the template for the relationship was set: impetuous, hotheaded action by Siegel; intervention and moderation by his more deliberate, thoughtful yet no less ruthless and cunning friend: the only man who could call Bugsy Siegel an idiot, a schlemazel, to his face and live.

Of course, Siegel was no idiot—meshugena, perhaps, but clever and smart, smart enough to realize that Lansky had not only guts but the brains and the judgment to offset Siegel's tendency to shoot first and think later. And Meyer was never as averse to strong-arm tactics as his carefully cultivated legend was later to maintain.

Upon meeting Lansky, however that meeting did occur, Siegel and his new friend formed a close alliance, their friendship forged in the streets between the years between 1916 and 1920 when their life of crime commenced in earnest. They were virtually blood brothers; their two-man crime wave soon became known as The Bugs and Meyer Mob. They built a reputation as violent shakedown artists, preying on Jewish moneylenders and shopkeepers as well as Irish and Italian merchants and gamblers. The gang they assembled consisted of close friends from the neighborhood, local talent they knew from childhood, who would mature into men of unshakeable loyalty and trust. There was Joseph "Doc" Stracher, who lived around the corner from Abner "Longie" Zwillman; both would become two of Lansky's closest confidants. There was the strange Toledo-born Red Levine, named of course for his hair color, a dangerous thug but a devout Jew who went to synagogue on Saturday and wouldn't kill on Shabbat; Lansky's cousin Irving Sandler, aka Tabbo; Yudie Albert, who ran some of the crap games Meyer had so closely observed, Dutch Goldberg and two figures who would go on to become highly feared and powerful mobsters in their own right: Louis "Lepke" Buchalter, and Arthur Flegenheimer, soon to be known as Dutch Schultz. And of course there was Lansky's younger brother, Jake, tall and broad as Lansky was small and skinny, who idolized Meyer to the point of deliberately slouching whenever walking beside him to, he reasoned, make his brother a little less conscious of his barely five-foot height. When the gang wasn't shaking down pushcart vendors and shopkeepers, pulling stickups and street robberies, they played basketball and swam in the East River like other kids—save for occasional violent encounters with Irish or Italian gangs.

Like so many unions of opposites, Lansky and Siegel together were a formidable team, a whole greater than the sum of the parts. They were shrewd as well as ruthless and violent, the most violent of the street gangs at the time. While Meyer was and has always been seen as the cold, calculating "brains" of the organization and somewhat of a bean counter, and Benny the volatile muscle, the reality was not so cut and dried. As Albert Fried takes pains to point out in *The Rise and Fall of the Jewish Gangster in America*:

> The commonly held view is that Lansky was the brains, therefore the senior partner. It is an impression deduced mostly from the contrast in their personalities. Lansky was (and is) the very model of conventional virtue.

Nightclubs and women and fancy clothes, the signs and baubles of success in the profession, attracted him hardly at all. He felt no need to
compensate by swagger and ostentation and a brave display of power
for his modest size and undistinguished looks. When not working he
usually stayed at home with his wife and children. He kept his own
counsel and spoke softly and to the point. He was the quintessential
gangster-bourgeois.

Siegel was truer to type. Nicely built, ruggedly good-looking, by the cinematic standards of the day, and always nattily dressed, he unfailingly
drew attention to himself wherever he went, whatever he did. He gam-
bled heavily and was an insatiable womanizer despite his wife and children. He was impetuous and quick to take offense, passing easily from
rage to violence. Now these personality differences, interesting in themselves and the source of much copy, should not deceive us. Both men
were exceedingly smart and exceedingly ruthless, and their friends and
co-workers knew better than to draw invidious distinctions between
them. Their qualities of mind and character, not the superficialities of
style and manner, accounted for the astonishing success of their joint
enterprise.[83]

The "Little Man" had a talent for organization, a genius for numbers and a mind like a steel
trap, but he could also beat the shit out of someone and had no compunctions about using a
blackjack or a gun when necessary. Siegel was indeed impulsive, hot tempered and prone to
violence as a default, but he could also be poised, dapper, witty and charming, especially with
the ladies. He was also fearless, a much appreciated quality in the underworld. Both Luciano
and Lansky later said he saved their lives on many occasions, sometimes by taking the kind of
violent, precipitous action he became notorious for.

Perhaps it was Lansky's experiences in Russia, or Siegel's impoverished upbringing, Austrian
heritage, or simply his volatile nature, but both men from the very beginning were tough, uppity,
badass Jews who would simply not take it lying down, Jews who would fight back; dangerous
Jews, Jews with guns and the balls to use them. Rich Cohen, in Tough Jews, describes how the
men of his father's generation, the generation that fought World War II, liberated the concentration camps and founded the State of Israel, paradoxically considered men like Lansky, his pal
Bugsy Siegel and other Hebrew hoodlums heroic, men who, despite their viciousness and
sadism, their ruthlessness and psychopathic lack of remorse, their criminality, stood up, fought
back and helped to counter the image of Jews as passive pawns and physical cowards, gentle
sheep, unwilling or afraid to use force, not even cognizant of the idea of resistance to the fiends
who led them to the gas chambers.

" . . .this is a lesson many Jews of my fathers generation took from the
war. Shooting is bad. Shooting is to be deplored. But if shooting should
break out, make sure you're on the right side of the gun. . . . Which is
one reason my father's friends cling to the romantic image of the Jewish
gangster. In their formative years, those following the Holocaust, as they
were faced with the image of dead, degraded Jews being bulldozed

into mass graves, here was another image, closer to home—Jews with guns, tough, fearless Jews. Don't let the yarmulke fool ya. These Jews will kill you before you get around to killing them. Bugsy Siegel, Abe Reles, Louis Lepke, antiheroes whose very swagger seemed to provide another option."[84]

Before World War II Lansky and his crew broke up German-American Bund meetings, decorated with swastikas and pictures of Hitler, up in Yorkville, a predominantly German enclave on the Upper East Side of Manhattan. According to Lansky, this was at the covert behest of a judge and important Jewish member of the Republican Party, the anti-fascist columnist Walter Winchell, and Rabbi Stephen Wise, activist founder of the Free Synagogue of New York, and the president of the President of the World Jewish Congress, with the caveat that no one was to be killed. But arms, legs and other body parts were broken, and the thuggery attracted the unwelcome attention of the news media, bringing Lansky's name to greater public consciousness than he cared for. He was soon asked to curtail these activities.

Far more significantly, along with Luciano, Lansky helped insure that there would be no sabotage on the docks of New York, after the burning of the French luxury liner the *Normandie*, slated to be converted into a troop carrier, by Nazi saboteurs on November 9, 1942—and for the rest of the war there was none. The enlistment and participation of Lansky, Siegel and Luciano in the war effort was sanctioned at the highest level of the American government, and their cooperation won Luciano a commutation of his 30-50-year sentence by the man who put him behind bars, Governor Thomas E. Dewey, in 1946. (Luciano was deported to Italy.)

Siegel's efforts in the war were even more colorful, indeed incredible, although unfortunately less fruitful.

In the late 30s Siegel, through one of his mistresses, the Countess Dorothy diFrasso, concocted a scheme to sell some kind of an explosive device to Benito Mussolini. The countess's husband was close to the Italian dictator and, though sale never worked out, on a trip to Italy in 1939, while staying at the DiFrasso estate, the crazy Jew from the Lower East Side was introduced to the corpulent Air Marshall Hermann Goring and rat-faced Minister of Propaganda Joseph Goebbels. Siegel said he took an instant disliking to the pair, supposedly for personal rather than political reasons, and in true Siegelian fashion planned on putting them out of their master race misery. He was only dissuaded by the countess, who pointed out that both of them would probably not make it out of Italy alive if Bugsy went ahead and bumped off the two upper echelon Nazis, who were personal guests of Il Duce.

Siegel also reputedly helped in the establishment of the State of Israel. The fighting spirit of the Zionists impressed Siegel; at a meeting with a representative from the Haganah on 1945, he allegedly asked the emissary, "You mean fighting, as in killing?" When told that was exactly what was meant, Siegel said, "Count me in," and thereafter a steady stream of suitcases filled with five- and ten-dollar bills, $50,000 in all, made its way to the Haganah.

In this context it is not difficult to see how, for Rich Cohen's father and his friends, these antiheroes became heroes. Cohen movingly describes the way his father and his friends, tough but legitimate businessmen and professionals, imitated LES gangster style: the clipped slang and cryptic lingo, the sharp way they dressed, the tough guy attitudes and the sinister panache and stoic realism they brought to life. They held the same perverse fascination for Jews of their generation and the generation after that Nicky Barnes and Frank Lucas held for the black hip-hop and rap community in the 70s and 80s. As precursors of the militant, postwar "Never Again" Jews, Lansky was at the top of the pyramid, combining brains, determination and the will to use whatever means were necessary, including violence in whatever measure, in order to achieve success in America—that success measured by standards that these Jews could understand and traffic in: money, power and, to some degree, fame, something Lansky was not really interested in, and in fact, abhorred.

Lansky and Lucky

Of even greater significance for the future of organized crime was Lansky's lifelong friendship and business association with Luciano, a bond cemented by an episode that illuminates the cunning, ruthlessness and ambition that characterized the operations of Bugs, Meyer and their mob.

In 1915 Luciano was set up by the 18-year-old son of an Irish cop and sentenced to a year in prison for selling narcotics. By then Lansky and Luciano were close, and through his relationship with Lansky, Luciano was tight with Siegel as well. Through Luciano, Meyer had forged a rough alliance with some of the Italian gangs, and his Sicilian friend valued Meyer's brains, nerve, even temperament, judgment and loyalty; to Lansky and Luciano, loyalty, though elastic in extraordinary circumstances, was nonetheless paramount. Released from prison after six months, Luciano vowed quick revenge; no doubt Benny was hot to help him take it. At this time, the Bugs and Meyer Mob ran street corner dice games, pushcart protection rackets and stolen car rings. From all accounts, contract killing was not yet part of their repertoire. Meyer told Luciano he and Benny would take care of the Irish kid, but that revenge is a dish best served cold. Prudence, and avoiding the electric chair, dictated that they wait.

A full year passed. Luciano left town on a "vacation," the details and documentation of which were precise and verifiable. The Irish kid disappeared, the body never found despite a massive search. Luciano was questioned but his alibi was ironclad. Besides, no body, no crime, no charges.

A decade passed. A woman surfaced who knew of the killing and who the killers were. She attempted to blackmail the trio, apparently not realizing just who she was dealing with. Bugsy, Lansky and Luciano paid a visit to her apartment and beat her savagely, but the melee attracted the police and the trio was briefly arrested. The woman, however, failed to show up in court. Eight years later she ran into Siegel in a bar and made the mistake of mocking him in public. Siegel followed her home and raped her; again Lansky stepped in and "persuaded' the woman not to press charges. Effective at both business and violence, these Jews knew how to watch each other's backs, and their loyalty and service to their Sicilian friend would be well rewarded. They had earned his respect, and his friendship.

The sheer gutsiness of Lansky and Siegel's young fuck-you attitude could also be measured in their initial run-in with the murderous figure of Old World Mafia Don Joe "the Boss" Masseria in

1919. During one of the first crap games Lansky and his gang had organized, six men burst into the tenement basement where it was being held and pounded the players, as well as their bodyguards and bankers, with iron bars, warning that next time somebody would get killed. Lansky, who had promised the players his protection, vowed revenge; when he tracked down the Italian thug who had orchestrated the assault, he learned it had been ordered by Joe The Boss. It was a message from Masseria: He was moving in on the Lower East Side. Lansky knew that if he let the Mafia leader "wet his beak" he would soon be taking a larger and larger bite out of every gambling operation he floated, that is, if he lived long enough to float them.

Lansky realized there was too much at stake to back down; who would ever show up at one of his crap games unless they knew Meyer and his gang could provide protection, both from the police and the Italians? Luciano, who hated the imperial and often needlessly violent ways of the old-line Dons, backed Lansky. With Bugsy Siegel and the rest of his gang Lansky found the Italian who had led the raid on his crap game, and beat the crap out of *him*. When the fight went to the street, Lansky was arrested and fined two dollars for disorderly conduct. But the biggest shock was that Masseria just let the incident pass. Inexplicably, there was no retaliation, even though he had more than 200 button men (you push a button, they kill somebody) whom he could have ordered to hit Bugs, Meyer, Luciano and the rest of the gang. Perhaps he thought he would bide his time, perhaps he respected, in some perverse way, the guts and gall of these aspiring gangsters. We know he was interested in luring Luciano away and into his organization. But for now, his refusal to seek the revenge Lansky, Siegel and Luciano were expecting gave the gang the confidence they needed to continue to expand their fledgling empire.

For a time, The Bugs and Meyer Mob, working with Luciano, laid low, running crap games, engaging in labor slugging and pulling stickups and burglaries, mostly uptown, as far as possible from their own neighborhoods. As Prohibition got underway, they graduated to car theft and hijacking, drawing on Lansky's expertise with automobiles. His tool and die apprenticeship was at last paying off. A legitimate car and truck rental garage fronted the operation; it also served as a warehouse for swag. Under Meyer's skillful management the legitimate front businesses, and the illicit enterprises they masked, both prospered. The gang became known as specialists in various forms of "transportation." They contracted out their other "services" at exorbitant, often extortionate fees—hijacking liquor shipments or providing protection against hijackers, whatever came their way, at whatever the market would bear.

Lansky also began to demonstrate some of the foresight and business acumen that would make him indispensable and irreplaceable. He persuaded Luciano to establish a special fund—a "Buy Money Fund," for buying police and public officials. Initially 5,000 dollars, it also bought interests in other gambling operations, and financed bordellos, one of Luciano's specialties, despite Lansky's distain for prostitution. Bribe money, the mother's milk of corruption, was liberally distributed to politicos through Charlie's close friend and trusted lieutenant Francesco Castiglia, aka Frank Costello, by the 1950s known as the "Prime Minister of the Underworld." While other gangs squandered the proceeds of their crimes, Lansky and Luciano began to think strategically. Shrewdly entrepreneurial, they developed business plans, infrastructure and financing, with long-term goals, a paradigm shift crucial to the re-establishment of organized crime as a sophisticated, tightly run national corporate entity, albeit with a violent logic and certain peculiar means and methods all its own. Lansky still haunted the libraries, reading anything that had to do with investment and finance. At one point he suggested to Luciano that they place their fund in a bank, where it could accrue interest and perhaps fend off the tax authorities. Siegel cased out a prospective institution and discovered that security—a lone, elderly night watchman—was less than adequate. Instead of making a deposit, Bugs, Meyer and cohorts made a withdrawal, netting around eight grand.

Lansky and "The Brain"

Sometime in 1920, shortly after his arrangement with Waxey Gordon, "The Brain" invited the young man he had met at the bar mitzvah in Brooklyn to dinner at the Park Central Hotel, his headquarters at 56th Street and 7th Avenue. Despite his agreement with Gordon, over the next six hours, Rothstein cut a deal with the "ambitious and hungry" young Jew and, in a subsequent meeting, his Sicilian friend, outlining to both men his plans for bootlegging on a massive, mind boggling scale. At first, the Bugs and Meyer Mob would provide protection, lethal, if necessary, for Gordon's liquor caravans heading to the city from the eastern end of Long Island. Hijackers would now have to contend with the likes of Louis "Lepke" Buchalter, Gurrah Shapiro, and Jack "Legs" Diamond, all fearsome graduates of Little Augie's Gang of LES labor sluggers, unhesitant killers who would later figure prominently in Murder, Inc. Bugsy Siegel, always eager for action, rode along, and when needed, Lansky as well, shotgun in hand.

The Brain would shrewdly keep the nervous system of various gangs and factions in line by dividing territory and profits among them. Violence, messy and counterproductive, attracting the attention of the police and the press, was deemed bad for business, to be used only as a last resort. Guns would give way—it was hoped—to negotiation, for the benefit and profit of all. Stacks of cold hard cash would keep the cops and the politicians at bay. Under Rothstein, who acted more as a guiding advisor and venture capitalist, everybody would make money, and making money, not the murderous politics of ethic domination or geographic territories, was paramount. For there was so much money to be made; there was be plenty for everybody; or so it was thought, though the motivating power of greed could never be overestimated and, in the end, overcome.

Rothstein's first lieutenants were mainly Jewish: Dutch Schultz (born Arthur Flegenheimer) would take over bootlegging operations in the Bronx and upstate New York. Lansky's close friend Longy Zwillman, would run North Jersey. Through Lansky's relationship with Luciano, Rothstein sought a tentative alliance with the rising generation of young Italian mobsters who were chafing under the harsh domination of the old Mustache Petes, primarily Joe the Boss Masseria and his main rival Salvatore Maranzano, who ran their gangs with rapacious greed and the ruthless authority of the mad emperors of Imperial Rome. Under Luciano these men, at least the ones who survived, would become the modern face of Cosa Nostra: the vain Guiseppe Doto, a.k.a. Joe Adonis; murderous Vito Genovese, Carlo Gambino (both models for Mario Puzo's The God-father), and the truly sinister Albert "The Mad Hatter" Anastasia, who became a co-director, along with Siegel and Lepke, of Murder, Inc. Rothstein ended his formal partnership with Waxey Gordon in 1921 and consigned him to his home town of Philadelphia; Luciano was given the first dibs on the high quality scotch—referred to as "liquid gold", which Gordon smuggled in from distilleries in Scotland; he scooped up every drop. Gordon was not pleased with the plan, viewing Lansky as the architect of the arrangement, but had to go along with Rothstein, Luciano and Lansky; Benny Siegel's muscle saw to that. This led to problems later, a "War of the Jews," which Lansky and Luciano ended with typical subtlety and cunning: In 1931, through Lansky's brother Jake, they leaked evidence to the IRS implicating Gordon in tax fraud, for which he went to jail.

Within a very short time after their meetings with Rothstein, Lansky, Siegel and Luciano solidified their own network of bootlegging operations, making alliances with other "importers" like Lucky Johnson in Atlantic City, Moe Dalitz and Johnny Scalise, of Cleveland, and Solly Weissman, boss of Kansas City. During this period, Rothstein acted as Lansky's mentor, introducing him to sophisticated business practices, emphasizing above all the importance of providing only top quality booze, the finest imported scotch and whiskey, unlike the amateurs in Little Italy who moved whatever bathtub rotgut or watered down liquor they could make, find or hijack. This reflected A.R.'s understanding of one of the most basic, yet subtle and all too frequently discarded economic principles: that people with means will always pay a premium for quality, quality being a reflection of their status; just as addicts will always absorb the cost of their fix, regardless of how high it climbs. Rothstein's superior product could be peddled at a spectacular markup to his high society friends, who had money to burn, and provided free or at cost to pliable politicians, judges and the police. Whiskey purchased from Scotch distillers at a little over two dollars a fifth—which included the cost of bribes and labor and shipping—could be sold in its original bottle at thirty to forty dollars a fifth. Even when the distillers raised their prices the profits remained astronomical. A case of liquor—twelve bottles—that cost twenty-five dollars would bring in more than a thousand dollars of pure profit. Under Lansky's direction (Benny being a loose cannon with whom Rothstein wanted little connection), the Bugs and Meyer Mob would administer A.R.'s liquor empire on the East Coast, making Lansky in effect Rothstein's operating manager.

In doing so Lansky and Luciano soon came up with some ingenious entrepreneurial innovations of their own. Alcohol was still considered by many, even in the medical community, to have health benefits; an exception was carved out of the Volstead Act for medicinal use (hence the origin of the wink-and-nod phrase "strictly for medicinal purposes" that accompanied many a shot). A doctor could write you a prescription for alcohol; many in fact did, and to supply the "medicine" the government sanctioned special factories to bottle the medicinal booze. So Lansky and Luciano went into partnership with these firms and rolled truckloads of booze through this loophole. Firms that resisted were made an offer you couldn't refuse. Since the product was being peddled as medicine, not cocktail sauce, Lansky would carefully have it watered down with prune juice, caramel, molasses or other additives that would preserve the color and taste of the real thing; chemists and other professionals he put on the payroll saw to it that only a connoisseur could tell the difference. In fact, shortly after his marriage Lansky formed a company with his new father-in-law, Molaska, Inc., to both provide the molasses while serving as a useful front for a variety of illegal activities.

One bottle of high quality Scotch could be morphed into three, thus tripling the profits. The scam was probably not revealed to Rothstein, and was practiced on a grander scale in Philadelphia by Lansky's nemesis Waxey Gordon.

Lansky's antipathy to Gordon (the two nearly came to blows at one point and had to be separated by Luciano) made for some sticky situations as time went on. While protecting shipments of liquor for Rothstein, Bugs and Meyer were certainly not beyond running a hijacking or two of their own, even—and especially—if the shipment belonged to Joe The Boss Masseria and was, behind Rothstein's back, intended for Gordon in Philadelphia. At bottom, Meyer and Bugsy were, of course, still criminals; cutting corners and double-crossing were still their modus operandi. When Siegel learned that a boatload of booze earmarked for Gordon was due to arrive in Atlantic City, he assembled a crew and went south to hijack the shipment. The ambush turned ugly: Three of Masseria's guards were killed and several badly wounded. Siegel and his men then gratuitously beat the rest of Masseria's men, who recognized him and Lansky and some of the other Jews from New York. Of course Gordon couldn't complain to Rothstein, because he had been dealing with Masseria behind his back. Rothstein hated the Italian; like Luciano, he considered him old fashioned and needlessly violent, and was plotting with Luciano to assassinate him. Masseria didn't retaliate, because he was trying to recruit Luciano as his second-in-command, and he held back because he knew how close Charlie was to Lansky and Siegel, whom he figured on eliminating later anyway. The hijacking was only part of a larger scheme devised by Lansky and Luciano to pit Masseria against his rival Maranzano and eventually eliminate both.

The growing Bugs and Meyer operation was run along the lines of any other large scale American corporate enterprise, with some important exceptions: All payments were made in cash; consequently the bootleggers paid no taxes. Profits were enormous. Public opposition was minimal: Most people wanted a drink and saw bootlegging as a public service, certainly not a crime, despite the Bible beaters and the government. Penalties for bootlegging were small, there were few arrests, and judges who drank and served alcohol in their homes were reluctant to jail the men who supplied them with their booze.

The public viewed bootleggers as outlaws, in the romantic American tradition of a rakish character who skillfully defies illegitimate authority, who lives with a certain integrity beyond the law; not as criminals, fiends who commit heinous acts outside the realm of decency and honor. As Al Capone put it, as quoted in *Mogul of the Mob*:

> "I made my money by public demand. If I break the law my customers, who number thousands of the best people in Chicago, are as guilty as I am. The only difference between us is that I sell and they buy. Everybody calls me a racketeer. I call myself a businessman. When I sell liquor it's bootlegging. When my patrons serve it on a silver tray it's called elegant hospitality.[85]

Of course Capone, who began his career on the Lower East Side, also said: "You can get much farther with a kind word and a gun than you can with a kind word alone." Along with Lansky, Siegel and Luciano, he practiced what he preached. Alphonse ascended to power in Chicago with the help of his Jewish pals in New York. According to Lansky, Bugsy Siegel's aunt once hid Capone, fleeing a murder rap, from the cops at her apartment on East Fourteenth Street. Siegel, Lansky and Luciano helped facilitate Capone's rise by sending Frankie Yale to Chicago to assassinate the main rival of Johnny Torrio, then Capone's boss, an old Moustache Pete named Big Jim Colosimo, who had once passed anti-Semitic remarks about Lansky and Siegel to Torrio. Frankie blew his brains out.

Before long Lansky and Luciano were awash in more money than they could keep track of. Lansky quickly mastered the intricate details of running a large scale bootlegging operation. Under his direction—or to use the modern term, management—the gang purchased real estate for cutting and packaging the product; bought a bottling company and a printing plant to make exact duplicates of Johnny Walker, Dewar's and Haig & Haig bottles, labels and packaging; expanded their shipping and trucking fleets; financed speakeasies and clubs; and pretty much grew his business the same way a conventional corporate enterprise expands, with the exception of certain less-than-legal practices such as bribery, extortion and murder.

All of this had to be done clandestinely, through dummy corporations and untraceable knockouts (techniques later adopted by the American intelligence agencies the Mob worked with during World War II and the Cold War); secret contracts often sealed with a handshake, in the centuries old manner of Jewish jewelry merchants; and coded account books, though it was said that Meyer kept the most important transactions in his head—one legend that may well be true.

Rothstein saw his emerging bootlegging empire as the forerunner of a national organization, a nationwide crime syndicate controlling booze, gambling, prostitution, labor racketeering and diamond and drug smuggling, which he also was developing a strong interest in via another Lower East Sider named Jacob Katzenberg. Katzenberg had begun importing heroin from Europe, which Rothstein then distributed in New York and across the country. Ever a visionary, Rothstein was positioning himself for the day when Prohibition would end and lucrative new illicit vices would take its place. It was a day The Brain would never live to see.

The Death of Arnold Rothstein

By the late twenties, bootlegging was big, big business, and of course where there is business there are business disputes, involving winners and losers; in conventional business the losers get kicked upstairs, get bought out or demoted or retire; in gangland they get killed.

Little Augie Orgen was such casualty. After Kid Dropper's murder in August of 1923, Orgen gained complete control over labor racketeering on the Lower East Side and throughout the city in general. But after Kaplan's broad daylight murder the heat was on, and the city mounted aggressive investigations into extortion and labor slugging. This was bad for business, and bad for Rothstein, who tried to minimize any police attention he couldn't pay away. Some say he dispatched Louis Buchalter, others say Lansky, to "advise" Little Augie to concentrate on infiltrating labor unions; Rothstein and Lansky preferred subtle control from within to outright, often messy intimidation from without. Orgen refused to "listen to reason." He was also moving into bootlegging. On October 16, 1927, while walking on Norfolk Street, Buchalter and Shapiro dispatched Little Augie in a drive-by shooting. Orgen received a Jewish burial from his father, who had disowned him after he had formed his gang "The Little Augies" in 1919.

A little over a year later Arnold Rothstein's number came up. On the night of Sunday, November 4th, 1928 he was found near the employee's entrance of his favorite haunt, the Park Central Hotel, shot in the abdomen. He was taken to New York's Polyclinic Hospital and operated on. He lingered, going in and out of a coma, speaking to his wife and his two brothers. Questioned by the police, Rothstein, a stand up guy to the end, replied, "I'll take care of it myself." He died two days later, on Election Day, 1928.

Who killed Arnold Rothstein? The standard theory is that during a marathon three-day poker game in September, Rothstein claimed the game was fixed and walked out, welching on the $320,000 he owed to three West Coast gamblers, Nate Raymond, Alvin "Titanic" Thompson and Joe Bernstein. The game had been organized by George McManus, a well-connected bookmaker and gambler, who had a brother on the police force. McManus assured the West Coast trio the debt would be paid. Nicky Arnstein, Fanny Brice's gambler boyfriend and a friend of Rothstein's, advised him to pay the debt regardless of whether the game was rigged: Nobody likes to look like a sucker. Rothstein refused and weeks went by. On November 4th McManus, drinking heavily and under pressure, asked to meet with Rothstein in Room 347 at the Park Central. Rothstein emerged from the room with a bullet in the abdomen.

McManus was arrested and charged with the crime, but there was no witness to place him in Room 347 when the shooting took place. He was acquitted. Some have always thought there was more to the murder than gambling debts; attention has centered on Dutch Schultz, whose friend Joey Noe had been killed by a Rothstein protégé, Legs Diamond, and who was intent on entirely taking over Rothstein's interests in the Bronx. Strangely enough, Meyer Lansky, Benny Siegel and Charlie Luciano, the men who stood most to gain by Rothstein's demise, and who inherited his empire and put many of his ideas for a national crime syndicate into play, were never considered suspects.

Rothstein's influence on Lansky and his importance to the history of organized crime can never be overestimated. "We all admired him," Lansky told Uri Dan in *Mogul of the Mob*:

> He was always totally honest with us and taught us a great deal. We got on well right from the beginning—like me he was a gambler from the cradle. It was in the blood of both of us. Rothstein seems to have had a gift for figures too, and he used to practice by asking his friends to fire off random numbers at him. He would multiply, divide, add or subtract these numbers and produce the answers instantaneously. He had an ice-cold nerve and even when playing for the highest stakes, with hundreds of thousands of dollars at risk, he never lost his head.[86]

Perhaps laying it on a little thick, Lansky painted a poignant portrait of Rothstein's last days as a gambler:

> The gambling fever that was always a part of Arnie's make-up appears to have gone to his brain. It was like a disease and he was now in its last stages. He gambled wildly—even bet a half a million dollars on the 1928 presidential election. His money was on Herbert Hoover to beat Al Smith, and of course he won. But this did not seem to help him. He started to look like a man suffering from some terrible sickness. Gambling really is a disease. It becomes part of a man and takes over his life even if he's winning. And there is only one way to win—and that is not to play. Every player, even Arnie Rothstein, king of them all, loses in the end. . .[87]

In the Jewish tradition, Arnold Rothstein was buried in an orthodox service the following day in Queens, wearing a white skullcap and a purple-striped tallis; his death cancelled the bet he had placed on the outcome of the election that was held the day he died. Had he lived to collect, the money would have been more than enough to pay off his debt.

The Castellammarese War and The Beginnings of the Modern Mafia

With Rothstein gone, the stage was set for a series of major upheavals in the underworld, in which Lansky, Siegel and their Jewish cohorts played critical and at times violent roles.

Employing all of the Machiavellian deception, Yiddish cunning and the ruthless intrigue they learned on the streets of the Lower East Side, Lansky and Luciano engineered the downfall of the old Moustache Petes, first Massaria, then Maranzano, playing each off against the other during the Castellammarese War of 1927-31. Named from the town in Sicily, Castellammarese del Golfo, where both men were born, the war was ostensibly between the two aging dons for control of the Sicilian Mafia in New York and the title of Capo Di Tutti Capi.—Boss of All Bosses. In reality the war spelled the overthrow of the old Moustache Petes and their Unione Siciliane methods by the Young Turks: Luciano, Costello, Lansky, Siegel and the rest of their generation, and the modernization of organized crime in America.

It would do well to take a second to appreciate that these men were not the doughy, wizened mobsters called to mind by sinister pictures from the 50s and 60s, well after they had entered middle age. In 1929 Meyer Lansky was 27, Luciano 32; most of their cohorts were well under 40, in their late twenties and early thirties. Save for their murderous ways and their illegal pursuits they were slick, clever and modern, like rising young adventurers and dynamic entrepreneurs of any era.

The first blow was struck at a meeting held in Atlantic City in 1929, a meeting that pointedly excluded Masseria and Maranzano. Major bootleggers, both Jewish and Italian, from across the country were represented, including Dutch Schultz from the Bronx, Waxey Gordon and Nig Rosen from Philadelphia, Moe Dalitz, Lou Rothkopf and Charlie Polizzi (actual name: Leo Berkowitz) from Cleveland, and "King" Solomon from Boston. The Italians were represented by Al Capone, Willie Moretti, Albert Anastasia, Frank Costello, Ace Mangano and others. The conclave was held primarily to iron out problems in the nationwide distribution of liquor and lay the groundwork for future cooperation, in gambling as well as bootlegging.

In addition to bootlegging, between 1925 and 1931 Lansky and Luciano revolutionized the business of gambling, expanding a variety of rackets that originated on the Lower East Side throughout much of the New York metropolitan area, and then out into the rest of America. Working with Frank Erickson, the late Arnold Rothstein's chief aide, as well as Frank Costello, plus Moses Annenberg from Chicago, Lansky helped turn the local bookmaking operation Erickson and Costello ran so profitably in New York into a national wire service equipped to handle large scale betting action, hundreds of thousands of dollars, even millions. This capitalized the Mob's future investments in race tracks and other sporting venues. Lansky, who probably understood the psychology and mechanics of gambling better than anyone who ever lived, then turned his attention to the creation and development of a number of new rackets—gaming innovations, mostly in the realm of bookmaking, the taking of bets on horse races, prizefights, base-

ball, football, basketball games and even elections, and other events with unpredictable out-
comes. The Lower East Side was Lansky's laboratory for these ideas. First, small neighborhood
shopkeepers who were taking bets and making modest payoffs on their own were placed on a
regular weekly salary to take bets exclusively for Lansky's organization; their phones were
installed for free so they could call in the action. Lansky and company would keep track of the
betting and pay off the winners, the shopkeepers would get police protection and a regular
salary: You take the bet, we do the rest. The shopkeepers were happy to be relieved of the burden of keeping track and paying off on bets, and having a regular weekly salary didn't hurt
either. Recalcitrant store owners were "persuaded" by some sinister shoppers or an unfortunate
fire or flood. Meanwhile the number of wagers Lansky's organization could take expanded
exponentially, as did the profits. Winners now knew they would be paid off promptly, and payoffs would always be made; in any gaming situation, Meyer Lansky was known to be scrupu-
lously honest and utterly reliable. Door-to-door peddlers were also recruited to take bets and
carry the betting slips back to Lansky's bookmakers. Lansky and Luciano established banks where
bookies could lay off large bets, spreading and lessening their exposure to big payouts. With the
cash flow from these enterprises, Lansky and Luciano opened elaborate "horse parlors," where
wealthy patrons could gamble in a luxurious environment not unlike that of the track:

> "We made these the finest establishments in America. We bought the best
> furniture, so the society ladies would be comfortable, and the atmosphere
> was like a living room in a rich house. We provided good food and
> installed telephones and loudspeakers. We even had some of the places
> painted and decorated to look like a racetrack, with fancy pictures of
> horses, and we installed betting windows . . . everything was legitimate.
> We never cheated the customers—we didn't have to. The minute the
> results of each race were known the management would put up the win-
> ning names on a board or announce them over a loudspeaker. We gave
> them the same odds as the track. We always had an excellent reputation.
> . . . There was no limit to the amount of money we made. Because book-
> makers never lose. Just the suckers who bet on the horses."[88]

But perhaps Lansky's most remarkable contribution to the culture of gambling was a betting system that became ubiquitous, (so ubiquitous it eventually had to be legalized and co-opted by the
state) especially in Harlem and other poor and minority areas of the city: the numbers, also
known as "policy," a racket that seems as if it has been around forever but has only existed
since 1925, when Meyer Lansky invented it. Every day there would be a three digit lucky number, called a combination. You would know where it came from: a horse race, a baseball score,
the last three digits of the Dow Jones Index at the close of the market—but the number could
never be predicted in advance and could never be fixed. It paid off 600 to one; you could bet
as little as a penny. The Moustache Petes ridiculed it: How could anyone make money with
nickel, dime and penny bets? The people of Harlem, and then Brooklyn, and then the Bronx
loved it. People bet every day, it was a daily diversion, an addiction that they could afford, and
one they refused to do without, despite the efforts of the police and the admonitions of preach-
ers. During the Depression it also proved to be a valuable source of employment for thousands
of people. Frank Costello ran it in Harlem, and Lansky and company spread the game throughout the rest of New York and across the country. It was another highly lucrative revenue stream
for the Lansky/Luciano Mob. It made them a fortune, and it drove the old dons crazy.

Charlie Gets Lucky

For Lansky and Luciano the biggest problem with Masseria, a boorish but deft Sicilian who had arrived in the Lower East Side in 1903, and Maranzano, a younger upstart sent in 1925 by the Don Vito Cascio Ferro of Castellammare to reassert Sicilian control over the American Mafia, was their provincialism, their blinkered, Old World way of conducting business: squeezing tribute from the poor and staging of never ending vendettas, murderous family feuds so costly in blood, money and morale. Then there was their obsessive, almost psychotic fixation on archaic Sicilian rituals: the pricking of the finger, the burning of vows in cupped hands, the kissing of the ring, the passing of sealed envelopes of money, all of which originated with secret societies like the Black Hand and the Camorra in Sicily, and seemed like something out of the Middle Ages (which it was) to the next generation of Jewish and Italian mobsters, especially when set against the fast tempo of modern life in urban America.

"It made me laugh when the older Italians I knew spoke about the Mafia and it's code of honor," Lansky told Uri Dan.

> . . .the idea that the powerful were helping the poor was a bad joke. I used to tease my Italian friends about the Mafia. They were so honorable that no one in the Mafia ever trusted anyone else. They lied to each other, cheated each other and killed each other. The crime in the Italian ghettos was in fact carried out by gangsters who called themselves the Mafia but didn't even know what it meant. . .[89]

Though Maranzano was younger, educated and more cultured he was no less murderous and no less wedded to the old Sicilian rituals. Both men also had no liking for Jews, and taking them in as equal partners was out of the question. This especially piqued Luciano, whose friendship with Lansky was not only one of genuine respect, equality and affection, but one that had always made him and younger Italian cohorts money—lots of it. That was the bottom line—all this crap interfered with making money, and there was a lot of money to be made out of Prohibition. Arnold Rothstein had shown them that money, and the ability to make it, was the great equalizer. "There's no such thing as good money or bad money, " Luciano once said. "There's just money." As Rich Cohen points out, Lansky and Luciano were way ahead of the rest of America in rejecting the small-bore prejudices that were so much a part of American life:

> In an era when much of the country was hyper-aware of background and religion, Lansky and Luciano got beyond that. They believed that in America your brother can be born to any parents, in any house. 'Gangsters who never made it out of high school broke social barriers thirty years before anyone else got near them,' Ralph Salerno told me. 'Much more than other people in other parts of society, gangsters are pragmatic and realistic.'[90]

Maranzano was a charismatic presence (he was fascinated by the Roman Empire, particularly Julius Caesar) and, backed with money from Italy, he rapidly set up a formidable bootlegging operation with a tough gang of young mobsters, including Joseph "Joe Bananas" Bonanno,

Joseph Profaci and Stefano Magaddino. Masseria eyed Maranzano's organization warily, and by 1927 open warfare had broken out. Masseria murdered major figures in Maranzano's gang, then ordered a hit on Maranzano himself. There were shootouts, hijackings, ambushes and bodies in the streets, and soon both men surrounded themselves with bodyguards and gunmen. Both, particularly Masseria, also put pressure on Luciano to sever his Jewish connections and merge organizations. For a time in the mid 20s Luciano allied himself with Masseria while still maintaining ties with his crew on the Lower East Side. Lansky advised him to bide his time, divide and conquer. Maranzano began to secretly approach key men in Masseria's organization, trying to undermine his rival from within. On Lansky's counsel Luciano stalled, and the Bugs and Meyer crew, with the help of Luciano's Sicilian allies (to prevent a war between the Jews and the Italians) arranged several "false flag" rubouts, killings that one boss would blame on the other, and perhaps avenge accordingly, thereby disrupting both factions. Meanwhile Luciano flirted with both men, but this game almost cost him his life: On October 17, 1929, with Lansky preoccupied with his wife's difficult pregnancy, Luciano met Maranzano in a deserted garage on Staten Island. Maranzano's thugs beat him to a pulp. The Don told Luciano he would be killed unless he agreed to kill Masseria and merge his gang with Maranzano's. His reward, strangely enough, would be to become Maranzano's second in command. When he told Maranzano to go fuck himself and his Sicilian honor, Maranzano personally gave him the scar that was to forever mar his face. Luciano was tossed on a beach and left for dead, but was found by the police and taken to a hospital, where he slowly recovered.

One might suppose that Charlie—now dubbed "Lucky" by Meyer Lansky —would seek immediate revenge, but Lansky and Luciano played the situation with their usual devious cunning, aware that their lives would never be secure unless both Dons were eliminated. As with the Irish informer, they would wait, letting Masseria and Maranzano dissipate their strength by murdering each other's bodyguards and top lieutenants.

By spring Luciano had recovered, and he again agreed to meet Maranzano, this time in public, at the Bronx Zoo, with Bugsy Siegel and friends along to assure his safety. Tossing peanuts at the monkeys, Maranzano and Lucky cut a deal in which Luciano would become Maranzano's number two, this time with his Jewish partners, and share in the proceeds of their combined rackets. Obviously, the first order of business was to eliminate Masseria.

A Leisurely Lunch and a Business Meeting

According to Uri Dan, Luciano went directly from this meeting on April 15, 1931 downtown to Masseria's office on Second Avenue. After detailing his plans to wipe out Maranzano once and for all, he suggested that he and The Boss celebrate by driving out to Coney Island for a leisurely lunch at the Nova Villa Tammaro, a restaurant owned by Gerardo Scarpato, a friend of Luciano's. A legendary glutton, for three hours Masseria gorged himself on giant portions of veal, linguini with clam sauce and other Sicilian delights, washed down with plenty of red wine. Afterwards, it is said, the two men played poker. When the crowd thinned out around three in the afternoon, Charlie went to use the men's room.

While Luciano pissed, a black sedan from Lansky's garage pulled up. Bugsy Siegel, Joe Adonis and Albert Anastasia, and some say Red Levine and Vito Genovese as well, ran into the Villa

Tammaro, guns blazing. They pumped six bullets into Joe The Boss, and left fourteen more in the restaurant. Supposedly Masseria died holding the ace of diamonds, face up. Rich Cohen says the card was ever after cursed, and receiving it meant you would soon be on the receiving end of a bullet. But Lansky told Uri Dan that the only thing Joe The Boss was holding was the tablecloth, soaked in his blood, which he pulled around himself as he fell to the floor.

Luciano finished his business, yanked the toilet chain, washed his hands, went out and called this shocking crime in to the police. When the cops asked where he was during the carnage, Lucky said he had been taking a leak. "I always take a long leak," he said.[91]

Maranzano declared himself the winner of the Castellammare War. He was now the most powerful gangster in New York. A few weeks after Masseria's murder, several hundred Mafiosi gathered at a banquet hall in the Bronx where Maranzano laid out his vision for the future of the Italian underworld, which survives, albeit in mutated, truncated form, to this day.

It was based upon the hierarchical structure of the Roman Empire. There would be five criminal families, each run by an underboss: Lucky Luciano, Joseph Bonanno, Joseph Profaci, Albert Anastasia and Tommy Luchese. The soldiers under their leadership would pay a percentage of their earnings—tribute—to them, and they would in turn kick tribute upstairs to Maranzano, the Capo Di Tutti Capo, Boss Of All Bosses. In return their illegal activities would be protected, mainly by bribes and graft. If that failed and they were arrested they would receive legal help; if they went to prison, their families would be taken care of. Maranzano also established certain rules: There would be no more unsanctioned killings: interfamily disputes were to be settled quietly, at sit-downs by the bosses, whose word was final; and there was to be no discussion whatsoever about the Mafia or its activities, including the fact of its very existence, to any outsiders, including wives. The punishment for violating these rules was death.

The ceremony was later described to Lansky by Luciano; both were disgusted by Maranzano's imperial pretensions—sealed envelopes of cash, ring kissing, a long lecture on Sicilian honor and Julius Caesar and other unreal Old World malarkey that Luciano found both condescending and crazy. But what really pissed him off was when Maranzano, naming him his number two, patted him on the head like a child.

Despite all the pomp and circumstance, Lansky and Luciano were well aware that in this arrangement their days would be numbered. Before long they learned the Boss of All Bosses had hired a crazy Irish hit man named Mad Dog Coll to murder Luciano, Frank Costello and Vito Genovese; and that was just the beginning: Maranzano's hit list also included Willie Moretti, Joe Adonis, Dutch Schultz, Al Capone and plenty of their men, and the rest of the Jews were next.

Knowing they had to kill Maranzano before he killed them, Lansky and Luciano devised a plan, much of it probably conceived in the back room of Ratner's on Delancey Street, over belly lox and bagels, corn beef on rye, or latkes with applesauce, followed by Danish and coffee. It proved to be one of the most audacious hits in gangland history, portrayed many times in fiction and film. Lansky assembled a crew of Jewish killers from across the country, men Maranzano and his bodyguards would not recognize, including Red Levine and Bo Weinberg, a gunman for Dutch Schultz. Led by Bugsy Siegel, they hid out up in the Bronx, awaiting Meyer's call.

On September 10, 1931, Maranzano asked Luciano up to his elegant offices at The New York Central building above Grand Central, at 230 Park Avenue. And by the way, said the Boss, could you bring along your pals Frank Costello and Vito Genovese to discuss business? We'll all have a nice lunch. Luciano knew exactly what that meant.

The recently built tower was then one of the most prestigious addresses in New York, and Maranzano had a real estate concern and an import export business on the ninth floor. They were legitimate businesses, and the Don took pains to see they were legitimately run. But lately Maranzano's offices were being paid occasional visits by the Treasury Department, especially since Meyer's brother Jake had tipped off the government that they might well find incriminating evidence about the Don's other, more colorful business interests there. The drop-ins became an annoying formality, but since everything was legit, Maranzano had no qualms about letting the agents in to examine his books. In fact, it was a point of pride for the elegant and unflappable Don that everything was on the up and up.

So when a group of men in overcoats and fedoras arrived, flashed badges, claimed to be Treasury agents and said something about a raid, they gained easy entry. Maranzano's bodyguards were quickly disarmed, some say tied up, others say held at gunpoint, while Red Levine and Bugsy Siegel took Maranzano back into his office. Levine stifled his protests with a knife; then he was shot four times. After blundering into a ladies' room while making their escape, they ran into Mad Dog Coll by the elevator and told him to beat it, the cops were on their way. Six months later, Coll was making a call from a Manhattan phone booth when Bugsy Siegel shot him to death.

The Combination and The Commission

After the dust settled, in November of that year Lansky and Luciano convened an underworld summit at the Franconia Hotel on West 72nd Street. The top East Coast Jewish gangsters—Jacob Shapiro, Louis "Lepke" Buchalter, Joseph "Doc" Stacher, Hyman "Curly" Holtz, Louis "Shadows" Kravitz, Harry Tietlebaum, Philip "Little Farvel" Kovolick and Harry "Big Greenie" Greenberg—were all in attendance, as well as their Italian counterparts from the Five Families and Mob organizations from outside New York State.

Lansky told the Jews that now that the Italian mafia was united, the Jewish mafia, through an alliance with Luciano, would form a confederation—a combination, a syndicate of national proportion—with the Italians. There would be no Boss of Bosses, no money in sealed envelopes, no ring kissing; bosses would be equal (although of course, it went unstated that Lucky Luciano was first among equals; and Lansky reportedly suggested to Luciano that the Italian mob could keep some of their silly rituals, if it made them feel comfortable. He agreed.) Like any major American corporation, they would now governed by a Board of Directors, a Commission, which would decide policy, make rules, issue edicts and settle outstanding disputes, albeit in their own unique way.

"The old Mafia traditions are fine for Sicily. But we are in America," Luciano told the assembled guests. "The idea of putting a crown on my head is kid stuff. It's time we grew up. We'll all work for each other, but each is running his own outfit." When the meeting ended, Bugsy Siegel proclaimed: "The yids and the dagos will no longer fight each other."

To guard against vendettas and to enforce the edicts of the Commission with a perverse degree of justice and gangland professionalism, the Commission established Murder, Inc. It consisted of hired killers, mainly from the Brownsville section of Brooklyn, but also from other parts of the country, led by Bugsy Siegel, Albert "Mad Hatter" Anastasia and Louis "Lepke" Buchalter. The group carried out hundreds of contract killings throughout the late thirties and forties. Murder's much feared lineup of killers, at least of the Hebraic persuasion, included Martin "Buggsy" Goldstein, Gurrah Shapiro, Abe "Kid Twist" Reles, Red Levine, Harry "Pittsburgh Phil" Strauss, Allie "Tic Tock" Tannenbaum, Seymour "Blue Jaw" Magoon, Mendy Weiss and Charles "Charlie the Bug" Workman, a family man who invited the whole gang to his son's bris, held in 1935 at his Lower East Side apartment, an event magnificently reconstructed by Rich Cohen in *Tough Jews*. (The Bug later went on to hit Dutch Schultz, on orders from the Commission, after the Dutchman vowed to kill Tom Dewey.) Once the Commission put out a contract it was irrevocable—the informant, embezzler or traitor was doomed. Often the killers and their victims were unknown to each other, the button man dispatched from another city with just enough information to find his victim. There were occasional mistakes, which made for bad publicity, but most hits by Murder, Inc., though garish enough to make the point to other potential mob transgressors, went unsolved. Like star freelancers, members were kept on retainer, and then received an average fee of between one and five grand for a hit. It was a very professional operation, although Reles, a sadistic psychopath, was known for his lethal use of the ice pick, killing his victim just for the fun of it, just for kicks.

But most of the operations of Murder, Inc. were nothing personal. They were strictly business, and confined to the mob, or those who had crossed it. As Bugsy Siegel put it to Del Webb, the contractor who built the Flamingo Hotel, when Webb expressed some uneasiness about the ominous number of monosyllabic men with concealed weapons loitering about the worksite, "Don't worry, Del, we only kill our own."

And so it was. Siegel was assassinated in 1947, a well planned hit approved by the Commission, including, reluctantly and after much anguished argument, his best friend, Meyer Lansky. It was again, strictly business; Bugsy Siegel had squandered millions of Mob money on the ber-luxurious Flamingo Hotel in Las Vegas: Construction materials had to be beought on the black market at enormous cost, each of the ninety three rooms had separate sewer systems, the boiler room and the kitchen were rebuilt several times, Siegel insisted there be a trapshooting range, nine-hole golf course, tennis, squash, badminton, and handball courts, as well as extensive landscaping with imported Oriental date palm and Spanish cork trees. The staff wore tuxedoes.

Despite millions in overruns, the hotel's opening was a disaster. Aside from astronomical operating expenses, the casino lost around $300,000 to gamblers in the first two weeks. Siegel had oversubscribed the hotel's stock, selling 25 percent interests to twenty people. But the topper was Bugsy's infamous mistress, Virginia Hill, the Flamingo for whom The Flamingo was named, whom Siegel had stolen away from Joe Adonis. Asked at the Kefauver hearings by a Senator why she had so many tough guy celebrity boyfriends, Virginia testified it was because she gave the best head in America. Hill had a history of being a courier for mob money, and was now suspected by the Commission of carrying suitcases full of embezzled Flamingo cash to Switzerland for Siegel.

On the night of June 20, 1947 at Hill's home in Beverly Hills, as he sat on the couch reading the Los Angeles Times, Bugsy Siegel was shot to death by a sniper. The thirty-caliber high-speed bullet that killed him went though the back of his skull and exited through an eye socket; the eyeball ended up on the other side of the room. He was perforated several more times, for good measure.

Today on the Lower East Side a Yartzheit (remembrance) plaque for Benjamin Siegel can be found in the Bialystoker Synagogue, on 7-11 Willett Street in Lower Manhattan. Above it, a plaque bears the name Max Siegel, Bugsy's father, who died two months prior to Bugsy's murder. His Hebrew name is "Mordechai Dovid Bar (son of) Beirush HaLevi. Bugsy's Hebrew name is Bairush HaLevi Bar Mordechai Dovid HaLevi. He was named after his grandfather, who had died shortly before his grandson was born.

With Meyer Lansky and Bugsy Siegel, the era of the Jewish gangster and his rise from the Lower East Side reaches its apotheosis and, especially after Siegel's assassination in 1947, begins its long decline and slow transfiguration into legend and myth. Lansky would go on to establish carpet joints (lavish nightclubs with all forms of gambling) in New Jersey, huge hotels and luxurious casinos in Cuba and Vegas, and important "business techniques" such as skimming—taking a cash cut off the top at casinos ("one for the government, three for the house, two for Meyer"). Perhaps Meyer's greatest financial innovation—enthusiastically adopted by politicians, drug cartels, and the CIA—was the art and science of money laundering, the avoidance of taxes through the metamorphosis of "dirty" money—cash from illegal activities—to "clean" money, by washing it through an impenetrable maze of legitimate businesses and banks.

The End of The Road and the End of Ratner's

 As Rich Cohen points out, unlike the Italians, the Jews for the most part, actively discouraged their children from continuing the underworld life they had led, the life of guns and bootlegging and gambling and drugs and cold cash that had brought them out of poverty and propelled them into the ranks of the wealthy, or at least the upper middle class bourgeoisie, to which they had aspired with so much sweat and blood. Now, with a solid foothold in the good life, there was no need for their children to maim and murder for money. As Luciano once commented, and as history has proven, one man with a briefcase can steal more than a hundred men with guns. Lansky's son Paul went to West Point and flew fighter planes in Vietnam; other sons and daughters of Jewish mobsters, with a few exceptions, also went legit, entered the "professions" and became the doctors, lawyers and businessmen their fathers had once dreamed, even fleetingly, of becoming so long ago in the past, when such dreams seemed daunting, if not impossible.

Throughout his life, Lansky and his pals would meet at the old Ratner's, the famous kosher dairy restaurant on 138 Delancey Street, between Norfolk and Suffolk Streets, up the block from the Williamsburg Bridge. Later on, in the 50s and 60s, when it stayed open all night, they would congregate - where else?—in the backroom, for business, of course, but also undoubtedly for melancholy frissons of nostalgia, along with a nosh. The waiters, famed for their insulting, no bullshit attitude, would bring split pea and matzo ball soup, Ratner's own onion rolls (10,000 baked on premises for the restaurant's famous Sunday brunch), bagels, blintzes, perogies, and latkes; but as the decades passed, it wasn't the same. Year in, year out the number of Jews on the LES dwindled as their children fled, abandoning the schmatta and hardware and dress businesses their grandparents had built, first for college, then for the suburbs of Long Island, Westchester or Connecticut. Urban renewal and the rising projects brought change. Blacks, Hispanics, Ukrainians, Poles, other new minorities, hippies and the few poor luckless Jews who couldn't escape now populated the Lower East Side, spilling as well up into the area from Houston to 14th Streets that real estate brokers eventually renamed the East Village in a long, and until recently, futile effort to upscale the market.

In the mid-90s gentrification finally began taking hold in what had once been one of the poorest and least desirable neighborhoods in Manhattan. Tenement apartments that in 1978 went begging now sell for hundreds of thousands of dollars, and boutiques and bistros have replaced discount fabric and hat stores. In 1983, Meyer Lansky died of lung cancer in Miami Beach. He was 80 years old. The FBI estimated that Lansky had stashed away $200 million in secret bank accounts; they never found a penny. Later, some biographers, particularly Robert Lacey, in his 1991 biography *Little Man: Meyer Lansky and the Gangster Life,* contended that Lansky died poor; that he was more of an accountant than an actual gangster, much less the secret mastermind, the hidden hand, the mogul of the Mob. It was all a myth, a joint fiction of the FBI, magazine writers looking for a quick buck, and the media looking for ratings.

Meyer Lansky once told the owners of Ratner's that he had spent so much time there he deserved a dedicated room. Fourteen years after his death, in 1997, the grandchildren of Ratner's founder, Jacob Harmatz (the restaurant was named for his brother-in-law on a coin toss) opened the *Lansky Lounge* in homage to the Ratner's most notorious patron. The Lounge, with lobster now on the menu, was an effort to attract the hipsters and well-heeled young professionals moving into the neighborhood, who were more into sushi and quiche than blinis and borscht. In 2002, the old restaurant closed and for a time, the Lounge took over the entire space. But not even the Lansky legend could save it; all that was left of Ratner's closed for good in 2004. Now Sleepy's, The Mattress Professional, occupies 138 Delancey; the franchise furniture store is sandwiched between a branch of Banco Popular, and a Donkin Donuts; nothing of Ratner's remains. Early in 2008, the postmodern, oddly shaped 16-story "Blue" Condominium, built on Norwalk Street, directly in back of what was once the restaurant welcomed its first tenants. It's occupants now sip their scotch high above the new Lower East Side, gazing though floor-to-ceiling turquoise tinted windows out over the Williamsburg Bridge, far into Brooklyn and beyond.

Timeline:

1880–1920 Era of massive immigration to America. By 1890 more than 190,000 Jews have settled on the Lower East Side of Manhattan; by 1915 more than 320,000, nearly 60 percent of the neighborhood's population.

Around 1895 Monk Eastman appears in Manhattan, becomes a sheriff at New Irving Hall; by 1897 he establishes his own gang, by 1900 it numbers around 1200 professional criminals.

1901–1903 Eastmans Gang fights The Five Pointers, led by Paul Kelly (Paolo Vaccarelli). Convicted of a botched robbery, Eastman goes to Sing-Sing for ten years. His deputy Max Zweibach – a.k.a. Kid Twist, a.k.a. Kid Sly Fox, succeeds him as head of the gang.

1905 Benjamin "Dopey Fein" forms a gang of pickpockets on the LES.

1907 Joe "The Greaser" Rosenzweig forms a gang of labor sluggers.

1908 On May 14, 1908 Zweibach and Vach "Cyclone" Lewis are murdered outside a Coney Island bar by "Louie the Lump" Pioggi.

1908–1912 Big Jack Zelig takes over the remnants of the Eastmans Gang; Benjamin "Dopey" Fine joins Zelig's gang as a labor slugger in 1910.

July 1912 Herman "Beansie Rosenthal, police informer, murdered outside the Metropole Hotel.

October 1912 Zelig is murdered on a LES trolley.

1909-1917 Era of labor strife on the Lower East Side from 1912 as Benny "Dopey" Fein transforms labor racketeering; period of the first The Labor Slugger's War (1913-1917) between Fine, Rosenzweig, Pinchey Paul, Paul Sirroco.

1909-1919 The longstanding rivalry between Nathan Kaplan (Kid Dropper) and Johnny Spanish ends in July 1919 with shooting death of Spanish on 2nd Avenue.

1920 Prohibition; the Volstead Act, banning the manufacture, sale, and transportation of alcoholic beverages, passed in 1917, ratified as the 18th Amendment to the Constitution, takes effect in January of 1920.

1911-1919 Arnold Rothstein establishes himself as a legendary New York gambler, stock swindler, racketeer and fixer. In 1919 he allegedly fixes the World Series.

April 1911 Meyer Lansky arrives in New York.

1914-1920 Meyer Lansky meets and forms lasting friendships with Benjamin Siegel and Charlie Luciano; Lansky and Siegel form the Bugs and Meyer Mob.

1920-1921 Rothstein makes deals with Waxey Gordon, then enlists Meyer Lansky and Lucky Luciano to initiate large scale smuggling of high quality liquor into America.

1923 Nathan "Kid Dropper" Kaplan murdered by Louis Kushner outside the Essex Market Courthouse, August 23rd; his labor rackets pass on to Jacob "Little Augie" Orgen.

1927 On October 16, as he walked on Norfolk Street, Little Augie is killed by Louis "Lepke" Buchalter and Gurrah Shapiro in a drive-by shooting.

1927-1931 The Castellammarese War between Masseria and Maranzano for control of the Silician Mafia.

1925-1931 Lansky and Luciano revolutionize the rackets, establishing a nationwide wire service and horse parlors, and inventing the numbers, also known as "policy."

1928 Arnold Rothstein shot at the Park Central Hotel; he dies two days later on Election Day.

1929 Major bootleggers, both Jewish and Italian, from across the country meet in Atlantic City;

Masseria and Maranzano are not invited.

1929 Luciano survives a near-fatal "ride" with Maranzano in Staten Island.

1931 On April 15th Masseria is gunned down in a Coney Island restaurant during lunch with Luciano; on September 10th, Maranzano is assassinated in his office above Grand Central Station.

In November of that year an underworld summit at the Franconia Hotel on West 72nd Street, led by Lansky and Luciano, establishes The Combination, a national crime syndicate, led by a "Commission" of bosses. Murder, Inc. is created to enforce the Commission's edicts.

1947 Bugsy Siegel is assassinated in Los Angeles.

David H. Katz is a writer, photographer and artist working in New York City. He has written for a wide variety of publications, including The New Statesman, High Times, the British fashion magazine TANK, The Villager, The Portable Lower East Side, Circus, Rap Express and London's Jewish Quarterly. His memoir, The Father Fades, appeared in Transformation, A Journal of Literature, Ideas and the Arts, Spring, 2005; subsequent issues have featured his fiction and art.

His artwork has been published in Zeek web magazine, and his work has been exhibited at Makor Gallery, Diamonds and Oranges Gallery, and Gallery 225 in New York. In addition to writing and editing, he maintains a website featuring his artwork: ZtakArchives.com, which hosts ongoing artistic projects. He lives on the Lower East Side of Manhattan.

---

[56] Rich Cohen, *Tough Jews* (New York: Vintage Books, 1998, 1999), p. 130.

[57] Ibid., p. 130.

[58] Jacob A. Riis, *How The Other Half Lives* (New York: Penguin Classics, 1997), p. 83.

[59] Albert Fried, *The Rise and Fall of the Jewish Gangster in America*, (New York: Columbia University Press, 1993), p.29.

[60] Ibid., p.32.

[61] Ibid., p.29.

[62] Ibid.

[63] Rich Cohen, *Tough Jews* (New York: Vintage Books, 1998, 1999), p. 46.

[64] Ibid.

[65] F. Scott Fitzgerald, *The Great Gatsby* (London: Penguin Books, 1926, 1990), p. 46.

[66] Dennis Eisenberg, Uri Dan, Eli Landau, *Meyer Lansky: Mogul of the Mob* (US, Paddington Press, 1979) p. 79.

[67] Ibid., p. 27-8.

[68] Ibid., p. 32.

[69] Robert Lacey, *Little Man: Meyer Lansky and the Gangster Life.* (Boston: Little, Brown and Company, 1991) p. 28.

[70] Ibid., p. 30.

[71] Dennis Eisenberg, Uri Dan, Eli Landau, *Meyer Lansky: Mogul of the Mob* (US, Paddington Press, 1979) p. 37.

[72] Ibid., p. 32.

[73] Ibid., p. 37.

[74] Ibid., p. 36.

[75] Albert Fried, *The Rise and Fall of the Jewish Gangster in America*, (New York: Columbia University Press, 1993), p. 229.

[76] Dennis Eisenberg, Uri Dan, Eli Landau, *Meyer Lansky: Mogul of the Mob* (US, Paddington Press, 1979) p. 52.

[77] Ibid., p. 53.

[78] Ibid.

[79] Ibid., p. 143.

[80] Ibid., p. 51.

[81] Martin A. Gosch, Richard Hammer, *The Last Testament of Lucky Luciano*, (Boston, Little Brown and Company, 1974).

[82] Dennis Eisenberg, Uri Dan, Eli Landau, *Meyer Lansky: Mogul of the Mob* (US, Paddington Press, 1979) p. 55-56.

[83] Albert Fried, *The Rise and Fall of the Jewish Gangster in America*, (New York: Columbia University Press, 1993), p. 231-232.

[84] Rich Cohen, *Tough Jews* (New York: Vintage Books, 1998, 1999), p. 20.

[85] Dennis Eisenberg, Uri Dan, Eli Landau, *Meyer Lansky: Mogul of the Mob* (US, Paddington Press, 1979). p. 86.

[86] Ibid., p. 103.

[87] Ibid., p. 105.

[88] Ibid., p. 149.

[89] Ibid., p. 119-20.

[90] Rich Cohen, *Tough Jews* (New York: Vintage Books, 1998, 1999), p. 61.

[91] Ibid., p. 63.

My Name is Ben

Ben Essex

Hi, my name is Ben. I was born at The Maternity Center, which is no longer there, on 94th Street, April 4, 1981. My mother lived on Essex and Stanton streets in the East Village.

At that time New York was a very scary place to live. There was a drug epidemic, particularly in the East Village, but to some degree I was impervious to that fact. My mother was a visiting nurse with the Visiting Nurse Service. She was involved with healing practices like massage and herbal supplementing as well as political activism in the community, nationally, and globally. She was a "real neighbor" as a friend once put it, so I felt very safe and loved as a child.

My school was across the street. Growing up I had the feelings that maybe a lot of kids but perhaps especially sheltered kids have: that other kids and people who don't know you will not automatically like you, be nice to you or be on your side! This was a very hard and sad feeling to live with so I indulged in fantasies of how things could be "better." Being from the city, I always fantasized about living in the sticks and being like a happy and healthy kid in the 'burbs. So naturally, I was all for the idea when my mothers' friends bought a house upstate in Monroe Woodberry and she wanted to do the same (fall of 1991).

Up there I experienced anti-Semitism for the first time. They called me mean names and I wanted to fight over it a lot but wouldn't always because I knew I would get my ass kicked or was afraid of the other person. After a while, I kind of accepted it from my so-called friends and it almost seemed endurable at times. It was the kind of town that had one black family in the whole place. You never saw them but when you passed the house, they would tell you a black family lives there! Everyone in the town had the same last name, Jones, and everyone was related. It was kind of like the white version of the projects.

There were Jews right outside of the town in their own community, isolated from everything not Jewish. Like the Jewish religion enforces. They would drive through the town in station wagons filled all the way with Hasidic Jews. My "friends" would tell me how if caught walking through, the Jews would be brutally beaten, which may or may not be true.

My mother kept her job with the Visiting Nurse Service (which she could not afford to lose) and commuted an hour and a half to New York and back everyday, which gave me plenty of unsupervised time to get into trouble. My mother had tried after-school programs for me, but I fought that relentlessly. I wanted to get out and get my own friends and do my own stuff, which to this day I find hard to do at school or work. At school, everyone is only there because they have to be. And nobody is friends outside of that.

I remember the first time my friend offered me pot. My best friend at the time was a kid in my class that I got in trouble with for disrupting class. His name was Greg but one called him "Headbanger" to make fun of him for liking heavy metal music and dressing in the style. Another group in school mostly liked rap and were dressing in those styles; but the kids from this area were straight-up rednecks, chopping firewood and driving tractors, so they made fun of those kids, calling them wiggers, which means "white nigger!"

Anyway, one of those wiggers told Headbanger (Greg) that he had an ounce of really crappy weed that he bought. It was mixed half and half with oregano from the pizza shop. Headbanger lit it up and offered me some. I said, "Hell no!" I knew, coming from the city, that drugs were for junkies and bums. But he assured me that if I ever changed my mind he would light me up.

Later on, I met these kids who were wiggers and I joined them. They immediately accepted me because I was from New York City. And they just assumed I had tried weed because of it, so I played along and told them I had. I then proceeded to Headbanger to get him to light me up. All of a sudden, he had turned cheap. He talked of not having a lot of stuff so I reminded him of his promise to me. He then rolled the smallest joint possible, which was literally the size of a pin. I then got really stoned but did not even know it. I just ate a very large pot of baked ziti (about five or ten bowls) and felt what I could only describe now as flush and maybe horny but with no girls around. I was eleven and had had crushes on girls, but never admitted to it.

Before smoking weed, I had tried cigarettes, which I was also against. Again, all of it had to do with a friend that I admired and wanted to like me. To get me to try smoking — he was older, my mother's friend's son — he showed me six packs of Marlboro Reds unopened in a drawer, like it was this fantastic secret, which I guess it was when he was thirteen and I was ten. They looked very attractive, fire engine red all in a row like that. I did not smoke at this time, just got let in on a secret.

I had made a fort out of this old steel shack in my backyard by laying carpet and putting in a couch we found on junk day, which was every spring when the trash collectors would pick up large furniture and carpets, etc. That's what we used to do upstate, build forts and treehouses and crap so we could smoke and drink safely away from adults.

My mother's friend's son from Pitt Street — the one with the Marlboros — came to visit us upstate. He proposed a very exciting idea: that we try to score Marlboros at a strange roadside gas station that I had never been to. W wrote a fake note from my fake father (I'm a single-parent child) who supposedly had a broken leg. He requested that the clerk sell me the Reds to bring to him. Miraculously, this worked! So we divvied them up and smoked them in the fort. He taught me how to inhale and all that. Anyway, jump ahead, my mother saw I was getting in trouble and she was getting tired of that long commute. At the same time, she learned that a friend of a friend, who had an apartment in the Seward Park houses, was moving to Massachusetts and that she could sublet the apartment so my mother jumped on it.

She had a friend who worked in the Sun Yat Sen Intermediate School (a big Chinese junior high school on Hester Street). I got into that school. It was 90% Chinese, 10% black and Spanish, and me and the Indian kid! That school was probably not the most dangerous but it was the worst one I had seen up until then. If I thought that small town anti-Semitism was bad; it was nothing compared to what I would experience now for being "white." I remember thinking that I can't win, that I would never belong anywhere. Pretty quick after I started at my new school, I got robbed on the way home for my backpack and whatever else I had in there. As one robbed me, I looked right into his eyes. He was an older Spanish boy, much bigger and stronger, even had a little teenage mustache. He told me if I didn't give him my stuff he would punch me.

I held my cool but when I got home, boy did I let it go. I told all the worst things to my mother you could imagine. I told her there should be segregation. She reminded me of my lifelong friend and her best friend's son (the kid with the Marlboros), who was half Jewish and half black. She says, what shall be done with him then, tear him in half?

Later on, I lost my virginity at twelve years old to a sixteen-year-old black girl who had made out with three of my friends. I lied even then. I told her it was not my first time and we should do it because we had both done it before. That's hilarious, but she didn't care. I think she really loved me a lot. I didn't wear condoms. I would try to pull out on time but sometimes I couldn't.

Back at school, I remember I saw this riot start. It was like an unofficial race riot because the lines were clearly drawn. All the Spanish and Black kids knew and joined each other but were very much outnumbered by the Chinese kids. It all started during lunch period in this very large room, which was the whole ground floor of the school. Kids would be scattered around in separate small circles sitting on the floor or just whatever, walking around. I see this Chinese gang member arguing with this girl who I knew who was half Chinese and half black but you know how that goes. (In America it doesn't matter what you are, if your skin is black, then you are Black. Same goes with you being white.)

Anyway the riot started with two people arguing over the spot. The Chinese gang member told the black girl she was in his spot so she got all in his face. The next thing you know there may have been everyone in the whole school, because the whole room was crowded with people punching and kicking each other. And remember, we're talking maybe ten or twenty black and Spanish kids and about fifty or a hundred Chinese kids. You could not even see much beyond the chaotic fight scene. But I remember just watching in awe, somehow never getting hit. I remember seeing the black girl on the floor getting repeatedly kicked in the vagina by the same Chinese gang member, and seeing my friend, Angel, who was this Dominican kid, jump up from the crowd with this huge smile on his face as he chanted, "I got a beeper!" He was holding the beeper up proudly and jumping up and down because, after all, what's a good race riot without a few looters!

Fast forward to me and my friend from the projects starting to cut school while my mom was at work, just staying home and literally doing nothing, watching videos, him watching me play with G.I. Joes on my couch. At twelve years old I had lost my virginity and I was still playing with little kid toys.

We started to venture out to the East Village once again. From ages thirteen to fourteen, I frequented this coffee shop on Third Street and Avenue A called Limbo. We would go to Limbo and meet all types of characters in the backroom that they allowed you to smoke in. I would draw in my sketchbook, drink café au lait and smoke Drum rolling tobacco.

I then went a little further up to Tompkins Square Park where I would find my social group, all my weed connects, and spend every free moment for years, ages thirteen to sixteen, '94 to '97.

There was a time when me and my friend from the projects would go back and forth upstate with my mom to the house and visit with my friend, Lucas, who I had met one day through head banger. Lucas was a real hippie from a real hippie family. His parents were Rainbows and went to Rainbow Gathering every year. We spent days and weeks at his house getting wasted, hanging out with characters, it was a blast.

The first time I got really drunk was over there. We drank a whole bottle of Seagram Seven whisky and chased it with Pepsi. I don't remember much of that night. The last thing I remember was being discovered in the woods by our parents because I could not stop laughing. After that, nothing, but when I came to, I was in a bathtub filled with my own vomit.

The last time I saw them they came to New York City and met in Tompkins Square Park. Lucas and his dad, Bruce, not his mom. They looked just like the homeless punks. They blended right in, complete with big hiking tent and backpacks. By this time I looked like a Puerto Rican thug, with a tucked-in polo shirt and a blowout with a temp fade.

His father had had some brain disease that made him do crazy stuff like expose himself and have paranoid and violent rants about conspiracy theories. I felt bad when I heard that some shitty kids from around there, that me and Lucas knew, beat him up and robbed him when they were chilling there with him smoking or something.

Me and my friend from the projects and this Irish-Italian kid Luke from Greenpoint used to take acid and smoke a ton of weed and watch this crazy animation movie called *Akira* in my mother's apartment. So we brought Lucas and his dad to my house and watched *Akira*. Lucas emptied the entire contents of a small organic jar of peanut butter onto two slices of bread. But I did not know he used the whole jar until they had gone and I found the empty jar. I saw the sandwich he was eating in my room and I asked him in a wise guy voice how much peanut butter he could eat. He laughed an evil laugh with crazy eyes and a mouth full of sandwich. When it was time for them to leave, Bruce asked me if they could stay with me and my mom but they could not. I felt bad later because, after all, I had stayed at there house practically for years. But now they were just a couple of crazy people on a random visit on short notice.

After junior high school, my mom decided she wanted me to try boarding school, I think maybe because the kid with the Marlboros was going. Anyway, I started out at the summer school to make up for failing 8th grade, then I would start 9th grade in the fall.

That summer I learned how to do a kick flip and "Ollie" a skateboard but I still don't do them perfectly. I also learned about Crips and Bloods. There was a Crip from St. Louis. His mom sent him there to keep him out of trouble. He was nice, nothing to prove to anyone.

I did pass summer school but when my mom came on the last day, I told her that to continue there would be a mistake. She told me that she was making me go. I fought her so much that, on the way home in the middle of nowhere on the highway between Connecticut and New York, she told me if I did not agree to go there, I should get out of the car right then. I said, "Fine," but she was going to waste a lot of money, my whole college fund, which was not enough to pay for four years of college but was enough for two, that is, 50,000 bucks. She would spend half of that on the dumb boarding school and half later for living expenses. (I don't care very much now. I don't regret the past.) I forgot to mention that the summer school was in Cornwall, Connecticut, and come fall the school was moving to the top of a mountain in Kent, Connecticut.

That fall I went back but to the new campus. The school was at the top of Skiff Mountain. We used to call it Sniff Mountain! But, yeah, Skiff Mountain. It would be raining and you'd get half way up the mountain and it would be snowing. A very beautiful campus that I should have taken full advantage of — not that I would do any better now.

Did I mention that they told my mother if I did well for that year we could get financial aid for the rest of the time? That may have been a partial scam with a partial opportunity, but I didn't know shit. I was a freshman in high school and the odds were highly against me.

The weird thing is that they never kicked out like a rich kid whose parents made large donations or like some sports hero. Mostly, they kicked out kids like me. They treated all the freshmen boys like total victims.

I almost said "losers" but that's dumb shit stupid motherfuckers from the suburbs would say. People in New York don't talk like that. Real people don't have time for stupid judgments like that. Whoa! Sorry about that, but, yeah, my peers and I were not given much respect.

At the end, we got hazed really badly one night. Scott, my roommate, my friend Alex, and I were cutting study period, when you were supposed to be confined to your room studying. We noticed the senior prefect and a couple of other bullies all sitting in the same room, where they had special privilege. We decided it would be funny to walk past the window and wave at them. They caught Alex and the senior prefect and lacrosse player Josh knee-dropped him in the chest. He coughed up blood. When they caught up with me, one person grabbed my legs, the other my arms. What seemed to be every boy from both dorms proceeded to give me pink belly, which, for those that don't know, means a slap on the belly. They all got in a line and took turns doing this. When this kid, Rob, had his turn — he was a real dick who picked on us a lot — he slapped my belly so hard I pulled both the kids holding me together so they smacked into each other.

Now there were about ten feet between me and about twenty boys who were all older and better, and I was telling them to come forward and get killed by me, cursing and screaming through tears and snot. When all of them dispersed, I noticed Rob's handprint was still there and actually raised on my skin where it would stay as proof for about two more hours that he had given me a good one.

One day me and Scott, my roommate, were cutting class, standing around in the dorm hallway with this semi-obese kid named Marc. Scott suggested that we dare him to break a reinforced window with a lacrosse stick. We both did so. He proceeded to smash the glass window.

Next thing you know we were sitting at dinner and this teacher, Mr. Bogartis, stood up and starts talking about how he came out of his room and cut his feet on the glass and if anyone knew who did it, they should come forward now.

Marc comes up to me after dinner in a fat boy rage and says, "Did you see how Scott broke that window hitting it OVER and OVER! That's so fucked up, I'm gunna TELL on 'em." So I'm thinking, "This double-crossing son of a bitch."

The next day Marc told and, just as we were on our way to his room to kick his ass, a teacher stopped us and forced us to stay in our rooms till it was time to leave. We were already on headmaster's probation for doing graffiti all over the dorms, so we were out.

The next school I went to after that was an alternative school that my mother had found. I guess she was still trying. I actually don't think she ever stopped.

That's where I met my friend Luke, the Irish-Italian kid from Greenpoint. We were the only two white kids in the school. At this time I was still in touch with my ex-roommate Scott and I used to sleep over with him in Massachusetts, where he lived. I did acid with him for the first time, orange fluff blotter paper tabs, then later mescaline microdots.

But the best acid I ever took was scored for me by Luke from this Greenpoint old-school raver Polish guy named ID. Actually he's an old school writer. Apparently there was an all-city crew of old school Polish writers from Greenpoint called ALIEN CREW or AC for short, which consisted of famous all city bombers like Rp3, Armia and ID. Anyway, ID had this shit called sunshine acid; one tab felt like you took a quarter ounce of mushrooms every single time. After you did one of those, you didn't need to do any more for a while. Luke didn't know ID well enough for him to sell to us so we had to go through this Polish skateboarder/writer named RAW who was down with AC.

One day me and Luke and Raw and my best friend from the projects were all tripping on that ID shit in my room and we were so noisy my mom kicked everyone out and told me I could go with them! So I did, but not without this Louisville slugger wooden baseball bat we had stolen from a shack in the baseball diamond behind the Con Edison plant on 14th Street prior to that night. It was raining but it was warm and we were tripping balls so we didn't care. We walked around breaking the side, rear and front windshields of expensive cars in the neighborhood. There wasn't a cop in sight the whole night but if someone came to find their car damaged and us walking around with a wooden bat filled with glass, they would have tried to kill us. It seemed we were the only ones in the streets for miles that rainy night.

We went to the back of the supermarket, Fine Fare, to seek shelter from the rain. There was an outdoor loading dock with an awning. We could sit on some plastic milk crates. We heard a sound coming from a shack back there with a light on inside. It was still pouring. We went over to it and there was nobody in it but the light was on and so was the radio, this little fucking shack had electricity, exactly four chairs and religious Christian rhetoric tacked on the walls. We took it as a fucking sign! And we chilled in there while Raw bragged about how he could write with Armia whenever he wanted.

At the time I was writing my name, Ben. Later, it would turn into Benone, but back then it was still just Ben. Luke was Cer, short for "certified" — not the Cer who is down with Inkheads, but they used to rag each other.

One day I was walking down the street to Tompkins Square when I met this English photographer named Simon Pentalton by bumming a Marlboro light off of him. We smoked it together, talked and exchanged numbers. We would smoke and chill often. He asked me if I would let him take photos of me and this Calvin Klein model who was very cute for everyone's portfolio. I agreed. We smoked weed and took photos. All his friends were there — hair and makeup artist friends, wardrobe friends with clothes on loan from Calvin Klein. They asked me to put my hands on her but I didn't think to grope, so I literally just put my hands on her. It looked like art or dance. The model smoked a one-foot grafix bong for the first time. She changed her shirt in front of us and she wasn't wearing a bra. She had the most beautiful little breasts. I didn't want to change in front of them so they called me shy. I guess I was. I was not used to that yet.

Later on he called me up and said he had a girl over who was looking at his pictures, saw mine and asked if he would call me. That girl was James King, the supermodel. I didn't know that she was really famous but she was talking about how well she did as a model. She was pretty impressive even back then. She talked of this famous network, Graff crew, SKE, and her boyfriend ARGUE, who had been killed. Her brother used to write KING and he was down with them. She talked about High School for the Humanities and how they all went there back in the day.

So guess where I wanted to go next, that's right, you guessed it. So I was off to Humanities. I did not live in that zone, so I almost didn't get in.

Around that time one day my mom was on the phone yapping for hours and I had to call my drug dealer so I went to one of my neighbors and asked to use the phone. There were two brothers, Dan, and the older was Asher. They were Jewish and got the apartment when their grandmother died. They don't live there anymore. I asked Dan if I could come in and use the phone. He invited me in. Some buddies of his from college were there visiting and they were up at 10 AM on a Saturday drinking forty-ounce beer bottles and playing Super Nintendo. He asked me who I was going to call. When I told him it was my weed dealer, he asked if I would get some for them. We chipped in and smoked at his place. We would do that for years and we got so close it was almost like WE were family.

When my neighbor Dan introduced me to another dealer, the dealer told me that either I would sell his shit for double buying weight and sell dime bags, buy more and more and become bigtime, like some other of Danny's custies had done.

So we went into business but I was just selling so I could use for free and he was just doing me a favor by meeting me for an ounce or two when he really dealt in pounds so he got pretty tired of that. I was selling weed in Humanities High School where kids would buy these fat nick bags from uptown, split them and sell them for five. The weed was okay for the money but it all smelled like roach spray. When I came through with that crazy-ass Danny weed, they wanted to rob me so bad. A couple tried. The rest just ended up paying me because that was the best shit that kids in that school had ever seen in their lives! Bunch of little tramps they were.

The next year I transferred out of there to an alternative school called Wildcat Academy that I heard about when Luke told me he was going there. But the motherfucker had transferred out because his dad sent his ass to Daytop. To my pleasant surprise, my boy Greg Burke from Humanities had transferred into there too (good times).

When we were there, Greg told me he had the okay to throw people down with 357, DE3's crew, and told me to push it. He told me all about his crew YBW and about BAF. He said his brother was one of the founding fathers of BAF, which stands for "blunts and forties." YBW stood for "you're being watched"; pretty creepy, huh?

Wildcat Academy was fun. They let us smoke cigs in the bathroom; can you believe that?

I made friends with this kid, Uli, a Jamaican kid from Queens with no accent, who had the best acid I had tried since the ID shit. It was called Beavis and Butthead and the tab had a picture of Beavis and Butthead headbanging. It was fucking awesome.

So one morning I see Uli coming in the same time as me and I bought one before we went up in the elevator. I popped that sucker right then and there. His eyes opened really wide. "You're gonna take that now!?"

"Don't worry," I told him. Those classes were so small and I was always such a little joiner that that had to be the scariest trip of my life but, surprisingly, I held it all together on the weirdest day of school possible. There was this big reenactment we had been rehearsing for months for history class. I was to play a witness in a famous court case. I had rehearsed it a 1,000 times, but for some reason, that day I forgot and popped some fucking acid before school! So I'm sitting there, waiting to go on, and the principal was sitting across from me. Now I must have been making one of those special-ed acid faces because when I came to, that motherfucker was looking at me like I had six heads! I looked back at him as if to say I was fine. When it was my turn to go on, everything we rehearsed went right out the fucking window. The other actor asked me to describe some shit on a secret map of a military compound, some shit I knew perfectly the day before, and all I could say then would become the most embarrassing phrase I would know for the rest of my life: "I DON'T KNOW." It was truly a life-defining moment.

I started hitting the streets harder then ever before, pulling all-nighters every night, writing "Ben One" all over the Lower East Side and downtown area with my two friends TORE and CRES from Smith Projects (not the TORE from the Bronx). I was doing lots of acid, tons of weed and coke, angel dust, a cocktail of party drugs and even started experimenting with sniffing dope.

I saw my old friend Darrel, also from Smith Projects. I knew him since we were twelve, one of my first friends when I moved back from Monroe. He was working out at the jungle gym bars in Columbus Park in Chinatown. (That's the poor man's work out gym—very effective.) Darryl had just got out on parole from doing a two to seven upstate for a robbery.

I was wilding out back then so I told him if he ever got back into it to give me a buzz. He assured me that probably wouldn't happen but Darrel had a girlfriend who loved to go shopping so, sure enough, next time I saw Darrel, it was on.

A lot of kids got busted in my neighborhood for robbing Chinese immigrants. It sounds horrible, but they are the most obvious victims when you're walking around Chinatown at five in the morning.

When we did finally get caught, it was robbing some Chinese mafia dude. We had just finished robbing two other vics. We had hundreds or thousands of dollars each, but it wasn't enough for us. We were after the brick. It was me, CRES and D. We caught this vic and he starts yelling at the top of his lungs, "OKAAAAAY! OKAAAAAY!" Shut the fuck up.

We threw him on the ground and took a $1,000 bracelet at least, a pack of Marlboro lights, and a pager, but he must have just lost all his money gambling because all this fool had was eight bucks. The most time one of those robberies should take is three minutes because police arrival is like seven, but we took way longer.

I see the cops running towards us from way down the street so I'm like, "Run!" D takes one of the guys' shoes and throws it over a fence across the street and we start running. This motherfucker starts hoppin' along after us and pointing. I'm following D and I see cop cars stopping short in all directions. When we turn the corner, this dude D straight slides across the hood of one of the cop cars as they get out. I jump this little fence into the lawn that's right in front of my building—but my foot trips on the fence, so I fall. If only I had just stayed down, but I thought for sure they had seen me, so I got up. Right when I look up I see all the cops turn around.

After I'm in cuffs, the cop punches me in the back but I barely even felt it. "That's for making me run." They even let the vic take a shot, but he was so shook he just tapped me with his fingers. They had gotten D but CRES was safe, watching the whole thing go down from underneath a car.

When D and I got to the precinct, they took everything, including our clothes—for evidence, they said—and gave us these paper gowns. We both talked before we got questioned about how they would try to turn us against each other and get a statement but we both agreed that we would take the fifth. So when I get in there, this guy tells me that a good Jewish boy like me shouldn't be in there and that "Leroy" over there probably made me do it and that if I didn't think "Leroy" wasn't over there trying to give me up, then I was fucking crazy.

I told him for words I take the fifth, which I learned later is considered an admission of guilt. What one should say is: "I can't give a statement without representation."

When I got to Rikers Island, everyone thought I was a rapist because of that stupid paper gown.

There was this one kid who seemed really smart and they were all Bloods, so I made the statement to them—after they said I was a rapist—that I know some shit goes down and there's always a "herb" (a victim) but whatever happens, I refuse to be the herb.

The smart-looking one ponders a moment and says, "What's your name?"
I told him, "Ben."
So he says, "You need something more gangster. We're gonna call you White Bread."
"White Bread!" I said, "Shit, more like Thoroughbred."
"Somebody got that already. White Bread it is."

I remembered that my mother told me if I got arrested she would not bail me out so I didn't ask her to, but I did call her to tell her where I had some money stashed and asked her to send some to my commissary so I could get cigs. This was before they banned cigs from the island.

I asked some kid in there for a bust down on a cigarette. He gave it to me, and another kid came over and tried to start a fight with me over it, saying that I didn't even know that kid and that since it was his friend, he was entitled to the bust. He put his hands up and I put both my hands on his wrists and looked him in the eyes. This defused him immediately but he told me to come to the bathroom. I don't know if he knew that I knew this meant a fight. My plan was to choke him unconscious from behind as soon as we got there, but on the way there, I looked at the kid who gave me the bust as if to say, I'm going to hurt your friend. So he stopped it.

We all went to dinner at the mess hall. We're waiting on line when I hear the Blood house was coming through. They came in, looking rowdy as hell, and started cutting the line, every single one of them. So I started moving down with them. I hear one say to the other, "This *something* was all in his *something*." I knew he was talking about me but I kept my head straight, but tilted enough so they knew I heard them. Then the other said to him, "I wouldn't fuck with him; he looks like he'll kill somebody." We were having hot dogs.

There was this older kid in the dorm who was mad because he turned nineteen and was supposed to get transferred to adults at that age, but they were keeping him in there because he was big enough that he kept the others in line. They respected him. He used to complain that he was tired of babysitting them and wanted to go with the adults. Anyway, he sat at my table and so did the kid I almost had a fight with. For some reason, I thought I was above eating those hot dogs so the older kid said, "I'll take them if you don't want them." So I gave him one. Then that kid who I almost fought started shit about he should get one, too, so I gave him the other one. I don't know why I gave anything to that stupid fuck but I guess I didn't think anything of it.

Dinner was over at 5:30 p.m.; lights out at 9 p.m. So in between we were socializing, doing push-ups and all that. This kid behind me pulls out a burger that he snuck from the mess hall. He says with a big happy smile, "I snuck it in my sock!" I thought it was gross. I noticed the kid had messed up teeth because he said he'd been shot in the tooth, so all his teeth were moving dramatically to the right, like some crazy ghetto orthodontics.

I remember we were all hanging out – me, the kid who named me White Bread, and some other cool kids I found interesting. The kid who named me, who was shot in the tooth, was telling us how he didn't think there was anyone in the dorm that could beat him in a fight and to stick with him to be safe. I believed him because he just seemed like a simple, nice kid who was really strong and could fight—not scheming after anything. So we sort of had a little crew in place.

At like two in the morning, I got woken up by a guard who told me to pack my stuff, that I'd been bailed out. I was ready in two seconds and they said I had to wait for my bus. That took about an hour or two.

When I got home, my mother told me that my lawyer had called her and told her it was better to bail me out if she could. Better to fight the case from the outside. She told me to go to school. I didn't understand why but she told me to do that, but I did.

Needless to say, I failed the 10th grade again at Wildcat. The first and second time was at Legacy, then Humanities. So my boy, a writer named Tore who was down with 333 and 2N (which stands for 2 Nice) was going to a school for kids with learning problems called Riverview High School on the top floor of Bellevue hospital. My learning problem would be that I was depressed and I was on medication and that was good enough to get in. Tore said all you had to do was just show up and you pass, which was literally true. But you had to go to the psychologist every week.

I continued to go to court and go to school. After a whole year of that, the judge gave me four months of weekend work release, which meant I would go in on Friday night and come out Sunday night.

I started the probation at 365 Broadway and the weekends on Rikers Island at the same time. We all wore these grey jumpsuits and all the regular population wore greens, which is a matching green buttondown short-sleeved shirt and pants. Everyone got these orange, slip-on Chinese shoes unless you had your own, but they wouldn't let you wear certain colors. They held my New Balances because they said the name stood for "new bloods."

I met this guy in there who was an ecstasy dealer named Zef. He was a real character but he was fun and I liked him. For a while he actually stayed with me at my mom's house. She liked him okay. He looked like a clean-cut white dude who dressed like a yuppie and wore J. Crew and Banana Republic. He was smoking weed but I was just doing the hard stuff like E, because that was out of your system in a week whereas weed stayed in your system a month. He was using other people's urine but I didn't have the balls to try that so I gave myself a week in between using and drank water till I was pissing clear.

My mother said he could stay there till his weekends were done. Normally he lived with his girlfriend, who was a vice president of one of the biggest TV networks, like NBC or ABC, one of those. I watched him do crazy shit. Once we went into the Rite Aid near my house where he stole a bottle of aspirin and emptied it into a baggy. Then he met this Spanish mafia dude that got out of a limo right in front of Rite Aid and bought $1,500 worth of aspirin.

One day he bought all this dope and held out on me, did it all, and pretended like he was sick while I took care of his ass. He left dirty tissues all over and broke some shit that had been in my house since before I was born while fucking around with me. I told him over and over to stop. It was a ceramic pot glazed and painted in the shape of a dog. I didn't realize how much I cared about it till I saw it broken. I still have holes in my closet door that he made banging it with a tennis racket.

We used to walk around the street with this video camera. One night we were up on the Brooklyn Bridge sniffing special K mixed with coke. My mother kicked us out of the house when she caught us cooking it because she thought it was crack — not that it makes much of a difference. So we are on the Brooklyn Bridge and he told me the reason why he bought the camera. He told me to imagine we're walking on the bridge, which we were, and a plane crashes into one of the Twin Towers. We would be there with the camera and get it all on film. That was in the summer of 2001, right before the towers were hit.

That day on 9-11, he calls me up and says, I heard you blew up the towers and I'm like, "What the fuck are you talking about?" And he says, "Yeah, BEN LADEN. That's a weird coincidence." I don't think he remembers the conversation on the bridge. I didn't even recall that till much later.

At around that time I had already given my PO dirty urine so she told me I had to find my own rehab or they would find one for me. At the time I was seeing an inexpensive therapist, Libby, at a community center in the projects called Hamilton Madison. She was an Orthodox Jewish lady with a wig and the whole nine but I guess in a way she was hip if she was working there doing that. Anyway, Libby found me a rehab. It was called Realization Center at 19 Union Square West. So I went. There all of my mother's suspicions about all the different drugs I was doing would be confirmed although she said she had no idea it was that much. Most of the kids there had no intention of ever stopping drugs and alcohol, including me, but we were all just doing what we had to do.

We had to give urine every group. So every Tuesday and Thursday I would try to have three days between my last drug. I wasn't smoking weed so it wasn't that bad. Sometimes I would smoke weed but every group I would take some kind of cover-up solution for my system, these things you can buy in head shops that also require you to drink water. I did every type of flush: vinegar, golden seal, but mostly drank water eight cups to a gallon to do it. I was probably hurting my system. But that was the least of my concerns back then.

The kids in the group would change a lot because most were sent by their parents or the court or something mandated them for a certain number of days. Since I was on probation I was there until the rehab said I was okay to leave, which would be never as long as Medicaid was paying for it

I remember I met someone in there who had tags and he had gone to Humanities. He wrote BLACK LF. LF stood for La Familia, which is Latin King or LK. La Familia is pretty well-known for being a gang but LF had a lot of tags in New York. Latin Kings had beef with Bloods in New York and probably everywhere else too. For this reason, they got along with Crips and strangely had some of the same mannerisms as Crips for being different races and all.

One day I almost got into a fist fight with this kid (who was a Crip) for using the "N" word, which I used to do every other word. I had picked it up in the mid-'90s in junior high school and never dropped it since it was used as a terminology to describe a man, whatever race, and the "B" word to describe woman. "NIGGAS & BITCHES." This kid was just trying to start a fight. He wasn't offended the first time. I apologized and said pardon me, but the second time he said "What?" I replied, "What the fuck did I say!" I was from the hood after all.

So he said, "Alright, we're gonna see."

When we came out of group into the waiting area, one of his gang affiliates had been waiting there for him. The kid from the group was talking to him about me and the other kid knew I wasn't a racist and looked at me as if to give me a chance to explain it to him so he could squash the beef, but I didn't want to explain anymore. If this punk ass wanted to bring people, I was prepared to do the same.

I went downstairs to wait for him and that stupid skateboarder kid made a wisecrack imitation of me to Ryan in front of me — "UM FROM DA HOOD!" — and laughed. I told him to shut up and I went into this deli to drain the lizard before I had to fight. It couldn't hurt but I told Ryan if they came out tell them I was in the bathroom. When I came back out Ryan and the other kid was still sitting there. I asked, "Did they come out?"

He said, "Yes."

"Did you tell them I'd be right out?

He said, "No! Why would I say any shit like that!"

I went home and called the counselor, Stacy, who had witnessed the argument, and told her that if he tried any shit I was going to fuck him up. She told me that that would not happen and that she had spoken to him already. She must have had something to him because he never said anything about it.

The next thing Stacy said was that I had to fill up this card with signatures from group leaders at Marijuana Anonymous meetings. When I went to this M.A. meeting for the first time, there was nobody like me but secretly I related to them, especially the ones I hated the most. I could only see what was different from me, like the Hasidic Jewish girl or all the middle-aged people. I thought, these people don't love weed like me. They're just such losers with nothing better to do. I needed those signatures to graduate the program.

At the time I was in this vocational program and during lunch I talked to this girl because she was like the only good one there. I started bragging to her about all this shit you don't tell a girl that you want to get to know, like I'm on probation for a robbery, I got three dirty urines and I'm still getting high, HA! Like that's cool or something.

Then she said something I did not expect. She said "I used to shoot special K in my neck, and I never left the house without coke and pills on me at all times." I did not expect this because she looked so straight. She told me she got clean in AA, which I had been hearing about. I was still trying to talk to her so I said that I try to just do the hard shit but I keep smoking weed, which stays in your system forever, that eventually I'm smoking it before it's even a thought in my mind. She responded by saying she relocated to get clean. She couldn't do it here because she was a bartender so she moved to Ohio or some shit.

"I need sober friends," she said, "not just sober but friends that used to get high and now they don't."

Then she talked about simple shit, like eating food and going to the beach, shit I hadn't done for my whole adult life, practically for ten years. I lived on Debbie Cakes and beer.

I wanted to do those things with her but she made it clear, for whatever reason, we could not. But I wasn't mad. When she left the program, I never saw her again. I don't even remember if she came back after that day.

For about a month I stayed off of pot and went to those M.A. meetings, raising my hand and counting clean days, but I really didn't have any because I was still using coke and whatever else.

Then one day I was at the club with this kid I knew named Josh, who was this really talented CRIP. So we're in the club sniffing bumps, and him and another kid get this bright idea to put the rest of the coke in the blunt!

The next day I went to the meeting and said I have one day and told the story of the night before. After the meeting, a guy gave me his card. He was an agent for professional boxing, an older Jewish guy in his thirties. I said, "I guess I'm supposed to get a sponsor."

And he said, "I could help you with that."

I wanted all new friends. My friends didn't care if I fucking went to jail or fucking died or anything. All they wanted to do was use around me. I knew I could find all the people I needed in the "rooms" and I didn't NEED anyone else. I had at least three dirty urines in two years and three years left of probation but I knew after I got in the program that I would complete the probation. Plus I figured whatever problems I did have, they couldn't blame it on drugs anymore. I got so sick of teachers, parents, and everyone else blaming EVERYTHING on that.

I hung out with my friends STINKY and CRES in this bike shop in Williamsburg that they worked in. At that time Williamsburg was becoming trendy so a lot of people who were young and good-looking and into fashion were coming in there. STINK got really into building, riding and collecting vintage low rider bikes. Sooner or later we all had one and rode around in a gang which consisted of me, PASER, BUBS, Al GUZ, NATE, BIKE DOC, GARY, STINK and CRES. If I forgot anyone, I apologize. One of STINK's best friends was this guy PORKCHOP, who worked at Mama's. There were a lot of great people who worked there. It was like a family of artists and bikers and we used to hang there every night after they closed.

Later I met this guy, Simon, who was in a well-known Lower East Side punk band called Simon and the Bar Sinister. He was a bike messenger and talked about surfing. I wanted him to teach me how to surf and he gave me a few lessons. I learned of a surfing community out in Rockaway where he lived.

I would see these guys hanging out at the bungalows and the parties on the beach. But Simon had nothing to do with STINKY or the others. There was the coincidence but not so much because bikers, surfers, graffiti people, artists are all in the same circles.

Simon was old-school New York from the '70s and '80s. His kid brother played Ramo in *Beat Street*, a legendary hip-hop movie staring Rae Dawn Chong. Simon was more rock but he was a famous guy who knew everyone, but was super humble — a bike messenger and a struggling musician who never got the break he deserved, like so many others, but continued to play with bands his entire life. He does well now since he retired from being a bike messenger, a twenty-year veteran of the streets and started to teach guitar full-time.

Simon had given me my first ten-speed Schwinn so that I could keep up with my friends at Critical Mass, which I used to ride in every last Friday of the month before it became this stupid poser political action for kids that couldn't change a flat tire. Don't get me wrong. I'm glad someone is doing something, but they ruined it in New York for real bike people who don't fight cars and cops. It was actually started by messengers in Chicago. Every artist is not a political activist; few really are.

Don't get me wrong. I love the anarchists, but the real political activists, the peace people and civil rights people, are not loud and obnoxious and usually fight within the law.

I started riding my bike everywhere since the train fare went up to $2. So I'm riding my bike when it hits me that I should do messenger. I asked Simon where I should go. He told me to go to Mother's Messengers and talk to Steve. That was like December '02. Steve hired me.

That winter, there was one of those really bad snowstorms that were happening every four years or so. I really proved myself that winter. I asked them about messenger names, so they gave me "Jewish Jet." Then Steve said, "Yamakazi." Mother's Messengers was a famous company since the early '90s for their rock star persona.

Simon once told me that I talked like Meyer Lansky, the Jewish gangster, and he used to call me that. He'd say, "Meyer Lansky, how ya doin?"

Simon was half Jewish, half Cuban from the Lower East Side and me and Meyer Lansky were both Lower East Side Jews as well. So one day, we had plans to meet in his neighborhood but we never did because I couldn't find the place. So I just walked around hitting tags, but instead of writing what I wrote at the time, I put up Lansky because I knew he would recognize that. That was way better than what I was writing, so I kept it. I was putting up several variations. I used to write out the whole thing, MEYER LANSKY THE JEWISH GANGSTER or just JEWISH GANGSTER or MEYER LANSKY.

I started putting that shit up all over. Spray paint tags, fill-ins and marker tags. All during the day and during work in front of everyone in midtown.

One day I was with Simon and he was talking to these two women, Kembra Pfahler and this John Waters actress, Moby Dick (Mo). Kembra and I became friends. She was a famous underground punk rock artist who was also in a band called The Voluptuous Horror of Karen Black. I had no idea how famous they were. Kembra and me started flirting and became lovers, then boyfriend-girlfriend.

At that time, STINK had started working at Mother's with me. One day I met him during work for lunch. Since I knew he was coming, I hit a fresh spray can tag on a clean truck so he could see it. He says, "You just did that now?"

So I went into this lot one night after I had already hit two trucks all over with fill-ins and tags. I said to myself, "Let me just hit one more." I rolled past this one twice but I didn't see the driver sitting in it. He was a very dark black guy and it was after dark. I'm trapped between three trucks and he was blocking the only way out. The security guy comes over and holds me there. I called STINK and told him to come get these two packages I was still holding, but I forgot to tell him they were doorman buildings so they could be delivered anytime that night so he just brought them to Mother's the next morning and said, "Ben got arrested with two packages!"

I would be finishing the probation in another month or two, so technically I could have been violated. I was sweating over that, so I did the only thing you could do in a situation where you're powerless: foxhole prayer. They let me off with a warning, praise Allah, and I lost the job at Mother's.

I called Mother's and Dee told me you know what has to happen now and I said, "Yes." The same day I called Mobile Messengers on 54th and 10th Avenue. Simon had told me he worked there before and that it was good but that he got fired because they found out he had a side gig at another messenger company. He said not to do that and that they didn't like it. I kept it in mind.

I was at the beach with Kembra at Coney Island in March and we took a cold dip. She said she was a polar bear once. So me and Kembra are at the beach, talking graffiti, and I explain that this crew is so-and-so's crew and that crew is this guy's crew and so she says, "What's Lansky's crew?"

I say, "What?"

She says, "If Lansky had a crew, what would it be?"

I figured that if I was putting in the work I may as well put together my own crew, rather than giving more fame to crews that are already famous. After a while, I figured it out: ADF, which is short for Angels with Dirty Faces, a famous mob movie staring James Cagney.

I want to start a new crew, which I'm making official right now. It consists of me and Clayton Patterson and any other bosses who wish to join me at the table with the board of directors.

I finally met one of the owners of Mama's through Kembra, who was friends with him. One day Kembra called me and said if I wanted to work there I should call them tomorrow. So I did. I called Paolo and started there the same night. Now I was working at both places, Mobile Messengers by day and Mama's food shop by night, but my work at Mobile was slipping. I think they caught on that I had another job because they made up an excuse to fire me and I started working at Mama's full time. The food there is like crack; people get addicted to it. It's like southern style home cooking: fried chicken, mashed potatoes, veggies, mac & cheese.

Since I was just doing food delivery in the Village it was not as hard as midtown traffic. One week Mama's got voted the sexiest delivery people in New York by some magazine, not too shabby!

While I worked at Mama's, I saw my friend Kikay, the tattoo artist and messenger, in front of a client's building. Waiting for work I chilled with him for a little while. He was working for Flash Messengers on Fifth and Bowery. He gave me the number. Mothers was low on shifts and I wasn't making enough as before so I went to Flash.

A lot of people I knew already worked there, like Philippe the King, Carlos Diablo, Ham, Quinn, Morgan, Leo, Bash, Victor, and Tadpole Ted. Carl hired me. Natalie was the other dispatcher and Doug filled in sometimes. Chris Flash owned Flash and ran an anarchist newspaper called *The Shadow*.

Chris Flash was going to do a concert in the park and asked if Kembra would do it. I asked Kembra if she thought that was cool, and she said it sounded fun to do a show in the park. The show got rained out, unfortunately, and she ended up moving the show to Otto's Shrunken Head. It was an awesome show; she sang a Jawbreaker song and Kembra's brother, Adam Pfahler, the drummer of Jawbreaker, played the drums.

I had been talking to Kembra's neighbors, Jack and Peter of Allied Productions Artist Group and Petite Versailles. They had an idea to get a grant to sponsor a graffiti artist to do a legal mural to promote affordable housing with the prospect of doing many community murals. They said I could get a friend to help me, so I included BZEE. I did a drawing of characters and a slogan and we put it on T-shirts. We've had to change the slogan a couple of times since so it looks like we will be doing more shirts.

For about two years now, I've been in a Beastie Boys cover band called Posse 'n' Effect. It began when my friend, who is an actor, started doing all three parts by himself at talent shows for fun. One day he had an idea to make the band and take it seriously. He held auditions and hired me to film them. I decided to try out since he thought I sounded just like one of them. So I did and I've been down ever since. We just did a show at Hell Gate Social in Astoria, Queens, and it was the best one yet. That's where we felt the love. You can see videos of us performing on the Myspace page by typing beastieboystributeband.com

Ben Essex, *born and raised on the Lower East Side.*

One Hundred Forsythe Street
(a famous shooting gallery)

Anntelope
January 2010

I met Jason one very cold afternoon during a panic when there were no drugs around. Every-body had closed up shop and disappeared into thin air, because the undercover narco cops were all over the place. I was too sick to wait, however, and decided to take my chances and trudge on in hope of locating something.

It seemed like I had been walking around forever; my feet and hands were frozen when, finally, I ran into someone I knew who was in need of three dollars and, in exchange for this small sum, was willing to introduce me to his connection who lived on Forsythe near Broom. He said the fel-low was white and older, a very eccentric Orthodox Jewish guy with a long red beard and an oversized overcoat who picked through the garbage cans in the neighborhood. We went and rang the bell to the building where Jason lived, but nobody answered. However, my friend was-n't worried. He said Jason never went anywhere too far and right he was, because as soon as we walked around the corner, there was Jason with his attention on the contents of a huge garbage bag he was rifling through.

My friend quickly introduced me to the red-bearded man and, after looking me over rather casu-ally, Jason invited me into his house to wait while he went and copped for me and a lady, Iris, I brought with me. Iris was adored by all who met her, and this time was no different as she even-tually became both Jason's and Robin's (Jason's girlfriend) adored friend but, alas, she wound up catching AIDS (I suspect from them) and died of PCP, which is a AIDS-associated pneumonia.

Jason was a strange fellow, VERY smart and also very Jewish. He considered going to temple a huge and extremely important part of his life. I will always remember how Robin would get him ready to go to the synagogue. They'd fuck around doing everything else until some mystical moment would suddenly arrive when they both decided it was TIME. That's when everything else stopped in that house and anybody was expected to either leave immediately or sit quietly and stay the hell out of the way, because both of them would charge around the place ninety miles an hour, doing this and that. It would take around twenty minutes for them to complete the ritual, but Robin always did manage to get Jason looking nearly presentable after which he'd leave and go to the temple.

I don't know exactly what he did there but he'd often come home with money so I imagine this was one reason besides religion that drew him to synagogue.

Jason was a funky fella and got turned on by some unique things. For instance, hearing a woman fart would immediately arouse him sexually. Of course, since being in withdrawal gives most people gas and since he had a lot of ladies coming over to cop and since they'd often be sick and in various stages of kicking, he had a lot of farting women around. I myself went over there one day really sick. Once again there was a small panic and nobody had any drugs except Jason, who claimed he did, although they were stashed down in the basement.   Okay, hoping hard and crossing my fingers, I waited while he clonked around down there for about 20 minutes, during which time, in spite of my best efforts to hold it in, a loud fart escaped from my person. I was embarrassed, of course, and apologized profusely, which was when he assured me that not only did it not offend him but it turned him on. Anyway, much to my relief, he did indeed locate the bags of heroin and sold me two, which I did up immediately.

One day I came over while Jason was sleeping so Robin went out to cop for me and as I was sitting in their living room very quietly. All of a sudden, I heard Jason in the other room. He didn't realize I was there and was apparently practicing for the day that Robin might die. She was very ill with AIDS and thin and run down, and I guess he was trying in his own way to prepare himself. He was saying very loudly over and over "Robin, speak to me.   Robin, don't you hear me? Robin, wake up!!"

I knew immediately what it was he was doing and, of course, remained silent. I don't think he ever actually realized I heard him since I never mentioned it and neither did he, but darned if it didn't come true just a few weeks later when sadly, the love of his life died and he was left alone in that big apartment that reminded me of a funhouse in the amusement park.

There were huge gas jets which came right out of the wall near the ceiling that had flames at least two or three feet long. This was the way they got their heat, which, of course, was extremely dangerous, but, somehow, it never started a fire and the house is still there, albeit renovated. I'm sure the yuppies now paying thousands of dollars per apartment have no idea what types of ghosts are probably milling about in their now upscale environment.

As I mentioned, Jason would often pick through the garbage and he found many treasures that way, amazingly enough. He certainly kept Robin well-dressed and, as much as the house was a wicked mess, it was not exactly disgusting since the couches and chairs and especially the beds were kept reasonably neat and clean with fresh sheets and pillowcases, also compliments of the Forsythe Street garbage cans. Oddly, in "their" bedroom they had bunk beds. Jason was on the bottom and Robin slept on the top.

I don't know what eventually became of Jason as I myself got off drugs around that time and haven't looked back, although I certainly will never forget this man. He had a decent heart for the most part, never ripped anyone off that I know of, and was never really mean or violent. Yes, he could get a bit cranky when he was coming down off coke but it was never too bad.

I wonder if he is still floating around the neighborhood - a red-bearded ghost combing through the garbage, finding treasures and bringing them to Robin, his angel.

Maybe I'll run into them someday on the other side.

Anne Lombardo Ardolino *is a songwriter and poet who has lived in the East Village for over 30 years. She also writes short stories and paints a bit. When she's not rescuing animals, birds or plants, she can be found at her website www.eastvillagepoetry.com.*

Part 2: Business

Jerry Cohen

Keith Staskiewicz

Jerry Cohen was born on the Lower East Side. One month later, he, his parents and his two sisters moved into a more accommodating apartment in Masbeth, Queens. He never lived in Manhattan again, but the Lower East Side would play a central role in his life.

Seventeen years before Cohen's birth, his father, in 1937, opened a small candy store on the corner of Essex and Rivington. By the time he was a small boy, it had grown into a local landmark, a confectionary institution with its stalls and shelves pushing out to the very edges of the sidewalk.

Every weekday after school, Cohen would take the bus from Queens to help out at Economy Candy. On weekends, he would get up early and wait by the door so his father would remember to take him to work with him. Doors opened at 7:00 a.m., and soon the streets would be bustling with Sunday shoppers and honking vehicles. Pushcarts dotted the corners, selling knishes and fruit to passersby. Numerous dairy shops signified that this area was still predominantly Jewish, and the Garden Cafeteria to the south was a hothouse of Yiddish culture.

In these days before outlet stores, Orchard Street was thronged with people purchasing clothing. Businesses like Economy Candy thrived in a constant stream of folks with their children in tow. Hershey Bars for five cents each, six for a quarter. Boxes of Cracker Jacks. Marshmallows. All the classic candies bought with the pennies and nickels found on the curb or slipped to them from a winking relative.

Around the corner, on Ludlow, a succession of toy stores catered to the less saccharine fancies of these little boys and girls. They also were the perfect arena for a young Jerry Cohen to spend his afternoons. When his father didn't need him to help out in the shop, Cohen could be found in any one of these eight stores, playing with the displays. The employees knew and loved him, and would permit him to walk out of the shop with a Tonka truck under each arm, knowing that his father would pay for it.

Despite the youthful demographic that frequented his father's store, Cohen never really bonded with the kids on the Lower East Side. He attended school at Yeshiva and although he sometimes wanted to play baseball, that was reserved for those who went to the nearby public schools. So instead of hanging around with the neighborhood youths, Cohen dedicated himself to the store. He helped out with all sorts of small tasks, although he wasn't above hitching a ride from his father on the store's handcart.

As a teenager, he continued to help out, diligently putting in three hours each day after school. At this point, the neighborhood had begun to change. In one way, things had quieted down. Less people strolled the streets on Sundays and the Orchard Street clothing stores drew fewer and fewer patrons. In another way, the quiet had just ended abruptly. Drugs and crime became commonplace and no one ventured even one block over to Norfolk Street for fear of their lives.

Although Cohen had spent a great portion of his youth helping out at the shop, his father was insistent that he strike out on his own and not enter the family business. After completing school, Cohen began work at E.F. Hutton as a trader. In 1977, however, the company was hit hard by the economy and he was let go in a wave a layoffs. He soon returned to the thing he knew best, and from that point on, the candy store was his first priority.

A year later after returning to the store, he met the woman who would eventually become his wife. She was also a Queens native, and she fell in love with the candyman's son when she was just 17 years old. Cohen immediately brought her into the business, and she would commute in with him and work at the store on Sundays. They were married soon after.

In the Eighties, Cohen eventually took over for his father, who retired to Florida. In the past two decades, he has seen the neighborhood, and his business, transform dramatically. As the drugs began to filter out and the streets became safer, the foot traffic that defined the area in his early years returned in a different form. Tourists and newer, younger, residents began trickling in, many of them a generation removed from the Lower East Side, returning to a candy store about which their parents and grandparents would often wax nostalgic.

With this change in clientele came the inevitable change in business model. Economy Candy used to be a store strictly for the neighborhood, selling oils, vinegars, jellies and jams for the locals alongside their sugary mainstays. But as retail food giants like Trader Joe's and Whole Foods crept in, they were no longer necessary. A few years ago, the store eliminated these items and replaced them with more tourist-oriented fare. T-shirts, chocolate Statues of Liberty and I Heart NY gift tins started stocking, and subsequently flying off, the shelves. Economy Candy had become a destination.

Visitors flock from places as far-flung as Australia, Africa and Japan, the last of which adore the near-Astro Boy aesthetic of the store's logo. *Budget Travel* listed it as the twelfth best thing to see in New York City. Although the location of the store has moved a few fronts in from the corner into a building the father bought, the crowds on a Sunday afternoon are reminiscent in number and flurry to those fifty years ago. Also like fifty years ago, Economy Candy remains an integral part of the community. They provide halvah for bar mitzvahs and weddings, they donate to local synagogues and charities and they hire exclusively from the area. Most importantly, they provide a window into a world that has all but disappeared, a brief respite from the modern world where one can chew on a Tootsie Roll and catch fleeting glimpses of what the Lower East Side once was.

The future of the store is in safe hands. Cohen is prepping his son, Mitchell, to take over the family business. Like his father, he was in finance with no intention of getting involved in the store, but also like his father, its draw was too great. Economy Candy will soldier on as it was and is, even as the world around it transforms, and it will continue to offer confectionary joy to anyone with a sweet tooth and a pocketful of *change*.

Keith Staskiewicz was *born (1985) and raised in New Jersey. He received his B.A. from Johns Hopkins University and is currently whiling away on a Master's in journalism at Columbia. He has written for nationally broadcasted children's cartoons as well as for ABCNews, both of which were surprisingly similar.*

Memoirs Of The Abogado

Ben Kaplan

I have always lived, and still live, in Brooklyn, and had never set foot in the East Village until I was told by a good friend that I should open a store front office in the "Gouverneur Hospital" area. I was looking for a suitable office and was driving down Avenue B at the end of December, 1961 when I saw a "For Rent" sign in the window of 30 Avenue B, and stopped to speak to Philip Stein, the landlord of the building, who had his real estate office next door. I was interested in the space because there was a "Centro Medico" at 28 Avenue B (I did personal injury cases) and a delicatessen at the corner of Avenue B and East Second Street.

I signed a two year lease at $100.00 per month at the end of December 1961, and after renovating the space and installing a new store front, I put up my sign "LAWYER ABOGADO" and opened my office at the beginning of January 1962. I know the date because we saved the bills for the office renovation and office equipment purchased to open my law office (Desk $110.00, Electric typewriter $105.00, renovations $700.00).

Carlos Ruiz and Guy Dellaria, the contractors who renovated the office by putting in wall paneling and installing a drop ceiling and florescent lights, were recommended to me by my new landlord Mr. Stein, and did a creditable job. It was only later that I learned that they met and formed their partnership while serving time in Rikers Island.

My lease expired after the two year period, and was never renewed. Any time my present landlord (the granddaughter of Philip Stein) wants me to vacate the office she will tell me, and, perhaps, I can retire, but here I am, 45 years later, still in the storefront.

At that time (1962) the neighborhood was ninety percent Hispanic, and I went to Berlitz School to learn Spanish. I speak it but do not understand it well, especially when it is spoken rapidly, but I do my best and usually get by. Now, though there are still many Hispanics in the area, Puerto Ricans, Dominicans, Cubans, Mexicans, South Americans, etc., the neighborhood is now less than fifty percent Hispanic. The rest are college kids, yuppies and young business people and entrepreneurs.

Mr. Stein introduced me to many landlords in the area and I soon became an L&T attorney, but also did personal injury cases, criminal cases and whatever came into the office.

In 1962, my neighbors were as follows—to the north of my office at 32 Avenue B was Benjamin's Shoe Store, owned and operated by Benjamin Kramer. Mr. Kramer sold quality shoes, and walked around in any pair of shoes purchased from him for several days to break them in (at no charge). To the south of my office was the Real Estate Office of Philip and Donald Stein, father and son, my landlord. To the South of their office was the Centro Medico operated by Dr. Salvador Beris, a Cuban refugee. Subsequently he gave up the office and worked for Gouverneur Hospital in the emergency room. Across the street was an Athletic and Sneaker store that was looted during the blackout of 1965, and never reopened. Down the street to the south was an upscale dress shop owned by Irving Cohen and known as Cohen's Dresses. He closed his store during the blackout but was not looted. My barber Mr. Velez was also across the street. His nephew is my barber now.

The neighborhood changed and the delicatessen went out of business, as drug dealers and drug addicts took over the neighborhood. The cop on the beat was transferred and never replaced. Landlords could not rent apartments because few wanted to move into the neighborhood, and many of my landlord clients, unable to rent vacant apartments and unable to pay taxes, simply walked away from their buildings and allowed the city to take title in "in Rem" proceedings. The buildings were impossible to sell without taking back a purchased money mortgage because banks had "red-lined" the area, and refused to give a mortgage to a buyer. Many times when I left the office to go home to Brooklyn between six and seven in the evening, there were lines of addicts in front of my office, waiting to buy drugs from the dealers. The dealers had sentinels watching from corner to corner and from rooftop to rooftop who would signal to them vocally, using words like "bajando," meaning they thought the police were coming, and calls like "blue," "red," or other colors signifying their wares. Often, I had to push my way through the crowd to get out of my office in the evenings. They did not bother me, and I did not bother them.

Then, in the early '80s, came "Operation Pressure Point." I knew nothing about it until I was walking back to the office from the subway station on Delancey Street and saw police cars—parked at both corners on Avenue B and East Second and Third Street—and light uniformed cops on the sidewalk. There had not been cops on the beat for many years.

With much publicity, the war on drugs to reclaim the Lower East Side (now called the East Village) had commenced. It took years of overwhelming police presence and involvement before the drug dealers and their customers were gone from the streets. The open-air drug market was gone, and the East Village emerged.

During the drug epidemic, I was offered the position of Section 7A Administrator of a building at 625 East Fifth Street, New York City, by Nancy LeBlanc, an attorney working for Mobilization for Youth Legal Services, whose office was on East Second Street between Avenue B and Avenue C. Not knowing any better, I accepted it. I had never owned or managed a building, but I ran this one—which was well on its way to becoming an abandoned building—for about five years and kept it alive. Eventually, the City of New York foreclosed on it for unpaid taxes, and soon thereafter it burned down. However, I did obtain my legal secretary out of the ashes. Nancy Rodriguez, the daughter of my superintendent Ana Rodriguez, commenced working for me, and has been my secretary for over thirty-nine years, running my office and running me.

The experience of running 625 East Fifth Street, New York City, taught me one thing: I learned that I would never make a good landlord. Though I was offered buildings at giveaway prices during the drug epidemic, I never bought any of them. Had I done so, I would be a rich man today, but I didn't and I am not.

Throughout the forty-five years I have learned at 30 Avenue B, I have had a few interesting cases. I won several felony trials, including an armed robbery case in the Bronx and a rape case in Manhattan (on the front page of *El Diario*). But my career as a criminal lawyer came to a crashing end in a murder case in Brooklyn when my client was convicted of depraved indifference murder. He fired a gun into a crowd of people; the bullet went through a man and killed his brother. My client denied it, claimed he was elsewhere, and we went to trial. I hardly slept during the trial—the pressure was that great—and I retired from criminal law after defendant was convicted. He got twenty years to life, but it was reversed on appeal due to prosecutorial misconduct, and on retrial several years later the witnesses disappeared and he was acquitted.

Most of my practice is now in Landlord-Tenant Court, and in that area I have represented both landlords and tenants (not in the same cases however). I won some and lost some, and settled ninety percent of them. This is about average in Landlord and Tenant court, since if the overwhelming majority of cases were not settled, the system would collapse. There aren't enough Judges or courtrooms to try much more than ten percent of the cases that enter the court system.

I have always attempted to keep a low profile as an attorney despite my prestigious address on Avenue B, but I did make the front page of the *Law Journal* once. The case involved a "Relocation Lien" placed upon a building in Chinatown when, as a result of the alleged negligence of the landlord, the City was required to relocate tenants into hotels following a fire in the basement.

We were able to prove that the whole thing was a scam perpetrated by the tenant in the basement, who rented it from landlord for light manufacturing use, kept it for several months doing no manufacturing, and paid the rent. On the day of the fire the tenant moved twenty-nine persons, all Chinese, into the basement, set them up with fake leases and receipts, then arranged for the "fire" and called the Fire Department. The City, having spent a great deal of money in relocating these "tenants" into hotels, wished to be reimbursed by the landlord and filed the Relocation Lien against the building.

After trial, the lien was vacated by the Trial Judge, because we proved that none of the relocated persons were "tenants," within the meaning of the Statute, and, therefore, none were eligible for relocation services. The City was scammed, but not the landlord.

In the course of years I have represented landlords who owned a few buildings, Hyman Kaplowitz, whose office was located at 188 Avenue B, was one of my first clients. He owned eight buildings in the area and eventually sold them, as times went bad.

We signed a contract to sell 224 Avenue B, but never closed title. By then, Mr. Kaplowitz was suffering from Alzheimer's Disease, believed he no longer owned it, and cut off the heat and hot water service to the building. City inspectors, responding to numerous complaints from tenants, inspected the building, placed many violations on it for lack of heat and hot water, and sent the required notices to his office at 188 Avenue B, but by then Mr. Kaplowitz had stopped going to his office and never knew anything about violations placed against the building. A Marshal arrested Mr. Kaplowitz at his home for contempt of court and took him to court in his pajamas and bathrobe. His daughter, who, understandably, was hysterical, went down to court to represent him and called me. Mr. Kaplowitz did not have a clue as to what was going on, and after a hearing was sentenced to prison for contempt of court, over my protestations. I immediately applied to the Appellate Term to release him, and was able to do so, but he died soon thereafter, and I never saw him again. My last recollection of him was seeing him being led away by the Marshal in pajamas and a bathrobe. He was in pajamas, not the Marshal.

Another landlord I represented was Morris Levine, known affectionately as "hammer," because he did his own repairs and walked around with a hammer in his hand, or dangling from his back pocket.

Once we were on trial in a non-payment action before Judge Milano, now a Supreme Court justice in Queens. The tenant produced a list of violations in his apartment as the reason why he did not pay the rent, and Mr. Levine jumped up and said in a loud, clear voice, "I don't know why the inspector wrote violations, I gave him fifty dollars." The room broke up, and Judge Milano turned his back to hide his laughter. I do not remember the outcome of the trial, but doubt that we prevailed.

As Alphabet City has evolved, most of the landlords I originally represented have either died or sold their properties, and I now represent landlords who own buildings from Washington Heights to Chinatown. No large landlords, few who do their own repairs, and none as colorful as Morris Levine. But I am still here.

Benjamin R. Kaplan, The Abogado.

Ben Kaplan, lawyer, born and raised in Brooklyn, New York. Undergraduate, Columbia College 1945. Graduated Columbia Law School 1951. Opened law office at 30 Ave B at the beginning of January 1962 and is still there.

Transformations

Deborah Fries

Growing up in the traditional middle-class Jewish world of the 1960s didn't lend itself to running an avant-garde art gallery on the Lower East Side of New York. It lent itself to being a teacher (they get two months off and all legal holidays) or if you were really smart, a lawyer, a doctor, or a dentist. If you were good in math you became an accountant. You never became an artist because, "What are you going to do with that?" and "How will you earn a living?" Besides, artists were "weird." You followed the formula and did what you were supposed to do. You went to college, became a professional, earned a "good" living and dabbled in creativity on the side, designing themes for your Purim baskets and your children's Bar/Bat Mitzvah parties.

As a child I remember being very artistic. I could and would draw for hours, with an affinity for using colored pencils. My little drawings were the constant decorations on my grandparents' refrigerator doors and cabinets. I wanted to participate in the Brooklyn Museum's weekend art program for children, but the classes were always held on Saturdays. My family was Jewish and traditionally observant (Modern Orthodox is the current term) and so those classes were out of the question. Eventually my interest in art dwindled to doodling in my notebooks. In my junior year of high school I applied and was accepted to the College of Health Professions program between Brooklyn College and Downstate Medical Center. My area of study was Laboratory Animal Science. It was interesting, I enjoyed working with animals and I would be able to earn a living as a laboratory technologist while my husband attended and finished medical school. Eventually I found a job working for a large pharmaceutical firm in New Jersey. I worked there until my husband began his residency and I gave birth to my first child, both events occurring virtually simultaneously.

I became a stay-at-home mother raising three children and living in the Modern Orthodox community of Flatbush, Brooklyn, New York. My children attended the local co-educational yeshivah and my life continued to follow the more traditional trajectory of doctor's wife and mother via shopping, socializing and volunteering at my children's yeshivah. My disenchantment with the community was already underway by the time my youngest child was in the third grade. The neighborhood locals had always considered me to be well left of center. I have thirteen ear piercings and I wore mini skirts, leather pants, leather jackets and Doc Martens boots. It was definitely *not* your typical Brooklyn mommy attire. It certainly wasn't what the other yeshivah mothers wore. Suffice it to say, I didn't have many friends among my children's classmates' parents. In fact, no one was in the least bit surprised when I went back to art school because, I was constantly told, I "looked like" I "go to art school."

I really enjoyed going to Parsons. I loved spending time in Manhattan. I was able to dress the way I wanted without fear of being criticized or talked about. Finally, at the age of almost 40, I was able to be myself without answering to anyone. It was very liberating. I befriended other women who, like myself, were looking to nourish their creativity outside the confines of motherhood. I didn't have to explain myself to my newfound friends. My religious beliefs were almost never an issue. My family always had one foot in the real world, unlike most of the other Orthodox families we knew. We had friends of all colors and religious denominations. We were traditional in our beliefs and practices but we didn't live our lives segregated from the non-Jewish and non-observant world. My sister and I attended public schools, not yeshivas. We were raised to believe that we could be observant and still live our lives participating in the society around us. I was and still am comfortable with non-Jews and non-observant Jews. It still always comes as a surprise when I tell people I'm an observant Jew. I'm not what they expect an observant Jew to be.

For my second semester at Parsons I ambitiously registered for three classes - Color Theory, Drawing II and Life Drawing. The scheduling was difficult because I needed to work my classes around my children, my weekly errands and housework. I preferred taking my classes during the day when the children were in school and my husband was at work. I also needed Wednesday and Thursday mornings free for the weekly errands and shopping for food. Friday mornings were left for cooking for Shabbos. That didn't leave me too many options. I was able to schedule Color Theory and Drawing II for Mondays and Tuesdays. However, there were only three Life Drawing classes offered. Two were offered only on Wednesday and Thursday mornings, which didn't fit into my schedule and required me to be in classes three days in a row. The only other Life Drawing class that was available was scheduled for Fridays from noon until 2:30 pm. That class was being taught by a man named Shalom Neuman. I could conceivably do all my cooking Thursday nights and early Friday mornings. Parsons was less than an hour's ride by subway, even with a transfer. Getting there on time would not be an issue. Getting home in time to light Shabbos candles would not be an issue either. I knew that the teacher would certainly understand my need to leave early for Shabbos given that his name was Shalom Neuman. I never envisioned that taking his class would put me on the path I now travel.

I was not the most talented student in Shalom Neuman's class. Not even close. I had no prior experience with art classes and I found manipulating charcoal to be very difficult. To make matters worse, Shalom liked to stand behind his students and watch them draw. It made me nervous. I pushed him away from my easel enough times to make him finally stop watching me. Despite my lack of talent I enjoyed the class, primarily because the teacher was so encouraging and helpful. His critique was never nasty or condescending. It made me practice harder.

The final class was to be held in Shalom's studio. I had never been to an artist's studio before. My expectations were, I'm embarrassed to say, sadly stereotypical. I expected a large room with canvases lining the walls, some draped and others ready for viewing. I expected tubes of paint lying around and an easel or two with work that was not quite finished. It was not what I expected at all. The studio was a former garage on Stanton Street between Forsyth and Eldridge

Streets on the Lower East Side. If you got off the F train at the wrong exit you'd never find it. It was one of those places that my father would describe as "you can't get there from here"—family lingo for any place out of the way. This place was both out of the way and way out. Most of the walls were lined with huge oil paintings on plywood, all of them containing what I now loving refer to as found objects. But in 1995 these objects (to me) were merely the detritus of city life, junk picked up off the streets. One wall contained two thirteen-foot welded sculptures that were painted in oils and wired for light, sound and movement. I'd never seen art like this. It blew my mind completely. When I arrived home after receiving my final grade (a very generous B+), my mother asked me how the studio visit went. I told her, "This guy is out of his mind."

I continued my classes at Parsons and I asked the administration's permission to take Shalom's class again. I desperately needed the practice and his class was very non-confrontational. However, I didn't want him to think that I was stalking him. I ultimately paid to take Shalom's class three times. By the end of that third semester we'd become friendly enough to share some conversation and coffee after class. At the time our friendship began, Shalom was doing commission artwork for a private hospital. He felt that my comfort around doctors and science could be beneficial to him. In exchange for my assistance with this project, Shalom offered to teach me how to use Adobe Photoshop software on a Macintosh computer. I was fascinated with Photoshop and Apple computers so it was an offer I couldn't refuse. I began working with Shalom in 1996, after completing my Illustration courses at Parsons.

Shalom was in the process of moving his studio from Stanton Street to a larger space in Bedford-Stuyvesant, Brooklyn. The Stanton Street space soon became a venue for a group of writers known as The Unbearables and to a group of international artists Shalom had been working with for close to twenty-five years. They were known as the Performing Artists Network (P.A.N. Group), started by Jean Voguet, a Paris musician and action/performance artist. P.A.N. soon joined forces with a similar group from Japan called MMAC. We began to organize festivals in New York to host the artists that Shalom met through his participation in these international festivals. We hosted performances by artists from France, Japan, Canada, Poland, Italy, Germany and China. We combined these international artist-driven festivals with readings by our poet friends. We continued to call the space FusionArts, the name Shalom had been using for his art since 1966 and for the Stanton Street space since he purchased the property in 1984. We had our first group art exhibit in June 2000. Shortly thereafter we began to explore the idea of starting a not-for-profit arts organization that would be dedicated to promoting and archiving multi-disciplinary art, art that we called *fusion* art because it fuses the various disciplines of painting, sculpture, text and spoken word, kinetics and audio into its own genre. The Stanton Street space was ideal for exhibiting this type of work because the front window could be opened to accept very large artwork. It was also ideal for our long-term goal of attaining permanent museum status. We received our 501(c) letter from the IRS in January 2004. It was our first step towards becoming a museum.

FusionArts Museum will celebrate its 8th anniversary in June 2008 as the only contemporary art space in New York City dedicated exclusively to the exhibition and archiving of multidisciplinary art. I am the director. I'm amazed to be running an avant-garde art gallery on the Lower East Side, where so many Jewish immigrants began their new lives in America, where my maternal great uncle Louie traded stories, watches and jewelry in Seward Park on East Broadway and Essex Street and where my maternal great-grandmother, who owned a dry goods store in Williamsburg, did business with other merchants on Grand Street with only a handshake. Her word was good enough in a time when money was so scarce for so many. Working on the Lower East Side brings me back to my family's roots. I feel as if I've come full circle.

I'm also amazed at just how far my friendship with Shalom has taken me. We have been friends for more than twelve years. Experience has taught me that deep friendships between secular and Orthodox Jews are rare because their spiritual beliefs are so diametrically opposed. There is often a lack of respect for someone else's point of view. I have witnessed the disrespect from both sides—as an orthodox woman who is criticized for archaic beliefs and as a woman considered not orthodox enough by her community. I have never experienced that in my relationship with Shalom. He respects my beliefs and I respect his. No apologies necessary. That's why it works.

I hope that my life teaches my children that you don't need to follow someone else's rules to be a good Jew. You simply need to be a good person to be a good Jew. It's the legacy left to me by my great-grandmother, whose honesty and integrity helped feed her family. It's that simple.

Deborah Lacher Fries *was born and bred in Brooklyn, where she shares a house with her mother, two of her three children (her son moved out) and six cats. She is the driving force behind FusionArts Museum, NYC's only contemporary visual arts space that is dedicated to multidisciplinary (fusion) art exclusively.*

Dr. Dave of the Lower East Side

Gerry Visco

Dr. David J. Ores, M.D., is a medical man decidedly in the minority and on the edge. For one thing, he's one of the few doctors in New York City who operates his business out of a storefront on the Lower East Side and who sees uninsured clients for reasonable rates. I dropped by to meet him the day after Thanksgiving 2007 with writer, photographer, and activist Clayton Patterson. Ores sat down with us in one of the chairs in his waiting room and we conducted a Q&A on his medical practice and his decision to locate it on the Lower East Side, a neighborhood with few medical offices. His odyssey to the storefront and on the ramparts of the community is a result of a strong sense of ethics and desire to help people. It is certainly linked to his family upbringing, since his parents became doctors after surviving death camps during the Holocaust.

If you're looking to avoid the interminable waits and the anxiety-producing bureaucracy plaguing emergency rooms at your average urban hospital, Dr. Dave's your answer. He can check you out in his storefront and at least give you a referral or recommendation. In addition to his general practitioner role, Ores has a steady business specializing in the laser removal of tattoos and electrolysis. Despite his unconventional style, which includes multiple tattoos on his back and arms and an unrequited love affair with motorcycles, his medical background is solid: he earned an M.D. at Columbia University in 1985, no doubt inspired by his parents, Richard and Celia Ores, both also M.D.s. Ores is on the verge of moving his practice from his current office at 15 Clinton Street nearby to a larger suite on the ground level of a new development complex on East Second Street between Avenues A and B. The five-story building with eight studio apartments and Ores' offices has been built to provide low-income housing for the community residents served by the Lower East Side Mutual Peoples Housing Authority (LESMPHA). Construction should be finished sometime during the spring of 2008. Ores will be adding a receptionist/assistant who will help him handle the patients in his larger quarters. He's also organizing a health care cooperative for uninsured restaurant workers who will, along with their employers, pool funds. He's been in touch with local restaurants and their employees where the program has, of course, been met with an enthusiastic response. Lack of health insurance is a major problem for the food industry and this could be a low-cost option, which would be suitable for non-unionized workers without benefits.

As mentioned, Dr. Dave's activism in the health care field was influenced by his physician parents' struggle to survive the Holocaust. They later immigrated to the States from Poland, after the war. Ores was born in 1958 in Mount Sinai Hospital on 90th Street and Fifth Avenue in Manhattan. He's the only son, the second eldest among four sisters—two half-sisters and the two sisters with whom he was raised. Sister Pauline works for IBM and younger sister, Michelle, is an attorney. Pauline has three sons and Michelle has two daughters. Ores' father trained as a pathologist and a psychologist and was the director of the VA Medical Center in Manhattan for thirty years. He was born near Warsaw and saw his family slaughtered in the Bergen-Belsen death camp. "My father's mother, father, sister, brother, his whole town was slaughtered. Everyone he knew was killed; it wasn't just one relative," Ores said. He was sent to Plaschow and spent six or seven years there in a concentration camp himself.

As the Germans retreated, his father was moved to Auschwitz until he was transferred to the camp at Dachau. "One day my father woke up in Dachau to find the Germans were gone. Two days later the camp was liberated by Americans," Ores told us. The Germans threw his father over a fence onto a pile of corpses. "The GIs came to put the dead bodies into a truck and burn them. When my father saw them, he said, 'Hello!' and the soldiers freaked out and ran away," Ores said. "They thought he was dead — he only weighed about 60 pounds, just skin and bones." His father was very grateful to his liberators. "He had a memory of this giant black guy who picked him up and carried him to freedom and has always had an affection for black people and vice versa," Ores recalled. Maybe as a result of his rescue, his father felt a strong bond with all kinds of ethnicities. "Veterans from the Korean and Vietnam wars, black, Chinese, Korean—they all loved him."

At the time, his father had tuberculosis and was barely alive. After a long ambulance ride, which he couldn't recall, he ended up in the American Hospital, which he often later said was the only reason he survived. After spending a couple of years in a military hospital in a displaced person's camp, his dad went to medical school in Berne, Switzerland.

His mother had a similar experience, but on the Russian side of the occupation. Her family was condemned to live in Siberia for six or seven years. Stalin and Hitler had split Poland in half by that point, divided between Russia and Germany. Ores mother escaped to the Russian side with her mother, father, and sister. Her father, Ores' grandfather, was a tailor, so when they arrived in Siberia, he was allowed to live because he made uniforms for the Russian officers. Unfortunately, Ores never got to know his aunt, because she contracted pneumonia and died. There were no medicines to treat her. "Because my grandfather was an expert tailor for the soldiers, he was given a piece of bread and cheese and my grandmother said, 'This is for your daughter, she might die.' But he brought it back to the group, sharing it with everyone," Ores told us.

Nonetheless, his parents met each other in medical school in Bern and eventually got married. They both went to medical school and had three kids, one of them being Dr. Dave. They came to Brooklyn for a little while, with his mother's parents. There was no one left on his father's side of the family—the Nazis exterminated all of them, and they had murdered else everyone he knew as well. Starting over in a new country and with a family of his own, his father rose to the position of director of outpatient medicine at the VA hospital on 7th Avenue and later kept the same job when they moved the entire hospital to a new building on 1st Avenue and 23rd Street. His mother became a pediatrician who specialized in failure to thrive and cystic fibrosis at Columbia-Presbyterian Hosptial.

Although he grew up in Leonia, New Jersey, until he was two or three, Ores often spent time down on the Lower East Side from when he was about four years old. His grandfather, the tailor for the Nazis, set up a tailor shop on the Lower East Side. Ores' own family had moved to West 96th Street. He'd visit the tailor shop in a neighborhood with mostly Orthodox Jews and it was a whole different world for him. In addition to his tailoring work, his grandfather stocked the shop with notions and fabric. "I found it mesmerizing when he'd take a flat piece of cloth and turn it into a jacket or a suit. It's like origami," Ores marveled. He used to take the boy along with him on button buying expeditions.

Unlike the Jews on the Lower East Side, Ores' parents were atheists. "It's tough to have any belief after surviving the Holocaust," he said. However, his parents have always been politically active, including with their patients. "They'd do anything to help their patients. They're really protective, like a bear with their cubs."

Ores later traveled down to the Lower East Side during the 1970s when he was in high school. Ores didn't feel adjusted at school. He had problems in high school and couldn't sit still in class for more than a few minutes without being disruptive. He was kicked out and sent to prep school for a year, later attending college at Wesleyan in Ohio where he earned good grades. He was admitted into medical school at Columbia and graduated in 1985. "Med school wasn't hard for me at all. I didn't go to class and read all my lectures in a few minutes. An hour lecture would be a three-minute read. I could finish the whole class in a couple of weeks, then I'd roam around the hospital with my ID badge doing whatever I wanted. I went to the psych ward, the ORs, the ERs. They'd say, sure, come on in, we're doing such-and-such today. I was learning an incredible amount of medicine," Ores recalled.

Ores became a surgeon but he hated it. "The surgery itself was fine, the science of it is fascinating, but when you meet your patients, they're either in a coma or you make them that way so you can operate on them," he said. "The second you're done and they're well, they're gone, so you have no interactions with them—just the other surgeons, and maybe their families." It's not a very social job and Dr. Dave is very social. "I'd make jokes and fool around and the other surgeons didn't find that amusing. And I didn't find them amusing either," Ores said.

He drifted into ER for a while, then after graduation did a year in residency. He was licensed by the state to practice medicine and be a doctor. He didn't do boards because he didn't want to be a dermatologist or a plastic surgeon. In retrospect, he wished he'd been on a medical board just before certifying. "It makes your life easier for insurance and payments," he said. But he is licensed to practice medicine in Manhattan. However, he began taking care of patients when they were sick in the Emergency Room but was unimpressed with "the circus" around him and became a guerilla doctor. "I worked in ERs and found myself helping patients in the waiting room. I was sitting in the ER with nothing to do. There's fifteen people out there with broken wrists, fevers, and I could fix them in minutes. I used to go out there with Post-Its writing, 'X-Ray his right arm, culture his throat, do a chest X-Ray on him.' They hated me. The other doctors got really angry," Ores recalled.

He'd broken the wall, the physical barrier between the patients and the doctors. The patients had no money, no insurance, and hadn't been checked in yet. "Once the doctor says hello and touches the patient, it's a legal connection. You can't discharge them. The administrator who works in the front declares them unfit to be seen. If they drop dead of an aneurism, it's not the hospital's problem. They never established a doctor-patient relationship. That's a legal tactic and it makes sense," he says. Hospitals do need to make a profit, after all. "I don't want to sound like Jesus, but I was simply frustrated. Sitting still is not my forte."

Ores spent his free time and excess energy going downtown. From 1981 until 1985 when he was in medical school, he visited the Lower East Side, just as he did during high school in the 1970s. Those were the days before AIDS, and the popular bars were the Paradise Garage, the World, Area, and the S&M clubs. Ores recalls the vibe then: "The gay guys were so friendly and fun and phenomenal. Not that you were homosexual with them. They slept all day. Imagine spending three months preparing for a party. Every time you went to a club it was like Paris in the 1920s; it was great. They would dress up with fruit on their heads. It was fucking crazy."

This was the atmosphere he felt comfortable in and it was only a natural progression for him to migrate to the Lower East Side to open his own practice. Though he initially worked for a doctor in Queens by the hour, five days a week, he'd work a couple of hours in his own storefront. He did house calls for the first year and from 1988 until 1990 didn't have an office at all since he had no money to pay rent, though he lived on Third Street between A and B. Eventually he rented space on the corner of Clinton and Stanton, working out of his house and doing house calls. Business came through word of mouth. "It was just like, hey, Steve told me to call you." And then he got this little corner place over an art gallery. He made a bedroom out of the office and painted it camouflage, which was where he saw his patients. From the beginning, he had a different attitude about health insurance. Indeed, he had no interest in taking it at all. "People came to me saying 'My hand hurts,' and I'd ask them what happened to it. 'I slammed a door on it.' I'd talk to them, tell them to get an X-ray. If they've broken the bone, they need to wear a bandage." When the patients asked how much, he'd say, "Forty bucks," and that was it. "It wasn't shady or anything—it was between me and the patient."

Ores makes it a point to help anybody who asks for help and who can't afford health care insurance. Most patients came to him to see whether they really needed a doctor or not. "They'd say, 'My stomach hurts. If I go to the ER, it's going to cost me a hundred bucks to find out I don't need a doctor.' It's either something serious or nothing." Usually Ores was able to help them without X-rays or blood work. He wasn't actually doing surgery, just basic ambulatory medicine. When he ordered X-rays and blood tests, it wasn't financially motivated. "I didn't get more money if they came back and saw me five times, I didn't get more money if I ordered expensive EKGs," he said.

Dr. Dave is outspoken about how being a doctor has changed dramatically. "It was once a profession. Now it's an industry, and it's horrible. Taking away profit would solve the entire thing. All the evil guys would go away. You could pay the CEO fifty million dollars a year to run the company. You could pay all your employees, all your nurses, a hundred grand a year, pay all your doctors half a million—I don't care if they make a lot of money, I'm not opposed to that, but no profit, no shareholders, no dividends, that's the evil."

Ores is not looking to make a profit, though he has to pay his rent and survive. His patients pay him what they can but he charges everyone the same rate—$350 per person and $250 for a follow-up, but he'll accept $60 as a minimum. "Obviously if they only have $5, they'll pay me back later. But I have no collection system and I don't go after anybody. Three times a week I'll be walking down the street and someone will come up to me and give me $20."

Not surprisingly, especially on the Lower East Side, patients sometimes try to score drugs from Dr. Dave but his solution is to not prescribe them. "I don't prescribe narcotics. I give them four Advils. Once the addicts know you're not going to give them any drugs, they go away and they tell their friends. If you help one guy, then you have a line out of the office. They'll say, 'I'm in horrible pain, my knee hurts, Doc, you've got to help me.' I say, 'Okay, I'll help you, let's call the ambulance.' They say, 'No no, not the ambulance.' I say, 'How about some Advil?' They say, 'How about some narcotics?' It's pretty obvious."

Ores tries to help drug addicts, but it's a huge problem he can't solve. "I never say, 'Go away, you suck.' I tell them there's Beth Israel, it has an outpatient program, they will give you pain medicines. I'm against methadone, but they'd give you morphine and help you." He says treating drug addiction is a challenge requiring a team of at least twenty—psychology, psychiatry, religion, medical, and so forth. "People who have chronic pain from car accidents and stuff, that's no joke. They become addicted to morphine and Roosevelt Hospital is the best pain control center in the country. They'll help them in a planned, controlled way. So, I say, 'Here's who can help you.' Like I would do with a heart attack. I don't do heart attacks. I give them aspirin and call an ambulance."

Ores has a list of specialists he uses for referrals. He referred one of his patients to a gastroenterologist who performed an $800 procedure for free. All the doctors he knows do many procedures gratis to those in need. "Even the rich ones. They do cleft palates for free; they really help people. It's a myth that they're all money-grubbing douchebags. I'm sure some people are, but not all of them."

Nonetheless, Ores doesn't know of other doctors with a similar practice in New York City. "It's because of rent," he said. Running a doctor's office in New York City requires a lot of money. "I'm not married. I don't have kids. I don't have overhead. I don't have any assets. I don't own a house. I don't own a boat. What I make in a month is what I use to pay for expenses."

Dr. Dave was about to leave town when he had to move from his old office on Prince Street. "Someone took the building away to make money," he told us. He was fortunate enough to meet Mary Spinks, the head of the Lower East Side Mutual Peoples Housing Authority (LESMPHA). The rent for this office is $750. "Because of Mary, who manages the building, that's why I'm here. If it wasn't for her, I'd be in some small little town." And then New York City wouldn't have Dr. Dave, the only storefront doctor on the Lower East Side.

Gerry Visco, *a freelance writer and photographer, has published in* New York Press, New York Sun, New York Magazine, New York Blade, Gay City News, Spread Magazine, Beyond Race, The Villager, Our Town, West Side Spirit, Chelsea Clinton News, Columbia Review, *the* Adobe Anthology, *and has forthcoming articles in* Fit Yoga *and* New York Megaphone. *She* *has an MS from Columbia's Graduate School of Journalism, an MFA from Columbia's School of the Arts, a BA from Columbia's School of General Studies, an AAS from the Fashion Institute of Technology, attended the French Culinary Institute, and is a certified yoga teacher-in-training from the Iyengar Institute in NYC. She's been gainfully employed as an editor, actor, secretary, model, teacher, and currently as the Academic Department Administrator at the Department of Classics at Columbia University. She's always lived uptown, first on the Upper West Side and recently the Upper East Side. She's organizing a radio talk show—let her know, if you have something to say.*

The Rivington Street Rav

Alan Jay Gerson

Rabbi Yaacov Spiegel greeted everyone with a twinkle in his piercing blue eyes, which reflected the sparkle of his soul. That sparkle reflected a genuine love of life in all its quirky dimensions, which made him the perfect religious leader for Rivington Street on the Lower East Side. There is a Jewish sentiment popularized by *The Fiddler on the Roof* refrain: "G-d would like us to be joyful even when there's nothing to be joyful for." Rabbi Spiegel maintained and spread to all whom he encountered his *joie d'vivre*, through trial and tribulation, good times and bad.

Rabbi Spiegel dressed always in the traditional garb of his Orthodox European ancestors (actually from Poland, not Romania, with a long rabbinic lineage)—black hat, cloak, with a white shirt. He rigorously observed Halakah, age-old Jewish law, in accord with Orthodox interpretation. Sustaining, perpetuating, and passing on Judaism to the next generation constituted the Rav's greatest passions in life, to which he applied the totality of his being.

> The Rabbi was a tall man, around six feet, with a flowing, mid-sized beard. He walked fully erect, with near-perfect posture, his head always held high. The Rav's gait and garb together reflected his pride in and commitment to his Jewish faith and heritage. Indeed, the Rabbi's charismatic personality came most alive when he was giving his Sabbath drush—an explication on the weekly Torah portion—or advising someone on a point of Jewish law—teaching lessons on Jewish law or faith, conducting a traditional Jewish ceremony or, perhaps most of all, when preparing a boy for his Bar Mitzvah.

> In this lifelong mission, Reb Spiegel was joined by his beloved partner, the Rebettizen, Honi Spiegel. The Rebettizen provided a visual contrast to the Rabbi's not always meticulous black-and-white garb. Rebettizen Spiegel's first and last priority was her family and her support of the Rabbi's work and congregation—but she also has had a beautician business on the side. She has always been striking in her poise and appearance—always perfectly dressed and groomed, with the latest of fashions, in keeping with halachic modesty requirements. The two enjoyed a typical Jewish marriage over the years. She would not hesitate to correct or

direct the Rabbi. He accepted this with good humor. The two supported each other's endeavors. Their love for each other was clear to all in their presence.

Rabbi Spiegel would be the first to describe his family as his greatest accomplishment—though he would give credit to his wife, in keeping with Jewish tradition. The Rav left three sons and many grandkinder. All three sons have become learned rabbis, married, with children. The three Rabbis Spiegel remain passionately committed to honoring and carrying out the Rabbi's legacy, including the rebuilding and perpetuation of the First Romanian American congregation. To see all his progeny grow up fully committed to traditional Judaism, and to the values and the projects to which Rabbi Spiegel devoted his life, was the Rabbi's the greatest covet and or honor, and indeed the greatest honor any father can receive.

Of course, after his family, the synagogue was the focus and locus of Rabbi Spiegel's spiritual activity and efforts to practice and perpetuate Judaism. Sustaining the synagogue was a constant struggle. The First Romanian-American congregation has lived on well past its immigrant heyday. Rivington Street's teeming Jewry; especially its Jewish Romanian immigrant population, had long been replaced by a mostly Latino, non-Jewish population. A synagogue where hundreds once worshipped saw these numbers dwindle to a few dozen. The decreased population made keeping up the synagogue's stately building virtually impossible, due to the cost of repair, not to mention electric, heating and other basic bills. The main sanctuary, with all its glorious echoes of days past, became boarded up, while the congregation worshiped and enjoyed kiddush and classes in the smaller sanctuary on the main level and the adjoining social room. Disrepair throughout was obvious, but no one realized the building's structural weakness until its collapse after a ferocious storm several years after the Rav passed.

Despite all the obstacles, Reb Spiegel almost singlehandedly breathed life into this synagogue. His unflinching commitment kept it from disappearing into history, where population shifts had long relegated it. The Rav would rise early each morning, cross Delancey Street, leaving behind the Lower East Side's remaining significant Jewish population along the Grand Street corridor, to reach the lone remaining outpost of Judaism in the Rivington Street area. He would open the shul early—before the hour for the morning service—to allow himself the time to recruit Jewish men from the area to make up the required minyan of ten. If they wouldn't automatically come to him, he would reach out to them. The same offer was often repeated later in the day for mincha and mariiv—afternoon and evening services. Rabbi Spiegel never tired, throughout the years of teaching classes in Mishna, Talmud, Ethics of the Fathers, or any number of other Jewish texts or scripture. In between services and classes, the Rabbi's day was spent caring for his congregants in their life and religious needs, and struggling to raise funds to pay for the synagogue's fuel, electric, and other bills, along with his own meager salary, always the bottom priority; paying visits and delivering lectures at other synagogues in need of a substitute rabbi or scholar, and pursuing a few very small business ventures to supplement his family's income. His three sons all attended Yeshiva and incurred all the other expenses of growing up and then starting out in life.

By sustaining the First Romanian-American congregation, the Rabbi provided a home away from home and a house of worship to many over the years who had no place else or could not feel comfortable elsewhere. With a smile and an outstretched hand, Rabbi Spiegel welcomed everyone—from all walks and stages of life, with all levels of observance. Each of us felt comfortable in, and indeed cherished his presence and his observance. The Rabbi embraced and brought out the spark of holiness present in us all. Himself rigorously observant, Rabbi Spiegel encouraged his congregation to move toward greater Orthodox observance, more through his life example than through didacticism. The Reb recognized the birthright of every Jew, irrespective of creed or level of observance, to membership in the Jewish community, and thus to full participation in the Romainesh Shul (as it was called). In the pews—within the separate men's and women's sections—we all sat together: elderly Jews still living in the changing neighborhood, and young hipster kids moving in; American Hasidim and non-observant Israelis; homeless persons and area businesspersons; and, in later, more gentrified days, accountants and artists, not to mention a fledgling politician.

The congregation maintained Orthodox separate seating for men and women. Rabbi Spiegel apologetically and politely declined, in keeping with Orthodox custom, to shake a woman's hand, by explaining that his wife would become jealous. Nevertheless, the Rabbi treated all women as his full equals, if not his superiors. He ministered to their individual needs and concerns, if anything, as a priority—in keeping with the traditional Jewish view of a woman's centrality in the all-important home. My mother, a true feminist, always felt comfortable and inspired by his presence and words.

Rav Spiegel took to heart Judaic injunctions to care for the poor. Working with area charities, he made sure the synagogue provided free Passover seders and a free-of-charge weekly Kiddush (a reception)—always with cholent (a kind of Jewish stew), which the Rabbi frequently prepared himself, for all to partake of. He worked to make the synagogue a daily luncheon site for free meals. The First Romanian-American congregation was a true house of worship of the Lower East Side. After struggling to maintain the synagogue for so many years, the Rabbi lived to see his struggle vindicated by the start of a Jewish revival in the neighborhood, with a growing demand for synagogue worship in the First Romanian-American congregation.

Rabbi Spiegel served, of course, as rabbi for all our life-cycle religious occasions—birth, Bar Mitzvah, marriage, and funeral. He was one of the first and most frequent visitors to someone in the hospital. He was also constantly available to all who sought him out for life's daily quandaries and periodic crises. Rabbi Spiegel provided true pastoral care, with his open ears and sage advice on all matters from personal to financial, business and political issues. The Reb took special delight in assisting in matchmaking, helping singles find their beschert. He of course made a special effort for his three sons. When I first met Rabbi Spiegel, his oldest son was married; the Rabbi was planning a trip to Liverpool to meet the family of middle son's fiancé; and he was focused on the effort to help his youngest son, Shmuel, find the right bride. Shmuel's marriage completed a major part of the Rabbi's lifework—though he continued to plunge his heart and effort into the ongoing work to find a match for the rest of us remaining single.

On all matters, the Rabbi seemed consistently to provide the right sounding board and the right advice to think through and figure out all life's conundrums. He could be brutally honest when needed. But then he inevitably instilled in us the self-confidence and provided us with the moral support to take a chance or make the effort or change we needed to make. He did so with an unbridled enthusiasm and optimism, undoubtedly born of his faith in Hashem, which negated any of our self-doubt. In his attentive pastoral care, Rabbi Siegel was literally a lifesaver to many. He extended a lifeline to many a desperate and despairing person, helping them through major depressions; bringing them back from drug abuse or some other abyss; and giving them hope or faith to continue on. In my case, Rabbi Spiegel's uncanny political analysis and advice helped guide the successful campaign of my mother, Sophie Gerson, for School Board, and my own later successful campaign for City Council. His support and encouragement helped me decide to leap in to the fray—for all the right reasons of service and making a positive differ-ence. Tragically, Rabbi Spiegel passed several months before the Democratic primary (the tan-tamount election day). But his advice and encouragement remained an integral part of my campaign, as it remains an integral part of my public service.

Rabbi Spiegel's pastoral concern and care extended well beyond his congregation and indeed well beyond the Jewish community. Reb Spiegel was the Rav of all Rivington Street. Judaism complements its particularistic injunctions to the nation of Israel with its universalistic perspective of all humankind as G-d's children and its vision for a future harmony and unity among all G-d's children. The prophet spoke of a future when "my house shall be a house of worship for all peo-ple." Rabbi Spiegel embraced and personified that universalistic vision, embracing people of all races and religions. He was proud of his friendship with the Latino owner of the local bodega. His synagogue was indeed a house of prayer and house of comfort for all—community residents of all backgrounds. The Rav welcomed everyone and anyone, of all faiths, races, and lifestyles to the First Romanian-American congregation. And over the years, everyone and any-one came for spiritual solace, for the Rabbi's advice, or just for a little nosh. The Rav clearly enjoyed the diversity of character and characters on the Lower East Side, as reflecting the won-der of G-d's creation. He extended his friendship to all—including the quirky but brilliant and talented photographer and chronicler of the Lower East Side responsible for this tome.

> The Rav's concern for individual well-being led to his engagement in civic and community affairs. He reminisced with me how, as a young rabbi, he marched with Martin Luther King Jr. In more recent times, he involved him-self in the rough and tumble of Lower East Side community affairs, includ-ing his service as a vice-president of the United Jewish Council of the Lower East Side. The Council, based on Grand Street, serves as the area's prime social service delivery organization. One of the Rabbi's unfulfilled dreams was the creation of a sister council, which would focus on the parts of the Lower East Side and the East Village north of Delancey Street. Rabbi Spiegel would have been a shrewd politician. He analyzed and understood what was really going on behind the scenes, the true dynamics at work. I, fortunately, was one of the beneficiaries of his inci-sive political acumen. In a neighborhood often dominated by "go-along-with-the-machine politics," Rabbi Spiegel stood out as a bit of an iconoclast. He welcomed a good political discussion. In the end, both pri-

vately and publicly, he called the shots as he saw them, and spoke up and out for the truth and for the community's well-being. He was to me and to many an inspiration as a beacon of integrity.

Rabbi Spiegel always found the time—as much as you needed—to fit you into his schedule. Yet he seemed always on the run. With his jalopy of a car, the Reb was constantly enroute—to a wedding here; another simcha there; a funeral service; a visit to his old Yeshiva in Lakewood; a rabbinic conference elsewhere; a business meeting in Boro Park; or a visit to family or friend in Midwood. When the Rabbi left the metropolitan area, if it wasn't to visit his in-laws in Liverpool, it was usually to embrace his two earthly loves, in addition to his family and congregation. First: Eretz Israel, the land of Israel. Rabbi Spiegel was the staunchest of Israel supporters. All other issues paled in significance for him. He recognized the ongoing threats to Israel's perilous security, and the imperative for all Jews to support, politically and personally, our Israeli brethren. I lost track of the number of times he visited Israel. Of course, Jerusalem was his favorite destination. One could feel his excitement before each visit. He came back each time literally glowing. His second favorite destination: the mountains. The Rabbi owned a summer house and an undeveloped lakefront plot of land in Woodburn, in the heart of the "Jewish Alps," also known as the Catskills. This was the countryside of his youth, and he fondly recollected youthful mischief on or near the lake. His modest home had a porch, which felt like a treehouse, being surrounded by magnificent trees. The Rav loved swimming in the lake. He inhaled the fresh mountain air with gusto; he achieved a level of serenity amidst the lush greenery. The mountains and nature seemed to invigorate his body and replenish his soul. Yet, even there, the Rav was a resource to his mountain community—conducting services, giving lectures, and being available to listen to and advise his neighbors.

But the Rav always returned to Rivington Street, the center of his geographic universe. It is ironically fitting that one of the Rabbi's last acts, almost just before his death, was officiating at a bris, a celebration of birth and life: The Rabbi loved life, lived life, and breathed life into his community and congregation and all who crossed his path. Rabbi Spiegel was a Rivington Street fixture—which we all somehow felt was as permanent as any street accoutrement. Indeed, he now is. Shortly after he passed away, the community, in a consensus unusual for the Lower East Side, took action to co-name the Rivington Street block of the First Romanian-American Congregation as Rabbi Yaacov Spiegel Way. When we had to decide the full street name, we had to decide how the street would be designated from among words like "street," "lane," "corner," or "place." We chose Rabbi Yaacov Spiegel Way, because we all agreed that, in so many ways, Rabbi Spiegel showed so many the way to live life, and epitomized the life of our community. In his remembrance and with this street name, Rabbi Yaacov Spiegel will continue to forever inspire his family, the countless individuals whose lives he touched, the Jewish people, and indeed the entire community of Rabbi Yaacov Spiegel Way.

Alan Jay Gerson *born NYC November 1, 1957. Democratic City Council representative for district 1. Elected 2001, lost 2010. Graduated Columbia Law School 1979. For 18 years worked for law firm Kelley Drye & Warren.*

How I Came to Be Here

Jennifer Blowdryer

In 1955, Sion Misrahi's father, Jay Misrahi, moved his pregnant wife and young son from Larissa, Greece, to the United States. A Jewish organization called "Join" helped them leave Greece, but at that time it was felt there were already too many Jews in the New York area, so they landed, confusingly, in Iowa.

"There were no Jews there," Sion points out. "I was going to Catholic school. So we went from one place with no Jews, Greece, to another place with no Jews. I was going to Catholic school, so I wasn't going to grow up to be Jewish and my parents wanted me to grow up to be Jewish."

The family was sent to Iowa as part of a grand plan to spread the Jews throughout the country, but, of course, the moment the bored and lonely Misrahi family was able to make the fare, by 1956, they promptly took a train to New York, and took up residence on Hegeman Avenue. Sion was six years old, and happy to be there, though the other children mocked him at first for not being able to speak English.

"We were so happy when we finally moved to Brooklyn. We lived across the street from the park, a state park. They used to have movies on Friday nights, and they had a pool there, this two-foot pool with a sprayer. I used to love it. I used to run around with my friends there."

Their new neighborhood, otherwise known as East New York, had a Sephardic Jewish community. Sion went to Hebrew school, every day after school, at 3 p.m. A self-proclaimed product of the public school system, Sion eventually graduated from Bernard Baruch College. Though his father, like many Jewish immigrants, had no more than a fourth grade education, he began working for a hardware store in Manhattan, before moving up to a more lucrative position working on Orchard Street for $30, two days a week, enough to pay the rent, feed a family of four, and buy a few pieces of furniture. Probably used furniture, Sion reflects, a true merchant of the old school. By about 1962, Sion's father was able to buy a place on Orchard Street with two partners for $6,000 key money, his life savings. His father and his partner opened up Daniels' Clothing, on Orchard between Delancey and Rivington and, at the age of fourteen, Sion started to work there on the weekends.

It was tough, as Sion was already a night person and grudgingly got up early, after a week of school, to learn to sell, but he soon became enamored with the art of the deal, Orchard Street Style.

"So I start selling and they put me with this guy who's really a tough salesman, that guy was great. Mostly men's suits, three-piece suits. A three piece suit was fifteen dollars. They would send it to the tailor across the street. Imagine you could buy a three-piece suit on the Lower East Side for fifteen dollars. One guy taught me how to bargain. How do you bargain on a three-piece suit? 'I tell you what, you say, how much can you afford, in dollars? I tell you what, leave me the vest; you got a two-piece suit.' Later on we'd sell the vest for four dollars! Then we started getting more sophisticated; we'd raise it to eighteen dollars and let them walk out for fifteen dollars.

"Everybody was happy—the customer with that eternal glow of the good deal, the guys at Daniel's Clothing who were getting the price of a suit plus a later profit on the vest. I liked it once I was at the store, but I'm a late riser so I hated—after going to school all week—getting up on Saturday to go to my father's store. It was a killer for me; I wanted to have a good time. I think it was the best thing that coulda' happened to me. I became a people person. When you start taking customers, one after another, one after the other, one after the other, you learn how to read people, look them in the eye, say the right words, the right inflections. You become a street person. Getting here was half the battle; once I got here I was a great salesman. I had the youth, the twinkle in my eye. The other guys were tired by 4 o'clock, but I was raring to go at 4 o'clock."

Sion has that New York thing I've recognized in former bosses, particularly in the nightclub industry, where they can size you up lightning fast. It's what a good American merchant has to be able to do. New York City is not a culture with a lot of second, third and first negotiations. You've got to get with it immediately, and these people can read a potential customer like nobody's business but their own. Always a fan of the hyper-vigilant, I have come to admire it.

Sure enough, in 1971, Sion started up his own women's clothing store, with his sister at his side.

"I was in the business, this was my calling; I wanted to be what my father was, only better. I admired what my father did, but I was dreaming big. It was a marvelous education. And so we opened up Jaiz Fashions in '72. A year later we opened up Breakaway. One store on one side was Jaiz, the other side was Breakaway. My father and his partner put up the money, I put in the labor. In six months, I gave them all their money back. They went berserk!" he proudly recounts.

"I had fifteen salesmen in an eighteen by twenty foot store. I started selling Little Lisa Sweaters. They were cute, little appliqués, cute design, puff sleeves, really nicely done. We were catering to a Spanish clientele, from all over. All the business owners were Jewish, all the customers were Hispanic, and then others followed. I learned how to speak Spanish on the sales floor. I learned how to sell in Spanish, and to this day I could probably sell a suit in Spanish to a customer.

"We started selling Little Lisa sweaters, and I noticed I had a good sales force so I started bringing in leather jackets. I was one of the first to bring in fur coats, full skin fur coats. I brought fur coats in like there was no tomorrow. Little Lisa, leather jackets, leather coats. Denim became hot so we added denim. Remember Faded Glory jeans? That was hot; all sorts of jeans became hot. Eventually I threw out all the jeans because I had coats and jackets, then I added fur collars, then section jackets with fur collars to make it look even more impressive, then I went to all fur and all leather and I became an outerwear business. One day, two stores, I took in $78,000— in two stores, not to be believed."

He still sounds happy, especially about the Little Lisa sweaters, which makes me immediately want one. I remember the Orchard Street of the '80s, when much of the display fashion had degenerated to tackily decorated sweaters with bits of fur hanging from them, very Boca Raton, extremely not cool.

With the proceeds, Sion built his first original building, now home to Misrahi Realty.

"The purchase price was legitimately earned from the retail business on the Lower East Side. I renovated it. It was so gleaming and shiny, everybody thought I was in the Mafia! I was a businessperson who was doing well.

"I realized that I had to own a building in order to secure the business. I bought it in 1979, I opened the business in 1982, and it was ready. On the ground floor it was a half-in, half-up type of building. I made it straight. Downstairs was Cooper, who had a grocery store with the beans on the outside. I bought it from him, renovated, made it gleaming, steel plated all the walls 'cuz I was gonna keep furs in here. This building is a steel box. We used to change windows on buildings, due to bullet holes. That's how a window broke in those days."

Misrahi's stores did well until the late '80s, when the growth of national discount stores and the end of blue laws—which had left the Lower East Side one of the only places in the city where you could shop on Sundays—were draining customers from the area. Then there was the crash of 1987, which left Misrahi, along with much of Manhattan, dead broke.

"In 1987 the stock market crashes. It's like somebody flipped a switch. Everybody stopped buying. My business went into the tank. In one year I went from being very prosperous to owing two million to Banco Leumi. I went to all my suppliers and said, 'Listen, guys, I'm in trouble. I owe you 300,000. This is what I'd like to do.' I gave them promissory notes that were cashable during my business season. They'd supply me with fresh inventory. '87 to '90: From four stores to three to two to one store. I'm in one store at 125 Orchard Street. During my heyday a woman called Lucy DeSantos walks into my business and says, 'Hey you, come here! My building's for sale; I'm bringing my landlord over; make a deal!'

"For $75,000 down, I got half of 179 Orchard Street. Lucy DeSantos came to me because she knew me, she knew who I was. Now I own my second building. $75,000 was peanuts to me. Listen carefully—the building was $375,000, a five-story building. Some of the rents used to be sixteen dollars a month.

"You know what,' I thought, 'I have all this money, let me buy something, another building, what can it hurt.' So when I finally closed my business, I had that.

"I closed my last store. I go to my landlord and say, 'I'm losing money on this store. My rent is $4,500 a month. I'd like to fix up the basement and get a new lease.' The landlord hands me a lease, saying it will be $7,500 a month for 300 more square feet of business space. I say, 'I can't pay this rent. I'm in the toilet!'"

For two years Sion stayed at home, trying to figure out what he wanted to do. Sheldon Silver suggested that, as the well-connected president of the local Merchant's Association, Misrahi could form a Business Improvement District, otherwise known as a BID.

"When Sheldon Silver brought up the idea of a BID, I realized that I knew 250 building owners or more, and 450 shopkeepers, so I became a broker. In 1994 I opened up Misrahi Reality. I bought up eighteen apartments and two stores for $275,000. I was out of work but couldn't resist it. I was eating my money fast, with a wife, two kids, but, thank God ... If you look around, there were a lot of people who stayed in the stores and lost all their money. I got out. When I got out, they thought it was nuts." Sion was able to take a longer view, however.

"If you're a renter in an apartment, you know that your future is owning a home. The same thing goes for the retail business. Your future is in owning the building, or putting the business somewhere you own eventually. Here's the problem—people get lulled by low rents. Let's say a guy pays low rent, sitting on a ten-year lease at $2,500 a month, and he's happy. He doesn't think about owning a building. He should be putting 2,500 hundred a month in a bank account, towards owning a building. I'm in business today because I own a building. I wouldn't be here if I didn't."

"Store owners should have been saving up to buy their business, and now it's too late for some of them. Here's the thing. I had a vision of what I wanted to do—run my own building. One person came to me and said, 'Take my building,' so we got into building management. Then we started having to fix these old buildings up because they were coming apart at the seams. Sagging, floors coming apart, decaying from landlords not fixing water problems, leaks, land sinking, hundred-year-old construction, etc., etc. We brought a crew in for that. Misrahi Realty has thirty-two people now. We have to take care of all the ins and outs of a building." Eventually, Misrahi Realty got into development.

"In 1994 I had a vision for that. I would go to a landlord who had a store downstairs, but his place would be vacant on top. 'I have the bank,' I'd say, 'the contractor, the architect. I'm going to run the job; you'll pay me to run it.' We did it to about twenty buildings, got the management of those buildings. The landlords said it's the best thing they've ever done.

"What we did was create a package for landlords who were not so sophisticated. They looked. They agreed. A lot of it they ended up doing without me. They knew they stole my idea, my contract—it didn't matter to me. I was busy enough. It's okay. I started the idea, got the contract, the architect. It became a renovation party after awhile. Monkey see monkey do, that's it. In the interim we're trying to run a brokerage business. On Orchard between Houston and Stanton, there are twenty-one vacancies. It's a ghost town. I go to all the owners of the building, I say, 'Listen, guys, I'd like to have an exclusive on the store rentals, merchandise the rentals, merchandise the block, fill up the entire block.'

"I started advertising. Restaurants and bars answered the ads, wanted cheap rent. All of that block became an entertainment zone. 192 Orchard, he was the first guy there, then came River Town, then came everybody else."

Sion still operated more like a quick-thinking merchant than a bureaucrat, which is probably how he came to bring in businesses like Babes in Toyland and the fetish store, Damask, places that would usually be in a more forward-thinking city like San Francisco, definitely not the old LES of the fur-decorated sweater.

"There were city and state regulations. I didn't know anything. You wanna open a bar, your credit's good, let me see your bankbook, you're good. You got the money, you got the know-how, you're a good person, you're in.

"A few people started to complain that there was noise outside, vomiting in the streets; it was a little rowdy, but you know what, we filled up the stores. Eventually, everybody got regulated; it became more reserved."

Neighbors complained about the rise of the puking NYU student, but Sion had a reason for not wanting the neighborhood rezoned to residential.

"What I'm pushing now is that this neighborhood from Houston to Delancey, and let's say from Norfolk to Allen here is the Downtown of the LES. We want to maintain it as the downtown, the shopping district. If they zone it as all residential, the stores disappear, they become apartments, and that's no good.

"With all the subways, it's beautiful here. Three blocks, you're in the subway. How do you build a 2nd Avenue subway line and then down zone it?! Let this be downtown, an Entertainment Zone, with hotels and restaurants. You know what we do now for residents? If you're in a place with a bar, rest, we put noise riders in every lease, and it's a condition. People know what they're getting into when they take an apartment here."

Misrahi Realty has come to have a bad reputation as a landlord, though they're primarily a broker—they make money when a place is first rented out, and there is often an absentee landlord. Businesses like realty companies can attract a certain kind of employee: transient, fast-talking, a bit crooked, and I believe that's what's happened in the past to tenants who've been fleeced for extra fees. It's hard to control a staff of thirty-two, especially with a few fast-talkers on board. Sion can have the vague quality of an artist, more than a micro-managing tycoon, which indeed he isn't. He brokers a lot of deals, but doesn't own the properties. I asked him how he felt about the easily bandied about term slumlord, one who is often accused of changing the face of a formerly quaint neighborhood.

"Well, we renovated every single building we have in our hands. 168 Ludlow, that building will be a new building eventually. The first floor is a restaurant space, the guy stays, and no one can throw him out. The other store, we have a lease for a European jewelry store. The upstairs will be all brand-new apartments, four per floor.

"I was the one that pioneered renovating all the vacant buildings, went from door to door, talking people into doing it. We brought life into the area. It was drug-infested, bombed-out. We advertised all the time to bring fresh money in, for fresh tenants to come in from outside the neighborhood.

"We have very tiny stores on Orchard Street. We don't have the big box stores. We'll never get the Gap. The Gap needs 5,000, 8,000 square feet. These big stores need footage. We have small stores. The store I rented on Ludlow is 400 square feet. No chain is going in 400 square feet. However, nothing is static. One thing is sure—that change is a certainty. How do we preserve what we have? We can't. It's gonna change. It has to change.

"I don't mind that they talk about me. I don't think I'm a slumlord at all. I think I've revitalized, breathed life into this neighborhood. It's vibrant now. If you asked a young person today, 'Where would you rather live, Upper East Side or the LES?' everybody would say LES. But twenty years ago, they'd say, 'The LES, are you kidding me?' No one felt safe. This is a fabulous neighborhood."

If he had his way and was able to pull off a Robert Moses style of visionary rebuilding, the desperately seeking same young tenants would not keep the area in the state of a highly sexualized college campus, something longer term residents have come to resent.

"They come here for boy meets girl, lots of girls, lots of guys, but when they have kids, they won't stay. I don't think so. They're gonna move on. The apartments are small. The stores are small. If they let them build large buildings where people can have children, they might stay, but they're not allowing that. My suggestion is: Let's pick a spot where they can put these tall buildings, a core downtown everybody can get to in a five-or-ten-minute walk, so there's no need for cars.

"We've got all these low-rise buildings. That 2nd Avenue subway's gonna need people to feed it. The Community Board is mostly against large places, though. The smaller apartments are easier to rent. What a person needs in Manhattan is a nice bathroom, a place to make a cup of coffee and a place to put their head down." As for preserving the quaintness of many of our grandparents' crappy lives by maintaining the structures they once inhabited, he's not in favor of the landmarking plan proposed by the Historic Districts Council.

"Landmarking is the last thing you wanna do. You want to change a storefront, it's gonna cost you $250,000. Your front window, twelve grand. Russ and Daughters have historic status, which is different from landmark status. I was the one who brought that in, the historic thing. It's a state historic thing. City landmark means if you wanna change a window, you have to hire an architect, submit it, Landmark looks at it, then they say, 'You know what? Change one window. Why don't you change all the windows?' That's 40,000 bucks!

"Historic status means it's voluntary. If you want a historic look, you can apply for tax abatement and they'll help you bring it back to an historic look. If you want to change a storefront, and start with, 'Here's a picture of 1934,' how do you do that?! It's lunacy. This is the last bastion of small landlords. You landmark this area, these guys can't deal with $12,000 windows, so they're gonna all sell to institutions. Then it's the end of the real LES. The big guys will start trading buildings, buy blocks, knock them down, bring in box stores. You gotta leave it alone. It's working."

I pointed out that Sion has been in the same two-block radius from the ages of fourteen to fifty-eight, on a near constant basis.

"I love this area. I feel for it. No one has a history of it better than I do. I've seen it grow and I've participated in the growth. Those people who haven't participated in the growth want it to be how it was. They think if the rent was $300 a month, maybe I could do something—but that's not gonna happen anymore.

"This is an immigrant neighborhood still to this day, the only neighborhood where you can open up a business if you have some credit. You can't open up a business on 42nd Street. If you are opening up your first store, they won't let you in. Unless you have three stores already, you can't open up a store in a mall. Uptown you have to have a lot of stores; you have to be a chain. Down here you can walk into this office. You don't have to be a chain. Probably the last place where you don't have to be a chain.

"I still meet wonderful people. On 179 Orchard Street we have Johnson, a clothing store, designer, very talented. Then there's Apollo Braun, and Café Chabon, that little French restaurant. Also, you got Sal. It takes a certain type of person to transcend this neighborhood. I tried and I fell flat on my face. I can't expand past the LES. My store on 57th Street was my model store. From there I was gonna open up other stores, go public. I was talking to Drexel Burnham. Remember they went bust? I was gonna open store after store after store. That's what I was shooting for and I fell flat on my face.

"There is a ruling class mentality, and I'm really merchant class. When you talk to certain people, if they feel you're part of their class, they'll trust you and work with you. If you're not part of it, they won't. I'm the bridge between people like that and a small business. I get along with them but I'm not really one of them. I like that. I don't mind that. I feel for the small business owners. I did not start as part of the ruling class, and I'm too old to transcend that now. Maybe my son will do it. If he can't, that's okay. Maybe my grandson will.

"This is still the place to come for entertainment. If you're young and have business in New York, you will you go to 42nd or come to a hotel here, or on Orchard Street, where you have a nightlife, stroll around the neighborhood, meet new people. If they leave this neighborhood alone, due to the sale of air rights, things will stay pretty much the same. Though the Rivington Hotel looks like it landed from Florida, they did buy up all the air rights around it. All the buildings have to stay at a certain height now. Even at 168 Ludlow, when the hotel comes in, they will own the air rights. If they leave it alone, they will have only a few highrises. All the small landlords are destined to disappear anyway. If they landmark everything, it'll happen in one generation. On its own, three generations. They've tried to call this neighborhood LOHO, for Lower Houston, and NOD, for North of Delaney, but I stick with the LES. The LES is still music to everyone's ears."

Jennifer Blowdryer is an investigative thinker who's written a few books, most recently The Laziest Secretary in the World - other books can be found online for .01 cent. She's lived in the East Village since 1985, and was conceived at the corner of Bleecker and Bowery, indoors, of course. Jenniferblowdryer.com, jenniferblowdryer.blogspot.com. She performs a lot. Who doesn't?

In Memoriam of a Mensch?

Margaret Santangelo

A landlord. An American. An Israeli. A cab driver. A Jew. A lover of lesbian crackwhores. A father? A grandfather. An investor. A real estate under-developer. A comedian. A gambler. A caretaker. A benefactor. A cantor. A payer. A debtor. A transgressor. Many descriptive adjectives, often contradictory, come to mind when attempting to describe David Shuchat. A Lower East Side landlord, he certainly was, but that lacks evocation. David's persona was emblematic of the unique and mysterious character of the Lower East Side: a dying breed of New Yorker, the type of man that at once defined and challenged preconceptions about the Jewish slumlord. It is precisely because of men like David that the Lower East Side developed the character and flavor that spawned a generation of artists, musicians, and freaks of every kind. Without the defining influence of weirdoes like David, the Lower East Side—so quickly disappearing—would never have been. His death in December 2006 marked the end of an era for the colorful neighborhood that is fast becoming a thing of urban legend. The creative energy that flowed so rigorously through the veins and arteries of the L.E.S. was pumped by the heart of landlords who chose a different path: They accommodated and gave sanctuary to crackheads, prostitutes, and broke artists.

This insane little man was in many ways larger than life, with a deep, loud laugh that could be heard for yards and yards from wherever he stood. He was the sun around which a cackle of crackhead chippies rotated, hoping for a $20 or $10 to sweep or mop the hallways of one of his buildings. If you asked him to, he would sing a Hebrew prayer in a throaty tenor, usually in a stairwell where the acoustics were best. Sparkling blue eyes, a determined jaw, and a decidedly large, oval head marked some of his physical characteristics. But more interesting and mesmerizing were his intangible qualities. Like the way he pretended to be mad at you but really wasn't. Like how he came up with little nicknames for his favorite girls, such as Chinese Apple, which he called you as he pinched your cheeks. How he shook his head and deemed a friend of yours "corrupted" when he fell prey to drug addiction. He had lots of things to say about his little family of tenants, but one thing he never did was judge. He respected—and loved—every one of his tenants and treated them like family. In the age of management companies and absentee landlords, having a landlord who lived down the street and was often sunning himself on the stoop on bright days was a pleasure. An acquired taste, but a pleasure nonetheless.

Landlord-tenant court was one of David's favorite locales, a place where he could exercise some of his power. He and his brother Nathan were affectionately called "Tweedledee and Tweedledum" by many of the court clerks and judges. Although he was always taking tenants to court for this or that, he rarely ever actually evicted any of them. Landlords like David Shuchat have contributed to the proliferation of art, political activism, and general challenging of the system by providing housing unprejudicially, overlooking potential tenants' appearance, income, generation, or simple lack of financial stability. They saw past the outer, culturally-defined requirements that shut these individuals out of all other neighborhoods, and provided a type of sanctuary in which these artists could feel safe and take refuge, mainly in their work.

My long-lost surrogate grandfather, my adversary in landlord-tenant court, a friend who genuinely cared about me—David represented a dying breed of seminal characters who through their very persona captured the essence of the Lower East Side. The Davids of the Lower East Side flouted convention, operated by their own rules, and chose to live on the margins of society just like their tenants, the self-declared societal rejects that made up the more flamboyant and readily identifiable characters that eventually came to represent the image of the Lower East Side. The similarities between these two seemingly disparate groups made for the perfect relationship. It was a mutually profitable affair: The slumlords got undeclared cash, got away with doing minimal repairs on their ramshackle buildings and could violate building codes without any outrage, while an artist community quietly began to flourish. David thrived on his role as landlord and enjoyed his work. He confided his own reasons for this to me, ones so incredible, I could scarcely believe they were true. They are indeed true, and what is even more significant: the reasons are so noble they wouldn't be believed by any cynical outsider. But to a Lower East Sider, it will no doubt make perfect sense and actually enlighten the residents who are now under assault by an unfeeling, greedy, and illegally run conspiracy of real estate developers, municipal officials, and real financial interests that threaten the continuance of the traditional Lower East Side community.

One salient memory is of the morning of 9/11. Nearly all the tenants of my building (most of whom did not have "regular" 9-to-5 jobs, because they were junkies, lunatics or both) were up on the roof, and, as the megalith being built on Ludlow on Houston was not yet there, we had a wonderful view of the top halves of the towers. The Bangladeshi storeowners from the bodega in the building had come up, too, and we all stood in wonder, horror, and awe. Within less than an hour, David had walked over from one of his dilapidated buildings, the one in which he lived, to watch the ensuing madness from our stoop (incidentally one of the last stoops without fencing or gates to hinder hanging out, or stoop-hanging, a dead New York tradition). He immediately began shouting racial epithets, along with my then-boyfriend Donny who was down there on the stoop with him. Donny cried, "Round up the cabbies!" while David shouted, "We're under attack! It's time to invade"—obviously meaning attack the surrounding Arab countries in which the Israelis have been embroiled in a bitter battle since the nation of Israel's inception. This was the first time I had seen Donny and David—like a mongoose and a cobra until then—agree on anything. The German-Jew dialectic fully operated between the two. But it was a begrudging respect that kept the relationship civil, most of the time at least. I digress. David shouted his racially charged observations to the dust-and-blood-covered New Yorkers making the long exodus from Ground Zero on foot past our building. He was a rabble rouser, a rebellious spirit, who wasn't afraid to voice his politically incorrect convictions and attitude—even while his Moslem tenants, the Bangladeshi store owners, sat alongside him on the stoop where you'd often see him.

Roosters crowing and awakening you from your sleep: An annoyance to some, but a wonderful cacophony that greeted me every morning, a perfectly inappropriate and foreign sound to regularly hear in Manhattan of all places. Visitors from overseas or out of town would wonder in amazement if I actually had a rooster, with his own apartment no less, living in my building. But that's the way it is, or was, in my building. David kept roosters and hens. He ate their eggs; in fact, I've eaten many a David kosher omelet. The rooster was kept here, with a dedicated apartment all his own, and was a part of 179 Essex for at least three years of my tenure. As I am a (spiritually) displaced lifelong New Yorker, the sound of a crowing rooster did not bother me. I spent lots of time in Pennsylvania, where all our neighbor farmers had roosters, so the sound was reminiscent of bucolic days in the rolling hillsides of Bucks County. To my neighbors, it was a nuisance. This in-touch-with-nature side of David harkened back to his days in Israel, where he was one of 19 children of Rebecca and Abraham Shuchat. The family settled just after WWII, and worked to build a home in their religious homeland. When he was 16, David Shuchat boarded a boat bound for New York, with eighteen dollars he had saved from his jobs in Israel as a carpenter, laborer, and other odd jobs. Half of his pay went directly to his father, a devout Jew who ran his large family like a military battalion. But he blessed his son as he set out to return to his native America to make his fortune.

David Shuchat was raised in the Upper East Side—actually East Harlem—before his father did his duty and moved the family to Israel in 1949 to help establish settlements in the newly formed Israel. David was thirteen at the time, and therefore had experienced both the hard life in the desert and the satisfaction of working the land, toiling and laboring for one's sustenance, a life experience few New Yorkers could boast.

Another interesting facet of David was the fact that he was a world-class tenor. He sang High Holiday services all over the Northeast, for "big bucks," as he often boasted. He would sing for me in our hallway, where the acoustics were great, for twenty minutes at times. I know I recorded it once or twice, but the tapes are somewhere in my jumbled archive. He played reel-to-reel recordings of some of his performances, recorded in the prime of his life (and the height of his vocal power), that were amazing to hear. Religious a cappella— especially Hebrew prayers—are some of the most intense vocal performances I have ever appreciated. I saw him perform live once, a fish out of water in a Lower East Synagogue, but welcomed nonetheless by the conservative Jewish congregation.

How David interacted with other religious Jews in the community was also interesting and quite complex. Although he was observant, he openly flouted the tenets of the strict sect of Judaism to which he belonged; nonetheless, he was a respected member of the Lower East Side community. Many recognized his eccentricity and accepted him for it, if not despite it.

Don't misunderstand—David was a tough guy in the tradition of Meyer Lansky, Bugsy Siegel, and other gangster-type Jews. He loved to gamble, womanize, and make money. All of his buildings were, at one time or another, bona fide drug spots; in fact, my building was half a whorehouse and shooting gallery for much of the 1970s. I was the first resident of my apartment since 1974. Before that, a dog named Shadow lived here—for five years. Before that, it was a WWII colonel who paid $54 a month rent. I actually found a rent receipt when I cleaned up the apartment when I moved here in 1994.

The reason that David was so sympathetic to the artists he housed, I believe, is because he himself was an artist at heart. His talent as a singer was undeniable—he was in high demand all over the country to sing High Holiday services, and was paid accordingly. This aspect of David's layered and multi-faceted personality reveals part of why he ran his buildings the way he did. He gave sanctuary to his tenants, allowed them to float and owe months of rent, and all the while threatened eviction, initiated court proceedings, and continually demanded his rent. But it was all a game to him: His buildings and their administration were his life; he loved to play the role he did in so many of our—his tenants'—lives. And while he threatened eviction and took tenants to court, he knew he could never win due to basic laws he was actually breaking.

It's a bit technical, but his buildings lacked Certificates of Occupancy and were not registered as Multiple dwellings with the HPD (Housing and Preservation Department). So, in effect, he could not win his cases, yet pursued them anyway. Each time I went to Landlord-Tenant court with him, whether I initiated the action or he did, I always prevailed. And in addition, our dealings were always amiable, unlike all the other disputes being settled at court. We sat together and joked while waiting for the case to be called, the clerks and judges affectionately ridiculed him, and Lower East Side lawyer Ben Kaplan rolled his eyes and sometimes purposely lost cases (in my opinion) because he knew that David was not going to evict the tenant. It was his way of interacting with his tenants, and reminding them that he was in charge. In fact, after our court appearances, he always treated me to a kosher lunch at the kosher pizzeria on Grand Street. The fellow diners not familiar with David always looked at us with interest, wondering why this shiksa was dining with two orthodox Jews. But all those who knew him—most of the patrons, in fact—were friendly and greeted him with the enthusiasm he invoked in almost everyone he knew. Those lunches are some of my fondest memories—that he allowed me into his crazy little world and shared himself with me was such a privilege.

David was one of the old school, an aspect of his character that I loved and reveled in. He demanded his rent in cash, gave no receipts, and wrote no leases. And although he played the court game with many tenants, don't misunderstand—when he wanted someone out, he got them out by whatever means necessary. He was at heart a tough guy, and you lived in his buildings on his terms. He rented to people whom he liked and interested him. I spent countless hours listening to fascinating stories about his life and all the adventures he had. His apartment on Ridge Street was less than humble; it was basically a hovel, disorganized and completely unrenovated, despite the fact that he was worth millions—not just in terms of his real estate equity, but also in his investments in the stock market. Yet he lived on $2 a day of expenses, and that's not counting his gambling habit.

He played scratch-off games at the deli in my building, for hours on end at times. However, to him, as he explained, he was breaking even—he simply spent the rent he charged the deli on his gambling habit. This was David: a player, a business mind oriented toward gaming the system and winning. He indulged his vices, yet remained a devout orthodox Jew. However, this central contradiction in his character seemed to make perfect sense; he was far from a hypocrite when it came to his religious values. Although he frequently flouted the standard tenets and laws of his religion, he had convictions in his own personal beliefs. He related to Judaism on a basic level; it was his identity more in a racial and social sense than in a conventional, orthodox manner. He identified himself as a Jew, an orthodox one at that, and despite his transgressions was still respected and accepted by the Lower East Side Jewish community. That he was able to walk the fine line between heretic and devout follower was one of the most amazing aspects of his ultimately unique character. But he pulled it off flawlessly—although sometimes he was judged by fellow orthodox Jews for his behavior.

Because he traveled all over the Northeast to sing at High Holiday services, he sometimes brought his Puerto Rican, Lower East Side girlfriends with him. He told me a story once about how he snuck one of these girls into the hotel provided by the synagogue despite the fact that women were strictly forbidden from staying with a man, especially gentile women who were not the man's wife. He warned her not to come out of the room, but a peculiar smell emanating from the room while he was at the synagogue drew the management's attention. When they investigated, they discovered David's down-low girlfriend smoking crack in the hotel and their horror at his impudence dumbfounded them. He somehow convinced them to let him finish the job, although he had to send his female companion home (he wouldn't put her up in another hotel, of course; the extra expense was not in his budget) and was begrudgingly paid for his services. The synagogue, however, did not call on him again, a fact he laughingly told me proudly. When the gig was up, it was up, and David was a free spirit who walked the limits and challenged the status quo, not only in his religious practices, but in every aspect of his life: how he ran his buildings, how he lived, and how he interacted with people.

David looked at his tenants and his entourage of drug-addled young girls as a family of sorts. Although he had actual relatives, he rarely spent time with them. Instead, he shared his daily life with down-and-out, broke tenants, drug-addicted girls ('corrupted' as he would call them), degenerate gamblers, and Lower East Side neighborhood fixtures. The entire neighborhood knew him, simply because his presence was larger than life: His stoop-hanging at 179 Essex was legendary. I would spend hours on that stoop with him, listening to stories, laughing with him, and just bullshitting. Eventually, he invited me to his home and he shared his life story with me, with which I was utterly fascinated. Pictures of him as a young man, an Israeli soldier, a baby, pictures of his parents, a family portrait of him and his eighteen brother and sisters, programs and newspaper clippings about his performances, his numerous pets, tours of all his empty apartments. He simply loved my interest and to hear him reminisce was truly an amazing experience. I regret not tape-recording or documenting these talks in some concrete way, and just before his death, I was negotiating a plan to do a documentary about him, in collaboration with Clayton. However, he wanted to be paid, of course, no less than $3,000. He was such a trip—he would tell his stories for free routinely to anyone who would listen, but his businessman instinct was not to give anything away on film for free.

He lived through the roughest days of the Lower East Side, and therefore, it is obvious that he was, no doubt, a tough cookie. Since he collected his rent in cash—no exceptions—he was often a target for drug dealers and junkies on the make. Whenever I paid him a large sum of money—and this was in the '90s, long after the wild, lawless days—my boyfriend and I would often walk or drive him back to his Ridge Street apartment, a gesture he quietly appreciated. He was robbed at gunpoint, shot twice, and stabbed once, so he was no stranger to violence. However, for all the attempts made to rob him, the thieves were most of the time unsuccessful. As he said, they would have to kill him to get his money. But this attitude was not about being greedy or money-obsessed. It was about his inner toughness, his pride in himself, and his refusal to be anyone's victim. This was a truly amazing, not readily apparent aspect of his personality—he was not afraid of anyone and he would never give in to anybody's attempts to control him.

This quality illuminates his seemingly flagrant disregard for orthodox Jewish customs: He did not believe in them, so he did not follow them. It was as simple as that. Yet he had conviction in his particular and peculiar set of beliefs, at least those he chose to follow, and followed them religiously. He could explain his approach to Judaism and his apparent flouting of its laws with a simple statement: "God made me to be who I am, and if I can't be true to myself how can I be true to my God." He accepted himself without question, and refused to be judged by anyone. His fellow Jews respected this about him, and he maintained his place in the community, whereas any other irreverent Jew would be shunned. This is because he was open and honest about his habits and his life. He didn't suffer a guilty conscience or feel ashamed of his lifestyle; in fact, he was rather a showoff when it came to his weird ways. He somehow resolved his inherently contradictory approach to life: Remaining a devout Jew while doing what he wanted and choosing which tenets to follow, an extremely difficult way to live. However, he did it, and happily. He enjoyed every minute of his life, and celebrated himself with passion and self-confidence. There will never again be one like David. He was one-of-a-kind and occupies a special place in my heart and, I believe, the hearts of many in the Lower East Side community. May he rest in peace, and be remembered for the man he was and the rebellious, legendary legacy he left behind.

Margaret Santangelo *Native New Yorker Margaret Santangelo, also known as Daisy, Day Zee, and Day Z., is a freelance writer and fourteen-year Lower East Side resident. She has written horoscope columns for a number of magazines, including* Guitar World, XXL, *and* Cosmo-Girl! *Her book,* Rock Stars: The Astrology of Rock and Roll, *will be released by St. Martin's Press in Fall of 2009. She resides in the Lower East Side with her canine familiars, Fafa and Lizzie.*

Alan Dell

Keith Staskiewicz

When Alan Dell was a child, his father would always tell him, "You're going to have a restaurant." Every time the two of them would visit Katz's Deli, his father would ask the owners if they were looking to sell. They always thought he was joking, but Dell was never so sure.

At this time, Dell's father was himself the proprietor of Club 28, a gay nightspot named for its 28th Street address. As with most gay-oriented establishments in Lower Manhattan back then, both the Mafia and the local police would stop by every so often. Words, and sometimes something more, would be exchanged and business continued as usual. It was one of the many traditions of the neighborhood in which Dell grew up. Dell's family roots dug deep into the asphalt and concrete of the Lower East Side. Dell was born to two of the many Jewish immigrant parents who called it home. Both his father and his mother grew up in the area, at some points only a few blocks away from each other. Dell's paternal grandmother came to the United States from Russia to escape the pogroms. Alone, she stowed away on a ship westward-bound, knowing only that she had relatives in New York. While aboard, she was forced to sleep with a man who kept her presence secret and provided her with desperately needed food. Once in America, she married and started a family.

Dell's father was only six years old when his own father died. Short on money, his family became monthly nomads, moving from apartment to apartment every thirty days, immediately before the rent was due. At age seven, his father began working his first job at a tailor shop. From these beginnings, he worked his way to sartorial success, and by the time he had a family of his own, he already owned a company that manufactured *shmatahs*, inexpensive house dresses for the women of the Lower East Side. Dell's mother was of Austro-Hungarian descent, and her side of the family was religiously orthodox. While his father was not religious at all, the family would still attend the synagogue on Fifth Street on the Holy Holidays. Later on, they would attend services at the Americana Ballroom, a space in one of the Grand Street co-op buildings that could be rented out for parties and celebrations. On the holidays, it would transform into a functioning synagogue.

For the first six years of his life, Dell lived with his parents on the ground floor of a Third Street tenement building between Avenues B and C. They had a backyard, but, even at such a young age, he wasn't confined to it. Back then it was safe for a six-year-old like himself to run around the block with his friends. His family then moved into the newly opened Hillman Co-op on Grand Street. His parents' friends thought them crazy for buying an apartment, but they saved their money, and purchased a four-and-a-half room apartment for $2,250, at the going price of $500 a room.

It was a true cooperative, but no one ever really thought of it politically. At this point in the Cold War, the co-ops were viewed more as neighborhood necessities than experiments in collectivism. During his youth, Dell always felt removed from the Jewish Socialist elements that had previously found a home on the Lower East Side, even though his mother worked as a secretary for the International Ladies' Garment Workers' Union, an institution with a rich leftist history. Everyone in the building paid monthly maintenance fees, but Hillman was unique among the co-ops in that it had its own power plant. A big brick square located on Lewis and Delancey, it provided free electricity to all three buildings. It also served a much more important function: when local kids played stickball on Lewis, a ball that hit the plant counted as an automatic out.

Although the area had been almost exclusively slums before demolition began for the co-op, everyone who lived in Hillman considered it safe, and tenants would often leave their doors wide open. There was no thought of crime or someone uninvited coming into your home, only the promise of a great cross-breeze during the hot city summers. The kids would return home from school, drop off their books, and rush downstairs to the twenty or so others who were waiting to play. The lower floors were primarily Jewish, but the building also had a surprisingly large contingent of Italians. There were so few minorities, though, that the only black man to live there is still remembered by name: Mr. Eugene Young. The building's demographic was not particularly representative of the neighborhood at large. There was a strong Puerto Rican presence even then, accompanied by a smattering of blacks. Racial tensions existed between the various ethnicities that cohabited in the region, but during the day it was far from a battleground. Everyone always knew which nights there were going to be trouble, usually taking their cues from the police, who could somehow anticipate the early rumblings of conflict with uncanny accuracy. The officers, spotting a handful of youths hanging outside of Florence Nightingale School on such a night, would get out of their green-and-blacks and rap the kids' knees with their nightsticks, shooing them back to their homes. A lot of the time, these nights coincided with a neighborhood-wide convergence at the amphitheater in East River Park.

The amphitheater was free and open-air, an attractive prospect especially during the summer months. The eclectic mix of the Lower East Side would represent itself in full at the events, and sometimes that allowed tensions to rise to the surface. But no one ever worried while they were there. They worried about coming home, sure, but never while they were at the amphitheater. The music was primarily golden oldies, but the concerts would still attract a healthy combination of old and young. Kids and adults turned out in equal numbers, and not just because parents were dragging their own along.

In those days, entertainment was not lacking for those who sought it. Countless movie theaters dotted the area, usually playing a minimum of three movies, including cartoons. At The Windsor on Grand, fifteen cents would buy you admission to a C-grade movie projected onto a pull-down screen reminiscent of those used in the local public schools. There was also The Delancey, a Hispanic movie theater, The Canal on Canal Street, and The Apollo on Clinton, sharing the block with the former precinct house for the Seventh.

Neighborhood teens of the opposite sex could get together at dances thrown by the Educational Alliance. The lights were low, the chaperones were few, and grinding was not unheard of. If nothing local was of interest to you, once you hit nine years old, you and a few of your close buddies could always hop a subway to Coney Island and its myriad distractions.

Alan Dell engaged in all these activities and more. When he was eleven, his Uncle Sidney took him down to Wall Street on Sundays to teach him to drive. There were no cars in the city then, and if you were stopped by a cop curious as to why a kid barely tall enough to see over the wheel was steering it, you'd just explain the situation and he'd smile knowingly and be on his way. At the same young age at which he was learning to maneuver an automobile, Dell was also learning to fight. Nestled among the artifacts of his father's many trades was a pair of boxing mitts. The older Dell was one in a long, distinguished line of Jewish pugilists who graced the ring in the first half of the 20th century, but Dell's mother forced him to give up fighting when they got married. This didn't stop him from passing along his years of bruising know-how to his son. Back then, people in the neighborhood almost never used weapons, so when there was a problem, your fists were all you had and you had better know how to use them. With his father's experience and a steady diet of Friday Night Fights, Dell had the distinction of being one of the only local Jewish kids who could stand his ground and hold his own in a fight.

As he grew older, new venues opened up to Dell. A man in the neighborhood whose less-than-legal dealings brought him a heavy cash flow would use his funds to buy out the entire second row at the Fillmore, every show. Dell went to all of them, and saw every musical act worth seeing for a period of years: Jimi Hendrix, the Who, everyone. You name it, he saw it.

Icons like Janis Joplin and Bob Dylan would play the Village coffeehouses, and he was there, too. He didn't smoke, but at these places it was necessary to keep a cigarette in one's mouth at all times anyway. It made you look older, and it was an unwritten requirement for the hip congregations that frequented the scene. For the preceding decade, the Lower East Side was the aortic center of the Beat movement, pumping the culture of its poets and hangouts directly into the American mindset. But as the Beat Generation slid into the Generation of Love, the hair grew longer, the colors grew brighter and those cigarettes were replaced by similar equivalents.

With a lion's mane of hippie hair, Dell flung himself into the movement. He and four friends piled into a VW van with flowers painted lovingly on its sides and drove across the length of Canada, twice. After receiving a math degree from City College, where he had originally enrolled to avoid the draft, Dell left New York bound for the Mecca of Hippiedom: San Francisco.

In 1967 he had gotten a job in the Bay Area with Pan Am as a computer programmer, working on PARS, their new reservation system. Capable of solving simple algorithms with only a few dozen punch cards, and so temperamental that a slight change in temperature could shut down the whole system, the computer Dell programmed was a product of its time. The memory room alone took up more space than three Katz's Delis. He was one of ninety employees who worked on the project, and who, once it was finally finished, were all unceremoniously fired. As a consolation, they received one year's worth of flight benefits, which allowed them to travel anywhere they wished. Taking advantage of this opportunity, Dell spent the next months trotting the globe. When his trip drew to a close, he flew back to San Francisco, resettling into the hippie lifestyle he had partly abandoned for employment. He joined a neighborhood friend from the Lower East Side at a commune in Bernal Heights, affectionately dubbed the "Captain America Commune," where he lived until 1968.

By the '70s, Dell was back in New York. The hair stayed, despite the change in decade and setting. The only reason to chop it off was to get a job, and Dell was going back to school. He attended Hunter College and took classes that interested him, eventually falling into the music program. During his time there and at the Manhattan School of Music, he learned ear training, composition, and conducting, and graduated with a B.S. in Music. Although he could play the piano and clarinet, and the guitar by ear, he was not quite up to the level of a professional performer. And as the old music school saying goes, those who can, do, and those who can't, teach band.

Dell was a student teacher at Stuyvesant before being offered a full-time position in charge of seventy students. After a year, he was transferred to Seward Park High. He lived across the street from the school, only blocks away from the Hillman buildings where he had grown up. He taught there for ten years.

In 1987, decades after his father's retrospectively prophetic statement, Alan Dell bought into Katz's Deli. At that point, the deli was only one year shy of its centennial, and was one of the most important historical and gustatory landmarks on the Lower East Side. But its quality, if not yet its reputation, had fallen into disrepair. When Dell entered the business, the deli was using whatever ingredients came cheapest. His first major contribution was ensuring the standards of the food served lived up to the deli's renown. They added more staff and cleaned up both the premises and, on some occasions, the clientele.

Despite these improvements, the first few years were dire. The closing of the Williamsburg Bridge for repairs and the recession that concluded the decade kept business dangerously slow. Dell, his brother-in-law, and his father had all hocked everything they owned to buy in, and they were saddled with a double-digit mortgage. Their success or failure depended on moving pastrami on rye. By the mid-'90s, things started to turn around. Katz's always had a loyal following, but they were still more of a destination place than a neighborhood agora. As the Lower East Side changed and opened more to fanny-packed tourists, egalitarian epicures, and even meandering uptowners, the seats steadily began to fill.

Katz's is equal parts deli and museum, thanks largely to Dell's idea of blanketing the interior walls with framed photographs. Some are of average customers enjoying their meals, others are a bit more eccentric. One was taken around Christmas time, when all of the Salvation Army Santa Clauses sat down for a meal, a sight that must have confused many a child. Another depicts Katz's filled with Catholic nuns, while yet another is soaked in the irony of the time. A large group of Palestinians protesters came to the deli for lunch. But by far the most abundant photograph type is the celebrity shot: movie stars like Ben Stiller and Billy Crystal, local legends like Joe Torre and Cousin Brucie, presidents, dignitaries, comedians and sports legends. They all come to Katz's and they all get their picture taken—most of them with Dell's smiling visage beaming alongside them. This is one of the perks of the job. His favorite celebrity encounter, like much about Katz's, is tied directly into a sense of nostalgic remembrance. As a child, Dell would tune in every week to *Lunch with Soupy Sales*, the long-running children's show hosted by the venerable, and often pie-faced, comedian. One day, when Sales stepped out of his past and into his deli, Dell was so overcome he immediately called his wife to tell her that *the* Soupy Sales had just arrived at Katz's. Nothing before or since has been as momentous.

Dell's anecdotes are as numerous as the photographs. During his twenty years at Katz's he has seen everything from junkies bathing in the bathroom to a lunch meeting between Vice President Al Gore and the Russian Prime Minister Viktor Chernomyrdin. One afternoon, when the United Nations Headquarters was once again engaged in heated debate over the issue of Cypriot independence, Katz's received a phone call from the Turkish delegation, informing them that their president was interested in dining there. The Turkish secret service scoured every nook and cranny of the premises before the president, flanked by machine gun-toting guards, entered and sat down at a table. Soon after, the phone rang again: it was a Cypriot representative. The president of Cyprus wanted to stop by for a meal. And so, the two presidents, far from the heated debate of the General Assembly hall, regarded each other coolly from across the room as each ate their sandwiches among their armed sentinels.

Katz's Deli is undoubtedly an integral fixture in the history of the Lower East Side, but it has also infiltrated the shared annals of American pop culture by providing the setting for one of the most memorable scenes in movie history. When Rob Reiner's mother uttered her line, Dell had no idea it would become such an important part of Katz's legacy. The release of *When Harry Met Sally…* did not immediately boost business. In fact, few people were even aware of Katz's involvement, since there was no mention in the credits and a book released soon after mistakenly identified Carnegie Deli as the setting. But now a sign suspended from the ceiling marks Table 10 as where Meg Ryan's orgasmic outburst set up the immortal punch line, "I'll have what she's having!"

In the past, the international renown of Katz's was pretty much relegated to the meats they sent overseas during WWII as a part of their "Send a Salami to Your Boy in the Army" campaign. Now, the age of globalization extends even to pastrami. Dell has been recognized in such far-flung locales as Rome and India, where people stop him and inquire about the well being of the deli. Working-class Europeans who have used their savings to spend their holiday in New York will stop by the deli for lunch, benefiting from a turbocharged euro. In a way, Katz's is still serving the people it once did; only now they come from around the world instead of around the block.

Katz's international popularity is helpful, but its owners still have to contend with the major costs of running such a place. An average deli's material costs are much higher than those of a restaurant, and Katz's are even greater. Service there takes longer and more staff is required to keep it going. Katz's setup is inarguably inefficient. Patrons receive a ticket upon entrance and pay on the way out. The food is prepared one at a time at the counter, and not in a kitchen. Waiting customers get an ample sample of meat while they attend their sandwich's construction.

But the appeal of the place is in the inefficiency. These are the aspects of Katz's that lends it its distinction and its tradition, and that keep people coming back to get a glimpse of a history that is quickly disappearing from the surrounding neighborhood. The menu has changed, including the short-lived and ill-thought-out addition of an "Oriental Chicken Salad," and the hours keep changing, but Dell and the other owners have made sure that they never messed with the fundamentals. Katz's Deli is practically the same institution it was twenty, fifty, one hundred years ago, and it represents one of the last standing bastions of the Lower East Side's rich Jewish heritage. Dell has helped to keep this landmark as he remembers it, and it stands as a testament to his roots in the neighborhood. But despite these grandiose implications, Katz's Deli is still as open and unpretentious as its owners, and its importance as a cultural touchstone hides behind the modesty of its slogan: "Katz's: That's All!"

Alan Dell proved his father right back in 1987, but the place he bought into was much more than just a restaurant. It was a piece of his own history.

Keith Staskiewicz: *Born and raised in 1985 in New Jersey. He received his B.A. from Johns Hopkins University and is currently whiling away on a Master's in journalism at Columbia. He has written for nationally broadcasted children's cartoons as well as for ABCNews, both of which were surprisingly similar.*

Part 3: Politics

The Many Recurring Dreams of Reason: the Motherfuckers and the Art of Rebellion

Malav Kanuga

Much has been made of the fiery retort that was 1960s-era militant political activity, not only of the overt groups and organizations widely recognized as the New Left but also their underground variants, whose analysis and tactics went beyond much of the Left at the time. Within the U.S. context, we are familiar with the posturing, infighting and eventual decline of the SDS, the dramatics of the Weatherman and their escalation of anti-imperialist strategy, as well as the revolutionary program of the Black Panther Party (formed in 1966), who would captivate a generation with their militant blend of Fanon-inspired internationalism and Black Nationalism.

A decade of struggle met increasingly intolerable forms of domination: for civil rights and self-determination against white racism, for socialist revolution against the 'paper tiger' of U.S. imperialism, for spontaneity and autonomy against the total administration and boredom of every aspect of life. These struggles were explosive not only because they threatened 'the system' with new social relations that irreverently dropped out of mainstream culture at the same time that they 'demanded everything': they were explosive because they ushered in new forms of creativity in resistance.

Nothing characterizes that struggle more than the Lower East Side group Up Against the Wall Motherfucker. And yet the whole story of the Motherfuckers is largely left out of the pages of history. You can find a few sketches on it – mostly by following these pages to the preceding volume, "Resistance," where Eve Hinderer, John McMillian, and Osha Neumann each detail the history and exploits of the Motherfucker. You can also find texts, manifestos, and ephemera across two other collections: BAMN [By Any Means Necessary] published by Autonomedia in Brooklyn, NY and Black Mask & Up Against the Wall Motherfucker originally published by Unpopular Books in the East London (slated for republication by PM Press), as well as a smattering of writings in various academic anthologies on 60s movement culture (much of which fails to grasp, or worse, tries to discredit the preference for direct action over 'strategy' that exemplified the Motherfuckers' approach to liberation).

Of the fragments that have been brought to public record, many rehearse the same conclusions: a sympathetic reading of the Motherfuckers suggests that they were an iconoclastic group of practitioners of a certain experimental freedom that nevertheless mixed enough volatile chemicals to set flames to their own laboratory. A harsher condemnation faults them for helping usher in the dark and nihilistic demise of 60s optimism—as if the Port Huron statement and a few feel-good festivals or marches were all that was necessary to overcome (never mind understand) the ruthless plunder of capitalism.

But what if we were to analyze the Motherfuckers' particular brand of collective rebellion in light of the postwar lessons of anti-fascism, mass mobilization, and political violence? These were of central concern to a number of dissident Jewish émigrés during World War II whose experiences with these matters framed much of their thoughts as well as left their intellectual legacy with their generational inheritors. If we look to the roots of the anarchist 'street gang', we see a direct connection to this legacy.

John McMillian ("Garbage Guerilla" in *Resistance*) offers a rare opportunity to hear Ben Morea's (the notorious 'leader' of the Motherfuckers) thoughts on their history after nearly 35 years of silence. John also points out that Osha Neumann is the only Motherfucker to write about the group in retrospect. It is from these writings, namely his unpublished memoir, that I reconstruct the history of the Motherfuckers via a journey through a rebellion that was as personal as it was social; as embodied in the legacy of Jewish intellectual resistance to fascism as it was a bodily rejection of his inheritance of it; as much a continuation of the anti-fascism of his parent's generation as it is a break with its rational form.

A Brief History of the Motherfuckers

The following account of the Motherfuckers and much of the anecdotal history in it relies heavily on the unpublished manuscript "Up Against the Wall M_ F_: A Memoir" by Osha Neumann.

In 1967, Osha (Thomas) Neumann became a founding member of the Motherfuckers. This was a career change for the self-described "nice Jewish boy with an MA in history from Yale."[92] According to Osha, the Motherfuckers were an unruly street-tough group of urban guerillas "swimming in the countercultural sea of freaks and dropouts who swarmed to cheap-rent tenements of the Lower East Side." Although this mass of dropouts was too vulnerable, too lacking in the resilience and self-certainty necessary for 'armed love', through cultivation and guidance they would ultimately form the base from which the Motherfuckers would organize for 'total revolution.' They developed amongst this base an anatomy of action predicated upon rallies, free feasts, raucous community meetings, and a steady stream of mimeographed flyers. Mimeograph or no, theirs was a propaganda of the deed, which, on the day to day, appeared to be an endless return to provocation with the police, an enduring spiraling in and out of control, through riots, arrests, protests of their arrests and arrests all over again.

By the beginning of 1968, the Motherfuckers had become a formidable presence on the Lower East Side, running free stores, crash pads, organizing community feasts in the courtyard of St. Mark's. They propagandized in response to the recuperation of hippy/countercultural lifestyle into the capitalist totality – at first the merchandizing of hip culture and then the full on absorption of counterculture into 'alternative lifestyles' within the capitalist fray. They attacked cultural capitalism to preserve the right not to be followed into their own exodus.

A Rebellion Against Spectatorship

Against the backdrop of police crackdowns that began to sweep New York streets of its dissidents, the Motherfuckers channeled their concern from guerilla art activity (most exemplary are the short-lived Black Mask days immediately preceding the birth of the Motherfuckers) into the more immediate political needs of survival, and ultimately elevated their focus to what they called 'total revolution'. Unlike previous incantations of the word, total revolution was not the apocalyptic class battle that pitted industrial workers against an international class of capitalists. No, for the Motherfuckers, that was white-collar leftist rhetoric—Leninism in all it's prevailing forms that at best mirrored 'bourgeois politics' with its representational delivery of politics to the people.

Instead, the Motherfuckers tried to intervene into the everyday. Their politics stemmed from a 'street-gang' analysis (as one SDSer put it) simply because those streets, the garbage strewn side streets of the Lower East Side in early 1968, were the very context for situating their lives. Contrary to Milan Kundera's somber proclamation, politics was not elsewhere. Indeed, politics could only be where the self was: in this case, it was dirty and violent, frantic and irrational. It smelled like garbage when the sun beat down upon it, and in all likelihood, kept a poor diet.

Nevertheless, the Motherfuckers did very much portray an avant-garde approach; they believed the path to vision was through the automatic. They would dive deep into private, spontaneous and irrational experimentation with life forms, and when they emerged, bringing to their analysis a sense of this suppressed unconscious, their politics blended with the 'impossible' and 'incoherent'. As Osha suggests, just as Dada was fighting for total unemployment in 1919 at the same instant the labor unions were fighting for better factory conditions, the Motherfuckers were fighting for exodus at the moment when the Left leapt with increasingly glee toward the cultural revolutions of Cuba and China. Their initiative was not for "Utopia" in the constructed socialist sense, but to begin with everyday life and pass beyond it: to go "beyond being drop-outs...the negative of the negative...to being free men with new life patterns."

Much like the novel autonomous experiences coming from the French of May '68, the Motherfuckers were decreasingly interested in engaging in what they called the 'VD of the revolution'—"'jive-ass honky leftist white collar radicals' who vacillate from TV armchair to auditorium armchair, lapping at the pool of politics from the high bank of organizational vanguardism." Osha makes the distinction that sums up the Motherfucker's scornful irreverence: as communists took jobs in factories to be close to the 'people,' Motherfuckers hung out on the streets to be close to *their* people. Communists went to work; they did as little work as possible.

Significantly, the Motherfuckers correctly assessed the prevailing condition of their time: boredom. Since most workers knew that their work was meaningless, a solidarity of disdain naturally arose from this realization. Whether such realization was the basis of any real alliance is another question (one of tactic and political strategy) all together. "We roamed the streets in dirty black leather jackets, carrying in our pockets thin, single blade 'K-9' folding knives which we practiced whipping our and flipping open with one hand." Far from the shop floors of the factories, the Motherfuckers would hang out in front of Gem's Spa, a narrow magazine shop with a soda counter on St. Mark's and Second Ave, passing out flyers and picking up gossip from the street before heading back to the cluttered store front office on Ninth Street opposite the park.

"We are fighting for ourselves/for our community/for our very lives. The issue is not something other than ourselves/we are the issue. It is the liberation of our lives that we are fighting for/to liberate ourselves from tight-assed bourgeois life, and it is our experience of the boredom and misery of amerikan life that drives us to destroy it anywhere it confronts us." - Up Against the Wall/Motherfucker

Osha collected rent money for their storefront by walking up and down St. Mark's Place carrying an empty toilet bowl, shouting "American shits money. Shit here!" A crowd gathered. A police officer approached demanding the plumbing. The crowd chanted, "Free the toilet! Free the toilet!" After Osha placed it gingerly in the trash container, the police officer smashed it to pieces with his nightstick before promptly arresting him for littering. These provocations were the excessive giving in to the irrational behavior that shrouded the authoritarian core of everyday life. It was the unreason of the deed that ridiculed the irrational rationality of the police, the rent-collecting property elite, bourgeois life, its state, family, political parties, etc. Moreover, according to Osha, "the toilet bust was fun." But fun was no ruse for the deeper levels of his fantasies – there was a air of danger in the liberation of fantasy that Osha was not fully prepared to given in to: "All power to the imagination" was a fine slogan," says Osha reminiscently, "but the imagination does not discriminate." At least, not the way reason might.

If much of the rebellious 60s was about grasping for Utopia, that great nowhere, the Motherfuckers felt they had a place—the Lower East Side. And yet, this was far from Utopia, for it was war-torn from daily street battles with police and real estate speculators. Perhaps it was a bit of both. As a Motherfucker broadsheet states, "My Utopia is an environment that works so well we can run wild in it." What else could describe, for the Motherfuckers, the Lower East Side?

But it wasn't simply exodus into the utopias of a liberated imagination they were after. If that were simply the case, their name would be a gross exaggeration of their ambitions. No, theirs was a vision of total destruction and total creation. The Motherfuckers had their roots in Black Mask and Angry Arts, two earlier manifestations of artistic and theatrical resistance who took inspiration from 1920s Dadaists of Paris and Berlin, as well as Italian Futurist Marinetti.

As has been frequently suggested, the unacknowledged leader and irreducible common denominator of these groups was Ben Morea, who grew up in Hell's Kitchen and lived all his life on the streets of New York. Hanging out in the jazz scene at clubs where heroin was hip, he got hooked. He was able to kick his habit in prison before being released, only to slip back into the coiling miasma of downtown desperation. It was around this time that Ben Morea met Judith Malina and Julian Beck, founders of the Living Theater.

"[They] were Ben's introduction to anarchism. After meeting them he joined a study group organized by Murray Bookchin [that] met at his apartment on 9th street east of 1st avenue. According to Murray, he would show up, listen impatiently for a while and then start screaming. He'd call everybody a petty bourgeois white honky and storm out. Everyone thought that was the last they'd see him, but the next meeting he would be back, and go though the same ritual."

In 1966, Ben helped launch Black Mask, a short-lived, crudely mimeographed arts magazine that he peddled in the East Village for a nickel. Later, he connected with a group of artists who were likewise politicized by the antiwar and black power movements. In October of that year, Black Mask handed out fliers proclaiming they would shut down MoMA. As their contingency arrived at the austere building, they were greeted with a wall of police and barricades and declared victory – without effort, they proved art's retreat from politics, its shunning of democratic engagement and now its complicity to authority.

A similar early action took place in January 1967 during a week of protest against the war called by Angry Arts. During a ten o'clock high mass, twenty-three agitators infiltrated St. Patrick's Church and unfurled posters depicting carnage from Vietnam to protest Cardinal Spellman's recent comment that "the war in Vietnam is a war for civilization."

Shortly thereafter, a group of artists in the Lower East Side meet to discuss continuing their agit-street theatre a la Angry Arts. They chose a name for themselves: the Motherfuckers, short for "Up Against the Wall Motherfucker" which they lifted from Amiri Baraka's "Black People!"[93]

One month later, in February 1967, Ben Morea and others announced another anti-war action. They demanded that Wall Street be renamed to War Street and, to this effect, donned black ski masks and marched through the streets carrying puppets with skull masks. A similar theatrical provocation targeted poet Kenneth Koch. Newark was in upheaval with riots and arrests, during which Leroi Jones/Amiri Baraka had been charged with illegal possession of a firearm. Black-maskers took the occasion to crash a Kenneth Koch reading with fliers with Leroi's picture on it and the words, "Poetry is Revolution." They came with a pistol that shot blank shots. Bypassing any appropriate register in which to condemn the esteemed poet, they simply "assassinated" him from the theatre's balcony and threw the fliers as they fled the scene. Witnesses were shocked and scandalized.

That March the Motherfuckers held a 24-hour Spring Feast on 89 East Tenth Street. As an undercover surveillance report by the police states, about 100 people showed up to the 'four-floor derelict apartment house,' with no light except candles and battery-operated lanterns. In October 1967, before the Motherfuckers were a fully congealed group, Ben and Osha and a few others went down to DC for a demonstration against the Vietnam War. Abbie Hoffman and Jerry Rubin declared that they would exorcise the pentagon of its war demons. Theirs was a spectacular fame that could (and would) be repeatedly spread, if not celebrated, through the sensationalist media. However much envy belied their contempt, the Motherfuckers rejected Yippie-media stardom in favor of real action. In any case, they preferred the hostile anonymity of an unmentionable name doing unimaginable deeds.

On the day of the demonstration, Ben joined a faction of militant SDSers who tore down a fence surrounding the pentagon before being beaten by a battalion of riot-troopers. Undeterred, they pressed on to a temporarily unguarded entrance. The small group, with Ben leading the charge, dashed inside before being beaten back again. For a fleeting moment, the Motherfuckers had ushered in the impossible: they penetrated the belly of the war machine. At the height of reign of death and destruction, a bellicose government swallowed its sword.

A month later, at a Foreign Policy Association banquet at the New York Hilton, the every-ready group that surrounded Ben hurled bags of cow's blood, splattering evening gowns and tuxedos.

And so went the many actions of this early phase of Motherfuckering.

In early 1968, the Motherfucker made their first public action. The Lower East Side was in the middle of a garbage strike, teeming with garbage piled high along the streets, festering and feeding the multiplying rats. Meanwhile, on the upper west side, Lincoln Center retained its pristine décor of washed windows and shiny marble. The equation was simple for the Motherfuckers. They heaped trash bag after trash bag into a truck that then met them uptown. A group of them boarded the subway, rattling pots, banging on drums, and blowing kazoos and pennywhistles while handing out fliers to subway patrons. The festival got off the train at 66th and Broadway, met the truck carrying the garbage, and wheel barreled it to Lincoln Center. In a sort of cultural exchange ("garbage for garbage," so the flyer stated), they dumped the mess of old garbage bags on the front steps, left the remainder of the fliers with bewildered onlookers, and marched away. The war against 'art for consumptions sake' had been a precept ever since Angry Arts. Here, the focus shifted scales onto a total war with 'the system.' The flyer expanded on its initial premise:

"WE PROPOSE A CULTURAL EXCHANGE

AMERICA TURNS THE WORLD INTO GARBAGE

IT TURNS ITS GHETTOES INTO GARBAGE

IT TURNS VIETNAM INTO GARBAGE…"

But the Motherfuckers' engagement in total revolution did not simply bounce from themselves to 'the system' in a performance of endless hermetic heresy. Their dedication to liberation through struggle expanded their notions of each. On April 23rd, 1968, a few weeks after Martin Luther King, Jr. was assassinated, a group of Columbia students led by SAS (Student Afro Society) coordinated a student occupation in an attempt to stop construction of a gymnasium in Morningside Park. The group was joined by members of SDS, who were protesting Columbia University's links to the US Department of Defense. Mark Rudd, chairman of Columbia SDS concluded an open letter written to the President of Columbia: "There is only one thing left to say. It may sound nihilistic to you, since it is the opening shot in the war of liberation. I'll use the words of LeRoi Jones, who I'm sure you don't like a whole lot: "Up against the wall, motherfucker this is a stick up."

The Motherfuckers indeed joined in the festivities and took the lead in building barricades. Osha's brother, Michael was also part of SDS at the time. In fact, he was Mark Rudd's roommate. But he did not participate in the occupations. He shared their stepfather, Herbert Marcuse's sentiments that universities were realms of relative freedom, and thus to disrupt them was counter-productive. But for Osha and the Motherfuckers, the university was no such safe-haven.

His brother, wrote him this:

"Take the specter of rationality and kick it around some more first until you are not afraid of it, until you realize it isn't what you thought it was… Reason isn't to whip people with, neither is what you do. Reason isn't a thing at all, forget it. It means doing things right."

The University, like his childhood home, was one more refuge of reason that Osha would contaminate with his Motherfuckering and he was all too aware of it.

In August '68, Chicago was overwhelmed with all strands of the movement who came to protest the Democratic National Convention. A large encampment of folks converged on Lincoln Park, strumming guitars were drowned out by the wails of police sirens. The police kept pushing the crowd back through the night. Law and order was eager to lose restraint and erupt in a fight. This was, in Osha's words, " an event made to order for the Motherfuckers, a tight-knit street gang [that] could take the lead in battles with the police. We had an opportunity to demonstrate to a nation-wide audience that neither the idle theorizing of SDS nor the Yippies "it's all fun and games" street theater was an adequate response to the brutal violence the System would unleash if it felt really threatened. The police beat heads and protestors chanted 'the whole world is watching.' And it was. But it did not see the Motherfuckers." Before the end of the week, Osha would give a speech to thousands of demonstrators encouraging them to break through police lines and take the struggle to the streets. This, in combination with him being the most visible Motherfucker in town, awarded him a co-conspirator charge in the indictment that launched the Chicago Conspiracy Trial.

Two months after returning from Chicago, Osha and the Motherfuckers initiated a campaign to get a free community night at the infamous Fillmore East, a theatre on Second Ave that recently opened up under Bill Graham's ownership.

"As we saw it he was making big bucks off our culture and it was time for a little pay back. We presented our demands...it did not go well...Bill wasn't impressed. The discussion got heated. We probably made threats. I remember Bill shouting at us that when he was a kid he'd crawl across Europe to escape the Nazis and if he'd survive Hitler, he'd damn well survive us. So that was it. To Bill Graham, born Wolfgang Grajonca, a Jewish Orphan born in Berlin, whose mother died in Auschwitz, I had become the equivalent of a Nazi."

As the campaign continued, Judith Malina and Julian Beck were scheduled to perform *Paradise Now* at the Fillmore East as part of an evening of radical theatre to benefit the striking Columbia students. The Motherfuckers found the perfect opportunity to escalate their struggle. Judith and Julian met with them and agreed that at the end of the performance, the audience would stay and hold the theatre. What began as 100 bodies "dancing, chanting, and stomping away," as the Village Voice described the affair, now swelled to one big body, circling and passing the pipe while neighborhood kids flitted about "whistling and shouting 'Naked City.'" It only took the theatrical prowess of Ben Morea's reach for the microphone to announce that on the behalf of the Motherfuckers, the Fillmore East had been liberated. A many hour standoff ensued with Bill Graham that repeated many of the arguments previously rehearsed, but now in front of a freaky audience. Much past midnight, Bill announced that he would hold a town meeting on their proposal the following week if the Motherfuckers agreed to vacate. The Motherfuckers mimeographed a response on the spot and left, insatiate.

Needless to say, the town hall meeting was teeming with anarchic energy. "The theatre stage was set up with a table, two microphones, and two folding chairs – it was to be a structured debate between Bill Graham and Ben Morea. Motherfucker events did not happen this way. There would be free food, spontaneous speeches, call and response." The night dragged on. The Motherfuckers again brought their mimeograph machine, this time cranking out responses to the proceedings as they happened. Ultimately, Bill conceded to free Wednesday night events for the community.

The first one took place that November. It was an enormous success. The place was packed. According to Osha, "it seemed as if Second Avenue had tipped over on its side and deposited its entire contents – human, animal, vegetable – into the theater. Discarded sandwiches, cigarette butts, cans and bottles littered the carpet. Much wine was drunk, much dope was smoked." After four short weeks, amidst police threats to shut the whole theatre down, Bill had enough. Threats continued—once again, their Church-donated Gestetner recorded the situation:

"Situation: Pigs and Bill Graham stop free night. Why? They say we smoke dope, but we know it's because they are afraid of us. Afraid that we'll learn it's ours. Afraid that we'll get together there to destroy their world and create our own.

The pigs threaten to close Graham down unless he stops our free night. He doesn't have to worry about the pigs. We'll close him down. No free night, no pay night…"

The day after Christmas, MC5 was to take the stage. Electra Records had rented it out and distributed free tickets through the radio stations. The Motherfuckers demanded 500 free tickets for the community. Bill Graham acquiesced, fearing the worst. On the night of the show, the theatre filled and a crowd quickly gathered outside, demanding to be let in. Bill stood across the doorway, blocking the entrance. A bicycle chain rose up from a neighborhood kid and slashed Bill across the face – blood poured down his face as he fell back.

The band took stage and began playing. Once again, the theatre was overcome with a throbbing jubilee mixed with irreverence. MC5 played their hit 'Kick Out the Jams, Motherfuckers.' The Motherfuckers followed suit, giving speeches. People rushed the stage and pandemonium ensued. The band, much to everyone's disgust, got nervous and made a quick getaway to their limousine. The night ended with a few more injuries and a hollow offer from Bill to help finance their search for another space. Nevertheless, as Osha states, "times were changing and the very brief heyday of the Motherfuckers was nearing an end. I had watched Bill get hit with a chain and felt a door open between our violent rhetoric and reality. It did not want to walk through it. The vulnerability of the flesh of my opponent gave me no pleasure."

This sobering epitome suggested a larger trend: by 1969, it became clear that something in the air had changed. On the streets of the Lower East Side, hard drugs replaced LSD. The crash pad the Motherfuckers had set up was teeming with drunks who would wake up in the middle of the night and go after each other with broken wine bottles. The stash of guns that the Motherfuckers had accumulated began to be a source of constant paranoia. They rooted around listlessly from hiding place to hiding place. Ben's life was threatened by a hired hit man one day as he was standing on 10th and 3rd avenue. At the end of countless police confrontations, Osha was arrested and taken to the Ninth precinct, where he was once again confronted with the fragility of his own body.

Looking back, Osha states,

"For me, the movement, whose project it was to tear off all masks had, itself, become a mask. I hid my fear, my insecurity, and my obsessions beneath a façade of bravado. The relation between mask and reality was reversed. In the rhetoric of the movement, the bourgeois values of American masked its barbarism. For me, my barbaric Motherfucker exterior masked my ambivalent relation to bourgeois values. I incorporated into my life, as a strategy for self-preservation, the split between the hidden private world and public persona that I had hoped to cure by immersion in radical politics."

All the while, more death threats came from 'rival' gangs in the neighborhood. More and more, older Motherfucker members drifting apart, to be replaced by new recruits attracted to the muscular violence the group projected. Violence, fear, and repression stormed the center of their utopia – and the center would not hold much longer:

"We continued to swagger, but the circle was closing in on us. I was not the only one who felt it…Other Motherfuckers drifted away. Ben made up his mind to change course. We had mined a thin vein. It was giving out. We were deep underground, unsure of the supports shoring up the roof of the mineshaft. The little canary that warns when the air becomes unbreathable was beginning to cough and wheeze. It was time to get out."

A few of them made the trip out to New Mexico where a hippie gathering of tribes took place. With no intention of joining "one of the blessed-out hippie communes proliferating in the dry windswept plains around Taos," they moved to Espanola, home of the Alianza, a militant Chicano movement for land rights. They set up camp and began their country life. It was from this geographic and psychic distance that they read about advances in the movement. "Isolated in our little home in the country we read about the formation of the Weatherman, about their Days of Rage, and how they put on helmets and fought the Chicago police. We read about the explosion in the Greenwich Village town house that killed three of their members who had been trying to manufacture a bomb. The Weatherman were the new Motherfuckers." A few months later, in the fall of 1969, Osha peered out at the immense sky of New Mexico and wondered how the group became so marginal.

Jewish Roots in Rebellion

When Osha Neumann moved to the Lower East Side in January 1967 and began Motherfuckering, he already possessed a stretched existential canvas as large as that New Mexican sky. Born in 1939, his psyche spanned the horrific 1930s of his parents' exodus from Nazi Germany, the dull suburban postwar years of his 1950s childhood, and that "aborted revolution of the sixties," where he, along with a great number of other people, attempted to make meaning of the high order of barbarism in civilization.

Despite the disparate worlds of his parent's generation and his own, the questions of his time marched side by side with his parents' questions:

"Why do the most atavistic forms of consciousness flourish in the midst of modernity? Why does reason appear powerless in the face of unreason? What should we have done differently? What is to be done now?

But as intellectuals in exile at American universities, theirs was a world insulated (to the degree that it was even possible) from the noise of war, by the familiar sounds of dinner table debate. Defeated by the failure of the working-class Left to prevent the rise of fascism, these intellectual émigrés resorted to thought, not mass action, as the means through which to understand and shape the world. What remained for them was to correctly analyze the events of the world and locate the "forces that represent humanity's hope for liberation and a just ordering of human affairs."

As Osha states:

"We grew up in a Manichean world. Fascism was the expression of the irrational; reason was its opposite. The distinction was clear and unambiguous...A clear line separated fascism, the embodiment of irrationality, from anti-fascism, the embodiment of reason. I wanted to be on the side of reason, but feared I did not belong there ...Auschwitz was the embodiment of irrationality. The embodiment of rationality was the scholarly community of exiled Marxist Jewish intellectuals who were my parent's friends and colleagues."

Thus, to be anti-fascist was to be committed to reason. In this analysis, passion, chaos, muscularity were all suspect—anti-fascism could only be the practice of reason, and the practice of reason was the only anti-fascism.

Recalling childhood moments of listening to LPs of songs from the Spanish Civil War, Osha caught a glimpse of a passionate and worthy time, of deeds that captured the imagination. "Our side has lost, but from the trenches dug deep into Spanish soil by the singers of those songs, hope rose like a rush of startled birds into the night sky...with such fantasies I struggled, not entirely successfully, to reconcile reason's strict demand to prioritize thinking over doing, with the unruly energies of my corrupt insistent body."

On Arlington Avenue in Riverdale, New York where Osha grew up (across a tennis club rumored to exclude Jews and Blacks), rationality found a safe haven. But this suburban slice of tranquility and bourgeois family life already ruptured a sense of cleanliness and order that Osha could not maintain. The overwhelming despair of exile, however much it was pacified by the dull calm of everyday monotony, could not help but make a deep impression on Osha. His inheritance was a dissident intellectual history that fueled a will and determination to persevere. Yet, the constant appeal to rational thought and intellectual analysis left him feeling fractured. Just how would debate and philosophical inquiry change the world? Where the heroic march of revolutionary history from barricade to trenches always aligned thought with action, how would reason alone overcome the barbarism of the world order? And what of the 'unthinking' needs of the body, not only the pleasure of the touch, but the ability to use one's body as well as one's mind to shape reality?

In fact, Osha grew up defining adulthood by the "ability to subordinate the passions of the body to the guiding hand of reason. But [his] body rebelled, clouding [his] mind with perverse desire." "For me reason spoke with a German accent. It was Jewish, and it was out of place in America, a stranger in a land it could never make its own."

In a world divided neatly along fascist and anti-fascist lines, he interpreted his disorder and bodily 'vileness' as being a fundamental if not irreconcilable split in his being, something hateful living under the auspices of well-ordered Jewish exile. For his parent's generation, the postwar sense of loss that many Jewish émigrés felt was immeasurable. Theirs was a total fracturing of a sense of place and belonging, and a forced reconstitution of life after death. Osha's world also constituted two: with one foot in the damaged life of Jewish exile, he also, like so many others in his generation, grew up in relative comfort while looking uncomfortably out to world he would inherit. Needless to say, his world, much like his parents, offered but a glimpse of the impossible possibility of reason and revolution.

In 1951, Herbert Marcuse came to live with Osha's parents, Inge and Franz Neumann, close family friends since their days together in Frankfurt at the Institute for Social Research. Soon, Osha came to recognize two paternal figures: "My two fathers, Franz and Herbert, and my mother were aristocrats of the intellect. I was their crippled offspring." While he had two fathers at home, one of those fathers became father to the entire generation of New Leftists. As Herbert Marcuse came to be regarded as a towering influence on new left thought, in so many ways, Osha Neumann's sense of being *their crippled offspring* transformed into the Motherfucker's transgressive rejection of much of the New Left as well.

The Dream of Reason

"-What is our Program?
-We'll know we've got it if it makes us feel good.
-Is there any place in the revolution for incoherence?
-Incoherence is the only place"
-Motherfuckers Manifesto

But could the search for higher reason in the turbulent postwar, cold war, segregationist and imperialist U.S be sustained, let alone legitimized? The rebellious sixties, for Osha and for many other participants, questioned the very *rootedness* of Reason in governing the affairs of daily life. To many, it seemed like one more 'given' form of monotonization, penetrating deep into the very desires to be free. Was reasoned resistance another bureaucrat of the Left, dictating how social transformation would transpire? Whatever the answer, the Motherfuckers were too impatient to inquire. In his memoirs of his Motherfucker days, Osha says, "Reason has got some of the same problems God has, too many people appealing to it for too many different purposes."

In describing the Motherfuckers, he nevertheless claims that they represented reason, just not in a rational form.

When we look back to their writings during the Motherfucker heyday, we see in their perception of the impossibility of reasoned thought the very retort that predicated their visionary alliance with the irrational:

"The real criticism must be total...western death trip must be fully opposed on all levels...the western so-called 'revolutionary' attempt cannot succeed to overthrow the death *root* of the western totality since it is a product of the same partial thought pattern. Western civilization has to be destroyed...and new life-forms created...the struggle is as total as life itself."

Hence, the Motherfuckers renounced their ties to ordered discourse, the "traffic in abstractions, respect for explanations, the demand for coherence, and the subordination of impulse and emotion, all of which [they] thought of as characteristic of a life committed to reason."

This early tension between Motherfuckerdom and Osha's upbringing within Jewish dissident intellectual circles only expanded and folded back on himself: he exiled himself from that life (a life already in exile) and became an 'anti-intellectual, heavy into running in the streets'. According to Osha, "We were repelled by the world our parents had, to one degree or another, accepted. And we were attracted by the promise of a better world awaiting." But where does this generational tension really lie? In many ways, Osha's interpretation of Motherfucker tactics situates their activism along the same sharp criticism that Marcuse makes in "One-Dimensional Man": the world is increasingly governed by reason, whatever its actual merits (here faith steps in for teleologic belief), that is increasingly being hijacked and dominated by technocratc, instrumental rationality. But while Marcuse in large part was content to document and criticize this phenomenon as symptomatic of post-war industrial society, the Motherfuckers had no need for documentation in abstraction. Their lives were proof enough of the alienation and boredom of technocratic society. The parade of images that marshaled its justification like a seductress in fact only added insult to injury. What else could the Motherfuckers do but adopt the stance that rebellion against a rationality increasingly colonized by instrumental calculation must, in the first instance, involve a spontaneous creation of other modes of thought. Reason, rationality and all its trappings were too vulnerable, too susceptible to cooptation, to be the durable plaything of a permanent rebellion against boredom.

One sees this realization (and its increasing distance from his fathers' generation) in Osha Neuman's private fantasies, as they took root in "unacceptable" reflections in his journal:

"...Beware of action! Beware of its temptations! Preserve the truth inside you! Publish it privately among your friends. Live by it secretly. Draw strength from it. Reveal it to broader circles only in veiled allegories. But do not act on it. Do not witness it. Deny it under oath.

And if the desire to act is too strong, do something half-hearted. Picket outside the cathedral. Run the peace-candidate. Proclaim the possibility and necessity of moral outrage (do not admit that you have passed beyond outrage to something harder, glittering, vicious). Do not show your teeth. Be very careful. Shake hands with the right people. Smile. But inside, keep the faith...

Ethics is a bog. They have made it an instrument against us. They have poisoned its waters. It is the most tempting part of their system and the most dangerous. In defense one must become inhuman. One must cling to one's inhumanity, spit full in the face of their poisoned platitudes so that the possibility of a true ethics that will exist not in the minds of the moralists, but in our mutual happiness.

A-men

Fuck off!"

This statement signals an almost complete inversion of the Left Jewish epithet of the perseverance of humanity despite the horrors of war. Here, we see only inhumanity as a way to persevere, and this time, triumph, in the face of the horrors of the everyday.

Pious reverence to reason did not satisfy the bodily urges for rebellion that fueled much of the Motherfuckers' engagement with the world. Reason need not be called upon to act as the rational guide toward a better world. The compass then, could not be scientific, but one calibrated by the vicissitudes of the desiring body, thinking through action. Once the mind equates reason with domination, then only the irrational and absurd can be liberatory. Yet it is not easy to broker a practical politics on this kind of realization. Here, indeed, lies the unfulfilled legacy of the Motherfuckers as well as the open question of liberation that Marcuse posed in his critique of reason. Nevertheless, with the help of mimeographed fliers, these private fantasies quickly entered public political discourse as Motherfucker propaganda that roamed the streets — and titillated the police "who picked up these ravings out of the gutter and preserved them in their files as evidence of the terrible menace the Motherfuckers represented."

In some ways the displaced Frankfurt School forefathers (including Osha's step-father Herbert Marcuse), with their focus on 'rationality' and the 'totally administered society' were unhappily wed to postwar America. But what familial relations could be said to exist between the exiled Frankfurt group and the Motherfuckers? Was their mix of irrationalism and analysis the schizophrenia of a child, looking to multiply its oedipal tendency, destroy both mother and father, and become free from it all? Or did it still linger in that Oedipal dream—to destroy rationality and retain the grittiness of the downtown New York experience, to be a 'Motherfucker'? As Osha recalls, "As a longhaired, bearded, dirty Motherfucker I looked in the mirror and saw, with some satisfaction, my mother's worst nightmare."

Moreover, "society was our mother, and in the revolution, we fucked her…Parental authority is writ large in the coercive authority of the state. It is easy in challenging the state, to fall into the role of rebellious child. If society is the parent, and specifically the mother, and we fuck her in anger, or in love, or in some inextricable mix of the two, do we desire to merge with her, to destroy her or to be destroyed by her?"

It is not clear if the "surface of [their] angry, anarchistic counter-cultural take-no-prisoners motherfuckering" as Osha describes it, is a wholesale rejection of the abusive mother-state, or if it is in some ways a longing for it. This question haunts many New Left experiments in rebellion. It also recalls Herbert Marcuse's question in *Eros and Civilization*: "In every revolution, there seems to have been a historical moment when the struggle against domination might have been victorious—but the moment passed. An element of *self-defeat* seems to be involved in this dynamic…it explains the "identification" of those who revolt with the power against which they revolt."[94]

In Osha's words, "We could always rely on the state to play the role of dominatrix, to beat, and to trounce her disobedient children. Our politics was a passion play in which the bad parent proved her badness, over and over, to our masochistic satisfaction, … Did we secretly identify with the hand that beats us?" This questioning opens up to a realization obtained perhaps too late: these ambiguities are characteristic of a certain style of predominantly male, radical politics. "It is a politics which, however worthy of its goals, is self-defeating and 'infantile' in that it repetitively reenacts the relation of child to parent. The parent restrains the child. He throws a tantrum. He beats his little fists bloody against the bars of his crib. He grows up. The bars of his crib become the bars of his prison. He continues to beat his hands bloody. The bars do not bend or even notice." But Osha warns that it is all too easy to arrive at this assessment of childish rebellion—indeed, that analysis constitutes most revanchist history of the 60s left. No, says Osha, "it's more difficult to disentangle, delicately, as one would a bird caught in a net, the genuinely radical and uncompromising elements in this politics from those which are self-defeating."[95] There is no doubt about the Motherfuckers' contribution to the vocabulary of dissension. Indeed, they further pushed the often times static relationship between "art" and "politics" by suggesting that both are only found in the motion of everyday experience, and that any attempt to treat the one without the other ended in the stale acquiescence to prevailing norms. Nevertheless, the question of how they were able to advance collective liberation still needs to be posed. It would not suffice to simply formulate this as a tactical question, but one that tarries with the very nature of desire and reason, of possibility in and through the context of existing domination. Indeed, these questions take on a further generational form. Our collective responses, like the Motherfuckers before us, must be rooted in the eternal struggle for order in chaos, reason in consummate passion, and justice in spontaneity.

Malav Kanuga *is a member of the Bluestockings worker's collective. Additionally, he teaches in the CUNY school system, where he is also pursuing his PhD at the Graduate Center. Bluestockings is a bookstore, fair trade café, and activist resource center in the Lower East Side. It is collectively owned and operated by its workers, without bosses or managers. It is also a volunteer/community-run project that invites your participation, either through nightly events or through other collaborations.*

---

[92] Unless otherwise noted, all quotes come from a transcript of Osha Neumann's memoir, "Up Against the Wall M_ F_".

[93] "…you can't steal nothing from a white man, he's already stole it he owes you anything you want, even his life. All the stores will open if you will say the magic words. The magic words are: Up against the wall mother fucker this is a stick up!" (as quoted in Osha Neumann's 'Taking the Plunge' in Resistance)

[94] Herbert Marcuse, Eros and Civilization. (Boston: Beacon Press, 1955), pp. 90-91

[95] "I am a Motherfucker no more, but I still love a motherfuckeresque politics of disruption and confrontation…I still define the essential struggle we are engaged in as a struggle against fascism, but I know that, despite what I assumed as a child, Jews are not always anti-fascist nor commuted to the universality of truth. The 1982 massacres of Palestinians at Sabra and Chiatilla by Christian phalange troops under the watchful eye of Israelis, awakened me from my dogmatic slumber on the subject of the relation of Jews to fascism."

Emma Goldman – First Slum Goddess of the Lower East Side

Tsaurah Litzky

" I don't want a revolution I can't dance to." – E.G.

Who was this woman, this anarchist, agent provocateur, this rebel girl, rebel rouser, rebel spirit, this brilliant bombshell who made her life's work resisting the tyranny of any form of government? Who was this petite truth seeker-truth speaker, freethinker and double-barreled orator who could move a crowd of a thousand workers, clapping and cheering, to their feet?

Who was this mighty mite, this not even five foot tall Mother Earth, this publisher writer, nurse, lecturer, colleague, comrade, friend to so many other questing souls? Who was this fearless, all-night dancing woman who could rock and roll before there even was rock 'n' roll? Who was this fierce advocate of birth control who gave out pamphlets about condoms and douches at her lectures when distributing such radical information was against the law? Who was it that went to jail to defend the right of every woman to determine what she wants to do with her own body? Who was this crusader, whose righteousness was strong as tempered steel? Who was this lover of life and believer in free will?

Who was this who collaborated with her lover Alexander Berkman to assassinate Henry Clay Frick? Who was the courageous young woman who tried to sell her body on the street to raise money for this attempt, but was so obvious a beginner, she found no takers? Who was this champion of labor and the rights of the worker? Who was this whose courage knew no bounds, who could not be made to shut up? Who was she who never ran from a fight?

Who was this prophet of free speech and free love inspired by Emerson, Thoreau and the great, great bard of New York, Walt Whitman? Who continued to maintain and proclaim her deep-set conviction that no person can "belong" to another person while suffering from intense jealousy when the love of her life, Ben Reitman, was unfaithful? Who was she who was only human? Who was the memoirist who wrote so tellingly about her feet of clay? Who continued to confess her physical dependence on Reitman and her other lovers while simultaneously struggling to hold aloft that banner of free love? Who was it who wrote "it doesn't matter if love lasts but one brief span of time or for eternity!"[96]

Who was this champion of exploited workers, poverty-stricken mothers, hungry, wild lovers? She was a true Loisada girl! She was Emma Goldman, Goddess of Life and Joy, long, lusty nights and human rights; she was also Emma Goldman, first slum goddess of the Lower East Side.

Emma Goldman arrived in New York City in August 1889. She was twenty years old. "All that had happened in my life until that time was now left behind me, cast off like a worn-out garment, a new world was before me strange and terrifying. But I had youth, good health and a passionate ideal. Whatever the world had in store for me, I was determined to meet it unflinchingly."[97]

Meet it unflinchingly she did. She looked up A. Solotaroff, a young anarchist she had once heard lecture in New Haven. He remembered her with warmth and that night took her to Sach's Café on Suffolk Street. Sach's Café was the meeting place and headquarters of the radical Lower East Side thinkers, the anarchists, and socialists, the Yiddish writers and poets as well as miscellaneous artists and characters of all stripes and persuasions.

Emma was thus immediately launched into the tumultuous waters of social and political uprising and change. This was exactly where she wanted to be; she had come to the city in search of such a political and intellectual community. The foundation for her Anarchist beliefs was laid during her childhood in Lithuania. Her father was an innkeeper who was authoritarian and often violent. She yearned for the life of an emancipated woman. The oppression of peasants and political rebels by the czars convinced her she did not want to live under such repressive regimes. She joined members of her family who had already emigrated to America in Rochester, New York when she was sixteen. She went to work in a factory and experienced first-hand the demeaning treatment of the workers by the bosses. She was also influenced by news of the Haymarket Massacre in Chicago. Police had opened fire on workers demonstrating for an eight-hour workday and many workers were killed. After a protest demonstration at the Haymarket, a bomb was thrown at the police. A number of leading anarchists, none of whom had been at the scene of the crime, were railroaded into prison on capitol charges. So, it was in the hopes of being able to work for the Anarchist cause that Emma left an unhappy marriage behind her in Rochester and came to New York.[98]

At the café, Solotaroff introduced her to the Minkin sisters, two Russian Jewish young women who did piecework in the garment trade. They lived with their father close to the Café and it was soon decided that Emma would move in with them. Once settled in, Emma supported herself by piecework and sewing.

She walked the crowded streets of the Lower East Side hearing Russian, Yiddish, Polish, English, German and Chinese spoken all around her. It is possible she stopped on Essex Street and bought a pickle for a penny from a barrel from one of the many merchants who sold pickles there. It is possible she bought a sweet potato for a nickel from a corner cart. The sweet potato vendor would wrap her purchase in the thin purple paper that all the sweet potato vendors used. He might hand it to her with a bow and a big smile because young Emma was blond and blue-eyed with a generous bosom and skin like ivory silk. At first glance, one might not easily guess that a pilgrim heart and prodigious, original intelligence lived within her small frame.

On the night of her very first visit to Sach's Café with Solotaroff, she also met Alexander, (Sasha) Berkman who was to become her lover and then her colleague in anarchism and her lifelong friend. Eventually Goldman, Berkman, Helen Minkin and Fedya, a young artist and anarchist, rented a flat on Forsythe Street. It was there that Sasha and Emma plotted an attempt on the life of Henry Clay Frick. Frick was the manager of the Carnegie Steel plant who initiated a bloody confrontation between Pinkerton guards and workers on strike in Homestead, Pennsylvania. Many workers died. Frick survived the assassination attempt and Berkman was sentenced to jail for twenty-two years. He served fourteen and when he was released his convictions were stronger than ever. He and Emma went on to publish *Mother Earth,* an anarchist journal of great depth and conviction.

Loyal to her lover, she was stirred to defend him. When Sasha was first jailed, Emma's former mentor, famous anarchist Johann Most, ridiculed Sasha's attempt to assassinate Frick as ill-conceived. Emma went to a crowded public meeting where Most was speaking; she had a horsewhip hidden under her long gray cloak. Uninvited, she ascended the stage. She demanded to know the grounds of Most's accusations against Beckman. When Most replied by calling her a hysterical woman, Emma whipped him repeatedly about the hands, head and face. Friends of hers, who were in the audience, had to pull her off him.[99]

I like to think of Emma Goldman as the first slum goddess of the Lower East Side. She was intensely passionate, honest, loyal and unafraid to act in defense of her lover, all attributes of my construct of the true slum goddess. She was fearless in making her convictions known and brilliant in defense of these convictions. No one could push her around. She lived in at least six or seven different addresses in the neighborhood, among them the apartment on Forsythe Street, a friend's apartment on Fifth Street off First Avenue, a rooming house on Fourth Street near Third Avenue and which she soon discovered to be a brothel. She did live in other areas of Manhattan, briefly in Harlem and on 42nd street, but she retuned to Loisada again and again. For a long time she maintained an apartment that was both her office and her home at 210 East 13th Street.

She had many lovers, another attribute I consider typical of the slum goddess. Besides Berkman, she was also lover to his cousin Fedya, a young artist-anarchist. She had significant affairs with Hippolyte Havel, a European activist, Ed Brady, a socialist scholar and many others. Brady, who was involved with her for several years, left her because Emma refused to have his child. She had decided to give her whole life to the cause of anarchism. At the core of her anarchism was an understanding of the evil of the corporate state and the edicts of religion. Her anarchism called for a re-evaluation of values and a reversal of conventional moralities, that morality should not be regulated by church and state, that the people should be free to mate with natural grace.

Thus it was Emma believed in free love, but at the same time, she was a gambler in love affairs. When she fell for someone, it was all or nothing. The most intense of these affairs was her long involvement with Ben Reitman, a young physician, activist and former hobo. He was an American whose companions in life ranged from tramps and derelicts to distinguished doctors. Eventually he became her manager, traveling with her on her speaking tours and becoming deeply involved in her life as a radical agitator. Emma felt she had found a man who would " love the woman in me and who would also be able to share my work. I had never had anyone who could do both."[100]

The relationship between Emma and Ben was a tempestuous one. Despite her belief in free love, Emma had a hard time accepting Reitman's many infidelities. While she struggled with the demons of her jealousy and her erotic dependence on him, she continued to believe in free love and fight publicly for birth control and the sexual liberation of women. Reitman became dissatisfied with their peripatetic life, the speaking tours, the time they had to spend on the road. He began to want a traditional home, a wife and children waiting for him by the hearth. They parted. Emma bore the pain of this separation with her usual indomitable spirit. Emma Goldman could not be crushed or beaten down, another exemplary slum goddess attribute.

She continued to work with Alexander Berkman and other colleagues. She used the proceeds from her lectures on modern drama to support Mother Earth. It was closed down by the government in 1917 because of the Espionage Act, which made it illegal to speak disloyally of the military. Emma continued to campaign against the draft, for which she was jailed repeatedly; finally, she was deported for speaking against the American entry into World War I. She lived briefly in the Soviet Union. After observing it firsthand, she came to see the Bolshevik revolution was a dismal failure. Emma lived for a while in Europe and finally found refuge in Canada, where she died in 1940.

Emma Goldman, alone among the anarchists of her time, insisted that women's issues be addressed immediately, a position adopted by the Feminists of the 1960s and '70s. During her long affair with Reitman, while she struggled with her personal demons, she never stopped fighting for the right of every woman to live her life as she sees fit. She was a woman who knew how to think for herself and she urged other women to do the same. Her autobiography, *Living My Life*, is still selling well today. Her rebel spirit survives!

Sometimes when I'm in Katz's Delicatessen eating French fries and arguing with my writer friends about the meaning (if there is any) of our lives—why, without any major recognition, do we continue to struggle and write?—I imagine her sitting at the next table, looking in my direction, her clear eyes urging me to speak my mind. She is my ideal, Emma Goldman, the first slum goddess of the Lower East Side.

Bibliography

Living My Life, Emma Goldman, Penguin Books, 2006 edition.
Emma Goldman, An Intimate Life, Alice Wexler, Pantheon Books 1984.
Anarchism and Other Essays, Emma Goldman, Mother Earth, 1910.

Tsaurah Litzky *is a writer of erotica, a poet and a playwright. Her erotic sensibility was awakened early on by the sweet and sour briny pickles her mother used to buy her on their Sunday shopping trips to the Lower East Side. Tsaurah's writing, erotic and otherwise, has appeared in over ninety publications including the* New York Times *and* Best American Erotica *eight times. Long Shot Press published her poetry collection,* Baby On the Water. *In addition, she has published nine poetry chapbooks.*

Simon & Schuster brought out her erotic novella, The Motion Of The Ocean *as part of* Three the Hard Way, *a series of erotic novellas edited by Susie Bright. Tsaurah's writing class, Silk Sheets: Writing Erotica, is now entering its eleventh year at the New School.*

---

[96] Emma Goldman, *Anarchism and Other Essays,* page 220.

[97] Emma Goldman, *Living My Life,* page 3.

[98] Ibid., p. x.

[99] Ibid., p. 73-4.

[100] Ibid., p. 443.

Yiddishe Bread & Roses – Stories of the Jewish Left on the Lower East Side

Elissa Sampson

"A body gets a few cents, buys bread and relishes it, but in a few minutes it's all forgotten and one is as blue and miserable as ever, but when one spends an evening in a brightly lit hall in the company of congenial people, a good floor and some music to help glide along, I tell you what, it acts better on one's spirit than any amount of medicine. And why should it be a shame to dance, even if we are out to strike for the last six weeks, are almost starved and don't know what we'll do for food next." - The Diary of a Shirtwaist Striker[101]

"I shall approach you for judgment and I will be an urgent witness against ... those who withhold the wage of laborer, widow and orphan" - Malachi 3:5

The story of the Jewish left in the Lower East Side is an integral part of the history of its larger Yiddish-speaking, Jewish immigrant community. Some of the characters central to the political debates of those times still seem to loom larger than life and have left their imprint in numerous ways that are reflected in neighborhood venues today. As an aside, it's worth noting that not every leftist helped the working class according to plan; Leon Trotsky, for instance, had a reputation for being a lousy tipper during his sojourn in the neighborhood.

The activists' legacy is felt broadly as well: today's workforce—both white collar and blue— is still indebted to their tireless advocacy for the then radical demand for an 8 hour workday and a 5 day week.

It's impossible to separate out labor history from the general history of Yiddish culture, literature and immigration. Over 750,000 Yiddish-speaking Jewish immigrants poured into the Lower East Side between 1870 and World War I as part of the larger migration of over 2,000,000 Jews from Eastern Europe to the USA in the 19th and 20th centuries. To explain why Yiddish speaking Lower East Side Jews should be the organizing focus of radicals and labor leaders, we can paraphrase Willie Sutton by saying: "that's where the workers were."

Yiddish culture spilled into the American labor and left movements and vice versa. One needed Yiddish to become a labor or leftist leader in certain cities and industries. The garment trade strikes were largely a Jewish affair with the majority of factory ownership in German Jewish hands. The working conditions that accompanied the rise of the garment trade where 75% of the immigrants were employed made the twinning of Yiddish with the labor movement seem inevitable and natural to its participants. The Yiddish radio station WEVD, "the station that speaks your language," was named for Eugene V. Debs, the Socialist party's perennial presidential candidate.

Committed leftists saw Yiddish as the chosen tool to change the world by helping downtrodden Jewish masses, particularly those who conveniently clustered in the Lower East Side. Jewish workers would traditionally march from Strauss Square to Union Square for May Day rallies where demands for the eight-hour day were heard largely in Yiddish. In 1911, the May Day rally attended by 500,000 workers had a phalanx formed by striking machinists and Kosher Butchers that started at their union halls. A second phalanx started at the Triangle Shirt Waist Factory to commemorate the immigrant workers who died in that fire. Yet a third phalanx took the traditional Lower East Side route.[102]

Activists formed or joined immigrant-oriented labor unions (such as the International Workers of the World, a.k.a., the Wobblies) and took on the established labor movement challenging its nativist insistence that limiting immigration would prop up the wages of American workers.[103] While the American Federation of Labor (AFL) pushed for an industrial or business unionism, which ostensibly meant staying out of politics, immigrant unions wanted to have a socialist political party represent labor interests. One of the great fault lines in American unionism is over this debate. The AFL's initial insistence on closing the gates of immigration from Eastern and Southern Europe became a further reason to look to join a union that worked with a socialist party— all the better if the meetings were in Yiddish.

Although some activists participated in Russian revolutionary movements (e.g., Menshevik, Bolshevik and the failed 1905 rebellion), typically if immigrants in the garment trade were radicalized prior to immigration, it was through the Bund. This was the case of Baruch Charney Vladeck, a well-known union organizer for whom Vladeck Houses on Madison Street was named.[104] The founding of the Bund in 1897 in Vilna (now part of Lithuania, then part of the Pale of Settlement) changed Jewish leftist politics. The secular Bund proclaimed Jews now part of a 'people' regardless of geography, advocated Jewish nationalism within the territory where Jewish masses lived, touted Yiddish as the shared Jewish language across various state boundaries and combined all of this with a full espousal of socialism. The use of Yiddish in the Bund as a tool to educate, contact and appeal to Jewish masses galvanized a new intelligentsia of literary and cultural figures who helped transform Yiddish into a 'world-class' literary language. In the Lower East Side this combined powerfully with the immigrant experience to produce a flowering of Yiddish culture in newspapers, poetry, song, art and theater, including a group known as the 'sweatshop poets.'

While the famous sectarianism of the Yiddish left has faded with time, in the 1920s it was in full bloom. The Lower East Side had three important partisan newspapers read by over a million readers: the Communist *Freiheit (Freedom, 1922)*, the Anarchist *Freie Arbeiter Shtimme (Free*

Worker's Voice, 1899), and the Socialist *Forverts* (*Jewish Daily Forward, 1897*).

The work and immigration experience combined to radicalize immigrants toward a variety of union factions and parties, often divided along lines of socialism, communism, and anarchism. This conjunction is neatly reflected in the name of the first Jewish union in the United States, the United Hebrew Trades and Socialist Labor Party (Fareynigte Idishe Geverkshaftn, a.k.a. the UHT) which was headquartered at 25 East Fourth Street. The UHT was a male garment-makers' union that Morris Hilquit helped found in 1888.[105] In a famous sectarian split, Hilquit and his colleague Meyer London, subsequently left the Socialist Labor Party to help found the Socialist Party.[106] London was elected twice to Congress on the Socialist Party ticket and "sponsored bills which were defeated easily, but became integral elements of the New Deal of the 1930s and Great Society of the 1960s, including the minimum wage, unemployment insurance, anti-lynching laws, and paid maternity leave."[107] Both men also made their mark on neighborhood real estate: the ILGWU (International Ladies Garment Makers Union) named two Grand Street co-op buildings built in the 1950s after them.[108]

The activists' relationship to religion ranged from simple rejection to complex use of its symbols; some participated in Jewish institutions whose views on religion evolved over time. For many who were deeply secular, the call for action against factory owners was also an explicit call for rebellion against traditional Judaism.[109] While some activists had the distinct goal of creating a new secular Jewish, socialist culture, others saw organizing Jewish immigrants as a temporary stage that would lead to the 'Jewish question' being finally answered by the dissolution of Jewish distinctiveness into a new utopia. Either way, one of the ironies is that activists of all flavors who battled so-called 'religious superstition' commonly ended up buried in traditional, kosher Jewish cemeteries, since these were the norm for those connected to hometown or political societies such as the Arbeter Ring (the Workmen's Circle which was connected to the Bund).[110]

The building of Yiddish culture with its aspect of peoplehood—based on an acknowledgement of a shared religious past—sometimes made for a more nuanced attitude to religion, particularly for those who wanted to attract and organize Jewish workers. A striking example of the effect this approach could have on organizing could be seen at an ILGWU rally held in Cooper Union in 1909. To spark the 'Strike of 20,000', Clara Lemlich called on fellow strikebreakers to take a oath in Yiddish whose words came from a text used to remember Jerusalem: "If I break my oath, may my right hand wither, may my tongue forget speech."[111] These oath takers were mostly women waistmakers who as part of Local 25 headquartered at Clinton Hall[112] went on to win the first major successful, sustainable garment workers' strike, with picket lines that held for fourteen weeks and contracts gained in 354 shops.[113] Their efforts were tragically vindicated two years later in 1911, when 146 women died in the nearby Triangle Shirtwaist Factory fire, a shop that had refused to unionize.[114]

The appropriation of shared religious symbols into a new Yiddish culture that was part of a forged socialist future could be best created and appreciated by those who were religiously educated—and, as such, were part of the shtetl's elite. Abraham Cahan was one of the foremost leaders of the Yiddish socialist movement. In 1897 he helped found the *Forverts* located at 173-175 East Broadway, and was its editor from 1902-1951. In *his Rise of David Levinsky*, Cahan presents a somewhat mixed yet sympathetic portrait of a poor, religious immigrant who becomes a successful garment shop manufacturer but fails to find love or contentment. Like his protagonist, Cahan came from an Orthodox family in the Pale of Settlement. Like a number of the other characters depicted in his novel, Cahan had been involved in Russian revolutionary politics and as an immigrant helped organize trade unions.

Writing in English, Cahan is at pains to explain to his American readers "what is the Talmud… it is at once a fountain of religious inspiration and a brain sharpener,"[115] and has his protagonist state "some of my classmates had a much better practical acquaintance with English than I, but few of these could boast the mental training that my Talmud education had given me."[116] Cahan well understood that the sentimental attachment to an immigrant's home encompassed religion. His protagonist declares, "I spent many an evening at the Antomir Synagogue, reading Talmud passionately. This would bring my heart in touch with my old home."[117] A similar ambivalence and pride in immigrant accomplishments can be seen elsewhere in his writings. Cahan proffers the notion that it was the improvements made by lowly Russian Jewish operators to the efficiency of the sweatshop system that allowed them the opportunity to supplant German Jews as factory owners.

Not surprisingly, leftist attitudes to religion were hotly debated in Yiddish theater and in newspapers. Religion was seen as superstition, but this dismissive view was mitigated by its nostalgic depiction as representing the 'old' culture that was disappearing due to poverty, immigration and anti-Semitism even as the new, 'socialist' future replaced it. The desire to mock, valorize, transform and recruit from religion were all present to different degrees.

Yiddish as an Eastern European Jewish lingua franca was transformed further as it filtered the American experience. The plethora of cultural productions of all sorts meant the fast evolution of Yiddish into a language of the arts and politics. Activists often condemned the well-attended 'shund' (trashy, common fare) shown in theaters and music halls, which remains the source of most of the popular Yiddish song tunes that we know today. These pundits hotly debated whether those who allowed shund should still be seen as political at all.[118] Equally debated was the propriety of encouraging Yiddish cultural creations such as poetry to develop independent of political currents and parties. Sometimes leftists who wanted to recruit from the masses recognized that cultural productions should also entertain and not alienate, as more conventionally uplifting, highbrow and 'politically correct' realism fare risked doing. 'Grine Kuzine' captured the popular imagination when bandleader Abe Schwartz coupled a lively melody to lyrics in order to tell the all too recognizable story of a lovely immigrant girl's rapid devolvement into a broken, factory drudge.

A typical Yiddish theater plot could certainly contain a fond, almost hallowed notion of the shtetl even as it poked fun at that world with comic songs about rabbis and others. Often plays would have a traditional mama, matchmaker, rabbi, all subjected to an idealized treatment, even as it was noted that the Americanized children must move on. In the Lower East Side during the heyday of Yiddish Theater, amidst the shund, Ibsen's plays alternated with those of Shakespeare and Shalom Asch whose characters included Lower East Side lesbian sweatshop workers. It could justifiably be said that Ibsen's plays translated into Yiddish were better received in the Lower East Side of New York[119] (they played at the Henry Street Settlement on 466 Grand

Street, as well as in the Yiddish Arts Theater on 2nd Ave and E. 12th Street)[120], than elsewhere in the city. The Yiddish Rialto on Second Avenue gave rise to the first theater union in America, the Hebrew Actors Union, founded in 1899, on 31 E. 7th Street.[121] Despite socialist admonitions to keep away from Shund, a second and very separate Variety Actors Union was then created for actors from the Yiddish music halls (including vaudeville), which was seen as a step down from its more illustrious and fussier predecessor.

Since much of this mix of art, modernism, realism, socialism and nostalgia felt 'natural' at the time, ultimately many immigrants became part of a loyal and yet partisan Yiddish theater public that saw famous actors in a variety of productions, some more explicitly sympathetic to political ideals. Nor is all of this gone: that Shakespeare in Yiddish was educational and 'improved' when it was all the rage on Second Avenue was not lost on Joe Papp and other directors. Some of the more topical, political adaptations by Papp's nearby Public Theater were inspired by the success these Yiddish adaptations had in making these plays speak directly to their public. And coming full circle, Shalom Asch's plays have recently replayed in the Lower East Side in English.

In a gesture straight out of Yiddish theater, the famous anarchist and feminist Emma Goldman wrote in her autobiography "at the age of eight I used to dream of becoming a Judith and visioned myself in the act of cutting off Holofernes' head to avenge the wrongs of my people. But since I had become aware that social injustice is not confined to my own race, I had decided that there were too many heads for one Judith to cut off."[122] As an adult, Goldman was a great believer in the "social significance of modern drama" and as a theater critic was well known for advocating social realism.

Goldman, a firebrand who, like Clara Lemlich, is intimately associated with rallies, marches and speeches in Cooper Union and Union Square, earned her living as a Yiddish speaking midwife in the Lower East Side. As an anarchist, she identified organized religion with tyranny. Yet upon arrival in Russia in 1919 where she was deported with Alexander Berkman[123], she joined with him in immediately reporting on pogroms taking place in the small, often religious shtetlech of the Ukraine during the Russian revolution. These accounts were further vindicated when Samuel Schwartzbard, the Jewish anarchist and French legionnaire was later acquitted by a French jury in Paris for his assassination of Simon Petliura, a hetman responsible for the death of 60,000 Ukrainian Jews.

The best neighborhood memorial to Emma Goldman is to be found at the former *Ahawath Jeshurun Shar'a Torah* synagogue, at East Sixth Street, which now serves as a community and garden center. The traditional marble memorial plaques have separate areas listed for men and women's names with spellings from three languages, Yiddish, Hebrew and English. The recently restored plaques form the base for murals from which pictures of neighborhood organizers such as Emma Goldman and Clara Lemlich spring to life. The caption for Emma Goldman reads: "She spoke wrote and conspired. Opposed the state, religion and capitalism. She fought for the right to abortion and the eight-hour day. Worked as a seamstress and midwife, loved dancing and theater, had many lovers."

The muralists who memorialized Emma Goldman on a 1961 synagogue plaque donated in Stella Roth's memory have also rescued from oblivion the name of that unremembered, presumably religious woman. This twinning seems particularly fitting in a neighborhood where recy-cled memory and its associations have become a type of currency, a part of the Lower East Side's evolution into the Naye Alte Heym (the New, Old Country).

The Lower East Side was the place where the New and Old World came together, the hotbed where activists of every political persuasion framed their debate and dialogue. In America, tikun olam—the notion of fixing what is wrong and broken in the world—is seen as a religious idea. Its secular counterpart, often described as social justice and advocacy, is commonly seen as an integral component of Jewish identity. In both strands, immigrant activists have left a healthy legacy of commitment to causes and arguing about them.

Bibliography

Cahan, Abraham. *The Rise of David Levinsky*, Penguin, New York, 1993

Cohn, Jesse. "Anarchy in Yiddish: Famous Jewish Anarchists from Emma Goldman to Noam Chomsky," Presentation given at Temple Israel Temple Israel, March 2nd, 2002

Cohen, Rich. *Tough Jews: Fathers, Sons, and Gangster Dreams*, Random House, New York, 1999

Ebest, Ron. "Anzia Yezierska and the Popular Periodical Debate Over the Jews (Critical Essay)," *MELUS*, 3/22/2000

Gold, Michael. *Jews Without Money*, Carol Graf, New York, 1930

Goldman, Emma. *Living My Life*, (Dover Reprint 1990), Autobiography, Tamiment Library and Robert F. Wagner Labor Archives at New York University,

http://www.nyu.edu/library/bobst/research/tam/yiddish/Englishbks/engworkslives.html

Howe, Irving. *World of Our Fathers: The Journey of the East European Jews to America and the Life They Found and Made*, Galahad Books, New York, 1976

Katz, Dovid. "Proletpen and American Yiddish Poetry," *Jewish Currents* (Part 1 and 2), November-December 2006, January – February, 2007

Malkiel, Theresa Serber. *The Diary of a Shirtwaist Striker. Fictionalized account of the great 1909 strike.* (Ithaca, NY: ILR Press, Cornell University, 1990)

Reizbaum Marilyn. "Yiddish Modernisms, Red Emma Goldman," *MFS Modern Fiction Studies*, Volume 51, number 2, Summer 2005

Roth, Henry. *Call It Sleep*, The Noonday Press, (Farrar, Straus and Giroux), New York, 1934

Slobin, Mark. *Tenement Songs, the Popular Music of the Jewish Immigrants*

Szalat, Alex. Film, *Clara Lemlich: A Strike Leader's Diary*, 2006

Whyte, William H. (Introduction).*The WPA Guide to New York City: The Federal Writers Project Guide to 1930s New York*, New Press, Reissue 1995

Wengrofsky, Jeffrey. *Berkeley Journal of Sociology*, "Holy Days and Hallowed Ground: An Episode of Symbolic Reconstruction in the Public Sphere, 1997-1998"

Warnke, Nina. "Immigrant Popular Culture as a Contested Sphere: Yiddish Music Halls, the Yiddish Press, and the Processes of Americanization, 1900-1910," *Theatre Journal* 48:3 (1006, 32-335, Baltimore, John Hopkins University Press, 1996

Music

Klezmer 1993, Knitting Factory Records, Shvitz AllStars (Frank London composer), 1993, track 8, Emma Goldman's Wedding," track 9; Allo Trehorn with Klezmatics, Ode to Karl Marx

Mandy Patinkin *Mamaloshn*, 1997, Noneshuch, "Motel The Operator," track 11

Metropolitan Klezmer *Mosaic Persuasion*, Rhythm Media Records, 2001, track 5, "Mein Rueh Platz" (Moshe Rosenfeld)

"Yosele Hill" – Joe Hill in Yiddish
Ikh leg mir shlofn do ba nakht
In shtib siz sha un shtil
Ikh efn op die aygelakh
Hoo ha do shtayt Joe Hill
Oy Yosele ikh sog tsu ihm
'Khob gemaynt du host geshtorbn
Makh tsu dayn moyl du narish khlob
Kuk ikh oys vie a korbn?
Die balabostn hobn dikh umgebrakht
Tsu hitn ihre raykh
'Svet zay gor nit helfn ven arbeter
Fun velt feraynigt aykh!
I dreamed I saw Joe Hill last night,
Alive as you and me.
Says I, "But Joe, You're ten years dead"
"I never died," says he. (2x)
In Salt Lake, "Joe by God," says I,
Him standing by my bed,
They framed you on a murder charge
Says Joe, "But I ain't dead." (2x)
"The copper bosses killed you Joe. They shot you Joe," says I.
"Takes more than guns to kill a man,"
Says Joe, I didn't die." (2x)

"Joe Hill ain't dead," he says to me,
"Joe Hill ain't never died,"
Where working men are out on strike
Joe Hill is at their side." (2x)
"From San Diego up to Maine
In every mine and mill
Where workers strike and organize"
Says he, "you'll find Joe Hill." (2x)
"Mein Rueh Platz" – Morris Rosenfeld, Sweatshop Poet
Nit suzh mich dort, vu mirtn grinen
Gefinst mich dortn nit, mein shatz
Vu lebns velkn bei mashinen
Dortn iz mein rueh platz (repeat)
Nit suzh mich dort, vu faygl zingen
Gefinst mich dortn nit, mein shatz
A shklaf bin ich, vu kaytn klingen
Dortn iz mein rueh platz (repeat)
Nit suzh mich dort, vu fontanen shpritzn
Gefinst mich dortn nit, mein shatz
Vu trerm rinen, tsayner kritzn
Dortn iz mein rueh platz (repeat)
Un libstu mich, mit varh libeh,
To kum tsu mir mein guter shatz
Un heiter oif mein hartz, dos tribeh,
Un mach mir zis mein rueh platz (repeat)
Don't look for me where myrtles grow green
You will not find me there, my dear;
Where lives are withering by machinery,
There is my resting place.
Don't look for me where birds sing
You will not find me there, my dear;
I'm a slave, whose chains cling
There is my resting place.
Don't look for me where fountains splash
You will not find me there, my dear;
Where tears are flowing, teeth are gnashing,
There is my resting place.
And if you really, truly love me
Then come to me, my treasure dear;
And help this gloom lift from my heart,
Make my resting place sweet.
The Cloakmakers Union
Version from "Elissa's Grandfather," Abe Hecht
The Cloakmakers union is a no good union,
It's a rat-fink union for the bosses
The right-wing cloakmakers, they are Socialist fakers

They are nothing but takers for the bosses
The Dubinskys and the Roses and the Thomases,
They makes by the workers false promises
They preach socialism, but practice fascism,
To maintain capitalism by the bosses
Wikipedia version
Oh, the cloakmakers' union is a no-good union,
It's a company union of the bosses.
And the Hillquits and Dubinskys and the Thomases
The right-wing cloakmakers and the Socialist fakers
They preach Socialism, but they practice Fascism
Are making by the workers double crosses.
Are making by the workers false promises, Hoo Ha!
To preserve Capitalism by the bosses.

The Cloakmakers Union – The United Hebrew Trades was established in 1888 in NYC, at 25 E. 4th Street. In its first year, its members set up the Cloak Maker's Society, which was then reorganized in 1889 and became the Dress and Cloakmakers' Union of New York.

Elissa Sampson *is a local resource on the history and background of the synagogues of the Lower East Side, both extant as well as those lost. She is a long-time resident and docent, with close relationships to many shuls, and like her parents who worked or grew up in the neighborhood, Elissa has always had deep ties to the Lower East Side. With her husband, Professor Jonathan Boyarin, a well-known Jewish anthropologist and ethnographer, they have raised their children to love the neighborhood and its traditions. Elissa has contributed to the design of the tours that the Lower East Side Conservancy offers and is always interested in finding out what visitors and neighborhood residents alike would like to learn about the historic and living communities of the Lower East Side/East Village. ejswoo@yahoo.com*

---

[101] Theresa S. Malkiel, *The Diary of a Shirtwaist Striker*. Fictionalized account of the great 1909 strike. (Ithaca, NY: ILR Press, Cornell University, 1990), p. 144.

[102] Ibid., p. 134.

[103] Circa 1910, "instead of seizing on the incipient political capital in this population, the AFL adopted a defensive and xenophobic posture", p. 126 from Jeffrey Wengrofsky, *Berkeley Journal of Sociology*, Holy Days and Hallowed Ground: An Episode of Symbolic Reconstruction in the Public Sphere, 1997-1998.

[104] Each of the four East River Houses on Grand Street which were built by the ILGWU is named after a labor leader. The Erlich-Alter Building, is named after Henryk Erlich and Victor Alter, leaders of the Polish Bund.

[105] Another of the four East River Houses union co-ops is named for lawyer and Socialist Party founder, Morris Hilquit.

[106] The Socialist Party was created in 1900 with a merger of a wing of the Socialist Labor Party into Eugene V. Debs' Social Democratic Party. In her fictionalized strike account *The Diary of a Shirtwaist Striker*, author Theresa S. Malkiel describes their support for striking garment workers: "In 1913, the Socialist Party and the United Hebrew Trades lead over fifty thousand workers in their marches to Union Square", p. 134.

[107] www.findagrave.com, notes by Bill McKern.

[108] One of the three Hillman buildings built by the ILGWU is named after Meyer London, socialist member of the 64th United States Congress; see footnote 105 on Hilquit.

[109] After World War II that changed somewhat since that rebellion was predicated on the existence of a shtetl world that had disappeared.

[110] The 'beis olam' [cemetery] had a central place in Jewish towns and villages in Eastern Europe. Being buried in a Jewish cemetery served as a strong marker of belonging to a community for secular Jews as well. For immigrants outside of New York, it was often difficult to find kosher cemeteries that maintained separate areas for Jewish only burials. New York's immigrant population density allowed hometown and other immigrant mutual aid societies (which included both religious and non-religious immigrants) to provide the necessary kosher cemetery plots. The 'unthinkable' didn't need to be thought through since the choice was automatic.

[111] Psalm 137.

[112] Located at 96 Clinton Street.

[113] A year later, 1910 the ILGWU's Cloakmakers' Strike of 60,000 took place at Cooper Union.

[114] The Triangle Shirtwaist fire is still commemorated in the Lower East Side where the victims names are chalked on the sidewalk in front of their addresses on the anniversary of the tragedy. A recent e-mail call for participants included the following: "On Monday, March 26, 2007, from 12noon-1pm, UNITEHERE!, the NYC Fire Dept., and NYC public schools will hold a public ceremony in front of the building, at the NW corner of Washington and Greene Streets".

[115] Rise of David Levinsky, Abraham Cahan, (Penguin, 1993), p. 28.

[116] Ibid., p. 129.

[117] Ibid., p. 109.

[118] "Cahan and playwright Jacob Gordin, who became the primary intellectual presence in, and reformer of the Yiddish theater, had been the driving force behind a campaign to transform the community's theatres from establishments for "lowbrow" entertainment into institutions for "highbrow" and cosmopolitan European culture. Nina Warnke, Immigrant Popular Culture as a Contested Sphere: Yiddish Music Halls, the Yiddish Press, and the Processes of Americanization, 1900-1910, Theatre Journal 48:3 (1006, 32-335, 1996, John Hopkins University Press.

[119] The Folksbiene (pronounced "Folks-BEE-neh," meaning "People's Stage") started on the Lower East Side in 1915, staging Ibsen's Enemy of the People in Yiddish.

[120] Now the Village East Cinemas.

[121] The Forward, Oct 13, 2006 "The first theatrical union in the United States when it was founded in 1887, the HAU provided an infrastructure for the Yiddish theater that flourished in playhouses up and down Second Avenue. Yiddish theater in New York was more than just a temporary diversion for Jewish immigrants at the turn of the 20th century. It was a beacon of hope, fueling the political, social and professional ambition in its audience members. Often barely eking out a living in a city that seemed determined not to welcome them, immigrant Jews were starved for the messages about poverty, assimilation and equality hidden between the lines of the plays, and they flocked to performances in droves. Setting rules for everything from working conditions to payment schedules, the HAU was a vital part of that theatrical movement."

[122] Emma Goldman, LML 370.

[123] Alexander Berkman's failed assassination of Henry Frick was one of the great soap operas of anarchist history.

An Interview with Carole Ramer

Romy Ashby
Edited by Foxy Kidd

"Free speech is the right to shout 'theater' in a crowded fire."

- A Yippie proverb

When Carole Ramer was almost still a kid, living in a tenement on East 17th Street, a guy she knew from a funky shoe store in the neighborhood told her there might be a job opening down at the Law Commune at Union Square, near Andy Warhol's Factory. The Law Commune was a group of radical lawyers who represented some of the most subversive and interesting people of the day. It turned out that Abbie Hoffman, a client of the radical lawyers, needed an assistant, and that ended up being Carole. She worked out of his pad on the roof of the Felt Building on East 13th Street near Third Avenue. One of the projects she worked on was *Steal This Book*, Abbie's famous handbook for "getting over," published in 1971. When the famous drug bust went down that sent Abbie underground for years, the consequences for Carole were immeasurable. Yet to this day, she remains absolutely loyal to Abbie and grateful for everything she experienced thanks to him. Since the late 1980s, she's lived on the corner of Third Avenue and 13th Street, just up the block from the Felt Building. She's among the last glamorous figures in the East Village. She speaks with a classic New York brogue and she's an excellent hairdresser. Any person who has not had their hair done by Carole Ramer has not lived to the fullest in New York City.

Did you know about Abbie Hoffman when you got the job?

I knew who he was but I wasn't a groupie, which was probably beneficial. He lived with his wife Anita in the Felt Building in a little three-room loft on the top of the roof. You'd walk in and there was a little living room and kitchen, then a bedroom and one other room. It was cute and homey and they had the whole roof. They were the only ones living there. The rest of the building was offices. They had a very cheap rent, but people used to say that Abbie lived in a Penthouse. He didn't, it was just the loft on the roof, very simple.

And what was your job like?

It was different every minute. He used to call me his Left Hand. I would sort out his day, take phone calls, go drop things off. We'd talk about his little antics and crazy schemes. I had to know everything he was up to. He was involved in everything. I met so many people. One day it would be one of the Black Panthers, or some crazy genius street person who had invented something. It opened up a whole world for me.

What was the place like where you lived at the time?

It was on 17th between Third and Irving right near Max's. I was subletting it. It had the bathtub in the kitchen—I've been in a lot of those places with the tub in the kitchen—and the toilet in the hall. It was a real tenement. I think I was paying seventy-five dollars a month, and that was being *overcharged*. The building still exists. It's all condo'd out now, but it was such a mess then that when I was leaving it, I wanted to give the apartment to somebody and nobody wanted it. Seventy-five bucks sounds cheap, but I wasn't making much. I even had a roommate for a while. I couldn't afford it by myself.

Did you like the East Village as it was when you'd come down to work at Abbie's?

Yeah, I did. It was a combination of intrigue and fear. Even in those days the West Village felt safe. It was gayer then. The Lower East Side was very iffy. But there was something great about it. It was great and scary at the same. I liked the fact that it was a little wild, and it was just so interesting. Even before I came to work for Abbie, I used to come as a kid and walk on Saint Mark's and see the Psychedelicatessen and all the little stores and record shops. I loved it. Everything was colorful; it was like a carnival.

In the early 70s, there was a big army navy store called Hudson's on 13th Street and Third Avenue that took up half the block. I used to shop there a lot. And Third Avenue was the pawnshop area. I never used one because I never had anything to pawn, but Abbie used to go to one in particular all the time. I think he got his gun there, the time I almost got arrested with it. My memory is a little blurry, but I think he sent me to the pawnshop to get it and I didn't know you were supposed to conceal the gun outside. That was the law. If you were walkin' around with a weapon, you could get arrested. Well, it was a rifle and it had a strap, so I was walking along with this big gun hanging on my shoulder, and the cops pulled up. It got cleared up because I was a kid and Abbie had the registration and all that stuff. I didn't even know I was breaking the law, you know, he didn't tell me that you have to put it in a bag or something.

What did he want it for?

Protection, I guess. He wasn't hunting, that's for sure. But it was a big old rifle. There was a pawnshop in the block where the movie theater is now, on 11th and 3rd. Abbie always used a lot of the local stores, the framer, the art supply store, and they're still there. I used to go to the post office on 4th Avenue to get Abbie's mail. Even 4th Avenue still had a roughness about it. Union Square Park had a little nasty thing going too, but it wasn't as rough as Tompkins Square and further east in Alphabet City, which it was called then, where they had crack houses and shooting galleries and the whole nine yards.

On 3rd Avenue, trannie hookers would parade up and down like the West Side Highway. That lasted up until the 80s but by then the hookers weren't trannies anymore, they were junkie hookers. Really bad junkie hookers. You'd see people in doorsteps with needles in their arms, nodding. That was very popular. That lasted for a long time. I don't remember being scared. I just remember knowing to avoid this block or that block. Certain blocks were worse than others. I'd get the "Hey, Baby", and this and that, but I was never mugged. I kind of walked around like I didn't care.

Did Abbie like the neighborhood?

Yeah, he loved it. He was always traipsing around and he knew so many people. The people from the Movement and the radical lawyers, Jerry Lefcourt and all those people from the Law Commune, they were mostly on the Lower East Side. The Captain Crunches, the subversives, the smart, nerdy types that came up with all those gizmos for Steal This Book, like the black box that you could use to get free phone calls.

Abbie used to go to Luchow's a lot, 'cause it was right across the street from his place. I thought Luchow's was a landmark too. Now it's a dorm. And supposedly, the post office on 4th Avenue is going to be a dorm. I remember that Abbie used to like a famous pickle guy down on the Lower East Side. All the things that I hated because my grandmother tried to force 'em on me, he kind of liked. Like pickles. I never liked pickles. But he was a pickle eater.

What did your grandmother force on you?

Well, she was the worst cook in the world. She was very into S&W canned vegetables. She thought S&W canned vegetables were the best, I guess because they were expensive. So she would overcook those to a mush, and minute steaks were her favorite and she would cook 'em till they were like shoe leather. She would make all kinds of Jewish food, which she forced me to eat. To this day I can't look at gelfite fish or any of those things.

Was that your mother's mother?

Yes. Nana. She and her brother came from Poland, I think. Sarah and Myron were their names. And Myron was actually a cantor. But he was a bit of a schnook and she was a bit of a weirdie. My grandfather had all kinds of different businesses and they had money at one point, so my mother grew up with help in the house and that kind of thing. But then they lost everything from really stupid business decisions. I don't know the whole story and now there's no one to tell it. But Nana and Grandpa ended up in the Bronx, in the projects. That was a nasty old neighborhood, it was scary. There were drive-bys, it was one of those kinds of projects. All I remember from my childhood were the holidays where everyone would get together there, my mother's brothers would come, and Nana would make four different main courses. It was a very Jewish thing. I remember the holidays being a time of getting together, eating bad food and fighting. All the family dramas would come out. My grandpa would just sit in a chair and sleep through the whole thing while my grandmother was there dominating. Everyone would nitpick and squabble and eat the bad food. She did great latkes though, my grandmother, she did great latkes and great fried potatoes and a good chicken soup. She would do the menorah thing at

Hanukah; she was that kind of religious. Not the going-to-temple, not-shutting-the-lights-on-Saturday kind, you know? We did have relatives who were orthodox, like my great Aunt Ida who lived in Monticello, but I only vaguely remember her.

What about your father's side?

My father was born in Harlem, in what was a ritzy white area at the time, in the 1920s. His parents had money and lived in the Bronx. He was an engineer, but he unfortunately worked for the city. He was the only poor one in his family, but he built a lot of bridges in the city. My grandfather had a hardware store once on Madison Avenue around 80th Street but by the time anyone told me about it, it wasn't there anymore. That grandfather had seven brothers and sisters and they all came to this country and made a lot of money. One of his sisters became a Madame in Iowa, one of the brothers was a rich queen somewhere, but they all had money and there were a lot of engineers in the Ramer family. And they were all brilliant Bridge players. They all sent themselves to college by playing Bridge. Had I known this! I used to be very good at math; I was supposed to be an engineer, too. I could have learned Bridge when I was young and maybe done the same thing!

Did any of your family live down on the Lower East Side?

No, but my mother's parents had some friends who lived in one of the projects on the Lower East Side. They had been in concentration camps. They weren't actually relatives but they were considered relatives because my grandparents knew them from way back. They had a son named Max. "Maxie." And he and I were supposed to end up together.

Whose idea was that?

Maxie's parents and my grandparents. I think we kissed once. Maxie's mother used to cut his meat up when he was a teenager. He was a real Mama's boy. His parents were the types who always wanted to give you everything. They would almost envelope you with too much affection. They were religious. I think what they had experienced made them more so. I think I went to Maxie's bar mitzvah. Eventually he moved away and became a foot doctor.

So you could have been married to a podiatrist?

Yes.

Are you sorry you aren't?

No.

How long have you lived in the apartment you have now, here on 13th and 3rd?

Twenty years. Since the late 80s. And even when I moved in here then, there were still certain blocks that were scary with crime and drugs. There were shoot-outs on 13th Street over there at the crack house between 3rd and 2nd. I wouldn't walk down that block. Nobody would, after a few shoot-outs. That crack house has been bricked up for years, and I have no idea why. They're knocking everything else down. I never would have thought this neighborhood would turn into what it's turned into.

Note: That crack house is the one at 222 East 13th Street, which was an SRO full of hookers and drug dealers until 1992, when the Department of Housing Preservation and Development evicted everybody and padlocked the building. As of this minute, it is still bricked up and padlocked.

Do you ever feel that some of the changes to the neighborhood are horrible in the opposite extreme?

Yes. I actually miss when all the homeless people were around, in a way. They used to sleep on my doorstep a lot. When crack was big all the crack addicts liked my doorway because there was a brick wall, and it was a good spot. My doorway is in Taxi Driver. In that movie you'll see the donut shop and Carmelita's and the Variety Arts Theatre, and the Harvey Keitel scene was on the next block near where the crack house shoot-out place was. And I remember the donut shop from the Abbie days.

You looked down on the roof of the Variety Arts Theatre from your windows. Did you ever go inside it?

Never.

Did you ever think they'd tear it down?

Never.

Did you think it would last forever?

Yeah, I thought it was landmarked! I think they just demolished it anyway.

Your windows now look right into the huge new glass building that replaced it. What do you think of it?

It's hideous. All those apartments, one on top of the other, and every apartment is exactly alike. They are all exactly the same. The light fixtures are the same, they all have cheap furniture and everyone looks alike: white people who all look like they're related. It's cheap and cheesy and they've all spent a million and over. I don't even want to look. I try not to look out my window. It's not as if there's anything interesting going on in there. As we speak, I'm looking. I see a few people moving around and nothing is happening.

It seems that a lot of the old Jewish culture in the neighborhood is just going. Does it seem so to you?

Yeah. There were a lot of Jews in the East Village. But most of them are gone, or real old now, and there do seem to be less Jews. There seems to be less everything. It's like Middle America came and took over. Maybe I'm just not so connected. It wasn't like I sought out Jews for friends. I went to synagogue a few times in my life, and that was either for a bar mitzvah or a funeral. But recently—you know the Jew Truck? That's what I call it.

You mean the Mitzvah Tank? The Winnebago full of Hasidim that you see driving around playing music from a speaker?

Yeah. One was parked out here and when I crossed the street they said, "Shalom!" They recognized me as one of their own. They spotted me.

Did it make it make you feel warm and cozy?

Yeah, I kind of liked it. Why not?

Romy Ashby and **Foxy Kidd** *interviewed Carole Ramer in 2001 for Goodie Magazine®, where she tells in detail the story of the famous drug bust and everything that came after. A book of essays by Carole is forthcoming from Panther Books. www.goodie.org*

Romy Ashby *has lived in New York City since the early 1980s, initially on the Lower East Side. Since 1999, she and native New Yorker* **Foxy Kidd** *have been producing Goodie Magazine, a little publication dedicated to celebrating authenticity, in its many manifestations through in-depth interviews, one subject per issue. Watching the relentless destruction of New York City—as its beautiful and complex culture disappears along with countless old and storied buildings—has made Romy and Foxy preservationists by default. They both say that making Goodie Magazine is what makes life worth living.*

Frances Goldin and Miriam Friedlander

Chris Brandt

This is about two Jewish women who have had an enormous impact on the Lower East Side: Miriam Friedlander and Frances Goldin. There have been a great many Jewish women of influence here, but these two are not typical. They reversed the usual immigrant pattern of using the Lower East Side as a springboard out of immigrant status. Friedlander and Goldin both came not from the LES but from the American middle-class mainstream of upward mobility and suburban dream, and made their mark right here. Before telling about their experiences, however, let's look at the history of the Jewish Lower East Side. It is one part of the history of the immigrant Lower East Side.

From the middle of the 19th century until quite recently, the LES is where the poorest of immigrants have come to get a start in their new country. (Sometimes it's been called a dumping ground.) Irish, Italians, Eastern Europeans, Russians, Germans, Chinese, Puerto Ricans, Dominicans, and African-Americans from the south's Black Belt—all have come to the Lower East Side. And in broad outlines, their stories are pretty much the same. They settle, get jobs, work hard, put their children through school so the children (some born in the old country or the old place, some born here) will have it better than they.

The children grow up American, speaking a language their parents often don't understand. Sometimes the kids are embarrassed by their parents' old-fashioned ways, and sometimes the kids refuse to learn the old language or the old ways, so they can put some distance between themselves and their stodgy ancestors. Then comes the actual distance—they move out of the Lower East Side, to Queens, to Westchester, to Long Island, to New Jersey. It's a statement— we're part of mainstream America now! Sometimes the aging parents come along with them; sometimes they stay behind. And as the older generations die, the old culture is lost, or becomes a museum exhibit.

Working-class Jews started coming to the Lower East Side in the late 19th century after the assassination of Czar Alexander in 1871 and with the increase of pogroms in Russia, Ukraine, Poland, and other Eastern European countries. Though most Jewish immigrants identified themselves as Jews, they also held on to their national identities as Ukrainians, Poles, Germans, and to their European sense of class. Middle-class and wealthier Jews did not settle on the Lower East Side; they went to the Upper East Side or the Upper West Side, just as the first generation of middle-class and wealthier members of most other immigrant groups did. So the Lower East Side filled with working-class people of all kinds, who brought with them their religions and their nationalities.

In the late 19th and early 20th centuries there were well-defined national and ethnic areas on the Lower East Side—Italian, Irish, Jewish neighborhoods. There were even individual blocks identified with ethnic groups. A friend's father who grew up here told how he had to avoid certain streets because as a Jewish kid he would have been, and frequently was, attacked for being where he didn't "belong." There are many histories about the waves of immigration to the Lower East Side (see endnotes for a random selection). But perhaps the best way to understand ordinary immigrant life here is to read fiction like Henry Roth's *Call It Sleep* or Milt Gross' *Nize Baby*, which paint fascinating pictures of life in the tenements; or to visit the Tenement Museum, where you can see how the immigrants lived; or to marvel at the displays on Ellis Island, which show what they brought with them; or to see the newly renovated Eldridge Street synagogue and museum.

Many of the Jewish immigrants (like many Irish and Italians, and others) also brought with them their political and economic class consciousness, forged by 19th-century European social upheavals. So it is that the Lower East Side was home to Johann Most, Emma Goldman, Alexander Berkman, Irving Howe, and many of the seminal activists and writers of the 20th century. And so it was that many of the most powerful movements of the 20th century, class-based movements for unions and social betterment, were born here.

Jews were prominent in these movements. There were anarchists, communists, socialists; they organized themselves or were recruited into settlement houses, mutual aid societies, political clubs and parties, and labor unions. One of the most important of the mutual aid societies was the International Workers Order. According to the entry in Wikipedia, it was a Communist-affiliated insurance and fraternal organization (landsmanshaftn) founded in 1930 following a split from the The Workmen's Circle/Arbeter Ring, a still-extant Jewish fraternal organization. After its separation from the Workmen's Circle, the IWO opened itself to Communists of all ethnicities, although its Jewish section, the Jewish People's Fraternal Order, remained the largest group in the Order, and played a dominant role throughout its existence.

At its height, after World War II, the IWO had almost 200,000 members and provided low-cost health and life insurance, medical and dental clinics, and supported foreign-language newspapers, cultural and educational activities. The IWO also ran a Jewish summer camp, Camp Kinderland. Additionally, the IWO owned and operated cemeteries throughout the US and Canada, a common practice among left wing Jewish mutual-aid organizations like the Farband and the Workmen's Circle.

The United States Attorney General placed the IWO on its list of subversive organizations in 1947. Though [it was] financially solvent and conservatively managed, the New York State Insurance Department contended that, since it was alleged to have engaged in political activity, which is prohibited to insurance organizations, it placed its members' interests in jeopardy, leading ultimately to its liquidation in 1954.

In addition to the progressive Jews who grew up on the Lower East Side and stayed here to carry on their struggles, there was a smaller current who grew up elsewhere and moved here precisely to join those struggles. Both Frances Goldin and Miriam Friedlander belong to that group. And both, when they came to the Lower East Side, joined the IWO.

Miriam Friedlander was born in Pittsburgh and grew up in the Bronx. She moved to the Lower East Side in the early '60s. "I was moving from the Bronx to Manhattan," she says, "and the Lower East Side was working class, so that attracted me, and I was also attracted to the area around Tompkins Square Park. This was the first place I looked." Part of the magnetism of the area, for her as for the many other political organizers, artists and young people, was its radical history. Growing up in a family of radicals—her parents were already members of the IWO's radical wing, especially in its cultural activities—Friedlander had been involved since childhood in organizing activists in the Yiddish chapter of the IWO, to which her father belonged.

What Friedlander found here was a rich ethnic and cultural stew, though by the '60s it was beginning to die out. Second Avenue had been the center of markets and the Yiddish theater, which played a tremendous role in Jewish life. There had been three currents in Jewish life on the Lower East Side for the previous 80 years—the theater, religion, and radical politics. The theater solidified the culture, melding the many currents of Jewish immigration both linguistically and in their love of art. Religion was less a common bond, for there was every kind, from the ultra-orthodox to the non-observant. Still, a shared history of religious oppression had made people tolerant of each other's beliefs.

Politics, however, was less unified. Grace Paley (who grew up in the Bronx in an extended Russian-Jewish family), when asked where her distinctive writer's voice came from, attributed it to "this big family [where] everyone was always yelling at everyone else." The Socialists were yelling at the Communists and the Communists were yelling at the anarchists and the anarchists were yelling at the religious ones, and so on. Within a family such divisions could be managed, but in a larger community, the national, political and class fault lines were more difficult to deal with. On the Lower East Side, the differences developed into two major tendencies. One, to oversimplify, was the trade union/middle class/reformist side; the other was the working class/radical/revolutionary side. The former took on tasks like building housing. Miriam Friedlander says that when she arrived in the neighborhood, "The Grand Street area in the main was people from the trade union group that had built the housing there. ... They were very strong, and contained even a religious element, but since they were union they were certainly a step beyond just religious—I guess mostly Socialist. And since they were union-based, they were more middle income."

The differences, she says, were between the more radical leadership, many of them communist, and the unions, which considered themselves Socialist but not Communist. Also, the more radical the group was, the more likely there were to be women in the leadership. "They weren't necessarily the name leaders," says Friedlander, "but they were very active." She became one of those leaders, and in 1972 she ran for the City Council seat in the district, and won. She ran as a Democrat because "by 1972 it was not possible to run as a Communist anymore. Before that, a few had."

Miriam Friedlander represented the Lower East Side with great distinction from 1973 to 1991, until she was defeated by the reactionary Democrat Antonio Pagán. Far from retiring, however, she began working to help unseat Pagán. She supported CODA, the Coalition for a District Alternative, and campaigned for Margarita López, who took over the seat in the next election cycle. This too is a legacy, and one of the best, of the radical Jewish Lower East Side—racial and ethnic tolerance. More than tolerance, it was the active promotion of diversity and the determination to help other immigrants, not only those of one's own group, to achieve independence in the new country.

Frances Goldin was born in 1924, in Queens, the youngest of three surviving children. In those days, Queens was still undeveloped and had dirt roads, and Frances' childhood in a loving family was full of adventure. But it was also lonely because of their isolation; theirs was one of the few Jewish families in the neighborhood. This led to one fight, with a girl down the block who said, "Kill the Jew," Frances recalled. Frances won the fight, so she never had to fight physically again. But she has learned to fight in other ways, and she has won most of her battles.

Her opinionated mother mapped out her career: she would study accounting, bookkeeping, stenography and typing, then get a job as a secretary. She did as her mother wished. Her second job was at the War Shipping Administration, where she met Morris Goldin, whom she later married. Many Socialists and Communists, mostly men a decade older than she, worked at the War Shipping Administration. That was where "I cut my eye teeth on politics."* These were lessons that have lasted all her life. Morris Goldin was a member of the Communist Party, and after about a year, she joined too. "I didn't know much," she has written, "but it was an exciting life. There were Blacks in the union, and there were Chinese. I was introduced to people who were not white. And I became very active in the union and in the Party." (During this period—in fact, from the 1920s into '50s—the CP was the only organization that consistently fought for civil rights.)

After they were married in 1944, Frances and Morris moved to the Lower East Side, where she discovered the First Avenue Tenant's Consumer Council. She volunteered to help and has remained active in the housing struggle ever since. At the time, there were many older Jews living here, and since Frances spoke Yiddish, she became their translator. Her housing activities led her to city-wide organizations, and her reputation as a successful fighter grew. In 1951 the American Labor Party asked her to run for the New York State Senate, as the only woman on a ticket headed by W.E.B. DuBois for U.S. Senator, an association of which she is justly very proud. They made a good showing, but lost.

Later, she left the CP because "it wasn't radical enough for me." Having been born after the Bolshevik Revolution in Russia, and having begun her political education in the 1940s, her allegiance was not to Mother Russia or the Comintern but to the goal of a revolution in this country. "My goal was a democratic radical U.S., sort of a Woody Guthrie-Eugene Debs-Marxist approach," she said. Meanwhile, her secretarial skills landed her a job with a literary agency, where she learned the publishing business that would sustain her from then on.

In 1959 came a major turning point. "It started because Robert Moses and the United Housing Foundation decided to take 2,229 families who lived between 7th Street and Delancey Street and kick them out to build a co-op that 93% of the people who lived there couldn't afford to move back into. When this was announced we said, 'Hey, we've got to stop this.'" The result was the birth of the Cooper Square Community Development Committee and Businessmen's Association, founded by Frances and four others. She was also one of the founders of Metropolitan Council on Housing. The Cooper Square Committee fought Moses and won—the only citizen's group to defeat the "master planner"—and became known simply as the Cooper Square Committee.

After Moses was defeated, the 100-year-old tenement buildings that had been condemned for urban renewal passed into the hands of New York City, and the long-term struggle began to preserve low-income housing in the area. Slowly, battles were won and lost—some of the losses resulted from internal political splintering—until finally, under the administration of Mayor David Dinkins, an agreement was signed (which even Rudy G. could not derail). Over slightly more than a decade later, the twenty-two old buildings were renovated and have become a low-income co-op, owned and managed by organizations set up by the tenants themselves: the Cooper Square Mutual Housing Association and the Community Land Trust. (This writer is one of those tenants.) No one person is responsible for this triumph, but without Frances the outcome would surely have been different. She was there for all the demonstrations, arrests, internal and external struggles, and negotiations with the city bureaucracy. At the age of eighty-three, she still sits on the Mutual Housing Association Board of Directors.

Meanwhile, Frances established her own literary agency (in 1977). She has cultivated an elite list of progressive and radical writers, including Barbara Kingsolver, Adrienne Rich, Martín Espada, Susan Brownmiller, and Martin Duberman. In the late 1990s, she received an unsolicited manuscript, essays by a prisoner on death row in Pennsylvania, Mumia Abu-Jamal. She sold the book, and four subsequent ones (so far), and she has become one of the principal organizers in Mumia's defense, an ongoing struggle against racism, police brutality and corruption in Philadelphia. It was Mumia's politics that were on trial—he was the Minister of Information for the Philadelphia Black Panthers when he was all of fifteen years old. He left the Panther Party at age seventeen when Nixon's COINTELPRO tore the Panthers apart, but as an activist journalist he remained a thorn in the side of Philly's status quo. This was a fight Frances could not ignore; along with the struggle for affordable housing on the Lower East Side, which continues full tilt, the fight to free Mumia has been a major part of her life for the past eighteen years.

*Quotes from Frances Goldin are from two sources: *Goldin Years*, a privately published 80th-birthday tribute to her, and interviews with this writer.

Some further reading on Jews in Lower East Side history:

Buhle, Paul, *From the Lower East Side to Hollywood: Jews In American Popular Culture*, Verso, 2004

Ewen, Elizabeth, *Immigrant Women in the Land of Dollars : Life and Culture on the Lower East Side 1890-1925* (New Feminist Library), Monthly Review Press, 1985

Glazier, Jack, *Dispersing the Ghetto: The Relocation of Jewish Immigrants across America*, Cornell Univ. Press, 1998

Herscher, Uri D., guest ed., *American Jewish Archives - The East European Immigrant Jew in America (1881-1981)*, Vol XXXIII No.I April, 1981

Hindus, Milton, *The Old East Side: An Anthology*, The Jewish Publication Society of America, 1969

Howe, Irving & Eliezer Greenberg, eds., *Voices from the Yiddish: Essays Memoirs Diaries*, Schocken, 1975

Howe, Irving & Libo, Kenneth, *How We Lived. 1880 - 1930. A Documentary History of Immigrant Jews in America*, Richard Marek, 1979

Howe, Irving, *World of Our Fathers*, New York University Press, 2005 (30th Anniversary Edition)

Lasky, Kathryn, *Dreams in the Golden Country: The Diary of Zipporah Feldman, a Jewish Immigrant Girl*, Scholastic, 1998

Metzker, Isaac, *The Bintel Brief: Sixty Years of Letters from the Lower East Side to the Jewish Daily Forward*, Schocken, 1990

Roskolenko, Harry, *The Time That Was Then The Lower East Side 1900-1914*, Dial, 1971

Schoener, Allon, ed., *Portal to America : The Lower East Side, 1870-1925*, Holt, Rinehart & Winston, 1976

Chris Brandt is a writer and activist. Also a translator, carpenter, furniture designer, and theatre worker. He teaches poetry at Fordham University. He is proud to have been found guilty on May 29, 2008, of exercising free speech at the Supreme Court, and sentenced to ten days (suspended) and a year's probation. His poems and essays have been published in magazines, journals, and anthologies, including Off the Cuffs: Poetry by and About the Police (Soft Skull, edited by Jackie Sheeler); Lateral (Barcelona); El signo del gorrion (Valladolid); La Jornada (Mexico); Phati'tude, Appearances; The Unbearables; National Poetry Magazine of the Lower East Side; and Crimes of the Beats. His translations of Cuban fiction have been published in The New Yorker and by Seven Stories Press, and of two volumes of Carmen Valle's poetry by the Instituto de Cultura Puertorriqueña. Seven Stories published his translation of Clara Nieto's Masters of War, a history of U.S. interventions in Latin America. Translations of contemporary Cuban poetry will be included in a Univ. of CA Berkeley anthology to be published in 2009.

Part 4: Art

Shalom Tomas Neuman - Celebration Of A FusionArtist

Merry Fortune with John Farris

"If our world is composed of overlapping stimuli which create constant sensory overload, then why should visual art limit itself to any one discipline such as painting, sculpture, print, video or computerized digital images? Is it true that imagery is inseparable from sound and evolution in time? Shouldn't art be a mirror that accurately reflects our environment, society and culture? Don't we gain more freedom by being inclusive and expansive?"

- Shalom Neuman

If somehow one day New York were to be rendered some kind of Atlantis, if years later artifacts were to surface and be found by what one would hope would be a species of continually evolving humans of some kind, if pieces of Shalom Neuman's works and structures were to appear lifetimes after their creation, whatever would be made of these fused, dimensional scriptures?

Art can be a way to simultaneously free emotions while gleaning a comforting order from an often indecipherable and violent universe. Out of the dark history of certain Germans and Jews Shalom instinctively began drawing and painting before years of formal training Creating art was his way of synthesizing trauma. Born on July 27, 1947 in Czechoslovakia—death and dying is already part of an infant's consciousness when nine family members are killed in the concentration camp of Auschwitz.

Before Shalom and his sister Channa were born, to escape the Nazi Germans, Shalom's mother and father Rudolph and Truda Neuman crossed the Czech boarder into Poland and Russia. Russia was hardly neutral or safe but there were not many options open to the family of Jews. Rudolph and Truda were given an ultimatum to become Russian citizens or to be arrested. Refusing to relinquish their citizenship to Russia the young couple chose confinement in a Siberian prison camp. Subsisting on bread and water, prisoners used exclusively for labor were forced to chop down trees to be contributed to Russia's timber industry. They could be killed at anytime.

Russia began losing the war and the prisoners were "freed"—utilized to fight against the Nazis. Rudolph assisted the Czech General Ludvik Svoboda to mobilize other Czechs, which led to the independence of Czechoslovakia, Poland, Hungry, Romania, Bulgaria—all countries occupied by the Nazis and home to refugees who fled their own country to avoid persecution and death.

General Svoboda later became a member of the Communist party and was "elected" President of Czechoslovakia on March 30, 1968. At the end of WWII the Communist Party asserted control over the newly independent [satellite] Eastern European countries. Within the Czechoslovakian government conflicts between the Democratic faction and the Communist party were mitigating any hope of peace and unity. Rudolph Neuman aligned himself with the Democrats and this alliance placed him on a death list. His knowledge of the details of the controversial death of Foreign Minister Jan Masaryk, son of professor and politician Tomás Masaryk first president of democratic Czechoslovakia, made certain that his life would be taken if he stayed.

In the middle of the night the family left their home in Prague, immigrating to the newly created state of Israel, the only place that would shelter Jews.

For many years the family lived in Kirayat Chaim, a little Mediterranean ocean village outside the major Israeli city of Haifa. The village was home to a mixture of a few hundred indigent and immigrant Jews of Sephardic and Ashkenazi descent many sharing similar stories. Geographically much of Israel was a desert and the climate was warm and mild. There was one single road in Kirayat Chaim and no sidewalk. The village is now a suburb of Haifa; there are many roads, the landscape is fertile, and most of the sand has been replaced by grass and trees.

Israeli leaders, determined to protect and assert Israel as a state, began the process of building a homeland for all Jews. Shalom's father and mother were on the manual labor end of this aspiration. His father worked in irrigation and fertilizer products. He would ride his bicycle back and forth from his work place, a makeshift garage where he and his partner enlisted modern technological formulas created by the Dutch for making fertilizing chemicals. Truda worked long hours for very little money as a seamstress to the privileged. Her father was a tailor and had taught his daughter his trade. When Truda was not sewing for others, she made clothes and knitted sweaters for her family. She also cooked, cleaned and maintained their home. Unfortunately for many resourceful, intellectual women in such situations, college was not an option as life was swallowed up and complicated by war activities. Before making a home in Kirayat Chaim, Truda spent a lot of time running from Nazis.

Shalom remembers life in Israel as being simple and "very primitive" and holds images of his mother going outside with clamps to bring in a delivery of ice for the icebox, and of walking around barefoot most of the time and having one pair of sandals. Tribes of Bedouins, nomads throughout their entire existence were themselves beginning to consider roots and civilization, if only theoretically. They began providing an inspired service to the citizens of the outskirts. Their donkeys and camels stocked with produce, the Bedouins made their way "every so often" through the village to bargain with the people. The people, anticipating the arrival of the Bedouins, would come out of their houses and begin a ritual of enthusiastic negotiation for fruits and figs "and a tomato or two" the Bedouins may have gleaned from an orchard a few miles away. The goods they brought were not products—but perishable, desirable local organic fare. Truda would sit sectioning the various fruits and the pieces would be shared among the family.

Because of the extreme heat, school would end at noon and Shalom would walk home on the flat ground along the coast. Though monetarily impoverished he did not feel poor or deprived and there was glamour in a simple existence. On the beach where he spent a lot of time, he could luxuriate in the unadulterated pre-industrialized beauty, the serenity of natural things. In school he enjoyed gardening and drawing classes. Each child was given a little plot, a small rectangle of land about six by four feet, "and we would plant seeds and nurture whatever plants we had chosen. I planted cactus and vegetables...we would eat cucumber, tomato and water melon."

With friends he played homemade games of ingenuity, process and skill—playing cards made from the front and back of hard cardboard boxes, specifically a brand of cigarettes known as *El-Al*. "We would collect the cards from garbage cans and each find of one would yield two cards—front and back! And we would use bottle caps like marbles...only you would *find* bottle caps whereas you had to *buy* marbles!"

Shalom did not want to leave Israel, especially the ocean. For his parents, however, making a living there was difficult and it did not seem like the family was going to be able to rise into the upper echelons. Otto Frohlich, Shalom's uncle and a known pianist, conducted the Wind Symphony. He was also a visiting conductor for the New York Philharmonic and had been living in New York with his wife Herta, Truda's sister. Blonde and fair, Otto had survived the war by hiding out in France and was now completely welcome in the States because of his celebrated musicianship. Otto and Herta convinced the family they would be much better off in New York and in 1958 the Neumans moved to an affordable apartment in Squirrel Hill, a residential area of Pittsburgh.

The family almost did not make it to the United States. In order to get a requisite green card one had to have a psychiatric evaluation. This rule was particularly strict where children were concerned. The initial psychiatrist determined that Shalom was mentally impaired. Knowing that was not the case, the Neumans were allowed to bring the child to a second, more open-minded person who found Shalom smart, charming and exceptional. Shalom says, "If that first shrink had his way, I would have been in Israel right now."

Induction into the United States was no freedom fries. Poor English usage inspired children of all descents to unite to effectively ridicule the young artist who acquired a stutter and was becoming withdrawn. Not a verbal sort even when expressing himself in his own Czech and Hebrew languages, attempts to communicate using a foreign language was an exercise in futility. American kids taunted and made fun of Shalom and he shrank, retreating deeper into artistic productivity, amassing hundreds of drawings. He remained an introvert and only when he began teaching in graduate school did he begin to open up and relax. So it could be said college life and its social milieu was very good for his sense of belonging. The life college provided was quite a contrast to the oppressive social angst he experienced upon first arriving. A self-professed great flunky but for art, much of that time, the formative wonder years of his teens, were spent repetitively visiting a child guidance center.

At First Temple University in Philadelphia, Shalom's tenacity and prolific creative momentum brought some positive attention, and through his undergraduate work he earned a fellowship. A desirable summer residency transported Shalom half an hour outside of Paris to Fontainebleau. The award made it possible for him to step into a world of lush beauty. Fontainebleau is one of the biggest, most magnificent chateaus second only in magnitude to Versailles. It is surrounded by a beautiful sprawling garden. In Shalom's enthusiastic memory the garden "just may have been half the size of Central Park" and the chateau itself "just may be the size of the Metropolitan Museum." He stayed in a pension, a small house with a courtyard. In this place of beauty, where Louis the XIII's mistress had lived and court artists had painted in another century, he had an art studio. One day after working he walked out of his door and saw a couple hundred soldiers on horses with Napoleon himself. A film was being shot and reality and sur-reality collided and, for a few seconds, Shalom was transported even further through time itself.

While at Fontainebleau he spent most of his time painting. Wanting to break from formal exercises and established methods he began a piece, a triptych titled somewhat ironically—*Classical Myth*. So began attempts to deconstruct and reveal the disparities of gods and religion, the meaninglessness of icons. His travels in France led him to observe the "many Mary and Christ paintings, each different. There were no authenticating photographs and none of the artists could possibly have known what Jesus or Mary looked like. In all the paintings they had white-blonde hair!" To Shalom it appeared that each artist created his or her own myth.

In *Classical Myth* it was Shalom's intention to reveal and convey absurdity. The Madonna is dark and the Christ child is Asian. The two appear in a painting at the top of the center panel. Also placed in the composition is a structure featuring a Muslim crescent. It is not exactly a wall Madonna and child hang on—but a thrilling, cloudy sky of either dawn or dusk that travels through a house, through open windows, and through the canvas panels themselves. Also present in the work are two youths: an African-American male and a light-skinned female with long dark hair and dark eyes. Their modern, integrated presence could be a negation of all religious pretense and absolutes as absurdity poses unresolved questions.

In the center panel the male and female appear together in the house. The female looks out the window on the left as the male watches her. The male appears again in the left panel, naked and wearing a cross, and the female appears in the right panel. The male is more warrior and perhaps ready to "take on" the world, whereas the topless female appears fatigued in her open blue jeans. Both figures appear stark and haunted to the core and the work resonates at once dreamy, specific, world-weary, intimate and optimistic.

At the bottom of the center panel there is a copy of the American publication *Time Magazine* sitting on a table. It sits in its traditional red border and the headlines read *American Jews And Israel*. It sits on a crooked table with a potted plant also on its surface. The table, magazine and plant are so far down as to appear to be falling off the canvas. Thinking in terms of fusion, Shalom melded a real flowerpot with the painted one, creating a dimensional form instead of a flat one. This gives the work a mystical but approachable, universal quality. The painting was completed at Carnegie Mellon University in Pittsburgh. The mysterious, unlikely elements have a consciously altruistic message; it is with certainty Shalom expresses that, "if we are to survive as a species we must regard each other and intermingle."

Still at First Temple, Shalom had begun a series of ballpoint drawings that inspired the Pittsburgh Ballet to commission him to illustrate for the cover of their catalogue. Abundant in wry political commentary, the animated collection—thousands of representational drawings—is allegorical, cynical and darkly lyrical. The work evokes the black and white lithographs of George Grosz and the emotional drawings of Kathe Kollwitz. Grosz, affectionately referred to as the "bright red executioner," embraced devastating subject matters and graphically depicted victims of the First World War. Kollwitz, considered by her century most excellent in her field, experimented with printing-making tools and was a fellow purveyor of truthfully explicit art in the form of lithographs, etchings and woodcuts.

Primarily residing at the time in New York City, Elaine DeKooning was a visiting professor at Carnegie Mellon and one of Shalom's favorite teachers. She believed New York was *the* place to be for experimentation. Taking her enthusiasm to heart, he left Pittsburgh. Shalom had accrued an inventive art aesthete and formidable craftsmanship. Upon arriving in New York he held a master's degree in painting and sculpture and was an excellent carpenter, finishing carpenter, welder, electrician and inventor—all traditions and skills that he would enlist in his evolving fusion art.

Somewhere in the Sixties, Ad Reinhardt, with passionate certainty and a degree of dogma, confirmed the advent of a popular form of art known as Minimalism, stating: "The more stuff in it, the busier the work of art, the worse it is. More is less. Less is more. The eye is a menace to clear sight. The laying bare of oneself is obscene. Art begins with the getting rid of nature." Shalom's desire for a materially all-inclusive way of working, an aesthetically chaotic recycling process, is distinctly antithetical to Reinhardt's: "I'm a maximist, a fusionist; I want to fuse *everything*. I don't want to exclude anything. Pack it all in! Because that's the way I feel in the city. That's the way I feel in this energetic capitalist culture overloaded with stimuli!"

By the 1980s the Lower East Side of Manhattan had come to resemble a moonscape of rubble-strewn lots. There existed whole blocks of burnt-out tenements. In front of them sat the steel skeletons of torched and scavenged automobiles mocking the American dreamscape. Housing stock abandoned and vandalized, population largely undervalued, marginalized by poor education and little or no economic resources—the area was left riven and shredded by the social upheavals of the 1960s.

Conversely, the imploding social situation created an opportunity for speculation. Sharp realtors with an eye to the not-too-distant future began the business of acquiring old buildings, storefronts and lofts. The little mom and pop store and the humble bodegas that characterized the area began to disappear, slowly at first. Artists desperate for affordable shelter began looking around the Lower East Side. The landlords, or at least the unethical ones, took advantage of the situation and continued to rent substandard, deteriorating, leaky, rodent-infested rooms that were often not in compliance with any existing regulations.

Experientially aware of the displacement his family endured for survival, freedom of expression and security of place were of great importance to Shalom. The rootlessness of fleeing has an indelible effect on one's own needs. While considering stability and the paces one goes through to merely rent, Shalom came across a building off the corner of Eldridge on Stanton Street. The building, number 57, was in sad shape. "As-is," the place and many like it were for the taking and he and his wife Karen were able to purchase the precious but dilapidated abode for next to nothing. Through a labor of love throughout the years, they brought their new home up to snuff and formal building code.

Directly around the block from Stanton Street on the corner of Rivington and Forsyth Streets was an abandoned lot that, through the communal efforts of certain artists, was transformed into a zenith, a kinetic center of creativity, and became formally known as The Rivington Sculpture Garden. The roots of this experimental ad-hoc endeavor are said to have began in 1985 when sculptor Ken Hiratsuka started carving a rock. Transplanted Texan Ray Kelly, a sculptor and welder, ran the show.

For the artists of the Lower East Side, the misfortunes and invisibility of a neglected and marginalized area created another kind of opportunity. The community, though in transition for better or worse, was still very much abandoned by government agencies and developers. This fact enabled the artist to take a peculiar form of license. One could easily tear open a fence and lay claim to a vacant lot and remain there, free to create for years at a time. Spaces such as these became known to some as Temporary Autonomous Zones or the T.A.Z.[124] and appeared in various forms throughout the Lower East Side.

The rock that Hiratsuka had carved metamorphosed into something euphoric and elaborate. The inspired structure became so imposing that it was a perfect stage for FusionArts events and Shalom joined in. "Rather than the two-dimensional canvases of the assemblists and the Russian contructivists," notes Shalom, speaking about his first event at Rivington, "the assemblage of a medley of recycled contemporary waste artifacts was embellished and punctuated by performances: poets, musicians, dancers, all vying—competing for the audience's attention. A welder in the background spraying sparks behind a dancer...to the left on top of the skeleton of a truck was heard the ranting of a poet...and at the same time to the right—the screeching of a singer...the dimming of lights fading in and out on portions of the scenario, the sculpture never subordinate to a narrative as might be props in a staged play. The Rivington School sculpture was on equal footing to the other disciplines that had fused into this mix."

Over those years, from that rock a slew of fusion-inspired events took place in the Rivington Sculpture Garden. The spirit of the participants and comrades was at once boyish, wild and renegade, but the technique behind the art itself was formal. Apart from these fusion performances the actual artwork generated was created from found *metal* objects—metal much the exclusive material of choice—and pure sculptors were the dominant creative and social force. Shalom built a tall outsized painted wooden sculpture, stepping outside the metal-only rule, and in his absence the group disassembled it. Three years later the garden had run its course and the realtors, sensing it was time for the strategic cash in, appeared ready to bulldoze, wreck or implode.

In 1987 composer/musician Charlie Morrow (Charles Morrow Productions LLC) and Shalom pulled together a large fusion-style summer solstice festival. Organized by the non-profit organizations New Wilderness Foundation and FusionArts—Morrow's and Neuman's respectively—the pair coordinated a series of performance events throughout the city's parks. Shalom organized the sculptors and welders (doing quite a bit of welding and sculpting himself), and Charlie Morrow organized the sound. The events were sponsored by The New York City Department of Parks & Recreation with support from the presiding Mayor Koch and took place in Tompkins Square Park, Battery City, Union Square and Central Park.

In Tompkins Square a split-level sculptural performance site was erected which took approximately two months to build. The structure featured a spiral staircase from one level to the next fused with colorfully painted found objects culled from dumpsite excursions. For the event Shalom had been given carte blanche to the city's dumps and metal scrap yards, specifically the luxuriously abundant Brooklyn facilities.

The idea was not to constrict creative individuals, but to set up a platform for them to do whatever they liked. Shalom explains: "There was no linear sequential progression, no dominant individual who orchestrates everything because that's essentially what a playwright or director does. So in [working] that way there is no room for anybody else; the statement is that of the playwright or director. In this type of production—it is truly free." The event was scheduled to begin at three p.m. and to end at eight p.m. Among the participating musicians were members of an '80s post-punk band who called themselves Demo Moe. For the evening they were known per orchestral instructions as "the metal bangers," as they would be banging on anything in the construction that was made of metal.

The finale of the event involved a musical deconstruction orchestrated to gradually subside and surcease led by the members of Demo Moe. The performance inspired people—anyone and everyone—to bang on various objects all over the park. Once the homeless contingent, the indigenous presence that was "tent city[125]," got banging in spirited union, the police seemed powerless to stop the spontaneous eruption of joyous noise. Says Shalom, "I was kind of happy about that...people were...enthralled given the chance to express and the infectious rapture could not be stopped." The reverberation did not remain confined to the event or even the park. It was said the percussive mayhem could be heard all the way up to Union Square and continued way into the night.

Light and motion lie at the core of human experience, and artists of the Bauhaus, Moholy-Nagy and like-minded groups embraced the invention of the electric light at the beginning of the last century. Their adventure was the marriage of art and science, of light and motion. Compelled by fantasy and the unrealized idea of multi-sensory environments where lights, sound, movement, visual imagery and sculptural elements merge, Neuman is continually drawn to experimentation with inevitably post-minimalist materials. Methods of working with lights and computers in the late sixties were a challenging adventure for which there was really no precedent because the technology had not yet arrived. Prior to the mid-sixties art technology did not include, for the most part, dimming systems, computers and projectors—all mechanical territories Neuman frequents, visits and revisits. At that time, even if one wanted, to one could not buy a computerized lighting system, and more specifically one that did not repeat sequential changes in light.

To realize his enhanced computerized dimming system Neuman studied the mechanics of rudimentary stage lighting and teamed-up with a number of electronically inclined individuals. While an undergraduate, a sophomore attending Carnegie Mellon, Shalom got some help from his good friend, a physicist/mathematician, Paul Szymanski. Szymanski was able to create a dimming system that could produce infinite variations and no repetitive pattern could be identified. In 1968 Shalom then had access to his conception—the very first computerized hook-up to lights. His newly designed dimming system made its more formal public debut at Shalom's first art exhibition at Kingpitcher Gallery in Pittsburgh. Featured were a series of three-dimensional sculptural light-boxes covered in overlays of representational images, the installed lighting altering the physical appearance of the boxes.

Initially beginning as a formalist interested in the theories of Kandinsky, Shalom began eliminating many chromatic registers from his palette except for the most opaque: blacks, burnt umbers and ultra-violet marines. Incandescent light fused directly into the work was compatible with such colors, and constructed shapes of wood and metal would often replace canvas. He began creating more and more assemblages that included found objects such as plastic toys. Focusing on the detail, you might locate the "Hulk" flexing his plastic muscle in an environment of industrial waste, or a tiny yellow incandescent bulb in a violet sky approximating a wan sun—Batman and the lights of the Batmobile itself, pinpoints of bright incandescence.

Art you can touch confounds the idea of art as precious object and can potentially defuse ideas of elitism and objectification. The idea that you can touch or play a painting is demystifying and may offend those who prefer the monied high-maintenance inherent in the order of a hands-off mystique. A collaborative piece between Shalom and Cincinnati artist Reed Ghazala features a circuit bent toy instrument, specifically a small keyboard. To create circuit bending, the electronic part of an instrument is cross-circuited, altering the connections to make unpredictable and skittering chance sound effects.

Shalom's works and structures could be held up as deviant artifacts accused of darkness, offensive rhetoric, toxicity, berated metaphor and careless love. They are of a kind of beauty that is truth, and often hard to take. The artist is the mirror, reveler, creator, historian and prophet. The artist with an eye on the transcendent and possible has generously given us a moment to reflect on a object to see what we are made of, what materials abound, what sensibility is prominent, what morality may not be exactly moral.

It is often Shalom's intention to put on display the nomenclature of current mythologies and in the translation, in the apprehension—the subject appearing where the subject is unlikely—through simple kitsch comes not so simple subversion. One could make a conscious, or even unconscious decision to stop at the surface. A look around FusionArts and one could very well selectively choose to remember only colors and iconography. Whether or not such things are a ploy is subjected information, but what comes to mind are the colorful toxic strains of plants and mushrooms; the fantasia of poisonous bugs, snakes and sea life and the stunning hues produced by something as insidious and non-glorious as common, now traditional pollution.

In Neuman's studio on Stanton Street exist semi-gargantuan colorful Fusion Golems, the creation of which began in the late eighties. Typically working on many, many projects at one time, the mechanical monsters took years and years to complete. They have been described by Fusion-Arts' director Deborah Fries as "robotic sculptures [created with] found objects, oils and incandescent lights." Enamored of the ideas of the Swiss Tinguely, Shalom produced this anthropomorphic-sculpted duo with audio capability, and their metal bodies contain depictions of various scenes of dystopia often in the form of cartoons. These mechanical figures might have their compliment in the motorized constructions of the Chilean Enrique Castro-Cid.

The Golem, thought to be the precursor to Mary Shelley's Frankenstein, is a kind of monster-like being said to be created from mud. Many variations of the story exist but the most popular is the narrative whereby one Rabbi Judah Loew, Maharal of Prague, creates the monster to defend the Prague ghetto of Josefov from anti-Semitic attacks. Situated in the back of the gallery the large, colorful, yet eerie combines do appear guardian-like; the average height of a Fusion Golem is thirteen feet. They talk and move and were designed to be projected upon and interacted with. Though still protectors of sorts, the monsters de-evolved and in the stream of creation they became bigger-than-life, guys with too much machismo. Somewhere in the creative process, the colorful pair's persona deconstructed and they became known as *Dick* and *Womanizer*, jolting and mechanical apparatus appropriately reflecting their fall from grace.

Currently Shalom is creating a series of dimensional panels: thirty-six sculptural full body "portraits" inspired by André Schwarz-Bart's novel *The Last Of The Just*. Schwarz-Bart's own parents were killed in an extermination camp.

"According to it [the tradition], the world reposes upon thirty-six Just Men, the Lamed-Vov, indistinguishable from simple mortals; often they are unaware of their station. But if just one of them were lacking the sufferings of mankind, [they] would poison even the souls of the newborn, and humanity would suffocate with a single cry. For the Lamed-Vov are the hearts of the world multiplied, and into them, as into one receptacle, pour all our grief."

Shalom's rescuers-of-the world are bold, sentimental characters you might come across at Coney Island; a Burlesque venue—Commedia dell'arte; a prison; a church; Beit Knesset; a gay bar; a haberdashery; a bar-bar; the supermarket; a Nick Zedd, Federico Fellini or David Lynch movie. All are colorful and celebratory, containing clues and details. Into the design has been devised lights, and a slowly creaking sound emanating from somewhere, an ominous squeak like a ghost rocking chair permanently perched on the porch of a deserted run down house moving mysteriously at high noon, a door being rhythmically open and shut by "the wind."

FusionArts is a celebration of innovative, inclusive realities and Shalom, proprietor and visionary, is the conduit, the heart and soul of this vast orchestration of detritus, diversity and human spirit. Under the direction of Deborah Fries since 2000, the FusionArts Museum received its not-for-profit-status in 2004 and has the distinction of being the only gallery in New York exclusively featuring multi-media artists. The modest rooms on Stanton Street have been continual stage and home to a free-flowing community of dedicated artists of all mediums, techniques, personal persuasions, backgrounds and class structures.

Apart from the immediacy of the local, there exists an international alliance of fusion artists, authors, performers, musicians—explorers of all social strata and premise.

Through an artist-driven international cultural exchange program, New York City artists who exhibit at FusionArts Museum are connected to a network of arts festivals held throughout Canada, Europe and Asia. In turn international fusion artists from participating countries are hosted at a New York-based FusionArts festival held annually at the end of the summer. Collectively these international fusion artists are from Japan, Italy, Germany, Canada, Poland, China, Russia, the Czech Republic and France. FusionArts supports a large number of artists whose work has never before been shown anywhere.

Shalom lives in New York and works out of his studio in Fort Green, Brooklyn. Currently he teaches at Pratt Institute's Manhattan campus.

Partial Exhibitions List, 1986 - 2007 [*solo exhibitions]:

5.07 Cargo Gallery - Paris France / 3.07 Pratt Manhattan Galleries - NYC* / 10.06 Ginza Art Gallery - Tokyo, Japan / 6.06 Chateau de Chevigny - Burgundy, France / 5.06 City Hall Paris, France / 3.06 Musee de l'Homme - Paris, France / 10.05 Creek Art Center - Shanghai, China / 8.05 The Ukranian Museum of New York - NYC / 7.05 La Galleria d'arte ARTantide Lugano - Lugano, Switzerland* / 4.05 Mishima Eco Museum - Mishima, Japan / 9.04 Innerspaces Museum - Poland / 6.04 Arsenal Galleries - Poland / 12.03 Zimmerli Museum - NYC / 9.03 Para Globe Gallery - Tokyo, Japan / 9.03 Aizu Art College - Tokyo, Japan / 9.03 Mishima Eco Museum - Tokyo, Japan / 1.02 Exit Art - NYC / 11.01 Casa Obscura Gallery - Montreal, Canada / 4.00 Tribes Gallery - NYC* / 12.97 Joseph Helman Gallery - NYC / 7.97 Cambridge Multicultural Arts Center - Cambridge, MA / 4.97 Kern Gallery - State College, PA* / 9.96 Penn State University HUB Art Gallery - PA / 4.93 Galerie De La Tour-Kabinet Groningen - Netherlands / 9.92 Parsons School of Design - NYC / 6.91 OK Harris Gallery - Soho, NYC / 3.91 Emil Leonard Gallery - Soho, NYC* / 10.90 Carton Gallery - Barcelona, Spain / 5.90 Anita Shapolsky Gallery - Soho, NYC / 5.90 Institute for Contemporary Art, PS1 Museum - NYC / 10.89 Blum Helman Warehouse - Soho, NYC / 8.89 Centro Cultural Museau - Buenos Aires, Argentina / 5.89 Diagnole Gallery - Paris, France / 3.86 Digital Art Exchange, Dax Group, Venice Biennale - Venice, Italy.

Partial Collections List:

Hamilton-Von Wagoner Museum - Clifton, NJ / Enrico and Roberta Baj - Milano, Italy / Estate of Elaine DeKooning / Galerie Art Temoin - Paris, France / Museum of Modern Art - Nice, France / Sandro Darnini, Plexus - Rome, Italy / Ivan Karp, O.K. Harris Gallery - NYC / Madonna - NYC / Elaine DeKooning - East Hampton, NY / Ann Gibson - Baltimore, MA / Museum of Modern Art (Library) - NYC / Kamin Foundation - Pittsburgh, PA / Whitney Museum of American Art Library - NYC / SUNY - Binghamton, NYC / Guggenheim Museum Library - NYC / Rosa Easman - UBU Gallery, NYC / Joseph Melamed, Carimor Galleries - Israel / South Nassau Unitarian Church - Freeport, NY / Arts & Crafts Center - Pittsburgh, PA / Museum Da Imagem E Do Som - Sao Paolo, Brazil / Paterson Museum - Paterson, NJ / Ellis Island Museum - New York / Paco Das Artes - Sao Paolo, Brazil / Paolo Martini - Rome, Italy / Museum of Modern Art - Buenas Aires, Switzerland / Josh Weiss, Spectra Digial Gallery - NYC / Willem Brookman - Amsterdam, Netherlands / Chemical Bank - NYC / *The Days and Nights of Molly Dodd* - NBC, Lifetime 1987 / *Crocodile Dundee II* - Paramount Pictures 1988 / Tyler School of Art - Philadelphia, PA / Dr. Maria Pulini - NYC / Manuel Cardia - Portugal.

Reviews, Interviews and Articles:

New York — MTV / Good Morning America / NY1 / WNYC / WFMU / *The Village Voice* / *New York Newsday* / *New York Guide* / *Red Tape # 7* / *Downtown Magazine* / *Art Times* /

The NY Press / Art World / Where In New York / Novoye Russkoye Slavo / National Poetry Magazine of The Lower East Side / Grand Street News / Where NY.

USA — Northport Journal / Newark Star Ledger / Fad Magazine / The Miami News / Antiques / The Arts Weekly.

International — Panorama Magazine, Italy */ Paris Free Voice,* France */ Folha De Sao Paula,* Brazil */ O Sao Paulo E Gol,* Brazil */ Arte Magazine,* Italy */ Say Magazine* and *Arte Al Dia International,* Argentina */ World of Art,* Israel */ Art In China / Ecologia Dell Arte* by Enrico Baj - Rizzoli books.

Merry Fortune *is an environmentalist, experimental poet and musician. A collection of her work titled* Ghosts By Albert Ayler, Ghosts by Albert Ayler *was published by Futurepoem books in 2004.*

John Farris *Poet and writer John Farris has contributed work to many anthologies and journals including* hokum, *an Anthology of African-American Humor;* The Outlaw Book of American Poetry; Up is Up But So is Down; A Gathering of the Tribes; Your House is Mine; *and* Between C & D: New Writing from the Lower East Side.

The authors wishes to thank Bonny Finberg, Deborah Fries, Shalom Neuman, Clayton Patterson and Noam Scheindlin.

---

[124] Temporary Autonomous Zone or T.A.Z.: A phrase coined by Hakim Bey (aka Peter Lamborn Wilson) defined as the socio-political tactic of creating temporary spaces that elude formal structures of control.

[125] Tent City: A term used to describe a variety of temporary housing situations often consisting of tents. The tent city referred to here is the large number of homeless citzens who, in the late seventies and eighties, had made Tompkins Square Park their home laying claim to their own temporary autonomous zone.

Shalom Amerika: Humanism in Exile

Robert C. Morgan

Shalom Neuman is an art world phenomenon. At first glance, his work may appear excessive, over the top, metaphysical. But there is more to it than meets the eye.

Shalom's work reflects the chaos of his early life. He was born in Czechoslovakia in 1947 to parents who were Holocaust survivors. In 1948, his father moved the family to Israel to escape the political chaos and uncertainties of post-World War II Communism. They remained in Israel until 1959, then immigrated to the United States through the help of an uncle, the composer/pianist Otto Frohlich. As a young artist in the late sixties, Shalom began traveling to Europe, only recently returning to what was once Czechoslovakia.

While many Americans tend to separate art from life, Shalom regards them as a whole. In a way, he is close to the early Rauschenberg who said it was important to work "in the gap between art and life." For many who have seen Shalom's work displayed at the Fusion Arts Gallery in the Lower East Side of New York City, the question may arise as to what his influences are. The brightly-colored plastic and found figurines that the artist employs in his work— the florescent lights and neon tubes, the expressionist faces—might suggest another era; perhaps the sixties, or the eighties, but we have to look deeper.

Shalom's work is closely connected to the way he thinks. It is a kind of symbolic exegesis, a Romantic enticement that goes beyond the banalities of American culture into the realm of mysticism, the Kaballah, and the survival of planet Earth. There is a dark side to his art that runs contrary to Puritanism, a dark side that is more comfortable with the Parisian underworld—Baudelaire, Verlaine, Rimbaud, Redon, and Moreau—than it is to the founders of Plymouth colony with their theocratic notions of good and evil. Shalom's "obsessive" art is reminiscent of a statement by the Surrealist Max Ernst, who was once asked in a television interview in the fifties with Roland Penrose, if the madness of artists was the same as those who invented weapons of nuclear destruction. Ernst replied emphatically, "No! It is a madness of a completely different sort." What Ernst meant is that artists tend to sublimate internal conflict as a source of human expression, even if, at times, it appears errant or distasteful to viewers. On the other hand, scientists who work on ballistic and nuclear "devices" tend to live in denial—consciously removed from the cause and effect relationship of what they are doing.

Whatever elements Shalom inserts into his assemblage/collage technique are there for a purpose. He is a kind of old-world symbolist in that his images are not merely decorative, they are compulsively literate. They do not disappear into the furnishings, but instead function semiotically as signs—like the work of any mature artist, whether it be Caravaggio or Picasso, Balthus or Lichtenstein. He structures his work according to his own vocabulary, hoping to illuminate the dark side of reality. It is a visual vocabulary, largely founded on global signs from Eastern Europe and the subcultures of New York. Shalom does not stop mid-way in the process of making his work. He goes all way, that is, all the way through it. His brilliant colors and hybrid discontinuous forms, his recalcitrant, blustering heads, busts, eyes, nostrils, are surrogate portraits—archetypes appropriated from the underbelly of society. Shalom's portraits have the capability of opening new doors of consciousness, of going beyond the trashed ideas of the eighties—but he is not a postmodern junkie. He is deeply committed to creating a vehicle for reliving the excess of two decades ago from a different line of sight.

I see Shalom Neuman as a kind of artistic renegade, as someone who wants to remain beyond the superficial machinations of the market. He would like collectors to buy his work, but he is repulsed by the notion that investors speculate on these sales. Shalom has put himself in another position—in a place that is excessive and incendiary. Like the famous song by the The Doors, he wants to light fires—to open doors to another form of consciousness, both cultural and political. Shalom accepts his art as a visionary statement. He is interested in illuminating the dark side of the human condition in order to force human beings to turn in another (opposite) direction. Shalom's art manifests a passionate concern about the environment. He is deeply concerned with how human beings are going to survive if the current political trends continue. He has stressed this point in his work, and also in statements going back to his early "Art Alchemy" pieces in the seventies while working in Paris in a collective of artists called P.A.N. (Performance Artists Network).

Yet, throughout his career, Shalom has progressed as an artist from the platform of classical painting. An early painting, Classical Myth (1969 - 72)—begun at L'Ecole des Beaux Arts in Fontainebleau when the artist was in his early twenties, and later completed in graduate school at Carnegie Mellon University—offers his statement on race in America, not from a negative or cynical point of view, but through life-affirming sexuality. Classical Myth is, in fact, a triptych: Images of the two characters—a black male nude and a bare-breasted white female—repeat themselves from the exterior flanking panels into the interior narrative. At the same time, the perspective is carefully rendered, so we end up focusing on the center panel. Here Shalom has depicted a black Madonna holding a white child in a room that appears to be an interior of a Venetian palazzo, provoking a sense of displacement. This is reinforced by two real wooden table legs that descend from the picture plane below the frame, thus entering into real space.

I mention the painting Classical Myth not only because it is the earliest painting included in this volume, but also because it is the launching pad—the perspectival index—from which Shalom proceeded into the future. Classical Myth revealed his extraordinary ability to distance himself from the subject matter that he paints. I mention this because some would argue that his recent expressionist assemblage "portraits" in "Amerika" lack this distance, that they are too internalized, as if verging on some weird solipsistic disintegration. But not every artist's distance—formally speaking—reveals itself in the same way. Shalom has never been an artist to conform to a trend.

I admire the fact that Shalom does not care about what everybody wants. Instead, he is focused on his own image-making process, on his own intimate intentions. Shalom's aesthetic/anti-aesthetic dialectic goes beyond the commonplace. By the mid-eighties, he was painting consistently outside his earlier classical style, and had moved into a different form of expression, what eventually became his "Toxic Paradise" series. He was still involved with social commentary in an existential way, but less from the position of classical painting and more toward a fusion of Pop and Surrealism, often in relation to shaped structures.

Shalom's irony is also evident—a persistent component in his work—as in the "Toxic Paradise" series. One painting reveals two organically bent twin skyscrapers that eerily evoke the World Trade Center towers in New York. Flanking either side of these Towers are American cartoon superheroes, which include Superman, The Hulk, Captain Marvel, and Spiderman. In another equally ironic oval-shaped canvas, a bright orange sunset glows on a polluted seascape with a molded frame that repeats the image of encircling dead fish.

From the eighties onward, the term "fusion" applies to most everything Shalom has done. While he sees the origin of his fusion approach as being within the realm of a theatrical collage—or assemblage mixed with environmental art and artifacts—it also applies to the content of his work. Even in "Classical Myth" we see the legs of the table coming into the real space/real time environment, meeting the viewer halfway. This continues with "Toxic Paradise" and, perhaps, most explicitly, in another major work entitled "Neo-Nuky Madonna" (1983-84). This multimedia work is a relief, comprised of mostly plastic parts. While the symbolic aspects of "Neo-Nuky" may appear obvious, such as the dead bird affixed over the Madonna's head or the brightly colored plastic detergent containers that appear as multiple breasts, the artist's originality is less in the parts than in the syntax of the whole. This is where Shalom's intuition—his imaginative power—brings everything into focus.

The performative ingredient in his work is an on-going interest. It is through performance that the recent series of faces, called "Amerika," came into existence. I find a curious resonance in these masks, even though they were not intended to be worn. They are less portraits than archetypes—composites of much of the weirdness that the artist encounters in human beings who hang-out around the vicinity of his studio in Brooklyn. I would not refer to the "Amerika" series as Surreal—in the way the "Toxic Paradise" paintings are Surreal—but more Expressionist. However, they are not Expressionist from the perspective of the New York School of the fifties as much as the Sturm und Drang of the German and Austrian painters of the early twentieth century. Shalom wants to imitate the color of plastic containers on supermarket shelves. However, he does admit a certain kinship with the Woman paintings of DeKooning, and with the early Leo X paintings of Francis Bacon.

Like Kafka, who was also Czech, Shalom's vision of reality is paradoxical: He offers a deeply intimate reality with an outwardly existential point of view. Again, like Kafka, Shalom's Jewishness cannot be ignored. One feels alienation and an infinite longing in the respective Amerikas of each artist. (It would appear that the title of these collective masquerades—America spelled with a "k"—has been appropriated from Amerika, the early, unfinished novel of Franz Kafka.)

Kafka, of course, never traveled to the United States so that everything in this novel was based on fragments taken from reading travel guides and on conversations with travelers who had been there.

"Shalom Amerika" has many indirect references to Kafka, but Shalom is a product of his own time. In this sense, Kafka and Shalom share the experience of alienation at different moments in history. Perhaps Shalom is the postmodern version of Kafka, who is inextricably bound to the first decades of Modernity. If these faces are archetypes of the present, maybe they are less about the Pop exterior than about the interior appropriation of what the eye/brain mechanism has absorbed. Like the work of the Dadaist Marcel Janco, they are therapeutic. As much as we may attempt to avoid them, they still confront us. This is when the gaze of the viewer turns to stone and when the soul of the "other" relinquishes hope. Yet there is a glittering, almost hedonistic aspect to these heads, surrounded by little plastic figures, symbolic sports figures, cheerleaders, heroes, and heroines—all plastic fantasies. For example, as I study the work entitled "Amerika #10," I see all its glittering seduction. It has an endearing aspect as well, a face that tells us to deflate in the process of recognizing the "other" as our gaze reverts inward.

Shalom probably would not object to the notion we all have fierce funny faces hidden somewhere within us, faces that are revealed secretly on the dark side of consciousness. This may be the real legacy behind "Amerika." Like democracy in the twenty-first century, we should not assume that our fierce funny faces are not a visual manifestation of divergent conflicts hidden somewhere within our American identity. In this instance, Shalom's "Amerika" becomes a mirror that reflects those conflicts, and that represents the identity we may refuse to see.

Robert C. Morgan is an international art critic, artist, and curator, who holds an M.F.A. and Ph.D. Author of numerous catalogs and books on contemporary art, Professor Morgan lectures regularly at Pratt Institute and the School of Visual Arts in New York.

High Art in the Lower East Side: The Early Days

Sharon Newfeld

For many decades, artistic activity has been and still is part of the landscape of New York's Lower East Side. Modern artists such as Marc Rothko, Jackson Pollock, Sol Lewitt and Brice Marden, to name only a few, lived and worked in the neighborhood well before they realized international success. One may wonder if there ever existed a group of artists that could be distinguished as specifically linked to the Lower East Side. If so, when would such a group have been active and what would characterize its members? Quite often our collective memory ties art groups to New York neighborhoods based on the artists active in their vicinities. Union Square, for example, where many of the Social Realists of the 1930s resided and worked, granted the Fourteen Street School its name. Works by African-American artists of the mid-twentieth century are associated with one another and to their place of production under the designation Harlem Renaissance.

History has already revealed that the Lower East Side is not a name for any regionalist group of artists. However, it should not be ignored that the formation of American art in the beginning of the twentieth century led to the diverse, ethnically colorful and politically charged Lower East Side. Another fact is that American art history of the early twentieth century and American Jewish history of that same period are also closely intertwined and indicate the centrality of the Jewish population of the Lower East Side in that process. Studying the Lower East Side as a starting point for artists could take more than these pages can incorporate. But a short history that would cover atmosphere, major institutions and some significant movers and shakers, would hopefully give a taste of a vast and fascinating period in the history of art and history in general.

The reasons artists become involved in a certain area of the city can be multifold. They could vary from good art training opportunities in the area, to ethnic strings, or simply to the artist's ability to afford living in one area rather than another. The reason can also be a combination of several factors and, in the case of the Lower East Side, should be examined first and foremost in the light of historical context.

The period we are looking back at is one of major demographic change in the U.S., and in New York City in particular. Starting in 1881 until the early 1920s, the Unites States of America took in hundreds of thousands of Jewish immigrants mainly from Russia and East Europe. Greeted by Lady Liberty, they set their foot on American soil either at Castle Garden at The Battery and later, starting in 1892, at the more famous Ellis Island. For them, it was a last stop in their long journey from a life of restrictions—to freedom. But it was also a first stop in their voyage to a much-anticipated yet unknown new land. For many of the newcomers, the Lower East Side was a designated destination, as they had family members or friends awaiting their arrival in the neighborhood's tenements. Others were directed there by immigration officials simply because it was the place they could join their ethnic group, much as Irish immigrants were likely to join Irish communities and Italians to join their own people. Over the course of forty years, among the approximately one million immigrant Jews, about half first settled in the Lower East Side.

The Jewish quarter of the Lower East Side may very well showcase a segregated community that by choice maintained, at the time, or at least tried to maintain, a distinctive identity. The new Eastern European immigrants who settled in the Lower East Side tried to live their lives as a remake of their religious ones in Europe. These "old world" Jews formed a semi-Shtetl with sweatshops, markets, pushcarts and peddlers. They filled the open-air markets with the sights, smells and sounds of their old countries. Most importantly, they brought with them rich cultural life. At the heart of the intellectual activities were Yiddish theatres, literary clubs and education societies. Platforms for exchange of ideas were also created. The "Jewish intelligentsia" was reborn on the Lower East side.

The Jewish community was greeted upon their arrival with the funding and support of a veteran community of German Jews. These "Uptown Jews," who originally resided in the Lower East Side back in the mid 1800s, were affluent and well assimilated. This meant that religious life was trivial for them and Judaism was no more than a faith. They welcomed the newcomers with open arms, generous financial support and a formula for quick integration. They were soon to learn that their Eastern European peers had a different agenda. The mental gaps were the source for conflicts between the two communities, who in a way represented two ends in the acclimation experience in the U.S. Jewish identity is a central issue to keep in mind while following the story of this chapter in Jewish American history. The tendency to ghettoize by Jews who never emancipated was alternately dismissed by secular Jews who were more liable to assimilate. There is no one pattern to generally describe the choices made by the immigrants.

This dual approach is no less a crucial component in the formation of the Jewish artists shaped by this reality. It was part of the vibrant atmosphere and activity in the Lower East Side, which unquestionably set the ground for original artistic innovation. It is a fact that by the 1920s, Jewish artists played an important role in the New York art scene and in future American art at large. It should be noted that these artists stand out not only for their unquestionable talent. In the case of those who grew up in foreign countries, many of them discovered art without being exposed to it in museums or by attending art schools. Those who were lucky to come to New York and grow up in the ghetto still had to rise above a beginning of poverty and alienation in order to follow their passion.

Many of the key American Jewish artists known today, in one way or another, passed by, lived in or absorbed the spirit of the Lower East Side around the turn-of-the-century. Each artist, some are better known than others, bears an element that might be rooted in their affiliation with people or organizations in the neighborhood. Some artists were born or raised in the neighborhood. Others, who did not find themselves in the Lower East Side out of circumstances or fate, "discovered" the neighborhood in other ways. Wandering the streets of downtown New York, some were drawn to the authentic subject matter found on the streets of the Lower East Side. Another great source of attraction were the classes given at the local Educational Alliance Art School, an institution that earned its reputation for art training of highest standards.

The Educational Alliance was a major contribution the German Jews bestowed the people of the Lower East Side. Founded in 1889, the cultural center launched its permanent home in 1891 on 197 East Broadway, in the heart of the Jewish Lower East Side. The German's intention was undoubtedly philanthropic but a quick Americanization process was also on their agenda for the newly arrived, old-fashioned immigrants. However, their initial aggressive approach soon softened as they realized that the cultural adjustment should be gradual rather than hasty. Their goal was redefined to find balance between assimilation and living a community life. Services to the community provided at the Alliance were available in other civic centers in the area as well. The Alliance, however, was the only institution to provide education as well as social and religious services under one roof. This fusion of many life aspects into one microcosm provided the people the assurance they needed in order to adjust, despite language barriers and economic difficulties, and an escape from their daily hardships.

Art classes started rather informally in 1895. Henry McBride (1867-1962), an artist and later an art critic for the *New York Sun,* was the school's first director. Attending a local school enabled the aspiring artists to pursue their dream and do so in a familiar environment, with no commute costs and without feeling embarrassed for being foreigners. Those who worked during the day could take evening classes.

Due to high volume of immigrants and limited resources, art classes were suspended in 1905. In 1917 the Art School reopened—this time on formal basis—led by Abbo Ostrowsky (1889-1975), who ran the school until 1955. Unlike his predecessor, Ostrowsky was, like most of his students at the time, a recent immigrant from Russia. Under Ostrowsky the school was dedicated to providing highly professional training for immigrants and children of immigrants. It encouraged its student to explore their cultural environment, somewhat in the spirit of the Ashcan School. Models in life drawing classes were Jewish quarter types—peddlers, scholars, merchants—invited from the street to the studio. It is important to note that the Art School was open to all. As years passed, the student body consisted of high percentage of non-Jews, mainly Puerto Ricans and African-Americans.

The Alliance provided its young Jewish and non-Jewish artists with a supportive base to freely express their cultural background as well as to find an independent path within the local artistic vocabulary. Openness to newly imported modernist styles—Abstraction, Cubism, Constructivism and more—further reflects on the liberal ambiance in the school. Critics followed curiously after the new "immigrant Art School." Soon into the twentieth century, critics enthusiastically praised the artworks produced by the students as equal—if not better than—to those produced in more reputable schools.

Many generations of this century's greatest artists participated in all sorts of classes—from drawing, painting, etching and sculpture to industrial design at the Educational Alliance Art

School. Numerous later taught at the school. Among them are Philip Evergood (1901-1973), Ben Shahn (1898-1969), Moses Soyer (1899-1974) and his younger brother Isaac Soyer (1902-1981), Jo Davidson (1883-1952), Abraham Walkowitz (1878-1965) and Chaim Gross (1904-1991). Women artists who studied at the school were also equally successful—Lena Gurr (1908-1979), Louis Nevelson (then Berliawsky, 1899-1988), Dina Melicov (1905-1967) and Ella Ostrowsky make only a partial list. Along with other alumni of the Educational Alliance, they comprise a long and distinguished list of leading American artists.

Attending classes at The Educational Alliance, as with any other art school, was not an easy thing for immigrant students. As personal stories exemplify, for those young men and women— coming from poor families, some of them hunger-stricken, going to art school was not the natural path for those young men and women. Many of them had to drop out of high school to help support their families. It is understandable that their parents expected them to learn a trade that would secure their financial future. Art training did not necessarily answer that requirement.

From early on, art events became dominant amid other cultural activities in the Lower East Side. Organizations based or active in the Lower East Side sponsored and hosted exhibitions displaying local artists, and at times curated by them. Among them were the Educational Alliance, the People's Art Guild and the Jewish Art Center. In the years 1892 to 1897, the Educational Alliance, in collaboration with the University Settlement, organized art exhibitions by borrowing artworks from collections and artists. In 1901, another show had the Lower East Side as its subject. The goal behind such exhibitions may be best understood from an announcement for an exhibit at the Madison House in 1913:

An exhibition of works by artists who are in sympathy with, or have found inspiration in, this section of the city. In addition to subjects of general interest, the exhibition will partly represent an artistic representation of picturesque features in which the neighborhood abounds.

Exhibitions like these also advertised to the public the artistic possibilities within the Lower East Side. They suggested taking into consideration the importance of preserving these authentic abilities of the immigrant artists regardless of the Americanization process. In other words, the goal was to let their voice be heard within American idealism rather than dismiss it in favor of local styles and themes.

Worth mentioning is that the Jewish audience was not accustomed to attending art shows since they represented a problematic issue in the Jewish faith. The hostility against plastic arts stemmed from the first Jewish prohibition to create graven images. However, the response to the exhibitions was surprisingly enthusiastic and records show unprecedented attendance. It was as if the conservative inhabitants were gradually opening their minds and training their eye to see art not necessarily of Jewish themes or by traditional media like calligraphy or engraving. Some would credit the Educational Alliance for not only training artists but also guiding the public to appreciate art. Referring to earlier exhibitions, Hutchins Hapgood (1869-1944), author of *The Spirit of the Ghetto*, explained in his book the attention and overvalue given to art created in the Lower East Side by the fact that it represented the "sordidness and the pathos of that part of the city." In a way he also implied that the picturesque quality the neighborhood possessed in his day was fated to disappear. The exhibitions later organized by the Guild or local settlement houses started to feature second-generation artists whose horizons exceeded the Jewish ghetto. Alternately, there were artists who did not identify themselves as Jewish artists to begin with. Jacob Epstein, for example, would not exhibit in occasional all-Jewish exhibitions claiming that artists should not band together in racial groups.

Sculptor (Sir) Jacob Epstein (1880-1959) is one of the most renowned artists to grow up in the Lower East Side. Years before he was knighted by the Queen of England, his country of residency for the majority of his adult years, his childhood neighborhood was the center of his world. Born on Hester Street, in the heart of the Jewish ghetto, Epstein grew up in a family of immigrants originally from Russia and Poland. It is not unlikely that his exposure to the atmosphere of his childhood surroundings was the foundation for his genuinely authentic drawings and later his skillful sculptures. For as long as he could remember, he had his sketchbook with him, in which he recorded with black crayon the people of the Lower East Side. He later wrote in his autobiography that although he took classes at the Art Student League and the Educational Alliance, his major learning was in the densely populated streets and mainly via its unique human subject matter, his utter interest.

Epstein's successful family business enabled his parents to move to a more reputable middle class neighborhood uptown. Epstein remained on Hester Street in a studio overlooking the market. Epstein was involved in the community and in 1898 organized an informal exhibition at the Alliance, presenting local artists. There he was noticed by journalist Hutchins Hapgood. Hapgood has written detailed records of the Lower East Side in a series of articles published in the *Atlantic Monthly* between 1898 and 1902. In 1902 the series was published in *The Spirit of the Ghetto*. Commissioned by Hapgood, all the drawings in the book, of rabbis, writers, socialists, poets and other Lower East Side types, were by Epstein. Hapgood also dedicated a section in his book to Epstein, himself a Lower East Side persona. In 1896, Epstein took sculpture classes at the Art Student League determined to focus on the medium, although he kept drawing for a living. With his four hundred dollar commission from Hapgood, Epstein could travel to Europe, where he met Rodin, Picasso, Brancusi and other avant-garde masters. He finally settled in England in 1905.

Epstein was not the only artist fascinated by the people of the Jewish quarter. Members of the Ashcan school, such as George Bellows (1882-1925), John Sloan (1871-1951), Jerome Myers (1867-1940) and George Luks (1866-1933) were known to roam the streets below 14th Street in search for "exotic" faces to paint. In a similar spirit, members of the movement known to us today as Social Realism also found great interest in the Lower East Side. It was natural for such a group to be active in a politically dynamic area like the Lower East Side. The authentic subject matter they could find there reinforced self-expressions of social narratives. They saw the great importance that art would convey meaning to the viewer and thus resented any form of abstraction. Their art during the 1920s carried social messages, protesting social injustice and aiming at increasing social awareness. Following international events, their activism was also starting to take universal directions. Some of the artists, who painted themes from around the neighborhood, also lived there or took classes at the Educational Alliance.

William Gropper (1897-1977), a cartoonist and a painter, grew up in the Lower East Side. A devoted Social Realist with pro-communist views, his strong social consciousness is intertwined with his life story of poverty, hardships and hard labor at a young age. The injustices he has witnessed entered his canvases with images as powerful as his memories. Gropper's peer, Ben Shahn, is best known as the painter of the Depression's social protest movement. Shahn originally started out as a commercial lithographer (i.e. a practical trade) and later decided to devote himself to painting. In 1911 he enrolled at the Educational Alliance Art School for evening classes and in the following years studied in other New York art schools and in Europe. As a Social Realist, he skillfully combined a cry for universal equality with the written word, which fascinated him—especially the Hebrew alphabet. His expressionist paintings advocating human rights protested specific events such as the trial of anarchists Sacco and Vanzetti. Later in his career he moved from social protests to psychological explorations. In the 1950s, he engaged traditional Jewish themes.

Three brothers of the Soyer family became artists. The Soyer household was highly intellectual, providing their children with good education and cultural enrichment. Despite teaching his children about old masters and taking them to Galleries in Moscow, Abraham Soyer was less than thrilled when his sons, twins Raphael (1899-1987) and Moses and younger Isaac turned to art practice. He saw in art a profession that might destine them to live as outsiders. But the Soyers and many others in their generation simply *had* to become artists. Raphael enrolled at Cooper Union, the League and the National Academy. Yet he lived and spent much time on lower Second Avenue. There he met artists and writers and looked for inspiration on the streets. After 1929, all his studios were around the Lower East side. Moses Soyer chose to study at the Alliance, possibly to allow Raphael and himself to explore their similar interests separately. They both, as well as their younger brother, painted in a realist style, and painted their close environment of family and friends. No less, all Soyer brothers identified with the political left and were active members in several organizations. They were not involved in Jewish organizations as they advocated minimizing racial and religious differences. Their views were expressed in writing as well as on canvas and their paintings are characterized by chronicling oppressed classes and minority groups.

At the Alliance, Moses Soyer befriended Philip Evergood, a highly trained painter who studied in the best schools in Europe and New York. Nonetheless his interest in human "types" brought him to the Lower East Side and to the Educational Alliance, where he studied in 1924. Born in New York in 1901 to a Jewish father and non-Jewish mother, Evergood was not raised on the Jewish faith. More than being interested in the Jewish community, he shared with Soyer an interest painting contemporary working class life. Like many other fellows in the movement, Evergood has also written in socialist publications to raise social consciousness and co-founded *Reality*, where he published views by many of his colleagues like Shahn, Edward Hopper and Soyer.

Socialist and communist philosophy was allegedly likely to materialize in the Lower East Side considering the background of its habitants. Current local and international events such as the rise of Fascism and Nazism in Europe also reinforced such views. In the US it was the onset of the economic Depression. Artists such as Gropper, Shahn, the Soyers, Marc Rothko and others, despite their different styles and subject matter, shared similar backgrounds as immigrants or children of immigrants. As such, they identified and sympathized with minorities and the underprivileged. Life in the Lower East Side also emphasized the concern with the human experience. Indeed, a great deal of art produced in or inspired by the Lower East Side entailed social commentary of some sort.

Nearly concurrent to the emergence of the Social Realist movement, a new direction in the local art scene was established, based on imported modernist styles from Europe. Members of the founding group included immigrants and first-generation American Jews, many of whom were natives or products of the Lower East Side.

It is interesting how artists of European origin, who turned their backs on Europe, returned to European cities for inspiration. After arriving in the US with no intention to go back, they still recognized that artistic breakthroughs were not happening in the US—at least not yet. At the time, modernists, whether Jewish or not, were considered outsiders. It is not surprising, then, that contemporary American artists, who carried out the cry for national spirit, were reluctant to acknowledge the right for immigrant artists to be considered American. Especially so with the Jews, who not only lacked American roots but also came to the US to escape persecutions and were not motivated by romantic ideals.

Modernist artists started to travel to Europe in the first decade of the twentieth century. Starting in 1922, the Educational Alliance sponsored artists with travel grants. Among the early travelers was Max Weber (1881-1961), who traveled to Europe in 1905 followed by his close friend, Abraham Walkowitz, in 1906. They not only encountered some of the most influential avant-garde artists of the era, but, on a personal level, they celebrated their freedom to paint what and as they wished. One may rationalize it as an extreme reaction to their past experience of oppression. This resulted in a burst of expression with openness to styles as radical as Fauve, Cubism and Futurism. Upon their return to the US, they introduced the new styles and thus encouraged a major outpour of creativity, later to be considered one of the most inspirational periods ever.

Walkowitz, who came to the US from Russia at age eight, grew up on Essex Street. Before leaving to Europe he taught at the Alliance. He returned to New York in 1907 and was considered among the first American modernists. Since no gallery showed any interest in his work, he arranged his painting to be hung at Julius Haas' shop on Madison Avenue in 1908. The show, which created quite a stir, was the first one-man show for an American modernist in New York. Further south on Fifth Avenue, Alfred Stieglitz's gallery "291" was also a partner to introducing New Yorkers to European modernism. Walkowitz was a member in Stieglitz's inner circle and had a one-man show at his gallery in 1912. He also participated in the legendary Armory show in 1913 along with other Lower East Side fellows such as William Zorach (1887-1966) and Bernard Gussow (1881-1957).

Lower East Side scenes were entwined into Walkowitz's stylistically and compositionally pioneering paintings. He depicted market scenes that were praised for their sincerity. He was faithful to his abstract style and, as in all his work, he accentuated the subjective in art. His body of work prior to the 1920s is considered his most significant. Walkowitz was also among the founding members of The Jewish Art Center, a club for writers and artists that during the 1920s was dedicated to promoting Jewish secular culture. Among the artists that granted an exhibition through the center were William Gropper, Moses Soyer and Ben Shahn. By the 1940s, Walkowitz started to lose his eyesight.

Max Weber was also one of the prominent modernists. He has lived in Paris and absorbed Cubism, Futurism and Fauvism to later fuse in his painted experimentations. His Cubo-Futurist abstractions repeatedly portray Jewish people and scenes. Weber represents an example for a product of the ultra-orthodox Jewish immigrant community, who chose a different lifestyle yet remained connected to his roots. Arriving in the US from Bialystok, Poland, at the age of ten and settling in Williamsburg, Brooklyn, the Weber family was deeply rooted in the Jewish faith. Unpredictably, his parents did not resent his desire to go to Pratt Institute to study art. Later, when Weber was no longer as observant, his childhood imagery from the temple, especially motifs from Jewish ceremonial artifacts, were still part of his visual language. As rumors came from Europe regarding the fate of the Jews under the Nazi regime, Weber and others were troubled by the question of whether it could happen in the US. Weber was mainly examining contemporary Jewish life from a nostalgic point of view rather than a religious perceptive. Gropper, alternately, created highly political expressions, while others, like members of the Ten, which will be discussed later in this essay, chose to keep their art devoid of direct political implications.

A third road was soon to be taken by Jewish American artists—along with non-Jewish artists— who formulated an artistic style regarded as essentially American. This group, soon later called the Abstract Expressionists, or the New York School, was the first movement whose leaders were dominantly immigrants and sons of immigrants. Jewish artists Marc Rothko, Adolph Gottlieb and Barnett Newman played a crucial role in its conception. They were inspired by the same historical events that motivated the Social Realist movement, yet redirected their expressions to personal rather than political means.

A distinct group within that tendency was the Ten, which was founded in 1935 and dissolved by 1939. This independent group was comprised of nine permanent artist members and one guest artist for each show. The core group included Ben-Zion (1897-1987), Ilya Bolotowsky (1907-1981), Adolph Gottlieb (1903-1974), Louis Harris, Jack Kufeld (1907-1990), Marc Rothko (1903-1970), Louis Schanker (1903-1981), Joseph Solman (b. 1909) and Naum Tschacbasov (1899-1984). Coincidentally, all founding members of the Ten were Jewish. This fact used to be taken for granted because by then, Jewish Artists were considered mainstream in American art. Nonetheless, in retrospect, scholars have speculated about their cultural upbringing, which may have had to do with their progressive theoretical thinking and mutual aesthetic ideology. Most members identified with the expressionist tradition. One of their foremost principles was the elimination of any political use in art, a complete opposite view from the Social Realists. This is not to say that they were not politically active. In fact, all of the Ten were members of the Artists' Union and the Artists' Congress, both instigated by the Communist party. Their focus was on artistic issues, mainly on exploring the picture plane and expressing complex thoughts in a simple way. In their credo they wrote: "we wish to re-assert the picture plane. We are for the flat forms because they destroy illusion and reveal truth." Many Ten members found subject matter in the Lower East Side similarly to Social Realists, yet scenes by the former group did not include figures and denied social or political connotations.

Russian-born Marc Rothko is best known for his 'altar-like' color-field geometric abstractions. His starting point as an immigrant in the US was in Oregon, far from his New York Colleagues. He studied at Yale but left after two years to travel around the US. After settling in New York in 1925, he decided to commit himself to art and took classes at the League with Max Weber. During the Depression, Rothko was employed by the WPA (Works Progress Administration) project as a muralist. His later tendency to paint large-scale canvases may be attributed to that period. By then Rothko has already channeled his art toward a spiritual realm. His renditions of religion-related symbols, however, are universal and don't necessarily refer to Judaism. When Rothko lived and painted in his studio on the Lower East Side, however, he was engaged with Jewish themes on occasion. It has been asserted that Rothko is very much a New York artist—an artist affected by the city and life around him—and these paintings reflect on that period in his life. Quoting art historian Werner Haftmann, Matthew Baigell indicates a Jewish factor even in Rothko's late style. He compares the monochromatic color blotches to draperies that cover the ark in a synagogue. This view may be questionable, considering Rothko's ambivalence toward Jewish mysticism. As a founding member of the Ten he called for separation of art and poli-tics—yet Rothko was involved in some radical organizations, mainly for promoting artists' rights.

Rothko's friend and fellow Ten co-founding member, Adolph Gottlieb, was a New Yorker from uptown Manhattan. He got his training at the League, Cooper Union, Parsons and in Europe as well as the Educational Alliance. He was mainly influenced by the Ashcan School at the begin-ning of his career. His experimentation in modernism began following a trip to Europe, where he was exposed to avant-garde styles such as German Expressionism. This trip also accentuated his resentment of American scene paintings. Gottlieb studied at the Alliance in the late 1920s and it is likely that it was the Lower East Side's bohemian appeal that attracted him to the neigh-borhood. Yet he was not engaged with the Jewish community. Although born Jewish and at times willing to accept commissions from synagogues, Gottlieb is an example for an assimilated American Jew. He viewed art as international, crossing all ethnic and religious boundaries. He was active in art organizations and unions without Jewish affiliation.

Barnett Newman (1905-1970), a teacher at the Educational Alliance, was in the social circle of Rothko, Gottlieb and other members of The Ten. Executing highly abstract color-field paintings, Newman was devoted to search the absolute. Thus, he avoided representational images not because of the religious prohibition but because he believed that the absolute cannot be ren-dered by an image. Newman was not a religious man but was fascinated by Jewish mysticism. His art is far from being removed from religious connotations. The mere occupation with the absolute corresponds to the Jewish imageless, abstract God. His titles also carry sublime asso-ciations and relate some ritualistic or biblical terms (*Voice of Fire, Abraham, The Blessing*.)

Throughout this historical chapter surfaces the dilemma between assimilating and maintaining one's own Jewish identity. This crossroad encountered by so many was crucial in reconciling a duality that for some could mean a life of contradictions. Each had a choice to make regarding what would best describe their identity—whether Jewish, East European, American or all of the above. It seemed that a new kind of identity was forming.

The artists among the immigrants in many cases used their art as a vehicle to express this unset-tled position. As described above, many adopted local styles and joined local art movements. Others chose more independent paths. What can be determined is that either way, no substan-tial group has come together to initiate an emergence or revival of Jewish art. Thus, the predic-tion of Hatchins Hapgood that a nationalist Jewish art is possible to emerge at the Lower East

Side evidently did not realize. Several reasons come to mind: First, the Jewish community did not nourish Jewish Art as much as it did Jewish literature and theatre. Second, artists who occasionally handled Jewish themes in their art did not form a distinguished inclination that can be called Jewish or National Art. They were aware of their heritage but it did not define their artistic identity. Third, the majority of the artists, including those who grew up in observant and even Hasidic households, later abandoned their religious ties and became secular in orientation. At least with the artists, it seems that the urge to fit in had the upper hand.

The tendency to withdraw from religious life only further shook the Jewish community that was still adapting to living in the US and threatened the unity that was for generations preserved by religion. However, Secular groups still attempted to preserve their Jewish identity as an ethnic unit. At any rate, the question of Jewish Art was raised in close conjunction with other identity complexities. It coincided with a broader debate about nationalism and art that was occupying America. As a result of the increasing American nationalist spirit, American artists were expected to adopt styles conforming to American Scene Paintings. For Jewish artists, this dictation was to further complicate pre-existing conflicts that had to do with the unsettled status of Judaism and art. Naturally, all these issues were brought to the table by Jewish organizations operating in the Lower East Side. Years later, critic Harold Rosenberg also discussed this matter in a notable symposium at the Jewish Museum in 1962.

Several factors played a role in alienating Jewish artists from their roots and rushed their Americanization process. One somewhat straightforward way to dissolve into the mainstream was to modify one's name. Marc Rothko, for example, was actually born Marcus Rothkowitz. It may as well be that the intention was simply to make the name more pronounceable. New chosen names may imply an attempt to put the past behind by accepting new identities, but it is not necessarily so. There are views regarding artists who embraced modernism as more apt to break free from their past and their religious leaning. But there is also a simpler explanation for this phenomenon. The first generation of artists that was united around the community, the synagogue or Jewish organization, was succeeded by a generation that was liberating itself from these ties. They were less connected to their Jewish heritage and became part of the American culture. As they felt more accepted they were more willingly Americanized. Their work, in turn, became gradually more rooted in the history of American art. In dealing with national and global events, they were on the American front.

Pressing national events have surely influenced some artists to aim their efforts toward a united American society. In the 1920s and 1930s the great economic Depression did not discriminate between Jews and non-Jews. All people found themselves united in the struggle to survive an era of unemployment and desperation. The central issue was no longer about ethnicity but about classes. For that matter, they were all American. The feelings expressed in art were of similar nature. It was an opportunity for them to mingle in the mainstream and take part in a national effort outside their minority group. Many of them joined left-wing organizations such as the John Reed club (founded 1929), The Artists Union (founded 1933) and The American Artist Congress (founded 1936).

In the following decades, as the New York art scene advanced toward abstraction, especially during the heydey of formalist movements, the emphasis was on subjectivity and individuality.

More than ever before, the idea of distinct Jewish identity in art was far from becoming evident. To (Jewish) critics Clement Greenberg and Harold Rosenberg, an artist's religion did not matter. In Rosenberg's words, assimilated Jews express themselves in the visual arts as individuals, not as Jews. Moreover, since the making of graven images is forbidden by Jewish law, and given the lack of a Jewish nation to stand at the basis of Jewish art, the term was in itself problematic. Like other minorities, Jews had no single community or geographical location, and thus, there was no established narrative to which "Jewish art history" could fit.

Despite being for a long period a dense and poor neighborhood, or maybe owing to that, the Lower East Side has been one of the most inspirational in art history. It was probably not for the crowded tenements and sweatshops but for the people who inhabited the neighborhood, coinciding with a seminal period in history, and the atmosphere it all created. Artists, native and immigrants, Jewish and non-Jewish, were drawn to the intense human experience. A great deal of that had to do with the immigrant culture and blend of mentalities. Jewish artists who were magnetized to the neighborhood could have potentially been imprisoned in the provincial, old-fashioned community. But on the contrary—artists who developed in the Lower East Side were nourished by it to later thrive outside the borders of the ghetto. In the Lower East Side they were compelled to deal with questions that shaped the type of person and the kind of artist they turned to be. They also had to define how strongly they felt about being Jewish. It turns out that the time span briefly surveyed here demonstrates a transition from a strongly congregated first generation to more liberal minded and assimilated generations to follow.

There are artists who are synonymous with the spirit of the Lower East Side to this day, while some of the legendary artists of the twentieth century left no trace behind the neighborhood. Either way, it is their experience of the Lower East Side that left a trace in their work. Indeed, much creativity was born on the Lower East Side and many schools of thought were consumed there. We will never know whether these artists would have grown essentially different had they not spend their formative years in the neighborhood during that crucial time. As Moses Soyer recalled in a catalog for a retrospective exhibition of Educational Alliance alumni: "We differed in all things. Only one thing united us—the consuming desire to become artists."

References

Joyce Mendelsohn,. *The Lower East Side: Remembered and Revisited.* New York: Lower East Side Press, 2001, 9.

Irving Howe. "Americanizing the Greenhorns" in: *Painting a Place in America*, Norman Kleeblatt (ed.) New York: Jewish Museum, 1991.

The Educational Alliance was founded in the spirit of the Settlement House Movement. The movement's theory was to settle students in slum areas to live and work alongside local people. Initially conceived in England, the idea spread to the United States and later to other countries.

In 1905, the revolution in Russia triggered a new wave of pogroms. This led to massive immigration. The number of immigrants arriving in the US that year was close to 100,000. The next big wave occurred as a result of Hitler's growing power in 1933-4. Only a few years before, immigrants were reluctant to relocate to the Depression stricken US.

Alfred Warner. "Ghetto Graduates", *The American Art Journal*, Vol. 5 no. 2 (November 1973): 77.

Henry Moscowitz. "The East Side in Oil and Crayon," *The Survey* 28 (May 11, 1912), 273.

Moses Rischin. *The Promised City: New York Jews 1870-1914*, 1962, 102.

Hutchins Hapgood, *The Spirit of the Ghetto*, 265.

Jewish artists were hanging around the same social circles and they were likely to be members in the same organizations. It may explain to a great extent that fact that groups dominated by Jewish artists conceived ideas and established schools of thought.

In an essay about the Jewish artists in New York by Matthew Baigell, included in the exhibition catalog, *Painting a Place in America*, the author discusses how Jews were linked to Modernism in Europe during the period Modernism was considered a threat. In the US, however, Modernism was not necessarily associated with Jews. See: Baigell Matthew, "From Hester Street to Fifty Seventh Street: Jewish American Artists in New York. In: Kleeblatt, *Painting a Place in America*, pp. 28-71.

A similar phenomenon occurred in the 1930s and 1940s. Artists arrived in the US escaping the Nazi regime, brought with them the latest artistic innovations from Europe. Furthermore, many of them were well-trained artists and did not require any educational investment. They immediately used the American platform to spread the new styles in America. See McCabe, Cynthia Jaffee. The Golden Door: Artists Immigrants of America 1876-1976, Washington DC: Smithsonian Institution, 1976, 20.

Among the critical attention the exhibition has drawn, some negative voices were raised against the immigrant artists. Critic Thomas Craven blamed them for impairing the American aristocracy by bringing foreign styles that are lacking method and perspective. The Golden Door, 28.

As political affairs in Europe further complicated, the weight that Paris had as an international art center began to shift to New York. When Paris was paralyzed during the years of WWI, it was American art that had its chance to provide an alternative. It was then that "real" American Art was starting to develop.

Diane Weldman, *Mark Rothko in New York*, New York, Guggenheim Museum of Art, 1994, 12. Baigell, 67.

The Golden Door, Ibid.

Some found Newman's implication by presenting the artists as a creator, similar to god, problematic and even unacceptable.

A partial list of Lower East Side artists who engaged in Jewish subjects would include William

Auerbach-Levy (etching instructor at the Alliance), Abraham Walkowitz, Max Weber, Louis Lozowick (researched the theme of the Jew in Art), Elias Newman (described in the Alliance exhibition catalog from 1940 as a "painter of Palestinian scenes).

Kampf, Avram. *The Jewish Experience in the Art of the Twentieth Century*, Mass.: Bergin & Garvey Publishers, 1984, 50.

Margaret Olin, "C[lement] Hardesh [Greenberg] and Company" in *Too Jewish? Challenging Traditional Identities,* Norman L. Kleeblatt (ed.), 40.

Sharon Newfeld *is an art historian, specializing in modern American art and a fine art appraiser. Educated in New York City's Hunter College and New York University, Sharon was trained at prominent galleries and museums. While living in New York, she wrote an art column for an Israeli newspaper. Sharon currently lives in Israel where she works as a specialist at an auction house.*

June Leaf, Hands at War

Jerome Poynton

Hands at war.

Hands to tear paintings apart and hands to sew paintings back together. Hands to bend metal and hands to shear tin into delicate figures. Hands to make tiny springs that add life to sculpture. Hands to dismantle an antique sewing machine and build a breathing head where a machine once stood.

Hands.

Hands to draw with and hands to be splashed upon with oil, gas and paint—seemingly any chemical necessary—only to be washed but never washed clean of the will to create that which seemingly doesn't want to be created. Fighting with tools, hand tools. Fighting with broken nails—on fingers and other nails—hammered into walls made of brick.

Hands that are not delicate but hands that make delicate work.
June Leaf's hands.

There is a history there. Her art has been exhibited worldwide and represented in New York for several decades by Edward Thorpe Gallery. June Leaf's paintings and sculpture have been— and will continue to be—written about and appreciated by academics and curators who have worldly art knowledge fashioned while employed at museums and universities.

For me, it is her hands—bred in Chicago, trained in Paris, activated on the Lower East Side.
June Leaf fights with her paintings and sculptures. Some good ones don't survive.
The ones that do are a triumph.
They beat her to submission.
She can fight them no longer. They have won.

Jerome Poynton, a former Men's Gymnastics Coach from the University of Michigan, worked with New York painters, film makers, writers, photographers and art collectors for a quarter of a century. He now spends most of his time in Italy talking with farmers and appliance salesmen.

On Steven Marcus

B.J. De Guzman

The Lower East Side of New York City has been a constant setting in the personal and artistic career of Steve Marcus. Having the LES in his soul, he is an advocate and true representative of the community. Steve has successfully translated the dynamic cultures, social movements, and general fervor of the neighborhood into his artwork and lifestyle, even learning to speak Spanish in the street. Many New York artists have displayed the gift of representing their environments effortlessly, regardless of the medium, and Steve Marcus is no different. He continues to use his paintings, graphic design, and cartoons to tell story after story inspired or about his heritage and urban home in the LES. Steve's art is both gritty and vibrant, humorous and introspective. It is an engaging combination of aesthetics and NYC reality that has led to many achievements in the mainstream and underground.

Steve Marcus' career officially started in 1989 when he was paid 25 dollars at the age of 19 to draw a small 1-panel cartoon for Al Goldstein's infamous publication, *Screw Magazine*. The following year he became the assistant art director, a tenure he describes as "memorable and unspeakable."

Steve's artistry was developed very early as a child growing up. His parents encouraged him to cultivate his talent and took him to art classes at the YMCA and to artists who taught art classes out of their homes. It was his main after-school activity outside of playing little league for one pathetic year as the deep right fielder. It was a time in Steve's life when bialys and bagels were hot out of the oven; pickles were still available in the barrel; family celebrations were held at the now-closed Second Avenue deli. He attended Hebrew school — after public school in which he was one of the only Jews — to prepare for his bar mitzvah; and his family bought him a bar mitzvah set on Essex Street where Judaic shops, now quickly disappearing, once lined the block.

Those simpler times soon gave way to adolescence as Steve, now a man after having had his bar mitzvah, ventured out into the world. He found himself religiously going to the Sunday Hardcore Matinees at CBGB's in the early '80s. The punk rock scene at CBGB's became a weekly spot to meet with other politically aware, socially conscious peers who were equally angry about the state of affairs in the nation. Steve finally found a place where people shared his strong beliefs about social issues, including class, poverty, education and the police state. Punk rock and his association with other leftist or radical movements led to illustration work with the

Guardian and *World War III Illustrated*. He remembers a *Guardian* editor, and homesteader in the Lower East Side, asking if he wanted the fee for his illustration tallied up quarterly or if he wanted to dedicate his art to the struggle. He chose the former so he could begin his path as a living, working artist, understanding he stood a better chance of helping others if he had food in his stomach. Still, he never lost his will to use and contribute his artwork to comment on social injustice, "My people have been involved in the Civil Rights movement, the anarchist movement, the socialist movement and the counter culture. … I feel like I continue the struggle for survival for us all as a soldier in the culture war. Instead of embracing values of the current system, I produce artwork without corporate sponsorship so that I can function in society without sacrificing my artistic integrity."

In Steve's continual development as an artist, he found that revolution and socialization could go hand in hand. While he frequented punk rock and hip-hop shows, he also discovered the after-hours clubs of the late '80s and early '90s. Clubs such as Save the Robots (on Ave. B between 2nd and 3rd) and Impala (on 1st St. between 1st and 2nd Ave.), run by characters with names like Frankie Splits, gave Steve the opportunity to connect with other crowds in the LES, living with the highest of the high and the lowest of the low, and experiencing a downtown party scene before it became corporate. Bags of weed and cocaine were sold out of bodegas and other spots amongst junkies, whores, and stick-up kids. He crept through the streets after dark, surviving the danger that lurked around every corner, danger that sadly took the life of his best friend in 1994.

Steve then moved into a storefront on Elizabeth St. between Prince and Houston. Now he was not only a living artist, but also an artist open to the entire community. Kids playing stickball, old hippies, Mafioso, artists, Latino, Italian and Chinese families, who he describes as "the most beautiful community I ever lived with," became Steve's audience and inspiration. He worked consistently and developed friendships and community bonds the city way, with open fire hydrants, block parties and by always being available to help out and be a good neighbor.

From his storefront, Steve became a regular cartoon contributor to *Stress Magazine*, creating *The People's Comic* and *B-Baby* comic strips, signing his name, The Reverend Steve Marcus. He became known just as The Reverend during those years for giving sermons and lectures out of his storefront to enlighten people to the current plight of the city. During *Stress*'s existence (1995-2000), the magazine became known as an advocate for prisoner's rights, political prisoners, and journalists of color, and a fighter against police brutality. Above all, the magazine gave the hip-hop movement an outlet for firsthand experiences by employing non-traditional writers and participants of the culture. In 1992, Steve created his first animations for MTV. They were very crude shorts of pop culture gags that ran for one year in Asia, Europe and the United States in constant rotation. A year later he was given the award for The Best of Political Comics because of his strip in *World War III Confrontational Comics*. In 1994 he was awarded the American Illustration Award, and published in its well-respected annual.

More visible than ever, Steve's storefront on Elizabeth gave him the chance to help younger artists coming up and striving for the same lifestyle, "I know a lot of young artists in my community. Some are privileged, going to private art colleges, and others are going to school while living in the projects and working two jobs. When I share my experiences with them, I keep it real and raw on the failures as well as the successes. I let them know they have to stay focused on their goals and be disciplined to make it."

That focus and discipline has led to various achievements over the years including: *Re-Mastered* – a coffee table book of 55 contemporary artists from around the world (Dec 2006) and participation in the group show to celebrate its release at Art Basel in Miami, *Flash Frames, The Best of Internet Animation* – a coffee table book and DVD (2002), International Adobe After Effect Animation Competition - Adobe Sample Reel (2001) which was given with every Mac sold that year, The Red Hot Chili Peppers' Californication Tour's projection animations - seen at The MTV Music Awards at Radio City Music Hall, and *Creative Review Monitor*'s Top Ten ad campaigns 2001.

Steve's latest project is a culmination of all his cartoon and animation work throughout the years. Many of the urban references are drawn from his life experiences, especially the cherished storefront studio days in the LES. *Three Thug Mice* is an animated cartoon series that follows the misadventures of three mice while shedding light on a tough but energetic period in the city that some people want to forget, and others miss dearly. It is an alternate Lower East Side universe filled with pig cops, homeless pigeons, cockroach gangsters and rodent thugs. It pays homage to the thousands of stories that give the Lower East Side its pulse. After all the different types of artwork Steve has created to push the boundaries of society and make a living, this project is the perfect opportunity to utilize all of the skills Steve has developed. He added, "The first cartoons [ever drawn] were political and published in *Puck Magazine* over a 100 years ago. They commented on the issues at a time when a lot of people understood issues through pictures, humor, and satire. I try to carry that torch."

It's hard to imagine that Steve Marcus could be anywhere but the Lower East Side. When he throws the key to the front door of his rent stabilized apartment out of the window, because the building's so old, it still doesn't have doorbells, it's hard to imagine the Lower East Side without Steve Marcus. His personality and artwork exude the hardship, survival, and tenacity of this small but highly influential neighborhood in New York City.

"I was born with this natural inclination or ability to be an artist but I believe artists can be a critical lens of our society and would like to believe that I have and will continue to be a critic of our society and system through my artwork and the way I live my life. I guess I would say that born artists are born rebels."

B.J. De Guzman *graduated from New York University with a concentration in Creative Writing. He has written for magazines such as* Complex, Vibe, *and* The Source. *He currently resides in Kingston, Jamaica, and is the Associate Creative Director of advertising agency Prism Communications.*

Check more of Steve Marcus' artwork at www.smarcus.com or www.threethugmice.com

From *The Masses* to *World War 3 Illustrated*: New York art as political street commentary; or, Seth Tobocman and the Lower East Side

Paul Buhle

My mother worked at the Henry Street Settlement House during the second half of the 1930s, and I am certain that it was the happiest time in her often troubled life. She was one of many thousands of rebel souls, reformers and radicals, who either grew up in New York or came to New York and felt instantly at home in the densely packed neighborhoods, full of vibrant life as well as misery. And as historically important as any neighborhood in New York or North America, for that matter: the neighborhood has been pronounced dead every few generations, uninhabitable by decent human beings, and yet a flash point of social struggles and visions of a better world.

The role of art, photography to painting, humor to expose, in all this, is a subject that has already filled good volumes and is destined to fill many more. My purpose here is to arrive at one artist, his political-cultural milieu, and to trace backward just enough to make sense of a continuing, vital tradition that, as comic art, largely remains to be adequately explored and appreciated.

The irony is several-fold. Comics have, arguably, come of age at last. Beloved for a century and a generalized New Yorkishness with the vibrant neighborhood—the printing district was a subway stop away—they are now, at once, simultaneously the subject of unthinkable adaptation and exploitation through mega-million dollar animated films based on comics characters; and hosted in museum exhibits as "masters," something equally unimaginable only a few decades ago. Amid this commercial and art-world excitement, other public qualities of comics as art, their multiple connections with the most vital moments of radical art in the US, barely gain credence. Does anyone remember that the *New Yorker*-style cartoon began in *The Masses* magazine, suppressed for antiwar art a decade before the world's most prestigious magazine began? Has anyone looked with particular care at the crossovers between socially critical posters, murals, graffiti and comics from the 1970s onward? We can only make a small beginning here, but we can at least identify and analyze the works of the artist most connected. He is Seth Tobocman.

Born in Texas in 1958, but grew up in Cleveland among a Jewish family that had known radicals in past generations but not among his parents, he was a boyhood comics lover. The familiar story is that young Seth and his close friend Peter Kuper wanted to publish a zine, met Harvey Pekar and through him R. Crumb, thus gaining the self-confidence (and the art originals) to launch a fanzine that led to... *World War 3 Illustrated*, launched in 1979 and now approaching its thirtieth anniversary as the radical comic magazine, more or less annual, arguably the most interesting political comics magazine printed on the planet.

The familiar story is bit off, as it turns out. Seth and Peter were already publishing a 'zine' (Gary Dumm, eventually to become a major artist for Pekar, was one of the zine's artists) when they met Pekar and Crumb, but these are details. The crucial middle term in the equation is a shift from Cleveland to New York's Lower East Side, at a crucial moment of artistic as well as social-political shift. Tobocman's work is part of a comic art phase that belongs to the last quarter of the twentieth century, a phase unique unto itself, but distinctly related to some key predecessors, politically and artistically. The precise particulars of technique, background and trajectory of the succession of artists will be covered lightly here, by way of a few examples. But the central issues of a comic art form emerging full-blown, no longer regarded as a juvenile form to be escaped by the artist at the first opportunity (usually for commercial advertising work), are crucial. An art was invented just about a century ago and in many ways, it has proved more lasting, certainly more politically vital, than nearly all its predecessors. It was always, in form as well as intentionality, more radical: it sought to be part of the new world that it was creating.

It would be easy, and not entirely mistaken, to begin our story chronologically at the Tompkins Square eruption of 1873. That is, to the "police riot" of head-thumping amid the worst Depression to that date, a move to end the mobilization of the city's unemployed and especially of German radicals with Irish working (or non-working) people, themselves led by one of Marx's key American devotees (later, founder of the Carpenters' Union and a staunch labor conservative). The moment produced a somewhat significant art, that is, newspaper sketches of half-human creatures threatening law and order. It would make sense to fast-forward to the 1890s because the streets of the Lower East Side were full of socialists and anarchists, and the marching orders of the fledgling unions were sometimes pronounced in rhymed tones: the poets, from the pages of the Yiddish press and from the rallies large and small, not to mention impromptu street gatherings, imploring workers to hold out a little longer, accept a little more misery until victory could be won. The artist, the word-artist, was already a factor on the side of justice. Thomas Nast alone had proved it, not always, by any means, on the side of the oppressed.

The visual artist is about to appear, but by roundabout means tied to the contemporary popular culture rather than arising out of radical circles. The burgeoning daily newspapers, meeting a new public, were discovering the sights and sounds of the great city. The artists who arose here and came to identify with labor causes while creating an art about the masses are the real precursors of the *World War 3* milieu, and of Tobocman himself. We are soon to hear more from them.

The dynamism and the radicalism of Big City art—radicalism of style and of message—is a familiar subject, almost too familiar in some ways. Many essays and several fine books have been devoted to the Ash Can Art of the 1910s, some of the best of it reappearing in *The Masses* magazine (1911-17), other books on the graphic realism of the 1920s-40s, much of it influenced by a very different political movement on the Left, and occasionally we find a continuation of this sweep concerned with the murals movement peaking during the 1970s-80s. Too rarely has the subject connected with comic art, and in a larger sense with the mostly unseen relations between radical high and low art throughout.

Rebecca Zurier, the finest scholar of the Ash Can artists and their sources of influence, has commented in her definitive study of the subject that "style," once the gospel of art history but recently neglected for the social history of art, richly deserves a return engagement for Manhattan and vicinity of the early twentieth century.[126] Against the impulse of the contemporary European artists like Manet and Degas who looked at the emerging society with anxiety and a sense of loss, US counterparts saw themselves instead surrounded by exciting developments, not only modern art but the labor movement, women's rights, and even the look of advertising, particularly of the street variety. (Hugo Gellert, the last survivor among the *Masses* artists, told me in the early 1980s that after he won a scholarship to study in Paris, he was more excited by the Michelen billboards than by the paintings in the Lourve.) The street, after all, was the locus of interest but also the chief locus of hope, the reconstituted village where people of every kind could gather, understand themselves in relation with others, and begin to construct the communities of a new world. Ultimately, in their own styles, they ran into the limits of artistic identification with the subject, even knowledge of what the artist's eyes could tell him about the subject. En route, they discovered more than anyone could have imagined before, and much that seemed to be lost afterward.

All inspiration for Ash Can, in deeply personal terms, goes back to Robert Henri, teacher and painter who gathered around him in 1890s Philadelphia a circle of the future greats. They shared his enthusiasm for moving beyond the mannered genre painters like Winslow Homer whose work, even seeking to capture the life around them, was (in John Sloan's words) "too tight and finished." They would see the world with different eyes and brushes. Henri's move to Manhattan in 1900 placed him centrally, and as Whitman (his favorite poet) might have ordered, the painter could capture the beauty of the commonplace much as if he were a newspaper reporter. Radical street artists thereafter could rightly claim Whitman's heritage as part of their New York.

The connection is critical twice over because, in fact, the Ash Can painters also made their living, early on, working for the daily press, they by supplying sketches: a form of visual reporting then new and fresh, markedly different from disasters or famous personalities in the steel engravings of the magazine era passing, but likewise different from the comic art emerging in the back pages of the advanced tabloids. Their famed leap into the spotlight of modern art was the 1908 show, Eight American Painters, well publicized and patronized (Gertrude Vanderbilt Whitney bought four paintings on the spot for her collection).

Their boosters were not, however, among the prestigious magazines (*The Nation* ignored them) or noted reviewers for the press. Their detractors would naturally attack their radicalism, in later years, but even as their appearance in *The Masses* created a following, cynical art world critics made it clear that Ash Can artists were insufficiently "modern," more a case of traditionalists smuggling modern subjects into their projects. The Armory Show of 1913, highlighting the contemporary art of Cubism (a *Masses* sight-gag envisioned a whole world of cubist objects) and the onset of Abstraction generally, placed an artistic avant-garde of a certain kind against Ash Can.

This distinction is a crucial one because upon it rests the burden of radical art for the rest of the century and beyond. "Figuration," the depiction of a recognizable human figure, would return to bedevil the New York style of Abstract Expressionism in particular at the end of the 1960s, mixing feminist (or women's) art hitherto unrecognized, with Pop Art, social satire in the mixed media style of Larry Rivers, and most definitely Underground Comix. Deep in their Cold War stance, Clement Greenberg's circle of critics raged at their loss of control in all directions to the peaceniks, the counterculture and the newer phases of art. But we are getting ahead of our story.

According to Zurier, even a good leftwinger like American Cubist painter Max Weber had something very un-Ash Can in mind, a state of mind rather than a symmetrical composition, shocking in form as the painting of a prostitute was shocking in content.[127] Weber would be more typical of a 1920s-30s where "political" art had become pretty much didactic, no less so for a WPA mural than a drawing in a Communist magazine, and for much the same reasons. And we are getting ahead of our story again.

What interests us now is the looming coincidence of *The Masses* and its Ash Can contributors to the attachments of the best contemporary comic artists in the vastly circulated daily English language press. These artists, too, were discovering the masses, with even more immediate purpose: they had no galleries or patrons to buy studio works, and they had to satisfy publishers who meant to satisfy the semi-literate, largely foreign-born audiences of newspaper readers. The better the comics, the bigger the circulation, by the current formula. All too soon, much of the early craziness would be gone, replaced by a formulaic pseudo-realism in whose narratives bold Anglo-Saxons conquered the world or at least kept it safe from the varied threats of exotics. In the early period, the reinvention of comic dialogue, or invention appropriate to comic art, might be said to rival the discovery of street talk in some of the *Masses* artistic drawings with slum-dwellers exchanging pungent phrases. (A child looks up in wonderment at the stars and declares them "as thick as bedbugs.")

Not only New York was being discovered, of course, but so was the Lower East Side. *Masses* artists seemed scarcely aware of Tompkins Square's past, of the furious Jewish radical-labor organizing of the suffering 1890s, or all the radical activities, personalities and conflicts that took new life with the rise of the Socialist Party after 1900. Not one of them drew for the *Forverts*, the most circulated radical paper of the district, and it is doubtful if any save Gellert could actually speak or understand Yiddish. (A comic artist or two was reprinted from *The Masses* into the weekly humor paper, *di Groysser Kundes*, mainly Art Young). But the Lower East Side was only a neighborhood or two over from Greenwich Village, and its inhabitants as well as its buildings offered a convenient site for life-in-the-slums drawings.

The *Kundes* was there already, with sketches of Jewish ghetto personalities modeled after European caricature, cartoons of epic class struggle "adapted" from European or U.S. originals (like Marx as Moses, leading the working class across the Red Sea, a sketch actually taken from a drawing of Europeans immigrating to the US!). Like the comic strips in Yiddish papers that never adopted the dialogue bubble, these were adaptations (*Simplissimus* and *Punch* would have been the great European models), but in their subject, artists, writers, strikes, assimilation or a survivalist Yiddishkayt, they were unique, and also literalist. They had, even in their frivolity, political purpose. The *Kundes* actually survived, much weakened, into the middle 1920s (it gave up the ghost in 1927). By that time, for the most vital milieux of the 1910s, purpose had fled. George Groz, Edvard Munch and Kathe Kollwitz, among other European artists, made the biggest impression upon younger American radicals, along with a few domestic counterparts, notably the work of Lynn Ward, European in form but acutely American in spiritual content (the son of a radical minister, Ward saw his protagonist upon a spiritual quest for wisdom, justice and artistic self-realization).

The scant and largely apolitical impression left by New York Dada (less self-consciously radical than in Europe, where its devotees were militantly antiwar), the paucity of a US response to the Surrealist emergence in Paris, underscored the particular character of the discoveries that swept across American Left artists during the 1920s. Artistic views hardened, if never entirely, along pro-Russian versus non- or anti-political artistic lines. The suffering of Sacco and Vanzetti, the great political event of the decade, was also the suffering of isolation for American radicals. The white working class as a heroic subject receded into suffering members of the unemployed and underemployed, sometimes into the face of a hateful Middle America eager to persecute those who looked and acted differently.[128]

The two stylistic developments of considerable importance that did take place are, however, of considerable interest. First, the lithograph provided a medium for radical artists to maintain themselves among working class and lower-middle class buyers as well as the financially comfortable progressive collectors, especially in Greater New York. Until screen printing and the anti-fascist propaganda posters of the 1940s, it was to be the biggest leap of the time. Second, comic art began to make a certain headway within Left publications. Brilliant but sparse beginnings before 1920 (mainly the IWW comic "Mr. Block," including *Crimes of the Bolsheviki*, 1919, the very first radical comic book-of-sorts) were followed by closer attention afterward. The *Daily Worker* did not actually boast a comic strip until the 1930s but the comic-strip work of William Gropper in *The Worker*, the magazine-format *New Masses* and the Yiddish counterparts, *The Morgn Frayhayt* and *Der Hommer*, was deep comic strip material with a political punch. Meanwhile, themes of radical art for the interwar period settled in. Artists like Gropper, Alice Neel and others, only a handful carried over from the *Masses* era, felt a compulsion to depict the proletariat and the sub-proletariat, most emphatically including nonwhite themes. This last was a considerable advance from the art of the 1910s, and if the images of African Americans in the South, for instance, seemed to look backward to another era of agricultural life (albeit without nostalgia), they were struggling with the necessities of the serious social artist. In fact, as scholars of the 1930s have observed, the portrayal of victimization seems central to even the most heroic conflicts of the early 1930s, the general strike in San Francisco but also struggles of miners and factory workers in those desperate time. As the look captured by photographers like Dorothea Lange most often exhibited weariness, the look of characters in mobs was the irrational if wholly justified uprising from misery to action bound to be repressed with violence. On the flip side, of course, WPA muralists looked to the productivity of the masses in field and factory, the seeming triumph of society at its best to overcome historical scarcity and lay the basis for a wholesome future. Underneath, or to the side, remained a sense of exclusion, for black workers in particular, and bitterness at the fate of ordinary people during the Depression. African-American painter Jacob Lawrence's paintings actually appeared in a Cleveland exhibit during Tobocman's growing years, and became part of the young artist's learning experience.

The rise of the comic books marks an almost opposite graphic, as if the art had been created for entirely different worlds (and children or young people buying comics were not likely to come from underprivileged homes with an unemployed parent), a fantasy creation of power amid widely acknowledged powerlessness reinforced by age and class. Small threads of class tension might be found before Pearl Harbor, in the villains of Metropolis, for instance. (Never as many as in B film Westerns, where the banker so often turns out to be the force behind the theft of the small ranchers' lands.) All this seemed to vanish with the salesmanship of patriotism. But from the end of the war onward, and in line with the sudden rise of film noir, the fascination of crime shifted from the creepy characters of Superman and Batman to the dynamic if ultimately doomed criminals of Crime Does Not Pay. No one would call it Realism, and, of course, non-whites were absent where not evil (Japanese) or servile and laughable (African Americans). No more than before the war did "class" exist in any recognizable sense, except perhaps in ragamuffin children of some comics.

The EC lines of war and action, 1950-56, mark unquestionably the high point of comic art realism. But it is interesting to note, with the traditional barriers between "real art" and pulp illustration intact, how little the marvelous artists of the EC milieu—apart from a formally trained figure like Bernard Krigstein—were influenced by modern art, in particular, how much they raised instead the hidden genius of the comics themselves up to new levels. Perhaps this helps explain how a highly stylized, not even slightly progressive comic art running contemporaneously and seizing the depleted field from the middle 1950s onward, with an aesthetic of violent action and super athletic feats (accompanied by mostly slight and largely banal dialogue, marking highly limited plot narratives), had a surprising role in the future of radical comics. According to the artist's own account, the contrast between EC and the Superhero mainstream is a bit schematic, and the gray area between the two, for artists struggling to make a living, worth more careful scholarly work. At any rate, Jack Kirby and Steve Ditko in particular had developed a formula for reducing the body to a set of interlocking geometric shapes, making it possible to draw characters in almost any position without reference to a live model or photo reference, while Jim Steranko's work taught the young artist practical ways to design a comics page.

We are by now back to Seth Tobocman, and, in some ways, the inherently grim, expressionist thread that runs from Batman to the Marvel superheroes is not so far as an art historian would imagine from the Middle European expressionists of 1900-1940. The revolt against earlier artistic conventions by figures like Kokoschka was arguably reshaped by response to the visible horrors of the First World War. Munch's "Cry" had preceded them by a generation, but already glimpsed what Grosz and Kollwitz were to elaborate. New York, after the hopeful 1960s, after the onset of the fiscal crisis that sent elderly social democrats into the arms of the bankers, felt like Berlin of the 1920s.

But in more than grimness, because the explosion of public art during the 1970s-80s, buoyed by gay and lesbian activism in particular but also by the Nuclear Freeze movement and, of course, ongoing gentrification, also had a remarkable impact. (Tobocman arrived in New York in 1976 and moved to the Lower East Side during 1978-79.) He looks to figures like David Woj-narowicz, the perfectly untrained genius, Richard Hambelton, best known for his "apocalyptic shadows" on public walls, and Keith Haring, who went from subway chalk-ups to global fame for accessible art—two of the three dead at early ages—for inspiration of rage and experimentation, not so much for style proper.

As Tobocman moved forward with comics but also with public art manifestations of resistance at many levels, with him came a blocky functionalism that evidently values ideas over atmosphere. His often extreme economy of means almost continuously reflects an urgency to communicate far beyond any existing arts community. Images are enhanced not with detail, but with strategically weighted forms. His preference for black and white over shades of gray suits his moral and political decisiveness, but also represents an aesthetic disciplined by the characteristic low-tech media of arts activism, designed for cheap offset newsprint, copy-shop fliers, but especially street stencils. These were oddly solid forms because they depended upon solidity rather than fine lines or subtle shades easily lost in production. There is an echo of the heroic worker of left-ist propaganda in Seth's everyman, but when drawing characters based on real people, collectivism bows to rugged individualism. Well-versed in comics from early fandom, his unique style results from looking outside the medium, to painting, posters and film, which he studied as an undergraduate, without bothering to finish a degree when he learned that storyboards meant more to him than artistic formalism of any kind.

The uniformly young artists of World War 3 Illustrated heavily influenced each other, especially in the first decade or so. Peter Kuper, eventually to become the most famous (thanks largely to his taking over the "Spy vs Spy" page in Mad Magazine) may be said to have lightened the expressionist tone with humor, Eric Drooker with shadowy form, deeper and deeper into the logic of 1920s Central European art and the wordless masterpieces of Lynn Ward. Tobocman was the most influential because his style reflected the drama of the political situation unfolding in front of the artists.

Like Kollwitz and others, these artists grew up in War (in their case, the Vietnam conflict) and faced the prospect of far worse war, the Armageddon that Ronald Reagan averred to, now and then, as Biblical fate. But it was the fate of the Lower East Side the loomed the closest, the villainy of the bankers, the heartlessness of the Yuppies, the pitiless fate of the poor and the fierce struggles of the squatters that excited their art, above all. The chance (but politically natural) meeting of Drooker with an aging, near-dead Allen Ginsberg (resulting in an illuminated volume of poems: their collaboration) might have been, in some sense, a revealed secret of radicalism and art combined over distances of generations and particular causes. By the third issue, in 1982, a stenciled cover, "Captive City," proclaimed the magazine to belong to those seeking to recapture their city, to make it their own again. It was a gesture that the Masses artists would have appreciated. They meant to fight for its destiny, above all in their own adopted Lower East Side.

Tobocman's first solo book, You Don't Have to Fuck People Over (first edition 1989) directly reflected these struggles, not in any distanced philosophical fashion but at the ground zero of the squatters Left and its supporters.[129] Almost poster art, page per page, it included directions for graffiti, along with enraged explanations of his own activity inviting arrest ("Because I hate screaming alone," quoting poet Maria Magenti), disillusionment with everything he had been taught in youth about the virtues of American society, and above all, a fierce determination to use every opportunity, every muscle, every ounce of life strength until it was used up. His idea of survival did not depend upon personal survival, after all.

Observers of comic art from the 1950s but especially those involved or in love with Underground Comix (at their peak, 1970-75) might ask why and how the "cartoony" versions of life with funny animals, retro faces and gags, had become invisible here. It's a good question. Another good question would be the absence of the self-conscious artfulness so obvious in the pages of *RAW* magazine (1981-91), the premier art comic of the time, an absence the more remarkable because guiding spirit Art Spiegelman himself contributed, during the new century, to *World War 3* from time to time. Why, indeed, apart from occasional jabs by Kuper, was there so little humor in *World War 3* and in Tobocman's drawings?

War in the Neighborhood (1999), Tobocman's second solo book, may be said to have answered these questions decisively—in the negative. Luc Sante, in a highly useful introduction, makes the point that the struggle over New York neighborhoods goes back to the earliest white settlers, that well-to-do artists were a vanguard of Yuppies snatching the Lower East Side by 1990, and that squatters ironically contributed to the intensity of the invasion by their lives and their art of the 1970s-80s, making a drug-filled and depressed neighborhood into a lively community as it had not been, perhaps, since the 1930s or before that, the pushcart days. Tobocman's story "of community forged and tested in the heat of emergency" is artistically stark but also efficiently candid. Among the squatters are screw-ups, men perfectly willing to bash women and children, hopeless drunks and druggies, and also incredibly courageous people of every race and origin. If the struggle for the neighborhood was lost (for a generation or two), this is the last look around at the promise of community, of what is possible in struggles against overwhelming odds and overwhelming PR.[130] Another critic noted that in the process, Tobocman's streets and buildings created a meta-narrative of their own, a possibility of many paths posing separate lives and purposes or coming together. His climax, a personal apotheosis of the artists who never stands far from his subjects, is "How else could we come to know each other?" Indeed.

Solo book number three (in addition, that is, to several *World War 3* anthologies, and a special historical volume made up very largely of *WW3* contributors, *Wobblies! A Graphic History of the Industrial Workers of the World* on the labor organization's centennial, 2005), now at press, offers a broader and perhaps more artistically challenging Tobocman. *Disasters and Resistance: Political Comics* collects material from his own *WW3* work, mostly from the recent past, and adds two remarkable color inserts, the first responding to the query, "If you want a new 'Sixties'" and the second the reflection upon the situation in the occupied West Bank, prompted by memories of his own Kindergarten year spent in Israel, decades earlier. It is an unforgettable volume in many ways, but for me the story behind the cover drawing, Tobocman's visit to New Orleans after Katrina, is a highlight of the artist's adventures. The "Battle of the 9th Ward" over housing under capitalism reprises, of course, the struggles of the Lower East Side, greed moving into every crisis situation, further marginalizing the poor, old and weak, who fight back well or badly as life and collective self-organization allow. It is a tour de force, and mirrors

Tobocman's trip back in history to the Lawrence, Massachusetts, 1912 "Bread and Roses" textile strike led by the IWW. Here, too, Tobocman actually made the trip—to modern-day Lawrence, a beat-up working class town abandoned by factories that made fortunes for the owners, and by as many of the descendents of those strikers who could get themselves out afterward, over the generations. Tobocman's history is history that does not end; there are no happy endings, but the conquest of greed is not final, either.

How far we have come, in this essay, from the days of Robert Henri's Whitmanesque vision of a metropolitan community where the ordinary citizens are no longer invisible and where (at least for his students) revolutionary mobilization is no less possible than birth control and free love? How much of this journey might, with effort, be more precisely measured around the Lower East Side? We leave these questions to future critics. Let's close with a few observations of the artist himself to interviewers.

I see politics as entering into art naturally. The interesting thing about a comic is that it's a simple form of communication that allows you to express complex ideas. It lends itself to a certain amount of intellectualization and symbolic representation that other forms might not. Simple black-and-white line drawings, stencils, and silhouettes can become symbols—and they can easily be attached to other symbols. But when you try to include symbols in a realistic color painting, it often doesn't work.

During the last hundred years America hasn't experienced war within its own borders. So in that way a lot of people in this country were somewhat naïve — they didn't understand what people in other parts of the world had gone through. After September 11 people in New York had an understanding of what it means to have a violent attack in your city. I think it was a chance for us to develop some understanding of people in places like Baghdad and Indonesia who have to deal with this all the time. Our country has been bombing Iraq for a decade. People there who have nothing to do with the government or the military have to deal with the bombing. There are hundreds of people dying — and that comes from us. Suddenly we have a window into this reality that could help us become more mature people in understanding the world.

We started the magazine in a very similar situation, which was mainly inspired by the Iran hostage crisis. The Shah was overthrown and a new regime came in and seized the American embassy and held a number of hostages. Everyone in America was shocked. They were wondering: How could they do this? Why are they so angry at us …Why would anyone hate us so much? We've been in isolation from our own foreign policy. The hatred comes from the fact that we have been acting as an aggressor and as the dominant imperialistic power in the Middle East since World War II. We've supported oppressive regimes. People there are living in horrible conditions. They see us as the cause of it, and they're angry.

We started at a time when there were very few adult comics, so there wasn't a place where comic-book artists who wanted to deal with serious issues could do so. We wanted *World War III* to give us a platform where we could speak our minds without censorship and develop our own ideas.

I want to contribute to a dialogue among many people about where society should go. I want to inspire younger people to start thinking about issues around them. But I don't want to convert people to my way of thinking — I want them to understand the way I see things and make their own decisions. The best art has an active role in society. It isn't intellectual — it's part of life. There's a sense that the world walks through our comic book: it's not safe. We are all part of the art we make, and it scares some people and attracts others. We're not just observers, we're participants.

Paul Buhle, *a Senior Lecturer at Brown University, founder of the New Left journal* RADICAL AMERICA, *the popular arts journal* CULTURAL CORRESPONDENCE *and NYU's Oral History of the American Left archive, has published 35 books as author or editor, including seven comic art nonfiction histories. He is the authorized biographer of Pan Africanist C.L.R. James and noir film artist Abraham Lincoln Polonsky.*

---

[126] Rebecca Zurier, *Picturing the City: Urban Vision and the Ashcan School* (Berkeley: University of California Press, 2006).

[127] Ibid., 41.

[128] See, e.g., *Debating American Modernism: Stieglitz, Duchamp and the New York Avant-Garde* (New York: American Federation of Arts, 2003), text by Debra Bricker Balkin. See also Franklin Rosemont's entry "Dada," in *Encyclopedia of the American Left* (New York: Oxford University Press, 1997 edition)

[129] *You Don't Have to Fuck People Over* (New York: Pressure Drop Press, 1989, second edition 1999, Soft Skull Press).

[130] Luc Sante, "Introduction," to *War in the Neighborhood: a Graphic Novel* (New York: Soft Skull Press, 1999), unpaged.

This Neo-Expressionist-Comic-Book-Artist So Far

Seth Tobocman

Family

I am told that my great grandfather shot two cops in Poland. The officers were threatening his family during a pogrom. The details are lost in the ambiguities of transatlantic immigration.

My grandparents' generation is less mysterious but of equally mythic stature. Exchanging certain oppression in Europe for an uncertain life in Cleveland, they were people of massive contradictions.

Small businessmen who dreamed of being big businessmen, they nonetheless sent their children to the Workman's Circle Yiddish schools, read the socialist newspapers, voted for F.D.R. and believed in the rights of labor. Aaron, my grandfather on my mom's side, ran a little candy store in a poor section of Cleveland. He continued to live and work there long after that neighborhood had transitioned from Jewish to Black.

Before I was old enough to know him, he was murdered by local teenagers trying to rob his store. Aaron's wife worked alongside him in the store, which was also their home. Both my mother, Edith, and my grandmother, Frida, held full-time jobs but never described themselves as feminists. Jacob, my grandfather on my father's side, was more successful. Starting as a roofer, then a butcher, he went through a series of financial misadventures in various cities until he wound up owning a small meatpacking plant in Cleveland. Late in life, he told his daughter, "Everything I have, I've earned. But that doesn't mean America is fair. Because there are black men who have worked just as hard. And somehow they don't have anything."

My grandmother, Helen, did not know her own birthday. She grew up in Poland with little education. In her own words, "We were like the cattle." But she had an incredibly dignified demeanor, commanding, almost aristocratic. She made damn sure her son became a college professor. In the end, what drove their progressive politics was the same thing that drove their desire to make money. They hated being poor. Their children, my parents, inherited this whirlwind of contradictions. When I say that my uncle was a member of the Communist Party U.S.A., the phrase "red diaper baby" pops out of people's mouths like projectile vomit. And "red diaper baby" is as sure as Shylock a Jewish stereotype. The fact that my mom's brother, Jack, a hospital worker in Brooklyn, was a Communist does not mean that my father, Bill, who was professor of physics in Cleveland Heights, shared his views. Quite the contrary, my Dad voted for Nixon, Reagan and Bush. While my parents met at the Workman's Circle Yiddish classes, their trajectory over the course of their lives took them further and further to the right.

What I got from this was exposure to diverse political ideas. On Sundays my father and his two sisters, Marilyn and Marcia, would debate the Vietnam War before sitting down to bagels and lox. I remember thinking that politics must be a pretty strange business if people could get this heated over it without taking it personally.

To his credit, when we were growing up, my father never pressured my sister or me to agree with him and always encouraged us to think for ourselves. Bill made you feel that if you didn't have an opinion of your own you were stupid. He loved a good argument and, because he was witty and, in his own way, well informed, he usually won. He was a strange type of conservative. He seemed to be in favor of every imaginable American war.

But he was also the one who informed me that Henry Ford had been a Nazi. Bill did show me that a man can love his work. After a day at the university, he came home to sit at his desk doing physics equations. It was often hard to pull him out of his study to have dinner. Then he would sit at the dinner table with a little notepad in his hands writing equations.

So there were Communists and Capitalists, Cop Killers and College Professors in this family. What there weren't were artists. Well, there was almost one. My uncle Phil had been quite the high school painter. His Ashcan school-style representations of the old neighborhood adorned the walls of our home in Cleveland Heights. But Phil had done the "sensible thing" and given up his dreams of being an artist for a more lucrative career in medicine. When Phil found out that I was drawing, he told me, "If you want to be an artist, then you can never sell out or you won't be an artist anymore." I have done my best to follow his advice.

Education

I started drawing before I could read and have never stopped for long. By the time I was in grade school, it became evident that I was lousy at sports and academics, but pretty good at art. I was one of these kids who gets beat up all the time. I was the constant target of bullies and class clowns. This is probably what drew me to comics. While the Marvel Superheroes are pure fantasy, they mimic the lives of young boys in some important ways. I stood a pretty good chance of ending up in a fistfight any time I walked out the door. So did the Incredible Hulk. Only the Hulk usually won. When I was about 12, my friend Peter Kuper and I started to publish a comic book fanzine and attend comic conventions. At that time, comic book fandom was very small and it was possible to know everyone. I met Jeff Jones, Vaughn Bode, Jack Kirby, Robert Crumb, Neil Adams. It was an amazing art education for a couple of junior high school kids to meet so many working artists. From this experience, I saw that my parents were wrong when they told me that it was impossible to make a living as an artist. Jones and Bode were particularly supportive of my work.

Around the same time, we also met a thirty-something comic book and record collector who worked at the local veterans hospital and lived in one of the few apartment buildings in our sub-urban neighborhood. This was Harvey Pekar. He had not yet begun to write comics and was trying his hand at jazz criticism. He was friendly to us but also opinionated. He felt we were reading the wrong kind of comics (superheroes) and listening to the wrong music (rock

and roll). Harvey introduced us to underground comics, which we were too young to legally buy. He showed me the first printing of Art Spiegelman's *Prisoner of the Hell Planet*. We intro-duced Harvey to a local cartoonist, Gary Dumm, and together they started Harvey's now famous neo-realist comic book, *American Splendor*!

As I got into high school, I began to notice that superhero comics ran the same five plot lines over and over again. The characters no longer seemed real to me and I lost interest in collecting comics but I continued to draw my own.

William Burroughs, Abbie Hoffman, Pablo Picasso, Henry Miller, Alistair Crowley, Patti Smith and Andy Warhol soon replaced Captain America as my heroes. I admired them for their lifestyles as much as for their accomplishments. My friends in high school were mostly gay kids. This was the only clique in which I found acceptance, and the first group of people I came to identify with. I sometimes came to school with my face made up like David Bowie. We felt we were constantly at war with the conformity of the suburban society around us. Perhaps as a defense, we affected a degree of sophistication completely unjustified by our experience.

Another member of this group was David Solomonoff, an aspiring abstract painter who later got involved in electronic music. David turned me on to notions of Modern Art. I drew a couple of experimental comic strips using Cubist influenced layouts where the panel borders themselves seemed to be exploding. One of these received high praise from Jones and Bode.

Unfortunately, this praise led to a kind of crisis for me. I wanted to produce another strip just like it, and couldn't. This was my first experience of writer's block. I have since concluded that the way to avoid writer's block is never to try to do the same thing twice.

The writer's block, along with the death of Vaughn Bode, led me into a deep depression. I gave up drawing comics, started to experiment with drugs, became morose and self-seeking. While I was under this dark cloud, my father convinced me to give up art and attend film school at N.Y.U. He was sure that I would never make any money as an artist. I remember him pointing to the credits at the end of a movie, the long list of grips and gaffers and gofers, and pro-nouncing "There must be room for you in there somewhere."

Film school was a disaster. I couldn't handle it. I couldn't deal with the backbiting competitive students or the bored distant professors. And most of all, I couldn't imagine myself in the strict hierarchy of filmmaking as it was in the 1970s. My sketchbooks from the time are full of unfin-ished pencil drawings of people with arms, legs or eyes missing. I did learn some things from screen-writing classes that I would later apply to comics.

I was thrown out of the dorms in a drug-related incident. Probably the only good thing that came out of this is that I moved into an apartment on the Lower East Side. I soon dropped out of school.

Then my old friend Peter Kuper showed up in New York. He had sold a comic strip to *Heavy Metal* magazine and was working for Harvey comics inking *Richie Rich* while taking art classes part time at Pratt and the Art Students' League. I suddenly remembered comics. I decided to follow Peter's lead and look for work as an illustrator while studying art. I did my first commercial art job for the *New York Rocker*.

Art classes were no panacea. Many of my instructors were hostile to all forms of representation. There is something weird that happens when Modernism becomes the Academy. It is one thing to say "You CAN throw paint at the canvas like Jackson Pollack" and quite another to say "You MUST throw paint at a canvas like Jackson Pollack." I did gain some skills out of art classes, particularly anatomy with Sal Montano.

My parents had different ideas about my future anyway. They wanted me to finish film school then go on to a graduate degree in law like my sister. I knew this was impossible for me. When they figured out that I had no intention of getting a degree, they cut me off financially. I worked as an usher, a messenger, a construction worker, at a moving company, but eventually got work as an illustrator for the *New York Times* and other papers.

I felt like at any moment the ground would open up and swallow me. But I was exactly where I was supposed to be. I was broke and living at the crossroads of international culture.

In 1980 graffiti-influenced neo-expressionism was exploding onto the streets and into the galleries of lower Manhattan. Just walking around on any given day, I could see stencils spray painted onto walls or sidewalks by David Wojnarowicz, Michael Roman or Anton van Dalen. Murals by Eva Cockroft, chalk drawings by Keith Haring, Hambleton's black figure paintings, posters by Barbara Krueger, Basqiat's SAMO rantings and, of course, all the graffiti artists: Phase, Futura, Dondi, Chico.

I liked this work for its directness, its fresh approach to representation, its desire to communicate with absolutely anyone. I became very interested in the neo-expressionists' attempt to create an image of a universal, unspecified person. I experimented with faceless characters in a number of comic strips and also tried my hand at stencils and graffiti. Under the influence of my contemporaries, my work became simpler and more sophisticated. I still consider myself to be a neo-expressionist comic book artist. For a while, Tom Keough and I worked for some Left-Catholic Maryknoll missionaries who had just come back from Central America. They had us illustrating a text against the C.I.A. From them I learned a bit about cold war politics and from the project I learned how to reduce political concepts to very simple symbols.

I also taught summer art classes to kids on 9th Street at Charas community center, along with Sabrina Jones, Fred Sieden, Lupe Garnica, Eric Drooker and Paula Hewitt. The kids we taught were living on the worst heroin block in New York City. They appreciated the art making so much that they would often stop us on the street corner and ask us when the next class would be.

One day a group of very small children walked in and sat down together. They were unusually quiet. Slowly, haltingly and with great consideration they began to speak to each other. They had found the body of a woman who had been decapitated. They were trying to figure out what this meant. They mouthed none of the clichés adults use to cushion terrible events. Eventually the oldest and most verbal of the children came to the conclusion that they were safe because their father was armed. I myself was speechless and could only hand out the paintbrushes. Then the smallest drew a picture of a horrible screaming face. I still have that drawing.

For me, this was a profound experience. It changed the way I would write and draw for many years to come. Throughout the '80s I would try to capture this amazing voice that came from these children. The voice of a small, simple mind trying to comprehend something huge. It was all starting to make sense.

World War 3 Illustrated

In 1980 there were, to my knowledge, four adult comic books being published in the United States: Ben Katchor's poetic and forgotten *Picture Story Magazine*, Art Spiegelman's *Raw*, Harvey Pekar's *American Splendor*, and our magazine *World War 3 Illustrated*.

Peter Kuper and I started *World War 3 Illustrated* as a response to the Iran Hostage crisis. Revolutionaries in Iran were holding the staff of the U.S. Embassy hostage. The response in American society was an orgy of jingoism. Dartboards with the Ayatollah Khomeni's face. Buttons and T-shirts emblazoned with the slogan FUCK IRAN. Peter and I agreed that the time was right for an antiwar graphics magazine. Helping us out on the first two issues were Ben Katchor, who assisted with the technical end of publishing, and a German conceptual artist named Christoff Kolhoffer, who was our bridge to the art world. The first issue was no big deal. Competent comics playing with vaguely left-wing politics. Neither aesthetically nor politically very adventurous. But our timing was important. At the very moment when Ronald Reagan was bringing the Christian Right to power, two young men had founded an antiwar comic book. It was as though we had raised a flag. All kinds of people rallied around that banner: political artists, Anarchists, peace punks, poster pasters, pamphleteers, Squatters, Race Traitors, Feminists, people concerned about political prisoners and people with AIDS. I learned from each of these people and the experience radicalized me. The magazine evolved and took on a wide range of issues beyond its original concern with nuclear war.

The art critic Lucy Lippard was very supportive, along with academics like Jim Murray, Tom Ward, Terisa Turner and Paul Buhle. At the same time, I began to develop some new aesthetics. I remember walking through the young artists section of a comic book convention. At each table a different artist was showing his wares. Most of these fellows could draw quite well, but they were all drawing the same thing. A muscle-bound guy with a hot chick, both in revealing costume and holding obviously phallic guns or swords. I came to the conclusion that if our criterion for inviting new artists into *World War 3 Illustrated* was "can he draw hands?" we could fill the magazine with this junk. I had to develop some other standard. I decided to judge work, first and foremost, on the sincerity of its content. I reasoned that it would be easier for a sincere person to learn to draw than for a slick superficial illustrator to become sincere. As a result, many artists took their first crude baby steps at *World War 3 Illustrated* and over time evolved into the great talents you know them as today. It was at first hard to get distribution for the magazine. Comic shops were not yet interested in alternative comics. Bookstores had not yet discovered graphic novels. The Punk scene came to our rescue. Josh Whalen hooked us up with Mordam records, a Punk distributor who carried such political bands as the Dead Kennedys and the False Prophets. We were the only comic book whose primary distribution was in record stores, but it worked. The Punks were totally hip to what we were saying, politically and aesthetically. We got amazing letters from alienated kids in small town and suburban America. These letters made me remember my own confused teenage years. I tried to produce stories that would have been meaningful to me back then.

Self publishing on a small budget, I became acutely aware of what type of art was easy to print and what would be more difficult. My work became sharper and simpler. As a result, activists began to use my pieces for leaflets and posters—everyone from squatters in New York to the African National Congress in South Africa. Peter Bagge, Milton Knight, Tom Keough, Sabrina Jones, James Romberger, Stephen Kroninger, Eric Drooker, Paula Hewitt, Aki Fujioshi, Brian Damage, Scott Cunningham, Kevin Pyle, Isabella Bannerman, Sandy Jimenez, Mac McGill, Siobhan Neville, Lawrence Van Abbema, Peter Plate, Josh Whalen, Fly, Nicole Schulman, Penny Allen, Rebecca Migdal, Ryan Inzana, Chris Cardinale, Kate Evans, Anton van Dalen, David Wojnarowicz, Baron Storey, Sue Coe, Ted Rall, Kyle Baker, Tom Tomorrow and Art Spiegelman are just a few of the artists who have worked with us over the years.

I was also fortunate to have much of my work from the first ten years of *World War 3 Illustrated* appear in my first book, *You Don't Have to Fuck People Over to Survive*. Published in 1989 by Pressure Drop Press later reprinted by Soft Skull and now due for a third printing from PM press. The magazine has continued to this day as an artist-run collective. There are now people working on *World War 3 Illustrated* who were fans of the zine as teenagers.

Lower East Side Politics

I think that Jews emigrating to America from Eastern Europe in the early 20th century had a special feeling about the need to be secure in one's home. In Poland, a Jewish person could live his entire life in a particular community, build a business and a set of relationships. Then, all of a sudden, the Christians decide that it's time to avenge the death of Christ. It's pogrom time. They raid the homes of their Jewish neighbors and force them to leave town with nothing but the little they can carry. From such experiences, Jewish immigrants developed a strong conviction that eviction was a great evil. During the Depression, housing activists like Francis Goldin and Communists like my uncle Jack would move families back into homes they had been thrown out of. The result of such popular struggles are the New York City rent laws that protect us to this day. I learned about those rent laws first hand when the landlord tried to impose an unjustified rent increase on the building where I live. The residents formed a tenant union, went on rent strike, took the landlord to court and won many improvements. That was my first real experience of political organizing. I became aware of the Lower East side as a place with many neighborhood organizations, homesteading coalitions, credit unions, and community gardens. Back in Cleveland Heights, my father had never joined a block association. I don't know that there was one. There was no sense of community. While the media portrayed the Lower East Side as a drug spot, I began to see it as, in certain ways, a healthier place than where I grew up.

One of the big concerns in our neighborhood was gentrification. Mayor Koch had announced, "New York is a city for winners" and threatened that poor people would be pushed into the East

River. There were many initiatives launched to preserve the L.E.S. as a place where working-class and middle-class folks could afford to live. One of the most inspiring was the squatters movement.

Throughout history, radical movements have promised to take the wealth that was being ware-housed and distribute it to the people who needed it. Often this was a hollow promise. But this was exactly what the squatters movement was doing. In the 1980s hundreds of city-owned, abandoned buildings sat empty while people were freezing to death on the streets. The squat-ters broke into these buildings and turned them into low income housing.

The squatters movement also tried to protect the rights of homeless people who lived in Tompkins Square Park and worked with other progressive tendencies, such as the antiapartheid struggle, ACT-UP, and the December 12th movement against police brutality. All of this activity led to an attempt by the city to crush the movement. But people fought back. From 1988 to 1992 there were a series of riots in the neighborhood, usually started by police attempting to run homeless people out of the park, curtail civil liberties or evict the squatters. The Lower East Side became the focus of an international struggle for human rights.

I decided to get more involved and so I became a member of Umbrella House, a squat on Avenue C. I worked on renovating the building and ran a printing press on the first floor with the help of Sarah Hogarth, who was an experienced printer. I was involved in defending the build-ing against an eviction attempt, which got pretty hairy.

I also worked on defending the other squats and participated in lots of other protests and actions. I was arrested about 20 times and convicted twice. Eventually my lawyer, Stanley Cohen, advised me to cool it. He said that the D.A. had just about had it with me and that if I continued the consequences would get a lot more serious. At about this time I also began to fall out with my comrades at Umbrella House. We disagreed about a number of internal issues. I decided to give up my membership in the squat and return to life as a cartoonist who supports radical movements rather than be a radical who occasionally draws cartoons.

My experiences in the squatters movement are the basis of my second book *War in the Neigh-borhood*. Describing these events required me to change my drawing and writing style. Whereas my work in the '80s had been ideologically driven, using broad allegorical figures and simple symbols, my new work had to be character driven and more realistically drawn in order to describe specific circumstances and individuals. Drawing and writing this book took me over six years.

Touring

Having two books out from small independent presses, I had an obligation to promote them. To this end, I put together a slide show of my comics and learned to perform my texts with the help of some very talented local musicians, Cybel Blood, John Wagner, Zef Noise, Steve Wishnia, Eric Blitz and others. This is an experimental form developed by Vaughn Bode, which he called a cartoon concert. I took this show on the road to promote my books. This took me all over the U.S., to Europe, even to the Middle East. It's an odd coincidence that these events coincided with the emergence of an international movement for global justice, so, traveling, I had the opportunity to participate in protests against the World Bank, the WTO and the FTAA.

Teaching

For the last five years, I have had the honor of teaching comics at the School of Visual Arts. I really enjoy teaching. It's a lot like political organizing. Your objective is to get lots of other people motivated to do something, not just to do it yourself. It occurs to me that I never took courses in comics and that much of my education was informal. I wonder how my life would have been different if I had had teachers who were more supportive of my desire to draw comics.

9-11

In the wake of the events of September 11th, there were a number of comics anthologies responding to that traumatic experience. *World War 3*'s 9-11 issue was the only such anthology produced from a leftist perspective. We were surprised at the favorable reviews we received, even from very mainstream sources. In the repressive atmosphere that followed

9-11, a number of very established cartoonists turned to *World War 3 Illustrated* as the place where they could publish radical material their normal employers would no longer handle.

World War 3 Arts In Action

When George Bush announced his intention to invade Iraq, it seems like everyone but the U.S. congress could see what a dumb idea it was. Well, not really. A lot of misinformed people bought it. But John and Hillary really should have known better. With this catastrophic blunder looming on the horizon, an antiwar group formed on the Lower East Side called NO BLOOD FOR OIL that included some of my old buddies from the squatter days. I was asked to form an arts committee for this group. But *World War 3 Arts in Action* quickly became an autonomous entity that worked with many different organizations. We made signs, banners, posters and street theater for many antiwar events. For me, it was a way of participating in demonstrations that allowed me to contribute my most valuable resource — my artwork.

Art on the Israel/Palestine Conflict

Here I will make few friends. Like most American Jews, I grew up thinking of the Israelis as the good guys. We practically cheered when Israel occupied large sections of its neighboring countries in the six-day war. A Zionist education gives you extensive information about the oppression of Jews in the diaspora, but very little information about the Arabs. There are prominent Jews who have made the embarrassing assertion that "there is no such thing as a Palestinian." In college I met students from Iran and Lebanon and began to understand that there was another way of looking at the situation. Eric Drooker introduced me to the cartoons of Naji Ali and I learned more. Then in the 1990s the Israeli government admitted what it had been denying for over 40 years: that in the war of 1948, the various Zionist militias had forced a large population of Palestinian civilians to flee their homes through a series of massacres in order to clear the land for Jewish settlement. They made it clear that this was not the work of a handful of extremists but a deliberate policy. In other words, the Jews had engaged in pogroms against the Palestinians. Still, I tried to stay out of this issue. I reasoned that I had no intention of living in the Middle East, so it was not my business. And there was plenty to do right here, dealing with the contradictions in my own community. But in recent years I saw that a lot of younger activists who I met through the anti-globalization movement were going to Palestine to work with the International Solidarity Movement (I.S.M.) and other groups. I felt that I had an obligation to check this out more closely and decided to go to Palestine. So I volunteered for a few weeks, teaching art and English to kids in a village that had been cut off from the rest of the world by Israeli roadblocks. I produced a book about this experience called *Portraits of Israelis and Palestinians*. It is apparently the most offensive thing I have ever created and it consists largely of pictures of children.

I then engaged in an even more offensive project. *Three Cities Against the Wall*, an art show by Israeli, Palestinian and American artists opposed to Israel's building of a wall through the occupied territories. As the name implies, the show was to appear simultaneously in Ramallah, Tel Aviv and New York. I worked with Ronen Eidelman, an Israeli involved with Anarchists Against Walls and Fences, and Sliman Monsour, a well-known Palestinian painter, to organize the event. It took two years for our organizing committee to raise the funds needed to pull it off.

Steve Englander, Danielle Sarah Frank, Terry Berkowitz, Fawzia Reda and Melissa Jamesson all did an amazing job on that committee. The show involved some of the most respected artists in all three countries. I suppose I should not have been surprised at some of the problems we had.

In New York, the openings at ABC No Rio and 6th Street Community Center were well attended due to extensive online publicity. But the newspapers refused to announce it or review it. In Ramallah, there was a lot of controversy. Some Palestinian artists felt that doing anything with Israelis amounted to collaboration while others wanted to participate; in addition, the work for the Palestinian show was held up in Israeli customs. As a result, the show did not open in Ramallah and was moved to the Palestinian University in Hebron. Oddly enough, only in Tel Aviv was this show well received. It was written up in *Ha-aretz* and the opening was a success. I was pretty frustrated with both of these projects and for the time being I am focused on other issues. History will decide whether we were naive or ahead of our times.

New Orleans

A few days after Hurricane Katrina hit Louisiana, a friend called me and told me she was going to try to get into New Orleans with two truckloads of medical supplies. That action was the seed, which grew into Common Ground Relief, a major mobilization of volunteers. Because I was still tied up with *Three Cities Against the Wall*, I could not get down there until January. What I saw was really inspiring. I felt like the activists of the anti-globalization movement had finally become grounded in something of immediate material benefit to people. They were gutting flood-damaged homes, providing emergency healthcare, really doing a lot to meet people's needs. The real estate issues were also oddly familiar. The powers that be were trying to use the disaster to gentrify this historically black city.

Some friends and I set up a group called *The Loisaida-New Orleans Caravan*, which has brought people from the squatters' movement with experience in the construction trades down to

New Orleans to fix houses.

I encouraged other *WW3* artists like Mac McGill, Chris Carcinale and Carlo Quispe, to get involved in this struggle as well, and we produced *After the Flood*, a comic book to raise funds for Common Ground Relief. This publication also included some of Francisco diSantis brilliant portraits of Katrina survivors.

In 2007 I worked with Jules Stack, a Mardi Gras float builder, to construct a float in support of New Orleans public housing residents who are fighting for the right to move back into their old homes.

Disaster & Resistance

Comic strips resulting from my experiences with the anti-globalization movement, Palestine and New Orleans, as well as discussing 9-11 and the war in Iraq, form the basis of my next book, *Disaster & Resistance.*

On Having Survived

Michael Stewart was an African American art student who worked at the Pyramid Club on Avenue A. He was only a few years younger than me. One night he was murdered by police as he tried to catch the subway at Astor Place. His name became a battle cry for many of us in the 1980s. If he were alive today he'd have gray hair. Too many of my contemporaries died young — Brian Damage, Keith Haring, Willie Butler, Terry Taylor, Brad Will, Grady Alexis, David Woj-narowicz, to name a few. Despite all that has happened, there has not been much progress. Like my grandfather, I am forced to acknowledge that whatever I have achieved is a privilege denied to others who were too black, too gay or too radical.

Only the Story So Far

One of my personal heroes, Francisco Goya, printmaker, painter, and cartoonist, did his best work between 50 and 80 years old. So it says a lot about our times that I am not quite 50 but Clayton Patterson has asked me to provide an autobiography to his book on Jewish artists in the Lower East Side. I plan to continue drawing comics and other pictures for the rest of my life

Seth Tobocman *In 1980 Seth Tobocman was one of the founding editors of the political comic book* World War 3 Illustrated. *This magazine challenged the politics and morals of the Reagan-Bush era. His illustrations have appeared in the* New York Times *and many other mag-azines. Tobocman is the Author/Illustrator of four graphic books:*

You Don't Have to Fuck People Over to Survive
War in the Neighborhood
Portraits of Israelis and Palestinians
Disaster & Resistance

He has had a one man show at ABC NO Rio and a two man show at EXIT ART gallery. He has

been in group shows at the Museum of Modern Art and the New Museum of Contemporary Art.

His images have been used in posters, pamphlets, murals, graffiti and tattoos by people's movements around the world from the African National Congress in South Africa, to Squatters on New York's Lower East Side.

Boris Lurie

Clayton Patterson
(with editing assistance by Jim Feast)

It was not easy to include Boris Lurie in this book. He belongs in here because, since the 1950s, he had a studio in which he often slept on the L.E.S. on 6th Street, between A and B. But I couldn't find an interested *American* academic or scholar or qualified admirer of Boris Lurie and No!art to write about Boris or the movement for this book.

I knew that in Sweden, Dr. Max Liljefors, born 1963, research fellow in the department of art history and musicology at Lund University, had written about Boris in his doctoral thesis. He said he would contribute an article.

The second person who could write about Boris was Dr. Staar, the curator of the 1998 one man exhibition – "Life - Terror – Mind" at the Buchenwald Memorial site in Weimar, Germany. Although English was not her first or second language Dr. Staar generously agreed to contribute an article on Boris to the book.

I physically got Boris to Buchenwald for his exhibition. Boris was a pleasure to travel with, we had a lot of interesting conversations with many topics covered, much about Boris. We, Dietmar Kirves, his son Martin, Boris, and I, were all put up in the comfortable officer's quarters at the camp. We had no problems, except one small one. Boris had to have the large private room.

Dr. Staar had created a powerful exhibition. Seeing Boris's work in the Disinfecting Room storage area, down the stairs in the low-ceilinged, spacious basement with its thickly coated, whitewashed walls, I felt it was a good fit. Staar had studied and absorbed Boris's content and aesthetics, picked all strong work, and Boris was pleased with how the show was hung. While we were at the camp, Staar and Boris had a number of intense conversations.

Dr. Staar was lean, then in her forties, with a short, blondish, neatly combed, practical haircut. She wore '50ish-style glasses like the kind a place like Woolco used to sell. She had a little trace of black eyeliner; almost invisible lipstick; muted, mostly brown, earth colored plain clothes. She was somewhat shy, friendly, and very proper in her sitting up straight posture listening attentively to what Boris had to say. She is an intellectual, and married to an intellectual, both having a reserved manner. She was passionate about her job, and treated all the museum objects as sacred. She was empathetic to Boris. The show she put together was a good reflection of Boris's work. Even though all the work the Memorial exhibits is done by survivors, Boris included in his exhibition a video of mine, about him. They paid me as well. Boris did things like that. Boris was a stand-up guy as long as the other guy was paying. He did what he wanted, not what he was told. Besides, once it was determined and set in stone that the exhibition was going to happen, he made it difficult to have this show. The Memorial had to go way over budget. This was the most expensive show that they had put on up to that date. Boris's work is confrontational, so is getting his work to an exhibition. It is like Boris wants them to make up in hardship and spending for what the Nazi's had cheated him and his father out of.

The opening started and you could feel the tension in the room, as the audience was a little nervous about how to react to Boris or how he would relate to them, especially considering how confrontational and aggressive some of Boris's work is. Boris's artwork, even years after it was made, still gets strong reactions. However, Boris put everyone at ease. He was friendly, open, and even jovial. He loved the attention. He was in his element, showing his art in the place that tried to kill him and his father. It was a walk of glory—I am still here. Watching Boris at this camp reminded me of the etching he made by forcefully multi carving the Star of David over the top of the Nazi Swastika. Boris is a very unusual person. He is a survivor not a victim. His work is political, powerful, jarring, disgusting, and meant, in a hard way, to be in your face. One of his ways of fighting back is for his work to stand up and be noticed. His work was here to be heard, and hopefully understood. So bring it on, but look at the art.

Dr. Staar gave private tours of Boris's work to the dignitaries who visited Boris's exhibition. She described in a letter to Matthias Reichelt and Curt Germundson, for their article called *The Reception of the Art of Boris Lurie and NO!art in the Context of the Holocaust Debate in Contemporary Germany, with corrections and short annotations by Boris Lurie*, 2002, page 1/22, www.info_no-art.info — "A major problem that visitors to the Lurie exhibition had is that he does not fit the conventional notion of victim. They are not comfortable with facing work by an 'angry Jew.'" Dr. Sonja Staar, curator at the commemorative site Buchenwald, described how several visitors did react more positively after taking part in guided tours and discussions: "We led guided tours through the exhibition. The experience was that for the visitors the knowledge about the biographical starting point of the collages was very important. In discussions, they reacted attentively and sympathetic to explanations and suggestions. Once one made clear to the visitors what kind of tensions and personal hardship led to these images, they found a connection to them." It took the German visitors, because of the museum context and an educated curator, to start to get a glimpse into what the work is reflecting, sadly, something that it not usually evident with Americans, who (it seems) will never get to that point of comprehension

I admire Boris's inner strength, absolutely. He is not the least bit submissive and he is shameless about letting others know about the suffering his people went through. He is not just arbitrarily breaking social taboos, for pure shock value, in some kind of juvenile delinquent, antisocial way. One thing he is doing is mixing primal emotions and energies that have been dislocated, parts destroyed, or severely damaged, and pushing them to the surface of his art. Face it. Get past the abhorrent surface and feel the pain, the suffering, the sorrow. Try and understand what he is trying to express. What? All the images of the period have to be white-washed, cleaned up and put into modern spectacular settings, or some kind of some Hollywood Walt Disney type settings? What happened was pure evil. Deal with it.

Study the art. He has been forced to be a lone voice screaming out in the vacuum where art is viewed as only a provider of social status, its worth based on an auction-house, monetary system, and pushed to the outside by historians, academics, critics, and dealers, who can only deal with what is in front of them by contextualizing art in relations to what has been established, certified, by those experts who have come before them. Problem is — Boris is an original. He carries that awful burden.

Dr. Staar lives in Weimar, East Germany, which is located 6 miles from the Buchenwald camp. She spent most of her life under the rule of the East German DDR. The Russians, in 1945 after WW 2, took charge of the camp — now called Special Camp No. 2 — and again, until 1950, Buchenwald was a place of unimaginable horrors. Special Camp No. 2 without missing a beat, under the Russian authority with East German workers, carried on its sick legacy of murder and human rights abuses.

The camp had that kind of repressive feeling one gets in the old gray East German communist towns, pre the Western makeover. The outside of the Buchenwald buildings all looked untouched since the period of their use. The buildings were the color of chicken fat, the inside colors were all earthy and muted, such things as technology, equipment, and so on were contemporary and utilitarian. Everything was clean, orderly, and in good shape.

Buchenwald means beech forest. The camp is surrounded by a beech tree forest, but did not feel bucolic or wild and inviting with adventure. Everything had stillness to it like a graveyard. One grassy knoll was a mass gravesite. The constant wind almost carried an audible weeping sound. The feeling of isolation was everywhere.

There were flowers, pictures, stones, markers, all new artifacts laid down by grieving friends, relatives, sympathizers or by those who are connected to humanity. They were carefully set down by places such as the burners of the ovens that cremated the bodies of the camp's daily dead and near graves of the dead. The enclosed prison yard, the size of several football fields, was laid out as a piece of formal landscape art: black, broken-rock rectangles indicating where the different ethnic living quarters used to be (there was a large population of Gypsies who were exterminated at this camp). The general color in the space was a grayish white, very stark, very organized. It felt like everything had been thought out: nothing existed that had not been gone over with human hands and thinking.

The whole camp had a heavy spirit. There was one place at the top of the hill, which had a lovely panoramic view of the surrounding rural area, what could be thought of as a beautiful vista, but it was dominated by a dark memorial sculpture commemorating the brutality and volumes of murders that took place at this camp. Death and the ominous feeling of the presence of the spirits of the dead were everywhere. The mood was not one of pleasure, but one of sorrow.

Nazis were good at keeping records. Much to Boris's surprise, Dr. Staar had the archival roll-call record book with Boris and his father named as prisoners at Magdeburg, an ammunitionsmaking work camp, a satellite of Buchenwald where Boris and his father had been slave laborers. And much to Dr. Staar's surprise, by pure luck and presence of mind, Boris was able to keep and hang onto one of his cloth clothing prisoner numbers.

In talking to and documenting both Dr Staar and Dr. Volkhard Knigge the director of the Memorial (both spoke English), I got the impression that they felt the extra responsibility of dealing with the emotional and psychological perspectives of the visitors. They needed to be seen as ethically and morally upstanding, serious people. They had to come across this way because of the responsibility they felt as the conveyers, as well as the keepers and protectors of the records, the legacy, the landmarks, the hard copy material, the films and all the documents and artifacts of the history of this ever so dark period in human existence. You could feel that they carry this psychological load, that macabre stillness, that a mortician or funeral home director carries.

While at the camp talking to Dr. Staar, I discovered the concentration-camp reproduced images, those Boris used in his collage art, in pieces such *Railroad Collage* or *Flatcar Assemblage, 1945, by Adolf Hitler*, originated at the time of the Buchenwald liberation. The documentation was taken by photographers who came in with the liberators, led by General Patton and his 6th Armored Division. These are some of the few existing photos documenting the horrors of the camp. Patton had the whole town march through the camp and witness for themselves the horrors of which they were living in denial. There must have been a number of town residents who made some kind of income from the camp, similar to those in the communities in upper New York state whose income is tied to prisons. One day a small group of us took a side trip to Mittelbau Dora Concentration Camp, a few hours' drive from Weimar. At the camp, because of Boris, our special guest, we had our very own serious, young, thin, bookish college student, who was well-schooled on the camp's history, as our camp guide. His English was better than what one normally hears in Manhattan; he knew all the facts, figures, and history of every facet of the camp. He was stoic, yet seemed to take a quiet pleasure out of understating, but expounding on and on, educating us on even the tiniest of details and nuances, as in saying. "Look over there" pointing to two hardly noticeable hooks on the heavily whitewashed wall. "There is where they hung the bodies of the beaten, nearly dead prisoners." I can still, in my mind's eye, see his pale boney finger pointing towards the wall where these gruesome hooks were sticking out. It was memorably morbid.

The day we were at this camp the weather was bordering on rain, just a light mist and a rolling drifting gray fog. The place looked barren, foreboding and desolate. Because of what kind of day it was, the first impression I got was the place had just been deserted. Left exactly as it had been. It was somewhat damp and chilly. Everything was pretty much OK. Boris was holding up, no problem, until we went from a gray day into a foreboding dark and dank hole as we entered the mouth of the tunnel and made the long trek into the belly of the mountain. It was like walking into a tomb, a mass grave, where thousands of slave labor prisoners died building this hole into hell, which sheltered a war factory. (One roll of photographs taken by a Nazi captain survived and gave an insight into the camp life.)

Another notable fact our young bright scholar pointed out was that one of Mittelbau Dora camp directors eventually became an eminent American space scientists. This was Dr. Werner Von Braun, the same Nazi specialist who was a collaborating sinister genius behind the making of the V-2 rocket meant to wipe out England and then came to America and worked for NASA.

The air in this tunnel was cold and damp. I have a memory of the oppressive feelings that arose from the minimal amount of light thrown by the chain of low wattage, incandescent, bare light-bulbs, which cast shadows on the walls of that dreary lonely expanse, cut out of the mountain's guts to make this hidden death factory. WW2 mining and V-2 wreckage lined the side areas of the tunnel. Mix all of this with the stark language and expressions painted by the guide, and it all became too much for Boris. This time the evil exuding from inside that mountain was bigger than Boris.

Boris, our conquering hero, our friend who could stand up to anybody or anything, had his shell pierced. Boris sank into a depression after this day. I saw when that accumulating black cloud enveloped him. He was struck by emotional lightening. It was like he was hit in the head. Mr. Nerves of Steel, in your face with his art, nothing can bother me Boris found that this experience was emotionally devastating. Beyond logical comprehension. Soon after, he developed back pains, leg troubles. However, he did overcome this period, and a few years later, because of smoking, he had a stroke. He got over this, but soon, there was a second round. He was house-bound, in his eighties, and people brought poor Boris cigarettes. This, in my opinion, led to his massive stoke, which put Boris into a coma and caused him to disconnect from this world. He left us.

The East German concentration camps at the time we were there were used as military educational centers for teaching young cadets about the history of the war. These buildings were museum pieces, still looking like what they must have when fully operational. They were kept up, but everything in Communist Germany looked poor, and, lucky for us, the bad economy meant the places were still grim and not yet sanitized or Disneyfied for the American tourist. These places still felt like camps. And in both Buchenwald and Dora, we would see troops of young army cadets, in uniform, visiting the sites.

Another big disappointment for Boris was that in the Magdeburg site, which by now had been completely obliterated: torn down, wiped out, washed clean, nothing was left. No memory.

In Cologne, Armin Hundertmark, a dealer and publisher of artists editions, through an introduction made by Dietmar Kirves, was ready to begin the slow process of getting Boris's work out to the public. Armin Hundertmark was the closest Boris got to the functioning art world/gallery system. Here was a real dealer who promoted his work. Part of Hundertmark's reputation came from making editions and showing the work of Joseph Beuys and Hermann Nitsch when they were unknown artists. Hundertmark published the first No!art book, designed by Dietmar Kirves, and Hundertmark made some box set editions. Not much sold.

In 1974, No!art –Bags was an artwork published by Edition Hundertmark

1988 FEEL-PAINTINGS - Gallery and Edition Hundertmark

1996 No!art multiple Box Edition Hundertmark (included myself and Elsa Rensaa)

Some of the catalogues and books published:

NO!art PIN-UPS, EXCREMENT, PROTEST, JEW-ART. Edited by Boris Lurie and Seymour Krim. Edition Hundertmark, Berlin/Cologne 1988. (This book was put together by Dietmar Kirves and Boris Lurie. As a protest, there is a white space in the book's credits which is where Dietmar's name would have been. The reason for the protest is explained in the end notes.)

NO! Catalog, Neue Gesellschaft für Bildende Kunst, Berlin 1995. (Dietmar arranged for this exhibition, then, out of an ideological dispute, backed out. His name is only briefly mentioned in the thank yous.)

NO!art Show N° 3 (America) catalog. Boris Lurie, Dietmar Kirves, Clayton Patterson, Wolf Vostell. July-October, 1998. JANOS GAT GALLERY.

Boris Lurie: Geschriebigtes/ Gedichtigtes, 1947-2001 catalog, eds. Volkhard Knigge, Eckhart Holzboog, Dietmar Kirves, Berlin. Eckhart Holzboog Verlag, Stuttgart 2003.

(Note the Gertrude Stein Gallery in 1964 published *No! Posters/Anti-Pop Show.*)

For Boris, having his work understood seemed impossible. In 1946, in America, Boris was probably the first, and certainly one of the most emotionally charged and hardest hitting artists dealing with the horrors of the holocaust. As Boris describes it, he was cursed by being years ahead of his time. After the war, America was about moving onwards and upwards. Nobody, especially American Jews, wanted to hear, go near or enter in a dialogue touching on the subject of the Jewish holocaust. Not in public anyway.

According to Boris, as he spoke with such disdain, the Jewish Museum was busy trying to fit into the "new" American upper-class stratosphere by showing works by exciting Pop artists including Andy Warhol, Frank Stella, and other contemporary favorites. Then, as the years rolled by, the holocaust eventually turned into an industry, again cutting out provocative, rude, caustic art that was as hard and confrontational as Boris's. By now he was old and out of fashion, and, as we know, trendiness and pretentions are important to museums.

Let me give an example, when Sarah Boxer from *The New York Times* (Feb. 6, 2002) discussed with Norman L Kleeblatt, curator of a Jewish Museum exhibition called *Mirroring Evil: Nazi Imagery/Recent Art,* what he didn't include in the show, he told her, "This exhibition will leave out Boris Lurie's *Saturation Paintings,* in which sexually suggestive photographs are mixed with pictures of concentration camps, and Anselm Kiefer's picture of himself giving a 'Heil, Hitler' salute under a piece of public sculpture in Cologne. They are simply too old."

Before going on, let me clarify something that is not made evident in the *Times* piece. Comparing Kiefer and Boris is something like mixing apples and oranges. Anselm Kiefer is a German who survived the war living in Germany. Boris is a Jew, who was taken as a prisoner to a German work camp. So, while both detested the Nazis, they came from different sides, one from that of the aggressors, one from that of the victims, and so their aesthetic and messages are completely different. Another point. To my mind, Mr. Kleeblatt is simply wrong about Boris being too old. I don't know what he means exactly, but if he is trying to say Boris's work is of no interest to young people, I know for a fact that is untrue.

I have shown Boris's work to this generation and seen that many young artists love his art. Ami Goldman got inspired enough when he saw this work to make a movie called *No!art Man*.

Truth is, to Boris, many of the current crop of younger writers about the holocaust tended to stereotype the Jews in the camps. Take the illustrated comic book *Maus*, which won a Pulitzer Prize. Boris hated it and works like it. As he said, "I am not a mouse. We were heroes. We endured. We survived." Indeed, for Boris, Spiegelman's lowly mouse with his heavy accent was insulting.]

I suppose this attitude stemmed from Boris, who came from an upper crust Jewish family, seeing himself as an aristocrat. In a way, even in America, with his cheap clothes and down at the heels look, he was one, with the bearing, the confidence, the poise, and the self confidence.

He had come from a privileged, educated, well-off family, who spoiled him. His father was a successful industrialist while his mother was a dentist. He went to good schools, traveled across Europe as a young student, and spoke several languages.

As David Katz put it in the *Jewish Quarterly* (Autumn 2005):

> Boris Lurie was born in Leningrad in 1924 into an educated, highly cultured Jewish community. He and his family moved to Riga, Latvia, in 1925-6, where his talent as an artist was recognized at an early age. In 1941, when the Nazis invaded the Soviet Union, Lurie and his father were taken prisoner. For the next four years, they endured a hellish passage through the ghettos and concentration camps of Riga, Salapils, Stutthof, and finally Buchenwald-Magdeburg in Germany. His mother, sister and grandmother were all murdered. These primal losses, the Holocaust and all its psychological ramifications became essential and indelible themes in Lurie's painting, sculpture, writing and poetry, themes that he neither sublimated nor shied away from.

One unusual story Boris used to tell was the thrill the people felt when the Nazi's showed up in Riga to take out the Russians, who were not liked, but then things turned. Boris also talks about how he had one sister, whom, pre-Nazi invasion, caused enough political trouble that the police warned her father to get control. She was sent to Italy, and there married a prince, becoming a literal Jewish princess. The family raised horses, eventually moving to America. She was the sole woman in the family to survive.

After Boris and his father were sent to Germany, they managed to stay together during years of imprisonment, not being separated, as Boris described it, until 1945. They were in Magdeburg and the war was coming to an end. It was chaotic in the camp and he got separated from his father. The word was out the Americans were coming. The guards left. Boris wanted to wait in the camp for Americans, but a friend convinced him to leave. It was a good thing they got out, because some guards came back and killed prisoners. Boris found a bombed-out building and slept there till his father found him. His father called him a "dumbkoff" for going to sleep. His father had found and moved into an SS officers' home. As you can see, neither Boris, nor his father in Magdeburg were as weak and sick as the prisoners in Buchenwald proper.

Soon after the liberation, Boris began working with the American intelligence corp. He had a car to drive around in. His father was back in business. Although they were doing all right, he eventually lost his job. Meanwhile, his sister wanted to reunite the family, so in 1946 Boris and his father came to America. His father by this time was in his mid fifties and, though he never regained his former wealth, he did amass a small fortune in NYC real estate.

The father disapproved of Boris's artistic career, particularly as he was unsuccessful. To him, Boris was "meshugena." After the father's passing, Boris began to learn about Wall Street, eventually becoming quite wealthy through investing.

After I'd gotten to know Boris over many years, and grew to appreciate his art, I found myself saddened and disappointed that Boris was not getting the art audience I felt he deserved. I did what little I could to try and find some attention for him. To me, Boris Lurie was one of the most inspired artists of the 20th century. And he was a close friend. That doesn't mean we didn't fight over aesthetic issues, but these dissensions were not carried out in anger, and they only made our mutual respect and friendship deeper. If you cannot fight and get past your differences, you cannot be real friends. Life is not all licking lollipops. At bottom, one thing that kept us close was that we shared a lot of the same No!s.

Although some people found him gruff and hard to take, in Boris I found a lot to admire: his artist voice, his methods, his point of view, his way of expressing himself, his self-taught style, his self-developed outsider art perspective. There was also his fighter's attitude. His desire to stand up and shock the world by using his art to make people think about what had happened to the Jews. There was his dedication to his philosophy and his worldview. His determination to preserve memories, to express ideas nobody wanted to hear, and to make art that was very offensive but stinking of truths. His desire to survive, to continue on, no matter what. His self-conviction and sense of being right, no matter what. His need to start his own direction, his own stream, called No!art. His moral and ethical character. His not being a victim. His fearless heart. His never forget, never give in, never give up, never say die. His lack of shame and his ability to present a harsh statement, with no compromises. His ability to carry on no matter how much criticism was thrown his way. His ability to carry on with little support or little reward. His bluntness. His gall at juxtaposing incongruous images in such a rude way that it caused outrage, yet done so that if one examined these images carefully, one saw the essence of tragedy. His need to have people look at what humanity is capable of: the horrors of war, the brutality, the insanity, the deviance that can manifest under evil conditions. His originality. His belief in the importance of his own lone voice, his subject matter, his mission, and it was a mission about inclusion, remembrance. His toughness. He was an emotional pioneer. When he had something to say, there was no way he would bend or change shape or alter, or make softer, what he meant to say. His brutal honesty. His art was deep and spiritual. Representational. To the point. He represented. Yet, with all of this heavy weight Boris carried, with his great and important message that the world just did not seem to get, he had a loving, carefree, humanistic, jovial section to his being. Boris made me think and was wonderful company. He was not dark or pessimistic. He was a great traveling companion.

He was also difficult, cheap, opinionated, intolerable, argumentative, closed minded, unbendable, self-absorbed, self-centered, spoiled, a poor dresser, aristocratic, chain smoker. He was an Israeli right-wing Zionist hawk. Outside of international politics, an area we did not engage in, I was local, he was international. We fought about everything. But I loved him dearly, thought highly of him, considered him a brother and fellow artist. Boris was an intellectual, read a lot about a wide range of subjects, the different militaries, history, war, holocaust. He was a Zionist from childhood. Buried in Haifa with his father.

If a viewer just bounces across the surface of Boris's art, he or she might read it as nothing more than transgressive, rude, and disgusting, obsessed with degradation and punishment, perhaps attempting to portray the inside of an immoral, authoritative, fascist, S/M disciple, Nazi's sick mind. Sex and death. Lust and death. Dishonor, degradation, and death. And death.

Looking further, though, it's possible to see some important tropes in his work. Note, his sado-masochistic images were appropriated from S/M erotic magazines. The S/M culture can be a highly sophisticated, involving intricate forms of rituals and agreements, bonds of trust and understanding, and worked-out master slave relationships. In this culture, there are alternative ways of thinking about sexual identity, fashion, and one's interplay with other people. BUT it deals with individual consent. Central to this society is the fact that it is governed by a consensually established set of rules and guidelines. It consists of a small social niche of like-minded people, who engage in these rituals/games.

When Boris appropriated these images from the magazines, he changed their meanings. The S/M in Boris's art is not consensual, but turned toward violence, suffering, pain — unrelenting pain — degradation and death. Always death. It has nothing to do with the ritual verbal exchanges of S/M, the "I will be a good boy," following which the slave is released. There is only death and pain. The images add emotional, physical, and sexual pain to the art's surface. Some images exude blood. The woman depicted are not beautiful or romantic. They are not feminine, loving, subjects of desire. They are mature, ripe, woman, who appear to be cheap, ugly prostitutes ready to give pain or disease rather than pleasure. Breasts and brutality and murder.

Boris spent his youth, his spring, the years most people are learning social behavior skills between men and woman, locked up in a segregated concentration camp. These are the experiences depicted in *The Murdered Woman* series. It is not a misogynist's look at woman because in such looks the woman is sexualized. In this series, Boris puts no erotic charge. The viewer is not a voyeur. The women are murdered in a way that has nothing to do with pleasure and sex, and everything to do with the fact that the precious women in his life were murdered. Boris had been a spoiled boy with two adoring sisters, a mother, and a grandmother. All but one of these women were slaughtered by the Nazi's.

There are a few American writers who have written about Boris, and they usually, for the sake of convenience and historical reference, call him a Dadaist. If one really looks at Dada, rather than using it as a convenient label, one sees that the classifying gesture that would put Boris Lurie in the Dada camp is outright wrong.

Think about the various streams of Dada. French Dada of the Duchamp and his pals' school is anarchistic, flip, coming from a position of privileged, upper-class, anti-authoritarianism. This stance is controversial — painting a mustache on the Mona Lisa — without containing important political or social content. For Boris, it seemed too insider, too tongue in cheek. Too foie gras.

The European Nordic Dada strain was more engaged and polemical. The artists in this group went about during World War I attacking the government of their own country for using war and aggression against their neighbors. These were artists using art to attack their own rich, the corporate and the industrial capitalists, assailing them for their insatiable appetite and limitless greed. They dared to throw horrific images in the power structure's collective face. Think of the work of George Gorsz and his images that criticize, make fun of, and exaggerate the immoral, decadent life the rich are leading. Or images that exposed the gross side effects of the government's aggressive behavior: seriously deformed war veterans whose medals did not get them their lives back.

That would sound more like Boris's cup of tea. But this was criticism from within, emerging from its own indigenous, ethnic, racial, cultural, social world. It was a dialogue in which Germans spoke to other Germans, not to, for example, the Turks who may have been born in Germany, but had no citizen rights. Boris, too, would have been excluded from this dialogue. He had no connection to the power that made the evil decisions. He came from another place, from the receiving end. Through his art, Boris becomes a strong, stand-up tough guy defending the innocent Jews.

Let me reiterate that point since it is necessary to grasp it fully in order to see how Boris has to be reclassified as an artist, and not thrown in the Dada camp. Boris was a Jew from first Russia, and then Latvia. His people had nothing to do with starting the war and were not profiting from the troubles. All the murder, mayhem, destruction, death, abuse, rape and pillage, torture, poisoning of land and every living thing in its path, had nothing to do with Boris or his family and neighbors. Why would he (in the manner of the German Dadaists) want to scream at these countries' leaders? Why not scream at the whole population? The German artists' cries were real, sincere, significant, important; but they were not the type that leapt from Boris's throat. He was not implicated in the crimes he denounced. In this sense, Boris is an innocent.

Perhaps, there was an implicit recognition of his exclusion from this German tradition that explains why the more contemporary German art stars, the ones academics are always trying to associate Boris with, I mean those who, like him, brutally rejected the country's Nazi era, did not do anything to help or support Boris. Did Anselm Kiefer or Joseph Beuys ever recognize Boris? I say No! The exception here was his friend Wolf Vostelle, who did show with Boris in a number of No!art shows although, to the best of my knowledge, he didn't include Boris in his own prestigious exhibitions.

The point here is not about recognition but that I believe these artists intuitively saw that Boris did not belong in this German tradition, though critics go right on trying to connect Boris to

Dada or any modern recognized artist. It just doesn't work. Boris was an outsider, a solitary man who stood alone, rejected even by the American Jewish art community.

I think Boris created the No!art group because he wanted to fit in somewhere. He needed the security of a group. He needed to feel he was not alone, although he was alone. The group idea was important to Boris, the idea of a brotherhood and a sisterhood. When he talked about it, I could see the ideal No!art group Boris created in his own head had a large ladies section. In any show Boris was involved in putting together, every artist involved was, as far as he was concerned, a No!artist, even if the artists did not realize he or she was. Still, Boris's artist friends Sam Goodman and Stanley Fisher were the original No!artists.

The group was an aesthetic, not political organization. Boris was never too deep into American protest politics though he appreciated and sometimes supported the art and the artists who were connected to this type of political protest. His real political concern was Israel.

Though not political in the common understanding of the term, No!art was political in terms of challenging of the art world status quo. Boris was anti-Pop and anti-abstract art as styles, and, moreover, against corporate pandering, that is, creating art that was corporate sponsored or that embellished corporate ideals. He also had disdain for the monetarily focused art market and the hyped-up commercial gallery world. To put it most broadly, he was not about art that compromised.

With such attitudes, it's not surprising that he surrounded himself with activists, idealists, dissidents, and questioners of authority. He liked those avant-garde artists whose creativity broke the rules and pierced barriers, especially work that had an anarchistic element. For example, Boris liked and showed the work of the French artist Jean Jacques Lebel, who had participated with the Situationists in the Paris May '68 protests.

At Boris's request, I met with Lebel in Paris. He was an interesting man, from a privileged background, creating intriguing art. Still, as I said to Boris, though he disagreed with my opinion, Lebel, like the rest of the art star types, would show with No!art when he could reap some benefit, but would do nothing to return the favors. Like other stars in the commercial firmament, Lebel enjoyed Boris from afar, but did not have the guts to step inside the circle, and let others know he was affiliated with Boris. Truth is, I didn't get Boris's need for these connections. It means nothing if the appreciation does not go both ways.

The only artists who publically connected themselves to Boris were Dietmar Kirves, Amikam Goldman, who oversaw Boris's burial in Haifa Israel, and myself.

It was when I was in Europe that I would do various favors for Boris, such as meeting with Lebel. I also made a special side trip from Austria to Berlin, to Buchenwald Memorial Camp, and to Paris for Boris. I was already on tour in Europe anyway, and the company I was working with would pay for a trip. I visited Dr. Knigge and the Buchenwald director; in Berlin stayed with Dietmar and Matilda; and in Paris saw the head curator of the Center Pompidou, to whom I gave a No!book. I enjoyed the trips and was enthused at planting seeds, building a foundation for Boris.

To return to my idea, as I see it, both by forming and pushing the No!art movement and by attempting to establish connections with museums and art stars, Boris was trying to promote a counter establishment to the reigning corporate one in the art world. And he not only put on shows and had exhibits, he created a history of No!art, showing its formation and membership, though, on this last point, some artists were adamant in saying they wanted no part of the movement. For years, Yayoi Kusema, for example, was opposed to being included in the No!art history. Boris included her anyway. Others like Herb Brown never knew they were No!artists until the books appeared. Brown, in fact, was grateful for the second wind in his career that No!art brought to him.

However, let me clarify something about how I understand the power of groups to (possibly) propel the involved artists to fame. To my mind, it all depends on the group being led by a keen strategist, the way the Beat writers were piloted by Allen Ginsberg. Back in the early 1950s, there were many Beats, and some were poets. Beats came in many shapes and forms, filled coffee houses, listening to jazz and poetry. Ginsberg, being media savvy, created the illusion that a coterie of writers embodied the movement. He brought in the poets, he drew the circle. He created what became the group known as the Beats. Without Ginsberg, I wonder, for example, if Gregory Corso would have been a well known and respected poet. Not speaking about the quality of his poetry, but about the fact that fame and inclusion is *engineered* and does not happen by chance.

In the art world, there is a romantic illusion, which is spread in art schools and other places of fabricated ideals, which holds that fame is achieved somehow by merit alone. The worthy person is magically engulfed in a mysterious golden pocket of air, which carries him or her up to the surface of public recognition. Out you pop, fame and all.

I bring this up because of a surprising inconsistency in Boris's outlook. Although in many ways, he acted as if he shared my feeling that recognition has to be orchestrated – after all, he did form a group and try to get the attention of curators – he still verbally held to the magical golden bubble theory of how fame can be effortlessly won.

Both of us could agree on many other aesthetic matters, such as the need for artists to leave a legacy, and that there can be a good reason for creative people to link up. We both saw the value of forming groups of like-minded artists, ones who have similar ways of thinking, a common goal, shared idealism, a sense of struggle, and who felt the need for art to have a purpose. We agreed on the ideas that an artist has to be dedicated to a purpose, that art can be used to help humanity, to educate, it can even be provocative, punching viewers directly in the face.

You must be starting to see how, despite our wrangling, Boris and I shared a fund of aesthetic positions. Boris's art, which was brutally up front about the holocaust, did not take this stance as an attention-grabber. In fact, it lost him more friends and supporters in the art scene than it could ever have attracted. But he felt an artist needs to carry on working whether the art is accepted, loved, appreciated understood, or not. To him, it was the work and what the work was about that was of critical importance, not the flames of fame.

And, in the same way, he realized that, while (as I brought out) an artists' group can be primarily concerned with engineering fame, it can (and it's better if it is) be primarily concerned with community, building a network of like-minded, sensitive creators. A brotherhood or sisterhood connection on this level can be deeper than an artistic association of, say, ethnic or minority group, which would ask, "Is the artist a Jew or not? Is the artist gay or not? Did he/she go to Yale?" An artists' brotherhood or sisterhood that is united on ideals can have a mystical and spiritual connection that is deeper than all others. When, in rare cases, such a brother/sister-hood forms, then a community arises that is helpful and supportive of the others in it, whether they are weaker or stronger, older or younger, healthier or not as healthy, more well known or less well known. None of that matters. The bonds are stronger and more important than the type that exist between those on a status plane or professional group.

(I can't help thinking of my dear friend Ron Kolm, who for many years has been at the heart of little-known (though profiled in these pages) dynamic, path-breaking – what other group went to *The New Yorker's* offices to demand they publish better poems – and humorous literary group, called the Unbearables. He explained to me that, in the early years, this group offered the kind of intense community, which Boris and I saw as vital for artists trying to resist the pull of the corporate realm.)

Let me lay it out plainly. For an artist, art is life and life is art. To be an artist is not a choice or a learned experience. One is not educated into being one. It comes from a drive, some kind of unstoppable internal force, some kind of spirit that guides you, bigger than who you are. And when one artist finds a fellow artist, one who doesn't separate him- or herself, but embraces the new acquaintance, a special bond forms, a smaller version of the one that links a brother/sis-terhood. When I met Boris, I formed such a bond.

Boris and I shared something that was, for me, almost indescribable, bigger than both of us. It was more intuitive than concrete. We were completely opposite in so many ways, yet so con-nected. I share such a bond with very few people.

And it is not simply that he was creating art, for, as I see it, there is an artistic way of living that transcends simply making art. Clearly, I am not talking about poseurs, "apes of god," who pre-tend to be artists, without real dedication or principles, but those who have the vocation and show it in every action. One can see this with such a person in a discussion or in how such a person makes connections between people, especially if that connecting results in something else happening, preferably a positive action. This "artistic" bringing together puts into contact different energies so that something, which would not have happened otherwise, happens, an act of creation. Those connections can change people's lives, can be mystical, unseen (before being put into practice) by anyone other than the person with the idea in mind.

Moreover, to touch on another thing that my relationship to Boris brought out, we shared the conviction that part of artists' struggles was to *not* be burdened by others' pre-conceived ideas of what an artist is. And this includes fighting to *not* be a slave to a market or to a job.

On the positive side, being an artist, we agreed, means working on a life philosophy, living by certain values, and allowing dedication to a thought. Moreover, it can involve going to bat for a dead or neglected artist who did not receive her or his due. On the negative side, it's about resisting being deterred by the fact of the public's incomprehension or rejection of one's project. One has to have the faith and the belief in the rightness of one's choices.

I may have argued with Boris about what I thought No!art should be or who should be in the group, but, these dissentions didn't stop me from supporting his struggle. I called myself a brother. Boris was making art when he struggled to save No!art from extinction. He was saving himself.

To be more specific, when I noted just above that, on the negative side, an artist had to resist lack of appreciation or even downright attacks on her or his work, I was thinking particularly of the way Boris kept going after the art magazine critics and academics who wanted to cut Boris's No!art throat in the mid 1960s. It was as if they decided that somehow he spiritually, artistically, and creatively just died, and, so, he never did another thing in his life. As they saw it, with his first scandalous works, his burdens had all been lifted. He had slain his demons and had nothing further to accomplish. A few might say he continued on with his writing and his Feel paintings, but these were dismissed as intuitive groping, blind, purely emotional work. But to say that No!art stopped and that Boris as an artist died in the early '60s is simply wrong.

I also mentioned a moment ago that part of being an artist involved going to bat for true artistic spirits whose work had been neglected or disparaged. I find myself in this essay and in other places willing to take up the bat for Boris in that he is still such a misunderstood, obscure artist, an artist who still must be recognized and given his proper dignified rightful and fully appreciated place in art history. In relation to this, he passed a duty, a torch and a responsibility onto me.

When I watched Boris standing up showing his art in Buchenwald, performing a No!art action, I realized how wrong were those critics who viewed him as simply slaying his own demons, laying to rest his memories of the camp. It was broader than that. He was bringing to the surface the damage that had been inflicted on not just him, but on all of society. His art went way beyond conquering personal demons to allowing others to think about what their own heritage (a heritage full of demons) was about.

So, I will continue to try and make his work known and, particularly, to get people to appreciate some of the unknown sides of his genius. In this case, I feel the action is reciprocal since when Boris asked me to be in one of the shows he organized or to exchange work with me, and I allowed him to choose among my pieces for what he thought was appropriate, he picked ones that no other gallery or fellow artist has shown interest in. These were the mystical works. As he saw things in my work that others missed, so I am hoping that I can bring my understanding of unnoticed elements in his creations to a wider light.

But to go back to my discussion of Boris and my shared understanding of the artistic personality, let me bring up how this (ambiguously) played out in his paradoxical antipathy to Warhol, who, not only in the fact that when it first became prominent, the American's style of Pop Art was being treated like it was as important as the election of John Kennedy while Boris's No!art was treated as if society was trying to bury its very presence.

Let me note some of the other oppositions. Boris had been brought up in an elitist, privileged home and social environment. Warhol's background was poor, working-class. Boris went to private schools. Warhol went to public schools. Warhol came across as insecure, and used his art as his way into the Upper East Side upper crust. Boris was self confident and was attracted to the working class Lower East Side. Boris's art was not of his choosing, at least so much as it stemmed from and meditated incessantly his forced incarceration by the Nazi's. It was as if his message and direction were forced upon him, and this alienated him from his social position. Warhol was the much loved and admired consummate insider, who seemed to glory in those around him on the higher rungs of society. Boris was the rejected-on-all-levels outsider. Warhol was the loved-by-all insider. Warhol was a practicing Catholic who went to mass on a regular basis, and who lived with his mother. Boris was a Jew who never spoke of G-d or observed religious practices or holidays. He was in a court battle, relating to his father's estate, with his step-mother, from the 1960's till the day he died. Warhol was gay; Boris was straight. Well-off Jews supported Warhol; few Jews purchased Boris's art, though that was not an anomaly, nobody bought or supported Boris's work. Warhol showed in the Jewish Museum. Boris was rejected by the Jewish Museum.

And although both of them made art that reveled in appropriation, there the similarity ended. Boris's art includes the real and deep cut to the bone pain and suffering he and others endured as captured slave workers, beaten and murdered. Although, it shouldn't be forgotten that Warhol also portrayed dark images, of electric chairs and auto crashes, his most iconic work, that which brought him fame and for which he is most remembered, is made up of Brillo boxes and Campbell's soup cans. These are light and lighthearted images. Lighthearted, but also empty-hearted, having no connection with suffering or distress, that is, with the human condition.

Another thing that linked the two of them was that both Warhol and Boris were collectors.

Warhol was very diverse in his collecting, which he took good care of preserving, so it has increased in value over time. Boris only collected art that was connected to what he saw as the No!art movement. The years and poor storage conditions have not been all that friendly to the collection or to Boris's artworks. His art should have been placed in atmospherically monitored, temperature-controlled, museum-quality environments, not interned in a basement tomb, boiling in the summer, freezing in the winter, with water dripping on them, mice and roaches gnawing, chewing, picking at the work, and leaving the resulting by-products of these meals dropped all over the work.

The difference in the fate of their collections parallels that of the placement of their work.

Warhol worked with dealer Leo Castelli to skillfully and mindfully put his art into important museums and private collections. Boris, although like any artist wanted to reach these havens, which can only be accessed through prestigious galleries, did favor artist-run galleries, such as found in the 10th Street coop gallery scene, because, as he said, there they had shows based on content not money. And yet, here we hit another of Boris's contradictions. While valuing these cooperative spaces, he prized more highly that he was accepted by a high-class, exclusive gallery. Between '62 and '64, he was in three shows in the uptown Gertrude Stein gallery. This gallery showed a highly valued and consistent art collection with some of the best examples of 20th century masters. Boris's work didn't fit, and the dealer, a friend of Boris's and a sophisticated, experienced dealer, who was an expert at selling established masters, could do nothing with getting recognition for an artist who is not already well known. She was not able to get Boris into the art market, and, consequently, his art has no market value and no auction record.

But, let's get back to Warhol and the point I made that he did occasionally depict horrific images, such as those of auto wrecks. But these depictions were not gripping or in your face. Done on stretched canvases made by paid, skilled shop assistants, the appropriated photo images were silkscreened, i.e., there were not brushstrokes, so as to give the impression they were not touched by an artist, appearing mass produced. And just as meticulously as they were created, were they aimed at a targeted audience. By making them with so little feeling, something indicated by the garish and flat colors and the clean, clinical looking style, even an electric chair or a deadly car accident looked unthreatening and, of course, hip enough to decorate a jet setter's cool wall. These works had no connection to Warhol's life. Was he for or against the death penalty? Who can tell? It's almost as if Warhol were saying he could make any subject inoffensive. These paintings purr like a fat, constantly patted, satisfied cat.

As you can imagine, when Boris painted such themes, they had no such dispassion. Boris's horrific paintings were wild, passionate, breathing fire, emotional, loosely painted, expressionistic, sometimes with acid-filled magazine images ripped out and collaged, added on guerrilla style. These were canvases made by Boris's unskilled-at-labor hands. The materials and gluing agents used in his combined work were often poorly conceived choices, without much archival merit. These works were forced up from the depths of Boris's injured soul. Angry. Sad. Upsetting. Disgusting.

To see the fury, you don't need to look at work that has dead bodies or symbols of death or sexual references, simply one in which he wrote the plain word No! It's a crude No! made with a knife or sharp object of some kind, put on panels composed of brutally torn pieces of old and breakable rotting linoleum kitchen floor tiles. The colors are not pleasing, but rather

ugly, jarring and disjointed. And when he included found objects, they were not like Duchamp's urinal, vulgar but humorous. Rather, as in the melted, red or yellow wax candle series, there were clumps of hair, which look like it had been ripped from some woman's head and left behind at some murder scene.

In looking at what they did overall, Warhol was all yes, yes, yes, sir. And Boris was No! No! No!- and forget the sir.

Yet one surprising element of this whole contrast was that they both became wealthy, and ended up both living on the same block on East 66 Street, just off Madison, almost directly across the street from each other. Boris, for all his iconoclasm, was a property owner, deep into the capitalist system, a successful Wall Street investor. Boris, like Warhol, at one time did fashion industry advertising artwork. Boris married a high-end fashion photographer.

What I've said so far about his being successful yet *at the same time* the producer of disturbing, splenetic art, should let you know that he was full of contradictions, and that, I think, is what brought him to the LES and kept him here. In fact, as time went on, he became increasingly immersed in the neighborhood, cutting many of his ties to the upper crust. He divorced the wife and gave up his social standing, becoming more of a struggling artist, living as he saw fit.

And like his fellow LES bohemians, he lived in a studio/apartment, which was messy, unkempt, and neglected by the landlord. His linoleum floor was so worn that it had a permanent grit like covering it, resembling nothing so much as a layer of sand. The larger back room of his first floor studio extended behind the rest of the building, and had a leaky roof. Consequently his ceiling was falling in and fixed. But, since the landlord tended to do a shoddy job, it would soon be falling in and again and need to be repaired again. Indeed, one of Boris's lifetime battles was with his Brooklyn-based, orthodox landlord. Even though Boris was the landlord of another building, he was a very difficult tenant. He constantly sued his LES landlord, as if he needed to go to court.

Also, like the LES artists he resembled, he kept his studio, spartan. His bed was about a foot off the floor. It was constructed from a piece of plywood covered with a 3-inch-thick layer of foam, covered with a couple of sheets, a blanket and a pillow. His desk was messy, filled with paperwork and old family photos. The second room in his studio apartment, again as with many LES artist's spaces, was a grimy workroom, filled with art on and leaning against the walls. A small toilet was jammed into an awkward, tiny hall space.

As I said, he gravitated more to his LES space than to his uptown apartment, but, after I visited the Upper East Side address, I found that it was not because he was shunning more luxurious digs. In truth, he had allowed that uptown space to deteriorate so that it wasn't much different from his other place. Uptown, Boris had gray, dirty walls, which had never been painted in 30 years. The stoves in both apartments were dark, burnt and grimy. Mice bred and ran free both uptown and downtown. The windows, in both, were covered or had shades pulled down. In other words, there was not much difference between the places, except in where they were geographically situated. No luxuries, none.

However, I've wandered off my comparison, to which I need to return for a few more paragraphs. Both Warhol and Boris made books and prints. Warhol became a publisher of his own work; Boris would never spend a dime on any kind of project like this. And even when others were willing to publish his work, Boris would tend to alienate them with his demands, such as his desire to use outlawed National Socialist-style typeface in one book or to use swastikas, another practice banned in Germany.

Another difference between the two artists is that Warhol's prints were made by fine art craftsmen. Warhol would draw an image to be used for a print, then it would be duplicated. That's the classy way to do things, but also one in which the artist him- or herself is intimately involved. In most cases, Boris would simply have his images photographed, and a print taken from them. Boris did have a lithographic Dance Hall series and the Star of David etchings printed by Martin Levitt, the LES fine art printmaker. And in 1964 he had a set of offset prints done with his original artwork, published by Gertrude Stein. I strongly disagreed with the cut-rate, shortcut method used for these latter prints, done via the photo method. This violated the ethics of print-making. I'm not saying, by the way, that such violations are never called for, if done for a specific artistic reason. But if it is done simply to get a product to market and damn the consequences as far as capturing the spirit of the artist, I think it violated the aesthetics and philosophical tenants of No!art.

I should add that Boris said he was not doing this, making prints, as a money-garnering scheme, but simply as a way to make his art available to the public. Fine. He had a reason. Albeit, a bad one.

But enough with the comparisons. There's another issue I want to bring up. When I first met Boris and recognized what I took to be his incredible artistic power as well as his quirky but authentic integrity, I decided in myself I would do what I could to promote his career.

I could see he was alienated from the art world, had zero options in terms of showing his art, and yet that he wanted to get his art out there so he could communicate. I did what I could for him.

In my life, I've been privileged to meet and befriend a few overlooked, unappreciated creative giants, who I appreciated and supported, having complete faith in their work and their need to be discovered. To mention three, there was Lionel Ziprin, extraordinary mystic, storyteller, thinker and writer, as well as savior of his grandfather's record collection, one that was recorded by Harry Smith. He's discussed in this book. There's also Nelson Sullivan, who is not Jewish so he's not in this book, although he does have a piece in companion volumes, which I also edited. In *Captured*, about LES film and video, he wrote an essay, and he is mentioned in *Resistance*, about the changing politics of the LES. To me, he is an unrecognized video genius. Third is Danny Stein, who has one of the most important and overlooked contemporary LES Orthodox Jewish community photographic archives. He also is completely unrecognized. I do what I can to keep these names alive, out there.

As to Boris, when I was touring in Germany and Austria, I brought along a box of Noart! And whenever I had time would drop off a free copy at a gallery or museum. Planting seeds. At the Clayton Gallery and Outlaw Art Museum, I gave him his first NYC show in about 30 years as well as including him in a group shows. In giving Boris the solo show, I knew he would never contribute one cent towards it nor extend a hand to help. As far as he was concerned, the gallery must handle all charges, all incidentals, all calls, all invites, and provide all services including alcohol. He wasn't distinguishing between the Soho and Upper West Side galleries, which had money to spend and personnel to spend it, and the more informal, low budget style of most LES galleries. And it was also a psychological thing. The idea if you do something yourself, it means you are not worthy, you have made a compromise.

Even with his less than helpful attitude, I pulled out all the stops in getting publicity. Fortunately John Strausbaugh, editor in chief, *NY Press*, wrote an extensive article, starting off with a reproduction work of Boris's filling the front cover, to a multi-page inside article. This was during the period when the paper was the best free newspaper in the city. John now writes a monthly column in the *Times*. Marvin Griesman wrote an article for the *Jewish Press*. Boris was also interviewed on the cable show *Conversations with Harold Hudson Channer*.

Such notice eventually led to a comprehensive article by David Katz in the *Jewish Quarterly*, and a number of pieces by Jan Herman in his web column *Straight up Arts, Media, & Culture*. After Boris's passing, Colin Moynihan, wrote a solid obituary in the *Times*.

I did all this work for Boris because I have faith once that his message is understood, someone will hear his voice and will step up and do the right thing, both in terms of getting him a wider hearing and showing the place his art can play in healing our fractured world. At the moment, however, I don't see much cause for hope. Aside from Boris's long-time supporter Dietmar Kirves, those who control his estate or are connected to his work haven't done much for him, at least, in my opinion. .

After he died, it was a typical situation of a storm of people wanting to take over and get a piece of the action. Boris, who had made some plans for his legacy, did not leave his affairs in the hands of righteous people. There was a lawyer he tried not to pay, who will not respond to questions. Another key person is a dysfunctional drunk. There's a dealer who did nothing for him in the past, and now is in control of key decisions. There's a career, mid-level bureaucrat in Germany, with all the myopia such officials generally display. Swirling around, I've seen a lust for money and imaginary art riches, but there is no thought or vision, and little love for what Boris was all about.

Boris had formed an advisory board, to which I was named. I thought the most obvious way to get his work noticed was to have a large retrospective. The response from others connected to Boris was, at first, warm, then lukewarm, then cold. An exhibition could have created an initial noise, and got the rhythm, and energy moving in the right direction. No one was really interested.

Still, as I said, I have tremendous faith. Eventually his voice will be heard and the message will be understood. I can't think of a better way to end this history and tribute than by citing a remembrance written for Boris by Aldo Tambellini.

To Boris

Remembering the many many times coming from Cambridge, MA, I stayed at your apartment on E 66th ST...the late evening & half of the nights, 2 artists talking about WWII-world politics-social issues-sometimes debating our beliefs in ART & yes, discussing the state of the ARTS-our long discussions on the phone-the many letters with clippings you sent me which led to even more discussions this old friend misses you, this poem for you, Boris:

the supersonic wind
blows creative thoughts
away from mental prisons to the sky
blowing past the planets
away throughout dark mysterious matter
echoing among galaxies
away where creative minds
burn their visions

with the energy of billions of fiery stars
As a kind of appendix to this article, I want to present a selection of Boris's shows, published work, and related events, and follow (to end this essay) with profiles of those who found something of value in his work.

2007 Screening *NO!art MAN* - The Third Ear-Screening rooms, Tel Aviv

2006 *SHOAH AND PIN-UPS* - Film by Reinhild Dettmer-Finke

2005 *WILD BOYS, BAD BOYS, OUTSIDERS* - a group show at Clayton Gallery & Outlaw Art Museum with Aldo Tambellini, Angel Orensanz, Boris Lurie, and others.

2005 THE 80's: 326 YEARS OF HIP - Clayton Gallery & Outlaw Art Museum. A Group Exhibition of Four Octogenarian Artists, Beach, Huncke, Lurie and Mead. Curated by Loretto, Patterson and Rasin. January 21st - March 31.

2004 THE HEAVY WEIGHTS - at Clayton Gallery & Outlaw Art Museum a group art show of artists who have worked on the LES for more than two decades, including Jim Power, Taylor Mead, Peter Missing, David Leslie, Spider Webb, Elsa Rensaa, John Penley, and Boris Lurie.

2004 FEEL-PAINTINGS/NO!art Show No 4 - Janos Gat Gallery, New York

2003 OPTIMISTIC - DISEASE - FACILITY - Boris Lurie, Buchenwald Weimar-Buchenwald Memorial (Germany)

2003 BORIS LURIE: GESCHRIEBIGTES/GEDICHTIGTES - 1947-2001 No!art in Buchenwald catalog with poems, images, and commentaries in German.

2002 NO!ART AND THE AESTHETICS OF DOOM - Iowa Museum of Art, Iowa City, IA

2002 NO!ART MAN - documentary film by Ami Goldman about Lurie

2001 NO!ART AND THE AESTHETICS OF DOOM - Block Museum, Evanston, IL

1998 LIFE - TERROR - MIND – SHOW - at Buchenwald Memorial, Weimar

1998 NO!ART SHOW # 3 - WITH Boris Lurie, Dietmar Kirve, Clayton Patterson & Wolf Vostell - Janos Gat Gallery, New York City

1997 NO!SHOW - with Mathilda Wolf and Dietmar Kirves, Clayton Gallery

1997 BORIS LURIE CONGRESS OF RESISTANCE, - New York

1996 146TH BOX EDITION, Hundermark editions - includes Boris Lurie, Wolf Vostell and, Dietmar Kirves

1995 BORIS LURIE und NO!art - Neue Gesellschaft für Bildende Kunst, Berlin

1994 NO!art - (with Isser Aronovici and Aldo Tambellini) - Clayton Gallery & Outlaw Art Museum

1993 OUTLAW ART SHOW - Clayton Gallery & Outlaw Art Museum, with G. G. Allin, Michael Cezar, Michael Wilson, Boris Lurie, and others

1989 GRAFFITI-ART - Nassauischer Kunstverein, Wiesbaden

1988 NO!art PIN-UPS, EXCREMENT, PROTEST, JEW-ART - book, edited by Boris Lurie and Seymour Krim

1978 COUNTERCULTURALE ART - with Erro and Jean-Jacques Lebel, American Information Service, Paris

1975 RECYCLING EXHIBITION - Israel Museum, Jerusalem

1974 BORIS LURIE AT INGE BAECKER - Inge Baecker Gallery, Bochum

NO!art-BAGS Gallery - Cologne

NO!art with Sam Goodman and Marcel Janco - Ein-Hod-Museum, Ein-Hod, Israel

1973 NO!art PAINTINGS seit 1959 - Gallery René Block, Berlin; Gallery Giancarlo Bocchi, Mailand

1970 ART AND POLITICS - Kunstverein Karlsruhe

1964 NO! POSTERS / ANTI-POP POSTER SHOW - Gertrude Stein Gallery, New York

1963 NO!SHOW - Gertrude Stein Gallery, New York

1962 SAM GOODMAN & BORIS LURIE - Gallery Schwarz, Milane

DOOM Show - Gallery La Salita, Rome

1961 PINUP MULTIPLICATIONS - D'Arcy Galleries, New York

INVOLVEMENT SHOW - March Gallery, New York

DOOM SHOW - March Gallery, New York

1960 DANCE HALL SERIES - D'Arcy Galleries, New York

ADIEU AMERIQUE - Roland de Aenlle Gallery, New York

LES LIONS - March Gallery, New York

TENTH STREET NEW YORK COOPERATIVE - Museum of Fine Arts, Houston

VULGAR SHOW, March Gallery - New York

1959 DRAWINGS USA - Museum of Modern Art, New York

1958 BLACK FIGURES - March Gallery, New York

1951 DISMEMBERED FIGURES - Barbizon Plaza Galleries, New York

1950 BORIS LURIE - Creative Gallery, New York

David Katz (New York, NY), wrote of him "I had the honor and privilege of meeting Boris through Clayton Patterson and interviewing him for *The Villager* and *Jewish Quarterly*. He was a profoundly human, deeply talented individual who had managed to retain his humanity and identity and talent despite the penultimate adversity and extreme horror of the Holocaust, and not only survive but create astounding works of art from his experiences. Boris was tough, opinionated, feisty, unafraid to shock or provoke, intellectually courageous, and, unlike many of the university trained, MFA generated artists of today, had never relinquished his anger, a quality I find in short supply in today's art world. He was not afraid to piss people off in an effort to make them think; he was not given to pretty pictures designed to soothe the sensitive bourgeois soul, or color coordinate with the new couch. He will be sorely missed by all who believe in the power of art to change the world."

Ami, born 1973 in Israel, created the first documentary film about the NO!art co-founder Boris Lurie under the title *NO!art MAN*. He lives in Tel Aviv.

Dietmar Kirves, born in 1941 in Fürstenwalde/Spree, Germany. Since 1964, he has done mixed media works with film, photos, music, sculptures and environments. In 1970, he created a media contact agency in Düsseldorf. He met Boris Lurie in 1975 and aimed to push the NO!art movement, helping publish in the NO!art anthology at Edition Hundertmark, Cologne. Lives in Berlin.

Much of the information presented in this essay came for the No!art books, from the Internet and from the years I spent hanging out with Boris. See my extensive archives http://www.no-art.info/text/attention.html

As an editor, **Clayton Patterson** *has published* Captured: A Film & Video History of the Lower East Side *(with Paul Bartlett and Urania Mylonas),* Resistance: A Radical Political History of the Lower East Side *both published by Seven Stories,* Wildstyle: The History of a New Idea *(ed. with Jochen Auer) Unique publisher, and* The Front Door: Photos & Other Artistic Reminiscences *O.H.W.O.W. publisher. He also has been the focus of a documentary by Ben Solomon, Dan Levin, and Jenner Furst:* Captured *(Video on Demand)*

Boris Lurie, NO!art and The Buchenwald Memorial

Dr. Sonja Staar, Curator, Buchenwald Concentration Camp

> I learned at Buchenwald the basics of my art education. First of all, you
> do not make art when you are in danger. You make nothing at all, except
> perhaps weapons. Secondly, Michelangelo disappears in the presence
> of a knife. – Boris Lurie

I first saw the art of Boris Lurie in December 1998. I remember being deeply and emotionally impressed by the radical nature of the collages, paintings, and objects.

Realizing that NO!art had no possibility of an exhibition in the German Democratic Republic or Former East Germany (GDR), I was extremely pleased the art of Boris Lurie could and would come to Buchenwald, the former Nazi concentration camp located in Weimar (Germany). The whitewashed rooms of the restored disinfection building of the concentration camp were to be filled with his artworks.

During the days it took to install the 2003 show at the Buchenwald Memorial, we wondered if Boris Lurie – a survivor of Buchenwald-Magdeburg – would be able to come to the inauguration of his show. But appear he did. This attentive, friendly and charming person was very interested in the reception of his art in Germany, especially after the German reunification of 1989.

In our correspondence since then, I learned a younger generation of immigrant artists in New York is interested in his work.

From Leningrad to Riga to Buchenwald to New York

Boris Lurie was born on July 18, 1924, in Leningrad (which is now known as St. Petersburg). He was the second child of merchant-father and dentist-mother. His family relocated 10 kilometers away to Riga, Latvia. It was in this location where he spent his early childhood and adolescence with his parents and two sisters. While there, Lurie attended the Ezra School where instruction was given in German. He was an active member of Jewish-Zionist youth and Maccabi Riga (a Jewish sports organization).

At the age of 11, he became curious about the art of the Belarus-born, Jewish-French artist Marc Chagall. Three years later, while visiting his married sister in Italy, Lurie saw an exhibition of

Renaissance painter Paolo Veronese's paintings; for some reason, they embarrassed him. Many years later, he tried to explain his feelings of that experience. Despite the colorful canvases, Lurie said, "The canvases smell of sweet-gray-pink death." By the end of World War II, he admitted that Chagall and Veronese were no longer of interest to him.

While in Riga, the Lurie family endured a series of social disruptions due to political changes: in 1934, the fall of the parliamentary-democratic government and installment of an authoritarian nationalist regime; in 1940, the invasion of the Red Army and subsequent Soviet occupation in Latvia; and, in 1941, the incursion and subjugation of Riga by German troops. Of the three, the latter was the most difficult for the Luries and their co-religionists. Latvian anti-Semites began their persecution by forcing the Jews from their homes into the Riga Ghetto with its double, barbed wire and electrified fence. Life in the ghetto was characterized by the struggle for daily survival. Almost 30,000 lived in 16 blocks. Its hospital was poorly supplied. Every morning, workers – consisting of men and adolescents – left the ghetto. During the day and upon their return, the Jews experienced degradation and attacks by the guards.

In late November 1941, the Riga Jews were told they would be moving again. They made the journey to the Rumbula Forest. On November 30 and December 8, about 1,000 to 1,700 men – comprised of SS officers, members of the Latvian auxiliary police and reserve, and the Latvian Special unit – massacred 28,000, almost every Latvia Jew. Among the victims were Boris Lurie's mother, sister, and grandmother. Lurie, his father, and others were spared in order to do work for the Nazis. Every day, though, these survivors were under constant threat for their lives whether they remained in Riga area work-detachments or had been sent to concentration camps.

On November 19, 1944, Lurie and his father were sent to Buchenwald-Magdeburg where they managed to stay alive until liberation in April 1945. As described by Eugen Kogon in 1946:

> [Buchenwald] was a city of its own, built solely by the labor of the inmates.... There were neither cars nor horses to pull the wagons.... There were barracks, detention cells, a central kitchen, laundry, bath facilities – modernly equipped, but without water. There were production work-shops, a sawmill, pig-breeding facilities, a vegetable garden, a brick-yard, quarries, a riding school, a zoo, dog breeding facilities for bloodhounds, an infirmary, a general records department, a depot, and a wood yard, hairdressers, guards and command towers, music bands, a sculptures workshop and a woodcarving shop.

By 1943, a railway line and armaments works had been constructed. That same year, Spanish writer Jorge Semprun was arrested in France for his Communist Resistance Group activities and sent to Buchenwald. In a fictionalized account of what it was like, written in 1963, the author further described the camp:

> Everything in Buchenwald is administered, classified, registered, invento-ried and initialed: the inmates' money, the number of articles manufac-tured in the factories, the number of working hours and leisure time, the

living and the dead, the cost of operating the crematorium, the homosexuals and the gypsies, the watches and the hair of the new arrivals, the
professional qualifications and studies of the deportees, the purchases of
beer and *machorka* [Russian tobacco] in the canteen, even the 'visits' to
the brothel. Bureaucratic order prevailed within the SS realm.

The everyday life of the prisoners was a radical change for the political inmates, Jehovah's Witnesses, persons with multiple criminal offence records (so-called "professional criminals"), persons regarded as "asocial" or "work-shy," homosexuals, Sinti and Roma [Gypsies], Jews, Dutch
inmates, persons from Czechoslovakia, Soviet prisoners of war and citizens, Croatians, French,
and Belgians, among others.

In 1946, Benedikt Kautsky – who was a prisoner in several concentration camps, added more
to the portraiture of this place of horror:

In reality, a concentration camp was a world [where] the feeble ones
were condemned to remain at the bottom forever and wait helplessly until
they were ground down to nothingness and there was no other place for
them but the crematorium. On the other hand, almost everyone who
could fight did fight – for a better position, for a bit of food, for a better
bed, for a less badly torn blanket, for a piece of soap, for a whole shirt.
It was every man for himself ... because what one person managed to
get, the other had less of, and fighting could only make the common cake
smaller, but never bigger.

One form of resistance in the camp was cultural activity. Prisoners created drawings and paintings; wrote and sang songs and other musical compositions; and produced plays and poetry.
Training and talent were was just one set of conditions for such. The artistic inmates needed
those who could find the necessary materials in the camp's offices, protect the artists, hide their
creations, make paper, or even smuggle work away from the camp. The discovery of a drawing
depicting the reality of the camp life could mean death for the artist. These works were dangerous, potential testimony and evidence for prosecution. They also represented traces of remembrance and epitaphs for the dead as well as affirmed the dignity of the degraded. These
artifacts existed because tiny cracks existed in the system of the terror.

Boris Lurie reminds us that concentration camp internees worked in 12-hour shifts. Without sufficient food, many died slowly of hunger. He says a few, however, endured the cold and were
treated relatively well as long as they didn't violate camp rules. This had to be some feat. In the
Buchenwald Concentration Camp, nearly a quarter of a million of people were tortured and
humiliated, and murdered.

Meir Levenstein in his German language book *You Shall Die and Not Live* (1993) reported in
the weeks before liberation in 1945, as Allied bombs were heard nearby, the prisoners lived
between their fear of death and their growing hope of survival. Some escaped the camp, only
to be caught, flogged, and shot. As Levenstein writes: "To run off the camp into this town was
pure suicide. The population acted, without exception, in a hostile manner. There was no hope
of getting help."

However, this was not strictly true in that Boris Lurie was a successful escapee. He didn't contact the unreliable townspeople, but found shelter in an abandoned house destroyed by bombs, staying there, where his father, who left the camp at another point, found him.

After the SS officers left the camp, the two returned there where they were, by his own account, "falsely liberated," which is to say, the troops were "liberating" them, but since their captors had already fled, there wasn't much to liberate them from.

Boris mentioned an example of bizarre and unbelievable behavior, which he witnessed at the time of the "liberation": "How does one make sense of the suddenly "free" prisoners who honored a "decent" SS officer by attempting to lift him onto their shoulders – as the first gesture of their liberation – although they were dehydrated skeletons?" When Edward R. Murrow reported for the BBC about the liberation, he reported a similar incident, albeit with a different honoree: "As I entered, I was surrounded by men who tried to lift me up on their shoulders. They were too weak. Many of them could not even get out of bed."

More than a year after liberation, in June 1946, father and son emigrated to New York City where 22-year-old Boris began a search for a way to express artistically the totality of the persecution experience. He asked himself several questions. How does a victim of violence survive when encumbered with painful memories? How does one endure ever-present photographic evidence of the concentration camps that was frequently published in weekly and monthly magazines? How does one deal with societal ignorance and indifference of their reality? By 1952, he added another question: How does one cope with the acquittal of those who had been responsible for murder in the Buchenwald Concentration Camp?

Lurie soon began to express his experience of the Holocaust in small format paintings. *Back From Work* (1946), *Roll Call in Concentration Camp* (1946), and *Entrance* (1946) are somber and depressing portraits of Nazi prisoners in the Stutthof Concentration Camp, which still manage to evoke the prisoners' grace and worth amid such despair.

From New York to Paris to New York to…

During the mid-1950s, Lurie tried living in Paris. After a couple of years, he returned to New

York with the reinforced moral imperative to "remind the world of much too much." In 1958, he created *Les Lions,* the year he also created *Adieu, Amerique [Farewell to America]*, which was intended to signal his next departure from the United States. These works, however, not only initiated a prolific artistic output, but kept the artist stateside. These collages combined girlie images cut from the then-current print media with photographs of heaps of corpses discovered when the Allies liberated the concentration camps. The pin-ups reveal the degradation and exploitation of a people, while simultaneously revealing these women's life, vitality, and power. The Holocaust photographs divulged the obscenity of humiliating, abusing, and destroying people, while simultaneously somehow revealing the victims' release by death, their testament (or proof) against lies, and – ironically – the preservation of a people. This paradoxical imagery, as Seymour Krim (1963) says, "screams, roars, vomits, rages" to enable viewers to express their own human emotions.

The years 1959-1964 were the best years for Boris Lurie and his friends, the artist Sam Good-man and the writer Stanley Fisher. Together, they founded the NO!art movement in cooperation with the now-defunct March Gallery (later called the March Group), on 10th Street in New York's Lower East Side. The March Gallery artist cooperative died in 1964, the same year Lurie's father died. In 1967, Sam Goodman died; 13 years later, Stanley Fisher died.

Though considered an important chapter of 20th century art, their work is not well known despite the efforts of a few art critics, gallery owners, and writers. Now, a half a century later, the NO!art movement is being rediscovered by a new generation and by those who wish to exhibit experiences and thoughts about the Holocaust. The disquieting images – with their espousal of violent expressionism – were conceived and executed in response to what he saw as the clashing cultures: postwar, frivolous consumerism versus the horrors of World War II and the Cold War's atrocities. Works like this are not easily viewed. And they were easily dismissed by the public and the critics.

In the first decades following World War II, Americans rarely discussed the Holocaust. Historian Peter Novick writes: "By the late 1940s and throughout the 1950s, talk of the Holocaust was something of an embarrassment in American public life... Between the end of the war and the 60s, as one who has lived through those years can testify, the Holocaust made scarcely any appearance in American public discourse directed to gentiles." He further explains that the fear of Communism, the political reactions to totalitarian governments, as well as the postwar opti-mism encouraged this silence. Furthermore, the American post-war society with its "booming economy that had avoided the widely expected postwar slump, [in what was] now by far the world's richest and most powerful nation" was looking forward, not backward.

Despite this American norm, Lurie produced a series of paintings between 1947 and 1959 enti-tled *Dismembered Women*. Through each different style, he decided to confront his life experi-ence against the principle credo of the then-current American way of life. In an interview with Dietmar Kirves, Lurie explained that artists have traditionally painted for two primary reasons: creating and selling. He and his NO!art associates added another: *destroying pretensions*. They put the claimed values in society about sex and art under the microscope. Lurie declared rebellion, protest, revolution, "guerilla fighting" as necessary and fundamental attitudes in life and in art. Merging life and art, NO!art had to challenge and provoke. Art had to become a space of refuge, a sanctuary, a place of desire and even a hell. In Lurie's mind, the NO!artist was a revolutionary in the real world and in art. Rejection of conformity, the "psychological falsehood," has to be radical if it expects to be true and convincing.

The medium to express his social criticism was found in 1959 via collages made of newspaper clippings and photos, which he partially covered with paint. These collages reveal the tragic, grotesque, and obsessive emotions and reflections that haunted (and still haunt) him. Placing girlie images on a canvas covering social and political issues gave the whole works ambiguity, tension, vitality, meaningfulness, and expressiveness. With these master works, Lurie became made himself an outsider as well as opponent to celebrated Pop Art where commonplace objects (such as comic strips and soup cans) were used as subject matter, created using com-mercial techniques (such as silk-screening), marking a return to more objective and recogniza-ble art (compared to the abstract art). While NO!art, like Pop Art, used reality for its compositions, NO!art rejected and criticized society; it had no desire to affirm society. In addition, the essential starting point for both artistic concepts – reality – was different for artists in both camps. As quoted above, Boris said, "The basis of my education in art, I learned at Buchenwald," in writing to art critic Thomas B. Hess in May 1966. In 1970, Lil Picard – who had been associated with the NO!art collective – in an address to an imaginary interlocutor, who rejects the tenets of the movement

> You tried to convince yourself that the cleaned-up "protest" is better than the rough and dirty form, because you want to escape the reality of dirty walls, dirty studio floors, dirty hallways, cockroaches, Bowery bums, the bloody mess of humans lying like shit on city streets and at the entrances of artists' studios, and the horrible images of war massacres and war-dead that bombard your visual senses in color every day on TV, from color pages in magazines, and in movies.

> Don't tell me today [the interlocutor would say] that "NO!art" is … more relevant to the issues of our time and could save the world from sick democracy and global destruction....

> [On the other hand, Picard says to refute the interlocutor] it might be that when the art history of the fifties and sixties will be written and evaluated in the relation to political and historical events, this specific political protest art [NO!art], post World War II protest art, could be the most significant expression of our so-called sick times.

Lurie, after watching the continuing racism and inhumanity in the world, said the job of counter-compliance artist is to upset the status quo. He quoted Russian poet Vladimir Mayakovsky, who in 1911 wrote, "Art is not a mirror to reflect the world, but a hammer with which to shape it!" So even after the demise of the March Gallery in 1964, the alternative art movement in which he was involved found an outlet by exhibiting in Italian, German, and American galleries.

By the mid-1970s, after visiting Soviet-held Latvia, Lurie developed a new cause. He complained about unmarked mass graves being used a garbage dumps. After the Union of Soviet Socialist Republics (U.S.S.R) collapsed in 1991, Latvia became an independent country. A year before, Latvia adopted a declaration denouncing genocide, war crimes, and anti-Semitism. It has since confronted crimes against humanity that had been committed under the Soviets and Nazis, and inaugurated events concerning Jewish genocide in Latvia. In 1990, it established the Jewish Museum of Riga.

Some of the reassessment carried out in Latvia also has occurred in Germany. In 1998/99, NO!art returned to its roots in a symbolic way: The Buchenwald Memorial organized a retrospective of Lurie's works which the artist attended.

The exhibition included the aforementioned 1946 concentration camp scenes, the dismembered women series, Lurie's 1970 series of *Feel Paintings* (which focused on libertine femininity expressed by burlesque dancers, dance-hall girls and pinups), and his *Candles*. Sculptures in the form of the NO!suitcase and the NO!bag, sold at the show, were covered with the images of Boris Lurie's art. Representing the artist's aggression and fury, the images served as epitaphs for those who perished more than 50 years earlier. The reception was held in the whitewashed, ugly, plain rooms of the former disinfection building where countless people were degraded.

In 2003, Boris Lurie published in Germany *Geschriebigtes Gedichtigtes* based on the 1998 exhibition. More than a catalog of his artworks, it includes a collection of texts, with essays by those who brought together the show, Lurie's poetry and verse, and also an interview of the artist by his friend and co-editor Dietmar Kirves. Each represents the tragic experience of the writer as well. Sometimes the words open the curtain over some terrible episodes and, surprisingly, some happier episodes occurring during his childhood. The prose, as in the section "Nacht, Stutthof" (1947), makes one hope for an autobiography.

Afterword

The Boris Lurie show at the Buchenwald Memorial owes it installation to a number of predecessors. It was also not the last done by survivors.

In 1990, we installed a permanent art exhibition with drawings and paintings created in the Buchenwald Concentration Camp and its sub-camps by survivors and members of the younger generation decades after the Shoah. This presentation was and still is the only permanent exhibition of its kind in Germany.

In 1991, we gave a show presenting the sculptures and paintings of Fischel Libermann, a survivor of the Buchenwald sub-camp Schlieben. Also a Yiddish writer, Liberman taught Yiddish at the Goethe-University in Frankfurt/Main and published melancholic stories that recalled the Piotrków Shtetl in Poland. Before the Buchenwald exhibition, he had only shown his works in Frankfurt.

In 1992, we collaborated with the Osnabrück Museum, which owns 170 of Felix Nussbaum's works, and presented some of his oil paintings and sketches. By his twenties, Nussbaum had successful shows in Berlin art galleries. By the early 1930s, he moved from Italy to France, then to Belgium to be a step ahead of the Nazis. In mid-May, when German troops invaded Belgium, he was arrested and sent to the Saint Cyprien Concentration Camp in Vichy France. A few months later, he escaped and returned to Brussels where he hid in a cramped attic, but managed to occasionally paint in a friendly art dealer's cellar. In June 1944, he was discovered and deported to Auschwitz, where he was soon murdered. His works, believed to have been lost, resurfaced in 1955 when they were revealed by friends who had safeguarded many of them.

In 1994, we collaborated again, this time with Yad Vashem, and showed the colored pencil drawings and watercolors of Thomas Geve who, as a teenager, survived the Auschwitz, Groß-Rosen and Buchenwald camps. After April 1945, in Buchenwald barracks, Geve drew for his father – who had emigrated to Britain before World War II – what life had been like in the camps.

In 1995, we dedicated a show to the graphic artist, painter, and sculptor Walter Spitzer, a survivor of the camps of Auschwitz, Groß-Rosen, and Buchenwald. In the camps, despite severe penalties if he had been caught creating art, Spitzer drew and exchanged his works for bread; these works are now preserved in the Ghetto Fighters' Museum in Israel. His sculpture *Musulman* (1994) is in our permanent exhibition.

In 1996 and 2005, we held exhibitions – of the graphic arts, sculptures, paintings and other objects – of the Polish stage director, scenery designer, playwright, painter, and graphic artist

Józef Szajna. The artist survived Auschwitz, Buchenwald and sub-camp Schönebeck. Two images painted on the wall of his barracks have been preserved and are now presented in our permanent art exhibition, together with his "Reminiscences" series created in 1969.

In 1999, we had a show with drawings of Nachum Bandel. By 17 years of age, he had experienced and survived the porom [the roundup of Jews to be sent to a concentration camp], Auschwitz, and Buchenwald. In Cyprus, on his way to Palestine, Bandel's artistic gifts were discovered and he received – with 25 others – art lessons. Once in Palestine, he used his spare time to sketch in ink and pen.

In 2003 we presented an exhibition of paintings of the Gypsy survivor of Birkenau, Flossenbürg, and Buchenwald: Karl Stojka.

Among several shows dedicated to younger artists were the installations of the American-Jewish artists Lisa Kokin ("Remembrance") and Edith Altman ("Six Million Almonds"), the British-Jewish artist Jenny Stolzenberg ("Forgive and do not Forget"), the Israeli artist Naomi Tereza Salmon ("Asservate"). Jenny Stolzenberg and Edith Altman, as daughters of Buchenwald survivors, used their art to examine and demonstrate the different symbols of victimization experienced by their fathers.

The 2006 video "Menschen.Dinge" [artifacts; that is, objects made or modified by a humans] installation was dedicated to Esther Shalev-Gerz who photographed objects found in the earth of Buchenwald, restored them, and asked people to discuss them.

Boris Lurie's art fits into the Buchenwald Memorial offerings by serving as a memorial and a stimulus to discussion about human intolerance and survival.

References

Kautsky, Benedikt. *Teufel und Verdammte* [Devil and Damned]. (Zürich: Büchergilde, 1946).

Kogon, Eugen. *Der SS-Staat. Das System der Deutschen Konzentrationslager* [The SS Community: The System of the German Concentration Camps]. (Germany: Karl Alber Munchen, 1946).

Krim, Seymour. *No Show*. (New York: Gallery Gertrude Stein, 1963).

Levenstein, Meir. Du Sollst Sterben Und Nicht Leben [You Shall Die and Not Live]. (Germany: Lit, 1993).

Novick, Peter. *The Holocaust in American Life*. (New York: Mariner Books, 2000).

Picard, Lil. "YES & NO Thoughts to the Issues of the Past" (http://no-art.info/_text/picard_yes-no.html, 1970).

Semprun, Jorge. *Le grand voyage* [The Long Voyage]. France: Gallimard, 1963.

Dr. Sonja Staar, *Foundation of the Thuringian Memorials Buchenwald and Mittelbau-Dora, born 1952, linguistic and art studies at the universities in Jena and Halle (Saale), promotion in literature sciences 1980, same year starting work at Buchenwald Memorial, there head of the art collection with artifacts from the concentration camps, survivors' art and contemporary art, collaboration in exhibitions on the history of the Buchenwald concentration camp, concept and organization of the permanent art exhibition, Means of survival. Testimony, Artwork. Visual memory. (Überlebensmittel. Zeugnis. Kunstwerk. Bildgedächtnis) 1998, research work on art about concentration camps.*

The Power and Challenges of Boris Lurie's Work

Dr. Max Liljefors,
Department of Art History, Lund University, Sweden

As I write, the ferry to Gdynia (Poland) passes across the bay outside into the calm dusk. We have had no real winter in the south of Sweden this year. The sea level is unusually high. The distance from my writing cabin at Cape Knösö to New York feels palpable. It is a twelve hours flight away. It is almost eight years since I was there. Then I was not yet aware of Boris Lurie's art; I encountered it for the first time shortly thereafter, in 1999 at the Buchenwald Concentration Camp Memorial outside Weimar, Germany. Weimar was the designated European Capital of Culture and a retrospective exhibition with Lurie's work was mounted in the former camp's disinfection cellar as part of Weimar's attempt to address its charged historical heritage as a symbol of humanity's potential for cruelty.

I visited Buchenwald as a member of a research group commissioned by the Swedish Prime Minister's Office to study German and Polish institutions for the remembrance of and education about the Holocaust, the Nazi genocide on European Jewry. "What is the best possible manner to extract edifying lessons from industrial genocide?" was the unrewarding question we were asked to ponder. Homeward bound, onboard the Gdynia ferry, still taken by the uncompromising character of Boris's art, I knew that I had to include him in the doctoral dissertation about art and the Holocaust that I was writing at the time.

As I communicated with Boris by mail, telephone, and fax, he initially seemed less than enthusiastic about my interest in his work. He, nonetheless, was willing to be interviewed. He never hesitated to counter any assumption of mine he considered premature or wrong. When I sent him the finished book, he doubly surprised me by being able to read some Swedish (a fact he never hinted at during the interviews) and by approving of my approach (although I am not sure he would agree with this description now).

It occurs to me now that I have always thought of him as a European artist.

History is repetitive. The hidden truth behind the erroneous idea that history repeats itself focuses on two aspects: The *writing* of history usually follows familiar narrative conventions that recount the past as "stories" with beginnings, middles, and endings. The *presenting* or *telling* of history is based on critical examination, evaluation, and selection of information from primary and secondary sources. The latter, however, requires the historian to extract material from so many events that – to satisfy both the demand for causal explanations and the desire for meaningful narratives – omissions become unavoidable. As the saying goes, you cannot have a story if you do not leave anything out.

To me, conventionality paradoxically appears particularly striking in a historiography concerned with tales about heroes and pioneering, masters and masterpieces, and struggles of a courageous few against the forces of nature or tradition – especially in the area of modern art. The variety of artistic expression that has evolved in this through modernity is commonly framed by modern art historiography as so many variants of the struggle of art against – and its victory over – bourgeois convention. Gustave Courbet's rejection of salon romanticism, Édouard Manet's scandalous *Olympia*, and Vincent Van Gogh's inability to sell fit perfectly into the frame story of modern art as revolt against convention. It also explains the embrace of what may be called "pejorative baptism" – originally scornful expressions by hostile critics, such as impressionism, fauvism, and cubism, turned into official modern art terminology.

Within this frame story, one narrative stereotype has gained particular momentum: The Discovery of the (Hitherto) Excluded Artist. Its foremost grace is its honorable intention to bestow fame on artists whose work has not, for whatever reason, been appreciated and studied sufficiently. While thus proposing an alternative to the mainstream art canon, though, this narrative also reproduces an essential component underlying that canon, since it is prone to argue that the artist in question was originally excluded for being too controversial even for an art world tuned to the unpredictability of the avant-garde. Clearly, what makes that argument so appealing is that it transforms the artist's exclusion into a "proof" of outstanding "quality," according to the criterion of the very system that excluded him or her.

However, I am skeptical. Firstly because an artist's omission from art history may depend on (any combination of) factors: structural hegemonies (class, gender, ethnicity); unrecognized genius; too little talent for making art or for self-promotion; too much talent for making enemies; and/or simply bad luck. Secondly, and this is worse, playing the too-controversial-card will too easily lead to a not-so-interesting, cut-and-dried, rebel-without-a-cause cliché, at worst relegating all other aspects from the scope of interpretation.[131]

Thus one was not very surprised to find in a recent major book about 20th century art (written by four of America's most renowned art historians and likely to become a standard university textbook) the complete lack of any reference to the NO!art group, active from 1958 to 1964 on the Manhattan Lower East Side, and to the group's "dominant male", Boris Lurie.[132] Lurie (b. 1924) founded NO!art[133] together with Stanley Fischer (1926-1980) and Sam Goodman (1919-1967). Apart from them, a number of artists partook in NO!art exhibitions and other activities, including names like Isser Aronovici, Allan D'Arcangelo, Herb Brown, Ferró (to become Erró), Dorothy Gillespie, Allan Kaprow, Yayoi Kusama, Jean-Jacques Lebel, Michele Stuart, Stella Waitzkin, and Wolf Vostell.

Initially called The March Group[134] after its first venue (The March Gallery), an artists' cooperative gallery on Tenth Street, the group later changed its name to NO!art after its war cry "NO!" often spelled out in Lurie's pictures. In 1963, the group relocated uptown, to Gallery 5 Gertrude Stein. Although diverse in style, most NO!artists applied a trashy, vulgar, anti-aesthetic mode of expression in their outspoken critique of American society in general and of the New York art establishment in particular. The titles of exhibitions – such as The Vulgar Show (1960), The Doom Show (1961), The American Way of Death Show (1964), and The NO!Sculpture Show/Shit Show (1964) – signaled their contempt for the aloofness of "high art".

The omission of NO!art from art historiography started already in the early 1960s. By then, the identities of the new and emerging art movements were far less clear-cut than they would later appear in the art history books. This becomes especially lucid when one considers the strained relation between NO!art and Pop Art, commonly described as opposites, even adversaries. In Lucy Lippard's well-known book Pop Art from 1966, NO!art is included, Lippard[135] explains, "only to dispel confusion by placing it properly outside Pop Art. [The NO!artists] are all that Pop is not.... They are anguished, angry, and hot where Pop is cool, detached, and assured."[136]

Two years earlier, though, art historian and critic Edward T. Kelly had argued that NO!art and Pop Art were essentially the same, and that both belonged under the heading of Neo-Dada. Each strove, Kelly thought, to purify the commercial consumer society through its own vulgar, superficial forms, albeit with a different "degree of violence". Kelly put forth his proposition in polemics against Peter Selz, curator at MoMA, who in 1962 had organized a symposium on Pop Art, which he inaugurated by explicitly rejecting the usefulness of the term Neo-Dada, since the original Dada "intended to change life itself" and Pop did not, according to Selz.[137] Lurie himself has stressed the antagonism between NO! and Pop in peremptory terms; yet the emphasis put on their being direct opposites surely indicates an elemental affinity between them (which, of course, one could say is a prerequisite for all comparisons). Still, despite support from a few influential persons like Thomas Hess, critic for Art News, and (somewhat belatedly, around 1974) Harold Rosenberg, prominent anti-formalist critic, NO! in the long run received little recognition, while Pop made art history.

Recent efforts to rehabilitate NO!art as a significant art movement have tended to foreground its marginalization, to the extent that exclusion in itself, as it was, almost appears as the true meaning of NO!art. For example, art historian Estera Milman underscores the uncompromising stance of the NO!artists in perfectly heroic terms, in a catalogue essay flanking a NO!art exhibition that she curated at the Northwestern University's Block Museum in 2001. Furthermore, Milman – in her own words, the "NO!art's 'designated' North American historiographer – describes the exhibition as a belated response to Rosenberg's challenge to the art world 30 years ago, to inscribe NO!art in art history.[138] And although I whole-heartedly applaud that endeavor, I cannot help feeling hesitant in the face of what I perceive as an exaggerated focus on NO!art's controversialism. Is there not a risk that such a focus reduces an inquiry into the meaning of NO!art to a mere search for a cause of its marginalization, and, accordingly, makes that cause appear to be the sole key to what NO!art "is about"?

More specifically, it is the Holocaust as subject matter in Lurie's and Goodman's art which, in Milman's view, explains NO!art's continued marginalization. Milman is not alone: the "rediscovery" of Lurie in the mid-1990s is primarily a discovery of him as a "Holocaust" or "survivor artist." His exhibition in Buchenwald in 1998-99 would hardly have taken place had he not been incarcerated in Magdeburg, one of Buchenwald's satellite camps, during World War II. (Born in Leningrad to Jewish parents, Lurie grew up in Riga. Several family members perished during the Nazi occupation of Latvia, while Boris, his father, and a sister were deported to camps in Lenta, Stutthof, and finally Magdeburg, where they were forced to work in the armaments industry. After the war, they landed in Italy and soon thereafter immigrated to the United States.) All reviews I have read from the Buchenwald exhibition describe Lurie's work as expressive of the concentration camp experience in his youth or as a working-through the trauma it induced in him. The same goes for the majority of the essays in the comprehensive catalogue to a NO!art exhibition in Berlin in 1995, the first major manifestation of the renewed interest in NO!art.[139]

In contrast, Lurie's personal history does not seem to have mattered much for the understanding of his work in the 1960s and 1970s. Despite Lurie's frequent use of the Star of David, the swastika, and documentary photographs from the camps, the Holocaust is rarely referred to in American texts from that time or in the Italian reviews of an exhibition that Lurie and Goodman showed in Milan and Rome in 1962. Instead, as mentioned earlier, NO!art was understood as dealing with contemporary political and social issues, rather than with history. In fact, I am aware of only one text about Lurie from the 1960s that focuses on the Holocaust. It is a review by Rosalind Wholden of a group exhibition in Los Angeles in 1964, to which Lurie had contributed an object called Immigrant's NO-box. Wholden, however, does not honor Lurie as a Holocaust artist.[140] On the contrary, she indignantly calls Immigrant's NO-box a "loathsome thing" and a "pestilence" for desecrating Hitler's innocent victims through its juxtapositions of concentration camp photos and pinup pictures. Wholden's characterization of the artist's conscience as "subhuman" (echoing the Nazi term Untermensch for "inferior people") lets us assume (or at least hope) that she was ignorant of Lurie's own Nazi camp experiences.[141]

Lurie's personal past was by no means a secret. He would refer to it occasionally in metaphorical comments about the New York art world. The general unconcern for his Holocaust experiences did not depend, then, on that they were not known, but on that they did not seem important for understanding his art, regardless of all its overt atrocity imagery. Milman is absolutely right in pointing to the heightening of Holocaust awareness that has occurred in the last decade as an explanation of the new readiness to appreciate Lurie's work today.

In the 1960s, not many artists were prepared to deal with the Nazi genocide explicitly, let alone incorporate photographic evidence thereof in their art. (The foremost exception is probably the Californian-based expressionist painter Rico Lebrun, who modeled his "Buchenwald Paintings" from the 1950s on atrocity photographs from the camps. Lebrun also participated in the Los Angeles exhibition reviewed by Wholden, and was criticized by her – although more mildly than Lurie – for displaying self-pity in his work.) And despite the increase of public interest resulting from the screen version of The Diary of Anne Frank in 1959, the publication of the Jürgen Stroop report in 1960, and, above all, the Eichmann trial in 1961, the Holocaust had not yet acquired the immense momentum in the historical consciousness that it has today. Therefore, it makes sense to say that the (art) world was not prepared to receive and assimilate the subject matter of industrial genocide that NO!art had put on the agenda.

However, there is another side to the matter. I do not think that the world has simply "caught up" with Lurie, and therefore is now able to recognize and respond to the Holocaust as subject matter in his art. Regardless of what one thinks about the causes behind the unfolding of contemporary Holocaust interest – does it represent a working-through of a long-repressed trauma as historian Dominick LaCapra suggests or is it the effect of conscious political choices as historian Peter Novick argues? – it has now established a culture of remembrance and education, governed by state authorities and manifested in museums, educational programs in schools, official ceremonies, etc., not to speak of the orchestration of collective emotion that is the privilege of popular culture. In one word, Holocaust memory has become institutionalized, and thereby contributes to how we learn to interpret and respond to the world. That is a quite remarkable development.

A quarter of a century has passed since the French philosopher Jean-François Lyotard compared the Holocaust to "an earthquake [that destroyed] not only lives, buildings, and objects but also the instruments used to measure earthquakes directly and indirectly".[142] Through that image he tried to evoke the sense of a catastrophe of such magnitude that it exceeds our faculties for judgment and interpretation. What has occurred since Lyotard proposed his metaphor is that the earthquake has been transformed into a building foundation, a base for consensual social values, similar to what Lyotard used to call a "grand narrative." For better or worse, the institutionalization of Holocaust memory also entails its domestication. For the history of industrial murder to be shaped into a compulsory school subject, a meaningful narrative must be extracted and indigestible implications filtered out. That entails, among other things, processing the unfathomable scale of genocide through the register of "personal experience," as evident in the sudden appreciation of survivor testimonies. And although Lurie, as Milman points out, hardly conforms to any victim stereotype, I believe that the new understanding of Lurie as a "Holocaust survivor artist" has sprung not only from the maturing of society to face the difficult subject of industrial genocide, but also from its codification of that event into something culturally meaningful.

And that is the point at which I hesitate. Not primarily because the category of "personal experience" is insufficient to harbor the implications of the scale of the Holocaust (no single victim could know, experience, or reveal that[143]), but because the interpretation of Lurie's work as "Holocaust art", expressive of his camp experience in his youth, brings a premature closure to what I regard as the genuinely questioning character of his work. In fact, I see that interpretation as an example of how the Holocaust has become a frame story, within which a reassuring meaningfulness can be ascribed to phenomena that, in actuality, is troublingly resistant to meaning. In what remains of this essay, therefore, I will try to consider Lurie's art in its openness, its refusal to answer questions.

In an essay from 1989, the American minimalist/postminimalist artist Robert Morris reminisces on his farewell to the traditional values of art in the 1960s, as he carpentered his minimalist pieces in his New York studio. His phrasing is worth quoting:

> When I sliced into the plywood with my Skilsaw, I could hear, beneath the ear-damaging whine, a stark and refreshing "no" reverberate off the four walls: no to transcendence and spiritual values, heroic scale, anguished decisions, historicizing narrative, valuable artifact, intelligent structure, interesting visual experience.[144]

In retrospect, Morris connects his "no"-experience to an undercurrent of negativity that he detects throughout 20th century art. Discontinuous and often overshadowed by formalism or by political ideology, the two dominant trends in modernist art, negativity has emerged irregularly at various moments in art history, Morris says, as a category always at risk of calcifying into form, gesture, or convention, it has manifested – if I understand Morris correctly – as a variety of (formally heterogeneous) ways to destroy or sabotage the beholder's act of reading or interpreting the work of art. An archetypical example is the Dadaist "simultaneous poems" performed by Hugo Ball and Richard Huelsenbeck at Cabaret Voltaire in Zürich in 1916, in which a poem was recited in several languages simultaneously, making any version of it incomprehensible – meaning eclipsed by an overload of information.

Despite the huge formal differences between NO!art and the minimalism that Morris represents, Morris points to what I see as a crucial feature in Lurie's art: a refusal to become imbued with meaning, a resistance to definite interpretation. Negativity, in this sense, is particularly strong in Lurie's collages and montages, where fragments of images and words and disconnected objects swarm and collide, but never merge into one unified sign – Lurie has described this artistic strategy as "simultaneity of attack."[145] The German art critic Matthias Reichelt has observed that Lurie's crude juxtapositions of attractive and repulsive elements – pinups and atrocity images – mirror the image flow of mass media society, where televised pictures of glamour and atrocity succeed one another incessantly.

While TV mediates its transitions between incompatible contents through cool wipes and vignettes, though, Lurie's coarse collages bring incompatibility to the front.[146] Indeed, in some works – like *Lumumba is Dead* – the grotesque plethora of pasted images resembles a time-span of TV, compressed into a single moment and stretched spatially across the canvas. As the American cultural theorist Fredric Jameson has remarked about the image-flow of television, no single sign in this picture-grove can dominate long enough to determine the signification of the other signs or of the sum of them all. Meaning, therefore, is perpetually postponed.[147] Collage, like television, is in this respect a genuinely modern mode of expression, difficult to imagine without the fragmentation of the semiosphere – the universe of signs – brought about by the proliferation of information technologies.

By definition, collage entails the violent forcing together of disparate elements that will always remain out of context, out of sync (or we would not recognize it as a collage). Through the invention of collage by Braque and Picasso in 1912, marking the transition from analytic to synthetic cubism, not only new but plebeian materials – such as newspaper snippets, mass reproduced prints – were allowed into the realm of high art. A break was also made with the paradigm of visual likeness in pictorial representation. For all its far-reaching abstraction, analytic cubism clung to the criteria of visual resemblance. Indeed, abstraction is ultimately nothing but a negotiation along the axis of resemblance. With collage, signification became radically arbitrary: Anything could now stand for anything else, given it occupied the right position in a system of relations, that is, the composition of the picture plane.[148]

To some extent, Lurie's shift around 1960 from his *Dismembered Woman* paintings to the collages echoes the move from analytic to synthetic cubism.[149] In the *Dismembered* paintings, abstraction conflates with the deformation of the female body (in principle not unlike Rico

Lebrun's *Buchenwald* paintings, where abstraction equals the material disintegration of the mass grave corpse), whereas the subsequent collages abolish the picture space altogether in favor of the superficiality of the image plane. However, this also has bearing on the significance of *paint* in Lurie's work. As the new, "alien" materials of synthetic cubism destroyed the taken-for-granted identity of the artistic image as one homogenous surface of paint, another consequence was the realization that paint itself was ultimately an alien ingredient, an intruder without birthright claim to the status of foundation – an insight which, somewhat belatedly, would spawn a far-reaching impulse to investigate painting as "an expanded field." In several of Lurie's collages, paint enters precisely as a foreign substance, as base and undifferentiated matter. It neither belongs nor yields to the levels of composition or signification, but operates on those levels solely through covering, erasing or dissolving any distinction set up at them. In works such as *Untitled*, negativity is manifested in its perhaps profoundest form, as monotonous matter spreading across the canvas, denying the validity of meaning altogether.

This aspect of paint as matter also sheds some light on what is probably the most (in)famous NO!art activity: the NO!Sculpture Show/Shit Show at Gallery Gertrude Stein in 1964.[150] Goodman, in cooperation with Lurie, filled the gallery space with painted plaster sculptures that looked like huge piles of human excrement, evoking strong responses from audience and critics. Even former Consultative Chairman of the Department of Twentieth Century Art at the Metropolitan Museum of Art Thomas B. Hess dissociated himself from NO!art at this point. The German art historian Georg Bussmann has described the Shit Show as the ultimate NO!art manifestation, since presenting shit as art, he claims, negates all expectations for sublimation and aesthetization in art.[151]

Indeed, but after 25 years of abject art – in the catalog to the "Abject Art" exhibition at Whitney Museum in 1993, Lurie and Goodman is mentioned as forbears to John Miller's "excremental" works of the 1980s – shit has clearly risen to become art. Ultimately, the disgust we may feel before feces emanates from the division of the world into the categories of "pure" and "impure," and the substitution of one for the other not only transgresses but can also ultimately uphold those categories. Far more profound is the nausea that overwhelms us when those categories are erased altogether, revealing art and excrement alike as nothing but neutral, indifferent matter.

To me, however, negativity is most strongly pronounced in the works by Lurie where only two or a few images are juxtaposed. In them, the inherent tension in collage as a medium, between the incongruity of its parts and the composition of the unified image field, is realized at its utmost. In *Lolita* from 1962, a torn poster for Stanley Kubrik's screen version of Vladimir Nabokov's novel *Lolita* faces a documentary photograph of dead Holocaust victims. Here, negativity dissolves meaning not so much through an overload of information as by short-circuiting two distinct and irreconcilable visual messages – attraction/ abjection, seduction/horror, culture/trauma.

Normally the two images belong to different cultural registers, e.g., "historical document" and "cultural expression," where each is processed according to its own parameters. And indeed, each image is troubling in itself. The *Lolita* poster, touching on the topic of pedophilia, provokes the viewer by positing him as the addressee of the girl's seductive gaze and thereby as a potential child molester. In extension, it brings up issues of sexualization, visual enjoyment, shame, and power in modern visual culture.

The atrocity photograph, in turn, brings to the fore the grave implications of the advent of industrial genocide in modern civilization. The picture was originally taken on April 16, 1945, in Gardelegen, eastern Germany, by the American soldier E. R. Allen. It depicts the bodies of three of the more than 1,000 inmates from the Dora-Mittelbau camp, who had been murdered by the SS two days earlier. Evacuated in the face of the Allied advance, the prisoners had been herded into an empty barn that was set on fire by the SS. Those trying to escape the flames were gunned down by the waiting guards outside – that is probably what happened to the man in the foreground of the photograph, who tried to tunnel under the door.

Separately, each image opens painful although quite different questions about ethical choice and responsibility; questions which for all their complexity can be, and are, worked- through by interpretative labor. However, in Lurie's *Lolita*, their forced immediacy locks them in a tense stalemate, effectively blocking all processing of them individually. I think it is important that this short-circuit of meaning is pulled off visually. The collision of the two visual signs is created by their co-existence within one image field as much as by the incompatibility of their content. Their difference would have little consequence, had it not been carefully organized into a relation of visual affinity. The hand that the Gardelegen corpse in the foreground seems to raise to his face, in an uncannily pensive manner, mirrors the erotically charged lollipop that slides between Lolita's painted lips. Even more effective, in this respect, is the overall composition: the shared horizontal direction of Lolita's and the corpse's head counterbalances the verticality of the picture field, which, in turn, is mirrored by the orientation of the Gardelegen photograph. Furthermore, the picture is divided horizontally into a lower part, dominated by the *Lolita* poster, and a smaller, upper part, dominated by the black-and white photograph. From this division, other proportional relations arise. For example, the proportion between the lower section's width and height corresponds approximately to the equivalent relation (although with height and width reversed) in both the Gardelegen photograph and the whole picture field. The vertical division of the upper section at the photograph's right edge corresponds, in turn, proportionally to the horizontal division of the entire picture.

In sum, the collage demonstrates a high degree of what in composition theory is referred to as structural simplicity: a limited number of *kinds* of relations between the constituent parts of the composition and between the parts and the whole picture. It is this compositional rigor which interlocks the two photographs, and their respective meanings, in a repellent, yet static – I avoid saying "balanced" since balance implies harmony – tension, like that of two magnetic poles of the same charge facing each other within a narrow frame.

In *Railroad Collage* from 1963, a single pinup photograph is crudely pasted onto a horrifying (and much-reproduced) photograph of a boxcar loaded with emaciated corpses, taken in Buchenwald in mid-April 1945. As revolting a combination as *Lolita*, this work merges its unsuited parts seemingly effortlessly, by a variety of aesthetic means. The similarity in scale and lighting makes it difficult to perceive the photographs separately as unrelated items. Almost filling the entire picture, the boxcar extends obliquely into the image depth, its direction supported by the eaves above, while the girl looks in the same direction. Moreover, the alignment of the upper edge of the photographs adds to this effect, as does the precise touch of the girl's right hand at the edge of the boxcar as well as the photograph's slight transgression of it, echoing the chain on the left side of the picture.

The exactitude of composition, so at odds with the incompatibility of contents, points to the critical role of beauty in Lurie's art. At first this may seem an odd statement to make, given the general rhetoric of "trash" and "anti-aesthetics" that surrounds NO!art. Beauty in NO!art, if mentioned at all, is usually described as accidental and insignificant, as when Thomas Hess remarks in passing that Lurie and Goodman "have stumbled into beauty" and that "art always sneaks back in to the studio".[152]

My opinion is quite the opposite. I find beauty absolutely decisive to the power of Lurie's work; however, I do not mean the weak and domesticated kind of beauty usually associated with ideas of "aestheticization" and "romanticization". No, I see in Lurie's art a relentless, unsentimental, sharp, and knife-like beauty, painfully precise, executed cold-bloodedly in the very moment of rage. It operates primarily on the level of composition, simultaneously simple and complex, adding precision to the sheer force of subject matter.

Max Liljefors is an associate professor in Art History and Visual Studies at Lund University, Sweden. He has published books and essays on the representation of the Holocaust in art and visual culture, on video art, and on visual culture in relation to the philosophy of history and the philosophy of law. He is currently pursuing research on contemporary scientific imagery and on the human/animal divide in modern philosophy and art.

---

[131] "It is extremely difficult to produce a kind of art that histories will pass over in silence, that the art magazines will dismiss, that will embarrass collectors and be offensive to most other artists. The Lurie-Goodman-Fisher activities in the March Gallery and later in the Gertrude Stein Gallery succeeded in achieving this large negative." Brian O'Doherty, "Introduction to a No!art Anthology," 1971 (www.no-art.info).

[132] Hal Foster, Rosalind Krauss, Yve-Alain Bois, and Benjamin H. D. Buchloh, *Art Since 1900*. London: Thames & Hudson, 2004.

[133] "We were opposed to the mute chest-beating of the Abstract-Expressionistic esthetic, to its refusal to be outspoken and concrete, to its romantic, ivory tower isolation fraught with ambitious power struggles. We were determined to cry out, to say everything at the expense of good table manners, to dispense with an idea of art that prevented action. We felt that the break had to be made absolute." Boris Lurie interview with Kathy Rosenbloom, 1974.

[134] Interviewer: "And what did you do in the March Group?" Response: "Exhibitions, exhibitions and once more exhibitions, actions and Environments for the people to get something to their eyes. You have to bring it vividly to their eyes. And if they aren't able to read you have to explain it to them like a graffiti on huge walls outside in the streets: MORT AUX JUIFS! ISRAEL IMPERIALISTE! In bloody colors if possible to express our rage. That's why we called our exhibitions DOOM SHOW, SHIT SHOW, NO!SHOW etc." Boris Lurie interview with Dietmar Kirves, 1995 (www.no-art.info).

[135] "I had a temporary job at the Museum of Modern Art where I met Lucy Lippard. She was not yet politicized and an advocate of socially conscious art.... I took her to the March Gallery. Riding in the elevator at the Museum of Modern Art, I overheard William Seitz, then the curator of modern painting, while looking over a list of shows for consideration: ''Not Lurie and Goodman – absolutely not!' Art history was being fabricated. NO!art was being dropped into the abyss, between hot Abstract Expressionism and freeze-dried Pop Art. The die was cast." Suzanne Long, "Erinnerung an die NO!art-Zeit" in NO!art Show Catalog. Berlin: Neue Gesellschaft für Bildende Kunst [NGBK], 1995, pp. 157f.

[136] Lucy Lippard, "New York Pop," in Lippard (ed.), *Pop Art*. London: Thames & Hudson, 1982 (1966), pp. 102f.

[137] Edward T. Kelly, "Neo-Dada: A Critique of Pop", *Art Journal*, XIII/3, spring 1964, pp. 195f.; 201. Also see Estera Milman, *"NO!art" and the Aesthetics of Doom*. Block Musem of Art, Northwestern University, 2001, pp. 15ff; 27, n. 26-29.

[138] Milman, p. 11.

[139] NO!art Show Catalog. Berlin: Neue Gesellschaft für Bildende Kunst, 1995.

[140] "What concerns me personally, I have been an artist since childhood. My imprisonment during World War II and its experiences certainly are a part of my personality, and it also enabled me to take a contrary [to art fads and fashions] point of view. But the NO!art that later followed was a direct result of the very tough circumstances in New York. It was only at the very beginning when I arrived in New York in 1946 that I did illustrational painting connected with the concentration camps etc. The Dismembered Women, though directly referring to New York, also had a war-content. And later, within NO!art (particularly after my first post-war visit to Riga in 1974), I included extermination-subjects [such as the Rumbula-boxes with torn pinups; Rumbula being the extermination spot in Riga]." Boris Lurie, interview with author, 2002.

[141] Rosalind G. Wholden, "Specters – Drawn and Quartered," in Arts Magazine, vol. 38, May-June 1964, pp. 17f; 115.

[142] Jean-François Lyotard, The Differend: Phrases in Dispute. University of Minnesota Press, 1988, p. 56.

[143] "Earlier, [Holocaust survivors] were told that even if they wanted to speak of the Holocaust, they shouldn't – it was bad for them. Later they were told that even if they didn't want to speak of it, they must – it was good for them. In both cases, others knew what was best." Peter Novick, The Holocaust and Collective Memory. The American Experience. London: Bloomsbury, 2000, p. 83f.

[144] Robert Morris, "Three Folds in the Fabric and Four Autobiographical Asides as Allegories (or Interruptions)," in Art in America, vol. 77, Nov. 1989, p. 144.

[145] Seymore Krim, "NO show at Gertrude Stein gallery", 1963. http://no-art.info/_text/krim_no-show_en.html.

[146] Matthias Reichelt, "Boris Lurie. Werke 1946-1998. Gedenkstätte Buchenwald im ehemaligen Desinfektionsbaude 15.12 .1998 – 10.5.1999," in Kunstforum International, no. 145, May-June 1999, pp. 391-394.

[147] Fredric Jameson, Postmodernism, or, The Cultural Logic of Late Capitalism. London and New York: Verso, 1991, pp. 87f.

[148] As Rosalind Krauss has pointed out, that is why cubism influenced the semiotic theories of the Russian formalists. See Foster, et al., pp. 112-117.

[149] "Cubism: Because of Braque, they started taking apart the painted object and trying to show if from different perspectives. So there is a NO! even in that. It was not a social or political NO! but one could extrapolate that and say that there was something even social and political about it. Actually, anything that is of any importance in art has to have a certain challenging element. It does not agree with everything." Boris Lurie, NO!art man, 2003.

[150] "These people are frustrating. They still won't come right out and be shocked. They, the culturati of the New York art world, look right at the mounds lying there on the floor and talk about them in terms of the usual, their mass, their tension, their thrust, their plastic ambience and so forth. Boris was outraged. 'These people are so intimidated by the aesthetics of modern art and all this aesthetic double-talk,' he said. 'They are afraid to look at it as what it is, which is dung. They just want to look at it as sculpture. They come in here and touch it and talk about form. I think they're too intimidated to express what they feel about a so-called work of art.'" Tom Wolfe, Interview: SCULPT & Local 1964, (www.no-art.info).

[151] Georg Bussman, "Jew Art," in NO!art Show Catalog, NGBK, 1995, p. 61.

[152] Thomas Hess, Introductory text to Shit Show, 1963.

An Interview with Tasha Robbins

Romy Ashby & Foxy Kidd

Did any of your family come through the Lower East Side and live there?

My great grandparents came from Russia in the 1880s, from Minsk and Pinsk. My grandmother was born in the 1890s and when she was a little girl, her family was located on the Lower East Side. Seventh Street was what I heard. My grandmother told a story about her little brother Henry taking a bagel and an apple and running away from home, which is where the Seventh Street reference came in, and that would have been before 1910. He probably sat on a stoop and ate the bagel and the apple and then went home. My mother's family spent a lot of their lives in Brooklyn, where they may have had furniture stores. Later on, my grandfather, who was a singer from Russia, ran a music store. He died in the sleeping sickness epidemic in the '20s.

Was your family observant?

We didn't keep kosher but we had that in the background. After my grandfather died, my mom grew up in her grandmother's house with her mother and her uncles and aunt, so she was in an orthodox household. I don't know if my father's family was very observant except for the Sabbath and the high holidays, but that grandmother could beat the hell out of a carp to make gefilte fish, and I used to watch her. So we had culture trickling in, but my dad was a real rebel. There was a lot of assimilation. I went to a Protestant prep school and I was a bit of a self-loathing Jew. I absorbed some of that.

When did you live in the old East Village?

I lived there the years that I was an art student, which was 1968 to the summer of 1971. First I came and I lived with Chaim and Renee Gross on LaGuardia Place. Chaim was a Jewish sculptor and a great teacher on the Lower East Side. He was involved with the Henry Street Settlement and the Educational Alliance on East Broadway. My parents and uncle were close with the Grosses; my dad collected his work and they had a great friendship. He was kind of a mentor when I was just starting to draw and paint.

After LaGuardia Place, I lived on St. Marks Place and on Sixth Street between Second and First avenues. I shared a two bedroom at 103 St. Marks Place, with a kitchen and another room, for about $150 a month. I got evicted from there because I let a musician crash with his girlfriend one summer. Then I moved over to a teeny-weeny apartment on Sixth Street. It was all one room, and sometimes I would have a roommate in the front and the roommate would sleep on this set of trunks with pillows on it. That was 75 bucks a month.

Nobody considered that dirt cheap down there then, did they? That was just what the rent was.

Yeah. I had an allowance, a few hundred dollars a month, and it was just the right proportion of what you're supposed to pay for rent.

I was at the New York Studio School for Drawing, Painting and Sculpture at 8 West Eighth Street in the old Whitney Museum. I had gone to a very academic undergraduate college in art history and the Studio School is based on atelier work. It was even more so then: paint draw, sculpt; paint, draw, sculpt, a lot of mentoring and great teachers.

I would walk home from the Studio School. I'd walk down St. Marks Place past the Electric Circus. I was much too shy to go inside; it never occurred to me. I was so preoccupied with learning to paint. It was crowded outside the Electric Circus and the crowds were not unlike the way they are now, only it was not a rerun. I'd swim home through the crowds at the Fillmore East. Odyssey House was across the street from me on Sixth Street. It was a detox facility for narcotic addiction, and they had these massive garage sales with clothes all over the entire block and you could go and roll around in the clothes and pick things out.

I spent a lot of time at the School, night and day, so it wasn't a very domestic scene. Groceries were from little bodegas, and if I *was* cooking at home, I'd make scrambled eggs with vegetables for people. We'd go eat at the B&H, and we'd go to Ratner's. There was maybe one Indian restaurant. We'd go to the Paradox on Seventh Street, right around the block, and that was a macrobiotic place. I ate there a lot. The food was healthy and cheap, fish and rice and brown rice, it was very yummy. I used to go to the Odessa on Avenue A with this crazy Russian boyfriend I had one winter. He had a place on Mott Street. Mott Street was quiet and full of snow when I went to see him. I remember the Peace Eye, Ed Sanders' bookstore at the northern end of Tompkins Park on Avenue A. I went in there a little bit. It was small with floor to ceiling books and packed with light.

Did you get to know Ed Sanders there?

No, I got to know him at Naropa about ten years later, as a scribe in his investigative poetry class. I eventually moved to California and came back to New York a couple times a year.

Did you meet Ginsberg there?
Yes, I studied with him there in 1976.
Did you ever work with him on any projects?

Yes. In 1977, I was studying poetics at Naropa and Allen was preparing to bring out the first version of his album *First Blues.* He needed someone to make a cover with which to submit it to Columbia records. I had given some of my gouaches on brown paper as presents (to Peter for his birthday, a kind of green gibbet in the clouds; and a blue window with a moveable scrap of cloud to Gregory). So Allen asked me to work with him on an album cover and we came up with a simple funky one with primary maitriya-like colors and the cloud image and his photo in an oculus on a black field on the verso; and we sent it off ... and waited ... Finally, a student who had a friend at Columbia gave her a call, and the report was that the whole caboodle was being rejected as "bad music and bad art"! I've always taken that as a great compliment; and *First Blues* later came out through John Hammond as the double album with Robert Frank's cover, which was brilliant.

In the Goodie *website Salon, we've featured some of Tasha's work, including several of her* Angel Alphabet *paintings. She created 22 of them, one for each letter of the* Alphabet Malachim, *which is an angelic script derived of the Hebrew and Greek alphabets, created by Heinrich Cornelius Agrippa, during the 16th century. She started this project in 1988.*

How did you come to do the series called An Angel Alphabet?

I started studying with the poets in Boulder at Naropa, with Allen Ginsberg and Anne Waldman, Diane DiPrima, Philip Whalen, Michael McClure, Gregory Corso and everybody that was around. And Diane DiPrima particularly would teach the connection between various forms of alchemy, spirituality, Kabbalah, this, that, and the other thing, in relation to romantic poetry and poetics. Later on, she taught workshops around the Tree of Life with the Ten Sephiroth, emanations of the unknowable. And she would lay Aleister Crowley cards out in those positions. It was very interesting. This was the late '70s. Having had a kind of assimilated-New-England-slightly-self-hating adolescence — I was a Hebrew school dropout — I was sort of brought back to this kind of work through Diane's teachings and the poets.

Around 1978 while I was at Naropa, George Scrivani and I made a weekend trip to Seattle to see *The Ring*. I found this alphabet in the back of a dictionary of angels where we were staying with a friend of his. Ten years went by and I started thinking about it again. I had done some costumes for a Michael McClure play in San Francisco with Peter Hartmann, and we played with some alphabetic/angelic script-imagery. Eventually, I started a painting project like a big unbound book of the angelic letters. In regular Hebrew, there is a correspondence for each Hebrew letter. Aleph is an ox and Beth is a house and Gimel is a camel, and it goes on and on. I changed those correspondences because it was my own personal meditation on the alphabet.

For the Aleph, which I painted late in the game in 1997, the traditional correspondence is an ox. I decided I'd do the honeybee for this one. It's a kind of work, what the bee does, and the ox is the worker vehicle. I was painting this right around the time Allen Ginsberg was dying. I didn't know he was dying, but it was in progress. The title of the painting is taken from Allen's poem called "Memory Gardens," and it goes,

Well, while I'm here I'll
do the work—
and what's the work?

to ease the pain of living.
Everything else,
drunken
dumbshow.

I was painting it at that time for my own reasons, and it was synched up as a farewell Allen gift. He died in April of that year, 1997. The Malachim are the angels of beauty, they live in the middle of the Tree in Tifereth and they fly around all the other worlds and they bring Beauty! Beauty! Beauty! like Gregory's line, "Beauty! Beauty! Beauty! I scream the name." And that's why it's a good, helpful alphabet.

I've shown bits and pieces of them in various places, at the Judah Magnes Museum in Berkeley, the Jewish Community Library in San Francisco, and more recently there were seven of them in a show about Kabbalah at the Gershman Y in Philadelphia.

When I started to paint the alphabet, I thought I'd better make a real practice out of painting the street, too, so I don't go flopping off into the great beyond with the mystical stuff. That continues. I've been working in acrylic since the late '80s, and my really favorite medium is cardboard from the street.

You like to paint street scenes.

Mm-hmm. People and things you notice out of the corner of your eye in the street, and the cracks in the sidewalk.

Did living on the Lower East Side when you did inform your painting as it is today?

Oh, definitely. The letter Teth in Hebrew, the 9th letter, means snake in the traditional correspondence. So how I figured it is as a spine. And curling through the spine is a curved column of air, which is the spirit, which is like travels of the Kundalini. And travels of the Kundalini was the information that was in the airwaves when I was a kid art student in the East Village. That's how it became part of my understanding of the meaning of the letters.

There are a lot of paintings about the street, and it was not that long after Claes Oldenburg did his big cardboard series that was *The Street*, which then became *The Store*, that I was being a student. And I took a big bite of that. The street as a mindset and as a long-term painting subject. I was very lucky to live in the East Village at that time. It was a syncretistic time with Baba Ram Das and Timothy Leary, psychedelic times, and there were a lot of swamis running around. I would say that was formative without my really thinking about it. Poetry was coming up out of the streets and the music was coming out of everywhere. It was what they call a TAZ. Temporary Autonomous Zone — Hakim Bey. It's a souvenir of a TAZ at this moment. Right now New Orleans is a sort of hanging-on-by-a-thread kind of TAZ, where the consciousness is free to go into the dangerous world of poetic-sense reality.

Note: Claes Oldenburg's Store *was located in an old commercial space at 107 East Second Street from December 1961 through January 31, 1962. He filled it with representations of everyday commodities, from ice cream sandwiches to stockings, which he made out of muslin, plaster and chicken wire, and painted in bright colors. There had been nothing like it before.*

At the time of Hurricane Katrina, Tasha was living in New Orleans, where she had gone from San Francisco together with the artist and poet Herbert Kearney. She, Herbie and a couple of other friends made it out hours before the storm, and found their way to New York, where they stayed the first couple of months at the apartment of a friend on Grand Street. After that, Tasha sublet a room from Jennifer Blowdryer at 155 East Second Street, blocks from where she had once lived, and just a few doors from where Claes Oldenburg had his Store, once upon a time. Many of Tasha's paintings are still stored in New Orleans, including some of the Angel Alphabet series. She is now working at the Studio School where she first went as a student in 1968, so in many ways, she's come full circle. But the old neighborhood isn't full of nooks and crannies to welcome artists anymore, so she took a room across the river in Brooklyn, in Bed Stuy.

In any way does Bed Stuy remind you of the old Lower East Side?

The population is different but it has the kind of energy of life to it that the Lower East Side used to have. I might have been a little hermit girl when I lived down there, but I could feel this consciousness revolution, this *life* going on in the Lower East Side. Fulton Street in Brooklyn, the bustly way it is right now, would probably be the kind of energy that in my grandmother's day was alive and well in what is now the home of the 15-dollar martini. The Lower East Side is a theme park now. The remnants are still there, but when the Second Avenue Deli, which I made a painting of when it was there, when they still had the Hebrew clock, when that becomes a *bank,* the picture is changing before your eyes.

Romy Ashby *has lived in New York City since the early 1980s, initially on the Lower East Side. Since 1999, she and native New Yorker* **Foxy Kidd** *have been producing Goodie Magazine, a little publication dedicated to celebrating authenticity, in its many manifestations through in-depth interviews, one subject per issue. Watching the relentless destruction of New York City — as its beautiful and complex culture disappears along with countless old and storied buildings — has made Romy and Foxy preservationists by default. They both say that making Goodie Magazine is what makes life worth living. www.goodie.org*

Tasha Robbins *is a prolific painter, much of her recent work capturing moments of street life and all its haphazard beauty in acrylic paint on cardboard. She was born in Worcester, Massachusetts, in 1946. She studied art history at Bryn Mawr College and then came to New York to attend the New York Studio School. She came to New York at a particularly vibrant time and lived in the East Village.*

Walking Tour

Richard Kostelanetz

Claw Money

Kathleen Osborn

Sitting on a plastic footstool facing an overflowing closet, Claudia offers up some peppermint foot scrub. This item had been long forgotten at the back of a closet filled with all means of toiletries and cosmetic swag from various photo shoots and industry conventions. I decline the scrub, but help myself to a sweeping look around Claudia's apartment that, like her closet, is like a swollen pregnant belly — that is to say, about to burst. Having been in her apartment many times before, I spy some of my favorite items. Her "PMS" cookie jar. A bric-a-brac welcome sign emblazoned with "Shalom." And her devoted dog, Peepers Saint Marie, better known as Peeps, a staple accessory of any room that Claudia occupies. Amid the trappings of domesticity in her Bronx abode, Claudia's life outside of cleaning reveals itself. Her glass cases lined with her vintage designer sunglass collection. A Claw-Money original tote filled to the brim with Rust-Oleum spray paint. Old MTA and NYPD warning signs painted over with the wild style of many graffiti greats hanging on the walls and propped up on the floor.

Claudia is better known (as Prince was circa 1993) by her symbol, the three toed claw icon. This legendary downtown graffiti artist is technically retired, but these golden years are busier than her partying days when she hung off rooftops and bridges dodging the cops and catching tags. Now she cuts her time between her titles as Fashion Director of *Swindle* magazine, designer of her own lines of streetwear and sunglasses, fashion industry "it girl" who everyone from Calvin Klein to Marc Ecko and Nike want to work with and mother (of Peeps), lover and friend to all who know her. But today she is her own cleaning lady.

Tidying up is not Claudia's number-one priority yet she and her fellow graffiti veteran fiancé spend the better part of their free weekends doing just that in their uptown apartment. While it may seem surprising that this street icon and fashion maverick would attend to such domestic needs, her non-stop weekly schedule makes a mess of her home. Since she moved out of her LES one bedroom that doubled as her office, Claudia's dwellings have experienced some growing pains. Her LES apartment-cum-office was splitting at the seams as her brand outgrew its origins. But taking the girl out of the Lower East Side does not take the LES out of the girl. While it was there that Claudia made the transformation from middle-class Jewish Long Islander to beer-slinging, spray-can toting, graffiti tough, her road was paved in that very same neighborhood by her Jewish ancestors that made the classical American dream transformation from persecuted immigrants to thriving American citizens.

In fact, when Claudia's paternal grandmother heard that Claudia had moved to the Lower East Side, she was appalled. Born and raised in the heart of the Jewish Lower East Side on Rivington Street, Bessie knew the neighborhood as a Jewish ghetto, overcrowded with war-weary European Jews filing off the boats and filling the tenements. But for both women the LES represented a new beginning.

Bessie knew of the sacrifices her parents made to birth her as an American. Her parents' marriage came at the expense of a one-way trip from Austria to New York. Bessie's mother, after having her heart broken by her young love, who came back from war married, had placed a price on her dowry. Her would-be husband must take her to the U.S. Bessie grew up on the Lower East Side, like many of her second- and first-generation immigrant counterparts, poor and in crowded living conditions. When she and Russian-bred Harry were married, they quickly settled in what were at that time the Jewish suburbs of East New York, where they raised their son, Bernard, Claudia's father.

Of immigrant origins also, Bernard understood the hardships that Claudia's mother, Denise Litman, had experienced in Nazi-occupied Europe. Denise's father, Charles, was raised in Russia but grew both his businesses in Belgium. He was a successful dry goods wholesaler who moonlighted in the diamond trade. At the outset of World War II, Charles saw the writing on the wall and one day after the Nazi invasion of Belgium on May 11, 1940, he packed up his wife and children and drove across the border into France. There he paid his family's way into Portugal, which did not prove a safe haven. There, Jewish refugees were often ferreted out by German agents and Nazi sympathizers. While visas for the United States were next to impossible to secure, Charlie held out hope that if he booked passage on a boat that had to dock in New York en route to Ecuador, his family might have a chance. Surviving the 10-day journey from Lisbon, the Litmans reached the shores of Ellis Island with little more than the name and a phone number of an American aunt. Hearing the pleading Yiddish voice on the other end of the line, Charlie's aunt immediately dispatched her sons to vouch for their family. After a few days and a cash voucher to grease the wheels, the Litmans became New Yorkers.[153] Narrowly avoiding the fate that so many of her relatives and peers faced in Nazi occupied Europe, Denise Litman would never forget the peril they escaped.

When Claudia hit the LES in 1986, she was breaking away from another form of Jewish oppression: Long Island. Claudia's father had a prosperous dental practice in Queens but he wanted his family to thrive in the suburbs. So while Claudia was in junior high, her parents moved from Queens to the burbs. In Long Island she spent the better part of her adolescence trying to escape the clutches of suburbia with all-night clubbing and shopping trips to Manhattan. Claudia would inevitably miss the last train home during these jaunts and end up sleeping in Penn Station. A self-identified underachieving charmer, Claudia managed to get accepted at the Fashion Institute of Technology

But all her high school reckless abandon had ended in her parents' refusal to pay for what they thought would be a wasted education. Out to prove them wrong, Claudia enrolled for her first semester of classes, landed a part time job, and found a cheap apartment.

To pay for FIT Claudia accepted a decidedly unglamorous position assisting her father's friend's son, Jeffrey Goldenstein, with his sweater business, or what Claudia with her best Yiddish calls the "shmate trade" in the garment district. At 20, living on her own in the city, Claudia enjoyed her existence as a wild child, and the reasons to fight to be in school were becoming less and less clear. So she dropped out of FIT in 1988 to work directly in fashion with Anne Klein's casual sportswear brand, Fortune Cookie. While her internship didn't exactly pay the bills, it did put her directly under fashion industry darling Narciso Rodriguez.

After being thrown behind the bar one particularly short staffed night at the LES establishment where she was a regular, she realized that walking out of the bar with $600 in her pocket after a night of bartending and revelry seemed to make more sense than sewing classes and running errands at the bottom rung of the industry. With her sharp dark looks and wild fashion sense, Claudia was easily drawn to the center of the famed Deb Parker's chain of innovative, themed bars on the Lower East Side, ones like No Tell Motel, Babyland, and later Beauty Bar and Barmacy.

At a time when the lower end of the east side and Alphabet City was a wasteland for night life, Deb Parker was single-handedly building the center and grungy aesthetic of New York downtown bar scene. While the epicenter of her landscape may seem unrecognizable today, crowded with blurry eyed, college baseball cap-wearing Midwestern NYU coeds, it was Deb who crafted the signature thematic décor and underground buzz for a downtown dive. And standing behind the bar was Claw. Deb as the ring leader of hardened downtown chic turned her long-time regular into a bartender at No Tell Motel, some nights bringing Johnny Depp and the Hell's Angels together. While Deb, despite having her hands full at the center of the revelry, running interference with cops and keeping the bar full by prolonging debauchery, helped keep Claudia in line while allowing her to be as surly to the customers as she desired.

As bartending paid the bills, it led to more time hanging out in bars and clubs where she met various mavens of the midnight hour, many of whom were graffiti writers. When Claudia met and befriended these writers, their stories of art in the streets struck a chord. On car trips into the city from Long Island, Claw and her sister used to count the three toed, quickly painted pieces known as "throw ups" all the way along the highway, done by '70s writer MIRAGE. As wide-eyed as when she was counting tags on the highway, Claw fell in with the downtown graffiti scene. Early on Claudia befriended famed train writer Zephyr, who would become her coach but never her midnight painting partner. A chance meeting with legendary graffiti writer Sane Smith on the rooftop of the infamous Flatiron club MK really got Claw started.

At the end of the 1980s as Claudia got her start, graffiti was entering a period of transformation of the New York City streets. While graffiti had experienced some cultural success in the mainstream with the rise of Keith Haring and train writers turned gallery darlings, graff's profile had embarrassed the city's managers. The MTA had struggled to find ways to maintain control over their fleet of trains, which had been taken over and christened anew with graffiti. Mayor Koch tried to contain the city through "quality of life" measures, one of which was the Clean Trains Movement, in an effort to quell painting on the trains. To this end, the MTA took the canvas immediately out of service once it had a fleck of paint on it. The train would not run and no one would have a chance to admire the art left behind. Train writers pronounced the form dead on arrival as painting trains ended almost over night. This measure coincided with the increasing success of the Vandals Squad, the special graffiti enforcement agency, which marked a turning point in New York City graffiti.

Claudia started out in one of the bleakest periods of graffiti history. Train writers disdained the street bombers, and the mainstream art movement had turned its back on graffiti. As New York graffiti had centered so intensely around the trains, it was the belief of the train writers that all other canvasses were weak copies of a pure authenticity. For those who continued to paint, it was very simply for the love of the game and the art form. While many old school writers will hold out that anything after trains is a sham, the late 1980s and early 1990s era of graffiti sought to expand its canvas and ultimately its sphere of influence. Street bombers went all city, systematically hitting every neighborhood possible. The streets, highways and rooftops opened up to the endless names of fearless bombers of the likes of REVS, RD, JOZ, VEEFER and, starting out, young Claw.

The peculiar insulated world of graffiti writing with its midnight missions to paint the town and the infamy garnered from an in-the-know crowd instantly appealed to Claudia. It was the opposite of anything she had ever known and she wanted in. She went painting in her early days with local Lower East Side writers DEVO KGB and with a young crew called the Violators. The LES writers that Claudia went out with lacked her tenacity and stamina for all-night bombing binges, content to be known only on the buildings and rooftops of their neighborhood. She would go out with ten guys and end up using all of their paint. A tantalizing one- or two-night adventure quickly turned into an obsession.

Graffiti writers gain satisfaction from the insider knowledge behind the anonymity of graffiti. But female writers gain an extra smirk of fulfillment from getting up when no one thinks that they can or would dare to. Claw did not want undue notoriety for simply being a female who paints. She had to be twice as fierce as any male writer. As defined by the battle cry of any Second Wave feminist brawl, she had to fight to get any credibility for every tag she copped and every piece she labored over. Being recognized as a woman on the streets at night can be dangerous enough. Claw's jumping barbed wire fences and climbing up to rooftops added insult to injury, as it were, as far as demolishing the stereotype of women being scaredy cats. And as she did this, she also had to deal with the bonus of being loathed and dubbed as a wannabe by her male counterparts. With all these stresses, there are few who could stay as tenacious and aggressive as Claudia. Yet this is all just a byproduct of being a woman in a man's art world. Claw's bent on having her art be a feminist message would become deliberate only in her later work. When she started, she was just trying to get up like any other writer.

For Claudia, graffiti was a form of self actualization. Seeing her name all over the city made her *feel* that she was actually there. Her tags were proof that she existed, seeing little bits of herself on New York's streets. No longer did Claw feel as she often had among her family; her art was her voice and she had a forum in New York's streets.

But her accession did not come without costs. Claudia explains that the ethic behind the practice and labor of being successful in graffiti is not unlike that of climbing the corporate ladder. A novice starts out at the bottom with no respect and little style, but with experience, daring and the tenacity for hitting prime spots where more people take notice of one's work, a writer eventually can get to higher plateaus with a burner in the not-so-distant future. For Claw, this underground work ethic is driven by a desire for notoriety, not mainstream success. Having come from a family that valued the mainstream accomplishments that they and their relatives had worked so hard to achieve in this country, her brand of independence had a guilty look to it. She worked diligently and adeptly at her very public art, a pursuit she had to hide from family and friends. For her, this lawless second-life provided a venue for her own self-styled achievement and validation under a new set of rules. Graffiti taught her how to work, and as such, she began at the beginning.

In her early days of painting, Claudia went out like any other graffiti novice to work on her own personal hand style. She mainly scrolled Claw, as it had been her long time nickname. The claw paw icon was an accident like many artistic epiphanies. Upon seeing one of her throw ups with the top half of her claw W covered over by a competing tag, she instantly saw the W bear its claws. Once she started embedding the nails into her throw ups and tags, it evolved into a single, clean icon that was readily accessible and remarkably original.

Claudia's relentless bombing earned her admittance into elite, male-dominated graffiti crews but it also caught the attention of New York's premier graffiti enforcement squads. By 1995 the hazards of painting in the streets from clashes with unsavory characters to heat from the cops and battles with graffiti writers had taken its toll on Claudia. After years of relentless painting in New York, Claw moved to L.A. to, as she said, "be in the movies." But as any diehard New Yorker knows, life in L.A. is not all the sun-filled, star-studded dream it is made out to be.

In L.A., Claw became disenchanted with graffiti as her efforts were frustrated by the city's strict enforcement of graffiti removal, which made toiling over a piece for naught. In addition, the distance from New York gave Claudia time to consider some of the troubles she had left there. She found that bartending didn't pay the bills in L.A. like it did in New York, so she found work as a stylist's assistant for music videos. She styled videos for the flavor of that late 1990s day for the likes of Bon Jovi, Korn and Hole as well as MC Lyte and Monica. Despite the career experience she was gaining in L.A., after two years she had had enough of her unemployed, live-in boyfriend, who only lifted a finger to a spray can.

Back in New York with no desire to paint and not wanting to be an assistant again, she fell back on bartending. Claudia's father begged her not to bartend as he thought it was a dead end. So, with her father's encouragement and financial support, Claudia launched her first clothing line. Claw Money started as a girls' casualwear line without a stitch of graffiti flare. Despite her padded start, her business suffered when Claudia failed to find buyers. She began to spend more time and money filling her alphabet city apartment with vintage designer monogrammed bags she bought on eBay and at thrift stores than designing her line. While Claw Money languished, Claudia sold vintage to the boutiques that were blossoming on the Lower East Side.

By this time Claudia was semi-"retired" from graffiti but when she met the intrepid bomber Miss 17 at a group magazine interview about New York's female graffiti movement, her comeback was not long in coming. As Miss 17 was relentlessly getting up all over the city, she offered Claudia constant reminders of what she was missing. After some friendly prodding on 17's part, Claw emerged from retirement for the love of graff and the opportunity to do it with another female graffiti writer. The claw icon began popping up all over the city accompanied by its 1-7 counterpart. It was an exciting new development in the city streets that had grown ever more sterile.

While these two did not have a specified feminist manifesto for their bombing, except for the fact that they didn't give a damn what anyone thought, many women responded to their work. In fact, many women remarked to Claudia that somehow they knew the writer behind the claw had to be a woman. Although there is nothing stereotypically feminine about the claw icon, being a female writer's stamp gives the icon a special fierceness. In some ways, the claw defies a sexual presence, as there is no name specified in its rendering. The claw is baffling because it denies access to information about the writer yet it is more accessible than most graffiti. Claudia has never allowed the icon to lose its edge just because the simple clean aesthetics of the claw are easily digestible. Each neologism she writes in the center of the claw icon elevates her tag with a sense of surprise and hardened wit. Claudia's wit knows no bounds as you can see anything from "shalom" to "boogie down," "crazins," "taco," "chicken-n-ribs," "pms," "flossy," to "get off my dick" splashed into the middle of her claw paw giving the reader an insight into her current mood or what she just had for dinner.

After being repeatedly asked by friends for a piece of the "claw" to wear, Claudia put it on some shirts as a joke between friends. To her surprise, the shirts instantly sold out when she hawked a few to downtown store owners she knew. Although Claudia was worried about letting the claw, that had been her lifeblood for so many years, be bought and sold, she quickly saw the potential in expanding its reach. To be sure she immediately trademarked the three clawed icon to make sure that it would remain her work.

Her brand is irreverently named "Claw Money," which sounds as if it were Claudia's cash moneymaking alter ego. The name alone is that in your face "I am going to say it before you" attitude that defuses any accusation that her art has been sold out. In the end, Claudia gets paid to extend her reach onto the very backs of her fans. Corporations will pay for the infusion of street cred and authenticity that her designs provide. Her brand has been incredibly successful in the five short years that it has been imprinting the "claw." She has done a limited-edition, graffiti-styled line of underwear for Calvin Klein to whom she shrewdly declined to license the "claw," as they didn't offer its true value. She also did a claw bombed exclusive for Ecko, who had the sense to fly her all over the world to paint their stores for the line's opening. Her claws have been splashed all over the walls of the set on the MTV reality TV series *Ego Trip's (White) Rapper Show*. Not to be left out, Nike came calling recently to have Claudia bless their swooshes with two series of sneakers, the classic Blazers and the appropriately chosen Vandals, the first female artist to do so. Most recently her work has been preserved and celebrated in her book, *Bombshell: The Life and Crimes of Claw Money*.

Claudia has helped give graffiti a wider presence, elevating its allure, legitimacy, and profitability. In many ways, she has been a midwife to graffiti's place in our time, explaining it to the mainstream while preserving its authenticity. She has successfully made graffiti profitable for the artist, holding at bay the full-fledged buy-outs that make slaves of so many artists to the will of the corporations. A claw tag on a T-shirt or tote bag instantly gives the wearer a piece of the street and access to her art.

Part of the Claw icon's success is that people, often shut out of the art of graffiti by the inability to read it, saw the claw icon and immediately identified with its striking symbol. The ease with which you can take in the artistry of the claw icon not only translated street graffiti for some, but put her standout mark on the map for all. Claudia literally is making a name for herself. Claudia as a white, middle class, Jewish woman betrays the Platonic ideal of a graffiti writer both for the mainstream audience and the inner graffiti micro-culture. Graffiti has often been spun as a representation of the "mean inner city," which is synonymous with communities of color. Despite the fact that graffiti continually refuses to fit this definition, people are consistently surprised by the face behind that so-called inner city grit.

Claudia has never let her heritage be masked by her street-made persona. While she may not go to shul weekly, Claudia wears her Judaism as a badge of honor, often rocking a heavy gold Star of David, big enough to put any crucified Jesus medallion to shame. Judaism isn't simply an accessory to Claw; her roots run deep from Austria to the Lower East Side to Queens and Long Island. Running the well traveled routes of the Jewish immigrant to New York, Claudia's faith-based immigrant background has had latent influence on her existence as an LES staple and fashion icon. Claudia's business has grown in part due to the strong foundation her father's advice and financial support and in no small part due to heavy installments of her mother's preservation mentality concerning her haunting Holocaust past.

One day when visiting her in the East Village apartment office that helped start it all, I remarked that her business resembled a sweatshop manned by child labor. Packed into a room jammed with boxes of merchandise and samples is a staff of two full time assistants, a graphic designer and two interns all under 25. "I keep them fed," Claudia retorts with a high-pitched laugh as she tends to a frying pan of bacon and eggs. You don't hear any complaints from this group who sit down to eat as they enthusiastically discuss the day's work.

That is exactly it. The thing about Claudia is that she is infectious—you can't help but hang on her every word, her laugh is ear splitting but intoxicating and you will leave any meeting with her, stealing her little sayings and in withdrawal that will only be satisfied by a fix of seeing a claw paw around town.

Kathleen Osborn *was born and raised on City Island in the Bronx, New York. Since graduating with a degree in Comparative Literature from Brown University, she has been working for Bill Moyers' production company, Public Affairs Television, currently, as a Senior Associate Producer. Kate's production work first hit the airwaves when her college radio program, Not Your Classroom, was featured on NPR. Since then she has worked on the EMMY Award-nominated documentary, Buying the War, and the weekly PBS news program, Bill Moyers' Journal. She continues to work as a freelance journalist out of Brooklyn, New York.*

---

[153] Information about Litmans' Ellis Island immigration originally researched and written about by Neal Hirschfeld. "Isle of Tears; For Immigrants Arriving on Ellis Island, Fear and Hope were Mingled in Equal Parts." New York Daily News Sunday Magazine, February 9, 1964.

Martha Diamond, Artist and Bowery Pioneer

Ilka Scobie

Painter Martha Diamond has lived in the same pristine, sun-filled Bowery loft for over 37 years. Known for her abstract cityscapes, she has exhibited widely and won prestigious art awards. As a pioneer of the Bowery and a member of the downtown cultural community, she spent a lot of time attending poetry readings at St. Marks Church and at the Eighth Street Bookstore. She showed in Soho galleries and taught at the School of Visual Arts and at Harvard.

Chuck Close has lauded her as an artist whose work is elegant, hip, contemporary and thoroughly modern.

Diamond, who was born in Manhattan, lived in Stuyvesant Town and attended kindergarten on Avenue B. Her family moved to Queens. After college, Diamond moved downtown when the Jewish presence was still a strong one. *I asked her about any of her own Jewish connections to the area.*

"I knew that my grandmother lived on Monroe Street, perhaps when she first arrived in America in 1904 or so. She'd been trained as a milliner. Maybe she worked in the Lower East Side, but I don't know that. She had a lot of style; her daughters were beautifully dressed (according to photographs) and she liked nice things. I got my love of transparent colored glass from glasses I saw in her cabinet in the dining room. I think my grandfather on the other side of the family had a jewelry store or watch store, way early in his career, near Bowery and Canal. For these connections, I was always sympathetic to the area.

"When I moved to the Bowery, I did a lot of exploring in the Lower East Side, which to me was an exotic area. Live theater. I also explored the fabric stores, especially Harry Snyder on Hester Street, who had extraordinary designer and imported fabric. I sewed my own clothes at that time. They were quite nice to me. I also remember having lunch at Ratner's, and Gertels Bakery, which I found out about from my Aunt Sylvia.

"I really didn't focus on it as a Jewish area, but I was quite comfortable there. I was never intimidated by the sales style. I was sort of amused by it."

Were there any particular Jewish cultural figures you were aware of?

"The Jewish cultural figures who were part of my life were, when I was young, The Marx Brothers, Hollywood movies, musicians ... And some relation on my mother's side was an opera singer. I was a TV baby, and loved the old Hollywood movies. As I got older, I realized how important the Jewish influence was in Hollywood. I guess it was only the shopping and the food that was part of my life as a young artist near the Lower East Side.

"And then there were the art museums, which were elsewhere. A different experience and a bit later in my life. I wasn't connected early on to art as anything Jewish. ... My parents thought my studying art and being an artist wasn't practical and far from essential. Later, I began seeing there was a Jewish connection. Hullo Gottlieb. Hullo Soutine."

Any statements about Jewish influence on art, culture?

"No. But where would life be without it?"

Ilka Scobie, *born in Brooklyn, lives in downtown Manhattan. She teaches poetry in the public school system. Her work appears in* Artnet, Italian Marie Claire, La Stampa *newspaper and small press publications. She is married to photographer Luigi Cazzaniga and is lucky to spend time in Italy.*

Jewish History and The LES

Efroim Snyder

Posted on a tree. It was uncanny to find such a "hip" drawing in the middle of "Jewish" Williamsburg. I had been living just across the bridge for a few years, never having purposefully ventured to explore the neighborhood where my grandparents once lived. They were a first generation of children born to Jewish immigrants who left Eastern Europe to escape pogroms and persecution. I was told by a relative that my great grandfather, Herman Hurwitz, did the initial electrical work to wire City Hall and scratched his initials into one of the basement beams. Now it was me, unknowingly, who was about to re-engage, the return of a "re-born" Jew (Bal Tshuva) to walk the same streets, to worship in the same synagogues. I began to scan the black-and-white photocopied image advertising for artists to exhibit in a Shul on 8th Street between aves. B and C in the East Village, aka, "Alphabet City." It was the "8th Street Shul," which was to become a legend in itself, having once been a house of worship, later a symbol of communal heroism, of urban ethnic flux and Jewish exile.

Interestingly, I never found anything particularly "Jewish" at all about the LES. For me it was about America: a place where many immigrants first came to settle upon their arrival here. It was basically a place to get work and cheap housing, just what was needed to begin a new life for those with fresh dreams of a better world. Like most other immigrant groups who at one time settled in mass in the LES and later moved on to establish larger communities elsewhere, the Jews did establish a lasting presence in the LES. The late Rabbi Moshe Feinstein's yeshiva, Mesivta Tiferes Jerusalem, aka "MTJ," and the "House of the Sages" where distinguished Jewish sages dedicate their days to immersion in prayer and learning sacred texts, are examples of such. The eager eye of any inspired visitor would surely come across many other "Jewish" landmarks, whether it be Gus' Pickle Shop, the Eldridge Street Shul, Kadori's Middle-Eastern Dried Fruit and Nut store, Nat Weisberg's Hebrew Religious Articles store or the Orensanz Center for the Arts on Norfolk Street. Most all of the Jews who came to settle initially in the LES would eventually move on to resettle elsewhere, being replaced by newer immigrant groups.

Connecting G-d and Art.

I jotted down the telephone number on the poster, eventually calling to speak with a secretary, getting directions and hitching a ride over the bridge to get to the 8th Street Shul. It was there that I met Ralph Feldman, Rabbi Isaac Fried, and Clayton Patterson. Although I was not interested in showing my work at the synagogue and never could have imagined ever praying in such a marginally "orthodox" (i.e., questionably kosher) environment, I was interested in trying to establish an active observant congregation that could justify keeping the once-abandoned building from being overrun by squatters and/or eventually sold for re-development. The initial effort to save the shul was by next-door neighbor Ralph Feldman, an artist and retired NYC fire marshal.   Living next door for many years, Ralph alone spent close to $100,000 of his own money and innumerable hours of his own time repairing the structure of the shul in addition to providing funds to feed the hungry and to establish an ongoing lecture series, which my wife and I would come to join. We tried on several occasions to fill in as surrogate Rabbi and Rebetzin figures, staying over Shabbos and bringing home-cooked food to feed the congregants and local guests, sleeping on a cold, unheated attic floor. We taught classes in both Yiddish and a basic introduction to Judaism for those testing the waters upon considering a return to observing the faith in the last synagogue left in a neighborhood, which was at one time packed with prayer and learning. I would eventually bring a rabbi and close friend of mine, Rav. Yehoshua Heschel Walhandler, from Williamsburg in an attempt to establish a guiding presence to rescue and revitalize the shul.

Despite encouragement and assistance from many others in the neighborhood, and the devoted help of LES community artist/activist and documentarian Clayton Patterson, Rabbi Issac Freid, Rabbi Walhendler and myself, Ralph was, after several years of long and persistent struggle, unable to put together a group of local residents who were willing to devote themselves to convincingly establishing a congregation that would justify a court order to prevent the sale of the shul next door. The neighborhood had changed and it just wasn't what is "used to be." The observant Jews who once filled the streets north of Houston and dutifully attended synagogue three times daily were no longer there to make the minyan (the minimum 10 men needed to initiate a prayer service).

What did happen to me was that this became the beginning of a relationship with Clayton Patterson, eventually leading me to my show my paintings in his "Clayton Gallery" (which would later become The Outlaw Art Museum) and eventually to develop and curate an exhibition of "Hasidic Art," working with gallery director Walter O'Neill at the Educational Alliance on East Broadway. Besides having been the first place to show my "Painted Streimel (fur hat) Boxes," it was there at Clayton's gallery on Essex Street where I would later meet and be interviewed by John Strasbaugh, the then editor of the *New York Press*, journalist Marvin Greisman from *The Jewish Press*, as well as independent filmmaker/writer Alan Edelstein, who would come to initiate an ongoing film documentary where he and I would be the two central subjects.   After spending just a short while with Clayton in his gallery, I came to realize that it was, in fact, a photocopy of his drawing posted on a tree in Williamsburg that led me back to the LES and began the process of my involvement in the community where my Yiddish-speaking great grandparents first settled.

Efroim aka Seth Franklin Snyder *The first person from the 'western world' known to have gone to Asia to study contemporary painting, Efroim aka Seth Franklin Snyder was born at about 6 am on Feb. 17, 1964 in White Plains, NY. In Seoul, between 1986 and 1990, he painted and exhibited the "Unbound Diary of Plankton's Tailor" a conceptual collection of images drawn and painted on green Korean paper ("nokji"). Efroim is perhaps best known for his painted streimel (fur hat) boxes. Along with inflatable artist Dennis DelZotto, he co-founded* *the "Lucky Structure Performance Project" an atonal, improvisational "music" ensemble which was one amongst a small group of artist/performers who pioneered the underground music scene in Williamsburg during the early 1990's. Snyder was awarded an honorary membership to the National Audobon Society after lecturing on his "Critical Re-Evaluation of John James Audubon's 'Birds of America' Paintings" establishing this important artwork as being a pivotal influence in the establishment of the environmental conservation movement. Efroim lives with his wife and family in a private Yiddish-speaking community upstate and works and paints in a remote cliffside structure at an abandoned 19th century iron quarry.*

Stanton Street Shul

Elissa Sampson

Other than those at the Stanton Street Shul, those at the Biaylstock Shul are the last of the traditional depictions of the months of the year that once adorned most Lower East Side synagogues and many of their antecedents in Eastern Europe. Seen as old fashioned rather than as folk art, many shuls simply did not value them from the 1950s on. These were lovingly and professionally restored in the 1990s and have become a visitor attraction as well as a point of pride for the shul.

Mazelos were constellations and the month one was born in was thought to be important in certain religious commentaries, including passages in the Talmud. The Jewish calendar is lunar, and it is stressed that stars and other celestial bodies are not to be worshipped. Full representation of the human figure was discouraged in traditional Jewish folk art and these mazelos not only have very specifically Jewish meanings, but are done in a way to show their differences from Greco-Roman or other astrological associations.

At the Stanton Street Shul, a.k.a., CONGREGATION BNAI JACOB ANSCHEI BRZEZAN (Sons of the people of Brezan, a town in a poorer province of Eastern Galicia) and historically one of the poorest Lower East Side shuls, they are crumbling literally into ruin and are the only other extant Lower East Side example.

They are representative of a generation of immigrants and particular to their interpretation of life in these places. For the month of Elul, the Virgo counterpart, is a B'sullah (a virgin) shown as the embroidered cuff and hand of a woman holding a sheaf of wheat (due to the prohibition on showing the face in traditional art), yet the embroidery is similar to that of a Ukrainian peasant blouse. There is also a lobster portrayed, perhaps due to a shared misunderstanding with the Biaylostocker Shul as to what a scorpion may have looked like (although they are assigned to different months).

If these disappear, it would be like having a page torn out of a history book that told the immigrant story. It's one thing to hear about the generation of people who migrated from Eastern Europe; it's quite another to see what they thought was pious art.

Elissa Sampson is a local resource on the history and background of the synagogues of the Lower East Side, both extant as well as those lost. She is a long-time resident and docent, with close relationships to many shuls, and, like her parents who worked or grew up in the neighborhood, Elissa has always had deep ties to the Lower East Side. With her husband, Professor Jonathan Boyarin, a well-known Jewish anthropologist and ethnographer, they have raised their children to love the neighborhood and its traditions. Elissa has contributed to the design of the tours that the Lower East Side Conservancy offers and is always interested in finding out what visitors and neighborhood residents alike would like to learn about the historic and living communities of the Lower East Side/East Village. ejswoo@yahoo.com

Lady Island: Agathe Snow

Mary Blair Taylor

Agathe Snow was born on the Mediterranean island of Corsica in 1976. Despite being a province of France, technically speaking, Corsica is a "territorial collectivity." This peculiar detail is an apt reflection of Agathe's style. Origins and geography are atypical and largely self-willed for her.

As a young child in the island community, Agathe's life centered more around a bohemian theater troop and her family's local restaurant than it did school, sports or other conventional institutions. Days were organized on a creative (and therefore unbound) front: eating and moving and performing.

In 1987, Agathe's family moved to the Lower East Side of Manhattan where her French-Tunisian mother, Martine Apparu, opened a tearoom and café called La Poeme on the corner of Prince and Elizabeth streets. Naturally, Agathe was a fixture at La Poeme, hustling around to help the restaurant and also learning the new feeling of the neighborhood. La Poeme was a nexus of local poets and artists seeking an unassuming spot to eat homemade food and exchange artwork.

A brief and bizarre interlude from 1995-1998 saw Agathe off to college in Montreal where she was both Pre-Law and a major in History. Many of us who know Agathe find this patch something of an anomaly, as does Agathe herself who remarks simply, "It was funny."

One lasting effect was a rediscovery of her Judaism. As she describes it, Corsica was oppressively Catholic, and though born to a Jewish mother, Snow's father was "a Polish Nazi." While the latter remark is to be taken with a grain of sea salt, Canada did (as usual) afford a pilgrim's dose of cultural shrugs and nods and, in Agathe's case, synagogues. Sure enough, after three years of Northern light, Agathe slipped back into the unchanged Manhattan enclave of La Poeme.

Asked whom she met during these early years, Agathe replies, "I met the oil, the vinegar and the salad." One of these early New York ingredients was Dash Snow, whom Agathe would marry in 1999. When they were first introduced, Dash was writing graffiti all over the city with the Irak Crew, a band of marauders making their mark as much and as often as possible, including around her mom's Nolita café. Agathe crept around writing with the boys, and then the gang would seek refuge from whichever descending authorities in the safe haven of La Poeme's basement. Thus began an underground operation.

At the turn of the 21st century, Deitch Projects art gallery put together an exhibition called "Street Market" in which artists and graffiti writers Barry McGee, Todd James and Stephen Powers "joined forces to recreate their version of an urban street" inside the gallery's space at 18 Wooster. The artists and their gallery opened the project up to include local street folks like the Snows and their friends (though Agathe says she was "just the lookout because they wouldn't let [her] touch anything").

So, fused art practice and street practice, and, as many 30-year-olds have joked in the last decade, sooner or later everyone became an artist. It was during this time that Agathe and Dash moved into an apartment on Avenue C and 4th Street where local companions included contemporary art stars Ryan McGinley and Dan Colen, the hardcore electro-rock band A.R.E. Weapons, downtown impresario A-ron "the Don" Bondaroff and fashion collective As Four.

Not long after this community of unprofessional professionals had formed, Agathe began *Feed the Troops*, "a nomadic feeding experience." Sunday's meal was at local bar, Sweet and Vicious. Fridays were "stoops and stairwells" nights, wherever she could set up. Full moons meant the East River Park Amphitheater, etc. Nobody had much dough, including Agathe, but people would pitch in a couple of bucks for her fresh meals as they could. Rita Ackermann brought Snow a Hungarian crock-pot. The cops, informed it was her birthday every time she encountered them, smiled and told her not to litter. Strangers on the Staten Island Ferry gave Agathe wary looks in exchange for her free hero sandwiches. No transaction was free of material.

On 9/11 Agathe was living on Hester Street in Chinatown where, along with most of her downtown group, being next door to Ground Zero meant that her view on the catastrophe was necessarily and literally obscured. Maybe at the time that moment couldn't even be felt as a watershed one after which the whole universe would change around them. Maybe it just felt like an ether to slip into, another portal like so many before and so many after.

Categorizing its immediacy is impossible, but the aftereffects were as long lasting and real as any they'd known. Agathe soon understood the need for creating something that could still be carefree. She began promoting parties around lower Manhattan where "it felt like the last party all the time ... nobody knew what to do."

For a soul like Agathe's a vacuum of energy is simply filled. More happens. As she says, "the last" is "all the time." Like T. S. Eliot of his *Waste Land*, Snow views her own apocalyptic visions as providing a new beginning.

In 2005 Snow staged the first official "Stamina" dance marathon not far from Ground Zero in a worn-out, 4-story building in the broken financial center. The idea was that we all come, do dance numbers, dine on a luscious spread, and boogie for as close to 36 hours as we dared. She installed 9 cameras (some handheld, some mounted) to document the unrelenting event, and as she points out that means 36 hours' worth of footage from 9 different vantage points that she may never be physiologically able to make sense of. But editing together a finished product is not her goal. "It's about moments, real honest moments where there's a certain trust that everyone has the same circumstance for that particular moment – but we all come from different things and then go back to different things. I really feel like a shepherd, where I get people together, but I'm always kind of separated from them."

In this natural way, Agathe's life began to assume what the art world would dub a performance aspect. Her relationship to others around her was so concerted and noticeable as to necessarily mean something to them. Even when Snow might not have been aware of her own impact, as in a recollection of a somewhat homeless moment, the community had to pay attention:

"I think that's important to realize that making art is not circumscribed by four walls; there's nothing different between living and working. It's all one thing. Especially in New York City, there's no division between personal space and general space. It's the only city where you can walk out on the street, and … really feel at home on the streets. Like when I decided to live in my studio, which was then on 39th Street, and I would shower on 36th Street. I remember once I was dying my hair, walking out on the street to go shower three blocks away – you know not a problem in my mind since I was still at home."

Did people notice?

"I mean people were really staring at me, but I was in my backyard."

It's not an easy transition from moving around however you will to having an industry of people codifying how willfully you move. Despite lifelong creative output, Agathe only began what she would term "calling herself an artist" about a year and a half ago, and when she talks about it I am reminded of movies in which actors "play" their own personae on-screen.

Her acceptance of having this role is always footnoted with that small space of an ellipsis, as in the closing credits: Agathe Snow… Herself.

I asked her once if it was a challenge for her to be a woman in the art world, a female artist in a crowd of men, and she responded, "The whole feminist idea – people ask 'are you feminist?' And really it was so hard to just become a human! To add this other thing?"

This question of how we become human is always at work in Agathe's art. In every object she fashions from materials salvaged from the garbage of her LES neighbors, pillaged from the park on Forsyth and Grand, recognized as valuable in a clog of valueless stuff, the bottom line is the destruction and resuscitation process. And the process itself is the point – the steps she takes to get through.

The object is a record of this becoming.

Most recently Agathe is devoting a year of her life to a current interpretation of Leonardo da Vinci's machines as she tries to locate a new American Renaissance. As da Vinci said, "Things of the mind left untested by the senses are useless."

For an upcoming show at the Jeu de Paume in Paris, she means to make an anti-gravity environment with no right angles to test our potential without the encumbrance of hard limits. She writes, "Call me naïve, but I think of his machines not in terms of function but resilience in the face of absurdity and the unknown. They are made of dreams and that's what I think of the make of America."

Instructions, guides, prescriptions, conversations, inductions, gatherings, offerings, pilgrimages, homecomings, home-goings. Agathe Snow is always moving, always bearing in mind and body an exchange of energy. This is the crux of her life project and art project, and she wouldn't have come to that crux without New York City. Agathe immediately knew that the streets of lower Manhattan's East side, the people, moments and materials she could find by seeking or by happenstance, would all be contributors and, in the true sense, part of her reason.

Mary Blair Taylor *was born in New York, raised in Boston, educated in California and has lived in Brooklyn for the last 6 years. She is NYC Director of Peres Projects, an international gallery representing many of the downtown artists who shape the city's contemporary art movement.*

Allure: The Circle Bait of Angel Orensanz

Donna Cameron

One senses that the greatness of Angel Orensanz in part consists in his being in synch with himself as his own director of his own visions. Orensanz's energies are channeled into the creation and installation of large, memorable, non-biodegradable and not politically correct (this, of course, being part of the message of Orensanz's art), plastic circles of bright texture and color, themselves a kind of displaced urban sculpture. These are an artistic return, of sorts, to the generic urban landscape of his dual studio residencies in New York City and Paris, France. Following his art on location is a curious way to follow Orensanz's oh-so-particular life.

Orensanz is a landscape artist. He approaches landscape as a reflection on the differences and the points of contact in the contemporary installation work of art as seen through such a classic genre as landscape painting, and as having a narrative potential with an ever evolving way of representing reality.

Orensanz's plastic circle symphonies conjure up a world of dreamscapes. They are stretched on skeletons of PCP piping, in which Orensanz himself, even as he is ever present as a recording artist and photographer of his own installations, exists as a small anthropomorphic creature whose figure moves from one circle to another and is finally, continuously, materialized in the "real world."

The emphasis is always on the notion of pictorial space. It is a space with a certain depth where a very "different" universe develops, one in which the radical figures of floating mannequins, flotsam and jetsam of urban garbage dumps and other miscellaneous items may surface, as in his piece, *Burning Universe* (2003), shown in the Venice Biennale of Art (2005), and New York City (2003). Or, as in his most recent installations in Moscow (2005), and Lisbon (2006), and Wales (2007), his circles, the exterior landscapes and interior architecture exist in five dimensions, in a time and space totally unconcerned with what is going on in the so-called "real" world, yet parallel to it. In his ethereal, snow-bound installation high in the French Pyrenees mountains, *Snow Sphere* (2004) or his earlier Toronto river bank installation, *Sundown Marshes* (1994), works which used clear plastics, muslin, tarpaulin and color pigment, the out-of-context fabrics and forms imposed evidence of human passage on the landscape in the form of non-biodegradable waste. In some mysterious way, the persistence of vision, itself a spasm of intellectual growth and a conduit of spiritual life, is included in the current color plastic circle metaphor. This may be interpreted as emblematic of greed, capitalist diplomacy, and contemporary industrial waste. (All of which you can't eliminate!)

It does not matter if the locale is Central Park (*Early Bloom*, 2005) or his own backyard (*Snow and Branches, Skull, Hand Series; L'Hay Les Roses*, Paris, 2005). Each Orensanz piece is not so much an assemblage of surface as a frontier between the world of appearances and the world of reality. Orensanz always shows us everything that is happening in front of and behind the color and geometry of the circle, the pedestrian and the landscape. We find ourselves always seeking a point of contact between what we are seeing (the viewer's vision) and what Orensanz intends for us to see (the artist's vision.)

Memory and the importance of an oral tradition are evident in the Orensanz aesthetic. As a fellow artist, as a filmmaker, I have easily imagined myself wandering from locale to locale with the PCP skeletons and environmentally unsound, colored plastic, as though I were part of a band of fanatics bringing a message of art and design to unknown inhabitants of wild and foreign places. Orensanz creates a familiar architecture of color and symbol in every unfamiliar landscape, and, as a result of historical data in my memory bank, I feel drawn to it, like to some kind of unnamable truth. This is iconic, religious impact. Perhaps it could be noted as religious impact indicative of a tradition. Perhaps it is a sense of wanderlust, of adventure. Those of us within the dictates of a Judeo-Christian ethos find self-same comfort in the displaced familiarity of many such secular icons. Is this a sensation or the memory of a sensation? My own take on Orensanz's art and his idiomatic circles of confusion is this: in the context of an artist such as Angel Orensanz, there is no question of the influence of an inherited family tradition. The fact is that Orensanz hails from a Spanish Jewish heritage. Yet, I do not. And he speaks to me, without my having to pose "the question." He speaks in symbols which are universal to all people. Nowhere is he quoting or referring to scripture. Anyone hungry for justice, truth and the survival of poetry, music and fine art finds solace in the Orensanz idiom, and invariably joins in, to wander in meditative thought, with the lost tribe.

One work which lives in such a sensation is the razor-edged position of multiple circle madness in the meticulously coiffed garden of the Palace Square, St. Petersburg (2003).

Contrasting this metaphor is another, which reflects the volatility of modern urban life in an ideal pastoral existence. This recent installation, *Do Sakuras Blossom in Winter?* (2004) takes place in the Japanese countryside in Akita, Japan. Orensanz has here advanced his archetypal vision of a primitive tribal fire of art, carried burning like an Olympic torch, unaltered by time, industrialization, and political transformations. His retreat to Japanese custom, landscape, and Zen thought, his self-confirmation in rites of passage through water and fire signal a poetic return to his mystic Spanish origins, his Jewish secular tradition and the Aragon countryside which originally inspired him. Here is art in which the symbiosis of the nomadic herder against the majesty of the land evokes images of stability, continuity, and cyclical renewal. There is an installation of color circles in an ancient gnarled tree. It is early winter, the branches are bare. Smoke rises from a fire lit at the base of the tree, as if in homage to some ancient deity, and nearby, on the river below, smoke burrows from another, stranger fire. This fire, burning through cardboard boxes aboard a makeshift sailing craft made of shredded sails and scraps of wood so as to call to mind the doomed vehicles in the film *Road Warrior*, stirs the mind. Is this where Art is going?

There is a sense of renewal as the burning sailing craft extinguishes itself in its own ashes, in the river water, with the tides then bringing it to a crashing toppling halt on the shore. And there above, the bonfire of the ancient tree vanity continues to smoke and burn. This Japanese installation is accompanied by a unique performance. Orensanz presents himself in a localized burlesque in the form of a photographic orgyman, created by himself, during which he explains in pantomime with camera, yet with intense gestural and emotional detail, everything that appears in the mountains and on the river and in the city and in a man's heart - there, on the banks of the River Omono in Akita, and, by virtue of that, everywhere, on every riverbank in the world.

Orensanz's installation art performances have been sponsored in most European countries, including at the Museum of Modern Art, Wales; Moscow and St. Petersburg museums and public spaces; in Baja, California and in New York City; in Tokyo and Akita, Japan, and in many other places. The tradition of landscape painting is radically transformed by classical modernity in all his pieces. This is a clenched fist that raps on the window of a familiar art history tenement. In the later 19th century, in the work of the Impressionists, landscape was turned into an artful construction that employed Nature merely as a stimulus for the formal arrangement of the picture.

The various approaches taken by Orensanz indicate to what an extent his visions of landscape evoke the mark of Impressionism, and challenge and upstage its now confining and ghettoizing structures, proving that vision such as that emblazoned by the early Impressionists has never died. Each Orensanz exhibition should therefore be considered metaphorically as a key to the artist's inner world.

If Angel Orensanz has expressed a sentiment that forms the emotional nucleus of art for the next several decades, it is this: his is a deep attachment to the land, to people, and to an art of meditation, self-renewal, and spiritual retreat. The circle is the most perfect form known to man. It is a symbol of eternity. In the circles of Orensanz, one finds the chance to live in a world created by spirit and dedicated to soul; present in the real world but removed as it were from all reality.

I call to mind the brilliant, immortal pictographs of his country of origin countryman, the Spanish painter Miro, who said, "I have withdrawn inside myself, and the more skeptical I have become about the things around me, the closer I have become to God, the trees, the mountains, and to friendship ..." And I wonder, is this metaphysical essence of Orensanz a Spanish trait or does it belong to a more global sensibility, the essence of Bauhaus and classic surrealist thought? Does it matter from whence and through whom it arrives?

What sets Orensanz apart is the clarity of his voice, a voice that drives individual meaning through the tough, opaque, idiomatic structures of his circle installations, his instrument of choice. Orensanz's art rings true in all of its cadences as an autobiography. Poetry is the substance of his life and hence of his creating, traveling in full circle, therefore, like and to his art. This phenomenon for me is best when, as in *Circles over Venice* (Venice Biennale of Art, 2005), it is about its own processes. In *Circles Over Venice*, several Venetian localities are geometrized, all of them with color arcs and sunlight, in windswept angles. One location, a walled area in a garden on the Grand Canal across from the Academia, was especially striking. The circles of Orensanz were lying flat against the walls, which in the sunlight were reflected in the Venetian tides as parallel to the surface of the water. Behind this flat maze of flowing water, another material color blazed from the hanging circles to form a vortex that seemed at once to recede and to rise up, like an abstract flame. It was as though Orensanz had, in a single work reinvented the illusory space of traditional landscape with his own meaningful methodology, so that everything was on the surface and at the same time bore no relation to the surface (which, after all, is never the philosophy of the landscape). Everything is inside and outside at once. And superimposed on the picturesque garden wall and its reflections were the devices of the most sophisticated tribal art. I experienced this wonderful exhibit on a crystalline June day. I crossed the wooden bridge of the Academia. The Guggenheim Museum on the other side of the bridge and, at my right, was mirrored in the blue pool of the Grand Canal (itself almost an Orensanz circle formation in shadow form) at the base of the ramp of its dock, making the museum's core a bright prism of light. On the bridge, under the blue sky, there were pedestrians, joggers, tourists, vendors, children, dogs. People were generally drawn to the Orensanz circles as they crossed the wooden planks of the Academia bridge. I imagined that they were filled with good humor at that sight, much like the sensation one has, passing through a surprise array of butterflies, resembling brilliant fish in tropical waters and, in an instant, disappearing over the rooftops reflected in the waters of the Grand Canal, as though turning unexpectedly over a most exotic coral reef. Not human, these tidal winged apparitions, but maybe humanoid, some coded display of procreative genitalia. The circles flowed at the water's edge, and like silk ribbons in a summer breeze, metamorphosed from ordinary plastic into an extraordinary organic substance, making Orensanz and his art part of neo-biomorphic dance.

Joy, light, color, humor, rhythm, meditation: these are the notes which characterize the visual music of the work of Angel Orensanz. His is a fundamental devotion to art.

Donna Cameron is a New York-based designer and journalist. She is an internationally acclaimed filmmaker and visual artist. Her films are collected by the Museum of Modern Art Dept. of Film & Media. The MoMA Circulating Film & Media Library represents her work. She holds a US patent for her invention, Cinematic Paper Emulsion. Cameron has served as senior editor of Manhattan Arts International Magazine, the Florida Keys correspondent for the Miami Herald newspaper, interviewer and essayist for exhibition catalogues for the MoMA, editor and graphic designer for the New York Film/Video Council Newsletter, and others. A book, Donna Cameron, about the photography and film paintings of Donna Cameron, was published in 2008 by Spuytendeyvil Press. Her documentary film collage, The Orensanz Portfolio, a developing compilation of the works of Angel Orensanz, was exhibited at the 51st Venice Biennale and is available for purchase or rental through the MoMA Film and Video Library. She lives in Brooklyn with her family, her cameras, books, paints, computers, garden and her Siberian husky, Snowflake.

His Son Was a Disappointment

Julius Klein

It was with the pointed finger of authority that my mother's boyfriend accused me of not being a "Practicing Jew." Being an adult of somewhat sound mind, I replied, "I don't need to practice being Jewish, I am Jewish."

Of course, I knew what he meant. I was not religious. I don't believe in an all seeing God, an entity that has my fate in its lofty hands, yet, even so, I pray. I don't follow the holidays, but I do remember them. If invited to a service, I might attend. I was circumcised, begrudgingly attended Sunday school and then Hebrew school, have been BarMitzvahed and always proudly identify myself as Jewish.

I am not a Zionist but, now that it is done, I support Israel. I also support the right and dire need for a Palestinian state. I don't see the Bible as a deed to land. "The Chosen People" and "The Promised Land" all seem to have worked to the detriment of the Jewish people throughout history. I resent the personification of history as in "what your people did to my people" or "when you enslaved us."

I didn't feel offended in the least when, while running for President, Jessie Jackson referred to NYC as "Hymie Town." He just as well could have said Darkey Town, Dago Den, Bodega Basket or Mick Stew. NYC is Hymie town… as well as all those other characterizations and more. That's why we have so many national parades on 5th Ave.

I like it when someone, someone who isn't Jewish, that is, tells me a Jewish joke (I don't look particularly Jewish). After the punch line is delivered, I inform, "Well, I'm Jewish." I like being "White" and a minority as well.

Living in Chicago, I had been getting comments like "You should move to NYC" for a while. At the commanding age of 23, it was not my intention to move to NYC. Why? Maybe to establish myself? Maybe I could live in both cities? I thought it cliché to be Jewish, in the ARTS, and move to NY, especially being from Chicago, the Second City, which for me wasn't lacking in any way.

If I were to move to another city, my sights were on Amsterdam or maybe Seattle, cities I'd hung out in, but NYC? Actually my sights, my ambitions, were the same as they are today and those are to make things that interest me in whatever medium seems best or that I can afford, and to participate in a creative and progressive environment.

It seemed that maybe those things could be facilitated to a greater extent in NY. Then again I was apprehensive. The first girl (my first true love) that I set up a household with when I was 18 moved to NY a few years before. I didn't want her to think I was invading her turf or that I was too dull to come up with my own exciting new place to be.

In '81, the young lady I was seeing that summer in Chicago lived in NYC, and went back to take up her studies at NYU. I'd also applied to NYU's grad program in film, and was accepted, although I never could get the financing together (I didn't try that hard). She thought I'd flourish in NYC, maybe our relationship as well. I felt the same way.

It was literally "Judaica" that brought me to NYC from Chicago – in the shape of a brand spanking new, right off the line, ambulance, donated to the state of Israel by the local B'nai B'rith of this or that town. It would have to be driven from Chicago to NYC, then loaded on a freighter bound for Haifa.

The drive-a-way service that I used from time to time for free car travel offered me the job. Unlike the standard deal, where you drove their car to a pre-set location, say San Francisco or New Orleans, in a reasonable amount of time and were responsible for the gas and most importantly getting the car there in good shape, they offered to pay a fairly good amount to drive, plus expenses.

Owing to the Hebrew lettering and Star of David insignias painted on the exterior, numerous ambulances had been vandalized along the way, so they wanted to take as many precautions as they could. I was to drive till the sun started to set, find a motel and park as close to the door of my room as I could possibly get.

I informed a couple of Chicago galleries that I'd be driving a van to NYC in the near future and if they needed any paintings delivered to let me know. That worked out. I posted a notice on a Ride Board for a passenger who could share in the driving. And that worked out. Arriving a day early, I couldn't deliver the ambulance to Brooklyn because we made the trip in one shot, to avoid the motel charge.

I delivered the paintings in Soho, dropped off my things at the sublet on Mercer and Spring sts. (a sub, sub basement without windows. but nice enough), then just sat in the front seat wondering what to do.

Two Hasidic men in full Hasid regalia approached and began to question me in very excited tones: "Where did I get the vehicle from?" "What was I doing driving it?" I had never seen a Hasidic man, maybe in old religious pictures? I felt similar to what bad ole A. H. Hitler observed in his *Mein Kampf*, where seeing a Jew dressed in such a manner he asked, "Is this an Aryan?" "This is more than an orthodox Jew," I thought, explaining the situation. One of them said not to worry, his cousin had a garage on 3rd Ave. and 15th St. He went off to make a phone call, returned and said it was all worked out, just drive over and they'll take care of you. And they did, no charge. Shalom. The next morning I picked the ambulance up, drove over the Brooklyn Bridge and delivered it.

That was Oct. 21, 1981. It was unusually warm for fall. I had a place to stay, a fine girlfriend to show me around, a couple of work opportunities. I felt great. I could taste the history in the facades of buildings, sidewalks and streets. I'd been here before, but now I lived here.

NYC offers a grace period to those who come with half-baked agendas or no agenda at all. It might be a month, a few months, usually not more than 6 months where everything connects; your accommodations are adequate or better, you're meeting fabulous people, famous people, work comes easily, you're in love, you're drunk without a trace of hangover and even if there is a trace, it feels poetic and romantic. Then it abruptly ends.

In my case, the grace period lasted three weeks. The sublet ended, the girlfriend ended and soon even the job ended, though I quit and was not fired, I have to say.

As I spiraled down, most of my time was spent wandering the streets, obsessively looking for a place to live. I found myself gravitating to the East Village/Lower East Side. I felt a sort of spiritual connection with the Hebrew lettering that appeared on signs and buildings, the vestiges of old Synagogues and tiny Schuls.

It had turned cold. I walked into an old Kosher restaurant at the corner of Ludlow and Grand, beckoned in by the steamy windows and the thought of a bowl of matzo ball soup, which was all I could afford. I pulled out my notebook and started writing.

The waitress brought a large bowl of pickles and pickled tomatoes. Surprised, I said, "I'm only ordering a bowl of Matzo ball soup."

"Dat's fine boychic," she replied in a warm eastern European yiddishy accent. "Und vhy you don't take off zat coat."

She brought me half a loaf of rye bread piled on a plate and a bowl of hot sauerkraut.

"Vat kind of dressing for your salad?" she asked.

"Oh, uh I didn't order a salad," I replied.

"No it comes vit de soup und zen a cup of tea or coffee."

At the end of my meal, she asked if I would like what was left of the bread, pickles and sauerkraut "to take home." It was all I could do to keep from crying.

It's fairly often when a situation will arise where I feel a distinct tug to return me to the fold, so to speak. Some years later, while looking for a new studio to work in, a friend had suggested that I contact a Mr. Silverman at a temple around Grand and East Broadway. Apparently, they had an unused room behind the Mikva, that I might have use of in return for light carpentry and general handy-man work.

I found the location, knocked on the door and waited. After a while I discovered a doorbell button and rang it, after a while I knocked on the door again. Giving up, I decided to leave my resume in the mail slot. As I turned to leave, the door creaked open slightly and a bit of the face of an old man peered out. I introduced myself and asked if Mr. Silverman was available. The door opened further to reveal an old, disheveled man who unknowingly had his foot on my resume. He instructed that I return the next day at one in the afternoon to speak to Mr. Silverman.

The next day, feeling a bit reluctant, I climbed the old stone steps and found the large wooden doors unlocked. As I stood in the musty vestibule, I could hear a service going on inside, yet very orthodox looking men seemed to be milling about, with their tallis draped over their heads, mumbling their prayers, dovening here and there.

A thin man in his 60s came up to me and introduced himself as Mr. Silverman, and continued to say that he was the head "Shamus" and had heard very good things about me. I would first have to meet with the "Rebbe." Did I bring my "Yarmulke and Talis?" He questioned.

"No," I replied.

With a reassuring pat on the arm, "Wait here," he returned with a Yarmulke and Talis, put an old prayer book into my hands and led me inside, showed me to a seat behind a table with several chairs, opened the book to the pertinent page, and left.

I sat and wondered what the greater significance of the situation was. I tried to follow. Long as I was there, might as well learn something, look for clues to why fate had brought me there? It was a long rectangular room with tables and chairs on the entrance side, and then several rows of chairs fronted by a small pulpit on which the ancient Rebbe sat surrounded by dovening-shawled men. Everything seemed faded and dusty, and there was a small balcony above.

The vast majority of the attending congregation were elderly men in dark rumpled suits, though there were a few more middle aged men in wrinkly white shirts, men I had seen hanging out in what still remained of the Jewish restaurants and on park benches in the neighborhood.

There seemed to be no direction to the service, no Cantor, everyone in their own state of chanting and communing with God. A fracas broke out when one of the younger men's guests, a broken down old bag of a lady, began giggling out of madness or morning drink.

"The men can't Doven with a lady present." I heard several of the men complain.

The matter was brought up with the Rebbe, who apparently pronounced that if she took a seat up in the balcony and behaved herself it would be OK. A man became indignant and slammed his prayer book on the table, at which time everyone's eyes became fixed on me.

I got up, slowly walked up to the man and said in the calmest of tones that maybe he should come back tomorrow; you know the men can't Doven. He grabbed her out of her chair by the shoulder of her coat; but she paused for a moment and gave me a piece of candy. They left, I returned to my seat and things continued along as before.

It didn't seem like there was a definitive end to the service, the men just left when they felt like it. It was becoming a bit clearer to me as to the subtle differences between a "Schul" (school) and a "Temple," at least on the Lower East Side, or, I'm sure, out in Brooklyn.

Mr. Silverman appeared ready to introduce me to the old Rebbe.

"Do not ask the Rebbe any questions, only answer the questions that he asks of you," he instructed.

"And" he continued, "don't extend your hand unless he extends his hand first." Now I was aware of the taboo of the ultra orthodox or Hasidim not to shake hands with women, but this I had never heard of.

"All right let's get this over with," I thought, knowing the situation was not for me. We met; I think he thought that I was applying for the super's job. I guess I passed mustard in that I was shown through the back, past the Mikva, which was steamy, moldy, greenish and smelled like piss, into to a small room that felt as if it had been locked up since the 1880s.

I left thanking Mr. Silverman but informing him that the situation would not work out for me. He seemed disappointed and that was that.

A similar event happened a few years later, while wallowing in confusion and self doubt, on a cold and clear afternoon at the Mars Bar, at the corner of 2nd Ave. and 1st St. As I sat getting drunk with a Native American friend of mine of Incan descent, a Hassidic man walked in and sat at the bar, something quite incongruous with the punky arty/farty temperament and post apocalyptic decor of the place.

We started talking, as it is always my inclination to make people feel welcome. He told me he was a Rabbi, which piqued my interest as to why he would feel the inclination to stop by such a place. It was just on the corner and he stopped in, he explained.

After a while I mentioned that my great grandfather on my fathers' side was, as I had been told, a noted Rabbi and scholar called Moram Schick. He jumped off his bar stool and said if, in fact, that was true, then I was a direct descendant of the great 12th century Rabbi, physician philosopher, none other then Maimonides. Well great for me.

He said that it was his and my fate that we should meet in such a place and proposed that we should pray together, if that was all right with me? I informed him that I wasn't religious and didn't feel comfortable anyway in that environment, although it occurred to me that I had some major unresolved decisions to make and anything that might bring me to resolution would be a positive thing.

So, yes, I agreed.

We stood in the northeast corner of the room surrounded by glass windows. As people walked by, he instructed me on how to put the Tchfilin on my left arm, put the little connected box on my forehead, put his Talis over my head and shoulders. My Indian friend laughed at first but then quieted. The bartender turned the music off.

The "Rabbi" pulled a bible out and after having me recite after him in Hebrew the familiar blessing I remembered from childhood, read another text, which I followed with Amen.

After, we shook hands and all in attendance seemed to feel better.

It has always been my inclination to balance situations, which is just my nature; if around macho men, I tend to be more effeminate, if around effeminate men, I tend to be more macho. The same is true with being with Jewish folk; the more Jewish they are, the more goyish I become. Many a time amongst older Jewish men, something I'm becoming myself, I observe the dropped head of one of them in response to the question of how this child or that child is doing?

"He has become a disappointment to me."

Julius G. Klein, born Chicago, Ill., June '57 BA, Columbia College/School of The Art Institute '80. Moved to NYC '81. Has partnered with Raken Leaves since '83. Ran "XOXO" '90-'97. Current Studio/Gallery is at, 44 E. First St. Continues to be afflicted, since his mid-teens, by the desire to exercise thoughts/feelings, through any medium at hand. www.juliusklein.net

Cartoon Jews on the Lower East Side

Eddy Portnoy

The Lower East, for most Jewish immigrants, was a place they wanted to get the hell out of. It was crowded, noisy and it stunk. Densely packed with over a half-million people to a few square miles, its streets filled with peddlers loudly hawking their goods, thousands of gallons of horse piss coursing through its gutters every day (not to mention the thousands of pounds of manure deposited on those same streets), and it wasn't fit for man nor beast. From the 1880s onward, as the "East Side," as it was known in Yiddish, filled up with Jews on the run from severe oppression and even more extreme poverty than they would know in America, the neighborhood became a little piece of *Yiddishland*, where the Old World mixed with the New and Jewish culture became Americanized.

Flapping in the wind like flags at the UN, sheets and underwear were the national symbol of the Lower East Side. Conversations were held through windows of adjacent buildings, or yelled across busy streets. Life was often lived publicly, especially in summertime, when doors and windows remained open and people slept on rooftops, fire escapes and on stoops to escape the stifling heat. Close quarters bred close friendships. It also bred contempt. It wasn't easy to be happy-go-lucky after working 12 hour days only to return to suffocate in tiny, airless apartments packed with kids. People knew their neighbors and they knew their neighbors' business as well. Angry outbursts, fights and crime were central to life in these conditions.

As much of this is replaced by chic boutiques and million dollar condos, the Jewish nostalgia industry, which has been promoting an urban *Fiddler on the Roof* type of Jewish shtetl on the Lower East Side, will become even more central in promoting the neighborhood's myths. 100 years ago, a gnarled, grimy hand plunged into a brine-filled barrel to get you a pickle. The nostalgia industry wants you to believe that today's pickle man, who wears surgical gloves and a white apron and whose plastic barrels are covered with Lucite tops, has some connection to the former. You want to believe him. It makes you feel connected. Maybe it does.

Life on today's LES is drastically different from the way it was when swarms of Jewish immigrants filled its streets. Life was lived out of doors. On sweltering summer nights, people would sleep on rooftops, fire escapes and even on the sidewalks. Shopping for clothing and food was done on the streets. Groups would gather in the dozens and hundreds to hear soapbox orators howl about anarchism, socialism, and religion. Thousands would wait up all night in Rutgers Square for the Jewish *Daily Forward* to put up election results in their windows. The *Forward* also used to show movies on the side of their building on hot summer nights. The streets were a stage: commerce was king, but a variety of different beggars, from fakes to cripples would perform for a penny.

The Jewish LES was one phase of many for the neighborhood. For the Jews, it was a kind of Ply-mouth Rock, the first place immigrants came to and settled en masse. There isn't much left of the physical LES – mostly synagogues. There's the Forward building as well. The clubhouses of *landsmanshaftn*, political organizations, youth groups, they're gone. The noises that resounded in their walls, the shouting matches and fistfights are also long gone. Jews don't argue anar-chism and socialism much anymore. Nor are there hysterical arguments over who gets what cemetery plot or who gets to sit near the eastern wall in the synagogue. These are some of the bits of history that don't get conveyed via traditional texts.

There are numerous iconic photographs of the LES. Jacob Riis's work in the neighborhood stands without parallel. The *Forward*'s Sunday rotogravure section also contains a fascinating look at LES neighborhood characters and the neighborhood itself. Photographs, however, are not the only form of documentation available. There are the famed Jewish artists of the East Side, Moses and Raphael Soyer, Abraham Walkowitz, Hugo Gellert, and Bill Gropper, to name a few. When considering the history of the LES visually, it may also be instructive to consider cartoons as well. Cartoons themselves are often an urban form. Outcault's *Hogan's Alley*, the first color cartoon, was a trip to the slums of New York City for better-heeled readers. They could look through a window at the pathetic ridiculousness of the poor without having to leave their living rooms.

A TURKEY RAFFLE IN WHICH THE YELLOW KID EXHIBITS SKILL WITH THE DICE.

New York Journal, November 11, 1896

Robert Henri and George Bellows, the founders of the Ash Can school and teachers of many modern artists, some of whom would go on to found important political/literary magazines like *Masses*, used to send their students to the LES so they could draw "life in the raw," a kind of Orientalist artistic exploitation of the immigrant poor. Coincidentally, a number of their students were immigrants who actually lived in this neighborhood. What did they make of their own lives "in the raw?"

One of these suddenly exotic students was Zuni Maud, a part time sweatshop worker and cigar roller who would go on to become one of the Yiddish press's most prolific cartoonists. The Yiddish press, after all, was the biggest institution the Jewish LES ever produced. With up to 4 dailies and dozens of weeklies and monthly publications, the Yiddish press had millions of readers throughout the US, but was centered in New York. It was the largest immigrant press in the history of the country. It is an oft forgotten fact that Yiddish media was far and away the largest Jewish institution ever created.

The Yiddish press of the Lower East Side was a national and international press. But, more importantly perhaps, it was a local press. For Yiddish speakers worldwide, East Broadway, which housed the offices of the *Forward*, the *Tageblat*, the *Tog* and a number of other, smaller newspapers and magazines, became the Fleet Street of the Jews. With the LES as its hub, it reported heavily on local matters and how they affected the neighborhood. Local reporting in the Yiddish press, from its creation in the 1870s until the *Forward* left the neighborhood in the 1970s, is very much a chronicle of the neighborhood in which it was situated.

One of the interesting aspects of the Yiddish press is the visuals it offered its readers. The *Forward*, famously, had its Sunday photo section, recently immortalized in Alana Newhouse's "A Living Lens: Photographs of Jewish Life from the Pages of the *Forward*." But Yiddish papers also contained visuals that have long been overlooked: cartoons. As historical documents, cartoons can be quite rich, providing insight into the lives and opinions of groups and individuals and, if they are particularly localized, they can offer a wealth of information on places whose voices don't get heard in the historical record.

On the whole, cartoons leave us with unusual notions of locale. Many take place in imaginary urban environments, many of them loosely based on New York City. The New Yorkishness of these cartoons is mostly a result of the City being the country's cultural and press center. But for the cartoonists of the Yiddish press, New York City wasn't just the backdrop of their work, but, in a more macro sense, it was the LES, the biggest and most important of the Jewish immigrant neighborhoods.

The information packed into a cartoon can vary wildly. They can offer a great deal of information or very little, leaving the reader to fill in the blanks. In Yiddish press cartoons, it is usually the latter. Typically, cartoonists focus on the speaking characters, leaving scant renderings of their locales. One useful aspect of Yiddish cartoons is the frequent constructions of LES – specific jobs, peddlers and street people, mostly. And just as there was once a wide variety of beggars, there were also different kinds of peddlers. That some of the earliest cartoons in the Yiddish press were of peddlers stands to reason, since peddling was such a common profession among the immigrant poor. The two images below, some of the earliest cartoons to appear in Yiddish, both deal with peddlers. The first one appeared in *Di nyu-yorker ilustrirte tsaytung* in 1887. Essentially an illustrated joke, the image shows a recent Jewish immigrant talking to an "American" as a black man passes in the background. The immigrant says, "That guy has been in America a long time." "How can you tell?" asks the "American." "He's become completely blackened." The joke here is that in Yiddish, the term "blackened," refers to an expression that means hard work causes one to become dark. More interesting, perhaps, than the joke itself, is the way in which the characters are portrayed. The immigrant, a peddler, as evidenced by the pots, pans and other items hanging from his clothing, is a stereotypical rendering of a Jew representative of 19th century caricature. The same goes for the black man. However, what is different here from typical 19th century caricature of African Americans is that this man is finely attired and walking with his head held high, a representation of a black man that was not typical in the general press. As to the background, there is a store with the concocted name of Kuni & Lemel, the name of a play written by one of the editors, an elevated track and buildings. It could be anywhere, but, as readers, we know that it is likely the Lower East Side.

Nyu-yorker ilustrirte yidishe tsaytung, 15 Nov. 1887

There is no background in the second image, which appeared in the humor magazine, *Der yidisher pok* (*The Jewish Puck*), in November 1894. It simply shows a peddler under attack. This was undoubtedly a common occurrence – peddlers alone on the streets getting rocks and such chucked at them by neighborhood kids. Though it is spare, it evokes a certain reality of life as a peddler on the LES.

Der yidisher pok, 29 November 1894

Another reality on the LES that has apparently been a constant is garbage picking. One item that no longer exists as refuse is ash. Up until the teens and twenties, many tenements were heated by coal stoves. As a result, ashes had to be thrown out every day. Sometimes, small lumps of usable coal would get thrown out with the ashes. The poor, who were desperate to heat their apartments, often went digging through the ash cans to find these lumps of coal. This cartoon, which appeared in the *Forward*, describes the practice. In fact, the caption says that a reporter happened to see people digging through ash cans and asked why. The response was that they needed the coal, but also included a complaint about how they were duped into thinking that America was the "Goldene medine," or the "golden land." The message behind the cartoon, that pre-immigration fantasies about life in the United States, in which it was imagined that the country's streets were paved with gold, were horribly wrong. There was poverty in New York, too. And lots of it.

Forward, 24 April 1904

As the Yiddish press grew, it would come to include more features, like cartoons, that had become popular in the English language press. The preceding cartoons were printed during a period in which cartooning had not yet become common in the Yiddish press. That would occur in 1908 when a humor magazine called *Der kibitzer* began publication. *The Kibitzer*, which bitterly mocked virtually every aspect of Jewish life, was instantly popular and begat several other Yiddish humor magazines, all of which contained numerous cartoons. These magazines, and, to a lesser degree, the Yiddish daily press, became the main forums for Yiddish cartooning.

Most of these periodicals were based on the Lower East Side and, because that's where their constituencies lived, the neighborhood was central to reportage. As a result, neighborhood politics, Yiddish press and theatre and whatever else fell under their purview became fodder for their satire. Part of this was the physicality of the neighborhood.

One of the prominent physical features of the LES was the neighborhood's one Jewish "skyscraper," the 10 story Forward building. The largest Yiddish newspaper in history and a cultural and political force to be reckoned with, the *Forward* was a huge organization. Under its sway fell its own Association, the *Arbeter ring*, as well as other institutions and unions. As such, the *Forward* was itself an institutional celebrity, a financially secure organization, which had the money and infrastructure to build its own building, which would broadcast its name across town in huge letters.

As a result of its success, the *Forward* cultivated a lot of enemies, mainly writers who thought the quality of prose in the paper was terrible, or socialists, who felt that the paper had betrayed socialism. The main forum for Yiddish cartooning in New York, *Der groyser kundes* (*The Great*

Prankster), which was populated with disgruntled writers and fiery socialists, had a field day mocking the *Forward* and did so in both words and image. One of their innovations was to create a cartoon character that represented the entire *Forward* organization. Cartoonists at the *Kundes* took the archetype of a fatcat *alrightnik* (a nouveau riche) in a top hat, which was typically used to portray an evil boss or a crass capitalist, and called him "Mister *Forward.*"

Der groyser kundes, 1 December 1912

But the portrayal of the *Forward* as a capitalist alrightnik was not specifically representative enough, and so cartoonists transformed the hat into the newly built Forward building, the most public face of the paper and the most recognizable symbol of conspicuous wealth and power on the LES.

אויפ'ן „פֿאָרווערטס"-באַנקעט

דער „פֿאָרווערטס" : אהאַ, איצט וועסטו שוין „סלושען" !
די „צוקונפֿט" (מיט חניפֿה און נע בעט): האַו, האַו, האַו !....

Forward, 3 May 1912

This capitalist alrightnik image of the *Forward* allowed cartoonists to vent their spleens regarding the paper's perceived hypocrisy in making large profits while espousing socialism. The image of the fat capitalist with the Forward building as his top hat became as recognizable a symbol for the *Forward* as the Uncle Sam for the United States and was drawn over and over in a wide variety of situations and commenting on a wide variety of issues by different cartoonists. Many of the basic issues remained the same: undue influence, betrayal of socialism, sensationalistic news coverage

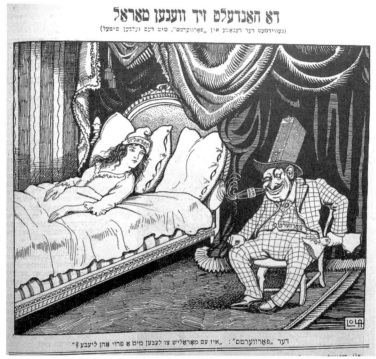

Der groyser kundes, 1 May 1911

No other building was as recognizable on the LES than the Forward building. Other buildings that show up in Yiddish cartoons tend to be less specific, mainly tenements or the front stoops of newspaper offices. Others portray neighborhood denizens, peddlers or specifically Jewish or local types of employment

The *Forward* itself published some of the most interesting cartoons to have appeared in the Yiddish press — but only between 1916 and 1920, when they allowed artist Zuni Maud to have free reign on a weekly humor page called, "The Stepchild." Maud had worked for the *Kibitzer* as well as the *Kundes* and was the in-house artist for an avant-garde literary group called Di yunge. On the pages of the *Forward*, Maud was to create cartoons that would appeal to the largest Yiddish readership in the world. The paper's print runs at the time were over 200,000, but the real readership was upwards of nearly three times that. Covering topics such as international and national politics as well as life in general on the LES, Maud created thousands of cartoons. Many of them reveal topics that deal specifically with the LES, such as the ubiquitous street peddler or pushcart salespeople.

Forward 8 October 1916

Forward 15 October 1916

These two street peddlers, one selling herring, the other "used etrogim" (which aren't worth much after Sukkot, the holiday during which they are used), were typical of those cramming the streets of the LES. There are many such images that chronicle the travails and mishaps of those who worked the streets or who worked in factories. One of the things these images don't convey is the cacophony of noises and myriad smells that assaulted people as they did something as simple as walk down the street or go shopping.

Forward 9 November 1916

The cartoon above shows a family with a weekly paycheck of $15 with a line of people to whom they owe money. From right to left, they are: the landlord, the groceryman, the butcher, the coal man, the milkman, the doctor, and the customer peddler. These were people that everyone met face to face on a regular basis. Today's bills are paid online or via mail. It's rare that we are approached in person and asked to pay a bill. There is a huge psychological difference in having to do so. The element of performing a negotiation with each person rarely exists in urban life. This aspect of life, along with many others, has disappeared.

Life in the tenements of the LES was cramped and often unpleasant. Typically 300 square feet, each tenement apartment was stuffy and noisy. Doors and windows were frequently open, and, as a result, conversations, disputes and fights that were meant to be private, became public. Neighbors, nosy or not, often heard everything in the surrounding apartments and the adjacent buildings, and gossip ruled. Below is a cartoon that evokes this feeling.

Forward, 10 December 1916

Read from right to left, the cartoon above shows a man and woman in three panels: before, after, and a bit longer after their wedding. At first, they're in love, after the wedding, they're not so much in love, lastly, they're viciously cursing each other as neighbors from the next building peer in and enjoy the show. This, no doubt, was not an uncommon sight in the tenements.

We can also see a bit of the reality of Jewish life of the period. Historians would have us believe that Jews were either in synagogues or at socialist meetings. The reality was that most Jews did avoided both places and were more likely to be seen at boxing matches, freak shows or the movies.

Even better, as the cartoon below shows, going to synagogue wasn't that big of a draw, especially when dance halls, pool rooms, and prostitutes beckoned. Published for Rosh Hashanah, this image shows a furious wife attacking her husband for even looking the way of the LES attractions available to him on the way to synagogue.

„יאנקעלע געהט אין שוהל אריין"

דאָס ווייב (כאַפּענדיג איהר יאנקלען מיט אַ „בעשערטער"): אָט אזוי, יענקעלע
ממזר, געהסטו דאָס אין שוהל אריין, האַ ?....

Der groyser kundes, 3 October 1913

As holidays go, Yom Kippur, when one fasts for 24 hours, is considered the most solemn. What are we to make of the cartoon below, which shows how the poorest and wealthiest echelons of Jews "fast" on Yom Kippur? Here the cartoon becomes a valuable resource, chronicling what would be impossible to photograph.

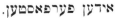

אידען פערפאסטען.

(1) אויף דעסטער קארנער עססעקס סטריט.

(2) אויף בראָדוויי, קארנער 42סטע סטריט.

Der groyser kundes, 10 October 1913

Another interesting aspect to these cartoons is how the neighborhood's Jews viewed themselves. Photographers and artists had a tendency to exoticize the Jews of the LES. Focusing on the poor, the infirm, and those in religious garb, they missed out on the very American story of an immigrant group becoming politically enfranchised. In the wake of numerous successful garment industry strikes in 1909 and 1910, the Jews of the LES were becoming an immigrant group with growing political and cultural clout. By 1911, the self image of the Jewish LES wasn't the pathetic beggar or street urchin. It was one of growing possibility and power. The cartoon below portrays this quite nicely. Published the week before mayoral elections in 1911, the caption reads, "When the East Side is in a good mood!" and shows the Jewish LES represented by a powerful woman in the style of the French Marianne or the American Columbia, clutching a sword marked "the Jewish vote," about to stab Charles Murphy, the leader of the Tammany Hall political machine. While representation of Jews in cartoon images was commonplace throughout the English language press, it can safely be said that they were only portrayed like this in the Yiddish press.

Der groyser kundes, 3 November 1911

It is impossible to imagine what life was really like in the tenements and on the streets for the millions of Jewish immigrants who lived or passed through the LES. The memoirs that have been passed down to us are inherently limited in their evocation of life. But they are probably the best we have. Cartoons, which also evoke certain aspects of life on the LES, are simply an unusual and mostly untapped source of historical media. What is interesting are the cartoonists' decisions to draw what they did. From the creation of the Forward Building as a caricatural icon to the variety of occupations – from peddler to landlord and everything in between, stands as a blatantly opinionated form of documentation of a neighborhood that has been nostalgized in an often saccharine way by some and overrun by others. What we have left to inform us are photographs and artistic renderings. We'll never be able to recreate the feeling of fear at the landlord's knock, the sight and smell of the dust explosion when a kid upends an ash can, the stifling stench from the heat of summer in the cramped tenements, the cries of a child being beaten, the smell of the steaming tar on the roof on a summer's night. There are million and one things we'll never know about life on the LES. The best we can do is find things that evoke the past as it disappears under new construction and a society that doesn't want to know everything.

Eddy Portnoy earned a Ph.D. in Modern Jewish Studies at the Jewish Theological Seminary. He teaches Yiddish language and literature at Rutgers University.

Part 5: Theatre

Under the World with Sholem Asch
(and a one act adaptation of his play *The Dead Man*)

Caraid O'Brien

When people ask me why I have a degree in Yiddish literature, I usually answer that my parents wouldn't let me major in theater, which is sort of true. It was actually reading an English translation of Chaim Grade's heart breaking memoir *My Mother's Sabbath Days* that created the desire within me to learn Yiddish and read Grade's masterpiece in its original. Having been born in a country (Ireland), where we all speak in translation (English instead of Irish), language has always been on my mind. My grandfather was a native Irish speaker from the Aran Islands, and my first language was a Gaelic sprinkled English as reinvented by the Irish, not unlike the way the Jewish immigrants to New York's Lower East Side created an American dialect molded by their Yiddish mother tongue.

When people ask me why I of all people became a historian of Yiddish theater, I point to Richard Ellman, a Jew from Missouri who became the greatest scholar of Irish literature, writing extraordinary biographies of Wilde, Joyce and Yeats, not that I would ever compare myself to him. It was as a student at Notre Dame Academy, an all girls Catholic high school in Hingham, Massachusetts that I first discovered Yiddish literature while reading the works of the Nobel Laureate Isaac Bashevis Singer in an American literature class. Never relating to the epic, adventure novels of Hemingway and Steinbeck, instead the works of Philip Roth, Bernard Malamud, Cynthia Ozick and Saul Bellow drew me in with their sly humor and intellectual heroes. I realized what I loved about American literature came from a very specific demographic within American society – Yiddish speaking immigrants and their Yiddish speaking (or somewhat Yiddish speaking) American children. When I discovered Yiddish literature, I felt I was connecting with the Ur text of the best of American literature. Not unlike the feeling I got while studying the Irish language literature of Ireland – from medieval poetry written by monks in the glosses of their copied biblical manuscripts to the modern Irish poetry of writers like Nuala Ni Dhomnaill.

Ever since James Joyce created Leopold Bloom as the hero of Ulysses, there has been a sense of literary simpatico between the Irish and the Jews. The Pulitzer Prize winning Irish poet Paul Muldoon, who is married to a Jewish American writer, frequently uses Jewish references and Yiddish words in his poetry. Almost every time I lecture to a primarily Jewish audience about Yiddish theater, one or two people will come up to me and say "I am you in reverse!" Recently while lecturing at the Beth Jacob Synagogue in Vermont, I met a Yiddish speaking accountant with a degree in medieval Irish literature. After a lecture at the Eldridge Street Synagogue in Manhattan, I encountered an Indian Jew, whose hobby was linguistics and who greeted me in Gaelic. One of my favorite Irish playwrights, Brendan Behan, wrote in both Irish and English and even created a Yiddish speaking character – never performed – after spending some time in New York.

Shortly after I had the idea to learn Yiddish and read *My Mother's Sabbath Days* in its original, I was walking the halls of the School of Theology at Boston University and noticed the phrase "Get Paid to Learn Yiddish" on a brightly colored poster advertising the summer internship program at the National Yiddish Book Center in Amherst, Massachusetts. I applied and was accepted. It was the first time my desire to learn Yiddish was taken seriously. We studied in the morning and unpacked and shelved books for the rest of the day. The experience of physically touching an entire literature that had been on its way to the dustbin was visceral and unforgettable. Unpacking boxes of books I wanted to read but could not, able only to decipher the author's name and sometimes the title; knowing where these books lived on the shelves was an incentive to quickly learn the language and be able to read them. Even today, when someone mentions a Yiddish author, my first thought is likely to be the size and color and smell of a dusty, worn book. Following my internship, I spent the next year studying Yiddish and Hebrew at the Hebrew University of Jerusalem, teaching Hebrew to Ethiopian monks who lived in tiny stone huts on top of the Church of the Holy Sepulcher in the Old City and performing Shakespeare in English directed by playwright Aron Coleite during a heat wave in the botanical gardens of Mount Scopus.

That was fun.

I returned to Boston University my senior year and through the introduction of Aaron Lansky, the founder of the National Yiddish Book Center, was able to take an inspiring class with Ruth Wisse on Yiddish theater. We read plays by the great Yiddish playwrights Sholem Asch, Peretz Hirschbein, Sh. Anski, Sholem Alechem, Avrom Goldfaden and Mendele Mokher Seforim in their original Yiddish. When I had finished my degree in Yiddish literature, I decided to move to New York to become an actress. My first day job was to write a now defunct Yiddish theater website for NYU. At the same time, I was acting in a storefront theater called Todo con Nada on Ludlow Street on the Lower East Side. I auditioned for its founder (and my future partner in life as well as art) Aaron Beall, who also created the New York International Fringe Festival, the largest theater festival in North America. For my first performance, Aaron cast me in a title role in Richard Foreman's *Rhoda in Potatoland* as one of six dancing potatoes.

Shortly afterward, I saw an abbreviated adaptation of Sholem Asch's 1907 drama *God of Vengeance*, a drama about a Jewish brothel owner and his quest for redemption. The version I saw bore no resemblance to the brave and glorious work that I read in my Yiddish theater class with Ruth Wisse. One of the most controversial Broadway plays in American Theater History, *God of Vengeance* was performed to great acclaim in a dozen languages throughout the world. Two years before Mae West was thrown into the slammer for jumping into bed with sailors in her racy farce *Sex*, Rudolph Schildkraut and Morris Carnovsky starred in the English language premier of *God of Vengeance* at the Apollo Theater on Broadway in 1923. The entire cast spent a night in jail charged with "lewd behavior" for performing in what was Asch's first full length play complete with Jewish prostitutes, a lesbian scene and a Torah hurled across the stage.

Watching the production I saw in 1999 which mocked not only Asch's genius but seemed to disregard the vast and sophisticated tradition of the Yiddish art theaters on the Lower East Side and throughout the world, I felt the spectral presence of Asch himself rise through the floorboards of the stage and hover in between the actors. With Aaron's encouragement, I translated the play and we staged it on the go-go stage of the world famous adult entertainment emporium Show World in Times Square, around the corner from its original Broadway venue. In our production, the Faux Real Theatre Company's Mark Greenfield played the brothel owner; Andrea Darriau his wife. Other actors in the show included David Pincus (Artistic Director, Workshop Theatre), storyteller Vered Henkin, Shane Baker (Executive Director, Congress for Jewish Culture), Naomi Odes, Mercedes McAndrew, Corey Carthew, Noah Kay, Shay Guttman, James Henderson, Maux Kelly, Lisa Syzmanski and others. The beautiful Canadian model Elizabeth Gondek played the lesbian prostitute who seduces the brothel owner's daughter. After seeing a rehearsal, the editor of *Popsmear Magazine*, Troy Fuss, agreed to be our stage manager after a half dozen others had quit. The show was a hit and we were sold out for our six week run.

Shortly after our production of *God of Vengeance*, believing Asch to be not only one of the most important Yiddish playwrights but one of the most brilliant American writers as well, Aaron and myself embarked on a mission to translate all of his 18 plays, many of which were written in New York City and at his estate on Staten Island. Originally coming to prominence in Europe, Asch's plays were first produced in America a hundred years ago by the impresario Jacob P. Adler, who steered the Yiddish theater toward literary drama. Born in Kutnow, Poland, in 1880, Asch dropped out of rabbinical school and spent a few years slumming in the Warsaw underworld writing plays and sketches before moving to New York City's Lower East Side. Second only to Bashevis Singer, Asch is among the most well known of Yiddish writers. His trilogy of historical Christian novels – *Mary, The Apostle,* and *The Nazarene* – published in New York in the 1940's, led to an attack by the Jewish press for his inclusion of Christian themes in his work. He was wrongly accused of having converted to Christianity and a defamatory book was published in Yiddish and English called *The Christianity of Sholem Asch*, denouncing his character. Asch responded with the essay "What I Believe," asserting his belief in Judaism and hope for improved Christian-Jewish relations. As a result of the attacks, however, Asch left New York and exiled himself in London and later Israel. He died in 1957.

His success as a novelist and the controversy surrounding his writings about Christianity overshadowed his work as a playwright, however, and most of his plays remain untranslated. We began our project by working on what we call Asch's Underworld Trilogy: *God of Vengeance, Motke Thief* and *The Dead Man*. Asch had been writing plays for over a decade when, in 1917, he decided to adapt his novel *Motke Thief* into a work for the Yiddish stage in New York City, where he was living at the time. An almost sequel to *God of Vengeance, Motke Thief* features some of the same characters (Shlomo, Hindl, Basha, Red) aged ten years. The play is a psychological portrait of a criminal that begins with the beating of an impoverished 12 year old boy, follows him as he runs away to the circus, murders a romantic rival and becomes one of the leading pimps of the Jewish ghetto. We staged the full text of *Motke Thief* with Jonathan Butler as Motke and also featuring Corey Carthew, Mark Greenfield, Laura Barnett, Aaron Beall, Caraid O'Brien, Ana Rita Da Piedade, Bern Cohen, Leah Emmerich, Marlene Hamerling, Penny Bittone, Devin Sanchez, Maureen Sebastian, Gurjant Singh and others at University Settlement in 2005. Uta Bekai designed the sets and costumes.

The third play in his underworld trilogy, *The Dead Man*, focuses not on the world of criminals but on that eternal underworld, the world of the undead. The battered survivors of a destroyed Jewish community gather together in the ruins of their synagogue in a Polish shtetl just after World War I. A debate ensues over whether to rebuild their community or immigrate en masse to America or Palestine. At the moment they decide to stay in Poland and rebuild their temple, a soldier thought to have been killed in the war, returns and tells his people of a new land where Jews aren't persecuted and where no one goes hungry. He urges his neighbors to follow him: "Down the road, past the field, behind the woods and over the stone." The children and the elderly, most eager to follow the soldier, begin to die. Finally, the leader of the community realizes that the soldier is directing everyone to the cemetery. A bleak statement on the future of Eastern European Jewry, but considering the further atrocities to come during World War II, Asch's vision can only be seen as prescient.

The Dead Man debuted in New York in 1919 at the 2,200 seat Yiddish Art Theater on Second Avenue and 12th Street (now a Loews movie house). The actor-impresario Maurice Schwartz, who ran the longest running repertory company in New York City's history produced the play on the occasion of the publication of the complete works of Sholem Asch in Yiddish. When *The Dead Man* was presented in Chicago a few years later, the Academy Award winning screenwriter Ben Hecht wrote of the play that "one comes out of the theater with a strange sense of understanding. The dead have spoken to one."

In 2004, our translation of *The Dead Man* received a new play commission from The Foundation for Jewish Culture. The following text is our one act adaptation of The Dead Man that we staged at the Eldridge Street Synagogue (Program Director Hanna Griff) in October, 2004. That production was costumed by Loren Bevans and directed by Aaron Beall. We performed the following text with a cast of 20 including myself, Ana Rita da Piedade, Neil Schwary, Robin Bloodworth, Anna Goodman-Herrick, Laura Zambrano, Maux Kelly, Paul Pierog, Marcy Rylan, Amitai Kedar, Liat Glick, Ruth Kulerman, David Zhonzinsky, Marvin Starkman, Vivian Akadamos, Moshik Cohen, Galit Levy, Alex and others. The original Sholem Asch text, the translation of which I am still working on, is in three acts.

Sholem Asch's *The Dead Man*
Translated and adapted by Caraid O'Brien. Dramaturgy by Aaron Beall.
Dramatis Personae
Crazy Man
Reb Nehemiah , a leader in the community
Efriam, the shopkeeper
Berish, the dissenter
Dobtshe, a young woman who has never been married
Shprintse, a woman whose son is missing
Lea, Shprintse's daughter
Khaya-Peshie, a woman whose husband went to America
Vela, an aguna (a woman whose husband is missing)
Reb Leybush, a scholar
Yankev, a butcher
Shlomo, his son

Moishe, a Zionist
Reb Honen, a Jewish official
Dina, his daughter
Yosef, a soldier just returned from the war
Frumme-Liebtshe, Yosef's blind mother
The crowd
Another child

Setting: a half destroyed synagogue in a Polish shtetl, just after World War I

The women are up in the balcony, the men are in the seats intermingled with the audience, everyone is dressed in black and white rags, their faces are whitened with black circles around their eyes, they do not speak to the audience but can stare at them if provoked, they look listless until the play begins.

Crazy Man (running up the aisle of the synagogue then speaking from the bima): Krank iz di alta velt, The old world is sick, es benkt der khola nakhn toit, the patient longs for death, nara-neem haltn zee ayn, fools hold her back, meshugim gayen faroyis, the mad men advance (repeat)

Reb Nehemiah (running up to the bima, pushing the crazy man off): Jews, what is happening to our shul? This is not a poorhouse but a place of worship. A crazy man speaks from the bima? What next, Jews? A woman? Pull yourself together Jews. The worst is over. The war is behind us. We must rebuild!

Efriam: How can we rebuild? Our homes are destroyed; our shul is in ruins; we have no business —

Berish: We don't know who is one of us and who is a stranger. I have lived here all my life and I don't recognize most of the people here in this shul. We have to make a separation between ourselves and strangers! Who is an enemy? Who is a friend?

The Crowd (looking around suspiciously at one another): Who is an enemy? Who is a friend?

Leybush: I don't even recognize you Berish! The war changed all of us forever; my own wife I don't even recognize and now that the war is over, we must welcome everyone. A stranger may be your brother or sister. Many of ours are still in faraway cities in Russia and Europe. We must welcome strangers as we would want our family to be welcomed…

Shlomo: He is right! My brother has been in Russia for three years. I am sure he is still alive, although we haven't a word —

Berish: What are you saying? We don't know who these people are! They are not your brother. Are they even all Jews?

Reb Nehemiah: This is a shul not a poorhouse, we must rebuild!

Shprintse: But we have no food –

Lea: I'm hungry, mama

Dobtshe: And our children are hungry –

Khaya-Peshie: And our men are gone –

(Vela wails.)

Reb Nehemiah: Jews, we need money to rebuild our community, who will give the first donation?

Shprintse: Who has money? –

Berish: We have no money

Reb Nehemiah: We must rebuild

Shlomo: We must go on!

Berish: Jews, we shouldn't stay here. It is only going to get worse! Why now would they stop
with the pogroms?

Shlomo: We should go to America. My brother, he lives near New York, in Brooklyn. He makes
a good living; he even sends home money sometimes. That was before the war, of course -

Reb Leybush: America! They don't believe in God in America. They walk around with their
heads uncovered; they never go to shul –

Shprintshe: And they forget their families in America. They go to an American rabbi; they get
an American divorce. Look at Khaya-Peshie, here beside me. Her man left her with 4 children,
5 years ago to go to America. He was supposed to send for them. He never did. I heard from
my cousin Chaim, whose wife's uncle is there, that he even married a woman in America, forgot all about Khaya-Peshie, never mind their children, nebekh. And Mentshn, his new wife, she
might not even be Jewish. (Khaye-Peshie wails.) There is no God in America!

Efriam: There is no God in Poiln. Jews, look around, look how we find ourselves -

Shprintshe: Tfu-tfu-tfu, how can you say such things? You are in a shul! This is not America!

Yankev: America! Jews listen! They have lots of money in America. My cousin built an entire
orphanage with money from America. They will send us money and we can rebuild our shul
here. I will send a letter to my cousin right away, and he will help us.

Dobtshe: What's a cousin? My own brother, he is in America, he will send us money, of this I am certain. I will ask my neighbor to write him a letter today-

Moshe: I don't care. I am not staying in Poiln any longer. I am a young man. Why should I wait to be killed in the next war, hm?

Khaya-Peshie: Maybe he is right. I think he is right. We should go to America –

Dobtshe: And where will you get money to go to America if even your own husband won't pay for you, huh?

Reb Leybush: No Jews, listen, I have heard that they are making a treaty in Paris to end all wars. They are all signing it. This was the last war

Moshe: The last war!

Shprintshe: Baruch Ha Shem, from your mouth to God's ears –

Berish: I don't believe it –

Reb Nehemiah: There will always be war –

Moshe: No, Jews, listen, I heard that they are going to make a Jewish state!

Crowd: No, no, it couldn't be true. But maybe it is? What if it is true?

Moshe: Yes, Jews, listen. In Palestine. There will be a Jewish state. The British are going to give Palestine to the Jews.

Berish: The British! What can the British do? Nothing! When was the last time the British ever did anything? It is only the Americans who can give Palestine to the Jews.

Moshe: It's true, the Zionists will get their way. There will be a Jewish state

Shprintshe: The Zionists are worse than the Americans! They don't even bother with a divorce. And they eat pig! Just ask Rokhel-Leah, her brother-

Dobtshe: Sh, sh, sha stil, it's not true –

Reb Nehemiah: Jews, this is our home. We will not be put into exile again. We have traveled already in the desert and until the moshiakh comes this is our home. They tried to kill us; they tried to send us away, but we are still here. We must rebuild –

Berish: I will give a wall, a wall from my own house, to rebuild the synagogue, I don't need it anyway, my wife and children are dead –

Efriam: I will give my roof. I will give my roof to the shul. I would give my walls, too, except that they are destroyed –

Reb Honen (moving up the bima): We must get back to life as normal. We have had too many funerals, We need marriages and births. This more than money will rebuild our community -

The crowd: True, true, he speaks the truth. Who can argue with that?

Reb Honen: And this is why I have arranged with Reb Yankev that my daughter Dina will marry his son Yitzhak.

The crowd: Mazl Tov. (Reb Yankev and his son walk up to the bima.)

Reb Honen: It is true, I have nothing left to give her as a dowry. The wedding would not be as my wife, oliah hasholem, Hannah's mother would have wanted it, but she is gone now and we must go on. They say Reb Yankev's Shlomo is still a little too young, but, Jews, we must get back to the business of living. Dina, my life, come down here.

Dina: (runs up to her father on the bima, and pushes Shlomo, a boy of about 16, aside): He is not dead, Tata. I know he is still alive –

Reb Honen embraces her tenderly.

Reb Yankev: He is dead. Berish's cousin was there when he died together with Vela's Chaim. He saw him being buried –

Vela (from the balcony): If he is not dead, then maybe my Chaim, too, is still alive, I don't know what to think. They tell me he is dead and then they say he is still alive.

Dobtshe: Don't listen to them Vela. Don't do this to yourself. He is dead –

Dina: But Yosef is not dead. He comes to me at night in my dreams and he tells me that he is still alive. I know that he is still alive.

Reb Honen: But, Dinale, we have not heard from him in two years and the war is over. He is not coming back, my child.

Dina: No, he is still alive, Tata. I am sure of it!

(Suddenly the door slams at the back of the shul. Yosef appears in a torn soldier's costume, his head bandaged.)

The crowd: Who is it? Who is it? Who's there? Another stranger?

Lea: Is it my brother?

Vela: Is it my husband?

Reb Leybush: Is it my son?

Shprintse: Is it my child?

Dina: Yosef!

Yosef walks up the aisle toward her. She runs down to him but stops instinctually, without touching him.

Yosef (stepping up to the bima): I told you I would come back for you Dinaleh

Dinale: O Yosef, they thought you were dead. I knew you were alive!

Honen: Where have you been? Why haven't you contacted us in all this time?

Yosef: I was in another land. The borders were closed, but they let me through, but not for long. I have to return –

Moshe: What land? Which land? Who are they warring against?

Yosef: In this land, there are no wars.

Shlomo: No Wars?

Khaya-Peshie: No Wars!

Reb Leybush: Didn't I tell you, the treaty in Paris, to end all wars!

Vela: Is my Chaim there? Is he still alive? Is he in this land with you?

Yosef: Yes, Vela, I have a message for you for Chaim.

Vela: He's still alive!

Yosef: He is waiting for you, for you and the children. He is preparing a place for you –

Vela: A house?

Yosef: Yes.

Vela: My poor Chaim! I knew it! You will bring us there? Where is the way to this new land?

Yosef: Down the road, past the field, behind the woods and over the stone.

Honen: Why have you not contacted us in so long, not even a letter?

Yosef: I told you, the borders are closed. You can go in but you can't go out.

Lea: Is there food? Is there food to eat in this new land?

Yosef: Yes. Any food you want.

Crowd: Any food you want? Milk? Fresh meat? Lamb? Kasha? Pierogi? Pickles? Potatoes? Sauerkraut? Borsht? Apples? Kugel?

Yosef: Yes. No one is hungry in the new land.

Lea (runs up and grabs Yosef): I want to go there. I want an apple.

Yosef (pushes her away): Go back to your mother. Shprintesele, take her away

Lea (running to her mother): Mama, I'm hungry.

Honan: Why do you look so weak, then, if there is enough food there for everyone to eat? You look pale, half dead, so thin –

Yosef: From longing, I am weak from longing for my home, for my mother, for my people, for my love –

Dinale: O Yosef!

Reb Leybush: Do Jews learn there? Is there a shul? A beis medresh?

Yosef: Yes, there is always a minyan in the new land. The shul is always full.

Reb Leybush: How do I get there?

Yosef: Down the road, past the field, behind the woods and over the stone.

Efriam: And how's business? Are there shopkeepers there?

Yosef: Yes, business is very good. There are many shopkeepers.

Efriam: How do I go there?

Yosef: Down the road, past the field, behind the woods and over the stone.

The crowd: Take us to this new land! We want to go! Where is it?

Yosef: Down the road, past the field, behind the woods and over the stone.

The crowd: When can we go?

Yosef: At sundown, I will show you the way tonight. Go home, prepare –

Honen: People, let's leave the young couple alone –

(The women disappear out of sight from the balcony. The men retreat to the back of the synagogue. Left alone, Dina kisses Yosef then pulls away.)

Dina: O you are so cold –

Yosef: I have come far for you, Hannah. We must leave and go back tonight.

Dinale: My father won't like me to leave him. Can he come with us?

Yosef: Eventually, but not right away. He has time yet.

Dinale: I don't know if he will let me go. Do you have a house there for us in this new land?

Yosef: Yes.

Dinale: Is it a big one?

Yosef; No, a little one, but just perfect for us.

Dinale: With a fireplace maybe?

Yosef: Yes, we will get married tonight, under a black canopy. Go home, get ready and tell my mother to come to me.

Dinale (about to go): Don't leave me.

Yosef: I won't. Hurry.

Dinale: I'll be right back.

Dinale leaves. The synagogue starts filling up again with people ready to travel.

Reb Leybush (with a religious book in hand): I am ready to go where I can learn with Jews all day. Show me the way.

Yosef: Down the road, past the field, behind the woods and over the stone. Look carefully. Do you see it?

Reb Leybush: Yes, I see it. I see the beis medresh. It looks just like the one where my father studied. And is that my brother, Yeshaya? He is already there! And Nasan and Reb Meir. I see it, illuminated by light –

Yosef: So go.

(Reb Leybush leaves.)

(A wail is heard from Shprintse. Berish and Efriam rush into the shul, followed by the rest of the crowd.)

Berish: People, Lea, Shprinstse's youngest child, has just died! And old Leybush! They too are gone.

Crowd: Oy vey. No, from hunger. They died from cold!

Efriam: We must hurry to the other land or we too will surely be dead!

Crowd: Take us to the new land!

Yosef: You can go. Down the road, past the field, behind the woods and over the stone.

(An old blind woman walks into the shul.)

Frumme-Liebtshe: Vu iz mayn kind? My son. Dinale told me my son has come home. Where is he?

Yosef: I am here Mama, come to me, Mama. (She walks toward the voice.)

Frumme-Liebtshe: I am blind and cannot see. You don't sound like my son. (She takes his hand.) Oh, you are cold. You don't feel like my son.

Yosef: It is me, Mama. I have come to take you home with me.

Frumme-Liebtshe: This is my home. All my friends are here.

Yosef: No, Mama, all of your friends are with me in the new land. Remember your first friend that you always told me about, Soreh Rokhl?

Frumme-Liebtshe: Soreh Rokhl! I haven't seen here since she got married. Her little house was right next to my mother's. We were so close as children. She is there?

Yosef: Yes, Mama, and Tata is there too.

Frumme-Liebtshe: Your Father! My Dovidl?

Yosef: Yes, Mama, he is waiting for you. Look, can you see, down the road, past the field, behind the woods and over the stone?

(Frumme-Liebtshe squints.)

Frumme-Liebtshe: I see nothing, my child. Oh look, the goat that was in our yard and Soreh Rohkl in her blue dress. I see. I see the sun, my child. Bring me there.

Yosef: No, Mama, you must go alone. I will be there soon.

Frumme-Liebtshe: But I am blind, child. I cannot go alone.

Yosef: You must, Mama. You can see. Walk toward the light. Do you see it?

Frumme-Liebtshe: My Dovidl, I see him. I am coming to you. (She leaves.)

(Vela enters holding a baby and followed by a child.)

Vela: Show me, Yosef. Show me the way to my Chaim.

Yosef: Down the road, past the field, behind the woods and over the stone. The child, are you bringing the child?

Yosef: They are too young. Send the children home.

Vela: I will not leave my children. Who will take care of them? They will come with me. Now show us the way.

Yosef (shrugs): Down the road, past the field, behind the woods and over the stone. Look, can you see it?

Vela: I see a little house, a chimney and some smoke.

The child: An apple tree! I can almost touch it. How do I get there?

Yosef: Down the road, past the field, behind the woods and –

Vela: And in the window, Chaim! My Chiamke! Run my children, go. (They leave.)

(Efriam runs up to Yosef.)

Efriam: Look, all what I brought with me to sell. (Shows him his wares.) Will I do good business in your new land?

Yosef: Yes. Better than ever before.

Efriam: So, tell me how do I get there?

Yosef: Down the road, past the field, behind the woods and over the stone. Look, do you see?

Efriam – I see the smithy where my father worked as an apprentice. I see a market, like the one my mother brought me to when I was just a boy. Do you think –

(Yosef, getting anxious, pushes him forward.)

Yosef: Down the road, past the field, behind the woods —

Efriam: And over the stone! I see it. (He leaves.)

Dinale enters. She is still dressed in rags but has made an effort to look her best. She walks up to Yosef.

Yosef: Come to me, my love. We will be married under a black canopy. Don't be afraid, my love.

Dinale: I am not afraid any longer, my love. I want only to be with you. (Two people hold a black sheet over their heads.)

(Dinale and Yosef hold hands under the canopy, looking at one another. Dinale begins to circle her Yosef as everyone chants in a growing whisper.)

Crowd: Down the road, past the field, behind the woods and over the stone (Repeat several times until:

Honen runs into the synagogue and rushes up onto the altar. He pulls down the canopy. Everyone stares at him.)

Honen: You leave my daughter alone. Don't touch her. (To the crowd, holding on to his daughter:) This man is not one of us! Look how many have died, Vela and her children, Shprintse's boy, Yosef's own blind mother – Frumme-Liebtshe, our learned Reb Leybush, Don't you see where he is telling us to go. "Down the road, past the field, behind the woods and over the stone." What is there? The cemetery, Jews, the cemetery. He is leading us all to the cemetery! (The crowd acts shocked.) (To Yosef:) If you are among the living, stay among the living. If you are among the dead, then go!

(Yosef walks out of the synagogue, as does almost everyone else including Hanahle, whom her father is forced to release. Reb Honen and the crazy man are the only ones left on stage. Reb Honen realizes everyone else is dead.)

Crazy Man (running up the aisle of the synagogue then speaking from the bima:) Krank iz di alta velt, The old world is sick, es benkt der khola nakhn toit, the patient longs for death, naraneem haltn zee ayn, fools hold her back, meshugim gayen faroyis, the mad men advance. (Repeat.)

END

Glossary:

shul – synagogue

beis-medresh - study house

nebekh – pity

Tata – father

mentshn – people

Poiln – Poland

Reb – mister

moshiakh - the messiah

Baruch hashem - Blessed be God

Vu is mayn kind - Where is my child

bima - synagogue pulpit

l'havdil - to separate the sacred and the profane

Caraid O'Brien *is a writer and performer who lives in Los Angeles. She received three play commissions from the Foundation of for Jewish Culture for her translations of Yiddish classics by Sholem Asch and David Pinski. She also arranged for the donation of several Yiddish theater archives to major universities and institutions. For three years, she directed* Bloomsday on Broadway *at Symphony Space, broadcast live on WBAI. She has lectured at many universities and institutions throughout the U.S. and her essays and reviews have appeared in books, magazines, newspapers, on the radio and online. Presently, she is writing a book on the Yiddish theater. www.caraidobrien.com*

Cafe Royal

Eve Packer

The Cafe Royal. I first heard those words from Leah, my grandmother, in the Bronx. Was she standing at the spotless stove flipping the lightest of blintzes or playing solitaire as she dipped two sugar cubes in her gluze tea? Or right after she shocked me, who knew nothing of her history, by getting up from her chair on the so-clean-you-could-eat-off-the-living room-floor, and performing, full-out and to perfection, the fat lady in the corset routine or ladzi—to be performed only, for the humor, by a slim lady, which she was. Later I saw Rita Moreno perform it, though terrific, she was no match for Leah—each tic and facial muscle calibrated minutely to comment and mock the epic battle between corset and body.

But, of course, my grandma, a sixteen-year-old actress running from sweatshop to theatre on the Lower East Side before World War I, had learned it from the European Yiddish theatre masters. And then she said, "We would all go over to the Royal." Because it turned out, the grandma I knew, the grandma whose fingers were bent backwards from arthritis doing piecework in the sweatshops, the grandma who sewed my clothes, who made the best brisket and blintzes, who was sharp and vinegary, whose house was eat-off-the-floor clean, that isn't who she was.

Indeed not. Until the aunt and uncle she lived with sold her to my grandfather. When, after all, do struggling actresses, even if doing piecework earn their keep?

I believe she hated him ever after. And after he died, she was free. Free to take in a boarder, to smile, to paint, even with crippled fingers, scenes of the Old World, and one Saturday afternoon to surprise and delight her granddaughter, by performing the fat-lady-in-the-corset routine. And then casually drop the name, the magic name, the Cafe Royal.

The Cafe Royal was hub and epicenter, backroom and promised land, of the vital and tumultuous Yiddish Theatre that was at the heart of the cultural life of the Lower East Side. It stood on the southeast corner of Second Avenue and 12th Street, now the site of the Japanese restaurant Shima Sushi. Opposite is the Multiplex, housed in what from the '20s to the '50s was Maurice Schwartz's Yiddish Art Theatre. But if you look above the marquee, you can see carved into the lovely yellow facade, the original Moorish type arches and, higher up, the small curved windows. Of the Royal, nothing remains. But in its heyday, it was the see-and-be-seen spot, the do-business locale, the hangout, the place to gawk or strut. All the great names stopped by: the older Goldfaden and Thomashefsky, founders of the Yiddish theatre, then Kessler and Jacob Adler (founder of the Adler theatre dynasty), Molly Picon, Joseph Buloff, Paul Muni; the politicians, Al Smith, LaGuardia; the labor leaders. In the '50s,

David Dubinsky would mention it with tears in his eyes. And no one was shy.

Thomashefsky wrote in his diary, "If Kessler wore a big hat with a long feather,

Adler wore a bigger hat with three feathers and a gold scarf."[154]

And, from the start, it was open 24/7!

So, here's the 4-1-1: The Cafe Royal was founded in 1911 at the southeast corner of Second Avenue and 12th Street as the Yiddish Theatre was moving north out of the Lower East Side, up Second Avenue from Houston to Fourteenth Street. Its founder, a Hungarian immigrant, lost it to his headwaiter, Oscar Szatmarie, in the Hungarian card game Klabyash. From the photos taken in 1930, we know what it looked like. It was modeled on turn-of-the-century European art nouveau style cafes: There were huge curved windows, with beveled glass bottoms, a tin ceiling, lots of curved wood, wood pillars with coat hooks. On the right was the bar. There were round and square tables with tablecloths, a front and back room. And the all-important telephone. Outside, by 1930, there was a neon sign, Cafe Royal, the top letters in script, the bottom, block print. In summer, the windows were removed for the open-air effect.

And, of course, the Cheese did not stand alone. Just below Houston on 2nd Avenue was the National Theatre, north of Houston, you could find Fred Spitz Florist, Rappoport's Photo Studio, the Second Avenue Theatre, and moving up the Avenue, other costume houses and restaurants. On East 7th, the Hebrew Actors Union, back to the avenue, Ratner's and Rappoport's Restaurant, the Yiddish Art Theatre, the Public Theatre at the corner of 4th, and just down the block and above the Royal, where the big actors lived: 166 & 170 2nd Avenue. The Royal was at the center of a matrix of life and work, shops and services, restaurants and nightlife centered on the Yiddish theatre. Even as the Yiddish-speaking population was moving out, the theatre and its world remained vital thru the '30s. The actors hung out at Boym's on Broome, the Monopole on 9th Street, Markiz' at Grand & 4th, Shtark's at Houston & 2nd Avenue, but the Cafe Royal reigned supreme.

So, what was on the menu? The menu looked a lot like the Veselka menu today, but more high-end, with its owner's Hungarian flavor. Palatschinken, a Hungarian crepe-like dish, was the specialty. Blintzes were featured, roasts with paprika, but, no kosher here. Also boiled ham and shrimp cocktail. You did not go to eat. Most ordered the very strong iced coffee with heavy cream and, even more, the least expensive, glezele tey. The menu was the least important feature: it was the power, the thrill, the shmooze, the business of see and be seen.

Essential elements in this mix were the members of the Hebrew Actors Union. This union, established at the end of the 19th century, was the first professional actors union in the United States. Located at 31 East 7th Street, east of McSorley's, just west of Second Avenue, its goal was to lift the actors from sweatshop to professional status. And it was tough. Entrance by audition only.

Maurice Schwartz auditioned three times in 1912, and was only accepted through the personal intervention of Abraham Cahan of the *Forward*. Later the building also housed Yiddish Artists & Friends. The beautifully proportioned grey stone edifice still stands. High on the front the words Hebrew Actors Union are carved, and the doorbells this spring (2007) still had the names of the Union and the Friends. The archive is now part of YIVO. There was a huge interplay of traffic and persona from cafe to union to theatre and back to the cafe.

And who did the serving? The waiters in black pants and jackets with rounded edges so as not to fall in the soup. Also bow ties. Very formal. They brought a glass of water to the table and the menu for a five-cent tip. The most famous waiter in the '20s and '30s was Herman Tantzer, who can be seen in the 1930 photo, stage center, hands behind back, ears sticking out. He also was the all-important bank and publicity service: If you wanted work or you name out there as a reminder to a producer or power, you phoned yourself from outside, and had Herman announce a phone call for you at the cafe. He also served as a bank, gave loans to theatres and actors, never said no, all for a nickel. Rumor had it that he was the only one out of the cafe who retired rich.

And then there was the pecking order. First, you were ushered in by Herman. Then guided to your 'spot' in the Cafe. Seymour Rexite, the last president of the Hebrew Actors Union, remembered the big front round table was for the writers; inside, back right, were the actors who had "made" it, the big names; on the left were working actors, writers, and the public. If an actor got a rave review in Friday's paper, he or she moved to the right side. Guskin, who was manager of the Hebrew Actors Union, had his regular table between two phone booths, on the side—this was his evening office.

Edwin Relkin, a non-Yiddish-speaking Jewish road manager, did business or betting there, so he had instant translation to and from Yiddish. Twenty-four-hour card games, klabyash, hearts, pinochle, and other games; betting, smoking, and gambling took place behind beveled glass in the back room. Once there was a robbery in connection to the high-rolling card game in the back; the only one holding real cash was the waiter, Herman.

Politics, socialism, theatre, writing, music, scandal, finances, gawking, all took place at the Royal, especially at night. On the tablecloths were the written remains of financial transactions, music notes, ideas. Lots of laughter, arguing, provocation. This was not a quiet crowd, or culture.

Here's a picture of an evening: Herman at the center. To one side, the Yiddish writer, Louis Freiman, negotiating a contract. I.J. Singer and Sholom Asch in conversation. The Yiddish composer Joseph Rumshinsky in collaboration.[155]

Everyone made an entrance. This from Oscar Leonard, a playwright whose family was part of Yiddish theatre: "The place was open all night and day. It never closed. You could always find actors as you walked in, sitting to your right, posturing and gossiping. In a back room pinochle was played in an atmosphere of smoke and intrigue ... it's just the way thing sorted themselves out ... one comedian, a Romanian named Aaron Lebedeff, had enormous energy and comic timing. He also had an ego you couldn't fit into the Coliseum. He loved to enter wearing a blue suit, white hat, white spats, and an unbuttoned cashmere overcoat around his shoulders."[156]

And all around, carpenters, house painters, seamstresses, theatre-goers, then one or several of the Adlers or Luba Kadisson, with her long dark hair and husband, the great comic character actor Joseph Buloff. And more. Kate Simon, who was taken to the Cafe as a child in the '20s, writes in *Bronx Primitive*: "Dazzlingly lit, noisy as a market, one tragedienne with a tall, blazing red turban, another with heavily kolh-circled eyes, a yellowed ermine capelet, hands buried in matching Anna Karenina muff."[157]

Ah yes! Everyone dressed: the men in suits, often pinstriped, long or bow ties, the faces at the window in fedoras, but men's hats hung up inside. The women with Persian lamb at collar and wrists or a turban or, in one photo, a tri-corner hat, pearls, necklaces, skirts, dresses, dark lipstick, heels, furs.

Some more stories: This from the early days, told by Lulla Rosenfeld, Jacob Adler's granddaughter: Around 1913, there was a bookish young man with glasses by the name of Bronstein who was a boarder in the Bronx. He read a lot, was a big fan of the Yiddish theatre and would stop by the Royal after the show. One night he told Jacob Adler that he was returning to Russia and so would be missing the theatre. Adler asked him what he was going to do there. He said, "We are going to overthrow the Kerensky government." Adler wasn't surprised. There were revolutionaries from Russia everywhere. Mr. Bronstein did go back. His real name, it turns out, was Leon Trotsky.

Much later, when Adler's widow, Sara, was in her seventies, she revived, directed and starred in a four-act play, *Homeless* (!). Then went and hung out till 4 a.m. at the Royal.[158]

After the heyday of the '20s, came the Great Depression, when the price of a theatre ticket, or a coffee, was impossibly steep. Then World War II. In 1942, Hy Kraft's Cafe Crown, based on the Cafe Royal's early days, opened on Broadway. Directed by the young Elia Kazan, it starred Jacob Adler's son, Jay, and a young actor from Yiddish theatre, Morris Carnovsky, who later did his own luminous Shylock. (During that production, at the Williamstown Theatre Festival, he advised my friend Robyn, "Duke, Duke, rhymes with puke.") In his scene notes, Kraft wrote, "The action takes place at the Cafe Crown, theatrical restaurant on Second Avenue, in NYC ... patterned after the Cafe Royal, the famous East Side restaurant...meeting and eating place for the Yiddish actors and actresses—the last cultural rendezvous of the Jewish-American."[159] It was a hit of the season. In 1988, Joe Papp, as homage — his own Public Theatre was so much a confirmation of the hopes and dreams of Yiddish Theatre — mounted a revival. Frank Rich wrote in the *New York Times* that is was "an occasion not just for laughter but for paying a grand departed theatrical universe final respects."[160]

In 1950, Maurice Schwartz' Yiddish Art Theatre closed. The Cafe Royal closed in 1953. Seymour Rexite, president of the Hebrew Actors Union till his death in 2002, said: "The Cafe Royal, that was the canary in the mineshaft."[161] And Harrison Salisbury wrote the eulogy in the *New York Times,* "And long since had vanished the youthful rebels, the brilliant socialists, the eccentrics and anarchists who poured their talents so lavishly into Great Causes like the Russian Revolution. You will look in vain for a restaurant that serves tea in a glass."[162]

Let's not end with a eulogy, but a photo, lines from a letter, and a salute.

The Hebrew Actors Unions archive has been acquired by YIVO, the Institute for Jewish Research, where the mostly unlabeled, correspondence, photos, and artifacts are being carefully sorted and archived. I was fortunate enough to have Ettie Goldwasser let me have a glance at a shoebox full of mostly unmarked photos. The one that really caught my eye, though not directly related to the cafe, but the care and spirit of the place and time, is a photo of a Maurice Schwartz' Yiddish Art Theatre's 1930 children's production (scribbled in Yiddish on the back), *The Tree and the Dreidel*. What's most astonishing is the number of kids—a huge number, both boys and girls, each dressed in fantastic costumes, each costume individual patchwork cotton, most playing musical instruments. The young princess, crown on head, was played by the very young Lillian Lux, later a leading light. You can bet they all went over to celebrate at the Royal.

Two stars of Yiddish Theatre in the 1920s were Joseph Buloff (who later played the peddler in the hit musical *Oklahoma!*) and his wife, Luba Kadison. For a while he tried to start a theatre in Chicago. This from a letter of his, 1928: "I am considered a simpleton ... despite my status as a star ... the simple reason ... I am a Talmudic scholar of sorts who believes that the theatre must be served with the same devotion as the Torah."[163]

Lila returned to New York ahead of Buloff, and wrote, "New York is still New York.

Same Second Avenue, same Cafe Royal."[164]

The last word from the Yiddish actress Rosetta Bialis, about to sign a movie contract with a British producer, "Meet me at the Royal."[165]

So, here's to you Leah, before family, the Bronx, reality, swallowed you. Here's to you, after dashing from sweatshop to theatre, rehearsing meticulously the fat-lady-in-the-corset routine, switching, way ahead of your time, into culottes and tam of your own design, sewn from remnants pilfered off piece work, making entrance, lighting a cigarette, dipping two cubes of sugar in glezele tey, at the table, taking your place on the scene, at the Royal.

Bibliography

Buloff, Joseph & Kadison, Luba w/ Genn, Irving. *Memories of a Lifetime in Yiddish Theatre.* President & Fellows of Harvard College, 1992.

Cypkin, Diane. *Second Avenue, the Yiddish Broadway*, Ann Arbor, UMI, NYU dissertation, 1986.

Kanfer, Stefan. *Stardust Lost.* Alfred A. Knopf, 2006.

Kanfer, Stefan. "In Lower Manhattan, the Echo of the Yiddish Stage Endures." http://travel.nytimes.com/2007/01/26/travel/escapes/26yiddish.html.

Kraft, Hy. *Cafe Crown.* American Play Co., 1942.

Nhashon, Edna. "The Golden Epoch of Yiddish Theatre in America: A Brief Historical Overview." http://www.jewishtheatre.com./visitor/article_display.aspx?article ID=1411.

Rosenfeld, Lulla. *Jacob Adler: Bright Star of Exile*. Thomas Y. Crowell, 1977.

Sandrow, Nahma. *Vagabond Stars, A World History of Yiddish Theater*. Harper & Row, 1977.

Simonson, Robert. "Where Have You Gone, Molly Picon?"

http://www.jewishtheatre.com./visitor/articledisplay.aspx?article ID=1784.

Terry, Michael. Yiddish Theatre Collection at New York Public Library. http://www.jewish the-atre.com./visitor/article_display.aspx?article ID=1865.

YIVO Institute for Jewish Research including: Cafe Royal photos., photographer, Eliot Elisofon, from *Life Magazine*, 1930.

Hebrew Actors Union, assorted photos, uncatalogued archive.

With gratitude and thanks to Ettie Goldwasser, Jesse Cohen, Irit Gafni-Pinchovski and the staff of YIVO Institute for Jewish Research.

Eve Packer, *Bronx-born, is a graduate of the University of Michigan, attended Girton College, Cambridge, received degrees from London School of Economics & NYU. She has traveled extensively in Europe and Latin America, and has taught at Queens College, the New School, for ll99, and is a Homebound Instruction teacher. An actress for many years, then performance artist and poet, she has been awarded grants from the New York State Council on the Arts, Jerome Foundation, Puffin Foundation, New York Foundation for the Arts, National Endowment for the Humanities, and a Time to Consider: the Arts Respond to 9/ll Award, & 2 Downtown Poet of the Year Awards.*

Her first book, skulls head samba, is from Fly By Night Press. In addition she has 2 single & 3 long-playing poetry/jazz CD's (w/Noah Howard): ny woman & window 9/ll & the long-playing CD's west from 42nd & cruisin w/moxie (Altsax, Northcountry), & that look (Boxholder). 2005 saw the publication of her second book of poems, playland, poems 1994-04, also from Fly By Night Press. She lives downtown, has one son, and swims daily.

According to Dennis Duggan (of Newsday) 'a woman of talent, imagination, and a mind that engages you in ways you seldom encounter.' And from Donald Hall (Ploughshares, spr '05)"..i salute her as the Weegee poet..."

---

[154] Kanfer, Stefan, "In Lower Manhattan, the Echo of the Yiddish Stage Endures."
http://travelnytimes.com/2007/01/26/travel/escapes/26yiddish.html., p.2.
[155] Much of the material in this section is gleaned from Diane Cypkin, *Second Avenue, the Yiddish Broadway,*

Ann Arbor. U.M.I., NYU Dissertation, 1986.

[156] Kanfer, Stefan, *Stardust Lost* (New York: Knopf, 2006), p. 207.

[157] Ibid., p.207.

[158] Rosenfeld, Lulla, *Jacob Adler: Bright Star of Exile* (Boston: Thomas Y. Crowell, 1977), p. 341.

[159] Kraft, Hy, *Cafe Crown* (New York: American Play Co., 1942), scene notes.

[160] Kanfer, *Stardust*, p. 290.

[161] Ibid., p.265.

[162] Ibid., p. 266.

[163] Buloff, Joseph, *Memories of a Lifetime in Yiddish Theatre*, (Luba Kadison & Joseph Buloff w/Irving Genn, President & Fellows of Harvard College), 1992, p. 73.

[164] Ibid., p. 79.

[165] Cypkin, p. 467.

Some Thoughts on The Lower East Side and the Jewish Community, Julian Beck and The Living Theatre, and Me

Tom Walker

I moved to the Lower East Side in 1972. I was crashing around New York at the time in order to remain in touch with The Living Theatre of Julian Beck and Judith Malina, which was then based in Brooklyn. 149 First Avenue turned out to be close enough. I had first seen the theater group in 1968 and 1969 during their American tour, and later in London in the summer of '69. I had finally worked with the group in Brazil in 1971 and had then spent two months in jail with it, for being in the presence of marijuana. It was a much better charge than sedition, which was a possibility under the military junta then in power. We were deported. The Living settled in Brooklyn near the Brooklyn Academy. I took some distance and began to live on my own for the first time, in the East Village on First Ave. The East Village was the right place. I lived in a building in which other members of my gay affinity group also had one room apartments. I had met Antonino Guerrero and Juan Carlos Vidal, my new neighbors, at the Living Theatre house. The Lower East Side environment of the Fillmore East, the hippy world, the Fugs, The Ridiculous Theater, political struggle, sexual experimentation, compromise and contradiction, swirled around me; it was a living theater.

Nearby lived veteran Living Theatre member Bill Shari and family on East 11th St. On East 4th, near La Mama, was Jim Anderson, another Living old-timer. With Jim, I worked delivering for food coops that he had set up. I rejoined the Living in the fall of 1973, eventually leaving New York in 1974 for an odyssey with the company, which took me to Vermont and Pittsburgh and on to seven years in Italy and Europe.

We returned to New York in 1984 for a brief run at the Joyce Theater and then Julian's cancer recurred, cutting him down in 1985. And then I was back living in the Lower East Side, on 10th St., barely half a block from where I'd lived in 1973. Soon a re-energized Living would be running a storefront theater on East 3rd St. at Ave. C (1989 – 1993), and performing in other Lower East Side venues such as CHARAS and Theater for The New City. Even during recent years of residency and touring in Italy, the company has continued to perform street theater in New York, sometimes in Tompkins Square Park. And now, in a significant mutation, the Living is opening a new space on Clinton St. And Judith Malina and partner Hanon Reznikov have taken up residence two floors above.

I asked Judith recently if she and her parents, father Max Malina, a rabbi from Kiel who had left Germany in 1928 and formed a congregation which had quarters in the basement of Central Synagogue, and mother Rose, had ever lived in the Lower East Side. No, she said, but her Wieseltier cousins were on Second Ave. and she was always over playing with them. She remembers being with her Aunt Jenny and playing in Tompkins Square Park. Later when her life grew more complicated, she remembers being arraigned with Dorothy Day at the Second Ave. courthouse, now Jonas Mekas's Anthology Film Archives. And the Becks, the Becks were all down on Grand St. and Essex; that was before Julian's father, Irving, started a family up in Washington Heights, eventually moving to West End Ave. Julian's mother, Mabel Blum, wondered why anyone would want to go back to the Lower East Side. And then Julian in the '47 and '48 had a cold water flat on lower First Avenue. There, he was the struggling emerging artist, before he married Judith and moved back uptown when Garrick was born. In the 80's and 90's, son Garrick Beck, resided on East 6th St. Garrick was and is a community garden activist and was a founding member of the large national Rainbow Gatherings. From '83 to '93, he and partner Joanee Freedom were involved in the East Village bakery, the East Village Baker's Dozen.

Of course, I was always aware of the Lower East Side being very Jewish. In the early 70's, I took it as part of the atmosphere. Everything was so new to me. I didn't think of the Living as being very, very Jewish, but it began to dawn on me that half the company was Jewish, and sometimes more than that. Working with the company in Italy, one wasn't so aware of everything Jewish. I knew *Paradise Now*, the iconic play from the '60's, was based in part on the Kabbalah. And every year we celebrated a liberation seder, Judith's adaptation, laced with the great poetry of Allan Ginsberg. But for years as I intoned the melodies of the Elders, acting in *Antigone*, I did not know that they were based on Jewish chanting. When we moved back to New York in the '80's and we did texts like *Poland 1931*, based on Jerome Rothenberg's work; *The Tablets*, based on a cycle by Armand Schwerner (both in adaptations by Hanon Reznikov), and *I And I*, by Else Lasker-Schuler, the Jewish roots of the Living Theatre shown more deeply for me.

I was a naïve guy, but I had faith and dedication. Julian Beck, I began to realize, had become my guru, or perhaps rabbi. Julian led the group with magnetic charisma. He was a great poet, writer, playwright, and actor, and he worked harder than everyone else. He was always with the last of us to leave the work place. And often the first one in. He made great public appearances, not just before audiences in the great theaters of the world, but before workers' meetings in France and Italy, students and the poor in Brazil, crowds in front of factories in Pittsburgh. Eventually, he was enshrined by Hollywood in *Cotton Club* and *Poltergeist II*.

Julian came from a well-to-do family and was brilliantly wise. Other geniuses sought him out, whether it was Allen Ginsberg, Pier Paolo Pasolini, John Cage or Peter Brook, or Tennessee Williams and William Carlos Williams (actually Julian sought out the latter, but was readily accepted), or the painters, Jackson Pollock (in youthful ferment), Willem de Kooning, Robert Rauschenberg, and Andy Warhol. Julian was on a level with all of them. But he was also a wanderer. And he was capable of great self-sacrifice, for his family and for his beliefs. His rejection of established theater cast a heavy weight on his shoulders. Michael Butler, the producer of *Hair* had offered to produce *Paradise Now* on Broadway. Julian said no, and instead, undertook a year later, in 1970, a five year experiment in working completely outside regular theatrical venues. Julian carried the well being of a company of from usually ten to twenty-five people on those shoulders as well. Year after year. His faith was strong and agnostic. He was influenced by Martin Buber and by Erick Gutkind, a family friend, and by Fritz Perls and Paul Goodman, collaborators in numerous projects. He knew he was right, but he knew he could fail. To me, now thirty-five years on, it seems to me so Jewish, and as a consequence it feels so appropriate and hopeful, remembering Julian, for his theater once again and always, to be found in the Lower East Side.

Tom Walker has been living in the Lower East Side off and on since the early 70's, a permanent resident since '84. A longtime member of The Living Theatre, he collaborates with other arts groups in New York and Europe, especially Italy. He paints, writes poetry, non-fiction, and theater pieces, and works as an archivist.

Memories of a German Jew on the Lower East Side

Judith Malina

In 1929 my parents brought me from Kiel, in Germany, to New York on the S.S. Lithuania. My family, imbued with the prejudices of our German-Jewish culture, excluded our settling on the Lower East Side and we first took up residence uptown in the German precincts of Yorkville. Later, we moved to the Broadway Central Hotel on Broadway between 3rd Street and Bleecker Street, and there we were certainly on the western fringes of the tenement quarter.

The Broadway Central was a relic of Stanford White's dream of grandeur, eloquently expressed in the grand marble stairway but, by the time we arrived, it had long been reduced to hosting conventions, bar mitzvahs, weddings and a big New Year's Eve bash.

On the eighth floor there were the Chassidim, a tribe apart. We only rarely went up to eat in their very strictly kosher restaurant. Sometimes I went up to play chess with the champion, Rzewski, who, it was said, would eat nowhere else.

The long, romantic history of the hotel ranged from its glory days to its use in the war as a headquarters for the W.A.V.E.S. and its final days as a S.R.O. flophouse until it suddenly fell down one night in the early 1970s. I went to see the pile of rubble that remained. I like to think that it was the prayers of the Chassidim that kept everyone safe during the horrifying collapse.

Just around the corner from the Broadway Central was the Falk's kosher restaurant behind which I played with my best friend, Rachel Falk, in a dirt-filled lot strewn with the refuse of several generations of sweatshop workers behind the windows above. Deeper down, there was a richer, black soil in which we futilely attempted to plant a garden. Now it's the entrance to a luxury apartment building and boasts elegant birch trees, as if our garden had finally come to life.

The members of my father's German-speaking congregation felt themselves in an awfully racist sense to be superior to the poorer, Yiddish-speaking Eastern European Jews. Later, when the Jews were hunted down in Poland, my father, who published a small newsletter called *Der Judische Zeitgeist*, rallied the community to their defense, insisting that even if our brethren are crude, dirty and illiterate, they are still Jews!

But it was taboo for me to venture east of First Avenue to enter the world which they rejected …

except when it came for the weekly shopping in preparation for shabbos, our ritual celebration of the Sabbath with its blessings, songs, candle-lighting and special foods like the braided challah. Every Friday morning my mother unfolded two re-used paper shopping bags and we boarded a bus for Orchard Street and environs. There we walked up and down searching out the best bargains among the pushcarts. We would buy the fish for making gefilte fish ("fresh-killed" – a horror for me). Rivington Street still is a magical name for me, sullied by my memories of the chicken-slaughtering and the smell of blood on the pavement. I took it all in, somehow, with a peculiar gusto, though I swore to myself from that early age (I was 8-10) that as soon as I was free of my mother's kitchen, I would break free of the cycle of carnivorous heartlessness. And yet it was clear to me that these were my people; these butchers and vendors, these children in clothes different from ours, these women with shopping bags were my *real* people, and the pretensions of the German refugees that made up my father's congregation were tragic masks. I had no doubt that I was part of Rivington and Orchard and Essex.

A short distance from the markets, the Jewish Education Alliance stood on East Broadway and stands there still today. The Edgies was our affectionate name for what is now called simply the Educational Alliance, having broadened its scope to a multi-ethnic constituency. It remains a real center for creative, cultural programs for young people. I expended much effort in trying to get into the Inters' (Intermediates') Room, eschewing the Juniors' Room which was bereft of the handsome Inter boys. Louis Eisenstein, who I think later, became a basketball coach, was my dreamboat. Sometimes we would go down to the benches by the East River and kiss.

There was theater, too, all kinds of theatrical efforts making an unending effort to rise above themselves. I recently participated on a panel at the Edgies, and as I sat in the auditorium, I was suddenly swept back into memory of the warbling children we had been on that stage, singing and dancing and acting out a play about Queen Esther, in which I believe I played one of Hamon's hanged sons.

The serious Yiddish theater, of course, was on Second Avenue. There were two rival masters at the time: Adler, founder of the dynasty that produced Stella and Luther, and Maurice Schwartz, founder of the Yiddish Art Theater. In around 1935, my mother and father took me to see my first play, *The Brothers Ashkenazi*, a family saga of three brothers who take different paths to success, at the Maurice Schwartz Theater. I was impressed by the grandeur, the vast stage, the mystery of the lighting. I supposed at the time that all theater must be written in the beautiful Yiddish language, which was entirely intelligible to my German-speaking mind. Some of the scenes are still vivid in my mind, though most of it has faded to a distant dream.

As with many contemporary Jews, the sound of Yiddish is profound for me. It seems the proto-language upon which all the others are built. Its singular feelingfulness – its kvetch of pleasure and its terrible oy veh! are unique and express the struggles of our suffering and our survival.

In 1945, Maurice Schwartz was rehearsing *Three Gifts* (*Drei Machtones*), gifts given by God to the rousing fanfare of angels. I auditioned and was cast as an angel and got to sing with the chorus:

We are the angels

We're singing, we're singing

> From Heaven we're bringing

> The gifts...

I worked for some months with this extraordinary company and then it came time for me to leave to join Erwin Piscator's Dramatic Workshop at the New School for Social Research, where I spent some years completing my theatrical training. But those months in the Yiddish theater still inform all my work.

And now when I'm past eighty, I've finally moved into the Lower East Side. We've opened a theater on Clinton Street and we have a little home above the store, so to speak. Our comrades in the neighborhood say that gentrification has destroyed the chaotic beauty of the neighborhood, but there are many of us here, still, with a revolutionary plan. Let's see how well we do our work.

Judith Malina *Born in Germany in 1926, the daughter of Rabbi Max Malina and his wife Rosel, Judith Malina came with her parents to New York in 1928. As a child she read poems at the anti Nazi rallies at Madison Square Garden, which her father was an active part of organizing. She studied acting with the great Erwin Piscator, who established the Dramatic Workshop at the New School. In 1946, she co-founded the Living Theater with Julian Beck, which became internationally famous over the next decades for the provocative, highly political and controversial performances they put on, such as The Connection, The Brig and Paradise Now. Julian and Judith found themselves in prison many times and prison was very much a part of their drama. When Julian Beck died in 1985, Hanon Reznikov, who had joined the company in 1977, "Took over the theater and took over me," as Judith says. She and Hanon married and ran the theater together until his unexpected death in May 2008. Judith continues to run the Living Theater in its present location at 21 Clinton Street on the Lower East Side, as always describing her life's work and philosophy as "The beautiful, non-violent Anarchist Revolution." In addition to her work as a playwright, actress and director of the Living Theater, Judith is also a writer, poet, artist, and highly regarded character actress often seen in films and on television.*

Judith Malina and the Miracle

Steve Dalachinsky and Jim Feast

On Dec. 24, 2007, the authors interviewed Judith Malina at her home. One of us (JF) transcribed, organized and (minimally) interpreted her words. (All interpretations are those of the authors, not Malina.)

Our purpose in this interview (in this book on Jewish culture) was to get at two relationships between Malina and Jewish tradition. The first is the influence of the Yiddish theater on her later productions. In covering that, which, as Steve says, is one of "the primaries" in the background to the Living Theater, we also get into the other main contributors to the organization's genesis, Piscator and Artaud. Our second topic is Malina and the theater's collective approach to creation and production of plays, a tack that is unusual in American dramaturgy, but, as we will show, a central component of Yiddish theater.

There's a Jewish saying. Although the Messiah hasn't come yet, the truth of god's promise is found in the (infrequent) occurrence of a miracle. There's another saying, this one about the tsaddik, or wise person. As the Messiah himself will be, the miracle is unnoticed or actively ignored by the busy world. Only a tsaddik can recognize a miracle. We end this interview with Malina's description of a miracle.

1) Yiddish Theater

In another selection in this anthology, Malina describes her brief time with Maurice Schwartz's Yiddish theater company. Here, however, she provides more background on the basic approach and emphasis of this theater. She begins:

> When I was 17, I was about to enter the Dramatic Workshop with Piscator, I met a friend who brought me to Maurice Schwartz. Maurice Schwartz was one of the two reigning figures [in the Yiddish theater in New York. He had] the Jewish Art Theater on Second Avenue, and I rehearsed there for *The Three Gifts*, but I had to leave because I had to start my studies at the Dramatic Workshop.

Jim

Did they teach...

Malina

They didn't teach anything. They rehearsed us. I was one of the chorus of angels. I was not a student but an angel.

I learned a lot. They had adopted something that was called the "Vilna technique." There was a company in Vilna that developed a certain kind of Yiddish style that contained our outcry of sorrow, our constant lament, we call kvetching, and the kind of joyousness that was the other side of this suffering. So we have the joyous music and we have the lament, and in some way the Vilna form, the Vilna technique, of theater is concerned very much with this highly emotional outcry and rejoicing.

She immediately linked this background to her own practice, by continuing:

And in some way I feel, you know in *Antigone* and *Paradise Now*, we have that way of taking the emotion very far, of not being afraid to express emotion.

2) Artaud

This brings up a second major influence, Artaud, who, like Schwartz, emphasized emotion. Now it may seem that all drama highlights feeling, but as Malina notes:

So many [acting] teachers teach that you have to repress emotion. Society represses emotion and you are playing a member of society who represses emotion. And that may be true. But somehow in the theatrical moment you want to break through that. From Meyerhold to Artaud, they taught us how to break through that. My experience at the Yiddish Arts theater on that score was very telling for me.

Of course, the Yiddish theater had a very distinctive genealogy in that, while its masters drew skillfully and knowledgeably on reigning modernist traditions (Sholem Asch worked with Naturalist structures while David Pinski used Symbolist forms, for example), they had a greater closeness to folk life than other major literatures of the time. The theater people in Eastern Europe, where Yiddish drama originated and thrived, were one remove from or had come from the shetl, and had no problem tapping the less refined, heartier emotions one associates with those who live in the countryside. Schwartz's theater conveyed these emotions to their New York City audiences, themselves probably immigrants.

This vibrant tradition is something which, for obvious reasons, the Living Theater could not reproduce since its diverse audience was far removed from the earthy emotional life that (we surmise) only comes from existing in intimacy with nature. Thus, to find a way to contact the deep emotion that came so easily (at least as long as it was in touch with Eastern European influences) to Schwartz's audience and troupe, Malina and her group needed to work with other sources. Chief here was Artaud, who also faced the problem of the vitiated emotional life of the capitalist cities.

Malina describes Artaud's quest in this way:

> Artaud analyzed the audience and how we could reach and affect them.

> Artaud felt we were all armored. And, in fact, every one of us is armored because we'd go to pieces the first day we weren't. You need to be armored to resist the onslaught of the world

> So Artaud said, "If we want to affect these people and they are all armored, how do we get through?" And he studied all the forms of theater that he could, Asian, Indonesian, all the forms that he could find. He came to this conclusion. He said, "There is one thing we all have in common; and I don't care who you are, rich or poor, beautiful or ugly, young or old, we've suffered, every one of us."

> And when I have young actors I always say, "Some of you are very young, and I know that you've suffered already."

> And they all say, "Yeah, sure I've suffered."

> Artaud wondered, since we have this in common—actors, audience, everybody suffered — how do we use this common ground? What he called the Theater of Cruelty — it's not a phase I like — is about being able to breach the armor of the audience by sharing our own true suffering with them.

> He was interested in the actor being able to express, not someone else's suffering, not some ideal of suffering or some remembrance of suffering, but our own real suffering. And when we play *The Plague*, we follow Artaud's description of the plague in the sense that we are playing our own fear and realization of our own death. In *The Plague*, we ask the actors to enact their own fear of their own death and to fight it.

> I think Artaud had a key to something, which was the truthfulness of trying to find your own reality and projecting that instead of some other [version], even [memory's]. Stanislavksy has the memory, memory of reality [as the basis], but memory, as we all know, is very highly edited. In some way, Artaud gave us the clue to enacting the truth about ourselves instead of the fiction about ourselves.

3) Digression on Childhood

It was hard, after hearing this, not to think of remarks Malina had made about her childhood perceptions, growing up as the daughter of a rabbi who ministered to a German Jewish émigré community. As she makes quite clear, each member of the congregation, for socioeconomic reasons, wore a mask instead of a face and thus was barred from direct emotional experience. It could be hazarded that this early observation sensitized Malina to the absurdity and harmfulness of burying one's emotions under a pretentious cover.

But let's hear her own description:

> I was the little girl of the congregation [of my father]. They were all German Jews that had had some kind of wealth that now were struggling, having either nothing, or having some relatives or having smuggled something in they could sell. It was a disaster to them and they tried very, very hard to keep up their elegance, their refined behavior, their aristocratic practice, and it was fake because they had to go to work at factories.
>
> In fact there's a funny joke. Two German Jews met each other in the street and they tell each other, "Ow, I used to be the owner of a factory in Hamburg."
>
> And [the other said,] "I ran a restaurant chain in Frankfurt and we were very wealthy."
>
> And there were two little dogs [with the men]. And one of them is a little tiny Schnauzer and it says to the other one, "I used to be a great big St. Bernard dog."
>
> So the fact that these were all people that came from a certain class and were struggling to stay out of a poverty class but were on the verge of it all the time made them particularly despise what they thought of as a lower class group, the whole Eastern European Jewish population, all of them.
>
> It was just a different world for them and it was not   helped but exaggerated by the fact that now they were poor too. Because they were thinking, "We're poor. We're not like that [like the Eastern European Jews]." You see, that's the whole racist part. "We're poor but we're not like that."

4) Piscator

To return to decisive influences, as Malina remarked, her sojourn with Schwartz was brief because she had enrolled as a student at Piscator's Theater Workshop. Although Piscator did not emphasize getting in touch with emotions, on the contrary, he did contribute another decisive piece to the theoretical infrastructure of the Living Theater. While both the Yiddish theater and Artaud (in this respect) centered their practice on the resurrection of hidden but existent emotional qualities in the individual, Piscator, like the Living Theater, would link any emotional opening within the audience to the nascent fashioning of egalitarian forms of audience/theater-ensemble interaction as prefigurative of a more humane, non-capitalist organization of social relations. Or, to be more precise about this last point, Piscator visualized but never directly carried out this fashioning. Malina describes how Piscator imagined the theater of the future:

> Piscator wanted the theater to be a forum. He said in the ideal theater every spectator would have a little desk and pencil. And, furthermore, [he'd say], "We [the spectators] are going to stop the performance at any point and say [raps] 'I want to ask a question?' And the play would stop."

> This is an ideal. This is not what happened. Ideally, the spectator could then ask a question. Someone comes on stage. And the spectator says, "You're wearing a very nice fur coat as a costume. Where did you get that fur coat? And how much did you pay for it?"

> And she says, "Actually I bought it at a thrift shop for $200. But I like to pretend it's a $1,500 coat because I want to impress the people in this room because that's why I bought this particular fur coat and even changed the label. All right, let's go on with the play."

> But Piscator never really had real audience interference. He talked about it, wrote about it, wanted to do it, His students did it, because he wouldn't do it.

Malina emphasizes, by the way, that her comment on Piscator's lack of follow-through in this area is not meant as a disparagement of his considerable achievement. Indeed, she is in the process of writing a book about him. She continues

> Brecht said of Piscator — and this is how I begin my book – "Piscator is the greatest theater man of our time and possibly the greatest theater man of all time." And that gives you pause. Now wait a minute, there's Aeschylus and Goethe. You've got a couple of biggies there. Why did Brecht say that? And my book is the response to why Brecht considered this relatively unknown director as the greatest theater man of all time and the book follows about how Piscator broke through all of the conventions or tried to break all the conventions, including this one of including audience participation.

But let's get back to Piscator's view of the audience member, which may not be clear at this point. In the example, our audience member discovered the actress was pretending, as did the German Jews of Malina's father's congregation, to a higher social station than the one she actually possessed. The audience member, through an astute inquiry, laid this bare. But what benefit is it for the audience to learn this or, more generally, to be able to interrogate the ensemble?

Malina notes that Piscator was obsessed with clarity.

> He wanted every play to have a narrator because he was afraid that the audience wouldn't understand. And the reason he believed the audience wouldn't understand is — he gave this as a terrible example — because you see the German people who were so highly educated, allowed Hitler to come into power, allowed the Third Reich to take place. So you've got to explain very patiently. He felt that you had to explain to prevent this.

 Okay, but what had to be explained? Not subtle turns of the plot or the depth psychology of the characters, certainly. No, what was of primary concern to the German director was the class position of the individuals represented and how each, from this position, played a role in the furthering or hindering of the progress of capitalist society. Malina notes,

> Piscator felt that the actor was duty bound to make his or her performance an explanation of this character's position in the social structure [and the characterization of that structure] always has to have a Marxist base. Piscator was a Marxist. He denied it but he was a Marxist.

> It was his way in [presenting] *Juno and the Paycock* to consider what O'Casey had to say about the lives of the working class and how that affected their character and whether it was successful or not successful and the whole economic structure. Piscator said this for every play.

> He believed that every play was a play about the social structure. That is, if I have a play about pretty chorus girls kicking their legs that's also about the social structure, because who the hell are they and why are they kicking their legs like that?

Steve interjected, "How do you feel about that?"

Malina's reply: "I feel, yes, the chorus girls do it for money and some of them love it and some of them hate it. Yes, the social structure's got us all in its claws."

We will return to the topic of the influence of the predatory commercial economy on artistic life below, but first let's look at the second major topic of this interview: the Living Theater's use of collective creation to hone a pacifist/anarchist/democratic ethos and how this is (if things work) passed to the audience.

5) The Yiddish Theater Emphasizes the Folk

This second discussion is not only important because it will reveal one of the most progressive and effective artistic processes yet devised for anti-authoritarian theater, one that is a true heir to Artaud and Piscator, and thus offers a template for any ensemble that wishes to go against the grain of commercial (i.e., hurrah for capitalism) drama, but because it links the Living Theater to the now-passed traditions of Yiddish theater, whose inheritance it also has treasured. The Yiddish theater, partly for reasons already explored, was collectively oriented like the Living Theater.

In a very different context, Chris Cutler (in *File Under Culture*) makes the argument that Black American music in the early 20th century, because it was actively segregated from most contact with the majority society, developed its key forms (gospel, blues, jazz) in close contact with the community, infusing this music with a folk spirit that gave it a vitality and authenticity that infinitely outshone anything created in other cultural channels. In the same way, Yiddish theater was imbued with the life of the people, those of the shetl.

Now combine this with the general orientation of Jewish life, which, contrary to common thought, is radically distinct from its Christian counterpart. As our friend, Jewish poet and literary historian Ivan Klein, said in conversation, "The hyphen that they put in Judeo-Christian to separate the two words should be replaced with a brick wall." The brick wall is explained by Joseph Landis in his introduction to *The Dybbuk and Other Great Yiddish Plays*, in a discussion of why Jews lack devotional poetry of the type so common in Christian folds.

> Devotional poetry must have at its heart the individual's personal relation to God and his concern for his personal salvation. Both of these are relatively unimportant to Judaism and its ethic, for it is the People with whom God made His compact, the People to whom he gave His Torah, and the fate of the individual becomes one with the destiny of the People. (7-8)

He explains further, "Redemption, insofar as it involves a Messiah, is entirely a social phenomenon. It posits the liberation of the Jews from exile and the attendant liberation of mankind from injustice and oppression." (4)

We mentioned Landis's characterization of Judaism to Malina and she concurred with his point, saying:

> We [Jews] have this [emphasis on the collective] in our liturgy too. We have the [part of the service concerning] the sins that I have committed. We beat our breasts and we say, "Forgive me for the sin I have committed by committing murder." "Forgive me for the sin I have committed by committing adultery." Maybe you didn't commit adultery or murder, but in the congregation you are speaking for everyone when you say the sin I have committed.

> It is a very important part of the high holiday, the Yom Kippur service. We confess our sins but instead of going and whispering to a priest, "You know what I did Thursday night," instead of doing that, we say, "Forgive me for the sin I have committed," and we're all saying the same words, "I committed adultery," and we're all saying it together.

A quick glance at some gems of Yiddish drama will drive home the point that, although the authors embodied the collective spirit in a very different (and perhaps less thoroughgoing) way than did the Living Theater, a focus on the lives the people, as opposed to that of the individual, was central to these works.

Let's take *The Dybbuk* by S. Anski, arguably the most famous Yiddish theater work. The story is that of a girl whose spirit is possessed by the ghost of a deceased, wrongfully rejected suitor. Yet, note, that all the events occupying the main characters occur almost on the margins of depictions of communal rituals.

Act One is set in a prayer house where a witty, learned discussion on the wonderworking powers of various rabbis is under way. Only in the last two pages of a 16-page act does the abused suitor, Khonnon, learn the woman he thought to marry is betrothed to someone else. Khonnon promptly drops dead, thus initiating the plot. Even more communally directed is the second act, in which preparations are going on for the reception of the bridegroom. The poor are fed and danced with, the to-be-weds are extolled, the bride, Leye, goes into the cemetery to invite her dead mother to the marriage, and so on. Only on the last of 10 pages does the plot reanimate, when Leye, who has been offstage for most of the act, returns from the graveyard possessed by a dybbuk.

Or we could take as an example H. Leivick's brilliant *Shop*, which indicates the same emphasis in a different way. The work concerns the doings in a garment factory before and during a strike. One looks in vain for a central character. The concern of the play is rather with how the 20-odd workers and two bosses anticipate the union's action, and then either scab or picket when the shutdown is called. The play explores (the chapter on Leivick in this book gives the details) how different people, in connection to the web of relationships they form, are inclined either to fight with their class for improved working conditions or side with the bosses so as, hopefully, to be able to curry favors and improve their lot individually. The play, then, surveys an array of conflicts in a cross-section of people, ignoring scrutiny of the personal salvation of any singular personage.

I've remarked that the Living Theater went further in the direction of emphasizing the collective than did the Yiddish theater. I meant, the group not only wrote dramas with a communal slant (as did Leivick and Anski) but made the writing of them, the performance of them and the viewing of these performances ways of democratically enhancing people's understanding of themselves as part of a community.

We now look at how this was done.

6) The Creation of a Play as a Collective Process

How did the Living Theater put together a play. Malina answers:

> We have a method that consists of talking together about what we want
> to say. What is the most important thing that the people in this room — if
> it was us three, it would be what do we three want to say — what does

this group want to say? What's important to us? Where could we have some useful input? Where do you think we could have some impact? Where do you think we can stir it up?

Then we talk about that for anything from a week to four years. Then we start to say how can we dramatize this? And we could end up with *Frankenstein*. If we want to talk about how society became mechanized and inhuman and all of those things, we get the theme *Frankenstein*.

And in that case we went from Mary Shelley's book, which we all read together a couple times and discussed at length, then we saw all the Frankenstein movies. We were in Paris. We were lucky. In Paris, the Cinematique had everything and they did a private showing of the whole slew, everything that was ever done on Frankenstein. And then we created a play together, collectively based on the studies that we as a group had done together, so that we were like a research team.

What is *Frankenstein* saying? How did Mary Shelley use it? How did the movies use it? Who the hell is Boris Karloff? Everything. And we put it together and we talked and we talked and we talked. It's a long process because it means everybody has to talk and everybody has to put something into it. Each rehearsal is a session of invention and writing I guess.

And at other times we may sit down and say, "What about opposing the war?" And we come up with *Antigone* and we do pretty much what Brecht wrote from his translation of Holderin who translated Sophocles. So that there was Sophocles, Holderin, Brecht, Malina; note the crescendo

That's a line from Pound, "Note the crescendo." He said that about someone.

Actually you could say we haven't developed a style. I think with every play, after we decide what we want to do. After we have decided on the idea and either decided that we had a text to work from or were going to create one, a text of our own, and then we say "All right, now what are we doing up there [on the stage]? How are we showing this? How are we doing it physically, verbally? Are we doing it vocally? Are we dancing? Are we singing? Are we talking? Are we playing relationships? What are we doing? Then, how do we get the audience involved?" That is a very important part.

Right now we're working on a play called *Eureka* based on an essay by Edgar Allen Poe, a wonderful work in which a hundred years before the right time he invented, he foresaw the discovery of the big bang. He describes the big bang and he describes how the creation and the

> moment of the creation continue now. And our hope is to get all the spec-
> tators to feel themselves part of the creation, which we are. Here we are;
> our speaking here, we're all as much a part of the creation as the big
> bang.

Malina has raised some important points for further reflection, but before letting her elaborate them, let's listen to more details of the creation of a play based on a text, given in an answer to a question on whether Piscator's demand to make the audience understand had affected Living Theater presentations. She said:

> Let me try to explain what actually happens in the play *Antigone*, as
> Brecht did it, as we do it. Brecht wrote a poem called *The Legend of
> Antigone*, which explains everything very precisely. And we took this
> poem and used it as a kind of subtitling, spoken by the actors themselves.
> In which [for example] I come forward at the beginning and I say, "And
> then Antigone went to gather dust to bury her brother, which the tyrant
> had thrown to the dogs and the vultures." And then we begin.

> When we did it — we did it in theaters all over Europe — we did these,
> what we called "bridge lines," which was the poem, verse by verse, dis-
> persed into the action, which he [Brecht] had used as titles for his direct-
> ing book which was…. a book of every action which the Berliner
> Ensemble did, using the lines from the poem of Brecht as a caption. We,
> instead of captioning it, had the actors come forward and speak it
> directly to the audience in the language of the country.

> Did we have trouble with the Greek. We were great with the Italian, the
> French, English, German, Spanish, Portuguese, that's fine. But some lan-
> guages were very difficult.

> Yes, [like Piscator], we do want to explain. In that particular play, since
> we are using that as an example, it has a narrative component, [that is
> conveyed] in the bridge lines. And if you look at the tape — there is a
> tape of this — you can see when the characters come forward and speak
> to the audience. Although the tape is all in English, it's much more in con-
> trast if I say it in Italian [and the rest is in English].

7) Group Creation and Audience, Theoretical

Malina noted that one of the major questions the company asked itself when preparing a play was: "How do we get the audience involved? That is a very important part."

Of course, all theater people want to have an effect on their viewers, but the Living Theater's desires in this direction are more politically charged than is the norm. As Malina expresses it:

> But we manage to steer a path where trying primarily to get the audience

to change or to open up to or to whatever they're up to. If they're up to making revolution or just up to thinking about it without prejudice or up to taking action or writing a letter to their niece saying she shouldn't be in the Ku Klux Klan. Everybody has a role

And in some way what we want to do is further the possibility of each spectator. In trying to invent a style, that's really what we are looking for: What will work for those people, change them? What will determine whether they vote or they don't vote or even who they vote for? What will give them hope?

Ultimately, politics, as far as I can see very personally, is whether you believe people are fundamentally good or fundamentally bad. I think [for] people who think people are fundamentally bad, we have a long educational job before we are going to win them over. We have to work first with our own sector of society, which is the group [that thinks] people are fundamentally good.

We've all been fucked up by the way we've organized things and by history. We can change that and we can change our antagonism into loving kindness. But it's a path.

For some people, it's very difficult. It's difficult for people that really think that we are sinners and that we are doomed; that we cannot be redeemed except perhaps by some special path and that path is very narrow and everybody that doesn't tread that path is doomed. These people are very hard to deal with. It's very hard to convince them of anything.

Following on these points, Malina became more specific about the relationship of the audience to the actors, in response to a question concerning whether she wanted to "grab" the audience.

We don't want so much to grab them as to make them feel that if they can participate in a safe place, a relatively safe place, and speak out and act and, this is a very important part of it, that they can change the action of the play.

I'm most interested in researching how to give them a real creative part, not only a supplementary part, but to make them really able to change what we're doing by their input.

We spent years talking about what is the difference between us and the audience. Why are we we and they they? Well, they paid and we are getting paid. That was the first economic level.

And then we started playing theaters and in the hospitals and on the streets and in the factories on strike, and we didn't get paid. And we didn't get paid and they didn't get paid, so that didn't make any more sense.

So what's the difference between us and them?

And after much discussion, which I won't go through now, we decided: We were prepared and they were not prepared. Now it is assumed that we who are prepared are in some ways superior to those who are not prepared. But this isn't true.

We may have worked a year and half on the subject and broke our brains on it, but what we don't have is spontaneity and diversity. Because they have all different ideas. We are all sort of anarchist pacifists and most of us vegetarians and all of us feminists. But they might be anything. So they have a diversity to contribute of different opinions, opposing opinions of energizing opinions.

They have also spontaneity. Even though we may do certain improvised things and, certainly, when we respond to a customer [in a question and answer session after the play], it's always improvising. But we have practiced even that. Even our inter-audience reactions we've rehearsed, with half the group playing the audience and half the group playing actors. We've learned to do these things. They haven't done any of that. They're fresh, different, they're new. They have a spontaneity that we have to learn to appreciate instead of saying we don't do that.

8) Group Creation and Audience, Practical Example, *Paradise Now*

Obviously, Malina has thought long and hard about the matter and, I daresay, this conceptualization has been enriched as it has strengthened in its turn by her participation in the extraordinary productions of the troupe. Let's look at how the Living Theater's quest to engage the audience in a way that became integral to a production by examining one major work, *Paradise Now*. In studying it, we depart from previous procedure (in this interview) in two ways. First, Steve (having watched the Living Theater in action since the 1960s) talks first, giving his own quirky and succinct reading of how the ensemble allowed audience spontaneity to enter the playmaking. Second, in Malina's lucid and moving discussion of the play, she looks beyond the (complex enough) question of how the audience was involved and renders for us the scene and context of one particularly explosive production that took place in New Haven.

Steve, first:

If I can say a word, it is set out in theory, and then if it works in practice, it's like good improvisation. Like Judith was saying. We [the theater ensemble] have our course charted and they don't, but once they come in, if they interact the right way, your ship's going to veer from its course while it's trying to maintain its stability. So, one way or another — whether it's the slightest tear in the fabric — something going to give.

Judith took this up, getting down to specifics.

In *Paradise Now*, there's nobody sitting in the seats. If they insisted on sitting in the seats, we ripped the seats bodily out of the auditorium and piled them on the stage. Which causes us any number of economic and police problems. But we tear the seats out from under them, so they just can't sit there, nobody can sit there.

In *Paradise Now* there were people that took off their clothes and got in a people pile. Audience members. In this people pile, they hugged and embraced and some actors even made love with the audience. I didn't but some people did. And we couldn't do that today. And that's really a tragedy of our time that you just can't make love to anybody anytime without worrying about certain health and certain inhibitions. The times are bad that way for sexuality.

At the end of the play when those who have stayed are very often without clothes, very often a whole portion of the audience was without clothes, then Julian Beck says, "The theater is in the streets." Then we go out. And it's an incredible thing that happens because it's then we get busted.

Obviously, this had the authorities up in arms, although perhaps not as much as their actions *after* the arrest.

When we come to a new town, like we come to New Haven or some place, the police ask us to come visit them, Julian Beck and I would sit with the Commissioner and have a cup of coffee and he'd say, "Look, kids" — then we were kids – "Look, kids, you can do anything you want in that theater. I don't care what you do in there, but don't come out in the street. Nothing out in the street. Whatever you do in there, I don't care what you do."

Well, we burned money; we made love in the aisles. We did all sorts of illegal stuff and that was all right, but then Julian said, "The theater is in the street" and out we'd go and the audience would come with us and they would get busted, too.

And they [the authorities] had to play their scenes. We, however, had our scene prepared. We had a wonderful scene when we got busted. To get busted in America, you know, you get a person called your arresting officer who is your baby till the day you're out of that case. And you and that arresting officer are in a very intimate situation because he wants credit for you. And you have another motive and you say to him "Look, officer, this is the final scene in our play which consists of this arrest and you and I are playing this scene."

And then he says something like, "Look, lady, I'm not in your play."

And then I say a thing that pushes his button. I say, "Boy, you said that so well. You're good at this. You could be a good actor."

He says, "Look lady, I'm not an actor."

"Hey, hey, you're doing terrific."

And then we are in a dialogue in which I'm praising him and he's resisting. And I'm saying we're playing a theater scene, and he's saying we're not playing a theater scene. And I'm challenging his reality.

But what I've also done … He is no longer in charge of me, I am in charge of him. And he feels that right away. That's why he responds to it so strongly. And that's another form of audience participation.

He is the audience. I'm working on him. And I'm going to work on him right until whatever court situation we're going to go into. Through the whole trial, like it was in New Haven, which was one of the funniest trials in the world. Jules Feiffer attended all the sessions and laughed his head off. The court is one of our best theaters.

It was in New Haven. A prosecutor asked Julian Beck, "Were your genitals exposed when you were arrested?"

Julian said, "Well, possibly."

And the prosecutor said, "Well, were you aware of your genitals?"

Julian rose in full Julian Beck dudgeon and hit the pulpit there "Sir, I am always aware of my genitals."

That was a very nice moment. We accept the court as a theater provided by the state for us to perform in and we usually do a good job.

9) Free Interaction of Interviewers and Interviewee

To give something of the flavor of the interview, which was much more give-and-take and informal that one might have expected with such a celebrated and wise interlocutor, we include some of the interaction between the three of us as we pondered the implications of what Malina had said about the *Paradise Now* production and thought about how the intercourse between viewers and stagers played out in other productions.

Jim

What she presented in *Paradise* is that you don't even have to convince the audience. The audience is asked: "Do I want to take off my clothes and jump in the pile?" If you do, you're already convinced. And if you, then, say, "I'm now going to walk out naked and get arrested." You've already become a pacifist anarchist by seeing a play.

Judith

I remember one night a soldier took his uniform off and got a big hand from everybody. He made a larger step of breaching what he was permitted.

Malina went on to note that some works did not come up to the level of audience interaction found in *Paradise,* but Steve came back with a counterclaim.

Judith

In *Frankenstein*, we played a lot in the theater aisles. We did arrests and beatings and stuff, but we hadn't yet caught up the audience in the action in *Frankenstein.*

Steve

But I also think one of the elements in every play is to do the aisles. In a way, even if you don't catch up the audience they're caught. I'm obsessive [when I see that kind of play] so I'm moving all the time. So, it's kind of interesting. I think the biggest hope for any of that is that the audience doesn't just become involved but there's that great artists' hope they take some of that home with them.

Judith

Which is the whole ...

Steve

Going in the aisles is also a major element in *The Connection*. They go out asking the audience for bread for drugs. I've seen the film and the film does not have that going out into the audience, freaking them out.

Like in *Mysteries*, to me, more important than the group hug, is when the people are dying in the audience. And even though the audience knows this is a play, when the actor is near you, this freaks you out. They're at your feet.

And I think that with *Maudie and Jane*, that young chick is always going through a dilemma and ... talking to the audience. She is almost talking to them from the first scene.

Then Steve points out that in productions, such as *The Brig*, which is set in a Marines military prison, and in which there is no overt interaction between the audience and the players, there is still a collective spirit.

Steve

It's that thing about the whole and the ensemble. It's like when you leave *The Brig*, you think: "Who's more important, the kicked or the kicker?" And you realize neither the guards nor the prisoners are more important. It's all about equal shares. It's such a collective *mentshelekhkayt* that [the roles are] almost inseparable.

Judith

It's also important to understand that in this cast everyone, except one, everyone who has played a guard has also played a prisoner. All the guards were prisoners, except one, he was a little too old. But that's a very important part of it. That *The Brig* consists of these guys and those guys and they're the same.

People in jail, the jails I've been in, the prisoners are always saying to the guards, "Listen, I'm gonna be out of here in three weeks and you're going to spend the rest of your life in here." Always a reproach to the guards, that's a common jail thing.

Thus emphasizing the commonality of fates.

We concluded this part of the discussion with some more far-reaching observations.

Jim

This perspective shows a basic difference from Piscator. He said, "Here's a play and the characters are in rigid social positions, which shows our society is frozen." Whereas in plays of the Living Theater, there is trans-formation, whether audience members joining the cast or actors chang-ing roles. That indicates a more hopeful view of society. If a soldier can strip his clothes off and jump into the people pile, maybe society is not as rigid as we've been told it is, and is indeed in many ways.

Further, since the theater evolves things collectively and works collec-tively, it must involve a different concept from a theater in which the play-wright, even Brecht, says, "Here's the piece. Do it this way."

Judith

I think it makes a lot of difference. I think the audience senses us as a group and senses our relation to each other.

I think it's part of our technique. Part of what happens is that we can demonstrate our collectivity and that we can communicate our collectivity and that, hopefully, ideally, it makes the audience want to function more collectively.

9) Trials and Tribulations

Given the reactionary current of our current (2008) administration in New York City and the country, a progressive and democratic company such as the Living Theater is going to travel a very rocky road. Yet, at the same time, as we will show in the next (concluding) section, only such an ensemble is open to the experience of miracles.

Here are some of the hindrances to the continued existence of the Living Theater, all of which, ultimately, translate as "the claws of the economy."

We can lead into the discussion by quoting Steve's characterization of what, at the time of writing, was their current production.

> You are taking a risk by having plays that are not necessarily popular. I mean *Maudie and Jane* has a lot of so-called popular qualities, both for the proletarian and the upper classes. And you don't only have class struggle in the play but you also have something that historically people love to see: the dialogue between two people, in this case two actresses, and how it develops and how the characters almost reverse by the end of the play. You're doing something that not only historically important because of getting the audience involved and trying to show the historical economic structure, but you're also doing something that, as we know, is completely against the grain when we look at what the grain now is.

A) The Foundations & Money Givers

Malina replies, broaching the subject of the obstacles to the Living Theater's existence in the course of her response:

> I'll tell you where the grain stops for me is that I have made an appeal to every viable foundation that supports all the art theaters, all the foundations that support, from La Mama, Theater For the New City, all down the line. I have made appeals to them. Some of them must know who the Living Theater is.
>
> And I've got straight zeros all down the line. "I'm sorry that the Schuberts can't afford to support you." "I am sorry that this or that foundation, ... we can't support all the people that ask us." "I'm so sorry. I hope you do well." I got straight rejection slips from every foundation.

I'm going to keep working on it. ... I've got a theater with thirty people.

Steve mentions Crystal Field, overall director of The Theater for the New City, as someone who seems to have mastered the art of fundraising.

Malina goes on:

> They work very hard and Crystal is very good at it, at raising money. I think it's a talent, like singing and dancing. Some people can sing beautifully and some people can study the violin for 20 years and not be able to play decently. I'm just not a good fundraiser and I'm working very hard at becoming a good fundraiser because I say, "Why the hell can't I play a good fundraiser as well as play Antigone? So now I'm going to play a good fundraiser." It hasn't worked yet but I'm working at it.

> I've love to [hire a publicist] if I had the money. I can't afford it. I'm looking for a publicist who'd consider working for a percentage of what he brings in and I can't find anyone. I've been looking for that for almost 10 years now. .... I want someone who can help but I never have the money to put into it. For me, it's a question of next month's rent. ...

> I spend more than half my time trying to raise money to keep the theater going and I think I spend more time trying to economically keeping the theater going than I can spend on actual plays and on actual work and that's also part of the economic pressure. And I feel myself repressed in a certain way because I have to spend my time not doing what is best for me to do but something else so that I can support even the possibility of doing what is best for me, because a lot of people would like to have their own theater and create their plays and it's a struggle to get myself in a position to do that

B) The Press

While the press has generally been supportive, with some few exceptions, this doesn't always translate into filled seats. Malina explains:

> And you say popular, Steve. *Maudie and Jane* got a terrific review in the *Times*. *The Brig* got a terrific review in the *Times*. And got all the awards and we still had five people in the audience.

> It's not that we're doing unpopular work. People come backstage. I meet with the audience. It's a small theater. I go out and talk to the audience. People are very enthusiastic about the play. Almost everyone that sees it thinks it's wonderful. I say, "Tell your friends to come please." Because last night we played for seven people.

Steve, however, remembered, with some bitterness, a misguided review in one paper, saying:

> And then there are ignorant people like the kid who wrote the thing in the
> *Village Voice* about *Mysteries*, which was that it was retro, that it's not of
> this time, that it's from the past. I mean that is the most absurd rhetoric
> imaginable. I mean, on that level, every time they play a Shakespeare
> play, they should say, "That's so retro." That was the most ridiculous
> review I'd ever heard. So people don't always get it.

Malina was more philosophical:

> I try to pay not too much attention to stupid reviews. Of course, in a way,
> I'm economically dependent on them. You can't expect everyone to
> understand everything right away. If a person happens to write for the
> *Voice* right now and writes this idiotic piece, I can't waste my energy wor-
> rying about this poor fool. Of course, he cost me a lot of money, but that's
> nothing I can do anything about. And I'm not going to waste my energy
> getting even as excited as you are.

C) Lacking Support for the Troupe

What is particularly frustrating about lack of funds is what it means for the fortunes of the actors.

> In New York we can't even pay actors enough. They usually have to do
> other work to [survive], which is a horrible thing that an actor can't
> devote himself to his work but has to go be a waiter and then he can
> come in and be an actor later. It's awful that we can't support the com-
> pany.

> I feel personally horrible in exploiting the people that you see about who
> do clean the bathrooms every day, clean the floors, make sure there's
> someone in the box office, pick up the phone, run the little coffee conces-
> sion that makes us a couple of dollars. They work very hard and when a
> set has to be built, they are there to build the set, and if the ceiling floods,
> they're there to hold the pots for the water.

> They are all actors. These are not street urchins. They were all in *The Brig*.
> They're all understudying and working very hard and running the lights
> and the sound, participating in the play. And we have nothing to give
> them but a split of the box office, which, when we have six people in the
> house, is pathetic. You can imagine. Do the arithmetic.

D) The Noxious Political Climate

Her discussion of the young people in the company glided into some thought on the political differences between today's youth and those of the 1960s when the company was starting out,

which brought up the current divisive social climate, which also has its effect on the theater.

Malina begins:

> I really feel that this generation is free of so much of the bullshit that pre-
> vented 1968 from becoming what everyone who was there then wanted
> it to become and that, for instance, had something to do with something
> as dopey as right and left.

> I am more right than you. I am more left than you. You are more right than
> me. You are more left than me. And who's lefter. In any gathering of five
> people, you could line them up from the most leftest to the least leftist and
> this was something we believed was real. I mean, Communism is real
> and the false hope of democracy is real, but the reality of our lives is not
> based on this kind of ideology.

> Now, of course, as a pacifist and an anarchist I except and say anar-
> chism is different But, of course, [as an ideology] it's not. Anarchism is
> also a form of thinking and a form of behaving.

Steve jumps in, "But don't we still have a situation of the liberals talking to the liberals and the
right wing talking to the right wing?"

Malina's response:

> I think it's gotten so bad that it's gotten good. It's like the old Bolshevik
> saying – "I'm not a Bolshevik" — but this is a good saying. The Bolsheviks
> used to say, "The worse it is, the better it is." Now, of course, that's dan-
> gerous because it might be making it worse.

> On the other hand, when it gets bad enough, people are just not so stu-
> pid they're not gonna say, "Stop." Unless we want to go into fascism,
> then we say, "Don't stop." And if the people don't stop it, it's going to go
> into fascism right now. All the way. Because the right is stronger than it's
> ever been. It's politically stronger.

> And talk about left/right. You've got the whole religious right. I wanted to
> talk about a Jewish problem. I think that the most dangerous thing that
> could happen is that the fundamentalist Muslims and the fundamentalist
> Christian and the fundamentalist Jews look at each other one day and
> [say,] "You know we're not each enemy. These people here, the progres-
> sives, they're the real enemies."

> If they ever get together and begin to persecute us, we're going to have
> a terrible holocaust. Because essentially those three groups could fight it
> out among themselves around a table. But here we are, messing up their

act, and if they ever realize that, they're going to wipe us out and we're going to have to find a tactic to overcome it.

We might assess the overall impact of these deleterious social conditions, such as the rise of the right, on the theater as, on the one hand, potentially very positive, in that the Living Theater is one of the few dramatic ensembles that, instead of offering light entertainment, grapples with the country's most pressing questions, such as the rise of fascism and increasing militarization. On the other hand, in the short term, the impact is not so good, because of the blistering wind of hopelessness these conditions produce, expressed through so many people's ties to self-wounding jobs and immersion in soul-destroying entertainment pabulum, from Hollywood films and TV to the hyper-commercialized, misogynistic sports contests.

Note, though, Malina's last comment. Her impulse, after realistically imagining that things may get worse, is to talk about new tactics rather than beat her breast. Such a forward-looking approach is rooted, I think, in what at the beginning I called the tsaddik's ability to discern the sudden shifting into radiance of a true miracle.

10) THE MIRACLE

Jim

Would I be right in assuming your actors, who don't simply appear in the plays but help create them, share your anarchist and pacifist philosophy?

Malina

Let me tell you about a miracle. This is my miracle.

We were rehearsing *The Brig*. It's hard to find actors who will work for so little money. At that time, we were paying a weekly wage while we were casting the play. We put in a notice in *Backstage* magazine, which is not a particularly political magazine. We advertised it in *Backstage* magazine when we were going to have auditions. People came in.

The audition consisted of only one thing, which is: Can they march? So we said, "Get up on the stage, attention, this is how you put your thumbs by the seams of your pants, chest up, chin up, listen to the rhythm, follow the rhythm. Right face, left face and all that." If they can march, they're in.

I never said to them, not to one of them, "Do you have any political philosophy? Are you an activist? Do you care about the poor?" I never asked any of them that. Then a miracle happened.

The miracle is that sometimes in order to draw audiences we give special performance with questions and answers afterwards for students. They come like from NYU and other schools, the New School, 10, 15 college students and we'll do questions and answers. I'm there to answer questions and so is *The Brig* cast. And they all sat round and these college students ask questions.

These people in the cast, who had never been questioned — they knew we were anarchists pacifists because the first rehearsal I made that very clear. They know who I was and they knew what the theater was because we told them, but we never asked them.

And when they had to respond to these college kids, and some of them [among the actors] were college kids and some of them … I doubt that they went through college, but they were so smart, that it was a miracle.

They understood things that intellectual actors from 1963 didn't know. For instance, I had to spend hours in the 1960s talking about why *The Brig* is a pacifist play to all those smart people, Steve Ben Israel and others, big brains.

But in 2006, none of those kids doubted it was a pacifist play. Of course, it's a pacifist play.

11) Coda

Steve

Can you say something about the Living Theater and sexuality?

Judith

I'm an advocate of free love. What else can I say. I think people should do what they like, enjoy what they enjoy and we should enjoy their enjoying what they enjoy. I don't know what else to say.

Jim

You said Piscator envisioned an audience of each member sitting at his or her desk, taking notes at this play. What would be the ideal audience member in the Living Theater?

Judith

I think they should run up on the stage, embrace us, make love with us and then run out and do immediately the beautiful, non-violent anarchist revolution. Ideally my idea is to get people to move out into the street with the enthusiasm that we feel in the theater.

Steve Dalachinsky *was born in 1946, Brooklyn, New York. His work has appeared exten-sively in journals on & off line including;* Big Bridge, Milk, Unlikely Stories, Xpressed, Ratapal-lax, Evergreen Review, Long Shot, Alpha Beat Soup, Xtant, Blue Beat Jacket, N.Y. Arts Magazine, 88 *and* Lost and Found Times. *He is included in such anthologies as* Beat Indeed, The Haiku Moment *and the esteemed* Outlaw Bible of American Poetry. *He has written liner notes for the CDs of many artists including Anthony Braxton, Charles Gayle, James "Blood" Ulmer, Rashied Ali, Roy Campbell, Matthew Shipp and Roscoe Mitchell. His 1999 CD,* Incom-plete Direction *(Knitting Factory Records), a collection of his poetry read in collaboration with various musicians, such as William Parker, Matthew Shipp, Daniel Carter, Sabir Mateen, Thurston Moore (Sonic Youth), Vernon Reid (Living Colour) has garnered much praise. His most recent chapbooks include* Musicology *(Editions Pioche, Paris 2005),* Trial and Error in Paris *(Loudmouth Collective 2003),* Lautreamont's Laments *(Furniture Press 2005),* In Glorious Black and White *(Ugly Duckling Presse 2005),* St. Lucie *(King of Mice Press 2005),* Are We Not MEN & Fake Book *(2 books of collage - 8 Page Press 2005).* Dream Book *(Avantcular Press 2005). His books include* A Superintendent's Eyes *(Hozomeen Press 2000) and his PEN Award winning book* The Final Nite *(complete notes from a Charles Gayle Notebook),* Ugly Duckling Presse 2006). His latest CD is *Phenomena of Interference, a collaboration with pianist Matthew Shipp (Hopscotch Records 2005). He has read throughout the N.Y. area, the U.S., Japan and Europe, including France and Germany.*

The Return of the Theatre

Gerrick Beck

When the Living Theatre returned from its "extended tour" in the winter of '83, the art scene in New York was a different place. The great playful art of the beatnik era had multiplied. And moved into different directions.

Instead of a few bold galleries hosting unusual painting, there were galleries from Harlem to Brooklyn, galleries on every block of the East Village. Action painting, collage, construction, abstract, pop, op, neo-this and post-neo-that. There were now thousands of struggling painters. And the original beat painters were being "inducted" into the lofty art history heights as the New York School, aka the Abstract Expressionists.

Instead of a few clubs with an open mic for spoken word, there were more venues than nights of the week to visit them. ABC No Rio, The Knitting Factory, The Fort, Gargoyle Mechanique, 8BC, Café Bustelo. Folkies playing folk, poets reciting, and performance artists carrying on by the hundreds. All adept, all heartfelt, all creative, some even bound for fame.

Instead of a few underground & FM radio late night jazz masters, jazz was everywhere. Uptown, downtown, out-of-town, everywhere. And even when some of the greats, Don Cherry trumpeter, came to visit the seriously underground East Village Shuttle Club. That was the exception. Jazz was everywhere; as well it should be, integrated into the mainstream sound.

The world of advertising had opened its doors to a new generation of graphics and video artists who easily appropriated the op, pop, surreal, dada, collage, paint-splattering styles. They made the innovations of the beat era painters commonly available and put them to use in eye-popping TV commercials and slick-paged magazine ads. But the audience-involving live action of the Living Theatre was light waves away from the remote controls that changed the channels in people's living rooms.

To most of these young graphic/sound/design/video artists, the beat era and its associated plays, poetries, performances were honored but bygone history.

It was a dance company that made the decision to bring the Living Theatre back across the Atlantic and produce "Le Living" (as they were called in Europe) at their own Joyce Theater. These were the people in the family circle of the Feld Ballet Company. They had converted an old "midnite movie" house on 8th Avenue, turning it into a beautiful jewel box of a theater. They remembered The Living from the strongest days of the Off-Broadway theatre experiments. Julian and Judith thought the time was right for a return to the city of their beginnings. They had played 44 countries in over twenty languages, bringing modern theatrical productions to South America, Africa, Scandinavia, Eastern Europe. They had played for free in churchyards, hospitals, school auditoriums and in the small theaters of countless towns of Europe. They had played the major theater districts of Paris, Rome, London. Often they would translate key passages into the language of the country they were playing. Or do as the playwright Brecht did: add a series of "bridge" lines that briefly described the action — like the side notes in Coleridge's *Rhyme of the Ancient Mariner* — which could be spoken in the language of the people in the audience. No other American theatre company, no other theatre company period, did anything like that.

The last time the company had been in the United States was a decade earlier when they had come for a season and created the play, *The Money Tower*. That outdoor epic was built around a five-story construction meant to be put up and played out-of-doors near factory environments. The top story had a giant revolving green neon dollar sign and that was the place of the "super rich." Each story below was broader so the whole thing was like a slender pyramid. The next floor down was the held by the military and the police. Below them were the white-collar workers. On the floor below that were the blue-collar workers and on the very bottom, the poor and the unemployed.

Paper money is dispensed from the top, fluttering to the grasping hands below. The play enacts many realistic scenes: the spiral of inflation, the pain of the underclass and the fear the employees have of losing their jobs.

The structure gets built in plain sight of the industrial zone where the performance is to take place. Then it's played in less than an hour during the change of shifts. So the factory folks have seen these beatnik actor and actresses building the steel construction all day long. Then the shift changes and play begins. In the middle of the construction is an elevator, well, really, a small dumbwaiter that brings people and props up and down the money tower. At the heart of the play, the elevator gets stuck, breaks and "kills" a performer. There follows a long argument on the money tower about what to do. The classic arguments:

"Forget about it. Just be more careful than he was when you're near the elevator."

"We should petition the management to put in a safer elevator."

"They'll never do that."

"We should strike if they won't give us a safer workplace."

"Do that and you won't have any workplace."

"There was someone killed last year too. In the same elevator. We gotta get some changes. Next time it could be me."

"Strike!"

"No way. No strike for me. I got a family I'm supporting. I'm not going to get fired, lose my wages."

And then one of the performers turns to the audience and says, "What do I know? I'm an actor not a factory worker. You, you tell me what we should do." Throwing the discussion open to the workers changing shifts. Real theatre.

Because of their "leftist" social leanings and willingness to criticize The United States, The Living Theatre got invited by the Italian Communist Student Arts League to do a tour in Soviet bloc Eastern Europe. They played in Poland and did *The Money Tower* in the shipyards at Gadnsk. Standing in that audience that day were the core of the early Solidarity Movement. Strike? What do you think?

What did they think! Months later they went on strike at those shipyards and the whole entire complex of the Soviet dominated domino states tumbled down. Don't ever let it be said that art does not walk hand-in-hand with history.

Coming back to the United States Julian and Judith and the 23-person company brought four plays. The classic *Antigone*, the anti-war masterpiece that simply won't go out of style. As long as we make wars, it just needs to be played. A revival of *Mysteries*, the trance-like production from the 1960s. A new production, *The Yellow Methuselah*, combining the text of George Bernard Shaw with the design and style of Vassily Kandinsky. The theme was the quest for immortality. Julian painted the largest-ever (at the time) canvas painting that ran as a slowly moving backdrop - from two gigantic rollers — across the back of the stage. An homage to Kandinsky's painting styles, it moved ever so slowly inch by inch behind the actors as they performed Shaw's play about the quest for extended life.

The fourth play, *The Archaeology of Sleep*, was something entirely different.

Julian wanted to do something more than tell another story in a beautiful style (or a poetic style) (or a political style) (or an audience-involving style) (or any regular tried-and-true dramatic style). The modern motion picture industry had become so adept at storytelling with all the available techniques and technologies. Theatre, live theatre is, of course, different. It has the power to affect us deeply. But how does live theatre do more than tell a story? How does a creator of theatre-type spectacle reach beyond the old-fashioned world of stage-play storytelling?

To do this Julian needed a theme that could be well-presented by the multi-layered possibilities: sounds, lights, songs, actions, acrobatics of actors and the extension of that energy beyond the stage ... so he chose sleep, whose dreams are themselves very like the kind of production Julian was envisioning. *The Archaeology of Sleep*, an exploration of the depths as Julian put it, "of the largest unexplored realm on Earth ... the sleeping mind."

The play's "plot" consisted of the dreams of the real cast members, mixed into the personalities of cats in an old-style sleep laboratory. The scenography of the play follows the true sleep cycle of the human being: alpha, beta, delta, gamma, the "REM" cycle, the stages of entering sleep, breathing cycles, twitching, dreams, and the cats and the cast enact dramas of great beauty and great terror, eros and wonder in a multi-imaged experience more like a trance than a play in three acts. Many of the dreams were so beautiful, like those tiny Christmas souvenirs that you hold in your hand and shake, and a scene of a city or cathedral is shimmering with tiny snowflakes, all in your palm, and chimes are softly gongalaling in the distance. But does it tell a story in the traditional sense? Well, there's a maniacal doctor (obviously, the evil authority figure) and certainly some animal rights themes, but a story? Only the stories of each of the cast member's dreams.

Just as Julian's collage paintings of the mid-1950's heralded a new multi-layered form of seeing into the canvas's depths, here Julian was making an overlay of images, one melting into the next to be presented to the spectator, live and coming from all sides, tantalizing, touching, inviting the spectators to join in. In several sequences, how the spectators choose or choose not to participate affected the course of the play's action.

The press in New York was abuzz. Every media ran stories about the theatre's history, its adventures, the foreign acclaim, the prizes, the causes the group had supported around the world. All good press. I gushed about this to Judith. She raised a warning eyebrow and explained how the press loves to put someone on a pedestal and then Whack! knock them off. "It's the reviews that really matter," she said knowingly.

We got the whole company housed in New York. The giant downtown arts collectives Charas and Quando opened up rehearsal space and set-building space for us and we hustled to get the four plays ready to open in rapid succession. My own experience on the farm gave me tool handiness. Joanee worked with Julian on the costumes. Languages were everywhere as the company spoke to each other in a pastiche of tongues.

The Joyce management was gracious and supportive. We loaded in the sets and began the run.

Opening was packed. The lights went down, the hush enveloped the room and the descent into the realm of sleep had begun.

Oh, how the press loved to hate us. First, they berated everyone's accents: Scandinavian, Eastern European, European, — this to a company that had brought Americanized English plays into countless foreign dialects.

But more important, much more important: They didn't get the imagistic, multi-layered live theatre experience. Where is the theater that used to discuss political ideas? Or where is the plot to this? What is all this supposed to be about? Who are they to be touching audience members? Asking us questions? The same old incomprehensible Off-Broadway stuff that we didn't like twenty years ago either!

A few of the small press and politically far left magazines had nice things to say — especially about the time-honored *Antigone* production — Judith's translation of Brecht's adaption of Sophocles' anti-war masterpiece — But the valuable New York "quotable" press that inspired box office revenue was simply not on our side.

The old friends of the theater all came to see the plays, of course. So there were endless reunions in the green room and lobby after the shows. Many of the old Beats were more staid in appearance; the academic look having overtaken the firebrand. Many still spoke affectionately of the dreams of a more poetic society. Some, like the early Hippies, were clearly astounded that the Great Changes hadn't already descended on all of us! Pretty much everybody was involved in neighborhood environmental or educational causes. And all were still relentlessly productive: music, writing, teaching, filming, sculpting, painting, et cetera.

Practically all of the City's young performance artists, the experimental visual and political artists came to see the performances. But that is not a large group, even in New York.

Beyond that? Into the masses of, say, college students or nightlife partiers, or well-off theatergoers or tourists who might get tickets to an Off-Broadway feature? Hardly. And that hurt. Because to sustain a run in the City you have to tap into those groups' economic power to survive.

The Empire of the West was going to be a harder nut to crack than the Soviet Union.

Gerrick Beck born on Manhattan Island 1949. Grew up in NYC acting in The Living Theatre founded by parents Julian Beck and Judith Malina. Moved out west to college in Oregon and then 13 years in the organic hippie farming and arts community outside Eugene, OR. Involved with the early Eugene Country Faires, Vortex Festival, endless anti-war protests, and then the beginnings of the Rainbow Gatherings which (I have)/(he has) stayed involved with ever since. Returned to NYC Lower East Side 1982 working with Trust for Public Land creating a Children's Gardening Program linking schools and community gardens. Currently living at a horse rescue shelter outside Santa Fe, NM.

Part 6: Film

Was

Margot Niederland with Merry Fortune

I grew up a cultural mongrel — American born, yet raised in a home oozing with Jewish and European influences: Goethe, Mozart, Brecht and opera colliding with rock & roll, cowboys and Indians, and American soap operas. Though I spoke English, my brain automatically would switch to understanding the German my parents spoke and the Yiddish my father threw in for emphasis. I was growing up American and at the same time I was sharing the Jewish immigrant experience with my parents. That's probably why I felt more at home on the Lower East Side than in any other neighborhood I have lived.

My *lower* Lower East Side is the area running from Houston south to the East River, and from Chrystie east to the East River. When I moved here in the 1990s, there were still buildings from the 1800s, glorious and sturdy brick structures featuring intricate carvings and details. There was also a large and vibrant mix of immigrants and first-generation Americans: Koreans, Dominicans, Chinese, Puerto Ricans, Mexicans, Indians, Italians and Jews. You could almost feel the stories of the past mingling with the new — all different, all individual. Underlining this great diversity was the unspoken gestalt of making a fresh start in a new country along with the fears and difficulties that come along with trying to assimilate.

For over twelve years I've been living on the Lower East Side and for the past nine I have been compulsively filming the disappearance of this historic heart of New York City. I now have over three hundred reels (100 feet) of 16 millimeter film and a huge credit card debt. It was only when I was asked to contribute to Clayton's book that I began trying to understand what drove me to continue filming for so many years without any consideration of the cost. The answer is that the melancholy of lost histories reverberates deeply in my DNA.

I come from a family of lost histories. A first-generation American, I am the offspring of immigrant parents who barely escaped the ovens of the Holocaust. My parents were born at the turn of the century: my mother in Leipzig, Germany, and my father in a small town near Vilnius, Lithuania. Later my father would live in Germany: first as a child with his parents in Wurzburg, then as a young professor in Leipzig.

My father came from five generations of orthodox rabbis and made extra money singing as a cantor for the High Holiday services. Yet, like his friend Kurt Weil and many other young Jews growing up in Germany in the 1920s, he desired to integrate into the secular world. Kurt Weil went on to write popular music, most famously *The Three Penny Opera* and *Mahogany*. My father went on to study at the Leipzig Conservatory of Music in hopes of becoming an opera singer.

My parents were in their thirties when they met in Leipzig and wed in 1936. Decades later as a child in upstate New York, I heard the stories of convolutions, eruptions and terror that marred and marked the first years of their married life in a Nazifying Germany. Their stories entwined in my mind with typical American childhood reading fare: *Dick and Jane* (and watching Spot run), *Little Women*, *The Bobbsey Twins* and *The Five Little Peppers and How They Grew*. Years later this surreal mixture found its way into my artwork. The strangeness in my style was noted by one reviewer of my photography exhibits, who likened my work to that of Diane Arbus, Lisette Modell and Elliot Erwitt.

Starting over in a new country with all its attendant complexity is part of my heritage. It's my family's history to be fleeing, immigrating and surviving in foreign lands. The Diaspora of my father's family began in the early 1930s when his youngest brother fled for his life, fearing retaliation for his political activities that defied the rising Nazi Party. When he arrived in Switzerland, the "neutral Swiss" government threatened to imprison or return him to Germany. He then snuck into British-controlled Palestine and succeeded in bringing his parents there as well. He became a dentist and lived in the newly created Israel until his death in 1967. My father's middle brother fled to Italy and earned his second doctorate in Italian. When Mussolini became prime minister, my uncle also had to flee, working as a ship's doctor, sailing to the Philippines. Eventually he relocated to New York City and, after getting his third doctorate in English, became a well known and revered psychoanalyst.

When my father saw his brothers' failure to find a safe harbor in Europe, he considered the possibility of coming to America. In the summer of 1938, after securing American visas, he, with my mother and her brother, visited my father's relatives in New York City. It was a kind of scouting exploration to see if immigrating to the States would be feasible. The American quota for Jews made it impossible. Their plea to American politicians was refused and they had to return to Germany. Several months later on October 27th, Hitler expelled 18,000 Jews of Polish origins from Germany. Although my mother had been born in Germany, her parents were from Poland and the Germans therefore considered her Polish. Separated from my father, she was forced onto a train along with her parents and younger brother and exiled to Poland.

My father was declared stateless and was allowed to remain in Germany. He was there on November 9th, the eve of "Crystal Night" or the "night of shattered glass." On this night synagogues were destroyed, hundreds of Jewish shop windows smashed and the shops looted, and many Jews were arrested and sent to concentration camps. Several days later, a neighbor warned my father that the Gestapo had been there looking for him. Immediately he tried to get a ticket on the next ship to America. His visa from the summer before was still valid, but at the ticket window he was informed that his passport had expired. So he went to the only place where one could get a passport extended, which was the Gestapo headquarters. When I asked him how he could do such a thing, walk into the belly of the beast, he answered simply, "What else could I do?! I either live or …" And he got his passport extended.

Unbeknownst to many at that time, the Nazis were being very practical and were letting certain Jews leave — those who could prove they were capable of exiting Germany and entering another country legally on their own steam. My father had unintentionally done just that. Some months after arriving here, my father was able to help my mother and her brother leave Poland and come to America on their visas. A few years later when the United States went to war with Germany, my parents were allowed to stay and eventually became American citizens.

Finding a job in the early 1940s was severely problematic for anyone with a German accent, and this was true even for German Jews. My father was now in his forties. Teaching in America as he had been doing in Germany was not an option; he looked into the possibility of turning his formerly part-time gig in Germany as a cantor into a full-time job in America. As a descendent of many generations of orthodox rabbis, he could read Hebrew fluently and knew the entire Jewish liturgy, the daily services, as well as those for the Sabbath and High Holidays.

After much searching, he got a job in a conservative synagogue in upstate New York. The pay was so low we were forced to live on the other side of the tracks away from most of his Jewish congregation. Nevertheless, my father threw himself into the work of recreating the synagogue's liturgical repertory to his liking. He had come here with a prodigious knowledge of cantorial music from the master Eastern European and German Jewish composers of the 19th century: Lewandowski, Naumbourg, Nowakowsky, Sulzer and others. He used some of their original compositions, tweaking, intermingling and embellishing them with riffs from classical music. He formed a choir of thirty voices from his congregation, which he simultaneously conducted while singing the cantorial lead parts in a lyric tenor voice. No cantor ever conducted and sang with the choir at the same time. The services were distinct and beautiful.

As much as I loved my father's services, I did not enjoy the strictures inherent in being a clergyman's daughter. So at seventeen when I left home to go to college, my life — like my father's as a young man in Germany — became more secular. I became a photographer, working as a photojournalist and exhibiting my work. While living in Cambridge, Massachusetts, from the mid '70s to the mid '80s, I worked in several film art houses. Over a ten-year period, I saturated myself with films: the French New Wave, the German New Wave, the Italian New Wave, along with Russian, Eastern European and American classics. In addition I managed a theatre, "Center Screen," housed in Harvard's Carpenter Center, where we primarily showed experimental and avant-garde films. I sat in on a film production class at the Massachusetts Institute of Technology given by Richard Leacock, one of the originators of "cinema verite." When I estimated that I had voraciously viewed up to 3,000 films during a ten-year period, I decided that my film education was complete! So in 1984 I moved back to New York City to make my own films.

Once in New York, securing shelter was not so easy or immediate. With great frequency I hauled my possessions from sublet to sublet, followed around by a feeling of loss and estrangement. The process of immigrating left an indelible mark. After much legwork and many false starts, I found an affordable apartment in Brooklyn. It is not surprising that for my first film I was drawn to the story of Arthur Wood, an artist soulfully involved in a labor of love that was to become his home which he has named Broken Angel. *Broken Angel*, Arthur's home and my first film, is a story of architectural poetry and tenacious vision sustained and realized against the grain. Arthur spent decades modifying, and constructing his hand-made home, using materials rescued and gleaned from the streets. Located on Quincy Street in the Fort Greene section of Brooklyn, Broken Angel has been called the "most-talked-about building" in Brooklyn. Clearly the subject matter of this short documentary is analogous to my family's fundamental struggle to create a sanctuary of their own.

In the summer of 1993 after my mother and father had died, I was at work on my second film. It was to be a film about my father. In 1995 a friend's apartment opened up on the Lower East Side. When walking through the neighborhood to my new home on Ludlow Street, I had a feeling of recognition. It was as if I were reuniting with the spirit of my Jewish roots. The old Jewish immigrant community that had been born here at the turn of the century was vibrant and active. The Forward Building, The Klezker Brotherly Aid Association and the old synagogues were still standing. Thriving Jewish enclaves surrounded me in abundance: Kosher delis, bakeries, butcher shops, restaurants, and stores selling Jewish books and religious items were fixtures throughout the charged immigrant landscape. I spoke Yiddish with the Jewish store keepers and befriended some of my neighbors, among them Bea Salwen, who owned the last remaining umbrella store in New York City. The store had been established by her husband's family in 1902 and then passed on to her. Two doors down from me was Sam Steinberg, who was born in the same building in which he lived for 91 years, and from which he ran his paper business. The neighborhood, the buildings and its people, became my new family.

A car accident in 1998 rendered me more or less house bound in my Lower East Side apartment. From my window, I began seeing construction men appear on a nearby rooftop on a daily basis. What I was seeing was a penthouse in the making. It was being constructed on top of an already existing building near the corner of Canal and Orchard streets. The building was being converted into condominiums selling for approximately $600,000 up to $1.6 million for the penthouse. I began filming from my window.

As I healed and started walking outside once again, taking a look around the streets, I saw more relentless changes happening at a disturbing rate of acceleration. Higher tops with added floors were beginning to appear on other buildings. Dozens of "for rent" and "for sale" signs waved from fire escapes. A formerly vacant lot was being dug up in preparation for a ten-story building. Each time I left my home, I would find some other area where more and more old buildings were being demolished. There was no indication of respect for preservation or landmarking, no consultation with the existing community. It is notable that while some of the buildings were in disrepair, many were simply financially viable commodities and it was open season. It was the beginning of the end of our neighborhood.

A friend observed that even 9/11 could not slow things down. The World Trade Center was sixteen blocks away and even such a nearby tragedy could not affect the developers' invasion. I perceived this onslaught as echoes of my family's past. The bulldozers, cranes, backhoes and scaffolds, and the constant daily noise of demolition and construction were an incursion — not of storm-troopers with guns — but of machines and money. Massive changes were coming and the people most affected by these changes were powerless, invisible and poor. I could do nothing to stop the metamorphosis of my neighborhood from a safe haven for immigrants into luxury homes and a playground for the wealthy. I had to do something; so I decided to save what I could, the only way I could, and that was by filming what still existed, before it disappeared.

When sunlight hits these old buildings, architectural details glow as if held within the light of memory itself. Using this beautiful light, I began filming the physical history of the Lower East Side: adorned cornices from the 1800's, chiseled ornaments around windows and doorways, Jewish stars and Hebrew letters on synagogues and walls, keystones and lintels with carved faces of men and women, real and mythic animals, gargoyles and angels. I filmed old store signs and faded ads painted on the walls of buildings. I filmed the daily signposts of the present immigrant history — laundry drying on rooftops, out windows and on fire escapes; dangling fish, hung on walls and out of windows to dry; murals celebrating the existence of culturally diverse community groups; and the myriad of creatively graffitied walls.

Recording the shattering of a beautiful old community is no compensation. As I went about filming, I also mourned the disappearing beauty of the delicate quality of light that still permeates these streets in early morning and early evening. As higher buildings rise on the Lower East Side, this luminosity will be shadowed and lost forever.

Much of what I filmed has already disappeared. This very special area, a two-hundred-year old sanctuary for immigrants is evaporating. The Lower East Side will no longer exist as an affordable place for those of moderate means. Not much of an inclusive community is left. The area is no longer a lifeline to new immigrants and artists. With skyrocketing rents, it's impossible for those who are here to remain much longer. As trendy bars, cafes, restaurants and boutiques continue to take over the local streetscape, it often appears that there is little or no respect for the historical environment or the surrounding community.

Newspaper articles about the Lower East Side's soaring celebrity have recently appeared. The Lower East Side has been lauded and promoted as "The New Bohemia," "New York's Groovers' Paradise," "Fashion's Frontier," "A Boulevard of Designer Restaurants," "The New Old World" and "Downtown's Hippest Address." The final blow — the last word and the worst stripping of my neighborhood's identity — has come from real-estate agents who have renamed the Lower East Side LOHO. As this community's name and spirit are gentrified, the message is clear; history is no longer of any importance.

Margot Niederland, *a first generation American, is an independent filmmaker, collage artist and photographer. She's lived on the LES since 1995. Her first film,* Broken Angel, *premiered at the Sundance Film Festival, followed by numerous screenings; around the world and in New York City venues including: The Metropolitan Museum of Art, the Museum of Modern Art, and the Pioneer Theatre. Since 1998, she's been working to capture visual historic remnants of the Jewish LES on film, before developers and gentrification destroy them forever.*

Merry Fortune *is an eco-centric poet, ghost writer, musician, and social activist of German and Native American descent. A new collection of her work titled* Poptones *is forthcoming from Straw Gate Books. A previous collection,* Ghosts By Albert Ayler, *was published in 2004 by Futurepoem books. She is a volunteer for the Leonard Peltier support group and is a registered Green. Merry was born in Brooklyn, New York, near Bergen Street.*

The Dream Life: The Lower East Side Jews In Hollywood

Rick Wirick

Between the wars, Jewish businessmen and artists converged upon the southern California land-scape like possessed daimons, ushering the region from an orange grove backwater to the transfiguring furnace of celluloid, the locus of what Norman Mailer called "The dream life of the race." Never had the diaspora been given such an empty, untested ground in which to work; never had a people so rich with storytellers been given the chance to do it with such enormous, inventive and transportable machinery.

Eight or nine Lower East Side immigrants effectively founded the modern film industry: Louis Mayer, Samuel Goldwyn, Joseph Loew, Carl Laemmle, Adolf Zukor, and the four Warner Broth-ers — Harry, Albert, Samuel, and Jack. They were fleeing not just their ethnic and historical ghosts, but were also leapfrogging the seemingly insurmountable professional obstacles domi-nating the East Coast movie-making business.

The cinema industry — though not large enough yet to be called that — was centered in New York City, and many of its shooting lots were near Ft. Lee, New Jersey. Epics were being churned out slowly and silently (the "talkies" were still a decade and a half away) on the cliffs of old mill towns above the Passaic and Kearny Rivers. (The most richly textured history of this time is contained in the anecdotes and asides of John Updike's novel *In The Beauty of The Lilies*, centering on the travails of a Mary Pickford-style silent screen actress who matrigenerates a film-making dynasty.)

There was one problem. Thomas Edison owned patents on the basic movie-making process, the manner in which a series of still photos were rapidly fed through projecting light plates to create the illusion of moving images. Edison's camera and projector manufacturers extracted punitive royalties on theater owners, many of them Jewish. It was before the Sherman and Clayton Anti-Trust Act, and the Edison Trust was, indeed, one of the country's first formalized restraints of trade, a truly ironclad, anti-competitive monopoly. At first these manufacturers banded together merely to enforce their royalty payments. But soon they resorted to threats, intimidation, and out-right brickbat violence. The Edison Trust was eventually shut down by federal marshals. But by then producers, directors and artists had been looking westward toward the Mexican border, contemplating escape from the Edison Trust's ferocious collection practices.

Thus began the small group of original production and distribution moguls. They ended up heading for southern California as a result of historical accident, intentional choices, and classic industrial war. The question became what they would do with it; how, exactly, would the East Coast Biograph model be transported to the reclaimed desert of the Los Angeles basin?

Another bit of happenstance gave a fresh boost to the Jewish businessmen who landed in Hollywood. After World War II, the French lost their short-lived monopoly on film production. French films, which had been widely circulated in the U.S., went on the wane. Each of the other world film capitals — Berlin, Moscow and Rome — was given an opportunity to model movie companies along the lines of manufacturers of large commodities and heavy industrial goods.

Movie production, then, could reorganize from its haphazard, tinhorn Biograph model to methodologies adopted by the makers of chemicals, steel, and other assembly-line paradigms. They could rationalize movies both for domestic and international sales. The early studio bosses saw how effortlessly automakers (and component part manufacturers) supplied materials to fulfill consumers' fantasies. But more importantly, they saw that design and content departments could literally *create* the yearnings of consumers. Electromechanical film and eventually celluloid would be the ultimate creator of imaginary worlds — not just of fanciful adjuncts, but of fantasies themselves.

1. The Technician: Marcus Lowe

One of the most representative of the Lower East Side Jewish businessmen was probably the least artistic and most commercial-minded: Marcus Lowe. But he fastened, with a vengeance, on those who were starting to Hellenize the industry with good writing and directorial vision. Lowe single-handedly, with a Zeus-like sweep, took vaudeville and early New York motion picture ventures into the first fully integrated film corporation. It was a company that became the primary vertically integrated entertainment conglomerate, if not in the world, certainly in the United States.

Lowe was born in the Lower East Side in 1870, the son of Viennese Jewish parents, with German ancestry on his mother's side. After quitting school and a brief run in the *schmata* trade, he joined up with an aspiring furrier, Adolph Zukor, who also had an interest in the cinematic experiments flowing from Berlin and Paris. (Zukor would later build Paramount, with its distinctly Hungarian executive beginning, but we get ahead of ourselves.)

Lowe and Zukor started the penny arcades of Times Square. They teamed with actor David Warfield to form the People's Vaudeville Company in 1904. They built four Manhattan amusement arcades, with a fifth in Cincinnati. The first cinematic presence in this author's home turf, the Cincinnati Penny Hippodrome, drew the largest crowds in the Midwest outside of Chicago, pulling in rivers of fans from northern Kentucky, Indiana, and the "sin capitals" of Parkerburg, West Virginia, and Steubenville, Ohio. Cincinnati, ironically, was the capstone in the (still) bicoastal empire Loew, Zukor and Warfield had sown the seeds for.

In 1919, Loew further expanded by purchasing Metro Pictures Corporation, which had been formed in 1915 to produce and market the films of fine small Hollywood producers. His link to the West Coast was established; the footprint that would change everything came down like a stamping boot in the basin dust.

Loew came to Hollywood on marathon train journeys with balance books spread out on his lap in the dining car. His meetings with accountants and bankers in these first trips gave rise to the new, reorganized Loew's Inc., which moved Loew full steam into the Western (soon to be the only) motion picture business. The first film he had his hand in, *The Four Horsemen of the Apocalypse*, starring Rudolf Valentino, was an enormous hit. Metro Inc. straddled the new "world of shadows" like a colossus.

By 1924, Loew had sufficient capital to acquire the foundering Goldwyn Pictures Corporation and Louis B. Meyer Productions. Goldwyn had an enormous studio in Culver City, and a supervisory production team that included the production wunderkind Irving Thalberg. On May 17, 1924, Loew's biggest subsidiary, Metro-Goldwyn-Mayer, was born into the incubator of a film-crazy, worldwide audience.

With the creation of MGM, the focus had shifted from theater ownership to the West Coast production facilities. The Culver Studio, begun by film invention wizard Thomas Ince in 1915, grew like a leviathan under Loew's management for the next seven years. Its forty-five acres of back lots became the largest self-contained production unit of the early studio era. It was also a bona fide industry with physical plant rivaling that of the Pittsburgh steel mills and the Northwest logging camps, carrying trolleys of people from location to location through the long Culver City afternoons.

Loew next brought out the silent *Ben Hur*, the film of which he was most proud. Within two years he would be dead, the first of the major Jewish film moguls to pass away. Nicholas Schenk succeeded him as president of the company from 1927 to 1955. But it was Thalberg that sharpened MGM into the most artistically and financially successful studio of the Depression.

2. "L.B."

Not far behind Lowe was Louis B. Mayer. Born in Minsk, his family immigrated to New Brunswick, Canada, where he attended the local schools. Louis was repulsed by the scrap metal business his father started, and set off for Boston in his late teens. With his first bit of savings, he bought his first movie theater in Haverhill and within a few years had the largest theater chain in New England. Mayer was impressed with the acumen of Dick Rowland, owner of numerous nickelodeon parlors (much like Lowe) in New York City, and teamed with him in 1916 to form Metro Pictures Corporation. Within two year, they had bought their first Hollywood studio.

Mayer stepped out of this partnership for a time to form Louis B. Mayer pictures, his own production firm, in 1920. Then came the inevitable collaboration with B.P."Bud" Schulberg and the formation of the Mayer-Schulberg Studio. Then, in 1924, Loew stepped in to buy Louis B. Mayer Pictures and as part of the deal made Mayer head of the new Metro-Goldwyn-Mayer.

That is all it took — L.B. was in the driver's seat. Once in California, which L.B. found particularly to his liking, he built MGM into the most financially successful motion picture studio in the world. The film industry, a respite for weary and hopeless workers in the midst of the Depression, continued to do well during those years and even paid dividends on its stock. MGM took on Irving Thalberg as production chief in 1932, lured by his promise of making the country's great literary works into equally salient celluloid monuments.

The problem was that Thalberg's fondness for Fitzgerald, Dos Passos, Dreiser and others did not result in "getting butts into seats" (Mayer's gospel tagline). Thalberg was unable to find screenwriters who could zest up droll fictions with sufficient box office appeal and make them "star vehicles" for the studio, a star reliant approach which his studio was the first to operate under and which would eventually threaten to ossify that system. When Thalberg had a heart attack at a fairly young age, Mayer grabbed the reins and had him ousted, then appointed himself production supervisor in 1936. By this time, the Dream Life was fulfilling America's escape fantasies with the "MGM Musical" that nearly made the two terms synonymous. Before that, and as the first studio chief making more that a million dollars a year, Mayer had signed — in serious dramatic and comedy roles — the likes of Lon Chaney, Joan Crawford, Hepburn and Tracey, Clark Gable and Greta Garbo.

Mayer had a Svengali-like, mesmerizing presence with many of the stars who signed with him, including with Katherine Hepburn, who personally negotiated her own contracts with him. A Bryn Mawr grad, she famously quipped, "I don't need a Philadelphia lawyer — I am one." Other female stars saw him as a father figure. Debbie Reynolds, June Allison and Leslie Caron used him as *pater substitutus* before embarking on the same course with their romances, resulting often in chains of disastrous marriages. Mayer was charming, genteel and dignified, an incurable flirt. And, putting aside the railroad and mining barons, he was the richest man West of the Mississippi.

Nicholas Schenk was brought in as president of Loew's, which technically owned MGM. As the '40s progressed and new, more upbeat appetites evolved in the post-war years, MGM suffered dropoffs in its success. Schenk made much of the fact that MGM had garnered few Oscars in the '40s, and none at all in the critical three years from the close of the war to 1948. As friction developed with Schenk, Mayer hedged his bets by promising to hire another "Big Idea Man," a "New Thalberg," who would make "message pictures" and tackle grave themes, in addition to making the "wholesome" pictures for which Mayer had become famous.

The "New Thalberg" was Dore Schary, a Yalie who tried to adapt some of the same classics to the screen that Thalberg had failed with. Schary wanted to scrap the "wholesome" menu of Mayer almost entirely, and soon the two of them could barely stand one another. Always open to brinksmanship, Mayer pushed and pushed for the "backlist" of musicals and romances he had given the public for 24 years. Besides, Schary was twenty years Mayer's junior, and had more fight in him than the old man could have anticipated.

When Schary moved for a new set of psychological thrillers and the first WW II pictures, leaving only one or two "light" Mayer-type items per year, Mayer decided to draw a line in the sand. He walked into Schenk's office at Loew's headquarters in Times Square and said of Schary, "It's either him or me." Schenk looked at the numbers and fired Mayer immediately. The latter's attempt at a boardroom coup failed utterly, and Mayer left the post he had occupied for nearly three decades.

Mayer was a richly rounded man, an eclectic, and the loss of his film empire did not at first seem to faze him that much. He had two daughters. They, too, were to follow into the Hollywood dynasty. The eldest(from a first marriage), Edith, married William Goetz, who went on to become president of Universal Pictures with some MGM seed money. (Mayer and Edie eventually became estranged, however, and he came to loathe Goetz; Edie was disinherited.) His other daughter, Irene, married David O. Selznick. She was an instrumental force in helping her husband propel Paramount to the forefront of the studios.

Mayer loved horses from his early years as a child going to Belmont. Soon after establishing his fortune, he bought a 504-acre horse ranch near Perris, California, some 70 miles east of Los Angeles. His biographer claims he "almost single-handedly" raised the standards of the California racing business to a point where the eastern horse racing establishment had to pay attention. He owned several Preakness Stakes winners, and in 1947, just before his precipitous fall with Schenk and to finance an impending divorce, he sold his nearly 300 horses for the then-princely sum of $4.4 million.

3. The Lone Wolf

Of the Big Three, Sam Goldwyn was the most fated for success, brimming with destiny, diving into the processes that would mold him. His New York drawl hung onto him like a cloak, a mantle of protection and rarefied direction.

Goldwyn was born in Warsaw in 1879, a child of the Pale of Settlement, who came to the Lower East Side at 13 in 1892. Like Mayer, his father was in the *schmata* trade, and he began his career in glovemaking and sales. He was fascinated by commodity volumes, the transfer of units of goods, and developed methods of custom glove fitting to special markets without sacrificing the overarching goal of volume and delivery velocity.

> The overwhelming goal was to get "hands in gloves" - - to deliver a kind of art, something delicate and beautiful, but to deliver it rapidly, massively, profitably.

Within a decade, Goldwyn found a "real filmmaker and producer," Cecil B. DeMille, and founded, with his brother-in-law, his first film group in 1916, the Jesse L. Lasky Film Play Company. The second company, Goldwyn Pictures Corp., merged with Metro, which in turn merged with the firm founded by Louis B. Mayer to become Metro-Goldwyn-Mayer. This "first trifecta" gave him the trajectory to become a studio mogul, which he most certainly was. But he was iconoclastic down to the last atom — he claimed if came from his family's resistance to Tsarist and Cossack occupiers. He was the ultimate studio man, but almost immediately defined himself as the anti-organization man; the embodiment of Kierkegaard's maxim that "the crowd is Untruth."

It was just that Goldwyn had the "lone wolf" in him down to the last corpuscle. He was also famously unable to get along with partners. His brother-in-law Lasky was difficult enough to deal with. Mayer was no easier. The large studio environmental carried along the Laskys and Mayers like sleepy surface fish, but for the "Goldfish," the deep, cold water was where good art and abiding entertainment would be found

By 1923, he had irritated his partners nearly to the point of being forced out of MGM. The only solution was to form Samuel Goldwyn, Inc., the first true "Indie" company that would form the mold for all future stand-alone producers.

When asked about his obsession with departures and thirst for independence, if not isolation, Goldwyn said, "I found that it took a world of time trying to explain my plans to my associates. Now, I have discovered I can save vast amounts of time and energy, and put it into making better pictures."

The Lone Wolf soon found fellow independent spirits and explorers of what he called [one of his many misnomers] the "inside landscape." Douglas Fairbanks, Jr., Charles Chaplin, and Mary Pickford had just founded United Artists, the ostensible reason for studio creation being all other studio's inability to pay the trios' collective or individual salaries. He loved Chaplin, welcomed Pickford's guarded flirtations, and valued what he saw of the businessman in Fairbanks, a thespian with strong vanities. By August 1925, he began releasing his films exclusively through United Artists.

After that point, Goldwyn stayed with independent production for a solid, successful 30 years. Iconoclastic spirits like Norma Shearer and Irving Thalberg saw him as Moses, the one who could part the bureaucratic, needlessly layered studio waters and get at the basic engine that could propel a picture forward. Many independents that followed, including David O. Selznick, Walter Wanger, and even Walt Disney, operated their business after the Goldwyn model.

In one form or another, the Sam Goldwyn Company lived through its eponym for another 35 years. It still exists, a tad under New Line and a hair above Fine Line, having outlived Global, Sirius, Canyon Films, Orion, and even Miramax, whose brother-founders modeled their first company on the industry's "great independent."

The most authoritative biography is still Scotty Berg's (the son of the ICM founder), where one can track Goldwyn's fascinating marriage to the much younger Frances Howard, and his desperate relationship with his two tortured children. Berg assesses him as an essentially self-educated (some would say uneducated) man who shuttled the most accomplished artists of his day into excellent pictures. Not only did he get the money, but he hired the most accomplished writers of his time: Sidney Howard, Ben Hecht, Robert Sherwood, and Lillian Hellman. He nurtured directors like John Ford, King Vidor, Howard Hawks, Rouben Mamoulian and William Wyler, the lot of whom opened their lenses on Vilma Banky, Gary Cooper, Merle Oberon, Barbara Stanwyck, Laurence Olivier and Danny Kaye.

When all was said and done, it was the Goldwyn logo that rolled up out of the darkness to promise brilliant, consistent quality: the gilded wreath, the roaring lion, and finally what we have today – the hammered gold and gold enameling of his signature, glimmering and alone in the new world.

Richard Wirick is the author of the memoir and story collection One Hundred Siberian Postcards, a London Times Notable Book of 2007, which has now been translated into four languages. His new collection, Kicking In, was published in 2009. He writes and practices law in Los Angeles, where he lives with his family.

The Given Word

Ken Jacobs

In the early '60s there was a middle-aged bohemian fellow I would sometimes chance to meet. Possibly a Jew like myself, but, if so, Jewishness was something long subsumed into his character; he was another art-minded intellectual at odds with capitalism and capitalist culture. I recognized this but had little patience for him, holding against him his determination to be interesting. Now I think how he had to have come up through the '30s and '40s, tough times, while I only had to endure rotten times, and how I could've been a bit more forbearing. He was a failure in my eyes because he was not so exceptional as to not need other people's approval. He urged me to see a storefront he was renting that he proclaimed, "sold nothing" — that was good — though it might eventually shape up as a coffeeshop (flash! East Village begins invasion of Lower East Side). He was paying neighborhood kids to bring him used coffee grounds – fifty cents for a one-pound can, pretty good money in those days – which he'd immediately pour out onto the floor of his no-merchandise store, there to dry and lighten in color. There was already a thick brown loam of grounds covering the floor, actually quite beautiful. It was, of course, an early dismissed-from-history earth-works and I'm not proud of myself for not valuing it more when seeing it then.

I was standing with my face in my reading on a crowded bus but I could see him working his way towards me. Not speaking while facing each other, we stood shaking and bobbing together to the irregular movements of the bus. Then, just before stepping off, he leaned towards me and whispered (I see his dopey smug face now), "The word is ... ineffable." I had a reaction of disdain, it was so arty a gesture. And yet there was no preventing it from sinking in and there's been no thinking of the word since then without thinking of him, and – curses – it's a word that someone in my line has to consider often. I'd been making *Baudelairian Capers*, determined to *allude to* and to not *say* things, and the ineffable was already much on my mind. What's called the Holocaust was still recent and many of us were still working at grasping its scope and reality. I wished only to *indicate*, only that was adequately respectful of what had happened, or conversely to lie big time (another fool had suggested I film "the revenge of Anne Frankenstein" and after the shock wore off, I decided to go with it) with the understanding that my blatant lie would be seen through and the unspeakable reality would surface to mind. This I was thinking is where art comes in, as a way to evoke or to pay homage to the unutterable, even by way of purposeful bad taste. Art is not expression but repression of emotion. The nerve then of this affected guy to position himself as angelic agent of something so crucial!

COMPRENEZ VOUS YIDDISH?

Flo and I often went to what had become the Village Theater before it further succumbed to the changes time had wrought upon the Lower East Side and became the Fillmore East. Management had dared to revive Yiddish vaudeville, alternating Yiddish-language movies with variety acts starring old-timers who had known the theater from when the clientele were just off the boat like themselves. There were also some young performers refreshingly disobliged from adherence to the Hebrew persuasion. The old movies only sometimes had subtitles so I would often be whispering rough and sketchy translations into Flo's ear, limited to a 7-year-old's vocabulary. My early years were in a Yiddish-speaking household in Williamsburg, where my grandfather took me by the hand to the Marcy on Sundays to see a Yiddish weepie double-billed with a Hopalong Cassidy. Though I'd often be playing under the seats during the features some had left impressions, mysterious disembodied cine-ghosts that I longed to meet with again. (A man has returned from prison to find the tenement gone that housed his family. He sits on the curb, head buried in his arms. Kids sit on curbs, not grown men. I learn this scene is from *Without a Home* and later, reading Hoberman's *Bridge of Light*, learn that it was the last Yiddish film out of Poland.)

The benumbed Lower East Side streets had begun flaming back to life. The '60s had just turned on (decades distinguish themselves when almost halfway through) and the streets were filling with young people dressed in thrift-shop outfits as their everyday party clothes. The dress-up, in-your-face street-theater Jack and I had fooled with (see *Star Spangled to Death*) was taking hold. I churlishly commented about how "things spread and sink" but lovely girls were everywhere, without bras, who directly met your gaze, while in the '50s I'd walked night after night through a sexual desert. This was better and do we miss it now, this widespread yen to achieve distinctiveness (if not personality, something reserved for genius). Second Avenue and Eighth Street was a hub with every sort of junk spread out for sale on Second both day and night. I'd meet Jack's creation Francis Francine (Frank DiGiovani, who had thrilled Jack with the anatomical trickery that had allowed him to pass sideshow inspection). Frank was selling his mother's old crap, having finally – in his fifties – broken the buck-and-a-quarter limit to his hourly earnings. *Flaming Creatures* had made him an Underground celebrity and he was in his element, excitedly bad-mouthing Jack about not seeing a penny from the film, hawking shmattas and imbecile knickknacks from a cloth spread flat on the pavement.

Things quieted quickly moving south to Sixth and away from the lights. People aged even more quickly, growing smaller and speaking quaintly. You could hear in their voices stickball Brooklyn during the Great Depression, Mayor LaGuardia, the famous war against fascism (had we only seen Bush-Cheney coming we could've surrendered then). A full house every time and it was a big theater. I may have been mature on Eighth Street at age 31 but we were both self-consciously young in this crowd, and exceptionally tall. English was spoken, murmured, but one could feel the hunger to again immerse in Yiddish. I knew these people, knew their ways; we had long rejected each other, at every bris, (before I refused to attend), bar mitzvah, wedding, where we'd been stuck with each other after an exchange of maybe 20 words. I also recognized them each and every one from waiting table upstate in the Catskills, with me returning to the city each time certifiably nuts. Flo would have to massage my neck and shoulders, talk me down from shouting. These were the people who thought art was fine but not something you did for a living. Now we were sharing a theater but a slight shift in time and space and we'd be interred together as per Hermann Goering's pronouncement, "I decide who is a Jew." That would've made me sulk but now they were okay, I had to admit, now that they weren't asking for more prunes.

1964 to 2007. They're gone now, too, but at least from "natural causes."

We loved the vivacity of the old performers, doing their stage-acts from when the Lower East Side had been a Jewish world complete unto itself. Back on their own stage-boards from when they'd been all piss and vinegar, they had to have known this was their last outing from the throwaway bin they'd been consigned to. Their sturdy routines still supported them. Jacob Jacobs in his seventies (it was announced) buck and winging – sort of – across the stage, arms flapping to busy the eyes so it wouldn't be noticed this was no dance at all. Leo Fuchs, still lean and dapper, our Yiddisha Fred Astaire. Miriam Kressyn was a regular at these shows with her truly beautiful voice. One imagined them performing one step in advance of their final heart seizures, plopping into offstage chairs to breathe, breathe … a little longer. They gave us all they had, wonderful mad egotists. Who could ask for anything more?

There was also The Fibbich Dancers, also regulars. Flo and I watched fascinated and appalled as each week these hopelessly sincere and maladapted young dreamers of a wonderfully ecumenical mix, some swishy, some black, did their enthusiastic versions of European folk dances. Camp beyond camp, because unintended.

Many in the audience left when the old movies came on. Too bad for them. Every one of the cheaply made and mostly awkward films was precious and revealing to us. After all, I was the champion of Oscar Micheaux, cine-blunderer par excellence, writing and directing his witless masterpieces under the tutelage of Sigmund Freud. Outstanding of course was *Green Fields* directed by Edgar Ulmer, *The Dybbuk* and *Tevye*. A surprise was *His Wife's Lover*, the first Yiddish talkie, a musical shot in 1931 right there on Second Avenue starring brilliant comedian Ludwig Satz and classic "Jewess" Lucy Levin(e) with her strong operetta voice. And with Isidore Cashier as a sort of Mephistopheles, "the man with no faith in women." Five years later, with my first paycheck from Binghamton University, I purchased a 16mm. print of it. (Joseph Seiden wanted me to buy one of his own directorial efforts. Addled by the recent loss of his wife, he'd already lost the storage ticket to another Satz movie and he scrapped the negative to this one after printing my copy.)

Allow me to explain my fascination with things Jewish: I despise, then as now, every manifestation of religion along with every other rigid ideology. When I chance upon some screwball or thug pushing religion on the radio or TV, I hear pathology. But Jews are a lot more than religion. I was shocked to learn about this minority-thing after growing up among Jews in Williamsburg, spill-off of the Lower East Side to just across the East River; I thought they were *people*. They were nice. Berry and South Tenth was crime-free; kids went out to play on their own as soon as they understood not to cross the street unsupervised. I saw my first cop at age five, a red-faced man from Mars all in blue. The synagogue was pleasant (though God went out of my life with the Easter bunny), the young rabbi concerned with real issues. A story he told probably decided my entire direction in life and I'll repeat it here. A man notices a boy with a mirror standing in the street every day at the same time. Curious, he finally asks the boy why he's doing this. The boy points out that the street, alongside a hospital, is narrow. His brother is a patient in the hospital. They are poor and the room he's in is always dark. But at this time each day he can reflect sunlight into his brother's room.

Around 1945 or '46 I found my grandmother tearful (but she was always tearful then). She'd gotten a photo from a cousin in Europe she was helping with money and packages. The photo was of a man and his young daughter, dressed neatly, staring ahead fearfully. They were living skeletons seated in front of a photographer's painted backdrop of swans in a lake.

Flo's Jewishness had in fact been a hurdle. Her too-familiar ways, problems, her parents, feh! I'd mostly gone with Italian girls, close enough to Jews to be understood yet at the same time coming from a whole other set of crazy-making strictures.

Religious study offers one significant historical fact: the theological recipe of the Jews, a conglomerate of near-Eastern lore plus monotheism, was grabbed up by Christians and later by Muslims with Jews being punished for not recognizing their savior in Jesus, as if that makes any sense. Jews remain a key to the understanding of the debacle of Western history at the same time that the minutiae of belief is a dead end, a morbid study (Freud got it right on this one) of hysteria, neurotic compulsion and murderous defensiveness. So for a long time, even as I was learning something of the mechanics of art and my mind was on abstract developments, Jews would enter into the work under cover of my subconscious. My first short was *Orchard Street*, 1954, when the outdoor market still had some of its cardboard signs handwritten in Yiddish. As late as 1986, I shot the material for *The Alps and the Jews*, a film I put aside when a European friend convinced me its message could make problems for people outside safe (for us) New York. But that's it, I neither seek out or avoid Jews for friends, don't put it on our kids to "remain loyal" in choosing mates, and the state of Israel –America's Igor – repulses me. As do most states but I'm as disappointed with Israel as with USA. Amy Goodman makes me feel good, the neo-cons lousy, meaning connection still exists. Jews *are* people, which other people want to draw a line around, and they're counter-fucked-up enough to again make the line a physical wall.

Exposure to the old performers got to me. If *His Wife's Lover* was the first Yiddish movie, I'd better be hurrying to make *The Last Yiddish Movie*. Jacob Jacobs was going to buck and wing right off the stage to his demise (only a few years later we did read of his dying). I'd film in 16, in-sync and non-sync, catch the old people on and off-stage, visit Miami where they could still get gigs in the nursing homes, catch them on film in and out of their personas. Study the animals in their habitat and go – cinematically – where chance/actuality led, juggling it all into shape on the editing table. But this was the last moment, while they still could be *impossible people*, not docile, not yet beaten.

Money. Underground filmmakers were getting some attention via Jonas Mekas's column in *The Village Voice* but Flo and I were still handsome and oddly well-spoken paupers. I thought that as irregular as the film I was groping towards might be, it would be heavy with truth and there was an audience out there that needed nothing less. I decided to go to the office of the Jewish Actors Union, where comparatively young Seymour Rexite was president. He was on radio then, WEBD (The Station That Speaks Your Language), daily, I think, with wife Miriam Kressyn. He had to have been involved in arranging the revivals at the theater. He was an energetic "macher," someone who made things happen, with his entire life in theater (he could be seen as a chubby distressed boy in the old movies where he was required again and again to emotionally spill his guts). The small office was – mmm – unprepossessing. There was one other person there who never spoke but looked at me fish-eyed. Neatly suited Rexite was being quick with me but I got out a description of the film I had (burning!) in mind. Then he asked – the only thing he asked – was what was my source of backing? I explained that was why I was seeing him, that with his backing I was sure money could be raised. He snapped, Come back when you have money." He turned his attention to fish-eye and I understood I was dismissed. Short shrift. Another nutcase he had to deal with. Couldn't he see something of my passion, that I was an artist? That there was a crying need for this documentation and it was now or never?

I began filming *The Sky Socialist* on 8mm Kodachrome with Flo playing Anne Frank, now that the obligation to preserve something of the past, or concern about any future for myself, no longer interfered.

Ken Jacobs: *Born, 1933, Brooklyn, New York. Studied painting with Hans Hofmann, 1956-57. Started making films, 1955. Created/Directed The Millennium Film Workshop, N.Y.C. 1966-68; started the Department of Cinema at S.U.N.Y. at Binghamton, 1969; Professor of Cinema 1974-2000; Distinguished Prof. of Cinema, 2000- ; Prof. Emeritus 2002*

Grants and Awards (a selection): D.A.A.D. 1986; Maya Deren Award 1994; J.S. Guggenheim Fellowship 1995; N.E.A. 1995; The Rockefeller Foundation special grant 1999; NYFA 2001; NYSCA 2001, 2007; NYSCA distribution grant 2002; Fund For Jewish Documentary Filmmaking 2003; Stan Brakhage Vision Award 2004; Los Angeles Film Critics Association - The Douglas Edwards Experimental/Independent Film/Video Award 2004 (for Star Spangled To Death); Il Cinema Ritrovato DVD Awards 2006 III edizione, Bologna (special mention/experimental for Star Spangled To Death); renew media (Rockefeller Foundation) grant 2007, Oberhausen prize of the Jury of the Minister President of North Rhine-Westphalia, May 2007; awarded Great Prize –15th Curtas Vila do Conde, Portugal, July 2007, Gran Prix (one of 3) 25 FPS Festival, Zagreb, Croatia, October, 2007; awarded Best Experimental short film Curta Cinema, Dec. 2007, Rio De Janeiro Int. Short Film Fest.; Tom, Tom, The Piper's Son named to the National Film Registry, Dec. 27, 2007

On Being a Jew On The Lower East Side

Jacob Burckhardt

A few years ago you invited me to write an article for the collection *Captured* about film making on the Lower East Side. I had a good story to tell (I think) about my experiences making a feature movie there in the eighties. Then you asked me to write about being part of the Jewish experience in the neighborhood, and I'm finding it more difficult.

For one thing, why did you ask me? Why did you think I'm Jewish? The sound of my name? Jacob Burckhardt is actually an old Swiss Protestant name. But it does sound Germanic and therefore maybe Jewish. Or do I act it?

I've always felt ambivalent about this issue, and this is a good opportunity to talk about it.

When I mentioned this to my mother, she said, "What do you know about being a Jew? You don't know anything. You don't even know what *Kaddish* is." Indeed, I have almost no first hand knowledge about it. I've never seen the inside of a synagogue, at least not during a service.

My mother's family were German Jews. My grandmother's grandfather sailed to California during the gold rush, got rich (not as a prospector but running a grocery store), returned to Offenbach, started a socialist newspaper, and lived into the early 20th century. My grandparents were completely assimilated members of the bourgeoisie – my grandfather ran a leather goods factory with over two hundred employees.

Then, late in the thirties, first my mother, then my grandparents and my uncle managed to escape (not without help from some German non-Jewish friends) first to England and then to the U.S., except for my grandfather, who died in England. My grandmother became a U.S. citizen, and never voted, never set foot in a synagogue again, yet never forgot or hid that she was both a Jew and a German. Until her age made it too difficult, she would travel to Europe every summer, visiting friends and family (my father's side) in Switzerland, Germany and Italy.

At first my mother hung around with German political émigrés here, but by then had became a confirmed artist. This is in the sense of a belief, or way of life, like being a Communist or a Buddhist. Her life has been centered on painting paintings, looking at and seeing art, and writing about it. She has an amazing recall of all the art she has seen in her life, and is writing an auto-biography that tells some stories of her travels in Europe before the war and more about her life in the New York Art world in the forties and fifties.

My father came from a Swiss Protestant family, but had left Switzerland to get away from all that, and to also follow the way of art. My parents met here.

By the time I started going to school, I went to Anglican church schools, not for religious reasons, according to my parents, but because they happened to be good schools. They and I also enjoyed the pomp of chapel every morning just like in one of the old paintings. I was in a boys' choir, and part of the fun of it was parading around the church in ecclesiastical drag.

So I was exposed to a lot of religion in school, enough to inoculate me against any religious fanaticism but, at the same time. I learned a lot of the old stories, and got a working knowledge of Judeo-Christian culture. However, I could never get myself to believe the central mysteries of religion, and now consider myself an Atheist.

So when someone asks me if I am Jewish, I have to answer, "Yes and no." Yes, because legally I am, as Jewishness is carried through the mother, and I certainly do not wish to renounce the distant relatives, including my great grandmother, who were killed; and no, because I've never seen the business side of a synagogue, not been bar mitzvah'ed, and, as I said already, I consider myself an atheist, and think that religions have been a source of a lot of bad things in history (but that's another story).

Once I was in Munich for a film festival. There was an opportunity to visit Dachau with some French Jewish filmmakers. I couldn't go because I knew, in some unexplainable way, that I would not be able to face my mother or grandmother if I had. Indeed, they did get furious at another family member who did.

How being this kind of Jew/Goy has affected my life on the Lower East Side? Not much – it's New York, nobody seems to notice.

One thing that does make me proud of being a Jew is the race's sense of humor, the jokes. Gary Goldberg, a great Lower East Side Jewish filmmaker, and I used to share a lot of Jewish jokes. Then one day, after we had been friends for years, he was amazed: "You mean you're one, too?" While until then I had never explicitly told him, I hadn't hid it from him. I probably would have felt more awkward telling him all those jokes had I been a goy.

The only time I remember denying it was when a couple of guys in front of a Mitzvah tank asked me, "Are you Jewish?" and I said, "No! I'm a Roman Catholic!"

As the dyslexic rabbi said, "Yo! Yo!"

Shalom! Jacob.

Jacob Burckhardt is a filmmaker who has been living on the Lower East side since the early eighties. He also mixes sound for movies professionally, and designs sound tracks for performance. He directed and produced two features: It Don't Pay to be an Honest Citizen (shot in pre-fashionable Red Hook Brooklyn) and Landlord Blues (shot all over the East Village in 1986). Both films screened at various international festivals and were distributed on video. In 1990 he and Mr. Fashion made The Frankie Lymons Nephew Story, and with Roy Scott, he made Louis the Fourteenth Street (2004), and a detective story, Tomorrow Always Comes (2006). Over the years he has made short, poetic, films such as Windmill for Polly (1976), Black and White (2001), Roma (2004), and The Surface (2007-8 and ongoing).

Part 7: Photography

Robert Frank, Gunslinger with Camera

Jerome Poynton
Edited by Loretta Farb

Robert Frank is generally not interested in being profiled in print. Publicity is a double-edged sword and when you've had your fill – it can often cut the other way – even a mohel's hand can slip.

In 1947 Robert Frank arrived in New York from Switzerland with his camera. His first photo job was shooting Moe, Larry and Curly – *The Three Stooges* – on a bus tour from high school to high school in Queens.

At each stop the Stooges disembarked to a throng of high school students and the Stooges would play their antics – punch each other's eyes out, pratfalls – etc. Back on the bus, Frank told me, the Stooges would speak of the boys and girls with absolute contempt.

Welcome to America.

Maybe it was this early exposure to the duplicity of success that framed Robert Frank's vision of America – and success – and gave him the necessary tools to remain an enigma sixty years later.

Frank received a Guggenheim grant on the recommendation of photographer Walker Evans in the '50s. With this honor in hand Frank set off on a road trip around, across and through the 48 states of the United States of America. Cameras were still not an everyday item for an American in the 1950s. Frank photographed with impunity – few sour glances – although several times he was asked to leave – once at the Ford Motor plant at River Rouge, Michigan, where a supervisor feared he might be a Communist.

After all, Frank did speak with an accent.

Father Coughlin, the Catholic priest in sync with Wisconsin's Senator Joe McCarthy, was based in Michigan and had a weekly radio address where he preached many of McCarthy's fears.

The Guggenheim introduction didn't look proper to people who listened to Father Coughlin or Senator Joe McCarthy. Frank was hustled off Ford's premises but not before he took some timeless portraits of life at River Rouge. It should be noted that at River Rouge Ford Motor Company incorporated all phases of auto production. Iron ore was shipped in to make steel, there was a glass making plant on premise and River Rouge had its own power and cement plants. Chemical by-products were sent to another part of the nearly 16 million square feet of plant space to produce paint. Over 90 miles of railroad track and conveyor belts connected the facility. Nearly every aspect of making an automobile was on-site.

Welcome to America in the 1950s.

Frank assembled his photos into a book with the simple title: *The Americans*. Robert Delpire, a French publisher, published *The Americans* in Paris in 1958. Frank asked Jack Kerouac to write an introduction for the American edition, published one year later by Grove Press:

"The gasoline monsters stand in New Mexico flats under big sign says SAVE – the sweet little white baby in the black nurse's arms both of them bemused in Heaven, a picture that should have been blown up and hung in the street of Little Rock showing love under the sky and in the womb of our universe the Mother – And the loneliest picture ever made, the urinals that women never see, the shoeshine going on in sad eternity –

Wow, and blown over Chinese cemetery flowers in a San Francisco hill being hammered by potatopatch fog on a March night I'd say nobody there but the rubber cat –

Anybody doesnt like these pitchers dont like potry, see? Anybody dont like potry go home see Television shots of big hatted cowboys being tolerated by kind horses.

Robert Frank, Swiss, unobtrusive, nice, with that little camera that he raises and snaps with one hand he sucked a sad poem right out of America onto film, taking rank among the tragic poets of the world.

To Robert Frank I now give this message: You got eyes.

And I say: That little ole lonely elevator girl looking up sighing in an elevator full of blurred demons, what's her name & address?"

— Jack Kerouac
Excerpt from The Americans

The photos in Robert Frank's *The Americans* are almost inseparable from Kerouac's introduction. At no point were two artists – one visual and the other literary – such a perfect match.

At the time of publication Kerouac's fame was skyrocketing from *On The Road* though his relationship with Frank was probably more grounding than what he had with others in his peer group. Frank and Kerouac were both outsiders. They were both second to the English language, yet they found themselves immersed in New York's premier literary society of the day – and quickly surpassed their peers.

After initial criticism, *The Americans* went through the cultural roof and has since become the standard from which all other photography books are judged.

Born in 1924, Robert Frank will be 84 years old on November 9, 2008. Kerouac will have been dead for 39 years from "the drink." While Kerouac never learned how to live with notoriety, Frank spent a lifetime avoiding notoriety's corrosive effect.

Frank joined Kerouac's marvelous use of language and Allen Ginsberg's penchant to play the lead in front of a camera in the 1959 film *Pull My Daisy*. Kerouac wrote the voice over and Ginsberg acted with fellow poet Gregory Corso, art dealer Richard Bellamy and painters Alice Neel and Larry Rivers, with a wonderful score by David Amram.

Pull My Daisy was co-directed with artist Alfred Leslie. Many of Frank's films were done in collaboration with others – Rudy Wurlitzer, Danny Seymour and Gary Hill come to mind – yet in the end they are all Robert Frank films. While collaboration is important to Frank as a filmmaker, he would never use collaboration to dilute the message, only strengthen the brew. (Wurlitzer's films, *Two Lane Blacktop*, *Pat Garrett & Billy the Kid*, *Candy Mountain*, *Walker* and others he scripted also carry a unifying thread.)

"There were moments working with him," Wurlitzer wrote in an e-mail, "that were totally and spontaneously pure and rare, as long as one sublimated oneself to his relentless will, and managed to sneak in a few contributions along the way. Not easy, but I'm grateful for the time we spent together, traveling and working."

"Robert always held to his own integrity," Wurlitzer continued. "He took no prisoners and dealt with the shadow world, loss and despair, friend and foe, with romantic and sometimes ruthless passion. One way or the other, he survived. Not a small feat given the casualty list in this end-times culture we're experiencing."

Robert Frank has lived the majority of these "end-times" on the Lower East Side. He escaped to the then desolate area – first the Bowery and then just a few buildings off the Bowery – after the dissolution of his first marriage.

Frank fit in to living on the Bowery, where restaurant supply houses stood next to hotels for the homeless and the alcoholic.

Walking along the street one day, Frank was approached by a Bowery resident. Frank was eating a sandwich.

"Where are they giving away sandwiches today?" the man asked Frank.

"I'll give you half," Frank replied realizing the similarity of their dress.

Years later, as the neighborhood began to gentrify, Frank began to be recognized.

"Hey," the garbage man said to Frank. "I saw you on TV last night. You're famous."

"So what?" Frank replied.

"Yeah, but you got a full half hour," the worker responded as the truck pulled away from the curb.

Robert Frank's films – *About Me, A Musical* and *Billy of the Bowery* – captured something of Bowery life. Many of his other films used the Lower East Side – *One Hour, Candy Mountain* – for primary locations. One of my favorites, *OK End Here*, was shot at the then new NYU housing on Bleecker Street off Mercer.

In still photography, Frank's images often capture the awkward moment in life, at a fork in the road, before a decision is made – *4 AM Make Love to Me* – and at other times capture his own deep romanticism as in *Sick of Goodbyes* or *Look Out for Hope*.

"You cannot compromise," Frank told me while filming *Candy Mountain*. "You compromise once and they [the producers] will come back and ask for more."

Another time during production, a location scout brought a selection of location photos for Frank to choose from for a scene scripted to take place in a lawyer's office. The locations were uniformly clean and sterile. There was a Wall Street office, a corporate boardroom office, a lawyer's office lined with books, etc.

"I have no objection to using a cliché," Frank said, flipping through the pictures, "but you have to give me a reason for it."

Every artist is exploitive of his own life and Frank's life is a document of both hope and sadness evidenced in the death of his daughter at an early age and his son's decades of living in a dark swirl of schizophrenia, which impacted every facet of Frank's family and professional life. There is probably no other artist who unabashedly looked inward to capture the intimacy of his life under such heart-wrenching circumstances.

Frank is a romantic in reverse and a consumer of non-consuming. He has the decadence of someone who can spend, but doesn't. He is a harmless man equipped with a flame-thrower, surrounded by parched earth. Frank's landscape is littered with singed court documents. Law suits. Judgments against adversaries and the many who have tried to rip him off. He once drilled holes through a foot-tall stack of his own prints, bound with wire, to settle one contractual agreement. The bundle of prints sat as a footstool in his basement for years. Later, he incorporated the bundle of damaged prints into a wall hanging.

Frank does not ponder to reconsider. He does not entertain the same question twice, particularly when it is rephrased. Artistic pathways do not cross his path; they end. The dark side of Frank is a blistering belligerence.

Frank is unafraid of conflict or upheaval. It is in the conflict, somehow, where he finds solace. At least one can see the problems – and photograph them if need be.

One day walking up 2nd Avenue in the early '90s with Robert Frank and Herbert Huncke, we stopped at the corner of 4th Street. An old Chevy was waiting by the curb for the light to change. The springs were gone and the shocks were shot – the muffler couldn't be heard over the din of music coming from the dashboard radio. It was a warm day and the car windows were rolled down. Inside, six Puerto Rican girls sat, three in the front seat and three in the back. They were the living, bouncing spirit of freedom teenagers have their first time out in a car without their parents.

We were standing on the sidewalk looking down into the car. Huncke was on one side, Frank in the middle and I on the other. The music had a steady beat and the car, an urgency of youth. Something all of us have felt once and then it is gone.

As the light turned green, the teenager seated in the middle of the front seat leaned over her companion's lap to the passenger side window and looked directly at Frank.

"Make a picture," she said. "Make it international."

With that comment the light turned green and the car roared through the intersection.

"She saw something," Frank said.

She didn't know who he was but she saw his eyes – and how his eyes looked – as if through a lens – ready to capture – the beautiful, the innocent and the broken in all of us.

Jerome Poynton, a former Men's Gymnastics Coach from The University of Michigan, worked with New York painters, film makers, writers, photographers and art collectors for a quarter of a century. He now spends most of his time in Italy talking with farmers and appliance salesman.

untitled

richard sandler

in september of 1956, when i was a lad of 10, my father introduced me to the lower east side. we drove from our spacious, greeny forest hills neighborhood to the gritty, grey immigrant streets where people lived in overcrowded tenements. this was to be a lesson. he wished to show me where we jews came from, but mostly he wanted to show me "poverty." i was a some-what spoiled suburban kid and this up-close viewing of the how the "have-nots" lived, he hoped, would prompt me into having a greater appreciation for our cushy life in the suburbs, but dad's plan backfired. ... all i wanted to do was get out of the car and play stickball in the streets that were teeming with kids. the place was so alive and i remember saying to myself, "i'd rather live here."

ten septembers later, i moved to 88 east third street to be part of the bourgeoning hippie coun-terculture. my native attractions were to lsd, free love, rock 'n roll, jazz and macrobiotics; and sources for all five were abundantly available and within walking distance. lsd was everywhere and defined our lifestyle's instant vision questing. sex and psychedelics were a potent brew; add to that, the first gigs of "the who" or the "mothers of invention" at the village theater, (soon to become the filmore east), add to that, the strobing psychedelic soul sounds of the chambers brothers at the "electric circus" on st. marks, add to that the blues of yussef latif at "slugs" on east third street, and you have a lot to "grok" as you read your "east village other" and chew on your brown rice at the "paradox restaurant," where eastern philosophies like zen and zen-macrobiotics and vedanta, mingled uneasily, with the ideas of older neighborhood politicos, civil rights and union activists, marxists, and "folkies," all of whom ate together nightly at the paradox's two long community tables ... where tea was always free and ditto for your second and third and fourth bowls bowls of un-polished rice.

in the spring of 1967, the owners of the paradox drank the kool aid and became hard core sci-entologists. at that moment the paradox restaurant changed dramatically. the first scientology church was housed above the restaurant, and quickly the paradox which had been a meeting ground for the neighborhood's rich ideological, racial and ethnic mix, was suddenly crawling with wild-eyed, former hippies zealots, but now wearing suits and talking about "getting clear."

to be fair though, there was a climate shift toward more conservative life styles at the end of the hippie years. trends such as the "back to the land movement," and the "home crafts movement," "scientology," "macrobiotics" and even renewed interest in "western religions" began in reaction to the excesses of hippie lifestyles..

on the day that 1968 reared its ugly head, i left the east village scene behind and moved to boston, to study with the renowned macrobiotic teacher, michio kushi. already, i had totally ceased taking any psychedelics or drugs of any description because food was the best medicine of all. i was living in a communal macrobiotic study house with others of like mind, who were also attracted to the exciting post-psychedelic culture that was growing there ... fast. many creative people from the former san francisco hippie scene made it to boston to study with kushi as well.

in rapid succession we started boston's first macro restaurant called "nowhere" and the seminal "erewhon trading company," which was to be the direct inspiration for its bastard child, "whole foods." i became the cook at "nowhere restaurant." (under pressure from a local business organization we had to lose the name "nowhere," changing it to "sanae restaurant," which means the first sprouts of grain).

in the winter of 1969 i moved back to new york to take a job as the head chef of a new macro restaurant on sixth street called "the caldron." i designed the kitchen, created the menus, and cooked there for a year, while training its owners, glory and marty schloss, in the ways of macrobiotic cooking. the caldron was quite an interesting scene, to say the least. its location near the corner of second avenue meant that it was a stone's throw from the fillmore east, and every night the restaurant would fill up with hippies getting a meal before or after the show. like "the paradox" restaurant on seventh street, it also hosted a whole spectrum of political and spiritually versed clientele. "the caldron" was a magnet for culture and an instant success, and since it was the very first restaurant to open on the whole block ... (there were no indian restaurants on sixth street then) ... it spawned a rush for restaurants wanting to locate there. the second and third restaurants on sixth street, "samsara café" (c.1971) and "ichiban" (c. 1972) were also macrobiotic restaurants and were started by the abehsera brothers: georges, (who was also one of the founders of commodities natural foods) leon, and michel. sixth street between first and second avenue became macrobiotic restaurant row.

the abehsera brothers are moroccan sephardic jews who grew up in an observant jewish home and who were beginning to mix macrobiotics with judaism. shabbat dinners at michel and claude abehsera's house were wonderful festive affairs. michel and claude abehsera wrote "zen-macrobiotic cooking," and "cooking for life," two of the first natural foods cookbooks.

in boston and in new york, many jewish macrobiotics were returning to, or experimenting with judaism in the early '70s. i would credit michel abehsera with this movement. bob dylan, for one, was often in crown heights for shabbat with the lubavichers. i also became an orthodox jew, and due to michel's influence, so did marty and glory at the caldron. the next chapter in the caldron's history became even more layered. the usual mix of east-siders, politicos, hippies and seekers now included a big influx of orthodox jews of every stripe. the back room at the caldron was a shoes-off, sit on the floor room, and was very relaxed. conversation at the caldron was often spicy and blunt though. the mixture of so many different people made for a joyous celebration of diversity, but come sundown on friday night until sun-up on sunday morning, the restaurant was closed for business, as is the jewish custom. the caldron operated as a "shomer shabbos" restaurant (observant of the rules of the sabbath) until it went out of business in the mid 1980s.

my work for the caldron was a labor of love ... it was "for the movement" .... and not about making money. of course, the cheap rents and low bills of those days allowed people to be more altruistic with their time and skills, which in turn built strong and connected communities. I returned to boston after the caldron was safely launched and i got married to connie frank, also a student of michio kushi. we had a son, benjamin sandler, born on 11/11/70. we three moved to state college, pennsylvania, and i enrolled in penn state night school, taking classes in anatomy and physiology.

from michio kushi i had become familiar with the concepts of oriental medicine. i decided to find a way to study acupuncture. i was fortunate to meet the english acupuncturist, j.r. worsley, in 1971 at a lecture he was giving in new york city. six months later I enrolled in his "college of chinese acupuncture," in kenilworth, england, where i subsequently got my degree and license to practice in england.

upon graduation from acupuncture school, i returned to boston yet again and started my acupuncture practice there in 1973. i practiced continuously from 1973 to 1978, making my living from it until spring 1978 when i started photography. in 1977 i was fortunate to move into a communal house in cambridge that was owned by mary and david mcclelland. mary was a great artist, photographer and art teacher at the friends quaker school. david was an eminent harvard psychologist and he was still teaching there when I moved into their house in 1977. Mary taught me how to develop film and print photos in her darkroom ... and just like that, i was bit by the photography bug and was now devoting all my time to learning its craft.

again, cheap rent figured into this change in my life as well. there were 15 of us living in their huge north cambridge mansion; our rent was a mere $30 per month and we all shared the costs of food. there would be nightly dinners around their large dining-room table. often there would be guests for dinner such as baba ram dass, john cage, gregory bateson, and buckminster fuller, to name a few.

shortly after i began still photography in 1977 i was able to earn my living as a photojournalist, working for boston area publications such as the boston phoenix, the real paper and boston magazine. all the while however i was making un-posed pictures of people on the boston streets and on the streets of nyc. at present i am a video and filmmaker as well as a still photographer.

my street photos are in the collections of the brooklyn museum, the new york public library, the museum of fine arts, houston, the dreyfus foundation and in many private collections. i started street video in 1992 and have made four new york city documentaries to date.

the gods of times square (1999) is about religious zealots in the fabled square and about the grotesque process of "disney-fication" there. gods chronicles the last days of the old times square and its traditional function as a place of free speech. the gods of times square has won a number of film festival awards including "best documentary" at the 1999 chicago underground film festival.

brave new york (2004) is a free-form documentary that loosely chronicles the last 12 years of intense change in the east village "hood." from the reopening of a newly curfewed tompkins square park and wigstock in '92, to the destruction of the cherished loisaida community gardens, to the yuppie invasions of the dotcom years, to the present era, indelibly stamped with post-9/11 grief, this durable, lusty neighborhood survives in spite of a real estate gold rush that has excluded all but the well-to-do. the movie's main voices are those of the artists and street people whose wisdom and commentaries upon the dominant culture give us pause amidst the speedy approach of a "brave new world."

SWAY, (2006) is a free-form documentary about the underground portion of the nyc subway system; edited from 12 years of daily shooting on the trains and on the platforms.

everybody is hurting (2006) is a documentary about the day of 9/11/01 in nyc, and the muscular debate and soul-searching that raged in union square park in the days and weeks after the attacks; the piece ends with a coda of contextual video of the world trade center towers from the previous 10 years.

i am in the final stages of shooting a documentary on film called *aka martha's vineyard*, which sees the lovely massachusetts isle from the perspectives of the wampanoag indian tribe, the islands' indigenous people. i recently finished another documentary called *the rocks of eternity: conversations with satish kumar*, (2007). satish kumar is an environmental and peace activist who walked for peace with no money, from the grave of mahatma ghandi to the grave of john f. kennedy, from 1961 to 1963. the purpose of the walk was to bring messages of peace to the (then) leaders of the four nuclear nations, the u.s.s.r., france, england and the u.s. satish is now the dean of schumacher college in devon, england, and the editor of *resurgence magazine*.

i won the new york foundation for the arts fellowship in photography in 1992 and 1998, and a john simon guggenheim foundation fellowship for filmmaking in 2006.

Richard Sandler, *a long time east village resident, is a film and video maker and a still photographer. previously, sandler was the first chef at the caldron macrobiotic restaurant (1968) and a licensed acupuncturist. he has been awarded two new york foundation for the arts fellowships in still photography, and a 2006 guggenheim fellowship for filmmaking.*

Maurice Narcis – East Village Jewish Artist

Rik Little

I think you had to live on St. Marks Place between 1st Avenue and Avenue A during the 80's Reagan regime to fully understand the beginnings of 'Amerika' today. That is where Jewish artist Maurice Narcis worked as a multidisciplinary artist, documenting the rise of the state and cultural doings in the neighborhood, which more often than not involved political artists who defined the times.

Maurice first introduced me to the band 'Drunk Driving' in 1982, whose Jewish lead singer, Peter Missing, went on to front 'Missing Foundation.' It was Maurice who photographed and videotaped these and other artists who defined the neighborhood as well as the rise of police power around Tompkins Square Park during the time. It was Maurice who first published my video work on his public access TV series 'On The Wire,' which led me to start my own public access TV series 'The Church of Shooting Yourself.' I can't think of a band other than 'Rik Little and the Loose' that had more gigs on the same bill with 'Missing Foundation,' and Maurice was always there promoting and documenting everything. Each venue Missing Foundation played was their last, from CBGB to the Kitchen to Danceteria, where I remember possessed Pete ripping off the doors to the Danceteria dressing room and the bouncers coming down to beat up Maurice and break his camera. In 1993, I was at Maurice's St. Marks apartment dropping off tapes when the news came on the radio of a fire at the World Trade Center. Although I had been awake for 24 hours, I spent the rest of that day documenting the 1993 WTC bombing in the fashion both Maurice and I had been taught, beginning with our school days together in 1972 at Buffalo State College.

Buffalo at the time (along with Ohio) was the breeding ground for artists that in the 70's would descend en masse on NYC and change the music and art scene in a new wave. When Maurice and I attended photography and film courses at Buffalo State, Maurice served as critic and commentator on artists in visual and aural mediums, and he has continued to this day as an inspiration and visionary definer of Art, as well as a creator of mind-blowing photographs in his own right. (Google them to find out more.) He was always 'right there.' Being from the Midwest myself, I had no idea what a Jew was until I met Maurice. He was from Sheepshead Bay (although he was actually born in Israel 'on a sunny day' as he likes to say), and my visits with him from Buffalo to his parents' home provided me with further insight into the world.

His brother had found a 8mm movie camera in his cab, and Maurice and I took it to Philadelphia to document the Bicentennial in 1976. Foregoing the tall ships in NYC, we rode the train while I filmed and Maurice provided audio and took photos. We documented a bicentennial parade in a sudden pouring rain, which caused the parade to scatter furiously against the buildings for shelter. A large plate glass window was shattered because of all the soaked people jamming up against it and blood was everywhere. People in revolutionary garb, Betsy Ross costumes, and one little kid with a flag were a bloody mess, as first responders descended to take control and clear the area. The parade was over and torrents of rain continued the afternoon in the City of Brotherly Love. We went to the Liberty Bell, which at the time was just a bell in a park. Unprotected, unnoticed and free to be rung with rocks by passersby like us. That night we documented a performance Sun Ra was giving in a little church. By the end of the night, everyone was dancing around in one line. All this footage was stolen from my apartment in the 80's, but this trip with Maurice remains intact.

Maurice and I became interested in the theme of microcosms in America at about the same time when we both first met with Robert Frank in Buffalo around 1974. His book about America, *The Americans*, was the most inspiring thing we had seen. Lee Freelander, Ralph Gibson, Duane Michaels, Stan Brakhage, Michael Snow, Kenneth Anger, Andy Warhol, Jackson Pollock, Jonas Mekas and one of our professors, Les Krims, had influenced us as well, but it was the presence of students at the college such as Cindy Sherman, Robert Longo, Kevin Noble, Mark Goldberg, Rubin Alspector and John Davis, who really inspired us and got things moving. Our best teacher was Alex Sweetman, an instructor at Buffalo State who could analyze a picture for content better than even Robert Frank. Also notable was Barbara Jo Revelle, who took the chances in teaching photography and film as no teacher has ever. It paid off. Harvey Weinstein at the time was running the 'Harvey & Corky Productions' theatre in Buffalo, producing musical events and enlisting Buffalo State students to run his shows, which Maurice and I were both involved with.

In 1974 Maurice and I were sent by the college to videotape NYC visual artists including Ralph Gibson, Jonas Mekas and numerous others in various disciplines. I was so pissed at Maurice, who told me he recorded over our tapes of these artists on the reel-to-reel Sony video camera by videotaping the Ramones at Moot Hall at Buffalo State in 1978. I realize now that Maurice was really on top of it. You don't get a Jewish artist (or any other, really) more important than Joey Ramone in his prime, as Maurice had the vision to see. Tape was expensive and choices had to be made.

I lived with Maurice in several houses in Buffalo. At the first was when he realized his lifelong dream to have a dog. He had no idea about dogs, and his first dog 'Jack' was an education that lead into numerous dogs well past the 90's of NYC until he got past it. There was another nine-person house we lived at in Buffalo, full of great artists including John Davis, Mark Goldberg, Arnie Shapiro, and Streetsheet. The house hosted many art events and collaboration. Maurice was always the critic and the force providing guidance and perspective to the often-crazy ongoings. Maurice has remained my friend throughout the years and has provided Jewish and human inspiration throughout.

Lately, Maurice has provided me support in the most unconstitutional and vile civil rights debacle to ever face American justice: the Family Law system. He photographed my daughter for one court event, helped me move out to PA after I was falsely charged with 'domestic violence' and downloaded Hannah Montana to the I-pod I gave my daughter (which I didn't know how to do). He is involved with the band Dufus, and has constantly involved me with this project as well as every other cultural vision he has appropriated. I take his vision very seriously, as that is my choice based on his track record. I could go on for hours about this man and his vision and choices, but I would like to expostulate upon the Jewish artists from the Lower East Side. Maurice is one of many.

The Lower East Side is historically a neighborhood of immigrants. The current demonization of immigrants totally fails to recognize the 'deviant' in the words of Lenny Bruce. The IDEAS of America all came from immigrants. This is not to short shift the Iroquois Nation on which our Constitution was modeled. Rather, it is to say that this country's ideas are based on the ideas of those Jewish immigrants and their offspring like Maurice Narcis. No one can tell me that I am not a Jew. God murdered everybody except Noah and his family because of his (or her) dissatisfaction with man. All the descendents are from Noah and if anybody is a Jew, then we all are Jews. If we are or are not all artists, then that is another matter. I thank Maurice Narcis. The rainbow was a promise, but NEXT time it will be by fire. Shalom.

Rik Little Musician, filmmaker, videomaker, photographer, writer, actor, composer, father.

NY Photographer

Sid Kaplan

For the last fifty-five years, Sid Kaplan, born 1938, has been documenting the life of New York City when it still had a 3rd Avenue El Washington Market, and hoards of kids playing on the sidewalks, stoops and gutters, unsupervised in the working class neighborhoods.

To finance his passion, he started working as a black and white photograph printer after high school in 1956, and in 1972 started teaching the craft at the School of Visual Arts in New York City. In the mid 1980's, he relocated to the Lower East Side after being gentrified out of his loft in the Flatiron District, and shortly after inherited all the family documents including his mother's birth certificate, with the address of the tenement building on Hester Street where she was born in 1905. When he went to look at the site, it was no longer there and he also noticed very few traces of what used to be a vibrant and thriving Jewish community. Those remaining remnants fueled a five year photo safari, from 14th Street to Brooklyn Bridge, 3rd Avenue and the Bowery to the East River searching block to block for any evidence of the past, and planning when to be there when the light is best with the proper equipment. In some cases when he got there the sites had been demolished.

At the two Shuls, the First Romanian at 87 Rivington Street and Sons of Moses at 135 Henry Street, he was known to drop in to help make a minyan, and photographed various events when permissible.

Currently, January 2008, he has been photographing upper 2nd Avenue, feeling the new subway construction will reinvent the character of the street. For the last few summers, he also has been photographing a small farming town in South Dakota, once with a population of two thousand people, now down to twelve. His work has been exhibited and published in America and Europe, and in private, corporate and museum collections in New York City, in the NY Library, NY Historical Society, MoMA, and the Museum of the City of New York.

A few of the people Sid printed:
Edward Steichen
Weegee
Robert Frank
Allen Ginsberg
Joan Roth

Sid Kaplan *Born 1938, South Bronx. Started photographing NYC in 1949. Runs his own professional black and white darkroom service. Sid has printed, in black and white, the works of some of the most distinguished American photographers of the 20th century. And still going strong with his photography as well as his darkroom work.*

Part 8: Loose Ends

Lew the Jew: Tattooist of the Mosiac Persuasion

Eddy Portnoy

With the alleged aversion of Jews to tattoos, it might stand to reason that there aren't a lot of articles on tattooing in the Yiddish press of the early 20th century. But there are a few and, as it happens one of them was written by Albert Parry, the author of one of the first seminal works on tattooing. Parry, one of the unsung documenters of American subcultures, wrote a small number of articles related to Jews and popular culture that appeared in New York's *Forverts* newspaper in 1927 and 1928. One of them happened to be a feature on the legendary tattoo artist Lew "the Jew" Alberts.

Of the dozens of texts that focus on Manhattan's Lower East Side, a giant urban sponge that absorbed millions of immigrants and which was bursting at the seams with Jews of all sorts during the early 20th century, not one mentions the fact that the southern edge of the famed Jewish neighborhood was pocked with numerous tattoo parlors, including those of famed artist/innovators Charlie Wagner and Samuel O'Reilly. Certainly, there have been many oversights in the historiography of this area, but this would seem to have been one of significance.

Part of the reason tattooing has gone missing from Lower East Side history is due to the perception that Yiddish-speaking immigrant Jews and their offspring were averse to tattooing, an urban legend that is only partially true. With a fair number of tattoo parlors and with a Jewish population of about a half a million milling about on the Lower East Side, it seems terribly unlikely that at least some Jews didn't wander in to get inked.

Evidence as to this fact crops up in reports like an 1899 *New York Tribune* article on Christian missionaries on the Lower East Side who would forcibly tattoo crosses on the arms of children. These extremely objectionable attempts to force children into Christianity involved tattooing a permanent cross on the child in hope that the child's parents would abandon him or her. Evidently not much of a success, the article also describes how a number of tattooed children had been brought to a Lower East Side doctor in order to have the crosses removed.

However, as Parry explained in his 1933 book *Tattoo: Secret of a Strange Art*, there is also evidence that some Jewish boys were not tattooed against their will, but did, in fact, wander into local tattoo establishments because they liked the ink they saw. Parry notes that the confluence of an increasing number of novice tattoo artists who needed practice on "live skin" and the desire of Lower East Side kids to get inked, made for a fair number of Jewish kids with tattoos.

A *New York Tribune* article from the fall of 1902 remarks on the number of Jewish boys who surprised teachers by arriving with new designs on their skin at the beginning of the school year. Jewish school kids on the Lower East Side spanned the gamut — from bookish nerds to neophyte gangsters. It's the latter group that most likely availed themselves of the tattoo parlors on Chatham Square. But cultural sensitivities should not have been dismissed entirely and when one tattooist inked a large crucifix on a Jewish boy's chest, he incurred the wrath of his parents. The Society for the Protection of Children got involved and the aforementioned Charlie Wagner was arrested. Only after he promised to keep the local kids out of his shop did the judge let him go.

The flurry of tattoo activity on Chatham Square brought the practice to the attention of the press and to local parents, none of whom were particularly happy with the results. Citing another *Tribune* article, Parry tells the story of a Jewish mother from Attorney Street, who bewailed the fact that one of the neighborhood's novice tattooists inked a scene of tombstones with the words, "To the Memory of a Beloved Mother Gone to Rest." Unhappy words to be sure for a mother who was still very much alive.

And, outside of curious kids, the kinds of Jews that got inked tended to be underworld characters: Parry makes mention of a Jewish racketeer who had his children's profiles tattooed on his arms. But he also claimed that American-born Jews did not have the aversion to the art that their parents had and that there were "Jewish salesmen, truck-drivers, chiropractors — and even lawyers" who had been tattooed.

Going further, Parry makes the claim that tattooing was quite popular among Jews, commenting that young, American Jews no longer care about the prohibition on tattoos, although he does also describe one young man who had to hide his "Harry-Goldie-June" (the names of his favorite Jewish boxer, his wife and his daughter) from his religious mother. And it was these mothers who invented the myth that a Jewish cemetery won't bury a Jew with tattoos.

While a variety of Jewish may indeed have gotten inked during the early 20th century, it is also true that tattooing was not normative in modern Jewish cultures, nor were Jews in America ever one of the more heavily tattooed ethnicities. But it can also be noted that, until recently, tattooing was only normative for criminals, gang members, bikers, and sailors.

And it was Jewish sailors who had fought in the Philippines during the Spanish-American war that happened to discover the art of Asian tattooing at the same time as their compatriots. One of these sailors was Lew Alberts, a Jewish kid from New York who had worked as a wallpaper designer before enlisting in the navy. Having seen it in the Philippines, and apparently been taken with the art of tattooing, Alberts quit the wallpaper business when he returned to New York and opened a tattoo parlor on Sands Street near the Brooklyn Navy Yard.

Working professionally under the name "Lew the Jew," Alberts built up a successful clientele among the sailors who were attached to the Navy Yard, eventually gaining significant fame among fighting men — in spite of the fact that some claimed his tattoos resembled wallpaper designs.

In a fit of innovation, Alberts began sending out sheets of his tattoo art to fellow artists who, in turn, put the art on their walls and offered their clients his designs. Known today as "flash," Alberts is regarded as the innovator of this idea: that the designs of various artists could be sent around and inked by any tattooist. The 1927 article that appeared in the *Jewish Daily Forward* noted that Alberts' flash could be found on the walls of tattoo parlors all over the West Coast and estimated that at least a third of American tattoo artists used his designs.

According to the same article, Lew the Jew was aware of Biblical prohibitions on tattooing and was very conscientious with Jewish customers, explaining the prohibition and often sending them away. He apparently lost a number of customers in this way. He also attempted to persuade other artists to turn Jewish customers away although it is not likely they complied. As a result, we end up with a missing piece in the puzzle of Jewish acculturation in America.

As the children of Jewish immigrants negotiated the twisted paths of ethnicities, traditions and their desire to be American, they often chose routes that were not necessarily in concert with Jewish law or tradition. Creating a new ethnic type was, and remains, a process that involves debate over what traditions will remain, what will be reclaimed, and what will be remade. For first generation American Jews getting inked was simply part of that process of cultural negotiation.

Eddy Portnoy *earned a Ph.D. in Modern Jewish Studies at the Jewish Theological Seminary. He teaches Yiddish language and literature at Rutgers University.*

Bill Heine and Anne Spitzer Remember
Thom deVita, Richard Tyler, and
The First Gnostic Lyceum Phalanstery Temple

As told to Anne Loretto

BILL HEINE: I met Thom deVita in New York around 1962. Thom had just gotten out of his one and only stint in prison, which was for a youthful indiscretion. He'd fallen into bad company where he grew up in Spanish Harlem, a neighborhood that at the time was all Italian, and he had tried an armed robbery at the age of 16 or 17, and had done seven years, I think. So he was still very young when he got out and came down to New York.

Thom's father was Italian, but his mother was Jewish, and she did all the cooking, so, remarkably, until after he got out of prison, Thom had never eaten Italian food.

He started out renting an apartment on Eighth Street: there was a long hallway, then a door with a huge padlock, and behind that was his place. You needed those locks back then downtown, that's how it was. The funny thing was, once you got inside, the apartment was furnished just like his mother's place, with pillows, drapes, doilies, all very lovely and formal and tasteful. Thom wasn't doing tattoos immediately. He had been getting some kind of income, I'm not sure from where, but after a little while, he decided to earn a living by tattooing. He met all the best tattooists he could find, and studied the old tattoo artists, and practiced on potatoes. His early tattoo device was rigged up somehow out of an electric bell ringer. Once he got going, he tattooed all his friends. He did this snake on my arm about two years after he first got started. He also pierced my ears, back in the early 60's. He had the flash sample pictures in his shop, and he had also studied the Japanese style of tattooing. He became a very good artist, and all the best artists, Japanese, Hawaiian, all the top ones, tattooed him, too, so that by the 1970's he became covered from his neck down to his ankles, and even, a little bit, his feet.

He had a great library of art books also, was very into Klee and also the German Jewish surrealist Felix Nussbaum, who died in Auschwitz. Nussbaum's last painting is called *The Triumph of Death*. It's really something.

ANNE SPITZER: I remember the first time I went over to Thom's apartment – I believe it was that first one on Eighth Street – he had beautiful framed canvases that he had painted of mysterious forest scenes, evenings in the forest, up on the walls. He was really a good artist. Thom loved dogs and would visit the Westminster dog show when it was in town. He would inherit dogs, too, from people who passed away. But he had one remarkable dog, back in the 60's, named Joe. Joe had a dark patch over his eye, like the dog in those old beer commercials, and Joe used to wander freely all over the city. You could meet that dog absolutely anywhere: Harlem, Battery Park, anywhere. I remember running into Joe up on 87th and 3rd with Thom nowhere near; Joe just loved to roam. He was a very well-behaved dog, knew exactly how to handle himself, and lived to be quite old. In fact, now that I think of it, I met Joe even before I met Thom.

BILL: After Eighth Street, Thom lived on Third Street, Fourth Street, then back to Eighth, all in the East Village. One of those places, the one on Fourth, was especially memorable in that the only way in to visit him was to get up a ladder onto the fire escape and then climb in through the window. For some reason, there was no access into the hall. Downtown being what it was, Thom had to hire a bodyguard after he started his shop, which had a big sign: TATTOOS. The guy's name was McKenna, a little guy from Hell's Kitchen, and he wasn't actually armed. He showed up with a pistol once, and deVita said "no" to that. But McKenna still managed to scare robbers away. This was especially important because, at least for a while, Thom didn't use a bank. A teller at his bank had reprimanded him for not having his bankbook with him, and Thom got mad and withdrew all his money.

A friend Thom made through tattooing was Richard Tyler, an artist who, at least initially, did only medicinal and magical tattoos, designs he would get out of books.

ANNE: In the mid-60's, Richard Tyler had inherited an extraordinary place from a rabbi, on Fourth Street, between C and D. He had worked for the rabbi as — I wish I could remember the proper word for this, because I know there is one — but some people call it the "Shabbas goy," the non-Jew who does the errands that observant Jews can't do on the Sabbath. Anyway, Richard and the rabbi became close, and when the rabbi died, he left Richard this house. Richard made his house into the First Gnostic Lyceum Phalanstery Temple. ["Phalanstery" is the term for a building housing a utopian communal group as conceived by the early-19th century French philosopher Fourier.] It was an ecumenical Lyceum Temple. Richard conducted elaborate celebrations of pagan and Christian and Buddhist holidays there. He had somehow become a minister, maybe through the mail, and a group of us was his congregation. If a member of the congregation died, for example, he would conduct the 49-day Buddhist Bardo ceremony for that person. Although Richard was open in observing several different religions, he was also quite traditional in following the rituals of each one. I liked the way he did things very much.

BILL: Richard was a little older than the rest of us. He had fought in World War II, had been a Marine in combat in the Pacific, and then after the war had graduated from the Art Institute of Chicago on the G.I. Bill. His wife, Dorothea Baer, had graduated from there, too. Richard used to do giant woodcuts in an Expressionist style; I especially remember one called *Welcome Death*. He would sell them from a pushcart outside the Judson Church. He taught art at Hunter College, and Dorothea taught woodworking.

The ceiling of his studio at the Temple was covered in samurai swords, memorabilia from the war, I guess. The staircase there was beautiful. And the place was filled with musical instruments as well. As many as thirty or more of us came over there for his Lyceum feasts, and Richard would record us playing the instruments – often people would play an instrument that they had never played before – and it sounded amazing. Dorothea would cook a beautiful meal for these Lyceum events. Being of German descent, she would do pig roasts, a whole pig with an apple in its mouth.

ANNE: Once I disappeared in the middle of dinner, and no one could find me, and I finally turned up asleep under the table! I'd had a bit of wine, and then I took one look at that pig, and it was too much for me! Richard's backyard at the Temple was full of strange found objects, like a Surrealist garden or a horizontal Guggenheim, very hard to describe. And there were two apple trees. The rabbi who left him the house had told Richard that children eating apples had planted the seeds about fifty years earlier, and two seeds had taken root, and so there were these apple trees, and Richard's curious, almost magical, object collection.

BILL: Richard tattooed a number of us himself: Anne, me, our friend Wade, some other people, with a dot on our hands. Having the dot meant you were an Agent. I still have my Agent dot, but Anne's has faded. Also back in the 60's, Richard drafted a letter to the federal government in his wonderful fancy calligraphy demanding that we be registered as aliens, meaning space aliens, from Uranus. A lot of us signed it, and he sent it in. He eventually received a response from the government stating that this couldn't be done because we had no papers.

ANNE: I'm sure Richard could have provided some papers!

BILL: I remember Agent Wade showing up stark naked at 14th Street and 3rd Avenue, sometime in the 60's, maybe the early 70's. That's the way it was. He had an immense penis.

Richard also tattooed Thom deVita with Tibetan mantras on his arms. Even before the days of AIDS and what we know now about diseases, Richard was extremely meticulous about cleaning his equipment. Later on, though, Richard was living down in the basement of the Lyceum like a mole, snorting cocaine and watching TV.

ANNE: We met so many of the people we knew in New York over at the Lyceum. The scene there started in the 60's and continued into the 80's. There was Thom, of course, and his brother Ron deVita, and Danny Baer, who wasn't a relative of Dorothea; the name was just a coincidence. There was a man named Smit, who was a really good saxophonist, and our friend Brett of Woodstock. And then there was a blonde woman, named Diana Johnson who had a tattoo of a beautiful cabbage rose and bluebirds on her shoulders. She said she was part-Indian, and that her mother had married a Swedish sailor. We roomed for a while in a house with her; she was living next door with a man called Big Mac, who ended up moving to California. Diana was using heroin most of the time. She was such a generous, just basically good person. We knew her about twenty years, and then she died, around 1988. She went into the hospital for a biopsy and didn't survive.

BILL: Thom deVita married his wife Jennifer in the late 80's and moved up to Newburgh and opened a tattoo parlor there. We drove down to visit him not so long ago, and we stay in touch.

ANNE: And Richard Tyler died while we were in retreat at the monastery. He had cancer.

BILL: That's the way it goes.

Anne Loretto *is a writer and independent film producer who lives in upstate New York. She has co-curated art shows including "The '80s: 326 Years of Hip," and "A Group Exhibition of Four Octogenarian Artists, With Boris Lurie, Mary Beach, Herbert Huncke and Taylor Mead" @ Clayton Gallery and Outlaw Art Museum. She has worked as an assistant to Jeremiah Newton and James Rasin, as well as being a producer for the movie Beautiful Darling. She developed the history and web-site of Bill Heine.*

Jewish Ink: A Telephone Interview with Stanley Moskowitz, February 18, 2006

Clayton Patterson and David H. Katz

Introduction 1 by David H. Katz

Stanley, with his late brother Walter, comprised the famous Moskowitz Brothers, pioneer tattooists who worked on the Bowery near Chatham Square in the 1940s, '50s, and on into the '60s, when they moved to Amityville to open up the first tattoo parlor on Long Island after New York City's Department of Health began closing the city's tattoo parlors.

The brothers learned the trade in their father Willy's Bowery barbershop from legends like flash artist Charley Wagner and master tattoo machinist Bill "Jonesy" Jones, and the pair supposedly alternated between inking skin at night and studying the Talmud at a Brooklyn yeshiva by day.

This back when the Bowery was known for bums, not boulevardiers; when the Third Avenue El rattled above, the tracks scattering Venetian slats of light and shade onto sidewalks populated by toughs, drunks, and hookers, sailors on leave and Marines about to ship out. No hotels with potted plants, no French-Asian-Hispanic-Greek fusion restaurants, no exclusive boutiques or backlit art galleries; just bars, barber shops, flophouses, pawn shops, kitchen equipment emporiums, and the Moskowitz Brothers, inking buxom bimbos onto Marine biceps for what would today be considered a pittance.

They are Jewish, of course, but in that classic, New York, Lower East Side way, less a religious identification, and more an ineffable cultural marker of a certain time and place: pre-hip, pre air-conditioned, pre-gentrified.

"Fights?" says Stanley. "Every day. If a day didn't go by there wasn't a battle or something or other. Every thief from every town across America came to the Bowery. They went down the Bowery under the El, drunks and thieves and murderers."

All gone, probably forever.

Introduction 2 by Clayton Patterson

It was important for me to get my friends the legendary Moskowitz family into this anthology. They represent the last of the old school tough guys, the last of the Bowery Boys, the end of the Golden Period of tattooing on the Bowery, and they are the token Jewish tattoo artists for the book. There have been many Jews who have made a noteworthy contribution to the world of tattoo.

The Bowery, like 42nd Street, always had its own unique, seamy identity and its own site-specific history. The Bowery represented different things to different people at different times. It has been a working-class entertainment zone, the location of a number of WeeGee's most memorable photographs, a haven of last chance hotels for lost souls and alcoholics who had reached their bottom. It was the demarcation line that firmly separated the Jewish, the Italian, and the Chinese communities from each other. It was a place people experimented with opening their first business or bought their first real-estate investment. On the Bowery and the street around Chatham Square produced some of the most well-known American tattoo heroes. This is where could be found legends like Charlie Wagner, Lew "the Jew" Alberts (who created flash-designs for tattoos), Samuel O'Reilly (who patented the first electric tattoo machine, thus revolutionizing tattooing), Bill "Jonesy" Jones (a maker of tattoo machines) as well as the place where tattoo artists Stanley and Walter Moskowitz, following in their father's footsteps, became known as the famous "Bowery Boys."

An article in the *Jewish Daily Forward* ("Tracing a Tattoo Dynasty Back to Its Bowery Days,"Gabrielle Birkner, September 19, 2003) quoted one of the brothers on the Jewish influence on his tattooing . "'Yeshiva taught me the value of putting in a long day's work,' said Walter, 66, a Reform Jew and Zionist." The piece continued, "Walter's work ethic proved valuable when he and his brother, Stanley, inherited the Bowery shop after their father's death in 1961."

Walter talked about being Jewish, Stanley did not.

Below David Katz and I talk with Stanley Moskowitz.

****

SM: So, what did you wanna know?

CP: We'll talk about the tattoo history, you know, when you got started and all of that. So, whereabouts were you born? You started off in East New York?

SM: I was born on 22 Amboy Street, Brownsville, Brooklyn. The war zone.

DK: Brownsville, Brooklyn. So you must have grown up with guys like Abe Reles [aka Kid Twist, of Murder Inc.].

SM: Yeah well, a little after that. My uncle was with those guys.

DK: My father came from Brownsville, actually. Did you spend your childhood there?

SM: Yeah, quite a bit. I went to school there. Around 13 years old I got wanderlust and I got locked up in South Carolina.

DK: You got locked up in South Carolina?

SM: Yeah, with a bunch of guys. Actually one guy that went along with us, we didn't know him that good. He had killed two guys. He was sixteen years old, murdered two guys and he was in jail with us. We didn't know it but one night he got up, he says, "I killed a man," like in his dream. He had this guy, this Southern guy, by the throat. His name was Nub, he had one arm. And we didn't understand that, you know. We didn't team it up with anything. But later on we found out he had killed two guys for no reason.

He was just some kid and someone had said something to him, a sailor. And he hit him with a tire iron and killed him. But they didn't know who did it. He killed some other guy in a bar or something, you know. He had some kind of mental disease.

CP: Was he from Brownsville?

SM: No he was down a little further in Brooklyn. You know like Dumont Avenue. Anyway he hopped a ride with us when we were going down south. We were looking for a job. Everyone said it was warm and it was like paradise. We got there and it was like snow and clay roads and, Jesus, we had no money!

When I got back, Jonesy, the guy that made all the machines for everybody, he was partners with my father, and he says, "Let's make a tattooer out of him."

CP: How old were you at the time? 16?

SM: 13.

DK: Was Brownsville really a rough neighborhood?

SM: Well, not really. It had only the first-born immigrants, you know, from the immigrant parents at that time. They were pretty good kids. You know there were gangs, but not vicious.

DK: These were all Jewish immigrants, right?

SM: They were Italians, Irish, Jews. It was a mix up.

DK: And when you started being a tattooer?

SM: Well Jonesy was there and my old man. And someone comes in and I'd work on 'em, you know.

DK: Were you religious?

SM: Well, they didn't have any religion, my old man. There wasn't much of any kind of religion [in the family]. My grandmother was half Inuit and half Russian; that's the Bering Sea.

DK: Was she Jewish?

SM: I don't know what the hell she was. My old man was a machinist in the war and then he became a barber. Because he was cleaning and he had his finger cut in half. With some power press or something.

DK: Wow. So he decided to become a barber and then he met Jonesy?

SM: He became a barber 'cause he figured it was cleaner, but he was [working] in a basement. He had to breathe the kerosene; you know there were no windows there and that probably killed him. He was sick when he was 49 or 50. But I was with him there tattooing. I knew how to work, you know. I was taught how to work, day and night.

CP: So your father worked in a barbershop.

SM: He owned the barbershop. [And it was difficult.] You had a lot of the Italian guys, with sticks, they'd open his lock. Barbers, [rival] Italian barbers. And my old man waited for them one night with a baseball bat. And he put of them in the hospital and then they never did it again.

Charley Wagner came over... you know Charley, the old chief of all the tattoists, came over and [dad] built him a bench and said, "You should [do] a little tattooing." [Dad] figured he would do anything to make a few bucks, he was poor. So it worked out for him, [though] he worked himself to death.

CP: Was this in Chatham Square?

SM: Yeah, right near Chatham Square. Under the El. [Manhattan's old Third Avenue elevated train system, demolished in stages beginning in 1950]. We watched it come down, me and my brother, when they had the welders up there and they were taking it down [around 1956].

DK: But you started this on Ludlow Street right?

SM: We lived there. We lived on Ludlow Street.

CP: So you moved from Brownsville to the Lower East Side?

SM: Yeah, because it was closer to where we was working. [I remember] there was a butcher shop there [on Ludlow]. The guy was carving meat and the guy's son stabbed himself in the belly and died. My mother was selling hooch you know, to make the rent. She did it in the bathtub, put tea in it so it gives it a color. The bums used to come and buy it.

As to who started my dad tattooing, it was Charley Wagner. Him and Jonesy. Charley was a terrific guy! He was terrific. [But,] you know, dealing with all these assholes, he became an alcoholic.

DK: What kind of people wanted tattoos in those days?

SM: Always Marines, guys in wartime. You know they're the guys who got the tattoos. That's where it really originated. You know, sailors. That was the origination of tattooing. Not like now [when] you got the starving artist puttin' all kinds of shit all over people.

This was the '20s. I was born in '32 and my old man was already doin' it so you know; World War I. Then there was World War II. It was mostly the wars when the guys were gettin' the real tattoos. Know what I mean?

DK: What would you see as the purpose?

SM: The purpose was he didn't know if he was gonna live or die, and you know he loves his family so he puts that on his skin. True love, Mother, hearts, crosses…

They didn't know if they were gonna get killed. It's like remembrance tattoos. Now it's glamorized into all kinds of horseshit.

CP: How old were you when you started tattooing?

SM: I was about 12.

CP: Had your father been tattooing for long by that time?

SM: Well it was at the tail end of the '20s and I was born in '32 so that was ten years… oh yeah, he was tattooing for a long time.

By '46, '47, I was already tattooing. I was helping my old man 'cause he was sick; he had no air down there. Then he moved up in '48 … onto street level. All the bums helped him; they were bringing up all that stuff. I was just a little kid watching. Then he had air when he came up. Under the elevated there. No sun. He went in the sun one time, it almost killed him.

He was at number 4 Bowery. That's where he moved up from, from 12 Bowery. He tried to buy the building but the woman didn't like him so she sold it to someone else. So we moved to this other building on 4 Bowery. That's where he saw the light of day anyway.

CP: Was that a barbershop in the front as well?

SM: It was always a barbershop and there was always a booth for tattooers.

DK: So when the guys came in, would they have something to drink?

SM: They were all drunk! In the heyday of that time, I would come in and there was 20 drunks, when I got done with them there was 20 more drunks. And the guys complained their back hurt, their this, that, asshole hurt. Me, I worked day and night. I had the stamina to do that. I was born that way.

DK: So a guy would come in and he would pick a design…

SM: It was all from flash at that time. Well, actually, the first guy [to my knowledge] to make flash was this guy Joe Liber. You know him and some other guys started to use a lot of flash. But other guys did it too.

[To do flash tattooing is to work with a set of standardized designs, a rose, for example. The customer at the shop looks at a set of designs and picks out the tattoo he wants. On a sheet, for example, may be a rose, an eagle, an anchor, a panther. It's because of flash that so many old school tattoos look the same; they all come from the same sheet. The sheets were sold to tattoo parlors. —CP]

Then it was wartime, so they all did a lot of wartime tattoos. You know, hula girls from Hawaii.

CP: Did you have to cover the pin-up girls nipples?

SM: No, not at that time. Afterwards guys would do that. Then they would stick the girl's ass out and the girl's tits. They do more now. Actually I'm makin' a book and I got some terrific pictures, but you know I got girls bent over and I don't know if the publishers gonna let me do that.

CP: How much were the tattoos?

SM: Eight bucks. You know, a whole chest piece, eight bucks. Not like these guys these days. We'd get 50 cents for a name. I had to work for my money, boy. Hard. Day and night.

[For comparison, now some tattoo artists charge up to $250 per hour. Many shops average $150 per hour. Also in the old days, tattooers worked fast, nowadays, with pay by the hour, some are known to work slow. The same price changes have affected the whole Bowery area. In the late '70s, early '80s, there was the 99-cent breakfast, now we have te $10 brunch. –CP]

CP: What kinds of businesses were on the Bowery at that time? Mostly Jewish shops I was told.

SM: No, no, no. Where did he get that from? There were all kinds of bars down there mostly. One bar after another. Then there was equipment: kitchen equipment, lighting equipment; that was on the Bowery. And there were barbershops.

DK: How come there's such a connection between barbering and tattooing?

SM: It was a man thing. No girls ever got tattooed except if some guy had a fetish he'd bring his girl in and they'd get all tattooed.

CP: When did your brother get involved?

SM: Walter came later. At least five years after I was tattooing. He coulda had a better job. He didn't really have to deal with that [tattooing] shit. But he came. He had a father-in-law with a giant printing place, who was gonna give him a job, but he picked us. Come with the old man.

DK: So you worked with your brother in the shop?

SM: Yeah, me and my brother, we worked for like 50 years. They put us out of business, and we went to Long Island and opened up. We were the first there. We were there 12 years before anyone else even opened up.

DK: When you say they put you out of business, I guess you are referring to when they passed a law against tattooing? [Tattooing was illegal in New York City from 1961 to 1998.]

SM: Yes. [And then they tried to outlaw it in Long Island.] My brother-in-law, Stanley Nussbaum, made the first health regulations in America for tattooing. [People in the government were trying to ban tattooing, and my brother-in-law and] the guys in Long Island beat them. Me and my brother beat them cause they said they were gonna put us out of business. All tattoos out of business.

Nussbaum was a dentist. We had to go to court and meet the doctors and the Board of Health guys that were invited from all over the country. And they wanted to put the kabosh on tattooing. We didn't let it happen. We fought them, you know. We put up like 20 grand at that time, all we had. We got together and we got that money and we got lawyers. And we went down to see what the hell they wanted to do to us. Because my brother-in-law says, he can't see [a reason for banning it], because tattooing's been going on for a long time and easily done, single service, the way he's got it figured out. So what could really be the problem unless they just don't like ya!

CP: What year was that?

SM: Somewhere like '68, somewhere in there. It was all doctors and board of health guys [against us], and we whipped their ass. That's why you got tattooing. That's why you're talking to me.

CP: But to backtrack a little, what was the effect when tattooing was made illegal in New York City in 1961? Everybody just shut down?

SM: There was nobody, nobody was alive. There were only a few people around.

DK: It had gone down in popularity?

SM: Not popularity. Nobody liked tattoos. They hated tattooing. Used any excuse, if they had any power, to put you outta business.

DK: The authorities tried to put you out of business?

SM: Every one of 'em.

CP: I don't really understand. In the '50s everybody hated it?

SM: Of course. They hated it before. They teamed it up with skid row and hepatitis and diseases and all that. [So, when it was made illegal,] that's it. So we went to Long Island, and we found a place up in a black neighborhood. That was the civil rights [era], the [neighbors] wanted to kill us. That was in Amityville. *Amityville Horror*... we knew those people.

DK: So did you find people on Long Island who wanted to be tattooed?

SM: Loads of 'em! Are you kidding, they were so happy when we got there. We worked day and night there too.

CP: By that time the prices were up, right?

SM: Not too much. We always worked on the very cheap prices. We knew how to work hard so we done it by volume.

CP: So what kind of tattoos were you doing by this time? The war was over, no more war tattoos …

SM: Yeah but then you got the sons of the warriors. They wanted what their old man and their uncles had. We made our own flash. But there was always guys wanting custom stuff you know. We always were able to do it, one way or another.

DK: Did you draw your own tattoos?

SM: Certainly.

CP: Who was the person who could draw the best?

SM: The best, the best... there was no best. Everyone's got their ideas. Hey, you hear that machine buzzin' [in the background]? That a machine [for tattooing] I made. Actually I make my own machines. Not many guys could make their own machine that'll really work right.

CP: You make many machines?

SM: Yeah, a few, occasionally. But Jonesy made them for everybody. See, Jonesy came out of the army, and he was deaf. He wouldn't even take a pension! Unbelievable. Jonesy was like a one-man show. He was unbelievable. His full name was William Jones. He was a Welch man. Everyone in Wales, in that area, is named Jones.

CP: Could he tattoo, too, or mostly just machines?

SM: He could tattoo. Flash, but very little.

CP: Did he have a mail-order business with the machines?

SM: Eh, a small one. [Take] the real big guys in the business. All of the [machine-making] work, or a lot of the work he would do for them. They'd contract him. They got the glory and he got balls. (laughing)

CP: Who would he contract with?

SM: All the guys. Zeist. He made parts of them, yeah. He made the — when Zeist was makin' the Bakelite machines, he made those plates; he did a lot of the things. Jonesy made his own pattern [for the machines]. Jonesy was a genius, a mechanical genius. He'd make the stuff to make the machines. Now I got a Coastal machine here, he copied Jonesy.

Huck Spaulding went down and tapped his brain. *My friend Huck.* Actually, Huck sued me. He was a good friend of mine too.

CP: What did he sue you for?

SM: He says we were usin' some of his stuff, actually he was usin' our stuff. He didn't know what the hell was goin' on.

CP: Did he ever tattoo in New York?

SM: He used to tattoo in our old place. My old man let him tattoo but he couldn't tattoo much. He wasn't too good at it. He'd come down on Saturdays but he was up in Catskill, New York. He tattooed his wife. I took her to a doctor who took all that shit he put on her off. Yeah, I gave him a chance. I took him to the ink business and everything when he was starving. I was friends with him.

You know what his real name is? Darwin Rose. He found that name Spaulding somewhere. And then he went down to Rogers and borrowed his name too! Spaulding and Rogers [for his business]. So he was smart enough to do that. It has a good ring to it: Spaulding and Rogers.

DK: Stanley, to change the subject a little, let me ask you a question. What about these guys who got tattooed from head to foot? How did that develop?

SM: We call them tattoo junkies. They just keep going. After a while, you don't know what's there anymore. They're basically pain freaks, you know. I have pictures of a guy my father started. He was a multimillionaire from Broad Street. He was the biggest exporter-importer of heavy machinery. And he was tattooed from head to toe; he just loved the feel of that machine. I got pictures of him. Actually there are books with pictures of him tattooed like that, and it says artist unknown. I'm the artist.

And I'm puttin' out a book with this. More of a pictorial type book with little comments here and there. Come down to Florida [to see it]. I'm in Tamarack, Florida. King's Point. Where all the old people are.

DK: You don't sound old. But I guess you've seen a lot in your years. You said there were fights?

SM: Every day. A day didn't go by there wasn't a battle. Every thief [and tough guy] from every town across America came to the Bowery. They came 'cause they're hidin' out. You're wanted in California, so you went to the other coast. Some guys went to Maine to hide out.

The type of people we work on, there was always battles, razor fights. You know at night all these wise guys and guys tryin' to intimidate ya [would come in]. Nobody could intimidate us, 'cause we'd pick up a hammer or a blade and that's it.

You know intimidators like to intimidate you slowly, but we'd attack 'em , beat the shit outta 'em. Even the Mafia guys knew that. We'd have battles down there with the sons of the big Mafia guys, the well-known ones. We'd kick the shit outta those guys.

[Nobody could cheat us.] Pay in advance. That was the thing. Actually, I just had a sign made so if I go out on conventions, I put it up "Bowery Style, Pay in Advance."

CP: None of that, "I'm just gonna go out to the car and get my wallet."

SM: Oh, they couldn't pull that shit with us.

CP: Who were the worst customers?

SM: The worst customers were neighborhood kids, like Bensonhurst kids. They were the worst cause their fathers were big shots, you know, Mafia guys. They were the worst, but they got what was comin' to them.

DK: What would provoke a fight?

SM: A guy'd jump right over and attack ya! So you'd stab 'em with a ice pick or you'd hit 'em with a hammer over the head and that's it.

A guy comes in with a Pagan [motorcycle club friend], thinkin' the Pagan's gonna help him [if there's trouble], and they both got the shit beat outta them. But we didn't just go out and do it, you know. The son-of-a-bitch jumped over the guy I was tattooing and was attackin' me. And I had a razor in my hand so you know what happened to his face. Hey look, they're gonna run or I'm gonna run. That was my place. They're gonna run.

CP: Was your father a fighter?

SM: My father would kick the shit out of anyone. Said one word out of the way that you should-n't and for no reason, he'd kill you. He was well trusted by the Mafia and Mafia cops. His mouth was quiet. Don't talk. He didn't talk to his family, he didn't tell nobody nothin'.

CP: Did your mother ever come down to the shop? [Her maiden name was Alfreda Crowell.]

SM: Nah. My father never told her nothing; he never brought nothing home. And I was the same way with my family. They don't know the first thing about anything that I ever did. If there were ever problems, any fights, I didn't bring it home.

DK: So would guys come in drunk to get tattooed or would you offer a cup?

SM: No, we didn't supply no drinkin' but there was bars all over. They were drunk and mean. We had 20 mean drunks waitin' for us. We had to tattoo them and then there were 20 more. And they wanna kill each other too. And kill us.

CP: Were there a lot of sailors in town in those days?

SM: Sailors, soldiers, marines... they hit the Bowery. Get drunk on the Bowery, get tattooed...

DK: What was your relationship with the Chinese?

SM: Chinese, they never got tattooed at that time, very rare.

DK: Same thing as the Jews right?

SM: Jews get tattooed. Lots of them. That's only a myth [that they didn't get tattooed]. I'm talking regular Jews, all kinds of Jews. Just like all kinds of Italians. Well, but the older Italians never got tattooed. Just young ones.

DK: So a young guy would come in to get a tattoo, a girlfriend's name or something like that?

SM: Yeah, that's usual, a lot of that. A lotta stuff with girls, girlfriends, mother, you know. That's what they all did at that time. Every old time tattooer, that was his type of customer.

CP: You have a lot of repeat guys? Guys hanging out?

SM: Yeah. There's guys that get one tattoo, there's guys that get 50 tattoos, there's guys that get 20 tattoos, you know.

CP: Would there be guys just hanging out in the shop?

SM: No, we didn't keep hang arounds. [We tried to keep things quiet.] You didn't tell nobody nothin'. You know you didn't want someone [finding out you were doing good business and so] openin' up next door like they do now. A guy has a good place and all of a sudden he's got 10 guys around him.

CP: Did you break anybody into the business?

SM: Never. Now it's all apprentice and, you know, cousins, uncles, everyone's a tattooer now. It was real tattooing at that time. Now it's all kinds of shit.

DK: And you got a lot of guys that tattooed their arm, their chest, but not their face much, right?

SM: Almost never. There was one guy here, a crazy guy worked for us. Jack Dracula he called himself. His real name is Martin Semnack. The guy worked for us and his grandmother sent him money. He's Polish.

CP: Did you tattoo him?

SM: Sure I tattooed him. I tattooed wings on the side of his head and he wanted me to tattoo his face but I wouldn't do it, so he went down to Coney Island to Junior Calantino and he tattooed his whole face. And he was a big handsome, powerful guy. Six foot four, giant, big black hair, good lookin' and everything.

CP: Why do you think he did that?

SM: Why, because he has mental disorder. With a mental disorder... Why a guy handsome like that, powerful and get his face tattooed? I wouldn't do that.

DK: What did he do on his face?

SM: He did all kinds of shit like eyeglasses and eagles on his face, on his forehead. Stupid stuff, you know what I mean?

CP: Did you get many sideshow people?

SM: Charlie Wagner was the champ of that. He tattooed all the sideshow women.

CP: That was before your time?

SM: I used to stop by when I was a kid. He would have these women that were all tattooed from head to toe, sideshow women.

CP: Whereabouts was he?

SM: Right on the next block. He was in Chatham Square. We were on the Bowery.

DK: I think that's great. Thank you.

SM: You got what you need?

CP: Yeah, that's really great. I'm sorry about your brother. How old was he?

SM: He was five year younger than me. He was 69. He had lymphoma. They got 'em out of it for four years, but when it comes back, there's no way out.

He never smoked, he never drank. I'm the smoker and drinker. It kept me alive, [that and] working on a farm. I had my own farm, and I worked day and night. I don't know how long I'll be around either. Nobody knows. You keep in shape and you live till you die, you know.

CP: Do you have any other tattooers in the family?

SM: Just my nephew, my brother's son. He's got the tattoo shop in Ronkonkoma. And my brother-in-law, he's dead, he was a tattooer. My son, he never went to tattooing.

CP: How many sisters did you have?

SM: One.

CP: Any other brothers?

SM: No, there was three of us.

CP: And your sister married the dentist?

SM: No, my sister married the tattooer. Also named Stanley. My wife's brother was the dentist.

CP: What was your sister's husband's name, Stanley what?

SM: Stanley Farber.

CP: Where did he tattoo?

SM: He tattooed with us and he tattooed down in Brooklyn and then he went into the air conditioning business, so that's where he stayed. [He tattooed with us] a couple of years. Also in Coney Island.

CP: How many years did you tattoo with your father?

SM: While he was still alive? Ten years, more than ten. I been tattooin' 62 years, 63 years. Since 1947. '47 I was already tattooing full time.

DK: Okay Stanley it's been an honor talking to you.

SM: Now, what are you writing?

CP: We're gonna put it in a book.

SM: You can send me a book.

CP: Sure, when it's finished.

SM: Finish it up already! (laughing)

David H. Katz *is a writer, photographer and artist working in New York City. He has written for a wide variety of publications, including* The New Statesman, High Times, *the British fashion magazine* TANK, The Villager, The Portable Lower East Side, Circus, Rap Express *and London's* Jewish Quarterly. *His memoir,* The Father Fades, *appeared in* Transformation, A Journal of Literature, Ideas and the Arts, *Spring, 2005; subsequent issues have featured his fiction and art.*

His artwork has been published in Zeek web magazine, and his work has been exhibited at Makor Gallery, Diamonds and Oranges Gallery, and Gallery 225 in New York. In addition to writing and editing, he maintains a website featuring his artwork: ZtakArchives.com, which hosts ongoing artistic projects. He lives on the Lower East Side of Manhattan.

Abbie Hoffman: American Dissident and Political Organizer Extraordinaire

Eliot Katz

One of the most well-known and influential American activists of the 20th century, Abbie Hoffman liked to call himself an American dissident and community organizer. As historian Howard Zinn has noted, Abbie's "community" at key moments in history extended to the entire country.

Abbie also liked to call himself a Jewish Road Warrior and he viewed his work in part as helping to carry on the radical Jewish tradition. In his autobiography (originally published as *Soon To Be a Major Motion Picture* and posthumously reprinted as *The Autobiography of Abbie Hoffman*), Abbie wrote: "Jews, especially first-born male Jews, have to make a big choice very quickly in life whether to go for the money or to go for broke....Wiseguys who go around saying things like 'Workers of the world unite,' or 'Every guy wants to screw his mother,' or 'E = mc2,' obviously choose to go for broke. It's the greatest Jewish tradition." (p. 14)

Abbie was intensely skilled at recognizing the political openings offered by different social contexts. As he put it in a 1987 speech to students at the University of South Carolina, "What kind of tactics you use to achieve social change depends on the historical moment." (*The Best of Abbie Hoffman*, p. 403) And as someone who had been influenced by the ideas of Saul Alinsky, Abbie understood that one key to fighting any City Hall is to speak in a language the people of that city understand.

Abbie moved from his hometown of Worcester, Massachusetts to 11th Street and Avenue C in New York City's Lower East Side at a particularly ripe historical moment—the fall of 1966 in the middle of the emerging counterculture. In the early 1960s, Abbie had worked in the free speech and civil rights movements, and he moved to New York to open Liberty House, a store that sold crafts made by black cooperatives in Mississippi. Recently divorced, Abbie met his second wife, Anita Kushner, soon after arriving in New York City. In early 1967 they moved into an apartment on St. Marks Place between 2nd and 3rd Avenues. Here is how Abbie described this move with Anita: "We had no way of knowing that we had just taken a $101-a-month front-row seat to the cultural revolution. The local counter-cultural institutions were all in a ten-block radius: Paul Krassner's *The Realist*, Ed Sanders and his Peace Eye Bookstore, resident poet Allen Ginsberg." (*Autobiography*, p. 92)

Abbie believed that political change and cultural change were inexorably intertwined. At Brandeis University, he had studied with Herbert Marcuse and learned how human psychology helped shape social dynamics. He had read C. Wright Mills, who argued for a New Left in which young people would play a prominent role and in which cultural forces would need to be addressed alongside economic ones. He'd studied Marshall McLuhan and grasped the powerful ways in which the medium of television was affecting public consciousness. In the social context of the last half of the 1960s, Abbie saw his main role as helping to move the blossoming youth counterculture into the broader social protest movement, especially the movement against the Vietnam War. As Zinn describes it, Abbie "helped turn the antiauthoritarian instincts of the younger generation into political resistance to racism and war." (p. 306, Afterword to *The Autobiography of Abbie Hoffman*)

It was from the countercultural vortex of the Lower East Side that Abbie—in collaboration with Anita, Paul Krassner, Ed Sanders, Jerry Rubin, Nancy Kirshan, Bob Fass, and others—formed the Yippies! and helped pioneer the use of humor, theater, and imagination as effective activist tools. With his unique blend of creativity and political insight, Abbie helped organize some of the most memorable protest actions of the 1960s, including dropping dollar bills onto the floor of the New York Stock Exchange, the "levitation" of the Pentagon, and the Festival of Life protests outside the 1968 Democratic Party convention in Chicago. Although later investigations blamed a "police riot" for the violence in Chicago, the "Chicago 8" (Hoffman, Rubin, Dave Dellinger, Tom Hayden, Bobby Seale, Rennie Davis, Lee Weiner, and John Froines) were arrested and put on trial. The ACLU called the legendary Chicago Conspiracy Trial "the most important political trial of the century," and largely because of the way Abbie and Jerry turned the trial into brilliant political theater unprecedented in American courtroom history, the trial is also one of the most dramatized trials in American theater and film.

It was during Abbie's years living on the Lower East Side that he wrote his classic books, *Revolution for the Hell of It*, *Woodstock Nation*, and *Steal This Book*. In his autobiography, Abbie offers a "must-read" description (see especially pages 87-100) of those Lower East Side years of the late Sixties, describing a thriving alternative culture filled with lively street theater, community medical clinics, volunteer lawyers, free food in the park, great rock & roll clubs, antiwar rallies, and local projects to plant trees and stop police harassment based on race or hair length. Abbie concludes: "It was a theatrical period, filled with rebellion, naive optimism, moral purpose, giddy sex, and cheap dope. (Believe me, you can do a lot worse!)...So we met, the times and me, down there on the Lower East Side. It was a nice fit; a great time to be alive." (100)

While the 1960s were the years in which Abbie made his most renowned mark on American culture, his lesser-known political and environmental work from the late 1970s through his death in 1989 proved his community organizing skills beyond a shadow of a doubt, and may yet end up proving just as influential since many of the young people who worked with and learned from Abbie in those later years are still active in various ecological, peace, health care, and global justice movements.

In 1973, Abbie was busted by undercover cops for acting as a middleman in a cocaine sale; the disputed details of Abbie's arrest have never been totally clear. In 1974, rather than face trial and the risk of a long prison sentence, Abbie fled underground. In Mexico, Abbie got together with Johanna Lawrenson, who would become his third wife, his trusted "running mate," and his talented co-organizer. Abbie and Johanna traveled the U.S. and the world, with Abbie taking on a variety of pseudonyms, disguises, and fake IDs. He also wrote and published dozens of articles for magazines, as well as three books, *To America with Love, Square Dancing in the Ice Age*, and *Soon To Be a Major Motion Picture*. While underground, Abbie also exhibited increased symptoms of manic-depression that would cause him (and occasionally some of his friends) considerable pain in those underground years and in the future.

In 1976, Abbie settled with Johanna in the scenic 1,000 Islands on the St. Lawrence River in upstate New York, at the Canadian border, in a cottage that had been built by Johanna's great-grandmother. Even though Abbie was still hiding from the law, when the Army Corps of Engineers announced plans to dredge the St. Lawrence River for winter navigation, Abbie and Johanna realized what an environmental disaster that would be and they decided to act. With local residents, they formed Save the River! and they began organizing door-to-door, which often meant traveling by motorboat among the islands in this traditionally Republican area. Using the name Barry Freed, Abbie had to work for the first time in years as a political organizer without the benefit of his name or fame. Save the River! was victorious, and even Senator Daniel Patrick Moynihan took a celebratory photo with fugitive "Barry," announcing at a large public gathering that they all owed a debt of gratitude to Barry Freed for his important work.

Abbie re-surfaced from the underground in 1980 in a national television interview with Barbara Walters and he was sentenced to three years, ultimately serving a year in jail and work release at a drug rehab program called Veritas, followed by two years on parole. Older, wiser, and as committed as ever to social justice, Abbie's activism on behalf of progressive causes never wavered. But his activist style evolved, as any good community organizer's would, in trying to stay relevant in changing times. Abbie maintained his great sense of humor, but without a large counterculture to work with, Abbie's organizing in the 1980s began to rely more heavily on reasoned discourse and long-range organizational considerations.

In the 1980s, Abbie led delegations to Nicaragua to show solidarity with the Sandinistas and to protest Reagan administration support of the right-wing Contras. In New Hope, Pennsylvania, he helped form DelAware to try to prevent a pump from being installed to divert large amounts of water from the Delaware River to a nearby nuclear power plant. In 1986, Abbie was arrested with Amy Carter (the former president's daughter) and over sixty others at the University of Massachusetts for a protest against CIA recruitment on campus. Fifteen of those arrested, including Abbie and Amy, decided to go to trial, pleading not guilty by using the "necessity defense."

At this CIA-off-campus trial in Northampton, which should be far better known than it is, the defendants claimed that their minor crime of trespassing was needed to stop the larger crimes of CIA covert actions in Central America and elsewhere. As witnesses, they called in Howard Zinn, Daniel Ellsberg, Ramsey Clarke, and former CIA agents to describe for the six mainstream New England jurors the interventionist history and immoral practices of the CIA. In the social climate of the Reagan years, Abbie decided on a courtroom strategy markedly different than his theatrical tactics in Chicago. Wearing a jacket and tie, Abbie represented himself and delivered a moving and well-reasoned closing argument in which he told the jury: "I grew up with the idea that democracy is not something you believe in, or a place you hang your hat, but it's something you do. You participate. If you stop doing it, democracy crumbles and falls apart." Invoking the best of America's radical and common-sense traditions, he urged the jurors to return a verdict of not guilty which would say to the students "what Thomas Paine said: 'Young people, don't give up hope. If you participate, the future is yours'." (*Best of*, 386-387) In a verdict that surprised many, the jurors did indeed return a verdict of "not guilty," demonstrating that fair-minded, mainstream Americans, even during the relatively conservative Eighties, could be convinced by rational argument and honest information that the CIA was indeed committing serious international crimes in their names, and that it was therefore justifiable for concerned citizens to oppose those egregious policies through principled stands (or, in this case, principled sit-downs) of civil disobedience.

I had met Abbie briefly in the early 1980s, but got to know him and Johanna in 1987 and 1988, when Abbie served as the major adviser for two student activist projects that I helped work on: National Student Convention '88, a conference which brought over 700 students from around the country to Rutgers University to discuss creating a new independent, multi-issue, and democratically structured national student activist organization somewhat modeled on SDS; and Student Action Union, one of several smaller groups that grew out of the convention and that at one time had chapters on over two dozen campuses. Because my partner at the time, Christine Kelly, was one of the lead organizers and Abbie's main contact in these groups, I was lucky to have had the chance to see the immense dedication, time commitment, and invaluable strategic advice that Abbie gave to these projects. Since it was important that these youth endeavors be seen as student-led, Abbie's help was usually behind the scenes, out of the spotlight. As a dedicated adviser, Abbie spent countless hours on the phone discussing potential resolutions to debates and obstacles that would arise. He wrote long letters brimming with organizing tips and helpful contacts. He helped recruit hundreds of students and other experienced advisers to join our initiatives. And he did college speaking engagements to help us raise funds. (He died with Student Action Union brochures packed in his suitcase for a scheduled campus trip.)

In his Eighties work, Abbie was committed to passing along skills and lessons honed through his decades of activism. He was also committed to using ideas and language that would resonate with the era. In a speech Abbie gave at the National Student Convention in February 1988, a speech that remains one of my favorite of Abbie's writings, he compared the political tone of the late 1980s with the late 1960s: "In the late sixties we were so fed up we wanted to destroy it all. That's when we changed the name of America and stuck in the 'k.' The mood today is different, and the language that will respond to today's mood will be different. Things are so deteriorated in this society that it's not up to you to destroy America, it's up to you to go out and save America." (*The Best of Abbie Hoffman*, p. 416) In that speech, Abbie also talked about the need to create long-lasting activist groups, to develop democratic organizational structures, to use majority decision-making rather than consensus when complex questions arose (because consensus could be difficult to achieve with FBI agents and schizophrenics in the room), and to be willing to work for social change both inside the system and out in the streets.

Near the end of his life, Abbie was splitting his weeks between Johanna's apartment in New York City and a room in New Hope, PA, where DelAware was centered. He died in his bed in

New Hope on April 12, 1989 from an overdose of phenobarbital and alcohol. I would argue strongly that his suicide was a result solely of the personal pain from his depression, and not a sign of political pessimism as some writers tried to claim at the time. Despite the fact that Abbie's depression resulted in moments of deep emotional pain, despite lingering physical pain from a bad car accident in 1988, and despite occasional expressions of frustration with the state of the American left, I don't believe that Abbie ever lost hope in the potential of young people to create a better world. His work with us proved otherwise. In that National Student Convention '88 speech, Abbie noted that young people have a particular quality that's essential for instigating political change: impatience. In a Walt Whitman-like catalog, Abbie told the gathered students: "There have to be enough people that say, 'We want it now, in our lifetime.' We want to see apartheid in South Africa come down right now. We want to see the war in Central America stop right now. We want the CIA off campus right now….This is your moment." (*Best of*, p. 418)

Abbie had the quickest and sharpest political wit that I've ever seen in a political figure of the left or the right. How I would have loved to see him alive into the 21st Century to debate the Bill O'Reillys and Sean Hannitys of the world on the current military disaster in Iraq and the Bush administration's serial violations of civil liberties and human rights.

Although the Bush years have taken us on a pothole-filled detour to the furthest edges of the American right, U.S. public opinion is thankfully once again swinging leftward as I write this piece in November 2007, with about 70% of the country having come to oppose the war in Iraq. And yet, there is still the need for impassioned and intelligent political organizing—still the need for an as-yet-undiscovered mix of inventive activist strategies—to force the new Democratic Congress and the next American president to set a tangibly different course for America's domestic and foreign policy, a path that honors our most progressive ideals and that addresses such deep-rooted problems as global warming, a still-escalating militarism, growing economic inequality with its attendant lack of affordable housing and health care, entrenched institutional racism, and the continuing assaults since 9/11 on our constitutional rights. Abbie Hoffman helped put imagination and fun into the recipe of American social activism, and his legacy—drawn from his work in the Sixties, Seventies, and Eighties—will continue to inspire young people to question authority and to believe that, by participating, they can change the world.

Eliot Katz is the author of five books of poetry, including Unlocking the Exits, and When the Skyline Crumbles: Poems for the Bush Years. *A cofounder and former coeditor of* Long Shot *literary journal, Katz guest-edited* Long Shot's *final issue, a "Beat Bush issue" released in Spring 2004. He is a coeditor of* Poems for the Nation, *a collection of political poems compiled by the late poet Allen Ginsberg, and his essay, "Radical Eyes," is included in the prose collection,* The Poem That Changed America: "Howl" FiftyYears Later. *Called "another classic New Jersey bard" by Ginsberg, Katz worked for many years as a housing advocate for Central New Jersey homeless families. He currently lives in New York City and serves as poetry editor of the online politics quarterly,* Logos: A Journal of Modern Society and Culture.

Copy Editors

Leonard Abrams was born in Brooklyn and raised in Spring Valley, N.Y. His maternal grand-mother was born in a building adjacent to the defunct firehouse on Broome Street (between Clin-ton and Suffolk Streets). He published and edited the *East Village Eye* magazine from 1979 to 1987, then created the multiracial hip-hop club Hotel Amazon and other venues from 1987 through 1990. After writing and traveling extensively in Mexico and Brazil during the '90s, he produced and directed a documentary film (*Quilombo Country*, 2006) about rural Afro-Brazil-ian communities. He is currently distributing and screening the film, developing a new docu-mentary project, and digitizing the *East Village Eye* collection for release on DVD.

Jennifer Blowdryer is an investigative thinker who's written a few books, most recently *The Laziest Secretary in the World*; other books can be found online for one cent. She's lived in the East Village since 1985, and was conceived at the corner of Bleecker and Bowery, indoors, of course. Jenniferblowdryer.com, jenniferblowdryer.blogspot.com. She performs a lot. Who doesn't?

The Leonard and Tobee Kaplan Distinguished Professor of Modern Jewish Thought, **Jonathan Boyarin** began teaching at UNC in the fall semester 2007. Boyarin, an anthropologist and lawyer, has served as visiting professor at Wesleyan University and Dartmouth College and came to Carolina from the University of Kansas, where he was distinguished professor of Mod-ern Jewish Studies. Boyarin received a J.D. from Yale Law School in 1998, after receiving his Ph.D. in Anthropology at the New School for Social Research in New York in 1984. His research and writing combine his backgrounds in anthropology and Yiddish culture to point toward new pathways in the study of Jewish culture.

His first book, as co-editor, was *From a Ruined Garden: The Memorial Books of Polish Jewry* (1983 and 1998), which served as an introduction for younger, English-speaking Jews to first-hand accounts of Jewish life in Eastern Europe. This was followed by *Polish Jews in Paris: The Ethnography of Memory* (1991), based on his dissertation fieldwork in Paris, and by a volume on the life history of Yiddish scholar Shlomo Noble. Further ethnographic and critical essays, including some dealing with the contemporary Lower East Side in New York, were published in *Storm from Paradise: The Politics of Jewish Memory* (1992) and *Thinking in Jewish* (1996). He edited and contributed to *The Ethnography of Reading* (1993) and *Remapping Memory: The Politics of TimeSpace* (1994). With his brother, Daniel Boyarin, he co-edited *Jews and Other Differences: The New Jewish Cultural Studies* (1997). His interest in Zionism, the Israeli Pales-tinian conflict, and revaluation of diaspora in contemporary Jewish life is reflected in *Palestine and Jewish History* (1996) and (again with Daniel Boyarin) *Powers of Diaspora* (2002).

His interests in the relation between Jewishness and legal theory resulted in a study published in the *Yale Law Journal* regarding a controversy surrounding a school board in a contemporary Hasidic community, in addition to a journal article on Jewishness, law, and psychoanalysis. He is currently working on a study and translation from Yiddish of the last book published by Abraham Joshua Heschel, while completing a manuscript on the relation between Jewish difference in late medieval Europe and the dynamics of the colonial encounter in Latin America. Boyarin has given guest lectures at a number of outstanding universities and has presented papers on numerous occasions throughout the United States, Canada and England. He teaches courses on a range of topics.

Paul Buhle, a Senior Lecturer at Brown University, founder of the New Left journal *Radical America*, the popular arts Journal *Cultural Correspondence* and NYU's Oral History of the American Left archive, has published 35 books as author or editor, including seven comic art nonfiction histories. He is the authorized biographer of Pan Africanist C.L.R. James and noir film artist Abraham Lincoln Polonsky.

Cate Corley is a resident of Clinton Hill, Brooklyn and a graduate of Columbia University with a M.S. in Urban Planning. From Midwestern ex-industrial cities, to the new metropolis of Los Angeles, and to New York, America's Greatest City, Cate has pursued her passion for refining the relationship between the urban environment and the quality of life of communities and individuals. The richness of this environment inspires her art, work, and daily life.

Loretta Farb happily exited the entertainment business for an interesting stint in politics and local government—though she sometimes takes issue with the description of politics as "Hollywood for Ugly People." Loretta plans to make her current business card last as long as her boss remains an elected official. She currently lives in Austin, TX.

Jim Feast (Ph.D, NYU, English, 1991) is a member of the Unbearables writers group and (with Ron Kolm) edited three of their anthologies, *Help Yourself, Crimes of the Beats, and The Worst Book I Ever Read*. He has also co-written a number of books with Gary Null, including *AIDS: A Second Opinion* and *Germs, Biological Warfare and Vaccinations: What You Need to Know*. With Ron Kolm, he wrote the murder mystery *Neo Phobe*, and, with the same Kolm, is directing the Autonomedia line of crime fiction. He writes book reviews for *Rain Taxi, American Book Review*, and *The Brooklyn Rail*, and *Evergreen Review* online. It was for Evergreen that he wrote a review of *Captured*, which first introduced him to these important and evolving records of LES history. He also writes for the Detroit political magazine *Fifth Estate*. From 1972-'75, he worked in Chicago as an aide in a nursing home and with Judy Sullivan and Bertha Harris worked on unionizing the largely Black female workforce. The three of them were fired when their campaign was exposed. Feast then took a job at the University of Illinois in Chicago while concomitantly working with the Vietnam Veterans Against the War. With the vets, he was involved in a counter Memorial Day march, sneaking into the VA to canvass for the group and in pickets. Ironically enough, in '75 he was clubbed and given a concussion by cops, then jailed in a protest against … police brutality. Mysteriously enough, he was not rehired at the university once his involvement with the vets became common knowledge.

Finding no work in Chicago, he moved to the Lower East Side, where, while working in a supermarket, he also got involved in tenant organizing with the CWP, although he did not share their Maoist philosophy. He began teaching in such schools as NYU, where he earned his doctorate, The College of New Rochelle, LaGuardia and, most long term, at Baruch. In the '90s, he became active in Adjuncts Unite, with Ingrid Hughes. The group fought to raise the status and benefits of adjuncts. Mysteriously enough, after working steadily at Baruch for 10 years, his contract was not renewed at the same time as his work in this organization became prominent.

Feast found more work as a free lance in the publishing. He worked as a temp at *Sports Illustrated*, the *New York Post* and *Women's Wear Daily*. He also worked, not always successfully, in helping with the memoirs of Barney Rosset (of Grove Press fame) and Gerard Damiano (of x-rated film fame). His most rewarding editing has been with Clayton Patterson on a series of books on the LES. His wife, in the meantime, published three memoirs in the New York Press about growing up in Saigon during the Vietnam war, one of which won first prize in a contest Describe the Happiest Day in Your Life.

Ari Fries was born in New York City and raised in Brooklyn where he currently lives. He graduated in 2004 from New York University with a B.A. degree in English and American Literature. He is currently working in marketing and writes short stories in his spare time. His grandmother also worked on articles.

Deborah Lacher Fries was born and bred in Brooklyn where she shares a house with her mother, 2 of her 3 children and 6 cats; her son moved out. She is the driving force behind FusionArts Museum, NYC's only contemporary visual arts space that is dedicated to multidisciplinary (fusion) art exclusively.

Jan Herman was born in Brooklyn in 1942. He lived on the Lower East Side in the early '60s, while clerking at the 8th Street Bookshop in Greenwich Village. He moved to San Francisco in the mid-'60s, where he was Lawrence Ferlinghetti's editorial assistant at City Lights Books (a.k.a. the Lower East Side west), and started a little magazine, *The San Francisco Earthquake*, with Gail Dusenbery. Later, he launched the Nova Broadcast Press. The Beat, post-Beat and Fluxus writers and artists published in the magazine or by the press included William S. Burroughs, Allen Ginsberg, Ray Bremser, Ferlinghetti, Bob Kaufman, Frank O'Hara, Sinclair Beiles, Alan Ansen, Carl Solomon, Dick Higgins, Wolf Vostell, Norman O. Mustill, Claude Pelieu, Mary Beach, Carl Weissner, Ed Sanders, Janine Pommy-Vega, Charles Plymell, Liam O'Gallagher, Nanos Valaoritis, Jochen Gerz, Richard Kostelanetz, Roy Lichtenstein and Edward Ruscha, among many others.

In 1972, Herman became editor in chief of the Something Else Press. As a journalist during the 1970s, '80s and '90s, he was a culture reporter and columnist at the *Chicago Sun-Times*, *New York Daily News*, and the *Los Angeles Times*, an arts journalism fellow at Columbia University, and subsequently a senior editor at MSNBC.com. He is the author of *A Talent for Trouble*, the biography of Hollywood director William Wyler, out in paperback from Da Capo Press. He is also the co-author of *Cut Up or Shut Up* and the editor of *Brion Gysin Let the Mice In*. His correspondence with writers and artists is in the cleverly named Jan Herman archive at Northwestern University Library. His blog, Straight Up, is posted at http:artsjournal.com. He lives in New York City.

Since 1999, native New Yorkers **Foxy Kidd** and **Romy Ashby** have been producing *Goodie Magazine*, a little publication dedicated to celebrating authenticity, in its many manifestations through in-depth interviews, one subject per issue. Watching the relentless destruction of New York City – as its beautiful and complex culture disappears along with countless old and storied buildings – has made Romy and Foxy preservationists by default. They both say that making *Goodie Magazine* is what makes life worth living. See www.goodie.org.

Eric Miller, Ph.D. is a native New Yorker transplanted to Chennai (on India's southeast coast), where he has co-founded the World Storytelling Institute (www.storytellinginstitute.org). His website is titled, Storytelling and Videoconferencing www.storytellingandvideoconferencing.com.

Timothy Moran: Writer, Editor and photographer born in Amityville, New York in 1958. Co-Author/Editor of Edie Kerouac-Parker's memoir, *You'll Be Okay: My Life With Jack Kerouac* (City Lights, 2007), author of *Jesus Lives in Taito-ku* (American Book Jam, Tokyo 1998). Contributor to numerous books and publications on and about Beat figures Jack Kerouac, William Burroughs, Allen Ginsberg, Herbert Huncke and Henri Cru. Photography credits include *The New York Times* and the permanent collection of The University of North Carolina. He currently resides on New York City.

Edward Mullany is an editor at *matchbook* and *Anderbo*. His writing has appeared in *Alaska Quarterly Review, New Ohio Review, Tampa Review, Keyhole Magazine*, and other journals.

Klara Palotai, a one-time member of the Squat Theatre, became an East Village resident for years after the theater moved out from their storefront building on 23rd Street in the mid-'80s. She works now full time at the Tisch School of he Arts. At the Angel Orensanz Foundation she manages their numerous websites and documents events for their weekly cable TV show. Klara has a Master's degree from the Sorbonne in Art and Archeology and is completing her second master in the Interactive Telecommunications Program at NYU's Tisch School of the Arts.

Canadian-born activist, archivist, and photographer **Clayton Patterson** came to New York in 1979 armed with college degrees in education and fine arts, and teaching experience in high school and college. With his partner of 37 years, documentarian filmmaker, writer and social commentator **Elsa Rensaa**, he has amassed an enormous photo and video archive – as well as ephemera – of the Lower East Side, including the videotape which became known as the 1988 Tompkins Square Park Police Riot whose clips have appeared on local television and around the world. In 1985, Clayton and Elsa devised and created appliquéd and embroidered baseball caps, known as Clayton Caps, which has since inspired a whole industry of decorated head coverings. Since 1993, the Clayton Gallery and Outlaw Art Museum (at 161 Essex Street) has shown important "outside" artist works including those of Boris Lurie and his fellow No!art artists.

As an editor, Clayton has published *Captured: A Film & Video History of the Lower East Side* (with Paul Bartlett and Urania Mylonas), *Resistance: A Radical Political History of the Lower East Side*, and *Wildstyle: The History of a New Idea. The Front Door Photos & Other Artistic Reminiscences* was just published. He also has been the focus of a documentary by Ben

Solomon, Dan Levin, and Jenner Furst: *Captured* (Video on Demand).

Bob Perl, a graduate of the University of Colorado at Boulder, is a broker and real estate agent/manager at Tower Brokerage on East 10th Street.

Ken Petricig, has lived most of his adult life on the Lower East Side. He is a musician, web editor, designer and project manager. He worked several years for the Columbia University Libraries and the Columbia Center for New Media Teaching and Learning. He also created the index for this book.

Eddy Portnoy earned a Ph.D. in Modern Jewish Studies at the Jewish Theological Seminary. He teaches Yiddish language and literature at Rutgers University.

Jerome Poynton, a former Men's Gymnastics Coach from The University of Michigan, worked with New York painters, film makers, writers, photographers and art collectors for a quarter of a century. He now spends most of his time in Italy talking with farmers and appliance salesman.

Elsa Rensaa; see the Clayton Patterson entry for information.

Elissa Sampson is a local resource on the history and background of the synagogues of the Lower East Side, both extant as well as those lost. She is a long-time resident and docent, with close relationships to many shuls, and like her parents who worked or grew up in the neighborhood, Elissa has always had deep ties to the Lower East Side. With her husband, Professor Jonathan Boyarin, a well-known Jewish anthropologist and ethnographer, they have raised their children to love the neighborhood and its traditions. Elissa has contributed to the design of the tours that the Lower East Side Conservancy offers and is always interested in finding out what visitors and neighborhood residents alike would like to learn about the historic and living communities of the Lower East Side/East Village.

Howard F. Seligman has been working as a self-employed financial and tax consultant since 1984. Howard's practice specializes in self-employed individuals in the arts and entertainment fields as well as not for profit cultural and literary organizations. He currently serves as the treasurer to more than 20 tax-exempt corporations. Mr. Seligman has taught accounting and finance at The Pratt Institute, The Taylor Business Institute and at the Newspace. Howard continues to pursue music and the performing arts as a "serious hobby" and a path to a "higher state of mind."

Multimedia artist and pilgarlic **Craig Silver** was happily domiciled near the Bowery for nearly 25 years until rising real estate prices drove him out. He recently completed writing a full-length musical about digital orgasms.

Monica Uszerowicz lives and writes in New York City. A graduate of Eugene Lang College at the New School for Social Research, she has been interning for Clayton Patterson for the past year. Recently, she has covered the changes in downtown New York City's art world for *The Villager* and edited and contributed a chapter to Clayton Patterson's *Front Door Book*, published in June 2009.

Victor Uszerowicz is an English professor at Miami Dade College and has written both fiction and non-fiction about the Holocaust. He divides his time between Ft. Lauderdale, Brooklyn and Los Angeles.

Alan J. Weberman studied at the City College in New York City. He worked as a researcher with Richard Schweiker and Henry Gonzalez that eventually resulted in the establishment of the House Select Committee on Assassinations investigation. With his co-author, Michael Canfield, Weberman published *Coup d'etat in America: The CIA and the Assassination of John F. Kennedy* (The Third Press, 1975). In the book they claim that E. Howard Hunt and Frank Sturgis were two of the "three tramps" arrested near Dealey Plaza just after the assassination. The authors were sued by Hunt but the case never went to trial. According to Weberman: "There was no way the CIA was going to let me win, it would have been very dangerous for this country as we were involved in a Cold War with the Soviet Union. The Agency went as far as drugging Congressmen Gonzalez and he started acting in a bizarre fashion and had to resign. Forget my bona fides, look at the info that I have brought together from telephone calls to Gerry Hemming, from documents, from court cases and from The Weberman Commission – where I used subpoena power to question Angleton, Helms, Barker, Sturgis, Liddy etc."

Alan J. Weberman is the author of the Coup D'Etat in America website. His latest book is the *Dylan to English Dictionary*. He is also active in the Medical Marijuana Movement and has just helped get that Hawk's nest restored in Manhattan.

Index

M

NOTES